Lecture Notes in Computer Science

Lecture Notes in Artificial Intelligence   14454

Founding Editor

Jörg Siekmann

The series Lecture Notes in Artificial Intelligence (LNAI) was established in 1988 as a topical subseries of LNCS devoted to artificial intelligence.

The series publishes state-of-the-art research results at a high level. As with the LNCS mother series, the mission of the series is to serve the international R & D community by providing an invaluable service, mainly focused on the publication of conference and workshop proceedings and postproceedings.

Abdulaziz Al Ali · John-John Cabibihan ·
Nader Meskin · Silvia Rossi · Wanyue Jiang ·
Hongsheng He · Shuzhi Sam Ge
Editors

Social Robotics

15th International Conference, ICSR 2023
Doha, Qatar, December 3–7, 2023
Proceedings, Part II

Springer

Editors
Abdulaziz Al Ali
Qatar University
Doha, Qatar

Nader Meskin
Qatar University
Doha, Qatar

Wanyue Jiang 🆔
Qingdao University
Qingdao, China

Shuzhi Sam Ge 🆔
National University of Singapore
Queenstown, Singapore

John-John Cabibihan 🆔
Qatar University
Doha, Qatar

Silvia Rossi 🆔
University of Naples Federico II
Napoli, Italy

Hongsheng He 🆔
The University of Alabama
Tuscaloosa, AL, USA

ISSN 0302-9743   ISSN 1611-3349 (electronic)
Lecture Notes in Artificial Intelligence
ISBN 978-981-99-8717-7   ISBN 978-981-99-8718-4 (eBook)
https://doi.org/10.1007/978-981-99-8718-4

LNCS Sublibrary: SL7 – Artificial Intelligence

This Springer imprint is published by the registered company Springer Nature Singapore Pte Ltd.
The registered company address is: 152 Beach Road, #21-01/04 Gateway East, Singapore 189721, Singapore

Paper in this product is recyclable.

Preface

The 15th International Conference on Social Robotics (ICSR 2023) was held in Doha, Qatar as a face-to-face conference on December 3–7, 2023. It was the first time that the conference was hosted in Qatar and in the Middle East and North Africa (MENA) region. The theme of this year's conference is "Human-Robot Collaboration: Sea, Air, Land, Space and Cyberspace", which emphasizes on all physical and cyber-physical domains where humans and robots collaborate. The conference aims to bring together researchers and practitioners working on the interaction between humans and intelligent robots and on the integration of robots into the fabric of our society.

This book constitutes the refereed conference proceedings. Out of a total of 83 submitted manuscript reviewed by a dedicated international team of Senior Programme Committee and Programme Committee, 64 regular papers and 4 papers in Special Session: "Personalisation and Adaptation in Social Robotics" were selected for inclusion into the proceedings and were presented during the technical sessions of the conference.

ICSR 2023 also featured two keynote, workshops, and robot design competitions. The first keynote talk, titled "Robotics Meets AI & 5G — The Future is Now!", was delivered by Professor Bruno Siciliano, who is a Professor of Robotics and Control at the University of Naples Federico II and a Past President of IEEE Robotics and Automation Society. The second keynote talk, titled "Perspectives and Social Impacts of Humanoids as General Purpose Robots", was delivered by Professor Abderrahmane Kheddar, Director of Research at the Centre National de la Recherche Scientifique, France. He is a Titular Member of the National Academy of Technology of France and a Knight of the French National Order of Merits.

We would like to express our sincere gratitude to all members of the Organising Committee and volunteers for their dedication in making the conference a great success. We are also indebted to members of the Senior Programme Committee and the Programme Committee for the hard work for their rigorous review of the papers. Lastly and most importantly, we are grateful to the continued support to ICSR by the authors, participants and sponsors, without which the conference would not be possible.

December 2023

Abdulaziz Al Ali
John-John Cabibihan
Nader Meskin
Silvia Rossi
Wanyue Jiang
Hongsheng He
Shuzhi Sam Ge

Organization

General Chair

Ali, Abdulaziz Al   Qatar University, Qatar

General Co-chair

Cabibihan, John-John   Qatar University, Qatar

Local Arrangement Chair

Mukahal, Waled   Qatar University, Qatar

Finance Chair

Sagheer, Mohammad Al   Qatar University, Qatar

Web Chair

Jabbar, Rateb   Qatar University, Qatar

Program Committee Chairs

Meskin, Nader   Qatar University, Qatar
Rossi, Silvia   University of Naples Federico II, Italy

Competition Chair

Pandey, Amit Kumar   Rovial Space, France; Socients AI and Robotics, France

Sponsorship Chairs

Sadda, Mohammad Al   Qatar University, Qatar
Jaber, Faisal Al   Qatar University, Qatar

Workshop Chairs

Qidwai, Uvais   Qatar University, Qatar
Erbad, Aiman   Hamad Bin Khalifa University, Qatar
Celiktutan, Oya   King's College London, UK
Ortega, Elena Lazkano   University of the Basque Country, Spain

Exhibition Chairs

Jang, Minsu   Electronics and Telecommunications Research
            Institute, South Korea
Chellali, Ryad   Moore Nanjing Robotics Institute, LLC, China
Staffa, Mariacarla   University of Naples Parthenope, Italy

Publication Chairs

He, Hongsheng   University of Alabama, Tuscaloosa, USA
Jiang, Wanyue   Qingdao University, China

Publicity Chairs

Belushi, Mariam Al   Qatar University, Qatar
Yafei, Ghusoon Al   Qatar University, Qatar
Rossi, Alessandra   University of Naples Federico II, Italy
Holthaus, Patrick   University of Hertfordshire, UK
Chandra, Shruti   University of Waterloo, Canada
Hart, Justin   University of Texas at Austin, USA
Taheri, Alireza   Sharif University of Technology, Iran
Shidujaman, Mohammad Independent University, Bangladesh

International Advisory Committee

Kheddar, Abderrahmane	CNRS-AIST JRL, Japan and CNRS-UM LIRMM IDH, France
Tapus, Adriana	ENSTA-ParisTech, France
Wagner, Alan Richard	Penn State University, USA
Agah, Arvin	University of Kansas, USA
Cavallo, Filippo	University of Florence, Italy
Feil-Seifer, David	University of Nevada, USA
Williams, Mary-Anne	University of New South Wales, Australia
Salichs, Miguel Ángel	University Carlos III of Madrid, Spain

Standing Committee

Ge, Shuzhi	National University of Singapore, Singapore
Khatib, Oussama	Stanford University, USA
Mataric, Maja	University of Southern California, USA
Li, Haizhou	Chinese University of Hong Kong, China
Kim, Jong Hwan	Korea Advanced Institute of Science and Technology, South Korea
Dario, Paolo	Scuola Superiore Sant'Anna, Italy
Arkin, Ronald C.	Georgia Institute of Technology, USA

Associate Editors

Mabrok, Mohamed	Qatar University, Qatar
Holthaus, Patrick	University of Hertfordshire, UK
Fiorini, Laura	Università degli studi di Firenze, Italy
Andriella, Antonio	Pal Robotics, Spain
Rossi, Alessandra	University of Naples Federico II, Italy
Nuovo, Alessandro Di	Sheffield Hallam University, UK
Gómez, Marcos Maroto	University Carlos III of Madrid, Spain
Louie, Wing-Yue (Geoffrey)	Oakland University, USA
Esposito, Anna	Università della Campania "Luigi Vanvitelli", Italy
Hindriks, Koen	Vrije Universiteit Amsterdam, The Netherlands
Bodenhagen, Leon	University of Southern Denmark, Denmark
Palinko, Oskar	University of Southern Denmark, Denmark
Fazli, Pooyan	Arizona State University, USA

Kwak, Sonya S.	Korea Institute of Science and Technology, South Korea
Tafreshi, Reza	Texas A & M University, USA
Meskin, Nikan	Qatar University, Qatar
Qidwai, Uvais	Qatar University, Qatar

Reviewers

A. Fiaz, Usman
Abdelkader, Mohamed
Abou Chahine, Ramzi
Aitsam, Muhammad
Alban, Ahmad
Amirova, Aida
Amorese, Terry
Andriella, Antonio
Angelopoulos, Georgios
Assuncao, Gustavo
Azizi, Negin
Barik, Tanmoy
Baroniya, Rupesh
Bello Martín, Felipe
Beraldo, Gloria
Berns, Karsten
Bevilacqua, Roberta
Bodenhagen, Leon
Bossema, Marianne
Boumans, Roel
Bray, Robert
Chandran Nair, Nandu
Chehade, Zeina
Cabezaolías, Carmen María
Cabibihan, John-John
Carrasco-Martínez, Sara
Carros, Felix
Chandra, Shruti
Chidambaram, Vigneswaran
Cuciniello, Marialucia
De Graaf, Maartje
de la Cruz, Andrea
Di Nuovo, Alessandro
El Khalfi, Zeineb
Ebardo, Ryan

Effati, Meysam
Elsayed, Saber
Esposito, Anna
Etuttu, Mariam
Fazli, Pooyan
Fernández Rodicio, Enrique
Fiorini, Laura
Fracasso, Francesca
Ghoudi, Zeineb
Gaballa, Aya
Ganti, Achyut
Greco, Claudia
Hedayati, Hooman
Hellou, Mehdi
Hindriks, Koen
Holthaus, Patrick
Kaman, Zeittey
Kang, Dahyun
Khan, Imy
Kim, Jaeseaok
Kim, Boyoung
Kim, Sangmin
Kwak, Sonya S.
Lacroix, Dimitri
Lakatos, Gabriella
Lee, Hee Rin
Li, Jamy
Lim, Yoonseob
Louie, Wing-Yue (Geoffrey)
Love, Tamlin
Luperto, Matteo
Mabrok, Mohamed
Maroto Gómez
Marques-Villarroya, Sara
Maure, Romain

Meskin, Nader
Minguez Sánchez, Carlos
Mohamed, Chris
Moros, Sílvia
Nesset, Birthe
Noorizadeh, Mohammad
O'Reilly, Ziggy
Osorio, Pablo
Palinko, Oskar
Paplu, Sarwar
Perugia, Giulia
Pramanick, Pradip
Preston, Rhian
Qidwai, Uvais
Radwan, Ibrahim
Recchiuto, Carmine Tommaso
Rehm, Matthias
Reimann, Merle
Rhim, Jimin
Romeo, Marta
Rossi, Silvia
Rossi, Alessandra
Staffa, Mariacarla

Sabbella, Sandeep Reddy
Schmidt-Wolf, Melanie
Seifi, Hasti
Shahverdi, Pourya
Shrivastava, Manu
Sienkiewicz, Barbara
Sirkin, David Michael
Sorrentino, Alessandra
Story, Matt
Tafreshi, Reza
Taheri, Alireza
Tarakli, Imene
Thijn, Jorrit
Uchida, Misako
Vagnetti, Roberto
Van Minkelen, Peggy
Velmurugan, Vignesh
Vigni, Francesco
Vinanzi, Samuele
Wang, Shenghui
Xu, Tong
Zeinalipour, Demetris
Zou, Meiyuan

Contents – Part II

Special Session Papers

Contents – Part I

Cultivating Expressivity and Communication in Robotic Objects: An Exploration into Adaptive Human-Robot Interaction

Pablo Osorio[1]([⊠]) [ID], Hisham Khalil[2] [ID], Siméon Capy[1] [ID],
and Gentiane Venture[2] [ID]

[1] Tokyo University of Agriculture and Technology, Fuchu, Japan
s202108v@st.go.tuat.ac.jp
[2] The University of Tokyo, Tokyo, Japan
{hishamkhalil,venture}@g.ecc.u-tokyo.ac.jp

Abstract. This work introduces a model to personalize 'robjects' - everyday objects with embedded robotic capabilities - using deep reinforcement learning (RL). The method creates user mood maps from emotional states and environmental conditions, allowing the robot to convey its status via light and movement. Two RL agents, with distinct reward systems, are deployed: The motor agent aligns the robot's expression with the human emotion, while the light agent correlates with the robot's expression adherence to the Pleasure-Arousal-Dominance (PAD) scale. The learning process establishes a base model for real-world use, starting with synthetic interactions in simulation. This model underwent a 10-day experiment aimed at assessing the model's reception and user experience. The model enabled continuous interaction; all participants reported a pleasant experience, expressing the desire to continue interacting with it. The robot's adaptivity is highlighted by a mean Jensen-Shannon distance of 0.334 between user emotion and the robot expression distributions, showcasing a responsive, adaptive model.

Keywords: Human-robot interaction · Intelligent robots · Adaptive robots · Deep reinforcement learning

1 Introduction

In our contemporary world, interactive technologies are increasingly becoming integral components of our daily lives, finding roles in homes and offices. However, over time, the novelty and engagement of these interactions often diminish, leading to the products being replaced, repurposed, or discarded [19]. This emerging pattern raises significant questions for social robots about the need for strategic human-robot interaction design that prevents monotony, fosters a gradual and sustained engagement over time, and maintains the robot's usefulness [13]. As Maze and Redström [24] astutely observe, understanding an object unfolds over time, necessitating that the object has sufficient time to reveal

Fig. 1. Experimental setup: On the left, the robot, Yōkobo, can be observed with its components labeled. On the right, a participant interacts with it.

itself to us. Consequently, individuals must actively use interactive technology to appreciate its value and capabilities truly.

The concept of fostering long-term interactions for reflection and introspection is prevalent in the fields of human-computer interaction (HCI) and human-robot interaction (HRI), partly due to the philosophy of *slow technology*, as introduced by Hallnäs and Redström [14]. This concept promotes the design of technologies that integrate seamlessly into people's daily lives for extended durations. Various interactive technologies, like Chronoscope [5], PhotoBox [30], and Yōkobo [9], embody this approach, evoking feelings of unity, nostalgia, and appreciation for memorable moments. These designs shift focus from functionality to understanding nuanced user experiences and interactions [29]. With many social robots envisioned to cohabit with us, a critical question arises: *How can these robots adapt, evolve, and mature in line with their users, given the continuously changing world and personal growth of users?*

Personalization is crucial in the evolution of social robots and interactive interfaces. Studies suggest that robots can enhance the user experience by incorporating engagement concepts, leading to heightened enjoyment and sustained interactions [11,32,37]. Robots can be gradually tailored to match user characteristics and preferences, optimizing the user experience [31]. Furthermore, personalization can boost long-term user engagement by adapting to users' personalities and likes and recalling shared experiences [33]. Tailored interactions can also enhance rapport and trust between users and robots [3,21].

Existing studies have focused on creating robjects within the animacy level of interaction, only displaying signs of movement, answering the question of whether its movements are autonomous or not [2,10,20]. In this work, we explore a method to move from this animacy level to a mental agency level within which the object's intention will reflect other users' interactions and its environment.

Previous research has fostered sustained interaction and engagement using adaptive behavioral techniques like deep reinforcement learning [1,39]. Specifically, Deep Q-Networks (DQN) have been shown to successfully associate environmental stimuli with robot actions inspired by biological behaviors [22]. Moreover, integrating emotions into reward systems has positive responses towards emotionally intelligent robots [27]. Thus, by incorporating reinforcement learning techniques into a robject, it is possible to obtain an adaptive system that can increase the agency level of a robject initially designed for a reduced set of communication capabilities.

The contributions of this work include the development of an adaptive model that enables robots, with a reduced set of non-verbal expressive mediums, to engage and adapt to their users through unscripted interactions over extended periods. The model continuously learns from the user's current emotional states and environmental conditions. Designed to evolve, the model is initially trained using a synthetic dataset of potential interactions, providing the robot with a foundational framework for adaptivity. Furthermore, we present an experimental protocol to assess both the instantaneous and long-term user experience under real-world conditions. Three participants in unscripted scenarios evaluate the model's user experience and evolution over time. This work unlocks a venue for fostering meaningful interactions with robots through a reduced set of non-verbal expressive mediums.

2   Extending Interactions for an Abstract Robject

This work enhances the interaction capabilities of a robject, Yōkobo, a dual-function robot acting as a key bowl and an interactive channel for household communication [4,9] (see Fig. 1). Using light and movement, Yōkobo interacts based on proxemics principles, with modes such as *Rest*, *State of the House*, and *Mimic*, reflecting house conditions or mimicking user movements [4,9]. Yōkobo's design comprises a base, a body, an apex, and a bowl.

Yōkobo perceives its environment using indoor and outdoor smart home system sensors (humidity, atmospheric pressure (AP), air quality (CO_2), and temperature) and an onboard camera for user body positions. There is potential for enhancement by integrating emotion recognition, allowing Yōkobo to understand user emotions and expand its communication capabilities, as emotions trigger a range of human actions [27]. Moreover, as presented by Wensveen et al. [38], systems must recognize emotional aspects to be truly adaptive.

Yōkobo, by understanding indoor and external environmental conditions, user body positions, and emotional states, constructs a 'mood map,' capturing the relationships between these data points. This map informs Yōkobo's behaviors while providing historical context.

By allowing the robot to learn independently from a given representation, it can develop its understanding of the world, leading to new behaviors. Initially, the robot's light and movement communication methods can be viewed as two separate agents, aiding in explainability.

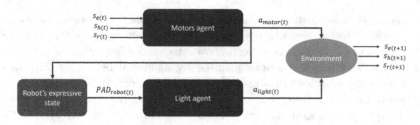

Fig. 2. Architecture of the adaptive model: This comprises three main components: the motors agent, the light agent, and the robot's expressive state. At each timestep t, the motors agent processes environmental signals $(s_{e(t)})$, human body position and emotional state $(s_{h(t)})$, robot's motor positions and expressive state $(s_{r(t)})$, generating robot actions $(a_{motor(t)})$. The robot's Pleasure-Arousal-Dominance (PAD) state $(PAD_{robot(t)})$ is computed in the Robot's expressive state block, serving as input for the light agent, which in turn, produces light actions $(a_{light(t)})$. These outputs interact with the environment, informing the state at the subsequent timestep.

2.1   Building an Adaptive Model

To address the high memory usage and computational complexity involved in environmental exploration, deep neural networks are employed for function approximation and data manipulation, enabling the management of complex environments. The DQN method [26] is chosen for its ability to learn the mapping between states and actions for both light and movement agents.

The adaptive model, shown in Fig. 2, consists of light and motor agents and the robot's expression. The motor agent receives an array of environmental data, including indoor and outdoor smart home system sensors, the user's emotional state, motor positions, the robot's current expressive state, and the user's trajectory estimation. The environmental data is used since it has a direct impact on the human's mood [35]. The user's movement direction, focused on the hip center, is estimated using a linear function of the two most recent positions, assuming users at home entrances move steadily. This linear approximation is suitable given that Yōkobo is designed for the home entrances. Based on this information, the motor agent determines the motor actions, maintains, increases, or decreases the motor positions, and the robot then adjusts its motors.

These actions are then transferred to the robot's expressive state component. The robot's expressive state is computed following the principles described in [6]. This involves correlating the PAD scale [25] with different motion elements. Pleasure is inversely proportional to jerk, arousal aligns with kinematic energy, and dominance corresponds to the robot's gaze.

Despite Yōkobo's lack of eyes, users perceive its apex as the head and the vent as *eyes* [4]. A lower apex implies lower dominance, meaning Yōkobo looking down, and vice versa. The PAD values inform the light agent, which maps Yōkobo's expression to brightness and color. The agent selects from ten colors, adjusting brightness accordingly. Table 1 outlines the relationship between the agent's color palette, PAD values, and expressions.

Table 1. Relation between expression, PAD, and color: The mappings are based on the sources [8, 12, 16, 25, 36], with exceptions for *neutral* and *curious* expressions. The *neutral* expression is associated with the null PAD value and is represented by white, a color traditionally considered neutral. As for the *curious* expression, there was no definitive color mapping in the literature. For this study, green was selected as the representative color for *curiosity*.

Expression	P	A	D	Color	Expression	P	A	D	Color
angry	-0.51	0.59	0.25	RED	violent	-0.50	0.62	0.38	RED
bored	-0.65	-0.62	-0.33	WHITE	sad	-0.63	-0.27	-0.33	VIOLET
curious	0.22	0.62	-0.01	GREEN	happy	0.81	0.51	0.46	YELLOW
elated	0.50	0.42	0.23	YELLOW	surprised	0.40	0.67	-0.13	WHITE
hungry	-0.44	0.14	-0.21	ORANGE	fearful	-0.64	0.60	-0.43	VIOLET
loved	0.87	0.54	-0.18	PINK	relaxed	0.68	-0.46	0.06	GREEN
sleepy	0.20	-0.70	-0.44	BLUE	neutral	0.00	0.00	0.00	WHITE

The emotion estimation algorithm used to identify possible human emotions understands four different labels: neutral, happy, sad, and angry. This algorithm is the emotion estimation method from the OpenVINO suite [15]. They must be grouped into the same four categories to correlate these emotions with the robot's expressions (see Table 1). This grouping uses the PAD values norm, aligning values closest to one of the four emotions.

The training process for the algorithm necessitates specific reward definitions for each DQN agent based on their assigned roles and interaction methods. For the light agent, the goal is to sync the light with Yōkobo's current expressive state. Thus, if the algorithm selects a color that matches the one that represents the robot's expressive state, as seen in Table 1, a positive reward is provided; otherwise, a negative reward is given. To prevent random or sudden color changes in Yōkobo, penalties are applied if the color varies at each timestep within the last five steps. Similarly, penalties are issued if the color remains unchanged, promoting the exploration of different mappings. Finally, a positive reward is granted if the new color is similar to the previous one (i.e. a transition from *green* to *cyan*). Table 2 summarizes the rewards. Through practical experimentation, these values were found to provoke an optimal response from the agent.

The motor agent learns to map internal and external state conditions to motor actions, using a reward system grounded in the robot's expressive state and the user's emotions. The objective is for the robot to reflect the user's expression over time. Rewards are calculated using the Kullback-Leibler (KL) divergence (refer to Eq. 1). The KL is used since it measures how different one probability distribution is from another. Equation 2 defines the reward $R_{(t)}$, which considers both Yōkobo's expressive distribution, $P_{r(t)}$, and the user's emotional data, $P_{h(t)}$ at time t for i expressions. As the two distributions align, the KL divergence value drops. To elevate the reward, the negative logarithm is applied to the KL divergence, which is then multiplied by a variable λ; set at 10 for KL

Table 2. The rewards of the DQN algorithm for the light agent.

	Continuous reward
The color matches with the PAD	3
The color does *not* match with the PAD	−3
The new color is close to the previous one	2
The color has changed each step for the last 5	−1
The color stayed the same each step for the last 5	−2

divergence values under 1 and 2 for those over 1.

$$D_{KL}(P_{r(t)}||P_{h(t)}) = \sum_i P_{r(t)}(i) \log \left(\frac{P_{r(t)}(i)}{P_{h(t)}(i)} \right), \tag{1}$$

$$R_{(t)} = -\log(D_{KL}(P_{r(t)}||P_{h(t)})) \cdot \lambda. \tag{2}$$

2.2 Model Integration with a Robject

Understanding the integration approach is essential to embed the learning process and agents into Yōkobo's software architecture. The adaptive model behavior is structured as a Finite State Machine (FSM) with states: *Idle*, *Online*, and *Dream*. The *Idle* state awaits activation commands for agent learning or real-time use. *Online* facilitates commands for both agents during user interaction, saving associated data. In the *Dream* state, agents learn from past interactions using stored sensor data and users' emotions. This FSM is depicted in Fig. 3.

Yōkobo's main FSM structure is based on proxemics, with each state corresponding to the user's distance from the robot. Further details of Yōkobo's FSM are presented in [4]. The adaptive model is designed to adapt to the user's mood map and operate within the inner circle of the interaction, close to the *Mimic* state-the most intimate state. The adaptive model's FSM transitions to the *Online* state to start the interaction when the RFID tag identifies the user in the *Mimic* state. The *Dream* state commences when Yōkobo is in the *Rest* state, allowing the algorithm to train without interruption. Otherwise, the algorithm stays in the *Idle* state. The NEP [7] framework was used for communication between different FSMs, onboard systems, cameras, and body position and emotion recognition algorithms.

3   Experimental Setup

To evaluate the algorithm's initial performance, reception, and user experience, an unscripted experiment for 10 day is conducted inside the laboratory space at the University of Tokyo (see Fig. 1). This time frame enables participants to bypass the novelty effect and become familiar with the robot's functionalities.

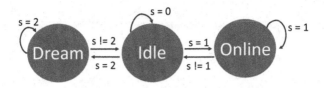

Fig. 3. FSM algorithm: Each state denotes a specific phase of the algorithm's behavior. The variable **s** symbolizes the command sent from Yōkobo's primary decision FSM. When the value of **s** is 0, it represents a waiting stage or *Idle*. The value of 1 is assigned when Yōkobo's FSM transitions to the *Mimic* state, whereas a value of 2 is given when Yōkobo's FSM shifts to the *Rest* state.

Moreover, participants were free to interact whenever, and however they seemed fit with the robot. Three participants were involved. This sample size is decided since, with this number, according to Nielsen et al. [28], more than 50% of all usability problems can be discovered. Furthermore, since the adaptive model must learn during the *Dream* stage the most up-to-date mood map of the participant, this sample size will enable hardware limitations to be bypassed and the model to converge without difficulties between sessions.

The qualitative methods of the User Experience (UX) Curve [18], and the Graffiti Wall [23] are used to evaluate the model's reception and the user experience with the robot. The UX curve enables users to draw and annotate their long-term experiences, capturing attributes like attractiveness, ease of use, degree of usage, utility, and general user experience. Moreover, it allows participants to reminisce about their experience with the robot and provides a tool for self-expression. The Graffiti wall allows us to capture instantaneous feelings that the robot might trigger. Three questions were asked to collect information regarding the perceptions of the robot's and the current participant's mood. This tool allows participants to express their impressions freely. The final tool is the UX Questionnaire (UEQ) [34]. It is applied twice, once at the beginning of the experiment after the first interaction with the robject and its adaptive model and a second time at the end of the experiment right after their final interaction. Applying the questionnaire twice makes it possible to measure the difference between the initial experience and how it evolved during the 10 days.

4 Results and Discussion

4.1 Learning from Synthetic Interactions

The training is conducted to obtain a base model using a simulation approach. This base model is desired for each agent to avoid random behaviors, setting up an initial interaction framework that regulates movement and light responses. The model is learned in simulation from synthetic interactions that mirror real ones. Each training episode, representing a single interaction, lasts 30 s to a minute, reflecting the average interaction time with Yōkobo based on prior studies [4]. The inputs for the adaptive model are generated by random sampling

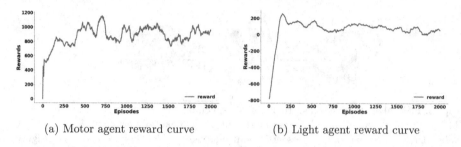

(a) Motor agent reward curve   (b) Light agent reward curve

Fig. 4. Reward of the models during training: Fig. 4a shows an increasing trend for the motor agent, stabilizing after 1000 episodes. In contrast, Fig. 4b displays a decreasing trend for the light agent after episode 250.

from predefined distributions. The user position, which follows a linear path, is either augmented or reduced by a constant factor linearly. The human emotion data is drawn from a uniform distribution, based on the four possible labels of the emotion recognition algorithm, across the entire training episode. The robot's expressive state, the motor position of Yōkobo, and the user's position are updated at each step, which are obtained based on the model outputs in simulation. Environmental conditions like humidity, air quality, temperature, and atmospheric pressure are predicted to follow a normal distribution, except atmospheric pressure, which is uniformly distributed. All environmental conditions values reflect the conditions of June in Tokyo, Japan.

Both agents are trained using a sequential structure, employing a two-hidden layer neural network featuring Leaky ReLU as the activation function. Stability in learning is enhanced through a t-soft update on the target network with $\tau = 0.005$ [17]. The DQNs utilize a learning rate 0.0001 and apply Huber Loss as the loss function. The discount factor is set as 0.9. Simulation training occurred over 2000 episodes with a random step length ranging between 300 to 500 to simulate the variability in user interaction time.

Figure 4 illustrates each model's cumulative reward across episodes. Both models indicate that as training proceeds, the reward increases, yielding a model that more closely aligns with the human expressive distribution, adequately recognizing the associated PAD, and effectively conveying the corresponding state through light. The learning curve of the motor agent, depicted in Fig. 4a, displays significant learning improvement over iterations, ultimately stabilizing after 1000 episodes. In contrast, Fig. 4b demonstrates stabilization around episode 250. Following training, both models are preserved and will serve as the initial version of the agents for each participant in the real-world deployment.

4.2   Long-Term Interactions

Once the base models were established, they were deployed for real-world experiments, allowing continuous learning from each user-robot interaction over 10 days. Participants engaged with the robot without set guidelines. On average,

interactions lasted six minutes, surpassing the typical 90-second interaction with
Yōkobo as noted in [4]. This extended time, they facilitated user familiarization
with the robot. Consistent interaction duration, as corroborated by participants'
UX curves for Degree of Usage (see Fig. 5b), ensured that the novelty effect dis-
sipated [19]. This allows innovative adaptive interactions to occur, given that
users were acquainted with the robot's motor movements and light changes.

After each interaction with the robot, participants provided feedback on the
Graffiti Wall, answering the questions "How do you feel today?", "How is Yōkobo
feeling today?" and "How do you feel after interacting with Yōkobo?". Early
feedback indicated initial confusion and intrigue, with some participants initially
unsure of the robot's actions. This uncertainty was reflected in the UX curves for
Participants 1 and 2, as seen in Fig. 5a. However, by day four, participants began
recognizing the robot's adaptivity, with remarks on the Graffiti Wall like "It was
exhausted like me!" highlighting its resonance with their moods. Participants
also noted a feeling of freshness, curiosity, and happiness after interacting with

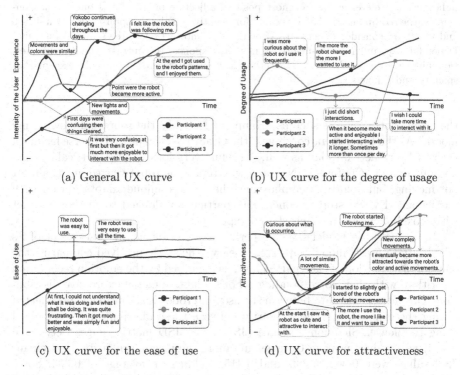

Fig. 5. UX curves by the three participants: This graphic shows the UX trend for all
participants, each denoted with a different color: light blue for Participant 1, red for
Participant 2, and green for Participant 3. Alongside the curves, participants' comments
at key points are also depicted. Figure 5a shows the general UX curve, Fig. 5b the degree
of usage, Fig. 5c the ease of use and Fig. 5d the attractiveness. All plots show a positive
trend, with most lines remaining in the positive area (denoted with a + sign).

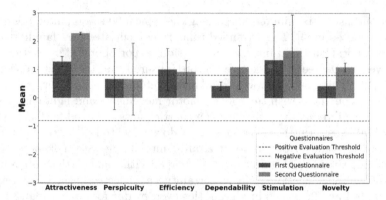

Fig. 6. Comparative analysis of UEQ scales across two questionnaires: This bar plot contrasts results from two UEQs: one following the initial robot interaction and another after the final interaction, displaying mean values and variances for each scale. The green line represents the threshold for positive results, with any value above 0.800 indicating a preference for the most positive adjective on the UEQ questions. Conversely, the red line marks the threshold for negative results. Responses between -0.800 and 0.800 are considered neutral. After the first interaction, three scales-Perspicuity, Dependability, and Novelty-favored a neutral response. In contrast, the second questionnaire, filled after the final interaction, saw improvements in all scales except Perspicuity and Efficiency.

the robot, noting points such as "Happy, it feels like the robot is following my mood." As the experiment continued, the Graffiti Wall captured diverse feedback such as "Very active today as well," "Feeling very 'otonashi' [quiet, calm], cute and quiet" and "Confused... Not sure why today the robot was so quiet, almost not moving, but colorful," emphasizing the robot's unique adaptation for each participant. By the study's conclusion, participants longed to further interact with Yōkobo, cherishing their shared experiences.

To evaluate the model's post-experiment performance, an assessment of its adaptivity to users' mood maps is necessary. The study involved comparing the emotion distribution of each participant, as identified by the emotion recognition algorithm, with their corresponding robot's adaptive model expressive distribution. This interaction data between the user and robot was continuously collected during the experiment. The similarity between these distributions was gauged using the Jensen-Shannon distance (JSD). The JSD metric ranges between 0 and 1, with values nearing 0 suggesting more significant similarity. Participant JSD values were 0.302, 0.286, and 0.415, yielding an average of 0.334. Some discrepancies can be attributed to neutral expression, which may be perceived as inactivity when exhibited by the robot. Though with occasional pauses, this led to a bias towards frequent movement in the adaptive model. Although the distributions are not identical, the JSD values below 0.5 highlight distribution similarities. Feedback from the Graffiti Wall and UX curves emphasized that participants felt Yōkobo increasingly resonated with their behaviors and moods.

The UEQ results at both the beginning and end of the experiment (refer to Fig. 6) bolster the slow technology concept, highlighting the progression from the initial to final interactions. Surprisingly, hedonic qualities, Stimulation, and Novelty increased their ratings, defying the *novelty effect*. The Novelty scale rose by 0.666 while reducing the variance by 0.870. Meanwhile, the Stimulation scale saw a 0.334 increment. The UX curves corroborate this for Degree of Usage and General UX (see Fig. 5a and 5b respectively). All participants reported improved general UX by the experiment's end, and all but one showed increased usage-the outlier maintained a consistent trend. Initially, interactions were deemed perplexing. Over time, the once monotonous interactions became "pleasant and elegant," akin to "watering a plant or observing art."

Regarding the UEQ's pragmatic qualities (Perspicuity, Efficiency, and Dependability), results indicated a modest rise, especially in the Dependability scale, which grew by 0.666. However, its variance also widened from 0.150 to 0.770, suggesting emerging consensus without unanimity. Notably, all these task-oriented metrics remained positive, except for Perspicuity, which was neutral. Participant feedback reflected this: initially uncertain of the robot's expressions, and they observed its range of motions, like single motor movements. Over time, as the robot adapted, its interactions diversified into intricate movements yet remained somewhat ambiguous. These outcomes align with Yōkobo's intent, which is not task-centric but designed for reflection and contemplation. Comments from the UX Utility curve reveal participants did not anticipate functional utility from the robot. However, over time, they began imagining specific roles for it, like cheering up or serving as a contemplative break. They felt the robot achieved these unintended functions. Additionally, the UX curve on Ease of Use (see Fig. 5c) demonstrated that interacting with the robot seamlessly integrated into participants' routines as the days went by.

The final UX quality, Attractiveness, showed significant consensus in the UEQ results. It rose by 1.000, reducing the variance to 0.040. As time progressed, participants found interactions with the robot increasingly appealing. One participant remarked on the UX Curve of Attractiveness (see Fig. 5d), "The more I use the robot, the more I like it and want to continue using it." Others echoed this sentiment, with their feedback highlighting the attractiveness of unscripted, free interactions. The adaptive model allowed diverse interactions, maintaining sustained allure over time.

5   Conclusion and Future Work

This work introduced a method for personalizing robots with reduced non-verbal expressive mediums. The adaptive algorithm takes as input its users' "mood maps", a collection of users' emotions, body position during the interaction, and the data from the environment surrounding them, and uses these historical data of interactions to reason about their behavior, adapting to them. By harnessing deep reinforcement learning techniques, we could couple our method with a robject, Yōkobo, enabling it to communicate its state effectively non-verbally through light and movement.

The approach provided a controlled environment for training robotic behaviors from simulation to the real world. We ensured a realistic base representation of human-robot interactions by crafting synthetic interactions to mirror real-life scenarios. After obtaining this base model, it is integrated with Yōkobo's existing framework to validate the adaptive model's user experience, reception, and performance. This experimental test consisted of a 10-day experiment with unscripted scenarios with three participants.

Our results, highlighted by the decrease in the JSD between the participants' emotions and the robot's expressive distribution, confirmed our approach's efficacy. The results from the UEQ showcase how the interaction improves over time, and the participants' feedback shows that they perceived the changes in the robot and how it manages to adapt to specific task preferences, even if it was not designed with that particular purpose. Moreover, the general user experience at the end of the experiment is positive, and the robject powered by the adaptive algorithm is easy to use and understand, develops over time, and enables a meaningful experience that participants noted they would like to continue having. The ability of our agents to adapt their behaviors based on human emotions and environmental conditions suggests a promising avenue for incorporating adaptive social robots in real-world, long-term settings.

Future work will delve deeper into refining these models, combining both agents into one, exploring other algorithms such as actor-critic or proximal policy optimization for continuous exploration, examining more diverse environmental conditions, user preference recognition, and testing with a broader range of human subjects and robots.

References

1. Akalin, N., Loutfi, A.: Reinforcement learning approaches in social robotics. Sensors **21**(4), 1292 (2021)
2. Anderson-Bashan, L., et al.: The greeting machine: an abstract robotic object for opening encounters. In: 2018 27th IEEE International Symposium on Robot and Human Interactive Communication (RO-MAN), pp. 595–602. IEEE (2018)
3. Belgiovine, G., Gonzalez-Billandon, J., Sandini, G., Rea, F., Sciutti, A.: Towards an HRI tutoring framework for long-term personalization and real-time adaptation. In: Adjunct Proceedings of the 30th ACM Conference on User Modeling, Adaptation and Personalization, pp. 139–145 (2022)
4. Capy, S., et al.: Yōkobo: a robot to strengthen links amongst users with non-verbal behaviours. Machines **10**(8), 708 (2022)
5. Chen, A.Y.S., Odom, W., Zhong, C., Lin, H., Amram, T.: Chronoscope: designing temporally diverse interactions with personal digital photo collections. In: Proceedings of the 2019 on Designing Interactive Systems Conference, pp. 799–812 (2019)
6. Claret, J.A., Venture, G., Basañez, L.: Exploiting the robot kinematic redundancy for emotion conveyance to humans as a lower priority task. Int. J. Soc. Robot. **9**(2), 277–292 (2017)
7. Coronado, E., Venture, G.: Towards IoT-aided human-robot interaction using NEP and ROS: a platform-independent. Accessible and distributed approach. Sensors **20**(5), 1500 (2020)

8. Demir, Ü.: Investigation of color-emotion associations of the university students. Color. Res. Appl. **45**(5), 871–884 (2020)
9. Deuff, D., et al.: Together alone, Yōkobo, a sensible presence robject for the home of newly retired couples. In: Designing Interactive Systems Conference, pp. 1773–1787 (2022)
10. Erel, H., et al.: Excluded by robots: can robot-robot-human interaction lead to ostracism? In: Proceedings of the 2021 ACM/IEEE International Conference on Human-Robot Interaction, pp. 312–321 (2021)
11. Gehle, R., Pitsch, K., Dankert, T., Wrede, S.: How to open an interaction between robot and museum visitor?: strategies to establish a focused encounter in HRI. In: Proceedings of the 2017 ACM/IEEE International Conference on Human-Robot Interaction, pp. 187–195 (2017)
12. Gilbert, A.N., Fridlund, A.J., Lucchina, L.A.: The color of emotion: a metric for implicit color associations. Food Qual. Prefer. **52**, 203–210 (2016)
13. de Graaf, M.M., Ben Allouch, S., Van Dijk, J.A.: Why would i use this in my home? A model of domestic social robot acceptance. Hum.-Comput. Interact. **34**(2), 115–173 (2019)
14. Hallnäs, L., Redström, J.: Slow technology-designing for reflection. Pers. Ubiquit. Comput. **5**, 201–212 (2001)
15. Intel Corporation: OpenVINO Toolkit (2021). https://software.intel.com/content/www/us/en/develop/tools/openvino-toolkit.html. Accessed 20 Aug 2023
16. Kaya, N., Epps, H.H.: Relationship between color and emotion: a study of college students. Coll. Stud. J. **38**(3), 396–405 (2004)
17. Kobayashi, T., Ilboudo, W.E.L.: t-soft update of target network for deep reinforcement learning. Neural Netw. **136**, 63–71 (2021)
18. Kujala, S., Roto, V., Väänänen-Vainio-Mattila, K., Karapanos, E., Sinnelä, A.: UX curve: a method for evaluating long-term user experience. Interact. Comput. **23**(5), 473–483 (2011)
19. Leite, I., Martinho, C., Paiva, A.: Social robots for long-term interaction: a survey. Int. J. Soc. Robot. **5**, 291–308 (2013)
20. Levillain, F., Zibetti, E.: Behavioral objects: the rise of the evocative machines. J. Hum.-Robot Interact. **6**(1), 4–24 (2017)
21. Ligthart, M.E., Neerincx, M.A., Hindriks, K.V.: Memory-based personalization for fostering a long-term child-robot relationship. In: 2022 17th ACM/IEEE International Conference on Human-Robot Interaction (HRI), pp. 80–89 (2022)
22. Maroto-Gómez, M., Malfaz, M., Castro-González, Á., Salichs, M.Á.: Deep reinforcement learning for the autonomous adaptive behavior of social robots. In: Proceedings of the 2022 International Conference on Social Robotics, pp. 208–217 (2023)
23. Martin, B., Hanington, B.: Universal Methods of Design: 100 Ways to Research Complex Problems, Develop Innovative Ideas, and Design Effective Solutions. Rockport Publishers (2012)
24. Mazé, R., Redström, J.: Form and the computational object. Digital Creativity **16**(1), 7–18 (2005)
25. Mehrabian, A.: Basic Dimensions for a General Psychological Theory: Implications for Personality, Social, Environmental, and Developmental Studies (1980)
26. Mnih, V., et al.: Human-level control through deep reinforcement learning. Nature **518**(7540), 529–533 (2015)
27. Moerland, T.M., Broekens, J., Jonker, C.M.: Emotion in reinforcement learning agents and robots: a survey. Mach. Learn. **107**, 443–480 (2018)

28. Nielsen, J., Landauer, T.K.: A mathematical model of the finding of usability problems. In: Proceedings of the INTERACT'93 and CHI'93 Conference on Human Factors in Computing Systems, pp. 206–213 (1993)

29. Odom, W., Stolterman, E., Chen, A.Y.S.: Extending a theory of slow technology for design through artifact analysis. Hum.-Comput. Interact. 37(2), 150–179 (2022)

30. Odom, W.T., et al.: Designing for slowness, anticipation and re-visitation: a long term field study of the Photobox. In: Proceedings of the SIGCHI Conference on Human Factors in Computing Systems, pp. 1961–1970 (2014)

31. Pollmann, K., Loh, W., Fronemann, N., Ziegler, D.: Entertainment vs. manipulation: personalized human-robot interaction between user experience and ethical design. Technol. Forecast. Soc. Change 189, 122376 (2023)

32. Ritschel, H., Aslan, I., Mertes, S., Seiderer, A., André, E.: Personalized synthesis of intentional and emotional non-verbal sounds for social robots. In: 2019 8th International Conference on Affective Computing and Intelligent Interaction (ACII), pp. 1–7 (2019)

33. Saunders, J., Syrdal, D.S., Koay, K.L., Burke, N., Dautenhahn, K.: "Teach Me-Show Me"-end-user personalization of a smart home and companion robot. IEEE Trans. Hum.-Mach. Syst. 46(1), 27–40 (2015)

34. Schrepp, M., Thomaschewski, J., Hinderks, A.: Construction of a benchmark for the user experience questionnaire (UEQ). Int. J. Interact. Multimedia Artif. Intell. 4(4), 40–44 (2017)

35. Spasova, Z.: The effect of weather and its changes on emotional state-individual characteristics that make us vulnerable. Adv. Sci. Res. 6(1), 281–290 (2012)

36. Sutton, T.M., Altarriba, J.: Color associations to emotion and emotion-laden words: a collection of norms for stimulus construction and selection. Behav. Res. Methods 48(2), 686–728 (2016)

37. Vigni, F., Rossi, S.: Exploring non-verbal strategies for initiating an HRI. In: Proceedings of the 2022 International Conference on Social Robotics, pp. 280–289 (2023)

38. Wensveen, S., Overbeeke, K., Djajadiningrat, T.: Touch me, hit me and I know how you feel: a design approach to emotionally rich interaction. In: Proceedings of the 3rd Conference on Designing Interactive Systems: Processes, Practices, Methods, and Techniques, pp. 48–52 (2000)

39. Zhang, Z., Jiang, W., Zhang, R., Zheng, Y., Ge, S.S.: Robot differential behavioral expression in different scenarios. In: Proceedings of the 2022 International Conference on Social Robotics, pp. 451–462 (2023)

Pepper as a Learning Partner in a Children's Hospital

Sara Zarubica and Oliver Bendel[✉]

School of Business FHNW, 5210 Windisch, Switzerland
`oliver.bendel@fhnw.ch`

Abstract. Social robots are increasingly used in learning settings. So far, the main focus of this has been in school lessons and teaching at universities. Another possible setting is the children's hospital. There, for example, young patients need to acquire basic knowledge about their disease so that they can deal with it appropriately. This should be done in a joyful, fun way, as the situation is stressful enough in itself, and so learning is also facilitated. The paper presents a learning application for diabetic children that runs on Pepper. This social robot was particularly well suited for this task because it has a large integrated touchscreen, similar to a tablet. A learning game is displayed on it that was developed especially for this setting. The children have to estimate the carbohydrate values of foods and meals or answer knowledge questions. The social robot gives verbal and gestural feedback in each case. The subjects responded overwhelmingly positively to the learning application. Pepper's visible and audible feedback plays a special role in this. Social robots like Pepper are an interesting solution for knowledge transfer in a children's hospital.

Keywords: Social Robots · Learning Application · Healthcare

1 Introduction

Social robots are used in a variety of ways in the healthcare sector [3, 4, 17], e.g., in nursing homes and homes for the elderly, and sometimes in hospitals. They are very important in the learning area [1]. Teaching of healthcare learning content occurs now and then. Mostly, however, these robots offer purely practical information to visitors and patients or encourage people in need of care to move and talk. Entertainment purposes are also not uncommon. Robots such as Pepper, NAO, and Robin are mainly used for information, animation, and knowledge transfer [2, 7, 14].

Diabetes mellitus type 1 is a common metabolic disease associated with insulin deficiency. It affects not only adults, but also children. If they are old enough, they can inject themselves with insulin. The required dose depends, among other things, on the amount of carbohydrates in the meals. However, estimating this requires some knowledge and a lot of practice. Therefore, it is important that children and their guardians and family members or caregivers receive training. In the diabetology department of the Children's Hospital in Bern (an Inselspital facility), nutritional counseling regarding

© The Author(s), under exclusive license to Springer Nature Singapore Pte Ltd. 2024
A. Al. Ali et al. (Eds.): ICSR 2023, LNAI 14454, pp. 15–26, 2024.
https://doi.org/10.1007/978-981-99-8718-4_2

the carbohydrate content of the diet takes place once a month [17]. This ties up staff and costs time and money. It would be desirable to have a learning application through which children could independently learn about diabetes, the dietary changes it forces, and the associated treatment. In this way, relevant knowledge could also be taught in a standardized way.

The School of Business FHNW approached the Inselspital Bern in March 2022 to inform them about the possibilities of social robots in the healthcare sector. The idea of using a model of Pepper from the Robot Lab of the university to teach about diabetes mellitus type 1 was initiated [17]. This social robot is suitable for interaction and communication with children due to its humanoid, cartoonish design, its size of 1.20 m, its large eyes and convincing eye contact, and its childlike speech. Its frequent use in different contexts also spoke in favor of Pepper, as did the fact that it is produced again after a break. Previously, other social robots such as NAO had been used primarily in this context [13–15]. The disadvantage of most of them is that they do not have a built in screen.

During its stays at the hospital, Pepper was supposed to offer learning software via its display in the chest area and to give verbal and gestural feedback to the children. The unit of Pepper and the learning software in combination will here be called learning application. The Inselspital took over the commissioning, the first author the project management and the application development (thus the contracting), and the second author the support and the consulting. The project started in April 2022 and lasted until August 2022. A prototype was created and tested on two small groups of children. In August 2023, the children's hospital was contacted regarding the actual use of the learning application.

This paper presents a learning software for children with diabetes that runs on the social robot Pepper. The second section lists examples of the use of Pepper in the health-care sector. The third section describes the preparation and implementation of the project in the children's hospital. The individual elements of the learning application – which contains a learning game that is, at its core, a quiz – are described. The fourth section is devoted to outlining tests with the groups of children in the children's hospital. In the final section, after a summary, an outlook is given.

2 Pepper in the Health Sector

Alongside NAO, Pepper is one of the robots that are used particularly frequently in the healthcare sector when information, communication, or entertainment are required [5, 14, 15]. Its natural language and gestural abilities make it a fitting candidate for these requirements. Three concrete examples of Pepper's use follow [17]. Two projects are mentioned that are specifically aimed at children and adolescents. The first one focuses on the information function, the other two on knowledge transfer [4].

In a study conducted at Townsville Hospital in Queensland, Pepper was installed as a concierge [9]. Its task was to provide patients and visitors with basic information about the hospital and to answer frequently asked questions that nursing staff did not have time to answer, such as how to get a coffee or where the exits are [11]. This corresponds to a partial automation of standard processes and information provision in the hospital.

Since early 2018, Pepper has been used as a caregiver on the Child Life team at Humber River Hospital in Toronto, Ontario [10]. Here, it serves to reduce young patients' anxiety about upcoming treatments, increase their comfort, and educate them and their families about the treatments. For example, children are encouraged to help measure their own blood pressure so they can gain their own experience with the equipment or are accompanied by Pepper into the operating room. Another model at Humber River Hospital has similar functions to the model at Townsville Hospital.

The PAL (Personal Assistant for healthy Lifestyle) research project supported by the European Union aimed to create a diabetes coach tailored to the individual patient by using NAO and Pepper [16]. This was designed to help sufferers between the ages of seven and fourteen with disease management through interactive learning programs. One option is a question-and-answer game in which the child can face everyday life situations, such as a child's birthday party or a dessert choice, and then be tasked with making the healthiest choice. It has been shown that patients who were involved in the PAL project were much more likely to come to the clinics for regular check-ups [16].

3   Realization of the Pepper Project

3.1   Foundations of the Project

The project goals were determined with the client in March 2022. Pepper was to become an interactive learning partner with which children at Inselspital could learn the basics of estimating carbohydrate values for the daily management of type 1 diabetes mellitus [17]. For this purpose, an educational software would be programmed that enables knowledge building about diabetes with the help of the display, complemented by the communication and interaction (such as gestures) of the social robot. The playful elements should turn the educational software into a learning game. The term "learning game" or "quiz" is used in the following for the educational software, not for the whole learning application, although Pepper also contributes to the playful character. The goal was not for Pepper to be autonomous. Rather, its actions and reactions were to be pre-programmed. The client also wanted the learning application to work without Pepper, i.e., as a learning game on an external tablet.

If one considers Sect. 2, it becomes clear that the project follows on from the uses of Pepper in the healthcare sector, with the European PAL initiative showing particular proximity. In addition, existing learning games and apps for children with diabetes, like Jerry the Bear (https://www.jerrythebear.com), Diapets (https://apps.apple.com/us/app/diapets/id1052313496), or mySugr Junior (https://apkpure.com/de/mysugr-junior/com.mysugr.android.junior), served as inspiration. The robot was extended with educational software of the type shown, precisely with the aim of imparting specific knowledge about their disease to the children in a playful manner and enabling them to administer the appropriate amount of insulin to themselves.

During its stays at the children's hospital in Bern, Pepper acts as an artificial learning partner who not only has learning software on its display (which the children can run through), but also gives feedback on the child's performance and at the end like a real person (Fig. 1). It thus simulates a teacher-student relationship or a tutor-student relationship, rather than a peer-peer relationship [2]. Moreover, this also means that one can adopt elements such as praise and blame in one's programming.

Fig. 1. The developer with the learning application

3.2 Implementation of the Project

This section describes the phases of implementation. A distinction is made between analysis, conception, and actual implementation (where the results are presented). The test phase has its own section (Sect. 4).

Analysis Phase

In the analysis phase, the developer defined the requirements for the learning application and performed an analysis of the technology stack [17]. First, she identified 15 requirements. Table 1 shows the one with ID 1, representing quiz question (1), where "ID" stands for "identification number". According to this scheme, all requirements were described, namely "Display answers" (2), "Query player name" (3), "Query age" (4), "Query which module to play" (5), "Query which question type to play" (6), "Display content based on selected settings" (7), "Show correct answer" (8), "Highscore per module" (9), "Ask if you want to play again" (10), "Greeting by Pepper" (11), "Reaction of Pepper to answer" (12), "Feedback from Pepper on score achieved" (13), "Cancel game" (14), and "Game length max. 5 min" (15). This is not a specific ranking, but an arbitrary order.

Table 1. Requirement 1 [15]

ID: 1	Classification	Explanation
	Name	Present quiz question
	User Story	As a player, I want the quiz question to be displayed so I can play the quiz
	Description	A text element for the question is to be implemented in the quiz view
	Dependency	–
	Story Points	2
	Priority	1
	Type	Functional requirement

Conceptual Phase

At the beginning of this phase, the developer researched what factors to consider when designing a learning game for children [17]. These include appealing colors, age-appropriate language, targeting a specific age group, cheerful atmosphere, and ease of navigation [6, 8, 12]. She created corresponding mockups, i.e., digital designs of a website or app, which are needed in the conceptual phase to visualize ideas and concepts. The mockups were presented to the client and the supervisor, who, together with the developer, selected the final design.

In the conceptual phase, the list of questions for the quiz was also defined [17]. The goal pursued with the educational software was that the children gain an understanding of the carbohydrate content of different foods and meals. Since this varies greatly depending on the amount and the children should have a rough idea of which meal has how many carbohydrates, the use of photos was appropriate. In order to have rights-free and consistent samples, the developer cooked the meals herself and photographed them. Fruit was placed on a plate and photographed as well. Knowledge questions were added as an extension of the questionnaire. These refer to the basic diabetes knowledge and serve its repetition. Furthermore, it was important to keep the wording of the questions simple. Those with higher complexity were only added for children over ten years of age. A total of 94 estimation questions and 52 knowledge questions were defined for the questionnaire. All questions were checked by a nutrition specialist from the children's clinic.

Last but not least, the developer designed a semi-structured written survey, which was also conducted with the help of a semi-standardized questionnaire and the results of which are still summarized [17]. The purpose was to determine the children's acceptance of the learning application. A collection of questions on 1) "General patient information", 2) "Quiz", 3) "Interaction with Pepper", and 4) "Design" was compiled. For 3, the aim was to elicit whether the children liked interacting with Pepper, whether they would learn and play with it again, and whether they preferred it with a display or an external tablet without it. In this way, the team wanted to find out to what extent Pepper, with its communication and interaction, adds value to learning. In order to evaluate the design of the learning software (4), the children were asked how much they liked it, without being presented with the above alternatives.

Implementation Phase

The implementation was completed entirely by the developer. In terms of architecture, a distinction must be made between the educational software on the display and the interaction and communication functions of Pepper [17]. The developer set up a web application for the learning game using JavaScript, HTML, and CSS. The code responsible for Pepper's actions is separated into two parts. One was created using the predefined elements in Choreographe and written in Python. This is where the setup of the learning application is done (displaying the web application on the tablet and starting face recognition and face tracking). It is also used to intercept and react to external events such as the wrong answer to a question. The second author programmed the other part in JavaScript. This has the advantage that it is easy to communicate between the web application and the interaction code for Pepper, since a JavaScript SDK is available ("SDK" stands for "software development kit"). It presents the events for the first part, stores the high scores, and generates voice instructions. The contractor deliberately separated the web application from the code responsible for the interaction so that it works without Pepper.

A more detailed technical description of the implementation is not given here. Instead, the typical process of the learning application is presented [4]. The whole process is divided into four phases for clarity. In the initial process (phase 1), Pepper is started up. The child enters personal information. Transport to the hospital, unpacking the robot in the next room, etc. are not considered.

- Pepper is positioned in front of the child and started up. It performs face recognition and establishes eye contact. From this moment on, it always follows the face of the person in front of it (face tracking). It greets the child in a general way.
- At the beginning, a cover page with the title "Diabeteslernspiel" ("Diabetes learning game") is displayed on the screen, which is supposed to invite the child to play (Fig. 2). Two children are seen as cartoon characters, male and female, black and white. As soon as the player clicks on the page, the next page is opened.
- On the next page, which shows one of the characters, the player has the opportunity to type in his or her name. What is meant by this is the first name, which the child also understands intuitively. As soon as he or she enters it in the field and clicks "continue", the next page is displayed.
- On the next page, which shows the other cartoon character, the player can enter his or her approximate age (under 10 and over 10). As soon as he or she has done this, the following page is called up.

In the next step (phase 2), one can choose the game and learning conditions. One can decide between estimation and knowledge questions and choose a module.

- Next, the player can decide whether he or she prefers to answer estimation or knowledge questions ("Estimation" and "Theory"). Once he or she has made a decision, he or she is taken to the next page. In the following, the "Estimating" strand will be followed up first.

Fig. 2. Starting page of the learning game [17]

– The player can now choose a module ("Breakfast", "Side dishes", "Meal", "Snacks"). On the next page, the game is started based on the settings made in the last three steps (age included).

Now, in phase 3, we move on to the actual quiz (Fig. 3). Photos of food and meals – related to the carbohydrate estimation – are shown and questions are asked about them.

– A quiz question ("How many carbohydrates does a banana have") is displayed with the corresponding four answers (given in grams). The player can select one of the answers and click on it.
– Pepper additionally reads out each question. Its childlike, robotic standard voice is used. It moves without distracting too much – after an initial familiarization – from the learning software.
– If the question was answered incorrectly, the answer chosen by the player is marked in red and the correct answer in green. In this way, feedback is provided directly via the learning software.
– If the question was answered correctly, the answer is highlighted in green. In this case, it is not necessary for another answer to be highlighted in red.
– Alternatively, "Theory" can be clicked instead of "Estimate". This starts another form of knowledge transfer.
– On the following page, one can answer a knowledge question – just within the theory part. Food and meals are not shown. Afterwards, it proceeds as above.
– Pepper gives verbal feedback and moves. The gestures are called up randomly, so they change again and again. It matches the wrong or right answer. For example, Pepper raises its arms appreciatively for a correct answer and shakes its head and body for a wrong answer. There are a total of five (wrong answer) or four (correct answer) movements.

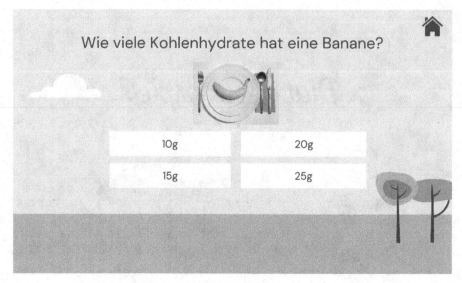

Fig. 3. A question in the learning game [17]

Now we move into the fourth, final phase of the learning application, the evaluation and feedback phase (Fig. 4).

- After the child has answered all the questions, the high score is displayed and there is an option to play the game again. In addition, a ranking list is shown to arouse ambition.
- Pepper gives overall feedback, mentioning the player's name again. For example, it says, "Oh, we're already at the end of this quiz. Well done, Sara! You got five out of eight questions right. Not bad!" (translation by the authors). As it does so, it moves its head, body, and arms.

4 Test Phase with Children

After finalization and system testing, which involved all components of the application, an acceptance test was performed [17]. In such a test, the delivered or provided software is included. It is primarily examined to what extent the tester (representing, for example, the client or the end user) gains confidence in the system. The detection of errors should already have taken place in the previous phases.

The learning application was made accessible on two half days in the pediatric clinic of the Inselspital in Bern [17]. The aforementioned survey was used. The number of participants corresponded to the number of children who had an appointment at the time of the acceptance test on site. A total of ten children participated, seven of whom were girls and three boys between the ages of seven and sixteen. The onset of diabetes of the children was between one and twelve years ago.

During the test, questions were asked about the level of difficulty and the comprehensibility of the questions in the learning game [17]. Seven out of ten children perceived the

Fig. 4. Ranking list of the learning game [17]

learning software as rather easy, two as medium and one as rather difficult. Therefore, it could be assumed that the questions are too easy. Surprisingly, the seven children who indicated a low level of difficulty answered only four and a half out of eight questions correctly on average. This suggests that there is a different problem here, such as lack of practice or estimating carbohydrates based on two-dimensional pictures. All children considered the quiz questions to be worded in an understandable way. Eight out of ten liked the interaction with Pepper very much and two children liked it moderately (Fig. 5, first tile, "Interaktion mit Pepper gefallen": "Liked interaction with Pepper"; "Sehr gut": "Very good"; "Gut": "Good"; "Mittel": "Medium"; "Geht so": "Just okay"; "Nicht gut": "Not good"). Nine would learn and play with the social robot again (Fig. 5, second tile, "Wieder mit Pepper spielen": "Playing with Pepper again"; "Ja": "Yes"; "Nein": "Nein"). Eight of the ten children preferred interacting with Pepper together with the tablet, while two preferred using the tablet alone (Fig. 5, third tile, "Bevorzuge das Spielen mit": "Prefer playing with"). The design of the learning game was liked by all ("quite well" was the best option), which is why this requirement was also met.

In addition, open questions were addressed to the girls and boys. They expressed their gratitude, for example, for the variety that the learning game brought to their clinic day. The oldest participant remarked in conversation that a tablet would be sufficient for him; in other words, he did not need a robot. One participant, who had also expressed her support for the tablet, did not comment further in conversation or free text.

It was observed that all children enjoyed the learning application. It was described as fun, interesting, and varied. Several children used the learning software repeatedly and would interact and communicate with Pepper again. They found the game and the whole setting to be an experience. An investment in Pepper, i.e., purchase or lease, would make sense for the children's hospital in that it would bring variety and joy to the otherwise rather monotonous hospital visits.

Fig. 5. Part of the evaluation of the learning game [17]

Although an evaluation with more subjects would be useful, it was not possible within the scope of the project. An analysis of the target group was not meaningful due to the small number of participants and test data. Therefore, the project refrained from doing so. In addition, it seems important to compare the use of Pepper with an integrated tablet to the use of an external tablet alone. However, there was no opportunity for this in the project due to time and cost restrictions.

The learning game was handed over to Inselspital at the end of the project. The social robot remained the property of the university. The learning software was used for some time, but never together with Pepper. Further tests of acceptance did not take place. A query to Inselspital in August 2023 determined what happened next with the learning application. Pepper was never procured due to cost. It was also feared that its use would have been too awkward. The learning game was also discontinued one day. Apparently, the people in charge were overwhelmed by it, despite its ease of use. They now prefer the monthly workshops, i.e., the traditional knowledge transfer.

5 Summary and Outlook

After a grounding in the first section and a list of application examples in the second one, this article described the preparation and implementation of the Pepper project (third section). In particular, it presented the individual elements of the learning application, i.e., the social robot and the learning game. In the fourth section, the tests with the groups of children in the hospital were discussed. In addition, the situation in the Inselspital, as it appeared one year later, was surveyed.

Pepper could be a learning partner for children in a hospital regarding various diseases, including inpatient stays [4]. It has the advantage over other models like NAO – which was used again and again in this context – in that it has an integrated touchscreen that can run educational software. It would be possible to "hire" it and involve it every day. One would have to keep in mind that bonds could develop between the children and the robot and corresponding jealousies. Supervision by an assistant or caregiver would be necessary and could help avoid such social conflicts. If the caregiver is allowed to do other tasks on the side, Pepper could be a supplement and relief for him or her.

The project demonstrated the possibilities of social robots in new learning settings. Pepper obviously motivated the children through its verbal and gestural feedback. However, it also became clear that practice can have different priorities. For example, Pepper was never able to show its qualities beyond the tests because it was not seen as available to the hospital. The initial effort to use a social robot for knowledge transfer is indeed high. In addition, there is the significant cost of models like Pepper. It needs to be investigated whether low-cost social robots are an alternative by embedding them in a learning environment and connecting them to external devices.

References

1. Belpaeme, T., Kennedy, J., Ramachandran, A., Fumihide, T.: Social robots for education: a review. Sci. Robot. **3**, eaat5954 (2018)
2. Bendel, O. (ed.): Soziale Roboter. Springer, Wiesbaden (2021). https://doi.org/10.1007/978-3-658-31114-8
3. Bendel, O. (ed.): Pflegeroboter. Springer, Wiesbaden (2018). https://doi.org/10.1007/978-3-658-22698-5
4. Bendel, O., Zarubica, S.: Pepper zu Besuch im Spital. In: Gransche, B., Bellon, J., Nähr-Wagener, S. (eds.) Technik sozialisieren? Metzler, Heidelberg, Berlin (2024)
5. Bendel, O., Gasser, A., Siebenmann, J.: Co-Robots as care robots. In: The 2020 AAAI Spring Symposium Series. ArXiv, 10 April 2020. Cornell University, Ithaca 2020. https://arxiv.org/abs/2004.04374. Accessed 14 Oct 2023
6. Bhagat, V.: Designing websites for kids: trends & best practices. https://www.feedough.com/designing-websites-for-kids/ (2020)
7. Csala, E., Németh, G., Zainkó, C.: Application of the NAO humanoid robot in the treatment of marrow-transplanted children. In: 2012 IEEE 3rd International Conference on Cognitive Infocommunications (CogInfoCom), Kosice, Slovakia, pp. 655–659 (2012)
8. Elrick, L.: Web design for kids: 10 tips for designing an age-appropriate website (2016). https://www.rasmussen.edu/degrees/design/blog/web-design-for-kids/. Accessed 14 Oct 2023
9. Fernbach, N., Rafferty, S.: Humanoid robot on the wards at townsville hospital. ABC News, 23 August 2018. https://www.abc.net.au/news/2018-08-24/townsville-hospital-trials-robot-helper/10157200. Accessed 14 Oct 2023
10. Fraser, L.: Meet pepper, Humber river hospital's Humanoid Robot (2018). https://www.hrhfoundation.ca/blog/pepper/. Accessed 14 Oct 2023

11. Griffith, C.: Next time you go to hospital or the doctor, look out for a robot named Pepper helping out (2019). https://www.kidsnews.com.au/technology/next-time-you-go-to-hospital-or-the-doctor-look-out-for-a-robot-named-pepper-helping-out/news-story/98aa96c738d9 8aadbd4dfabd80997f6a. Accessed 14 October 2023

12. Gross, R.: Designing websites for kids: trends and best practices (2022). https://www.canva.com/learn/kids-websites/. Accessed 14 October 2023

13. Lau, Y., Chee, D.G.H., Chow, X.P., Wong, S.H., Cheng L.J., Lau, S.T.: Humanoid robot-assisted interventions among children with diabetes: a systematic scoping review, Int. J. Nurs. Stud. **111** (2020). https://www.sciencedirect.com/science/article/pii/S00207489203 02352. Accessed 14 October 2023

14. Nalin, M., Baroni, I., Sanna, A., Pozzi, C.: Robotic companion for diabetic children: emotional and educational support to diabetic children, through an interactive robot. In: Proceedings of the 11th International Conference on Interaction Design and Children, IDC 2012, pp. 260–263, June 2012

15. Neerincx, M.A., et al.: Socio-cognitive engineering of a robotic partner for child's diabetes self-management. Front. Robot. AI **6**, 118 (2019)

16. Wallenfels, M.: Humanoide Begleiter stärken jungen Diabetikern den Rücken. Aerzte-Zeitung.de, 11 September 2017. https://www.aerztezeitung.de/Wirtschaft/Humanoide-Beglei ter-staerken-jungen-Diabetikern-den-Ruecken-297713.html. Accessed 14 Oct 2023

17. Zarubica, S.: Entwicklung einer auf dem humanoiden Roboter Pepper lauffähigen Lern-software für Kinder. Bachelor Thesis at the University of Business FHNW. FHNW, Olten (2022)

Teachable Robots Learn What to Say: Improving Child Engagement During Teaching Interaction

Rachel Love[1]([✉]), Philip R. Cohen[1,2], and Dana Kulić[1]

[1] Monash University, Clayton, VIC, Australia
{rachel.love,dana.kulic}@monash.edu
[2] Openstream, Inc., Deer Harbor, WA, USA

Abstract. Teachable robots are a promising technology to promote engagement in the classroom for young students. They are capable of displaying and adapting different social behaviours and characteristics, such as speech, gaze, and vocal pitch, to personalise the teaching interaction, and sustain interest for students over time. Research in this field shows a growing use of reinforcement learning to achieve this adaptation, however there is limited research on adaptive dialog behaviours for teachable robots. Our work proposes an adaptive dialog selection algorithm, implemented using Q-learning, which aims to personalise the dialog choices of a teachable robot in order to optimise for task engagement, measured by the time taken per teaching input, and the amount paraphrasing in the user's response. We investigate the effect of this approach in a case study with children aged 9–10 years old. The results show that this demographic responds positively to the teaching interaction, and provide useful insights into their preferences and abilities.

Keywords: Teachable Robots · Child-Robot Interaction (CRI) · Engagement · Adaptive Behaviours

1 Introduction

Social robots are a promising technology in education, and through personalised, one-on-one interactions with students have been shown to improve their engagement [13] and learning outcomes [3]. Social robots show particular potential when acting as a novice [3], where students learn new material by teaching it to the robot, taking advantage of the Protégé effect [6]. The additional responsibility of learning material for the benefit of someone else may improve learning outcomes [4], prolong engagement, and increase motivation [11]. Teachable robots have been deployed in classroom settings with children for a number of applications, including handwriting skills [8,13] and language learning [21,23].

Engagement is a key outcome for successful applications of social robots [19], and also in education, where it is a useful metric for predicting motivation and academic skills in the student [10]. In the field of education, engagement is a term which captures behavioural, affective, and cognitive aspects of a student's

A. Al. Ali et al. (Eds.): ICSR 2023, LNAI 14454, pp. 27–37, 2024.
https://doi.org/10.1007/978-981-99-8718-4_3

experience [7]. Zaga et al. develop a definition for task engagement that synthesises the three dimensions of student response to a learning task: attention (cognitive), emotional response (affective), and performance (behavioural), and uses it while investigating the effect of a robot's role in an educational setting [24].

Social robots possess characteristics and exhibit behaviours that may be adapted to better meet the needs and preferences of different users, which can assist in sustaining interest in the interaction over time [1]. Reinforcement learning methods are commonly applied in social robotics to learn such adaptations [2,20]. These methods have been applied to optimise for learning outcomes by adapting the robot's motivation strategies for second-language learning [9], and its story selection policy for vocabulary learning [15]. When also considering engagement, a robot tutor's help actions have been adapted within a long-division solving task [16]. The current work is limited to applications where the robot is the teacher. However, adaptation of dialog choices for a tutoring robot indicate that this approach may also be promising in the learning-by-teaching paradigm.

The Curiosity Notebook is a customisable web application that supports learning-by-teaching interactions with a teachable agent [12]. Users teach the agent about a classification task, with the teaching content aimed at children 8–12 years old. Teaching conversations are conducted as a series of teaching actions, where the agent poses a question which the user responds to (teaching input) using information in the source material. The flexibility of the platform allows for many different configurations of the teachable agent, including its embodiment and behaviours. Prior work has focused on configuring the dialog of the teachable agent, including comparing different styles of humour, as communicated through dialog choices, on user perceptions and outcomes [5]. This study used fixed dialog choices for a given user. Another study used reinforcement learning to adapt the dialog choices for a teachable robot in a group interaction to dynamically influence participation in group discussion [17].

We propose an adaptive response selection algorithm for a teachable robot, which learns a personalised policy for individual users to optimise for their task engagement. We apply this algorithm within a teaching interaction in the Curiosity Notebook, and estimate task engagement via the amount of paraphrasing between the user's teaching input and the source material, and the time taken to provide the teaching input. Prior work has been conducted using this algorithm, which investigated the effect of the proposed approach with adult participants [14]. The results of this study show that the adaptive approach was able to learn to select more rewarding actions over time, and to personalise to the individual user. In this work, we evaluate the proposed approach in a user study conducted with a small number of children aged 9–10 years old, the target demographic for the Curiosity Notebook content. The implementation and experimental protocol remain constant, where the proposed method of response selection is compared against a method of selecting responses at random. This is an exploratory study which aims to provide insights into the responses of the target demographic to this proposed approach, and also into their subjective experiences of the teaching interaction overall.

2   Adaptive Response to Teaching Input

Within a teaching interaction with a teachable robot, the user organises and presents information to the robot to promote their own learning. In turn, the robot can make numerous dialog choices in order to sustain and direct the conversation, and contribute to supporting the user's learning. The available choices are common among intelligent conversational agents, and include continuing or changing the current topic, asking for more information, or revisiting earlier topics. The most appropriate dialog choice may depend on the conversational context, and on the needs and preferences of the individual user. Additionally, the effect of the robot's choices may vary between users as a result of these individual differences. This motivates the use of an adaptive response selection algorithm in order to personalise the teachable robot's dialog behaviors.

We use a reinforcement learning approach in order for the teachable robot to learn which follow-up response(s) to provide after teaching input from the user. The algorithm is rewarded based on metrics related to task engagement. This implementation is presented in full in prior works [14], and is summarised in the following sections.

2.1   Adaptive Response Algorithm

The proposed approach uses Q-learning [20] to learn an individualised policy for each user to select follow-up responses, with the aim of maximising task engagement. Each user begins with a policy, $Q[s, a]$, which is initialised at random. The policy is updated each time the user provides teaching input.

State Space defines the conversational context in which an action is chosen. This comprises (1) the conversation type that the follow-up response is occurring after, (2) the last action taken, (3) the user's progress through the given topic, and (4) whether their teaching input contained recognisable features.

Action Space defines the dialog choices that are available as after the user has taught something. In this teaching dialog, the robot can ask the user to (1) rephrase the last thing they said, (2) ask for more information on the current topic, (3) confirm whether a fact that had been taught previously is correct, or (4) conclude the current teaching action. Up to three follow up responses can be given in a row before the teaching action will automatically be concluded.

Reward Formulation combines two proxy measures for task engagement: the user's attention to and performance in a learning activity [24]. In response to a follow-up question, the user may choose (1) to answer it, or (2) to reject it. If the user answers, task engagement is estimated via (a) the amount of paraphrasing

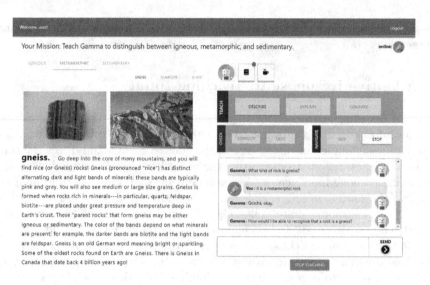

Fig. 1. The Curiosity Notebook interface, where the teachable robot has requested that the user teach a feature of Gneiss

in the teaching input measured as the semantic distance between what the user wrote, and the source material that their answer came from; and (b) the time taken to provide a teaching input. In the reward formulation, more paraphrasing is rewarded more highly, as this indicates a more thorough engagement with reading and processing the material, and faster response is also rewarded more highly, to represent greater attention and focus [7]. These two components are weighted at 80% and 20% of the reward total, respectively. Rejecting a follow-up response provides a direct feedback that this action is not preferred by the user, and incurs a highly negative reward to accelerate learning.

2.2   Curiosity Notebook Teaching Interface

The teaching interaction takes place via the Curiosity Notebook, a learning-by-teaching web application where users teach a robot called Gamma on a classification task on rocks and minerals. The Curiosity Notebook interface is shown in Fig. 1. Images and articles, split into three categories, are provided for each rock, containing information on the rock features. Teaching buttons are used to direct the conversation, which occurs via the chat window. The *Teach* buttons initiate dialog routines where the user teaches Gamma information on a rock, including descriptions and explanations of features, and comparisons between rocks. The user and Gamma take turns in deciding which of these to do next.

The user provides a teaching input by reading the source articles, and typing their response in their own words. This input is parsed by a natural language model implemented using Microsoft Language Understanding Intelligent Service (LUIS), a cloud-based, natural language understanding API. This model uses machine learning to identify intents and entities in the user's input which correspond to known rock features. Features identified with a confidence of 20% or greater are added to Gamma's notebook.

2.3 Teachable Robot

Users interact with the teachable robot, Gamma, and in this work we use the Yanshee, a humanoid robot manufactured by UBTECH Education [22]. Yanshee has a metallic build, and stands approximately 37 cm tall. It uses a Rapsberry Pi as its development platform. The Yanshee receives the text responses generated by the Curiosity Notebook via a socket connection, and the Google Text-to-Speech API is used to generate audio files for each utterance, as they are received, and then played aloud. We customise the voice to a male, Australian accented voice to increase the familiarity of the robot for Australian children. We also slow the speech down slightly, and show the robot's utterance in the chat transcript after it has been spoken to aid in understanding. Small arm gestures occur before speech to include liveliness and movement to the robot's embodiment.

2.4 User Study

We conducted a user study with children, who are the target demographic for the Curiosity Notebook teaching content. The aim of this study was to examine the effect of the proposed approach for selecting follow-up responses to teaching input on participant's engagement in the teaching task. This user study was reviewed and received ethics approval through the Monash University Human Research Ethics Committee (Project ID: 35097).

Participants. Children were recruited in collaboration with STEM Incubators, a non-profit organisation in Melbourne. Four participants took part in the study Female = 4, Age = 9.25 ± 0.5), and were randomly assigned to an experimental condition, with two participants assigned to each. Participants did not know which condition they had been assigned to until the end of the study.

Experimental Conditions. The experimental conditions corresponded to the method by which Gamma selected its response to teaching input provided by the user. Our proposed approach was compared to a control condition which used a method of selecting responses at random (up to three before concluding the teaching action). This method was chosen as the control because it represents the initial state of the Q-learning algorithm policy.

Procedure. Children took part in this user study while attending a STEM Incubators workshop, and were individually called aside to a quiet space to complete the experiment. Parental consent and the child's assent was obtained prior to the start of the study. Participants were told that they would be helping

Gamma prepare for a test. They were seated in front of a laptop showing the Curiosity Notebook, with Gamma next to the laptop. The researcher stayed in the room to answer any questions. Participants completed a Demographics survey, a Pre-Test on rock classification, and watched an instructional video on the Curiosity Notebook. They could then teach for as long as they wanted to. A Post-Test and User Experience questionnaire were completed afterwards.

3   Results

These result include a discussion of the individual participant's task engagement metrics over the interaction, their subjective ratings, and qualitative feedback. No statistical analysis was conducted due to the small sample size.

3.1   Task Engagement

We measure task engagement by analysing the change in total reward and its components over time. For the adaptive condition, we use rewards obtained during the interaction, and for the random condition we calculate the reward components post-hoc from the participant's teaching data. The rewards have been split into time intervals (n = 10), corresponding to the minimum number of rewards (min = 10, max = 32, mean = 17). The values in each interval were averaged and fitted with a linear trend line. These results are shown in Fig. 2.

Participants in the adaptive response condition show two different reward trajectories. P3 generally responded positively to the proposed approach, with a positive trend for the total reward (slope = 0.012) indicating that the algorithm learned to select more rewarding actions over time. P3 also received the highest number of rewards (n = 32), providing the algorithm with the largest number of opportunities to learn. The effect of this learning is largely seen in the paraphrasing component (slope = 0.024). The amount of paraphrasing increased by 26.7% over the interaction, from a cosine similarity value of 0.69 to 0.42. The teach time reward decreased slightly (slope = −0.0026), which corresponds to a 3.8 s increase in teach time, from 35.2 s to 39.0 s. The paraphrasing reward component is weighted more highly, which helps to explain this difference, and suggests that the algorithm allowed for p3 to spend more time crafting better paraphrases.

In comparison, p4 shows a decrease in task engagement, and a high degree of variance in reward values (slope = −0.082). P4 received a small number of rewards (n = 10), thus limited learning opportunities for the algorithm, where the majority of actions taken are exploratory. The trajectory of the paraphrasing component shows the largest change within the possible range of reward values (slope = −0.087). The amount of paraphrasing decreased by 97.5%, from a cosine similarity value of 0.089 to 1.06 (this final value is outside the possible range for this metric). The teach time reward also decreases (slope = −0.01), corresponding to an increase in teach time of 15 s, from 66 s to 81 s. These teaching times are longer than for p3 overall, as well as showing a larger increase over the interaction.

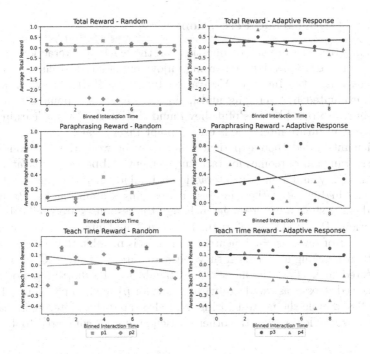

Fig. 2. Rewards shown over time, for random (p1, p2) on the left, adaptive response (p3, p4) on the right. A linear trend is fitted to the averaged values of the total reward (top), paraphrasing component (middle), and response time component (bottom)

Participants in the random condition show changes in task engagement that representing existing adaptation in user behaviours over time. For p1, the amount of paraphrasing increases over time by 27.8% (slope = 0.025), from a cosine similarity of 0.88 to 0.61, an increase comparable to p3, although paraphrasing is lower overall. The trend has been fitted from only three data points which limits the conclusions that can be drawn. This may result from inputs that could not be parsed by the language model, or from follow-up responses that did not ask for new teaching input. P1 is the only participant for whom the teaching time reward increased (slope = 0.0059), decreasing from 53.0 s to 44.2 s.

P2 is the only participant to utilise the rejection option, shown in the three highly negative values in the total reward. When including these values the reward increases over time (slope = 0.030), but when considering only the reward for questions answered, it decreases (slope = −0.018). The reward components show opposite trends. The amount of paraphrasing increased by 34.7% (slope = 0.031), but as for p1, only three data points inform this trend. The teach time reward decreased (slope = −0.017), an increase from 37.6 s to 63.3 s.

3.2   User Attitudes and Perceptions

Participant's responses to survey questions on the teaching interaction are summarised in Table 1. Questions regarding enjoyment, perceived effort, and perceived stress used the Intrinsic Motivation Inventory (IMI survey) [18]. Each metric is evaluated by averaging multiple questions on a 5-point Likert scale. Participants also rated how helpful they found the interaction for learning, and their interest in future interactions on a 5-point Likert scale.

Participants rated their experiences similarly between the two conditions, despite the range in outcomes for task engagement. All participants rated their enjoyment highly, and found the interaction helpful for their learning. Uniformly, participants highly rated their interest in teaching Gamma again. Ratings of perceived effort show a wider range, although the responses are similar between the conditions. P3 rated their effort the lowest at 3, and interacted for the longest time (number of rewards = 32, nearest n=16). It is possible that p3 was able to sustain their teaching for longer if they felt it required less effort. Conversely, p1 and p4 rated their effort the highest, and taught for the shortest periods (n = 10). Perceived stress was rated comparably low for p1, p2 and p3, while p4 rated stress at 2.8, double the nearest rating, and also rated their interest in learning more about rocks lower than the other participants, at 3 compared to 4.

Table 1. Metrics of user perception and attitudes towards the teaching task, grouped by condition. Instances where no response was given are indicated by a dash

	Random		Adaptive Response	
	p1	p2	p3	p4
Enjoyment	4.75	4.5	4.5	4
Perceived Effort	5	3.75	3	4.25
Perceived Stress	1	1.2	1.4	2.8
Learning Help	5	–	5	4
Teach Gamma Again	5	5	5	5
Learn More Rocks	4	4	4	3

3.3   Qualitative Feedback

The participants' free form feedback can give context to the quantitative results, and provide insight on their experiences when learning and teaching. They were very enthusiastic overall about teaching Gamma, were comfortable with using the Curiosity Notebook interface, and recognised that in the process of teaching they were also learning, making comments such as "I loved it! I could learn more about rocks as well!" and "I even learnt about rocks!."

We see that the rejection option was not readily adopted by most participants. Responding to a question on how much they enjoyed teaching, p2 commented "I loved teaching gamma but he was asking alot [sic] of questions." Their results show that they were able to reject questions they did not want to answer, however they were the only participant to do so. The limited use of rejection for this demographic may suggest that children are less confident controlling the conversation in this way, by directly declining to answer Gamma's questions.

We also see that some participants had difficulty in understanding Gamma's questions. Responding to a question on whether they felt they were good at teaching, p4 commented "Some times [sic] I got confused on how to answer his questions and sometimes he didn't understand me." P4 did not reject hard to understand questions, but may have taken longer to consider how to answer. P4 also gave highly paraphrased responses at the start of the interaction, and trended towards very limited paraphrasing as the interaction progressed. This change in behaviour may have been prompted by their highly paraphrased responses not being understood by the language model. This suggests that children may benefit from additional instruction on paraphrasing strategies.

4   Conclusions and Future Work

We propose an adaptive dialog response selection algorithm for a teachable robot with the objective of increasing task engagement metrics. We conducted an exploratory study to evaluate the proposed approach with a small number of children aged 9–10 years old. Our findings suggest that the proposed approach can be successful in improving task engagement for this age group, with more positive results for participants who interact for longer. We also see that despite some challenges, participants enjoy interacting with the teachable robot, and recognise the benefit of this kind of interaction for their learning.

The study reveals key differences in the response of this demographic compared to adults, and highlights areas for future development. Adult participants see a more pronounced effect of our approach compared to children, which may be attributed to longer interaction times, and more frequent use of the reject option which accelerates learning. Adjusting the presentation of the rejection option may have an impact on children's confidence in their role as teacher, and encourage them to take greater control of the interaction. Improvements to the language model and to the experimental protocol may improve confidence and success in providing teaching inputs. Accelerating learning via other mechanisms may offset the shorter interaction time for younger participants. The results of the case study show large variability due to the small sample size, thus experiments with a larger group of participants are needed to confirm these findings.

References

1. Ahmad, M.I., Mubin, O., Orlando, J.: Understanding behaviours and roles for social and adaptive robots in education: teacher's perspective. In: HAI, pp. 297–304. Association for Computing Machinery (2016)

2. Akalin, N., Loutfi, A.: Reinforcement learning approaches in social robotics. Sensors **21**(4), 1292 (2021)
3. Belpaeme, T., Kennedy, J., Ramachandran, A., Scassellati, B., Tanaka, F.: Social robots for education: a review. Sci. Robot. **3**(21), eaat5954 (2018)
4. Biswas, G., Leelawong, K., Schwartz, D., Vye, N.: Learning by teaching: a new agent paradigm for educational software. Appl. Artif. Intell. **19**(3–4), 363–392 (2005)
5. Ceha, J., Lee, K.J., Nilsen, E., Goh, J., Law, E.: Can a humorous conversational agent enhance learning experience and outcomes? In: CHI, pp. 1–14. Association for Computing Machinery (2021)
6. Chase, C.C., Chin, D.B., Oppezzo, M.A., Schwartz, D.L.: Teachable agents and the Protégé effect: increasing the effort towards learning. J. Sci. Educ. Technol. **18**(4), 334–352 (2009)
7. Fredricks, J.A., Blumenfeld, P.C., Paris, A.H.: School engagement: potential of the concept, state of the evidence. Rev. Educ. Res. **74**(1), 59–109 (2004)
8. Gargot, T., et al.: It Is Not the Robot Who Learns, It Is Me Treating Severe Dysgraphia Using Child-Robot Interaction. Frontiers in Psychiatry 12 (2021)
9. Gordon, G., et al.: Affective Personalization of a Social Robot Tutor for Children Second Language Skills. Proceedings of the AAAI Conference on Artificial Intelligence 30(1) (Mar 2016)
10. Hoffman, B., Nadelson, L.: Motivational engagement and video gaming: a mixed methods study. Educ. Tech. Res. Dev. **58**(3), 245–270 (2010)
11. Jacq, A., Lemaignan, S., Garcia, F., Dillenbourg, P., Paiva, A.: Building successful long child-robot interactions in a learning context. In: HRI, pp. 239–246 (2016)
12. Lee, K.J., Chauhan, A., Goh, J., Nilsen, E., Law, E.: Curiosity notebook: the design of a research platform for learning by teaching. Proc. ACM Hum.-Comput. Inter. **5**(CSCW2), 1–26 (2021)
13. Lemaignan, S., Jacq, A., Hood, D., Garcia, F., Paiva, A., Dillenbourg, P.: Learning by teaching a robot: the case of handwriting. IEEE Robot. Autom. Mag. **23**(2), 56–66 (2016)
14. Love, R., Law, E., Cohen, P.R., Kulic, D.: Adapting a teachable robot's dialog responses using reinforcement learning in teaching conversation. In: ROMAN (2023)
15. Park, H.W., Grover, I., Spaulding, S., Gomez, L., Breazeal, C.: A model-free affective reinforcement learning approach to personalization of an autonomous social robot companion for early literacy education. In: Proceedings of the AAAI Conference on Artificial Intelligence 33(01), pp. 687–694, July 2019
16. Ramachandran, A., Sebo, S.S., Scassellati, B.: Personalized Robot Tutoring Using the Assistive Tutor POMDP (AT-POMDP). In: Proceedings of the AAAI Conference on Artificial Intelligence 33(01), pp. 8050–8057 (2019)
17. Ravari, P.B., Jen Lee, K., Law, E., Kulić, D.: Effects of an adaptive robot encouraging teamwork on students' learning. In: ROMAN, pp. 250–257 (2021)
18. Ryan, R.M.: Control and information in the intrapersonal sphere: an extension of cognitive evaluation theory. J. Pers. Soc. Psychol. **43**(3), 450–461 (1982)
19. Sidner, C.L., Lee, C., Kidd, C.D., Lesh, N., Rich, C.: Explorations in engagement for humans and robots. Artif. Intell. **166**(1), 140–164 (2005)
20. Sutton, R.S., Barto, A.G.: Reinforcement Learning, 2nd ed.: An Introduction. MIT Press (Nov 2018)
21. Tanaka, F., Matsuzoe, S.: Children teach a care-receiving robot to promote their learning: field experiments in a classroom for vocabulary learning. J. Hum.-Robot Inter. **1**(1), 78–95 (2012)

22. UBTECH Robotics, I.: Yanshee (2021). https://yandev.ubtrobot.com/
23. Verhoeven, G., Catala, A., Theune, M.: Designing a Playful Robot Application for Second Language Learning. In: Brooks, A.L., Brooks, E., Sylla, C. (eds.) Interactivity, Game Creation, Design, Learning, and Innovation, pp. 385–394. Social Informatics and Telecommunications Engineering, Springer International Publishing, Cham, Lecture Notes of the Institute for Computer Sciences (2019)
24. Zaga, C., Lohse, M., Truong, K.P., Evers, V.: The effect of a robots social character on children task engagement: peer versus tutor. In: Tapus, A., André, E., Martin, J.C., Ferland, F., Ammi, M. (eds.) Social Robotics, pp. 704–713. Springer International Publishing (2015)

Social Robots in the Wild
and the Novelty Effect

Merle Reimann[1] , Jesper van de Graaf[2], Nina van Gulik[1],
Stephanie van de Sanden[2], Tibert Verhagen[2], and Koen Hindriks[1]

[1] Vrije Universiteit Amsterdam, Amsterdam, The Netherlands
k.v.hindriks@vu.nl
[2] Amsterdam University of Applied Sciences, Amsterdam, The Netherlands

Abstract. We designed a wine recommendation robot and deployed it in a small supermarket. In a study aimed to evaluate our design we found that people with no intent to buy wine were interacting with the robot rather than the intended audience of wine-buying customers. Behavioural data, moreover, suggests a very different evaluation of the robot than the surveys that were completed. We also found that groups were interacting more with the robot than individuals, a finding that has been reported more often in the literature. All of these findings taken together suggest that a novelty effect may have been at play. It also suggests that field studies should take this effect more seriously. The main contribution of our work is in identifying and proposing a set of indicators and thresholds that can be used to identify that a novelty effect is present. We argue that it is important to focus more on measuring attitudes towards robots that may explain behaviour due to novelty effects. Our findings also suggest research should focus more on verifying whether real user needs are met.

Keywords: Novelty effect indicators · Socially Assistive Robots · Retail

1 Introduction

We developed and deployed a wine recommendation robot in a supermarket for three weeks and conducted a preliminary study with the aim of evaluating its design and user experience. The primary aim of conducting this in-the-wild study was to gain insight into and explore how the intended audience, i.e. wine buying customers in a retail setting, would interact with the robot, how they would perceive the usefulness of our wine recommendation robot, and whether there could be any novelty effects biasing the results. We found that customers who did not buy wine engaged with the robot rather than the intended audience. Out of the 265 customers who interacted with the robot, only 44 (16.6%) also bought wine. It appeared that interaction was initiated more out of curiosity than out of a need related to the purchasing activity of customers. Because robot interaction may have largely been driven by curiosity, a novelty effect thus may have been at play. We also noticed that the overall positive survey ratings that customers gave seemed to markedly differ from what the behavioural data that we collected suggested. This raised the question of how to explain these findings. Why did wine buying customers not engage with the robot? Why did behavioural data paint a different picture of what was happening than the survey data? We believe that our findings suggest that field studies on human-robot interaction should more seriously take into account that most people are still unfamiliar with social(ly assistive) robots, and that well-defined indicators are needed to be able to identify to what extent a novelty effect is present in the studies we perform. In this paper, we explore these topics using the findings of our study as a starting point, and investigate the following main research question:

RQ. Which indicators suggest that people are engaging with a socially assistive robot out of curiosity rather than a user need? Or, in other words, how can we identify whether a novelty effect is the main reason for robot interaction?

As [9] suggests, lack of familiarity with a robot may provide a barrier to initiate interaction with it. This raises the question of how to eliminate such barriers that may lead to low acceptance or negative perception of social robots. We therefore will also try to explain why the intended audience did not engage with the robot, to gain a better understanding of how we can motivate people with a real need to make use of a robot that can assist them in fulfilling that need.

2 Related Work

Social Robots in the Wild. Previous work [10] has advocated that social robots should be observed in real world environments with untrained interactors, which allows for collecting a richer and more diverse set of behavioural data. People interact differently in natural settings than in laboratory settings [9] and performing studies in such settings enables researchers to gain insights into how the intended audience interacts with the robot in their natural environment. For example, service or socially assistive robots used in retail stores, can show how real customers interact with the robot [3]. Other example application areas where robots have been moved out of the lab, to mention just a few, include robots for way finding in office buildings [2], and servicing in malls [4] and airports [15]. Performing studies in these contexts is challenging, as there is typically only very limited control over who will be participating and how participants behave. Natural environments, moreover, vary greatly. For example, when conducting studies over extended periods of time, repeated encounters in certain environments are rare (e.g., airport) while in others they cannot be excluded (e.g., supermarket).

One interesting finding of prior studies has been that groups (of two or more people) are more likely to interact with a social (humanoid) robot in a public space than individuals. [6] reports that 67% of the time, children interacted with a robot with their friends. [10] reports that in a reception hall, there were more interactions with their robot involving two people (37%) than one person (20%), which might have been due to the crowded setting. However, [10] also notes that some people were showing off to their friends, while others were explaining how the robot functions to their group members. [11] reports that 63% of all visitors that came in pairs interacted with the robot, while only 43% of visitors that came alone interacted with it. [9] analysed various aspects of groups interacting with robots in more detail in a hospitality context. None of these works present a detailed analysis explaining why groups appear to be more willing to interact with a robot than individuals.

The Novelty Effect. Deploying robots in real-world settings means that people, who would usually not interact with robots, are confronted with them. It has long been recognized in the field that the novelty of social robots may give rise to curiosity and exploration of a robot's ability by testing it [2]. Interestingly, [2] also comments on the need to distinguish between a real user need ("genuine requests for directions") and curiosity driven interactions, which has been one of the main motivations for writing this paper. Of course, novelty may also give rise to anxiety and avoidance behaviors [12].

[12,13] argues that instead of assuming that novelty of social robots is "noise", novelty could also be viewed as a phenomenon shaping social robot interaction. The papers argue that social robots are a radical novelty, understood as a profound disruption of sense-making, and that studying novelty effects related to social robotics may increase our understanding of how pervasive these effects really are within the field and challenge our assumptions about, for example, how observations of people treating social robots should inform the design of them. If this is the case, then strong reactions of curiosity and exploratory behaviour instead of anxiety and avoidance behaviour are also to be expected.

However, to increase our understanding of novelty effects, we also need a toolbox to be able to identify to what extent novelty effects are present in our studies of social robots, and develop measures to assess how strong these effects are. As far as we know, a well-defined set of indicators for novelty has not yet been proposed for social robotics, and is one of the main contributions of this paper. This is not to say that the proposed measures themselves are new; in the literature, similar measures have been reported on. For example, [7] mentions the amount of time that users spend looking at a robot, while [10] reports that only 27% of people who looked at the robot also interacted with it. However, whereas [10] suggests this may be due to the fact the robot was already in use for years, such findings can also be interpreted as a sign of novelty (at least in certain circumstances, as we will argue below).

3   Method

The study took place in a small supermarket of a well-known chain in The Netherlands, where a Pepper v1.8a was positioned in an aisle next to the wine (Fig. 1).

Participants. 1396 customers were observed in the aisle where the robot was located, of which 265 initiated an interaction with the robot. Survey results indicate that slightly more female (55%) than male participants interacted with the robot. To ensure compliance with legal restrictions on buying alcohol, none of the participants were under 18. We computed an estimated mean age $M = 44.3$ ($SD = 14.7$) from the age bins used in our survey. As customers repeat store visits and the study duration was three weeks, it is likely that some customers have been observed multiple times.

Fig. 1. Pepper in the wine aisle

Design. We ran an exploratory study in the supermarket with the aim of evaluating user experience of our socially assistive robot designed to recommend wines, by means of both behavioural and survey data.

Materials. A Pepper robot was programmed to assist customers by recommending a choice of wine out of all wines available in the supermarket based on a brief interview asking for customer input, including constraints such as price, type of wine, and a request to match with food (by ingredients). The robot then would display three choices (names, categories, prices and pictures of wine bottles) on its tablet and would ask for more input if a customer was not satisfied with the choices offered. After an interaction was finished, the screen returned to the start screen. The robot was programmed to perform small, random movements and follow customers with its gaze, to appear more lively. We put effort in communicating the robot's main function of recommending wines, by putting up a poster on the wall above the robot, designed to incorporate the distinctive colours associated with the supermarket, ensuring visual impact and brand coherence.

An observation scheme was used for classifying engagement behaviour and identifying purchase intent. See Table 1 for the categories that were included in the scheme. To compute the dropout rate, the number of customers walking away while the interaction task was not completed was also kept track of. The robot automatically logged the number of interaction sessions and task completion.

A survey was used which included an item on age range and one on gender, and nine 5-point Likert scale items about, a.o., the robot being helpful, interaction performance, ease of use, and positive feeling towards the robot ('strongly disagree' to 'strongly agree'; see Table 2 for items), and a subscale of 5 items about the general attitude towards the store ($\alpha > .95$). We did not collect any privacy-sensitive data that would enable identification of customers.

Procedure. In order to start the interaction, a participant had to press a clearly visible start button on the robot's tablet. The robot then would greet the participant and ask them what kind of wine they were looking for. After finishing the interaction, one researcher asked participants for consent and to complete a small survey. Since week one raised questions about how many of the wine buying customers were interacting with the robot, in week two we started also counting customers who bought wine to gain more insight in this. In week three, we started actively asking customers to interact with the robot to be able to collect more data about how customers experienced interacting with the robot and how they assessed the recommendations made. A second researcher, standing in the same aisle as the robot at a distance of approximately 10 m, filled in the observation scheme, and restarted the robot when there were software issues.

4   Results

We collected data over a three-week period, for five days each week from 9:00 to 14:00 outside peak hours from 15:00–18:00 because the supermarket did not want a robot occupying part of the somewhat narrow aisle during these hours.

Stopping Power and Dropout Rate. We found an overall *stopping power* of 19% (customers interacting with the robot), which is similar to rates found in public spaces elsewhere, e.g., [4] reports that about 15% of passers-by initiated interaction. In week three, when customers were actively approached and asked to interact with the robot, Table 1 shows the number of interactions almost doubled compared to the weeks before. Compared to the stopping power, a slightly higher percentage of about 23% of customers stopped to look at the robot, but did not interact with it. We counted someone as stopping at the robot when they stopped walking within a distance of 3.5 m of the robot (within the 'social zone' [5]) and appeared to look at it. We found a high overall *dropout rate* of about 30%. In week 1, 58 out of 70 participants ended interaction early (before task completion, by walking away; 83%); in week 2, 12 out of 55 dropped out (22%); in week 3, only 9 out of 136 dropped out (7%). The much higher dropout in week 1 can be explained by software issues, while the much lower rate in week 3 is likely due to actively asking customers to interact. It is plausible therefore that the dropout rate of week 2 is the most realistic estimate given our design.

Table 1. Classification of engagement behaviour and purchase intent

Observation	Week 1	Week 2	Week 3
Customers walking past the robot	275	323	216
Customers stopping at the robot	122	114	81
Customers interacting with the robot	70	59	136
Customers buying wine without interacting	–	130	21
Customers buying wine after stopping	–	12	15
Customers buying wine after interacting	–	4	40

Key Finding 1: The Intended Audience Does Not Engage with the Robot. Out of all 929 customers that were observed in the aisle in week 2 and 3, 222 (24%) bought a wine. The data in Table 1 for these weeks clearly shows that few of those 222 customers (less than 20%) interacted with the robot. Of the 59 people interacting in week 2, only 7% bought wine. In week 3, this percentage increased to 29% (we note again that in week 3 customers were actively asked to interact with the robot, which likely explains the increase). Overall, out of the 195 participants interacting with the robot in week 2 and 3 only 44 (23%) bought wines.

Although we did not keep track of exact numbers of people grouped around the robot during an interaction, from our observations we know that most of the time 2 or more people were grouped around the robot and individuals were less frequently interacting with the robot on their own. In such group settings, however, most of the time only one individual in the group was interacting (did the talking) with the robot. It was also noticeable, in contrast, that most of the time customers buying wine were individuals shopping by themselves.

Table 2. Mean and standard deviation of survey item ratings

Survey items	Mean (SD)
The robot is helpful	3.72 (1.02)
The robot reacts quickly	3.31 (0.94)
The interaction with the robot runs smoothly	3.31 (0.97)
In general, I am positive about how the robot helps	3.67 (0.89)
I feel satisfied with the wine recommendation	3.63 (0.93)
The robot is easy to use	3.56 (0.92)
The robot is useful	3.77 (0.93)
I feel positive about the robot	3.81 (0.93)
I trust the robot	3.94 (0.94)

Survey Data. We collected 131 completed surveys (49% of participants who also interacted with the robot). All individual items (see Table 2) are rated above 3.5

except for the items asking for reaction time and smoothness of the interaction, which can be explained by some of the early software issues we had in week 1. The items overall give a somewhat positive impression of the robot with the item on trust being rated most positively with $M = 3.94$ ($SD = 0.94$). We also asked participants to rate the supermarket store, which received a rating very similar to the rating of robot trust but with a lower standard deviation ($SD = 0.6$).

Key Finding 2: Behavioural Data Paints a Different Picture than Survey Data. While results from the survey suggest that participants think the robot is helpful, feel positive about its help, think it is easy to use, useful, feel positive about the robot, and indicate that it is trustworthy, the results from the behavioural analysis paint a rather different picture. First, the number of customers who stopped at or simply passed by the robot is much higher than the number of customers who interacted with it. Although there are many reasons why a customer may decide not to engage with the robot, one explanation that we should consider is that customers did not feel comfortable enough to engage with the robot. When people were asked why they did not interact with the robot, they mentioned having no time, but also that they wanted to have nothing to do with the robot. The latter response is markedly different from those obtained through the survey, and we cannot exclude that this sentiment is representative of a larger segment of customers passing by. Second, it is hard to explain the high dropout rate of about 20–30% given the survey results. Dropping out suggests the robot is not helpful or useful, or not that easy to use, which contrasts with the positive ratings of the related survey items. Third, a striking difference is that participants are satisfied with the wine recommendation, which suggests the robot satisfies a user need, but we know from observations that most did not buy a wine at all.

5 Discussion

Explaining Key Finding 1: The Intended Audience Does Not Engage with the Robot. Most participants who interacted with our wine recommendation robot did not belong to the intended audience of wine-buying customers, for which our robot was designed. This function was also clearly communicated by means of a poster above it. However, robots are not a common occurrence in supermarkets, which may have led to people being curious about what the robot can do and interaction may have been due to a novelty effect. A plausible explanation of our finding thus is that participants interacted with the robot more out of curiosity than out of a need. Further support for this conclusion comes from our observation that groups interacted more with the robot than individuals. The robot may become a talking point in groups and promote curiosity about how it functions [9], also allowing one group member to show off to others as found by [10].

Although the novelty effect may offer a plausible explanation why customers interact with the robot (16% of customers passing by), it is noticeable that this effect seems almost completely absent for the intended audience of wine-buying customers (only 3% of customers passing by who also bought a wine). Why did the intended audience not engage with the robot? Apart from indicating to have no time, customers also said they wanted to have nothing to do with the robot. As we found that most wine buying customers were individuals, perhaps anxiety of interacting with the robot played a role. As [9] suggests, groups may decrease fear and make people feel more comfortable to interact with a robot, while individuals may have felt stronger feelings of embarrassment about interacting with a robot as reported in [1]. While human-like features (e.g., talking) can benefit customers in terms of ease-to-use, it can also result in emotional stress when interacting with a robot [8]. In our case, by talking with a robot, people may have been afraid of being outed as a non-knowledgeable wine drinker. [3] suggests studies on social robots (in retail) should assess "negative consumer perceptions towards robots in retail" more.

Lessons Learned from Key Finding 2: Behavioural and Survey Data Suggest Different Attitudes Towards Robots. The different picture that emerges from behavioural data highlights the importance of conducting in-the-wild studies. It is difficult, however, to provide a good explanation for these differences. Perhaps participants who were willing to fill in our survey were more positively minded. However, given that these participants were also willing to comment on satisfaction with the wine recommendation made by the robot, while they did not have any intent to buy wine (64%), suggests that survey items may also have been rated based just on a more general (positive) attitude of participants towards the study. We believe that our results show that researchers should be more critical about survey results, and in particular should not draw conclusions too quickly that people have a positive attitude towards robots based on survey data only. Such conclusions should be supported also by behavioural data that is not easily explained otherwise (e.g., interaction duration with a robot, used in e.g. [4], by a group is likely to be longer than by an individual). We propose that the dropout rate measure is useful for this purpose, as it is a simple measure indicating how often interaction breaks down. More generally, behavioural quality of task and interaction measures should be used to validate that self-reported attitudes match with observed behaviour.

Measuring the Novelty Effect for Socially Assistive Robots In-the-Wild: Our results can be explained by a novelty effect, but also suggest ways to measure to what extent such effects are present. We derive a set of indicators from our findings and suggest thresholds for several parameters for identifying novelty in social robot interaction, answering our research question:

- A substantial percentage (>15%) of passers-by stops to look at the robot, but does not interact with it;
- A substantial dropout rate (>20%) that contrasts with more positive overall survey results on perceived usability and attitude towards the robot (e.g., >3.5 ratings on a 5-point Likert scale);

- Passers-by that have no need for the robot's assistance interact more with it than passers-by that have such a need;
- Groups interact more with the robot than individuals.

We do not think that any of these indicators by themselves can be used to identify a novelty effect, but when taken together there is strong reason to believe a novelty effect is present: the first indicator suggests unfamiliarity with robots, the second suggests expectations are violated, the third suggests people interact out of curiosity rather than need, and the fourth suggests that people feel more comfortable engaging a robot together for various reasons (see also Sect. 2).

The threshold for the first indicator is derived from our findings (about 20% stopped and looked every week) but reduced as we feel that even lower numbers would already suggest people are (still) largely unfamiliar with but showing reserved interest into social robots. The threshold for the second indicator is based on the dropout rate we found in the second week. We think this is the most reliable figure to base the threshold on, as there were robot interaction issues that we resolved in the first week and in the third week we actively asked people to interact with the robot, which may have lowered dropout significantly. The first, second, and the last indicator require an observer that counts passers-by and the number of people that take part in a robot interaction session. The second also requires asking participants to complete a survey. The third requires counting people too, but also requires a measure for assessing a need for assistance (such as buying wine as an indicator of purchase intent). We believe that identifying user need should be taken into account more in social robotics research, and, related, that papers should discuss the task or function of a robot in sufficient detail to understand how it addresses such needs. Also, dropout rates are rarely reported. If [12] is right about social robots being a radically novel technology, it is important to report more on these measures to check for novelty effects.

How Can a Socially Assistive Robot Effectively Engage the Intended Audience? There does not seem to be a readily available answer to this question. We still need to gain a better understanding of the willingness of people to engage with socially assistive robots and, more specifically, how this relates to their needs. It is more often than not difficult to establish that participants interact with a robot because of a real need they have for the assistance that the robot can offer. For example, for a guidance robot that remains stationary as discussed in [4], it would be difficult to check whether a real need has been addressed by the direction-giving behaviours of the robot (checking if participants actually went to a place they asked directions for is not feasible in practice). As discussed above, ratings on related survey items should not be taken for granted. In our study, there was a rather straightforward way to check whether a user need was being addressed, but the results were quite different from what we were expecting.

Our findings also raise questions about the contexts where social robots can be usefully deployed; a small supermarket which people (presumably) repeatedly visit (and thus know well) and are focused on collecting purchase items based on a (presumably) more or less similar routine each time may not be interested in assistance from a social robot (or any other device for that matter).

Limitations. The study was conducted in a supermarket that is frequented by a lot of students. The supermarket is small, and placing it in a narrow aisle may have been less than ideal for social robot interaction. The indicators and thresholds proposed are based on boundary conditions derived from findings in a single study. More research is needed to validate these thresholds, and it is important to explore whether our findings can be replicated in different contexts.

6   Conclusion

Well-known technology acceptance models suggest that adoption of a new technology depends on key factors such as perceived usefulness and ease of use, largely ignoring affective components such as anxiety, fears, interest, and joy [14]. While participants agreed the robot is useful and easy to use in our study, behavioural data in contrast suggests a very low adoption rate. Our results suggest that participants who engaged with the robot mainly did so out of curiosity (novelty effect) and not because of a real need the robot was designed to assist them with. In order to differentiate willingness to interact based on novelty versus need, we introduced a set of indicators for identifying a novelty effect, based on behavioural engagement and task-related measures. Future work should validate the usefulness of these indicators for measuring novelty effects as well as the thresholds for some of the parameters that we proposed. Our results do not provide any insight into if and how the novelty effect wears off over time. Future longitudinal studies could shed valuable insights into the evolution of the novelty effect and its impact on customer behaviour over time. More generally, our work also shows that it is important not to rely on survey items only and makes clear that we should instead focus more on collecting behavioural, task-related performance measures (e.g., dropout rate) and indicators of user needs in field studies that aim to validate socially assistive robot designs in real-world settings.

Clearly, there must be other factors at play that can explain why the intended audience did not engage with a robot designed to offer them assistance. More specifically, for our retail context, we need to better understand why individuals with a purchase intent do not interact with the robot. A key question to investigate therefore is whether this is due to contextual or product-related factors, or because of (negative) attitudes towards the technology used (a humanoid robot that talks). The latter is in line with [9] which also advocates to put more effort into examining the attitudes towards a robot immediately after interaction.

Acknowledgements. This research was (partially) funded by the Hybrid Intelligence Center, a 10-year programme funded by the Dutch Ministry of Education, Culture and Science through the Netherlands Organisation for Scientific Research, grant number 024.004.022, and the RAAK-mkb project De toegevoegde waarde van sociale robots voor mijn winkel funded by the Taskforce for Applied Research SIA.

References

1. Bartneck, C., Bleeker, T., Bun, J., Fens, P., Riet, L.: The influence of robot anthropomorphism on the feelings of embarrassment when interacting with robots. Paladyn **1**, 109–115 (2010)
2. Bohus, D., Saw, C.W., Horvitz, E.: Directions robot: in-the-wild experiences and lessons learned. In: Proceedings of the 2014 International Conference on Autonomous Agents and Multi-agent Systems, pp. 637–644 (2014)
3. De Gauquier, L., Brengman, M., Willems, K.: The Rise of Service Robots in Retailing: Literature Review on Success Factors and Pitfalls, pp. 15–35. Retail Futures, Emerald Publishing Limited, Berkeley (2020)
4. Fraune, M.R., Šabanović, S., Kanda, T.: Human group presence, group characteristics, and group norms affect human-robot interaction in naturalistic settings. Front. Robot. AI **6** (2019). https://doi.org/10.3389/frobt.2019.00048
5. Hall, E.T.: The Hidden Dimension, vol. 609. Anchor (1966)
6. Kanda, T., Hirano, T., Eaton, D., Ishiguro, H.: Interactive robots as social partners and peer tutors for children: a field trial. HCI **19**(1–2), 61–84 (2004)
7. Leite, I., Martinho, C., Paiva, A.: Social robots for long-term interaction: a survey. Int. J. Soc. Robot. **5**, 291–308 (2013)
8. Lin, H., Chi, O.H., Gursoy, D.: Antecedents of customers' acceptance of artificially intelligent robotic device use in hospitality services. J. Hospital. Market. Manag. **29**(5), 530–549 (2020)
9. Preusse, H., Skulsky, R., Fraune, M.R., Stringam, B.B.: Together we can figure it out: groups find hospitality robots easier to use and interact with them more than individuals. Front. Robot. AI **8** (2021)
10. Sabanovic, S., Michalowski, M.P., Simmons, R.: Robots in the wild: observing human-robot social interaction outside the lab. In: 9th IEEE International Workshop on Advanced Motion Control, pp. 596–601. IEEE (2006)
11. Schermer, J., Hindriks, K.V.: Interviewing style for a social robot engaging museum visitors for a marketing research interview. In: 29th Int. Conference on Robot and Human Interactive Communication, pp. 1000–1005. IEEE (2020)
12. Smedegaard, C.V.: Novelty knows no boundaries: why a proper investigation of novelty effects within Shri should begin by addressing the scientific plurality of the field. Front. Robot. AI **9** (2022)
13. Smedegaard, C.V.: Reframing the role of novelty within social HRI: from noise to information. In: Proceedings of the 14th ACM/IEEE International Conference on Human-Robot Interaction. HRI '19, pp. 411–420. IEEE Press (2020)
14. Taherdoost, H.: A review of technology acceptance and adoption models and theories. Procedia Manuf. **22**, 960–967 (2018)
15. Tonkin, M., Vitale, J., Herse, S., Williams, M.A., Judge, W., Wang, X.: Design methodology for the UX of HRI: a field study of a commercial social robot at an airport. In: International Conference on Human-Robot Interaction, pp. 407–415 (2018)

Ethical, Legal, and Social Requirements for Assistance Robots in Healthcare

Marija Radic[✉] [iD], Agnes Vosen, and Sarah Kilz[iD]

Fraunhofer Center for International Management and Knowledge Economy IMW, Neumarkt
9-19, 04109 Leipzig, Germany
marija.radic@imw.fraunhofer.de

Abstract. According to forecasts, in 2050 more than 600 million persons world-wide will be in need of care. In many regions of the world, the healthcare sector suffers today already from a shortage of skilled workers, so innovative approaches are required. One possible solution with high future potential are assistance robots that provide support with everyday or work tasks. The aim of this study is to investigate the ethical, legal, and social aspects of the use of assistive robots in clinics and care facilities. Using an online survey, we address 279 decision makers in clinics and care facilities throughout Germany with respect to the ethical, legal, and social implications of the use of assistance robots in healthcare. The results show that the respondents of the study do not see any absolute exclusion criteria for the use of assistance robots regarding ethical, legal, or social issues. The majority of participants are not concerned that robots will replace jobs in the healthcare sector, but rather see them as an opportunity for relief. Especially the personalized communication with robots is viewed positively. The respondents see assistance robots also as an opportunity for more patient autonomy. Regarding data protection, data security and the human contact as a consequence of the introduction of assistance robots, the participants are divided in their opinions. About half of the respondents also expect a change in behavior due to the presence of a robot.

Keywords: social robotics · healthcare · ethics · user acceptance · data protection

1 Introduction

In view of the increasingly aging society and the simultaneous emergence of a shortage of skilled workers in the care sector, assistance robots can be a building block for relieving the healthcare system. This opinion was expressed in the study conducted by Klein et al. [1], who see great potential in the increased use of robotic assistance systems. At the same time in many respects the right framework conditions still need to be created in many respects. Numerous studies address the acceptance of robotics in healthcare and nursing such as the study by Meyer [2] which shows that there is a great openness for various robotic scenarios among nursing staff. In addition to technical functionality, social acceptance is decisive for the diffusion of robots into everyday care. In this context, the ethical discussion as well as legal and social implications play a major role. The basis for the present study was a comprehensive literature review of ethical, legal, and social

A. Al. Ali et al. (Eds.): ICSR 2023, LNAI 14454, pp. 49–58, 2024.
https://doi.org/10.1007/978-981-99-8718-4_5

requirements for robotic solutions in healthcare from the perspective of the end user. Different aspects emerged that form the basis for the present study: The dominating topic is the issue of data protection in the use of robots [3–7]. *Data protection and security* are at the same time important legal topics, which have been extensively discussed by Bender et al. [8] for Germany. The primary focus here is on the problems that can arise regarding data protection. How the data protection problem is viewed by end users receives little attention and thus represents a gap in the literature. There is also the *danger of reducing human contact* by using robots [3, 7, 9–11]. It is argued that the person in need of help is degraded by the robot to a problem that can be solved by technology. According to the study by Meyer [12], however, the reduction is not a mandatory consequence. German users, for example, see activation robots as an additional and not a substitutional offer in care. From the perspective of the caregiver, there is also the *risk of job loss* because of the robot [10, 12, 13]. Replacing the position is unanimously described as unethical. However, the robot's influence on the workstation can also be an opportunity if the robot supports the caregiver and thus improves the work situation [5, 10, 14].

The aspect of *patient autonomy* is also investigated dealing with aspects such as independence and self-determination [6, 7]. Furthermore, the question also arises as to *which role the robot* assumes. In a study by van der Plas et al. [15], different roles such as "the robot as slave" or "the robot as fellow human being" were defined in focus groups with technical experts and users. The role is expressed specifically in the communication between robot and human. In this respect, Meyer's study documented the desire for a "silent servant" [2]. To this end, research is also being conducted into the extent to which assistance robots should have a personality [16]. A study in which various participants such as robot manufacturers, university staff and end users as well as trade union representatives discussed the self-image of human-robot collaboration in the context of a workshop raised another question [5]: To what extent does the use of robots lead to a *change in the behavior* of nursing staff and patients? To the best of the authors' knowledge, only a limited number of empirical studies exists which comprehensively focus on the ethical, legal, and social requirements for assistance robots in the healthcare domain. The objective of the paper is to close this research gap through an online survey among German decision makers in clinics and care facilities thus covering both the inpatient and outpatient setting. The paper is structured as follows: After the introduction, we present our methodology and empirical results and close with a discussion and conclusion.

2 Methods

The results of the literature review served as the basis for the derivation of the questions and response options in the online survey. The target group of the online survey were decision makers in the healthcare sector throughout Germany due to their central role in investment decision in their institutions. The online survey was conducted between May and July 2021. Participation in the study was voluntary and without compensation. In addition to the content-related questions, we collected information on the participant's position, type of facility, facility size and state.

Table 1 provides descriptive information on the participants by type of facility. A total of 279 persons participated in the survey. The participants were recruited by email based on over 5,000 addresses that were identified nationwide through company databases. This approach was flanked by a cooperation with different healthcare associations which distributed the survey information through newsletters to their members. More than 46 percent of the participants work in inpatient care. More than 30 percent are assigned to outpatient care and 20 percent to clinics. A comparison with the actual number of facilities in Germany in 2021 shows that clinics are significantly overrepresented [17], whereas outpatient care is significantly underrepresented. The proportion of inpatient care in the sample is relatively representative of the actual number of inpatient care facilities [18].

Table 1. Study participants by facility type

Type of facility	Number of participants	Relative proportion in %
clinics	63	22,6
inpatient nursing facilities	129	46,2
outpatient nursing facilities	87	31,2
total	**279**	**100,0**

Regarding the size of the facilities, the entire range from less than 10 to more than 500 employees is represented (Table 2). Only around two percent of small companies with fewer than 10 employees took part in the study. Small and medium-sized facilities with 10 to 250 employees make up the largest share with 65 percent. Almost one-third are large facilities with more than 250 employees. Since only just over 60 percent of respondents provided information on the size of their facility, it is not possible to make a statement on the size-related representativeness.

Table 2. Study participants by facility size

Size of facility	Number of facilities	Relative proportion in %
less than 10 employees	2	1,2
10–50 employees	47	27,2
50–100 employees	38	21,9
100–250 employees	29	16,7
250–500 employees	14	8,1
More than 500 employees	43	24,9
total	**173**	**100,0**

Geographically, study participants from all 16 German states are represented in the sample. However, various German states are over- or under-represented, so that overall geographic representativeness is not given.

3 Empirical Results

In the following, the results are structured along the questions in the online survey on the various ethical, legal, and social aspects.

3.1 Danger of Job Loss or Chance to Relieve Workload

Robotic assistants are designed to support and not replace humans. This is an essential prerequisite for acceptance as several studies show. We therefore asked, "Do you think that assistance robots will replace jobs in healthcare, or do you see them more as an opportunity to relieve staff?" The response options were "I am very concerned", "I am more concerned", "I am undecided", "I see it more as an opportunity", and "I see it as a great opportunity." We modified the Likert scale to contrast the two positions whether assistant robots are a replacement for professionals or an opportunity to relieve the workload in one question. Figure 1 shows the results: Robotic assistants are more likely to be perceived as an opportunity to relieve the workload. Clinics show little to no concern about job losses. Greatest concerns are seen in outpatient care.

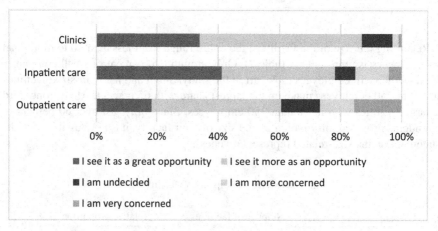

Fig. 1. Danger of job loss or chance to relieve workload (n = 248)

3.2 Recognition and Personalized Address

Studies such as e.g. Hebesberger et al. [19] show that a good communication capability of the robot is crucial for its acceptance. However, there are also contrary observations [2], that robots should "serve in silence". The next question relates to this: "How do you find it when the robot recognizes you or a patient/resident and addresses you in a personalized way (e.g. "Good morning, Mrs. Doe!") as opposed to a purely anonymous interaction?" The response options were "Not good at all", "Rather not good," "I am undecided," "Rather good," and "Very good".

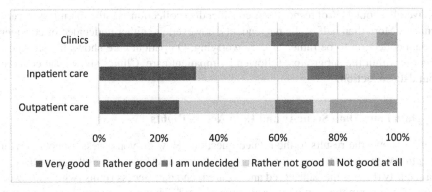

Fig. 2. Recognition and personalized address (n = 248)

Figure 2 shows that while more than half of the respondents find the recognition and personalized approach "Rather good" to "Very good", almost a quarter of the respondents also find this function "Rather not good" to "Not good at all". Outpatient care shows greatest skepticism regarding the function of recognition and personalized approach, followed by clinics. Inpatient care on the other hand shows greatest agreement with the function of recognition and a personalized approach. These results are not surprising since patients in inpatient care usually live in a care facility for a longer period.

3.3 Data Collection from a Data Protection Perspective

In ethical analyses of robotics, data protection as a safety factor plays a key role [4]. Data from surveys about data protection, however, is still very limited. The objective of this study is to make a contribution to close this gap by asking the participants the following question: "To be able to e.g. communicate with persons, the robot assistant needs cameras and microphones that are permanently in use. How do you assess this from a data protection point of view?" The response options were "Very worrying", "Rather worrying", "I am undecided", "Rather harmless ", and "Very harmless" (Fig. 3).

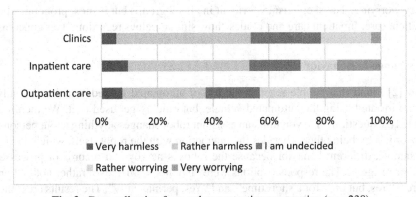

Fig. 3. Data collection from a data protection perspective (n = 238)

Overall, about 41% of respondents consider data collection as rather harmless or very harmless. More than half of the respondents, however, are either undecided or consider the data collection to be rather or very worrying. Outpatient care shows the strongest concerns within the subgroups, followed by inpatient care. Clinics show least concern about data collection.

3.4   Data Flow, Data Security and Data Access Rights

Figure 4 shows the results to the related question "How do you assess aspects of data protection with regard to data processing such as data flow (where does the data flow to), data security (how is the data stored and secured) and data access rights (who is allowed to view the data) in the context of assistance robots?" The response options were again "Very worrying", "Rather worrying", "I am undecided", "Rather harmless", and "Very harmless".

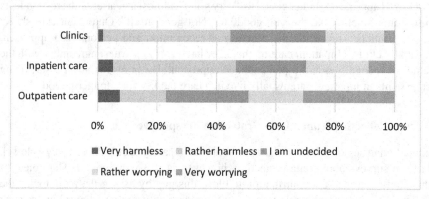

Fig. 4. Data flow, data security and data access rights (n = 235)

The results are similar to the previous data collection question, but the concerns are more pronounced: 61% of respondents are either "undecided" or consider it as rather or very worrying. The skepticism is evident in all subgroups but is most pronounced in outpatient care. Inpatient care and clinics show similar values regarding their concerns.

3.5   Change in Behavior

Meyer [2] found that people react to the use of automated guided vehicles. Initially, they are irritated using the automated vehicle, but quickly get used to it. We therefore included the question: "Do you think an assistant robot changes anything about persons' behavior just by being there (besides the interaction with the robot itself, which means, for example, different behavior because the robot is nearby and records or processes sound or image)?" The response options were "No, not at all", "No, rather not", "I am unsure", "Yes, but only for a short time", and "Yes, permanently". The results are rather unclear (Fig. 5). 35% of respondents think "Yes, but only in the short term", while 23%

answer "No, rather not". Outpatient care least expects a change in behavior triggered by the robot assistants. About 50% of the participants from the inpatient and clinics sector expect a permanent or a least temporary change in behavior.

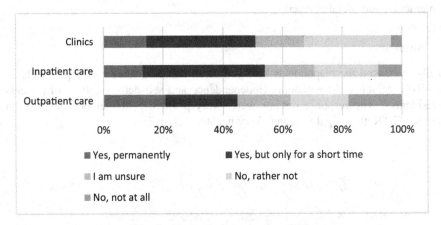

Fig. 5. Change in behavior (n = 235)

3.6 Reduction of Human Contact

In the ethical consideration of the use of robots in healthcare, the amount of human contact is considered decisive [7]. Therefore, the following question was included:

"Do you think that human contact is reduced by assistance robots or is it rather an opportunity to initiate more interaction and social contact?" The response options were "I see it as a great opportunity", "I see it more as an opportunity", "I am undecided", "I rather expect a reduction", and "I expect a reduction in any case".

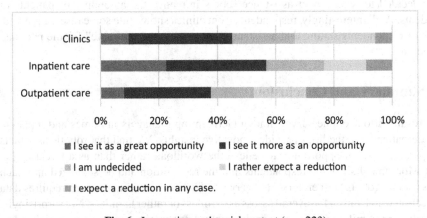

Fig. 6. Interaction and social contact (n = 223)

Figure 6 shows that, overall, 49% of the respondents see assistance robots rather or as a great opportunity for more interaction and social contact, while 32% of the respondents expect rather or in any case a reduction in interaction and social contact. Inpatient care shows the greatest optimism, whereas outpatient care expects most a significant reduction in interaction and social contacts.

3.7 Autonomy

Finally, we asked the respondents "Do you think that assistance robots positively or negatively influence the autonomy (independence and self-determination) of patients or residents?" The response options were "Very positive", "Rather positive", "I am undecided", "Rather negative", and "Very negative" (Fig. 7).

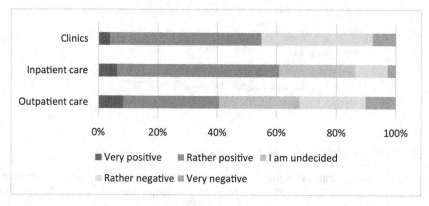

Fig. 7. Autonomy (n = 220)

The effect on autonomy is assessed as rather positive by the majority, specifically by inpatient care. However, almost one third of the respondents from care facilities is undecided to what extent assistance robots influence the autonomy of patients or residents. And, interestingly, respondents from clinics show quite some reservation with 37% of respondents stating that assistant robots are "rather negative" for the patients' autonomy.

4 Summary and Conclusion

The results of our online survey among German top managers in clinics and inpatient and outpatient care facilities provide innovative insights. We find that robotic assistants are perceived as an opportunity to relieve the workload rather than as a threat of job loss. More than half of the respondents find the recognition and personalized approach of assistance robots "rather good" to "very good". This function, however, requires data collection which only 41% overall assess as harmless or rather harmless. Not surprisingly, the values are similar for questions on data flow, data security and data access rights thus underlining the need of manufacturers to address these questions thoroughly in the technical design as well as when approaching healthcare providers. In terms of patients' or residents' change in behavior, about half of the respondents think that the presence of assistant robots changes the behavior. About the same number think that assistance robots are a great or rather great opportunity for more interaction and social contact. An even slightly higher number states that assistance robots can have a positive effect on patients' or residents' autonomy.

In terms of differences between the three subgroups, we find that clinics fear job losses the least. Inpatient care facilities have overall a rather positive attitude towards the potential of assistance robots. They see a high potential of the function of recognizing and personally addressing residents, a great opportunity for more interaction and social contact and higher autonomy of residents. Overall, the outpatient sector is most skeptical with respect to assistance robots which might be due to several reasons: To the best of our knowledge, there are not many economically sustainable robotic solutions for the outpatient sector yet. This on the other hand might be a reason why the outpatient sector had less opportunity in comparison to clinics and inpatient facilities to test and use robotic assistance in practice which is an important factor for user acceptance. The study shows that from the point of view of management in clinics and care facilities, it is necessary to specifically resolve legal issues relating to data protection and security. This is an important task for both policymakers and robotics manufacturers.

To the best of our knowledge, this is the first comprehensive empirical survey on ethical, legal, and social requirements for assistance robots in healthcare. Moreover, while there are plenty of studies that focus on patient and professional acceptance, there are hardly any studies which have top managers as the ultimate decision makers in healthcare facilities as target groups. Our study has several limitations. First, due to the page limitation, we present descriptive information only. Another limitation of our study is certainly its focus on Germany. While the results can be transferred to other European countries [20], it would be interesting to learn to which potentially different conclusions future cross-country studies specifically in other regions of the world arrive. Finally, future studies should differentiate the results along different types of robotic solutions that e.g. Radic et al. [21, 22] performed.

References

1. Klein B., Graf B., Schlömer I.F., Roßberg H., Röhricht K., Baumgarten S.: Robotik in der Gesundheitswirtschaft: Einsatzfelder und Potenziale. medhochzwei, Heidelberg (2017)
2. Meyer S.: Mein Freund der Roboter: Servicerobotik für ältere Menschen; eine Antwort auf den demografischen Wandel? VDE-Verlag, Berlin (2011)
3. Kehl C.: Robotik und assistive Neurotechnologien in der Pflege – gesellschaftliche Herausforderungen, Vertiefung des Projekts „Mensch-Maschine-Entgrenzungen. Büro für Technikfolgen-Abschätzung beim Deutschen Bundestag (TAB), Arbeitsbericht Nr.177 (2018)
4. Körtner T.: Ethical challenges in the use of social service robots for elderly people. Zeitschrift für Gerontologie und Geriatrie **49**, 303–307 (2016)
5. Nelles, J., Bröhl, C., Spies, J., Brandl, C., Mertens, A., Schlick, C.M.: ELSI-Fragestellungen im Kontext der Mensch-Roboter-Kollaboration. In: GfA (eds.): Arbeit in komplexen Systemen –Digital, vernetzt, human, pp. 1–6 (2016)

6. Nylander S., Ljungblad S., Villareal J.J.: A complementing approach for identifying ethical issues in care robotics-grounding ethics in practical use. In: IEEERO-MAN: The 21st IEEE International Symposium on Robot and Human Interactive Communication. IEEE, Piscataway, NJ, pp. 797–802 (2012)

7. Sharkey, A., Sharkey, N.: Granny and the robots: ethical issues in robot care for the elderly. Ethics Inf. Technol. **14**, 27–40 (2012)

8. Bender, N., von Maltzan, S., O'Connor, R.J.: Ethische, Rechtliche und Psychosoziale Implikationen im Bereich Reha, Gesundheit und Heim-Robotik. RoSylerNT_Kurzstudie (2018)

9. Banks, J.: The human touch: practical and ethical implications of putting AI and robotics to work for patients. IEEE Pulse **9**, 15–18 (2018)

10. Ethikrat, D.: Stellungnahme Robotik für gute Pflege. Deutscher Ethikrat, Berlin (2020)

11. Sparrow, R., Sparrow, L.: In the hands of machines? The future of aged care. Minds Mach **16**, 141–161 (2006)

12. Stahl, B.C., Coeckelbergh, M.: Ethics of healthcare robotics: towards responsible research and innovation. RobAutonSyst **86**, 152–161 (2016)

13. Vallor, S.: Carebots and caregivers: sustaining the ethical ideal of care in the twenty-first century. Philos. Technol. **24**, 251 (2011)

14. Decker, M.: Caregiving robots and ethical reflection: the perspective of interdisciplinary technology assessment. Ai Soc **22**, 315–330 (2008)

15. Van der Plas, A., Smits, M., Wehrmann, C.: Beyond speculative robot ethics: a vision assessment study on the future of the robotic caretaker. Account. Res. **17**, 299–315 (2010)

16. Mayer, P., Panek, P.: Sollten Assistenzroboter eine Persönlichkeit haben? Z. Gerontol. Geriatr. **49**, 298–302 (2016)

17. Statista, Anzahl der Krankenhäuser in Deutschland in den Jahren 2000 bis 2021. https://de.statista.com/statistik/daten/studie/2617/umfrage/anzahl-der-krankenhaeuser-in-deutschland-seit-2000/. Accessed 19 Aug 2023

18. Statista, Anzahl von Pflegeheimen und ambulanten Pflegediensten in Deutschland in den Jahren 1999 bis 2021. https://de.statista.com/statistik/daten/studie/2729/umfrage/anzahl-der-pflegeheime-und-ambulanten-pflegedienste-seit-1999/#:~:text=Im%20Jahr%202021%20wurden%20deutschlandweit%2016.115%20Pflegeheime%20und%2015.376%20ambulante%20Pflegedienste%20gez%C3%A4hlt. Accessed 19 Aug 2023

19. Hebesberger, D., Körtner, T., Gisinger, C., Pripfl, J.: A long-term autonomous robot at a care hospital: a mixed methods study on social acceptance and experiences of staff and older adults. Int. J. SocRobot. **9**, 417–429 (2017)

20. Carros, F., Störzinger, T., Wierling, A., Preussner, A., Tolmie, P.: Ethical, legal & participatory concerns in the development of human-robot interaction: lessons from eight research projects with social robots in real-world scenarios. i-com **21**, 299–309 (2022)

21. Radic M., Vosen A., Graf B.: Use of robotics in the German healthcare sector. Application scenarios - drivers and barriers – time savings. In: Salichs, M., et al. (ed.) Social Robotics. ICSR 2019. LNCS, vol. 11876. Springer, Cham. https://doi.org/10.1007/978-3-030-35888-4_40 (2019)

22. Radic, M., Vosen, A., Michler, C.: On the way to the future—assistant robots in hospitals and care facilities. In: Cavallo, F., et al. (ed.) Social Robotics. ICSR 2022. LNCS, vol. 13818. Springer, Cham (2022). https://doi.org/10.1007/978-3-031-24670-8_29

Emotional Understanding and Behavior Learning for Haru via Social Reinforcement Learning

Lei Zhang[1] , Chuanxiong Zheng[1] , Hui Wang[1] , Eric Nichols[2] ,
Randy Gomez[2] , and Guangliang Li[1(✉)]

[1] Ocean University of China, Qingdao, China
guangliangli@ouc.edu.cn
[2] Honda Research Institute Japan Co. Ltd., Wako, Japan
{e.nichols,r.gomez}@jp.honda-ri.com

Abstract. As a new type of human companion, social robots are becoming more and more popular and expected to being fully integrated with human daily life in the near future. Being able to correctly perceive the emotions of users and react to it can increase the sense of trust, affinity, and social presence of human-robot interaction. In this paper, we propose a human-centered reinforcement learning strategy to train social robots to achieve autonomous emotion understanding and behavior shaping. Our whole study was conducted on the social robot Haru, which has a large library of routines to express different emotions. Our experimental results show that autonomous emotion understanding and behavior shaping of social robots can be achieved through continuous interaction with humans.

Keywords: Emotional understanding · Behavior learning · Human-centered reinforcement learning · Human-robot interaction

1 Introduction

Social robots are becoming popular due to their human-like characteristics and are gradually appearing in many daily life scenarios, such as the classroom. In order to make social robots more human-like, realize more natural human-robot interactions, and to improve the individual and group well-being, first, social robots need to better and deeply understand users it is interacting with. Appel et al. proposed that robots that can empathize with humans are more trusted and welcomed by users [1]. Previous studies also show that social robots that can understand human emotions during interactions with humans will increase trust [2] and participation [3] in human-robot interaction. However, natural interactions between robots and humans require the robot not only being able to understand human emotions properly and but also respond to the human users in an appropriate way [4].

In order to achieve a natural interaction between the robot and the child, Filippini et al. [5] introduced heat signals to analyze the child's emotional state. Melinte et al. developed an end-to-end pipeline for a NAO robot to interact with people, using a

© The Author(s), under exclusive license to Springer Nature Singapore Pte Ltd. 2024
A. Al. Ali et al. (Eds.): ICSR 2023, LNAI 14454, pp. 59–70, 2024.
https://doi.org/10.1007/978-981-99-8718-4_6

deep convolutional neural network to implement emotion understanding [6]. Eyam et al. tried to facilitate the collaborative robot Cobot to understand human emotional states with electroencephalography (EEG) signals, and allowed robot to adapt to the human user's emotional state [7]. However, in most cases there are many expressions that do not belong to a certain category and expressions might be understood differently by different people (e.g., anger and disgust).

In this paper, we try to formulate human understanding (in terms of predicting human emotional, mental, social state) into a reinforcement learning problem and try to improve human understanding via online social interactions. We present a framework for social robot Haru to learn to autonomously understand human emotional states and react according to the human user's preference via human-centered reinforcement learning. Our study on social robot Haru shows that Haru can realize autonomous emotion understanding of human users via continuous social interactions and learn reactive behavior for recognized emotional states from evaluative feedback provided by the human user.

The rest of this paper is organized as follows. Section 2 reviews the most related work. Section 3 describes our proposed framework. In Sect. 4, we introduce the robotic platform used in our study and the experimental setup. Section 5 presents and discusses the results. Finally, Sect. 6 concludes.

2   Related Work

Automatic emotion understanding for social robots plays an important role in many scenarios, such as assessing students' participation [8], improving expression generation for autistic patients [9] etc. Liu et al. [10] proposed a human-robot interaction system based on facial emotion understanding for a NAO robot. The robot not only can recognize human emotions, but also can generate facial expression to adapt to human emotions. Fukuda et al. [11] developed a robot system that can recognize human facial emotions and express intentions via facial expressions. Leo et al. [12] developed a facial emotion understanding system with the R25 robot to accompany children with autism.

Robot emotional understanding can enable more natural and efficient human-robot interactions, and has been a long-term goal for realizing meaningful and comfortable interactions between robots and humans. A four-stage human emotion analysis algorithm is proposed and applied to the NAO robot, and facial muscle movements are acquired using facial action coding system (FACS) technique to understand human emotions [13]. May et al. [14] proposed a fuzzy cognitive map-based architecture for robotic emotion understanding to achieve a deep and continuous understanding of the user's emotional state. Heredia et al. [15] proposed a robotic emotion system, which was shown to enable multi-modal emotion understanding and trigger some robot behavior changes with predicted emotion. The above previous approaches mainly use extracted features to detect human emotions. With the advancement of deep learning, the raw facial emotional images can be directly input to a deep neural network for prediction without extracting features in advance. The accuracy of predicting emotions for social robots has also been improved as a result [16–18]. For example, in order to give users a better sense of the robot's friendly behavior, Bagheri et al. [19] proposed an automated cognitive empathy model that can continuously detect the user's emotional state through a network of stacked autoencoders. Their experimental results show that the proposed model allows the robot to respond appropriately to the detected emotions. To achieve dynamic emotion recognition in human-robot interaction, Chen et al. [20] proposed the AdaBoost-KNN algorithm using dynamic adaptive feature selection and direct optimization to train the robot. Their results show that using the proposed algorithm enables robots to understand dynamic human emotions, making robot-human interactions in a smoother and more efficient way. To enable better emotion understanding in robots and address the issues of learning efficiency and computational complexity of deep learning networks, Chen et al. [21] proposed a deep sparse autoencoder network (SRDSAN) for learning facial emotion features, which achieved a high average emotion understanding accuracy.

The previous above work generally used a pre-trained classification model to predict expressions. However, in most cases there are many expressions that do not belong to a certain category and expressions might be understood differently by different people (e.g., anger and disgust). Therefore, in this paper, we propose a human-centered reinforcement learning method to facilitate our social robot Haru to learn emotional understanding and corresponding reactive behaviors via online interactions with human users, which is expected to provide a personalized and friendly human-robot interaction experience.

3   Methodology

Our goal is to allow Haru learning to understand different emotional states of human users autonomously and learn reactive behavior for each recognized emotional state. The proposed framework consists of two models: one is the emotion understanding model and the other one is the behavior learning model, as shown in Fig. 1. To be specific, Haru will first sense the user's facial emotional state through the sensor (RGB camera), and take the raw images of human user's facial expressions as input. Then, Haru will both learn to understand human emotional state and empathic reactive behavior based on its emotion understanding of human user via human-centered reinforcement learning.

The emotion understanding model is pre-trained with a small dataset for Haru to get some basic understanding of human emotions. Then, Haru will improve its emotion understanding by further learning from human provided evaluative feedback via the DQN algorithm [22]. The recognized human emotions will be taken as input to the behavior learning model for Haru to learn corresponding reactive behaviors from human evaluations via a Q-learning algorithm [23].

3.1   Emotion Understanding Model

The mechanism of Haru's emotion understanding model training is shown in Fig. 2. Specifically, at time step t, Haru detects the user's current facial emotional state s_t and selects an action a_t (i.e., predict the user's emotion) with the loaded pre-trained model. Then Haru will speak the recognized emotion to the human user based on the performed action a_t. The human user will provide a feedback R_e according to her judgement on the spoken emotion recognized by Haru. For example, the human user will give Haru a

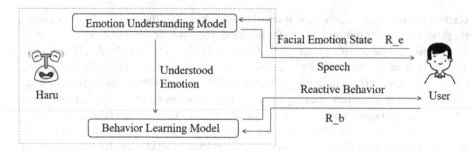

Fig. 1. Proposed framework for social robot Haru to learn emotional understanding of human users and reactive behaviors.

positive reward $+1$ while she thinks Haru correctly understands her emotion, and will provide a -1 reward while she thinks her emotion was incorrectly understood by Haru.

The sample (s_t, a_t, R_e, s_{t+1}) obtained from Haru's interaction with the user is stored in a replay buffer. Haru randomly selects a batch of samples from the replay buffer to update the Eval Net via gradient descent according to the mean squared error loss function:

$$L(\theta) = E[(R\_e + \gamma \max_a Q(s_{t+1}, a, \theta') - Q(s_t, a_t, \theta))^2], \tag{1}$$

where s_t is the current human emotional state detected by Haru, a_t is the action that Haru chooses to perform based on the greedy strategy, s_{t+1} is the next state, γ is the discount factor, and R_e is the evaluative feedback received from the human, θ' represent the parameters of the Target deep Q network and θ represent the parameters of the Eval deep Q network. The parameters θ' of the Target deep Q network are updated with θ every intervals and held fixed between updates. Both Eval and Target net have the same network structure, which consists of two convolution layers, two max-pooling layers, one fully connected layer and two dense layers.

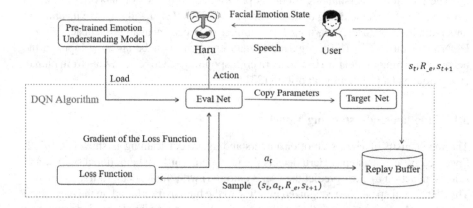

Fig. 2. Illustration of mechanism for training the emotion understanding model.

3.2 Behavior Learning Model

In the behavior learning model, Haru takes the predicted results of emotional understanding model as state inputs and uses the Q-learning algorithm to learn reactive behaviors. First, Haru receives the output of the emotion understanding model as the user's
current emotional state and selects a reactive behavior with the initial behavior learning model. After Haru completes performing the selected behavior, the user will give
feedback R_b according to her preference. She will provide $+1$ to encourage Haru to
perform the behavior when detecting the same state next time, and give -1 to discour-
age Haru to select the behavior next time.

The Q value for the selected behavior is updated as below:

$$Q(s_t, a_t)_{new} = Q(s_t, a_t)_{old} + \alpha(R\_b + \gamma \max_a Q(s_{t+1}, a) - Q(s_t, a_t)), \qquad (2)$$

where s_t is current emotional state which is the output of the emotion understanding
model, s_{t+1} is the next state, a_t is the performed action by Haru, α is the learning rate,
γ is the discount factor, and R_b is the received feedback from the human user.

At next time step $t + 1$, Haru receives another state output from the emotion understanding model s_{t+1} and will select the action with the largest Q value:

$$\pi(s) : a \leftarrow \underset{a \in A}{argmax} Q(s_{t+1}, a), \qquad (3)$$

where A is the action set of possible actions that can be performed by Haru and s_{t+1}
is the next state received by Haru. Haru updates its behavior learning model when it
receives feedback from the human user until the user is satisfied with Haru's learned
behaviors for all detected emotional states.

4 Evaluation

We evaluated our proposed framework by performing a study with human subjects
using the social robotic platform Haru.

4.1 Robotic Platform

Haru is an experimental desktop robot designed to study emotional interaction and
social engagement with users [24]. Haru has 5 degrees of freedom including base rotation, neck tilt, eye rotation, eye tilt, and eye stroke, which can be used to express different emotional routine behaviors by combining different facial and body movements and
voices [25]. At the same time, Haru's eyes have a 3.3-inch display in each eye and are
equipped with built-in stereo speakers to complete the expression of different sounds.
Examples of Haru's affective routine behaviors are shown in Fig. 3.

4.2 Experimental Setup

Our aim is to enable Haru to gradually understand human emotions and learn corresponding reactive behavior for the understood emotions with received human evaluative feedback according to her preference. To this end and as a first step, we used three

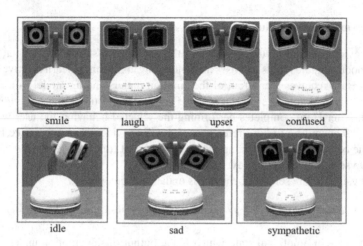

smile   laugh   upset   confused

idle   sad   sympathetic

Fig. 3. Examples of Haru's affective behaviors (i.e., actions to perform).

most common human emotions: happy, neutral and sad, as human emotional states in our study. Haru has a rich set of routine behaviors to respond to the different detected emotional states. We select 7 of them as possible reactive behaviors for Haru to learn from. The human emotional states and Haru's possible reactive routine behaviors are shown in Table 1.

We recruited 10 subjects from a university campus for our study and all subjects have some background in robotics and machine learning. In the study, each subject was asked to express the three emotions in a random order and Haru can sense and detect the subject's facial emotional state through the RGB camera with its own recognition module. Then, Haru will choose and perform a reactive action from the set of possible behaviors with an initial policy. The subject observed Haru's enacted behavior and then provided evaluative feedback. Haru's behavior model will be updated using the received evaluative feedback. A new cycle of detecting subject's new emotional state, performing reactive action with updated behavior model and receiving evaluative feedback starts, until the human subject is satisfied with Haru's learned behaviors for all detected emotional states.

Table 1. Emotional states of human user and possible reactive behaviors of Haru.

Emotional States	"happy","sad" ,"neutral"
Haru's Actions	"smile","sad" ,"idle",
	"laugh","upset","confused" ,"sympathetic"

In our study, subjects were allowed to give feedback within 3 s of observing Haru's action. Before learning from human users, Haru will first load a pre-trained initial emotion understanding model to get basic understanding of human users. Then, Haru will interact with human user and update its emotion understanding and reactive behavior learning models. It is worth noting that only when the emotional understanding model is trained to a certain level, the behavior learning model starts being trained by the human user.

5   Results and Discussion

5.1   Emotion Understanding

The emotion understanding model was pre-trained with a small dataset consisting of 150 color images of the three human facial emotions: happy, sad, neutral, with 50 images for each emotion. The dataset FER2013 [26] was used as the test dataset. Figure 4 shows the training and testing accuracy in pre-training process. From Fig. 4 we can see that, the training accuracy can real close to 1 while the average testing accuracy is around 0.4, with the prediction accuracy for the 'happy' emotion to be the highest of all three emotions. This indicates that the pre-trained emotion understanding model can get a basic understanding of human emotions but cannot correctly predict them yet.

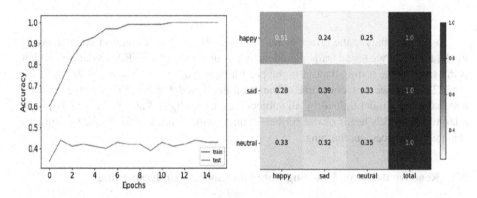

Fig. 4. The training and testing accuracy in pre-training process of the emotion understanding model (left) and tested accuracy for each emotion (right).

The pre-trained emotion understanding model was further trained with real emotions of subjects in the study via human-centered reinforcement learning. Figure 5 shows the final prediction accuracy of human emotions of the model trained by one subject. From Fig. 5 we can see that, the understanding of human emotions by Haru can be further improved by learning from human provided evaluative feedback during online interactions, with the prediction accuracy of 'happy' emotion increasing the most — from 51% to 77%, and 'neutral' emotion increasing from 35% to 59%, 'sad' emotion increasing the least from 39% to 47%.

Table 2. Accuracy and F-score of testing the trained models by all subjects on the FER2013 test dataset.

	Pre-train	P1	P2	P3	P4	P5	P6	P7	P8	P9	P10
Accuracy	0.43	0.63	0.51	0.59	0.42	0.59	0.60	0.61	0.38	0.61	0.60
F1_score	0.42	0.61	0.48	0.57	0.37	0.60	0.59	0.59	0.39	0.61	0.58

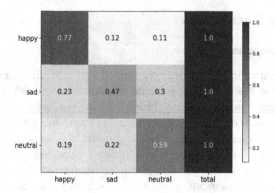

Fig. 5. The final prediction accuracy of human emotions of the model trained by one participant with real emotions of the experimenter.

To further analyze the effect of human rewards on Haru's emotion understanding model learning, we tested trained models by all subjects on the FER2013 dataset, which is the same as the testing dataset in the pre-training process, as shown in Table 2. From Table 2 we can see that, compared to the pre-trained model, the accuracy of the emotion understanding model trained by all subjects (except Subject 4 and 8) was improved to a large extent as a result of the further training with evaluative feedback via human-centered reinforcement learning.

5.2   Reactive Behavior Learning Based on Emotion Understanding

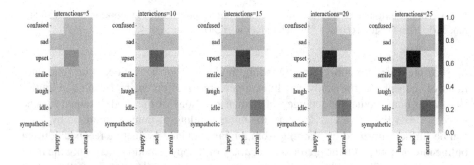

Fig. 6. Visualization of the Haru's reactive behavior learning process for each recognized human emotional state based on its emotion understanding model.

Haru will learn reactive behaviors for each recognized human emotional state based on its emotion understanding model. The reactive behavior model was also trained via human-centered reinforcement learning with human evaluations on Haru's performed action in each recognized human emotional state. We visualized Haru's learning process via a heat map, as shown in Fig. 6. In Fig. 6, the horizontal axis shows the 3 emotional states and the vertical axis shows the 7 routine behaviors to be selected in each state.

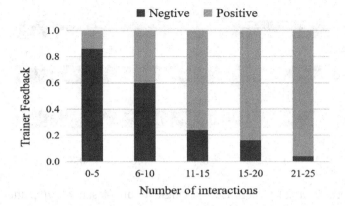

Fig. 7. The ratio of positive and negative feedback provided by all subjects every 5 interactions during the training process.

Each block shows one Q value corresponding to one routine in one emotional state. The darker is the block's color, the larger is the Q value. From Fig. 6 we can see that, Haru can gradually learn reactive routine behaviors for each recognized human emotional state via the emotion understanding model after 20 interactions.

We also computed the proportion of received positive and negative feedback by Haru every 5 interactions for all subjects during Haru's behavior learning. As shown in Fig. 7, the proportion of positive rewards increases as the number of interactions increases. During interactions 21–25, almost all received feedback was positive, which indicates Haru has learned the behavioral preferences of human users in the three emotional states. This is consistent with the results in Fig. 6.

We found that all subjects were trying to personalize Haru's behavior to meet their preferences. Meanwhile, subjects generally trained Haru to learn reactive behaviors similar to their emotional states. Figure 8 shows Haru's fully learned behaviors for the

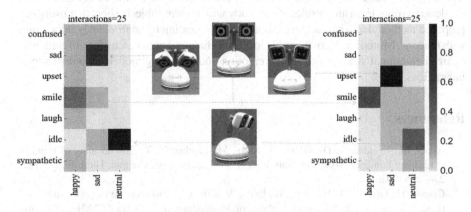

Fig. 8. Visualized heat map of final Q values and reactive behaviors for all facial emotional states trained by subject 9 and 10.

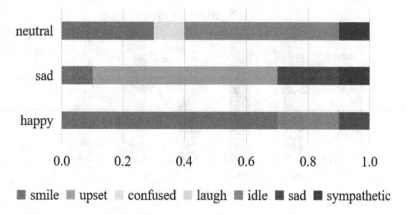

Fig. 9. The percentage of each optimal behavior trained by the 10 subjects for all emotional states.

three emotional states trained by subject 9 and subject 10. Figure 9 shows the percentage of final optimal behaviors for all three emotional states trained by all subjects. For example, as shown in Fig. 8, Subject 9 and 10 shared preference for the emotional state 'happy' and 'neutral', but have different preferences for emotional states 'sad' . In addition, from Fig. 9 we can see that, most subjects trained Haru to be 'idle' for the emotional state 'neutral', 'upset' for the emotional state 'sad' and 'smile' for the emotional state 'happy', which is consistent to the common sense of human beings.

6 Conclusion

In this paper, we propose a human-centered reinforcement learning strategy to train social robot Haru to achieve autonomous emotional understanding and behavior shaping. As different subjects provide different reward feedbacks, the robot learn personalized emotional understanding and behavioral preferences. We evaluated our method on the desktop robot Haru and results of our study with human subjects show that using our proposed method, Haru can achieve emotion understanding by continuously interacting with humans. Moreover, Haru was able to learn behavioral preferences for different recognized emotional states based on the emotion understanding model via online social interactions.

References

1. Appel, M., Izydorczyk, D., Weber, S., Mara, M., Lischetzke, T.: The uncanny of mind in a machine: humanoid robots as tools, agents, and experiencers. Comput. Hum. Behav. **102**, 274–286 (2020)
2. Cramer, H., Goddijn, J., Wielinga, B., Evers, V.: Effects of (in) accurate empathy and situational valence on attitudes towards robots. In: Proceedings of 2010 5th ACM/IEEE International Conference on Human-Robot Interaction (HRI), pp. 141–142. IEEE (2010)

3. Leite, I., Castellano, G., Pereira, A., Martinho, C., Paiva, A.: Empathic robots for long-term interaction: evaluating social presence, engagement and perceived support in children. Int. J. Soc. Robot. **6**, 329–341 (2014)
4. Merla, A.: Thermal expression of intersubjectivity offers new possibilities to human-machine and technologically mediated interactions. Front. Psychol. **5**, 802 (2014)
5. Filippini, C., et al.: Facilitating the child–robot interaction by endowing the robot with the capability of understanding the child engagement: the case of Mio Amico robot. Int. J. Soc. Robot. **13**(4), 677–689 (2020). https://doi.org/10.1007/s12369-020-00661-w
6. Melinte, D.O., Vladareanu, L.: Facial expressions recognition for human-robot interaction using deep convolutional neural networks with rectified Adam optimizer. Sensors **20**(8), 2393 (2020)
7. Eyam, A.T., Mohammed, W.M., Lastra, J.L.M.: Emotion-driven analysis and control of human-robot interactions in collaborative applications. Sensors **21**(14), 4626 (2021)
8. Whitehill, J., Serpell, Z., Lin, Y.-C., Foster, A., Movellan, J.R.: The faces of engagement: automatic recognition of student engagement from facial expressions. IEEE Trans. Affect. Comput. **5**(1), 86–98 (2014)
9. Cockburn, J., Bartlett, M., Tanaka, J., Movellan, J., Pierce, M., Schultz, R.: SmileMaze: a tutoring system in real-time facial expression perception and production in children with autism spectrum disorder. In: ECAG 2008 Workshop Facial and Bodily Expressions for Control and Adaptation of Games, vol. 3. Amsterdam (2008)
10. Liu, Z., et al.: A facial expression emotion recognition based human-robot interaction system. IEEE CAA J. Autom. Sinica **4**(4), 668–676 (2017)
11. Fukuda, T., Tachibana, D., Arai, F., Taguri, J., Nakashima, M., Hasegawa, Y.: Human-robot mutual communication system. In: Proceedings of 10th IEEE International Workshop on Robot and Human Interactive Communication (RO-MAN), pp. 14–19. IEEE (2001)
12. Leo, M., et al.: Automatic emotion recognition in robot-children interaction for ASD treatment. In: Proceedings of the IEEE International Conference on Computer Vision Workshops, pp. 145–153 (2015)
13. Göngör, F., Tutsoy, Ö., Barkana, D.E., Köse, H.: An emotion analysis algorithm and implementation to NAO humanoid robot. In: Proceedings of International Conference on Technology, Engineering and Science (IConTES), vol. 7. https://www.researchgate.net/publication/321704164 (2021)
14. May, A.D., Lotfi, A., Langensiepen, C., Lee, K., Acampora, G.: Human emotional understanding for empathetic companion robots. In: Angelov, P., Gegov, A., Jayne, C., Shen, Q. (eds.) Advances in Computational Intelligence Systems. AISC, vol. 513, pp. 277–285. Springer, Cham (2017). https://doi.org/10.1007/978-3-319-46562-3_18
15. Heredia, J., Cardinale, Y., Dongo, I., Aguilera, A., Diaz-Amado, J.: Multimodal emotional understanding in robotics. In: Workshops at 18th International Conference on Intelligent Environments (IE2022). IOS Press (2022)
16. Zhu, X., Lei, Z., Yan, J., Yi, D., Li, S.Z.: High-fidelity pose and expression normalization for face recognition in the wild. In: Proceedings of the IEEE Conference on Computer Vision and Pattern Recognition, pp. 787–796 (2015)
17. Polyak, A., Wolf, L.: Channel-level acceleration of deep face representations. IEEE Access **3**, 2163–2175 (2015)
18. Li, S., Deng, W.: Deep facial expression recognition: a survey. IEEE Trans. Affect. Comput. **13**(3), 1195–1215 (2020)
19. Bagheri, E., Esteban, P.G., Cao, H.-L., Beir, A.D., Lefeber, D., Vanderborght, B.: An autonomous cognitive empathy model responsive to users' facial emotion expressions. ACM Trans. Interact. Intell. Syst. (TIIS) **10**(3), 1–23 (2020)

20. Chen, L., Li, M., Su, W., Wu, M., Hirota, K., Pedrycz, W.: Adaptive feature selection-based Adaboost-KNN with direct optimization for dynamic emotion recognition in human-robot interaction. IEEE Trans. Emerg. Top. Comput. Intell. **5**(2), 205–213 (2019)
21. Chen, L., Zhou, M., Su, W., Wu, M., She, J., Hirota, K.: Softmax regression based deep sparse autoencoder network for facial emotion recognition in human-robot interaction. Inf. Sci. **428**, 49–61 (2018)
22. Mnih, V., et al.: Playing Atari with deep reinforcement learning. arXiv preprint arXiv:1312.5602 (2013)
23. Watkins, C.J., Dayan, P.: Q-learning. Mach. Learn. **8**, 279–292 (1992)
24. Sandry, E., Gomez, R., Nakamura, K.: Art, design and communication theory in creating the communicative social robot 'haru'. Front. Robot. AI **8**, 577107 (2021)
25. Brock, H., Sabanovic, S., Nakamura, K., Gomez, R.: Robust real-time hand gestural recognition for non-verbal communication with tabletop robot Haru. In: Proceedings of 2020 29th IEEE International Conference on Robot and Human Interactive Communication (RO-MAN), pp. 891–898. IEEE (2020)
26. Goodfellow, I.J., et al.: Challenges in representation learning: a report on three machine learning contests. In: Lee, M., Hirose, A., Hou, Z.-G., Kil, R.M. (eds.) ICONIP 2013. LNCS, vol. 8228, pp. 117–124. Springer, Heidelberg (2013). https://doi.org/10.1007/978-3-642-42051-1_16

Talking Like One of Us: Effects of Using Regional Language in a Humanoid Social Robot

Thomas Sievers[✉] and Nele Russwinkel

Institute of Information Systems, University of Lübeck, 23562 Lübeck, Germany
{sievers,russwinkel}@uni-luebeck.de

Abstract. Social robots are becoming more and more perceptible in public service settings. For engaging people in a natural environment a smooth social interaction as well as acceptance by the users are important issues for future successful Human-Robot Interaction (HRI). The type of verbal communication has a special significance here. In this paper we investigate the effects of spoken language varieties of a non-standard/regional language compared to standard language. More precisely we compare a human dialog with a humanoid social robot Pepper where the robot on the one hand is answering in High German and on the other hand in Low German, a regional language that is understood and partly still spoken in the northern parts of Germany. The content of what the robot says remains the same in both variants. We are interested in the effects that these two different ways of robot talk have on human interlocutors who are more or less familiar with Low German in terms of perceived warmth, competence and possible discomfort in conversation against a background of cultural identity. To measure these factors we use the Robotic Social Attributes Scale (RoSAS) on 17 participants with an age ranging from 19 to 61. Our results show that significantly higher warmth is perceived in the Low German version of the conversation.

Keywords: social robots · human-robot interaction · regional language · communication · cultural identity

1 Introduction

Social robots are coming into more and more contact with people in everyday life. Therefore, it is becoming increasingly important for human-robot interaction (HRI) to find ways for acceptance, good cooperation and collaboration.

In their research van Pinxteren et al. [1] focus on anthropomorphism as a central concept in HRI. According to theory, human-like features of the robot facilitate anthropomorphism [2]. And more than 80% of respondents surveyed by TU Darmstadt on the robotization of office and service professions believe that robots can show feelings [3]. So people tend to think of robots as social beings. This suggests that for a robot to be accepted by people as something to be involved with, it is important to have a suitable personality and appropriate manners.

© The Author(s), under exclusive license to Springer Nature Singapore Pte Ltd. 2024
A. Al. Ali et al. (Eds.): ICSR 2023, LNAI 14454, pp. 71–80, 2024.
https://doi.org/10.1007/978-981-99-8718-4_7

Winkle et al. expect carefully designed *social identities* in social robots for maximized effectiveness [4]. They conclude that the deliberate use of anthropomorphic social behaviour in a social robot is essential for good functioning and carries relatively low ethical risks. It is therefore important that a robot addresses people and engages with them in an appropriate manner, not least because many people are still surprised that they can communicate with a robot in a natural way using natural language [5]. Robots will be most successful in being accepted if they meet expectations through aesthetic characteristics that engage users within a clearly defined context [6]. Everything from the robots appearance to the visual design and the sound of voice hold semantic value. Previous work has also provided insights into the effects of language and cultural context on the credibility of robot speech [7]. The way robots express themselves to build credibility and convey information in a meaningful and compelling way is a key function in creating acceptance and usability.

In this paper we investigate the effects of spoken language varieties of a non-standard/regional language compared to standard language. We focus on the effects that these two variations of robot talk have on human interlocutors in terms of perceived warmth, competence and a discomfort in conversation. The regional language provides a cultural identity and serves as a variable for examining the influence in the perception of the robot's personality.

2   Preliminaries

The results of a survey conducted by Foster et al. [8] concerning expectations for conversational interaction with a robot confirm the significance of accent and dialect. They aim to develop a robot capable of fluid natural-language conversations in socially and ethnically-diverse areas. The circumstances regarding the differences in accent, grammar and vocabulary in their study environment in Glasgow, Scotland, between Scottish English and standard language seem to be similar to those in our environment with Low German and High German.

Low German is a West Germanic language variety spoken mainly in northern Germany and the northeastern part of the Netherlands. It is closely related to Frisian and English, with which it forms the North Sea Germanic group of the West Germanic languages. Low German has not undergone the High German consonant shift. There are about 1.6 million speakers in Germany, mainly in northern Germany. Low German is part of the cultural heritage of northern Germany and complements some of the characteristics and stereotypes people have in mind when they think of a typical northern German person, such as taciturnity, sarcasm and aloofness.

So our research question is to what extent the human perception of a conversation with a social robot speaking in Low German differs from the perception when the robot speaks the standard language regarding warmth, competence and discomfort. Linguistic variation in cultural context has not been well studied in human-robot interaction to the best of our knowledge. With our work we want to take a step forward on this path.

3   Related Work

As research has shown, people tend to treat machines like robots and computers as real social beings [9]. This behavior includes gender stereotypes and social role models. Nias et al. discuss how speech and dialect shape one's identity and state the importance of a culturally rich engagement experience between humans and social robots that respects diversity in experience, culture and language [10]. In their paper they focus on education and schooling, but we think this statement could be generalized. Obremski et al. discuss the representation of multiple cultural backgrounds in one socially interactive agent and how an agent is perceived speaking in a none-native accent [11]. They partly observed a transfer of stereotypes and a difference in the perception of the robot.

Personality can be manifested in voice and language and according to the principle of similarity-attraction a person tends to like others with similar patterns. This hypothesis is explored by Pazylbekov et al. who let humans choose between robots with different dialectal features of the language [12]. They suggest that dialect and language patterns are important in improving people's sympathy for robots.

Lugrin et al. investigated the effects of a regular language compared to High German [13]. They used recorded human voices with a robot and had the participants listen to the robot. The text was recorded in three different speech styles: High German, Franconian accent and Franconian dialect. They expected effects on perceptions of competence, social skills and likability. However, these effects depended on whether the participants themselves spoke dialect or not.

4   Humanoid Robot Pepper

The social humanoid robot Pepper, shown in Fig. 1, was developed by Aldebaran and first released in 2015 [14]. The robot is 120 centimeters tall and optimized for human interaction. It is able to engage with people through conversation, gestures and its touch screen. Pepper is equipped with internal sensors, four directional microphones in his head and speakers for voice output. Speech recognition and dialogue is available in 15 languages.

Since research has generally shown that anthropomorphism improves social interaction [15], a humanoid social robot like Pepper is a good choice for HRI experiments. A human-like face and body language, the use of voice and a name of one's own are considered beneficial to the human relationship with the robot.

The robot features an open and fully programmable platform so that developers can program their own applications to run on Pepper using software development kits (SDKs) for programming languages like C++, Python or Java respectively Kotlin. This approach allows the development of robot applications for a wide variety of scenarios in a development environment familiar to most developers.

Pepper's German language package and built-in speech recognition is used for understanding and talking with the user. When speaking in Low German,

Pepper's synthesized voice, though not perfect, is clearly recognizable as speaking Low German. For robotic conversation we created topics, which are a set of rules, concepts and proposals. These elements, written in QiChat syntax as shown in Fig. 2, set the template for the conversation flow.

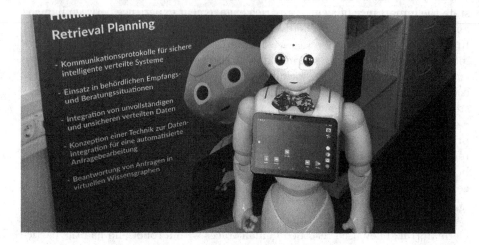

Fig. 1. Humanoid Robot Pepper

5 The Survey

To measure possible effects that the two different ways of robot talk (High German vs. Low German) have on a human interlocutor's judgement of social attributes of the robot we use the 18-item Robotic Social Attributes Scale (RoSAS) [16]. It comprises three underlying scale dimensions – the factors *warmth, competence* and *discomfort*. RoSAS is based on items from the Godspeed Scale [17] and psychological literature on social perception. It is considered to be a psychologically valid scale of robotic perception.

We assume that a robot speaking Low German in an area with a corresponding cultural identity should make a difference in how it is perceived by human interlocutors. If so, the inclusion of cultural identity traits could make a difference in personality perceptions of a social robot.

5.1 Experimental Setup

We used a within-subject design where all participants had a conversation with the robot both in Low German and High German. The 17 participants in our study came from different walks of life and were aged between 19 and 61. We had 9 female and 8 male participants. To eliminate ordering effects we mixed the order of Low and High German for different participants. Thus, nearly half of the

Fig. 2. Dialog topic file

participants first spoke to the robot in Low German, followed by an interaction in which the robot used High German. For the other group, it was the other way around. Apart from the order, the experimental scenario was identical for all participants. The topic, content and course of the dialogue were also the same for everyone. The robot started the conversation with a greeting, asked for the name of its counterpart and then asked questions on various topics, mostly closed questions to which the human interlocutor could express agreement or disagreement. The name given by the human was repeatedly incorporated into the robot's speech in order to create a more natural conversation. Participants could also ask a few predefined questions.

Before interacting with the robot, each participant filled out a questionnaire that included questions about gender, age, place of origin and knowledge of Low German. All participants in the survey lived in the northern part of Germany and were more or less familiar with Low German, but most of them did not actively speak the language. We had 7 participants who rated their knowledge of Low German as good to very good. The other 10 participants had little or no knowledge of this regional language, but could mostly guess the meaning. In any case, the participants had to speak High German because our Pepper robot did not understand Low German.

After each dialogue session with the robot, the 18 items of the RoSAS were presented to the participants. They were asked, *"Using the scale provided, how closely are the words below associated with your perception of the robot?"*. The participants responded using a 5-point likert scale from 1 = *does not apply at all* to 5 = *applies*. Every RoSAS factor comprises six items. For the factor *warmth* they are: happy, feeling, social, organic, compassionate and emotional. *Competence* includes: capable, responsive, interactive, reliable, competent and knowledgable. And *discomfort* comprises: scary, strange, awkward, dangerous, awful and aggressive. Each factor consisting of six items could therefore receive a total of between 6 and 30 points, with a score of 6 representing the lowest agreement and 30 the highest.

5.2   Results

We used a t-Test to determine whether there is a statistically significant difference between the perception of the conversation in High German versus the Low German variant in the mean. Figure 3 illustrates our results. In general, it can be seen that perceived warmth and competence tend to be high and perceived discomfort tends to be low.

The test showed in detail that participants perceived significantly higher warmth in the Low German version of the conversation (p = 0.027). Figure 4 illustrates the result of the perceived warmth. For the competence factor, there was hardly any difference in perception (p = 0.378, Fig. 5). Finally, discomfort was perceived slightly less in the Low German version, but this cannot be considered a statistically significant result, as the p-value of p = 0.056 is somewhat above the significance level of 0.05. Figure 6 illustrates this result. But in our opinion, this result can still be understood as an indication of an influence on the factor discomfort. Table 1 shows the results as mean values for the 18 RoSAS items divided into areas of the three factors *warmth*, *competence* and *discomfort*.

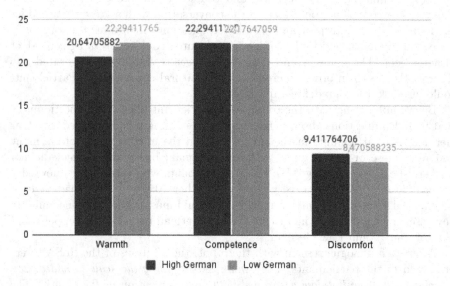

Fig. 3. The results of the perceived warmth, competence and discomfort of the High German or Low German speaking Pepper Robot.

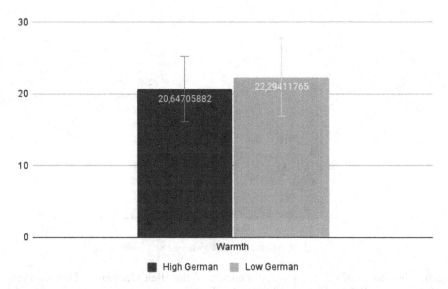

Fig. 4. The results of the perceived warmth of the High German or Low German speaking Pepper Robot. Error bars show standard deviations.

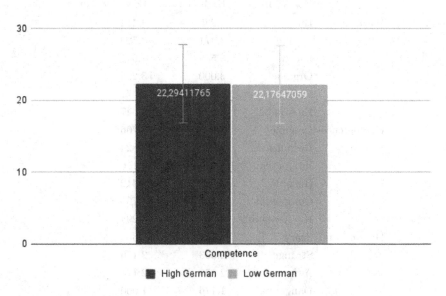

Fig. 5. The results of the perceived competence of the High German or Low German speaking Pepper Robot. Error bars show standard deviations.

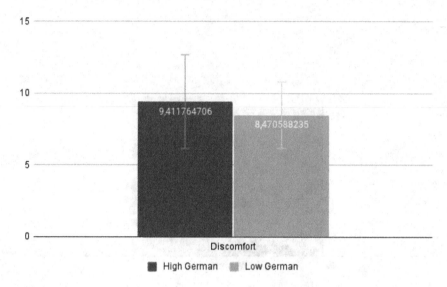

Fig. 6. The results of the perceived discomfort of the High German or Low German speaking Pepper Robot. Error bars show standard deviations.

Table 1. RoSAS items and their mean values for High German and Low German

	RoSAS item	High German	Low German
Warmth	Happy	4.235	4.412
	Feeling	3.471	3.529
	Social	3.588	3.941
	Organic	3.000	3.294
	Compassionate	3.059	3.471
	Emotional	3.294	3.647
Competence	Capable	3.588	3.706
	Responsive	4.000	3.824
	Interactive	3.941	4.176
	Reliable	3.588	3.412
	Competent	3.882	3.765
	Knowledgable	3.294	3.294
Discomfort	Scary	1.588	1.353
	Strange	2.353	2.176
	Awkward	2.176	2.118
	Dangerous	1.176	1.000
	Awful	1.118	1.000
	Aggressive	1.000	1.000

5.3 Discussion

For our study, we used a real robot that engages in dialogue with humans using a synthetic voice, while many similar studies use virtual robots, pictures of robots or a robot saying something on video with pre-recorded human voice. This certainly has an impact on the perception of the conversation because the physical presence of the robot has a much more immediate effect.

Some of the participants were not used to the Low German language and, although they could mostly guess the meaning of the words, did not speak it at all. Some knew Low German as the language of their grandparents from their childhood. Perhaps that is one of the reasons why it is associated more with warmth or perhaps coziness than High German. As suggested in previous work, a regional language seems to increase perceived social skills as well as likeability and could reduce people's discomfort. It is perhaps somewhat surprising that the use of a regional language in our experiment had no effect on the robot's perception of competence, as Lugrin et al. mentioned previous work indicating a possible decrease in perceived competence with non-standard language [13].

6 Conclusions and Future Work

In this paper, we present the results of a survey that asked whether a social robot speaking in a regional language is perceived differently in conversation in terms of warmth, competence and discomfort than when using the standard language. Our results suggest that the inclusion of cultural regional aspects, as found in languages, has a positive impact on the perceived personality of the robot, especially in terms of perceived warmth and discomfort in conversations.

In future work, the robot should also understand Low German, so that a dialogue is also possible with people who speak in this regional language. Gestures and body language as an essential part of expression should, if possible, also be adapted to regional characteristics and examined in their effect within the framework of a cultural identity.

References

1. van Pinxteren, M.M.E., Wetzels, R.W.H., Rüger, J., Pluymaekers, M., Wetzels, M.: Trust in humanoid robots: implications for services marketing. J. Serv. Mark. **33**(4), 507–518 (2019)
2. Epley, N., Waytz, A., Cacioppo, J.T.: On seeing human: a three-factor theory of anthropomorphism. Psychol. Rev. **114**(4), 864–886 (2007). https://doi.org/10.1037/0033-295X.114.4.864
3. Stock-Homburg, R.: Denn sie wissen nicht, was sie tun - Studie der TU Darmstadt zur Robotisierung von Büro- und Dienstleistungsberufen. Transnational Study series "Robots@work4.0" (2016). http://www.tu-darmstadt.de/universitaet/aktuelles_meldungen/archiv_2/2016/2016quartal4/einzelansicht_162880.de.jsp

4. Winkle, K., Jackson, R., Bejarano, A., Williams, T.: On the flexibility of robot social identity performance: benefits, ethical risks and open research questions for HRI. In: Conference: Workshop on Robo-Identity: Artificial identity and multi-embodiment at HRI (2021)
5. Gardecki A., Podpora, M., Beniak, R., Klin, B.: The Pepper humanoid robot in front desk application. In: Conference Paper: Progress in Applied Electrical Engineering (PAEE) (2018). https://doi.org/10.1109/PAEE.2018.8441069
6. Diana, C.: My Robot Gets Me: How Social Design Can Make New Products More Human, pp. 218–228. Havard Business Review Press, Boston (2021). ISBN 9781633694422
7. Andrist, S., Ziadee, M., Boukaram, H., Mutlu, B., Sakr, M.: Effects of culture on the credibility of robot speech: a comparison between English and Arabic. In: Proceedings of the Tenth Annual ACM/IEEE International Conference on Human-Robot Interaction (HRI 2015), New York, NY, USA, pp. 157–164. Association for Computing Machinery (2015). https://doi.org/10.1145/2696454.2696464
8. Foster, M.E., Stuart-Smith, J.: Social robotics meets sociolinguistics: investigating accent bias and social context in HRI. In: Companion of the 2023 ACM/IEEE International Conference on Human-Robot Interaction (HRI 2023), New York, NY, USA, pp. 156–160. Association for Computing Machinery (2023). https://doi.org/10.1145/3568294.3580063
9. Nass, C., Moon, Y.: Machines and mindlessness: social responses to computers. J. Soc. Issues **56**(1), 81–103 (2000)
10. Nias, J., Ruffin, M.: CultureBot: a culturally relevant humanoid robotic dialogue agent. In: Proceedings of the 2020 ACM Southeast Conference (ACM SE 2020), New York, NY, USA, pp. 280–283. Association for Computing Machinery (2020). https://doi.org/10.1145/3374135.3385306
11. Obremski, D., Friedrich, P., Haak, N., Schaper, P., Lugrin, B.: The impact of mixed-cultural speech on the stereotypical perception of a virtual robot. Front. Robot. AI **9**, 983955 (2022). https://doi.org/10.3389/frobt.2022.983955
12. Pazylbekov, A., Kalym, D., Otynshin, A., Sandygulova, A.: Similarity attraction for robot's dialect in language learning using social robots. In: 14th ACM/IEEE International Conference on Human-Robot Interaction (HRI), Daegu, Korea (South), pp. 532–533 (2019). https://doi.org/10.1109/HRI.2019.8673232
13. Lugrin, B., Ströle, E., Obremski, D., Schwab, F., Lange, B.: What if it speaks like it was from the village? Effects of a Robot speaking in Regional Language Variations on Users Evaluations. In: 2020 29th IEEE International Conference on Robot and Human Interactive Communication (RO-MAN), Naples, Italy, pp. 1315–1320 (2020). https://doi.org/10.1109/RO-MAN47096.2020.9223432
14. Aldebaran, United Robotics Group and Softbank Robotics (2022). Pepper [Online]. http://www.aldebaran.com/en/pepper
15. Fink, J.: Anthropomorphism and human likeness in the design of robots and human-robot interaction. In: Ge, S.S., Khatib, O., Cabibihan, J.-J., Simmons, R., Williams, M.-A. (eds.) ICSR 2012. LNCS (LNAI), vol. 7621, pp. 199–208. Springer, Heidelberg (2012). https://doi.org/10.1007/978-3-642-34103-8_20
16. Carpinella, C.M., Wyman, A.B., Perez, M.A., Stroessne, S.J.: The robotic social attributes scale (RoSAS): development and validation. In: 12th ACM/IEEE International Conference on Human-Robot Interaction (HRI), Vienna, Austria, pp. 254–262 (2017)
17. Bartneck, C., Kulic, D., Zoghbi, S.: Measurement instruments for the anthropomorphism, animacy, likeability, perceived intelligence, and perceived safety of robots. Int. J. Soc. Robot. **1**, 71–81 (2009). https://doi.org/10.1007/s12369-008-0001-3

Robotic Music Therapy Assistant: A Cognitive Game Playing Robot

Jwaad Hussain$^{(\boxtimes)}$, Anthony Mangiacotti, Fabia Franco, and Eris Chinellato

Middlesex University, The Burroughs, London NW4 4BT, UK
j.hussain@mdx.ac.uk

Abstract. Music Therapy is a non-pharmacological treatment used to maintain/enhance cognitive abilities, on the basis that music is able to simultaneously activate multiple brain functions. In this paper we propose the combination of Music Therapy (MT) with cognitive training games administered by a humanoid robot (QT robot of LUXAI). This intervention is intended to mitigate cognitive decline in individuals with mild cognition impairment, while reducing the load on therapists and care staff, by offering MT to a larger population. The four implemented music-themed cognitive games elicit activation of different sets of cognitive functions, producing an overall multi-domain treatment, and adapt to subject's preferences, skills and progress. We present here results from two pilot studies on our robotic-aided MT setup, and identify key factors necessary to increasing the success and feasibility of the approach.

Keywords: Social robotics · human robot interaction · cognitive impairment · music therapy · cognitive stimulation

1 Introduction

The average age of populations is rising worldwide, and more and more individuals are at increased risk of developing age-related cognitive impairments (e.g. dementia) [18]. This continual rise in the number of affected will carry over to the economical and societal impact that neuro-degenerative disorders have.

One preventative method to mitigate the loss of cognitive and emotional abilities associated with ageing is to play *serious* or *cognitive* games [22]. In the context of cognitive rehabilitation, these games are used to stimulate the brain in a targeted manner, applying loads to specific mental processes, with the intention of increasing or maintaining the related cognitive functions [25].

Music Therapy (MT) is a non pharmacological intervention wherein a trained music therapist uses musical themed activities to help patients maintain and improve their well-being and cognitive-psychological health. MT has been shown to reduce or mitigate loss in cognitive functioning in older adults [17]. MT requires specialised professional staff who are usually only employed for a few hours a week, making it difficult to extend to a large population.

Research Funded by Dunhill Medical Trust. Grant number: RPGF2006/241.

In recent years, quality of life of the ageing population has been improved by the growing use of socially assistive robots (SAR) [6]. Studies usually report positive reception from the older adults, and there is agreement on the potentials of SARs, albeit with attached concerns and considerations [20].

In this paper, we aim to make MT more accessible by combining it with cognitive games to be hosted by a robot. We aim to utilise the ease of distribution and wide accessibility of gaming, while eliciting the personal reaction that individuals have with music, through novel *music-cognitive games* (MCG). We expect that this will produce a successful and enjoyable cognitive game-playing experience, to be used as part of MT treatments. The inclusion of robots should allow reach of a wider population with the same amount of therapists and/or prolong therapy sessions without charging further on the care workers.

This study is intended to validate this approach, as well as the personality and hosting style of the robot. We will use the data and feedback to improve the intervention. This is in preparation for a further 8 week study to be performed in care homes with individuals with mild - moderate cognitive impairments (Mini Mental State Examination score of 14–23).

2   Related Works

2.1   Robots and Cognitive Training

Of the many studies investigating role of robots in care homes and community centres, some include the use of cognitive games as a feature of deployed robots. Andriella *et al.* used a robot to train participants to perform simple cognitive game included in the traditional SKT test (Syndrom Kurztest neuropsychological battery) [1]. The robot was able to demonstrate the test to participants, as well as actuate the physical blocks to assist in the completion of the task if needed. This displaying of agency is important as it possibly acts to increase engagement as a showcasing of the robot's practical ability and a reminder of its physical presence. Authors concluded that robots can be suitably employed to train and evaluate participants, but only simulated experiments were performed, without the involvement of actual human users.

A related study involved a robotic device (upper limb exoskeleton) that played cognitive games with patients who had suffered from stroke, and was instrumental in improving their cognitive test scores [2]. Another robot was used in a care-home to act as both a pill reminder and a host of cognitive games amongst other features [4].

Unique in form amongst other robots is the Tangibot, which has a paddle interface that allows it to play a cognitive game with participants, and appears suitable in the cognitive rehabilitation of people with mild to moderate symptoms of dementia [13]. An additional feature of this work was the multiplayer possibility, which exploits social interaction as a contributing factor in the reduction of some problematic behaviours in people with neurocognitive decline [8].

Another small anthropomorphic robot, Eva, was used to play cognitive games, both musical and non-musical, while doubling as an exercise coach for the participants [9]. The results of this study showed that the robot-led therapy sessions were able to decrease the problematic behaviours (e.g. agitation, delusions) of some of the participants, but only short term benefits were observed.

2.2 Robots and Music Therapy

Few robots have been used in conjunction with MT, and most were intended for autistic children. A NAO robot helped in MT sessions by dancing with the participants [3], thus giving the therapists a better chance to observe and evaluate the children's behaviour, by reducing their involvement in multiple activities. Another study utilised the NAO robot as a performer during MT sessions, by playing the xylophone together with the children who played improvised music [12]. This application of NAO could be considered a success as it was able to increase motor skills of most of the 9 participants, though they did not seem to improve in adhering to the robots cues. However, the intervention they showcase only has a single game, additionally, the target population were children with autism and of those participants, only 1 was female. As for the use of robots in music therapy for older adults, the only instance we are aware of shows a bio-mimetic humanoid robot playing a music themed cognitive game with the users [23]. The robot was used for a long term intervention, spanning 6 months that showcased its ability to play musical games successfully and helped supporting the use of SARs for interacting with participants with cognitive impairments. As is the same with the previous study, this intervention only featured a single game, which was a song recognition task. While the demographic were older adults (70+) with mild - severe cognitive decline, there were only 4 total individuals.

3 Cognitive Game Design

MCGs are intended as an additional rehabilitation tool in the arsenal of music therapists. The robot can be deployed where it is needed, for example while the therapist is seeing another group of patients, or when human-human contact is not viable, effectively doubling the therapists' outreach. It is important to clarify that the robot will not be alone with the participants in any case, as it needs someone to mediate in case of confusion and to set it up and prepare its instruments and environment, and monitor the session progress.

The robot we have chosen as MT helper is LuxAI QTrobot[1], approximately 1m tall and displaying a friendly humanoid aspect (Fig. 1). QTrobot offers a number of hardware and software features that makes it particularly suitable with a neurodiverse population, and has been successfully employed in education and rehabilitation, particularly with vulnerable groups, such as autistic children and older adults.

---

[1] https://luxai.com/.

Fig. 1. Example setup during one-one intervention. Left: camera angle of robot, Right: Camera angle of participant.

3.1 Experimental Setup and Role of the Robot

As illustrated in Fig. 1, QTrobot is placed on top of a table or desk, to be visible to participants seated in front of it. Users complete the interaction through the touchscreen interface of a tablet computer wirelessly connected to the robot (see example interface on Fig. 2).

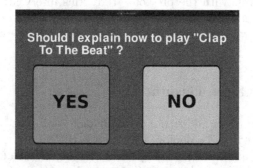

Fig. 2. Example screen on the tablet interface.

QT robot uses Text-to-speech (TTS), gestures, and emotes to convey instructions to the participant, in a jovial manner. It is required to encourage users to adhere to the games, as well as admit their focus back onto what the game requires, should it be the tablet screen, or the robot itself. QT robot introduces games and levels, providing tutorials when needed, and help when asked for. The robot also records user performance for each game and provides feedback on task completion. Explicit negative feedback is avoided wherever possible, to increase feelings of competence [5].

3.2 Game Design Choices

In the creation of the games, we identified aspects which we consider vital to the success of the intervention, explained below.

Engagement. We refer to engagement as a measure how much users' attention is focused on the game that they are playing. One way to maintain engagement is offering levels of increasing difficulty for each game. In this way, users are always challenged, but not so much as to engender frustration. This is often referred to as being *optimally challenging* [15], and strongly contributes to continuous engagement. Difficulty levels also introduce a sense of progression, with each level completed being an advancement towards a goal. This feeling of progression can contribute to feelings of competence and overcoming challenge, while also giving a tangible measure of improvement [7].

One feature of MCGs promoting engagement is that they utilise the relationship between music and memories, by offering music that individuals would likely have an emotional association with, thus making for a more enjoyable experience. In addition to the above, we can also exploit the characteristics of QT robot, which, as a facilitator of this intervention, can monitor user-activity and ensure focus. To this goal, the program reads and estimates user-engagement by way of mouse inputs, and QT uses this information to refocus the user by reminders or hints after periods of inactivity or distraction.

Accessibility. Paramount to the creation of MCGs are the user interface (UI) and game structure. The intended demographic of the intervention are individuals over the age of 65 who suffer from mild to moderate cognitive decline, who have often limited experience with digital design elements that have become common place and thus go usually unexplained (e.g. swiping movements, or typical icon symbols such as the gear for customisation) [24]. It is thus necessary to avoid interface elements that are not strictly necessary, as well as design features that rely on intuition and on previous game play experiences. Additionally, one also needs to account for the added complexity of varying levels of cognitive impairments, such as memory or attention deficits.

Our MCGs achieve this by having the music therapist or caretaker help in customising the game play experience alongside the user. Moreover, the general design style is to have a stripped down UI, that contains only the main required elements, while still allowing for customisation of the games.

Multi-domain. In a multi-domain approach, each game is intended to target various cognitive abilities, or domains, allowing for a more complete rehabilitation solution. This means that, while games will focus on exercising one or two cognitive functions, they will also require some effort in other domains at the same time.

An intervention that has multiple of such overlapping domains would allow users to be selective towards games, since others can cover the same cognitive skills. We have designed our games so that, whilst they address complementary cognitive skills, their offers overlap and intersect, allowing for personal preferences and experiences. Furthermore, games selection can be personalised based on user profiles, such that individuals who suffer from declining memory, will be suggested to play more memory games than someone with healthy memory abilities.

Familiarity. For older subjects, and especially when cognitive impairments are involved, game playing and user interfaces could result challenging and unfamiliar. For this reason, alongside the robot's tutorials and encouragement. Playing mechanisms and UI must be kept consistent so that they can be learned easily, and switching between games fast and seamless.

To this effect, each game uses the same interim screens - such as loading screens, as well as share a similar use of colours - such as green being yes/confirmations, and yellow being "help". Moreover, the games explanation, methods of choice selection and requests for help, and general game experience are consistent across games, as much as their different nature and cognitive targets allow.

3.3   Input from Music Therapists

We conducted a practical workshop and focus group with practising music therapists with at least 5 years of experience in care home settings $(n = 4)$, during which each game was demonstrated and discussed individually. In addition to the game-specific evaluation, we also gathered opinions about the robot's behaviour, MCG as an intervention, plus potential further developments and additions.

The therapists gave positive optimistic opinions, and helped clarifying ways in which the robot could interact with recipients and help therapists and care staff. Valuable and concrete oral and written feedback was given, in regards to how the robots behaviour could be more in-line with their expectations, and also how the games could be improved. Feedback was implemented to as close to their requests and suggestions as possible.

4   Game Description

All games are built on a common software platform. They all share the same type of configuration file for setting difficulty, song name and other parameters.

The graphical interface, playing experience and level transitions are also consistent across games. As illustrated in Fig. 3, all games share certain screens, shown in green, which serve to breakup the flow and give moments of rest between levels, as well as create a recurring pipeline that players come to expect.

Each game is described in detail below.

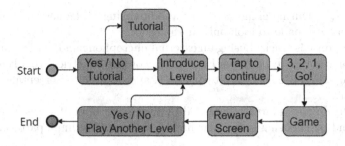

Fig. 3. Program architecture. Each box represents a screen/interface that is presented to the user.

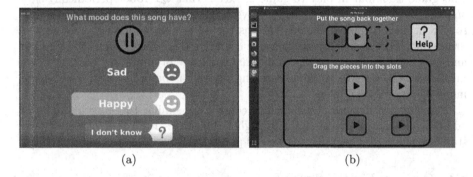

|(a)|(b)|

Fig. 4. (a) Main game play screen of Game 1: "Guess the mood". (b): Main game play screen of Game 4: "Fix the Song".

4.1 Game 1: Guess the Mood

This game is based on an exercise seen in music therapy, where participants are asked to say the mood of a certain music. Players are made to listen to a recognisable section of a song, while presented with different emotions to select from, in the form of text-based buttons (Fig. 4a). The user choice and response time are recorded. Only one choice is considered correct, but there is no negative feedback in any case, to avoid undermining participants' motivation.

As users progress through levels, they are presented with more emotion options, and with more subtle choices (e.g. from {happy, sad} to {angry, happy, confused, wistful}).

To our knowledge, within the field of serious games there are no studies that use music to train older individuals in emotional recognition, which has mostly targeted facial expressions and predominantly focused on autistic children [11].

4.2 Game 2: Clap to the Beat

This game is intended to target attention and motor function, and is based on a visuomotor synchronisation task, where users hear music and see that QT robot is drumming along. The user is prompted to either tap, clap or click their fingers along with QT. During game play, the accompanying tablet screen is blackened so that users are made to look only at the robot.

User response is tracked using an external microphone and performance measured through sound recognition. From this recording 2 metrics are taken: timing - the average response time to hit each note, and accuracy - percentage of beats hit correctly.

Difficulty in this game is controlled by increasing bpm of songs as difficulty goes up, and by choosing songs that have a less clear rhythmic pattern.

4.3 Game 3: Simon Says Clap

This game is similar in play to game 2, except that QT robot periodically says *stop* and stops all movement, until it says *start* and begins drumming again The song continues to play, but users are instructed to clap only when the robot is drumming. This game targets the same cognitive functions of game 2, attention and motor control, but has the additional challenge of inhibitory control. Users must resist the urge to continue clapping, as well as be prepared to start again immediately when QT does.

Performance metrics and difficulty control are similar to Game 2, with the addition of stop interval length: in higher difficulties the robot can start and stop frequently and abruptly, as well as pause for either longer or shorter times.

4.4 Game 4: Fix the Song

In this game, a song is split into 2 or more segments, and players must use the GUI to place the song back together in the correct order. The targeted cognitive functions for this game are working memory and executive functioning. Figure 4b shows the screen displayed once the song has been sliced.

Users must drag and drop song segments into the correct slots, and can listen to segments anytime by tapping on them. Should they drag a segment into an incorrect spot, QT robot explains that there is an error and the segment is moved automatically back to its initial location. Once a segment is in the correct slot, it can't be moved, but it can still be tapped on to listen to. Once all segments have been placed in the correct slots, the level is complete.

The difficulty of this game is controlled by how many segments each song is split into, as well as how easily recognisable different sections of songs are (e.g. songs with lyrics vs. instrumental). For the performance evaluation, we track how many times pieces are placed into the wrong places, how many times "help" button is pressed, as well as the time taken to complete the level.

5 Experimental Validation

Two pilot studies were performed at different stages of game development.[2]

---

[2] This study was performed in line with the principles of the Declaration of Helsinki. Approval was granted by the Ethics Committee of Middlesex University (28/01/2022/number 14845). All participants provided written informed consent before taking part in the study.

5.1   Questionnaire and Interview

Both pilot sessions used a very similar post-session questionnaire with 5 open questions and 36 (pilot 1) or 32 (pilot 2) Likert-scale questions from *1 - completely disagree* to *5 - completely agree*. Content validity of the whole questionnaire was assessed by experts on robotics, UX design, music psychology, music therapy and cognitive psychology. The experts judged whether the questionnaire items were essential and representative to assess the aim of the study. The final questionnaire was modified accordingly with their suggestions.

Categories of questions included in the questionnaire were the perception of the robot, e.g.: *the robot is cute*, as well as questions about the robot's behaviour, its ability to explain the games, e.g., *the games were easy to understand*, and about the interaction as a whole. The open questions provided context for the Likert-scale ratings, as well as have the additional benefit of contributing to user-centred design.

The semi-structured-interview allowed for even more nuanced feedback. Participants were asked if they had a favourite game, as well as about design elements they struggled to understand or others that they enjoyed. They were also asked about their experience with technology, amongst other questions that served to gather more details on the characteristics of the demographic.

5.2   Setup

Pilot 1 was conducted as a collection of 30 min one to one sessions, with participants sitting in front of the robot while researchers sat 2 m behind. Researchers were there to both observe the interaction and mediate should the program or robot fail to explain tasks properly. Sessions were recorded using 2 separate camera angles, one was showing robot and screen, the other the participant, as shown in Fig. 1. This was done to register positive or negative reactions as well as general engagement, like maintaining eye contact with the robot, or looking elsewhere.

Pilot 2 was conducted after feedback from pilot 1 and more suggestions from expert consultations were implemented into the games. Game 4 was also added for pilot 2. Due to the limited availability of participants from the first pilot, 4 out of 6 participants were included into a group session instead than individual. Participants sat around a 3 m × 2 m table with QT standing on top, and the tablet computer in front of it, clearly visible to everybody.

Procedure. In individual sessions, interactions started when participants first tapped the tablet screen. The robot began by introducing itself and expressing joy in playing games with the user. The actual game playing followed, with participants interacting both with the robot and the tablet screen, as instructed by the robot and GUI. Once they played all games, participants were made to fill out the questionnaire. After this, they were invited to have a semi-structured-interview inviting them to provide more detailed feedback about their experience.

In the group session in pilot 2, participants played a game each, with input from the other participants. All participants filled individual questionnaires. The role of the researcher did not change.

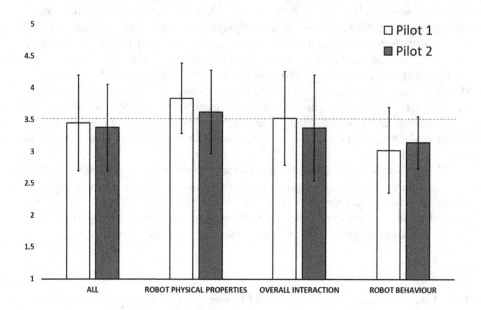

Fig. 5. Pilot 1 and 2 results.

Results. Pilot 1 had 5 subjects (75+, 4 females, 1 male). All participants agreed to take part in the interview after their session. Pilot 2 had 6 subjects (65+, 4 females, 2 males). The interview that followed was conducted in the same group settings.

We grouped the Likert-scale questions into three categories (robot physical properties; overall interaction; robot behaviour), inverting responses to any questions that were negatively presented. We thus produced normalised mean scores for each category, and for the whole question set (ALL), as illustrated in Fig. 5.

The small sample size and changes in procedure make a direct comparison between both pilots difficult, but the score similarity between categories implies a general impression of how the robot is perceived. The robot physical properties scored relatively highly between both groups, while robot behaviour scored lower. The latter improved for the second pilot, whilst the former got a lower score, even though the robot physical properties did not change. We thus consider the result consistent across pilots, and generally positive towards the exercise.

Feedback from open questions and interviews included: "robot voice is OK, but would be good to customise it"; "interaction requires the presence of staff, and would not be possible independently". Suggestions that referred to possible, implementable improvements will be taken into account in the new updates of the games.

6 Discussion

6.1 Ethical and Safety Considerations

The intervention is intended for use with individuals with mild - moderate cognitive impairment, and as such, all participants have been and will be required to provide informed consent, and are free to drop out at any stage, especially in the event of distress or discomfort from interactions with the robot.

The MCGs create user profiles and thus store data based on performance and some basic user information (full name and date of birth). This data is only stored locally and backed up through physical hard drives, in line with the General Data Protection Regulation (UK GDPR).

While the robot itself is not a significant threat to physical safety of the participants, there are certain precautions taken to ensure smooth and safe operation. Firstly, the robot is placed out of reach of the participant, so that its movements do not endanger the user, and the user can not attempt to reach out to touch the robot. Secondly, the user is always accompanied by a caregiver, who is trained on how to act in the rare event of robot malfunction. Lastly, the caregiver is also informed that the user is under no pressure to complete the session, and that in case of distress, the session should be ended immediately.

6.2 Limitations

Robot's Limitations. QT robot of LuxAI has been used in many studies involving autism in children [10]. It is also similar in design to NAO robot, which has been used in a multitude of studies with older adults, even those who have cognitive impairments. On this basis, we reason that QT robot is also suitable for use with older adults [19]. However, it is not a perfect candidate for the use in MCGs. While QT does come equipped with a 3D camera, it is unable to rotate its head downwards past a certain degree, limiting the usability of computer vision for tasks requiring discrimination between objects or colours. Furthermore, QT robot is not a mobile robot. While that does simplify stability and can make the robot partially safer than others, it also reduces the robots agency. Coupled with the fact that QT's hands are not actuated, but are rather clasps, it is unable to equip itself with instruments, or position itself in front of the participant, thus requiring some setup by a helper, likely a caregiver. This is likely to have some implications in the user's opinion of the robot [14].

Study Limitations. Although this pilot was received well by participants, a significant attribute of the intended end-user is that they will have some form of mild to moderate cognitive impairment. While we did consider design elements to best accommodate these deficits, it is difficult to say whether or not these measures will be sufficient with the intended users, as participants recruited were all of healthy cognition.

Additionally, this pilot was only a single session and focused on usability and suitability. As a result, there was no opportunity to measure cognitive ability, nor validate the use of these specific games in the increase or maintenance of these abilities. However, this pilot served to validate the use of this robot as the facilitator of MCGs, and the reception of these games with older adults. These findings will be built upon in a future 8 week long study in care homes.

6.3 Conclusion and Future Work

In this paper we described a novel application of a SAR as a facilitator of a combined intervention. Based upon related works and pilot results, this robot and the set of developed games appear to be suitable to facilitate Music Therapy sessions. The robot is perceived favourably by our sample of the demographic, and its physical form is adequate as per our Likert-scores and thematic analysis. We plan to further improve the *robot behaviour* rating obtained in the two pilots (mean = 3.1), with the collected feedback by users and therapists.

While the robot's behaviour is important, the embodiment of an actuated and capable agent has been shown to passively contribute to its appeal when compared to a tablet app or equivalent avatar [26].

Additionally, while this pilot was successful, it does little in the ways of predicting long term engagement and usability. As per the well documented novelty effect, the positive reception of this robot is very likely to decrease with time before stabilising once the user is accustomed to the robot [16]. We plan to further assess such factors with a future 8 week study conducted in care homes.

The intervention showcased in this paper is not limited to use with QT robot. As the games themselves are run on an accompanying tablet screen, the intervention is easily adaptable. While we find QT robot is a sufficient host for these games, we hold that many other commercially available robots, humanoid and otherwise, can be effective. However, form factor should be taken into account to fit the role of being a teacher or host, as physical characteristics are also important [21].

In summary, this paper presents a robot that is fit in form and has the potential to be successful at playing music-themed cognitive games with older adults, as seen in similar studies showcasing robots in care scenarios. It was received well and was successful in enabling older people to engage with computer programs.

References

1. Andriella, A., Alenyá, G., Hernández-Farigola, J., Torras, C.: Deciding the different robot roles for patient cognitive training. Int. J. Hum.-Comput. Stud. **117**, 20–29 (2018). Cognitive Assistants
2. Aprile, I., et al.: Robotic rehabilitation: an opportunity to improve cognitive functions in subjects with stroke. An explorative study. Front. Neurol. **11**, 1498 (2020)
3. Beer, J.M., Boren, M., Liles, K.R.: Robot assisted music therapy a case study with children diagnosed with autism. In: 2016 11th ACM/IEEE International Conference on Human-Robot Interaction (HRI), pp. 419–420 (2016)
4. Broadbent, E., et al.: Robots in older people's homes to improve medication adherence and quality of life: a randomised cross-over trial. In: Beetz, M., Johnston, B., Williams, M.-A. (eds.) ICSR 2014. LNCS (LNAI), vol. 8755, pp. 64–73. Springer, Cham (2014). https://doi.org/10.1007/978-3-319-11973-1_7
5. Burgers, C., Eden, A., van Engelenburg, M.D., Buningh, S.: How feedback boosts motivation and play in a brain-training game. Comput. Hum. Behav. **48**, 94–103 (2015)
6. Carros, F., et al.: Care workers making use of robots: results of a three-month study on human-robot interaction within a care home. In: Proceedings of the 2022 CHI Conference on Human Factors in Computing Systems, pp. 1–15 (2022)
7. Clarke, G., Kehoe, J., Broin, D.Ó.: The effects of gamification on third level intrinsic motivation towards studying. In: European Conference on Games Based Learning, pp. 953-XX. Academic Conferences International Limited (2019)
8. Cohen-Mansfield, J.: Nonpharmacologic treatment of behavioral disorders in dementia. Curr. Treat. Options. Neurol. **15**(6), 765–785 (2013)
9. Cruz-Sandoval, D., Morales-Tellez, A., Sandoval, E.B., Favela, J.: A social robot as therapy facilitator in interventions to deal with dementia-related behavioral symptoms. In: Proceedings of the 2020 ACM/IEEE International Conference on Human-Robot Interaction, pp. 161–169 (2020)
10. El-Muhammady, M.F., Zabidi, S.A.M., Yusof, H.M., Rashidan, M.A., Sidek, S.N., Ghazali, A.S.: Initial response in HRI: a pilot study on autism spectrum disorder children interacting with a humanoid QTrobot. In: Jo, J., et al. (eds.) International Conference on Robot Intelligence Technology and Applications, vol. 642, pp. 393–406. Springer, Cham (2022). https://doi.org/10.1007/978-3-031-26889-2_36
11. Elhaddadi, M., et al.: Serious games to teach emotion recognition to children with Autism Spectrum Disorders (ASD). Acta Neuropsychologica **19**, 81–92 (2021)
12. Feng, H., Mahoor, M.H., Dino, F.: A music-therapy robotic platform for children with autism: a pilot study. Front. Robot. AI **9**, 855819 (2022)
13. Garcia-Sanjuan, F., Jaen, J., Nacher, V.: Tangibot: a tangible-mediated robot to support cognitive games for ageing people—a usability study. Pervasive Mob. Comput. **34**, 91–105 (2017)
14. Kwak, S.S., Kim, Y., Kim, E., Shin, C., Cho, K.: What makes people empathize with an emotional robot?: The impact of agency and physical embodiment on human empathy for a robot. In: 2013 IEEE RO-MAN, pp. 180–185. IEEE (2013)
15. Larche, C.J., Dixon, M.J.: Winning isn't everything: the impact of optimally challenging smartphone games on flow, game preference and individuals gaming to escape aversive bored states. Comput. Hum. Behav. **123**, 106857 (2021)
16. Leite, I., Martinho, C., Paiva, A.: Social robots for long-term interaction: a survey. Int. J. Soc. Robot. **5**, 291–308 (2013)

17. Lyu, J., et al.: The effects of music therapy on cognition, psychiatric symptoms, and activities of daily living in patients with alzheimer's disease. J. Alzheimer's Dis. **64**(4), 1347–1358 (2018)
18. Nichols, E.: Estimation of the global prevalence of dementia in 2019 and forecasted prevalence in 2050: an analysis for the global burden of disease study 2019. Lancet Public Health **7**(2), e105–e125 (2022)
19. Olde Keizer, R.A., et al.: Using socially assistive robots for monitoring and preventing frailty among older adults: a study on usability and user experience challenges. Health Technol. **9**, 595–605 (2019)
20. Pino, M., Boulay, M., Jouen, F., Rigaud, A.S.: "Are we ready for robots that care for us?" Attitudes and opinions of older adults toward socially assistive robots. Front. Aging Neurosci. **7**, 141 (2015)
21. Schaefer, K.E., Sanders, T.L., Yordon, R.E., Billings, D.R., Hancock, P.A.: Classification of robot form: factors predicting perceived trustworthiness. In: Proceedings of the Human Factors and Ergonomics Society Annual Meeting, vol. 56, pp. 1548–1552. SAGE Publications Sage CA, Los Angeles, CA (2012)
22. Susi, T., Johannesson, M., Backlund, P.: Serious games: an overview. Technical report, Institutionen för kommunikation och information (2007)
23. Tapus, A., Tapus, C., Matarić, M.J.: Music therapist robot for individuals with cognitive impairments. In: Proceedings of the 4th ACM/IEEE International Conference on Human Robot Interaction, HRI 2009, pp. 297–298. Association for Computing Machinery, New York, NY, USA (2009)
24. Wandke, H., Sengpiel, M., Sönksen, M.: Myths about older people's use of information and communication technology. Gerontology **58**(6), 564–570 (2012)
25. Wang, G., Zhao, M., Yang, F., Cheng, L.J., Lau, Y.: Game-based brain training for improving cognitive function in community-dwelling older adults: a systematic review and meta-regression. Arch. Gerontol. Geriatr. **92**, 104260 (2021)
26. Zhexenova, Z., et al.: A comparison of social robot to tablet and teacher in a new script learning context. Front. Robot. AI **7**, 99 (2020)

Empowering Collaboration: A Pipeline for Human-Robot Spoken Interaction in Collaborative Scenarios

Sara Kaszuba[1]([✉])(iD), Julien Caposiena[2](iD), Sandeep Reddy Sabbella[1](iD), Francesco Leotta[1](iD), and Daniele Nardi[1](iD)

[1] Department of Computer Control, and Management Engineering (DIAG), Sapienza University of Rome, Via Ariosto 25, Rome, Italy
{kaszuba,sabbella,leotta,nardi}@diag.uniroma1.it
[2] CPE Lyon, 43 boulevard du 11 Novembre 1918, Villeurbanne, France
julien.caposiena@cpe.fr

Abstract. In the context of collaborative robotics, robots share the working space with humans and communication between the two parties is of utmost importance. While different modalities can be employed, speech represents a natural way of interaction for people. In this paper, we introduce a speech-based pipeline for collaborative robotics, specifically designed to operate in the context of precision agriculture. The system exploits frame semantics as a modality-independent way of representing information, which allows for easier management of the dialogue between the robot and the human. One of the key features of this pipeline is the utilization of various techniques from Natural Language Processing (NLP) to extract and manage frames.

Keywords: Human-Robot Collaboration · Human-Robot Interaction · Natural Language Processing · Precision Agriculture

1 Introduction

Collaborative robotics, a specialized subfield within Human-Robot Interaction (HRI), encompasses situations in which robots, commonly referred to as *cobots*, either share a workspace with humans or operate in close proximity to them. Although manufacturing is a typical application scenario, cobots demonstrate their versatility in various domains, including precision agriculture and robotic surgery.

Modalities in collaborative robotics encompass a spectrum ranging from direct physical contact to indirect methods such as speech, gestures, light, and sounds. The selection of specific interaction channels is typically influenced by the particular application scenario, as discussed in [7]. Among these modalities, speech holds a prominent position [8], as it aligns with humans' natural way of

---

S. Kaszuba and J. Caposiena—These authors contributed equally to this work.

J. Caposiena—Work done while the author was interning at Sapienza, University of Rome.

© The Author(s), under exclusive license to Springer Nature Singapore Pte Ltd. 2024
A. Al. Ali et al. (Eds.): ICSR 2023, LNAI 14454, pp. 95–107, 2024.
https://doi.org/10.1007/978-981-99-8718-4_9

communication. Recent advancements in Natural Language Processing (NLP) techniques have further facilitated its integration into HRI, reducing associated constraints.

In this paper, we present a speech-based communication pipeline designed for mutual interaction between humans and robots. Our focus is on its application within the context of precision agriculture, particularly in the CANOPIES project[1]. One of the salient features of the proposed solution is that it is fully based on the so-called *frame semantics* [5].

Frames are linguistic structures that describe real-world situations, and they are identified in sentences through specific words (verbs). These frames include semantic roles called *Frame Elements*, which provide relevant information about *"Who did what to whom, when, where, and how?"* [6].

Differently from some other works that rely on hardcoded rules for extracting semantic frames from human speech, our approach leverages modern techniques from NLP. The task of automatically recognizing frames and their associated arguments in a sentence is known as Semantic Role Labeling (SRL) [10]. Recent advancements in Large Language Models (LLMs) have enabled the development of highly accurate SRL techniques based on Deep Neural Networks (DNNs), as demonstrated in works such as [2,3,16].

Utilizing frame semantics enables a focus on the transmitted information rather than specific utterances used to convey it. Specifically, in Human-To-Robot communication, SRL is employed to extract frames and frame elements, whereas in the Robot-To-Human communication phase, frames serve as a basis for reasoning. The specific sentences generated by the robot using Text-To-Speech technologies can be freely modified and updated without affecting the underlying reasoning task.

The paper is organized as follows. Section 2 introduces relevant related works. Section 3 describes the proposed architecture and the specific modules. Section 4 reports performed experiments. Finally, Sect. 5 concludes the paper.

2   Related Work

In recent years, the significant interest in Human-Robot Collaboration (HRC) led many researchers to study and investigate the most suitable interaction modality to adopt when human workers and robots have to collaborate together. Spoken communication has been identified as the most appropriate, intuitive and natural means for exchanging information in such scenarios. To this aim, the majority of the developed robotic systems, for both indoor and outdoor environments, employ speech as the primary interaction channel.

The spoken dialogue capabilities and design choices of the Hygeiorobot are discussed and motivated by Spiliotopoulos et al. in [14]. In this work, the authors present the architecture of the dialogue manager with the objective of ensuring that the user is aware of the robot's understanding of the utterances provided as

---

[1] https://canopies.inf.uniroma3.it/.

input by humans. Therefore, they develop an online spoken HRI system capable of performing hospital tasks, such as message or medication deliveries through speech.

A software interface facilitating voice control for lightweight robots has been implemented and evaluated by Deuerlein et al. in [4]. They proposed a system in which spoken commands are transformed into machine-readable code after performing cloud-based speech recognition. Consequently, the system recognizes the intent and populates the slots, enhancing dialog interaction and enabling the robot to execute linear and circular movements in a two-dimensional industrial environment.

Similarly, Bolano et al. explore the potential of speech as a hands-free communication medium in industrial HRC in [1]. They investigate potential issues associated with speech recognition, aiming to propose a modular system that enables robust and natural speech interaction in acoustically challenging environments. Their approach operates offline and shows promise in improving intent recognition and productivity. Moreover, by enhancing multimodal HRI, the system has the capability to control multiple robots through speech in challenging conditions.

An Edge-IoT online framework is described in [11] by Nambiappan et al., wherein users communicate speech commands via smartphones to a robotic system. Once a task is completed, the MINA Robot, consisting of a Franka Emika Panda Arm mounted on a Summit-XL Steel Mobile Base, sends a task completion notification back to the human. The authors demonstrated the proficiency of the Edge-IoT framework in managing multiple sequential or simultaneous requests and its effectiveness through a task validation experiment. In this evaluation, the robotic arm moved objects on a table from an initial to a final position.

In [9], Merge et al. introduce a human-robot interface called TeamTalk, designed to interpret spoken dialogue interactions between humans and robots in both virtual and real-world collaborative settings. The system focuses on goal-oriented dialog within a search domain referred to as the "Treasure Hunt", in which a team of humans and robots collaborate to locate color-coded "treasures" scattered in an indoor area. Communication is achieved by sending speech commands from user smartphones to the robotic platform. TeamTalk incorporates dialog managers for each robot, modeling the conversation state and task progression. Various levels of instructions are also supported by the system, ranging from high-level tasks like exploration to low-level turn-by-turn commands.

Despite the existence of several applications aimed at addressing spoken HRC, the challenge of identifying a robotic system encompassing all the following functionalities: multilingual capabilities, multi-user interaction, offline functionality, robust data logging, safety mechanisms, and modularity, still persists. Given the specific requirements within the CANOPIES project, where the system needs to operate alongside other modules like perception, motion, and manipulation on a real robot, we opted to design a more lightweight pipeline. This system does not rely on LLMs for generating robot sentences. However, we

have kept the option open for potential inclusion of LLMs in the pipeline.
In essence, we have developed a comprehensive and versatile system that can be eventually employed in any real-world collaborative environment.

3 Proposed Architecture

The developed spoken pipeline for empowering collaboration between humans and robots in outdoor environments, specifically in table-grape vineyards, is presented in Fig. 1. The system has been implemented with a special emphasis on the following features, which are especially important in the context of the CANOPIES project:

- **multilingual**: the user has the chance to engage with the robot using any of the following supported languages: English, French, German, Italian, or Spanish. The android will communicate using the same language spoken by the human.
- **multi-user**: the robot can manage requests from multiple users by recalling who made each request.
- **offline**: no module within the speech pipeline necessitates an internet connection, making the system fully operational in an offline capacity and viable even within environments featuring limited internet connectivity.
- **robust**: data logging is pivotal in robotics, enabling transparency and informed decisions. Hence, the implemented logging strategy is straightforward yet effective. Every module input is logged, safeguarding against communication disruptions between nodes by ensuring swift troubleshooting and seamless operations. Each log is saved in a dedicated JSON file, to facilitate efficient retrieval and analysis.
- **safe**: the system preserves human safety by notifying the user about criticality issues when unexpected situations are encountered by the robot.
- **modular**: each module of the pipeline has its own dedicated ROS package to allow future changes and improvements.

The developed system consists of 7 modules, for each of which a dedicated Section is devoted to motivate the implementation choices and provide further details. The communication between modules occurs through the use of ROS topics. As anticipated in Sect. 1, the pipeline is strongly rooted in frame semantics, so we have identified a set of predefined frames, which include both generic and domain-dependent predicates. Additionally, we have also delineated an intuitive collection of predetermined frame elements, such as "Theme", "Location", "Attribute", "Possessor", "Time", and more, so to minimize the users' effort in interpreting the robot's understanding [7].

3.1 Speech-To-Text

The identification of the most suitable tool for the Speech-To-Text (STT) module is of fundamental importance to ensure stable and robust communication

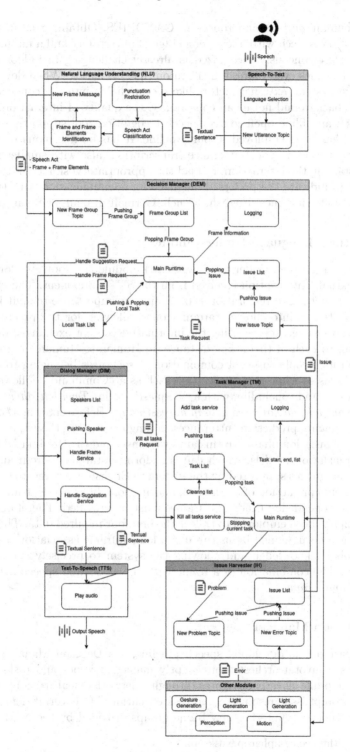

Fig. 1. The proposed architecture.

between human workers and robots in CANOPIES. Obtaining accurate transcriptions from speech with a low percentage of uncertainty and a minimal number of words erroneously recognized is already challenging in indoor environments. It becomes even more difficult in outdoor scenarios. When developing a voice-based system, external factors like an unreliable internet connection and disruptive background noise can compromise the quality of interaction. To this aim, Vosk[2], an offline open-source speech recognition tool supporting multiple languages, has been employed in our pipeline. It has been demonstrated to be particularly precise in vocal utterance transcriptions also with smaller models. Prior to starting the interaction, to load the appropriate Vosk model, the user is requested to indicate the preferred language for communication with the robot among the following ones: English, French, German, Italian, or Spanish.

3.2 Natural Language Understanding

The Natural Language Understanding (NLU) module is responsible for analyzing the textual transcription received from the STT component. Therefore, the process of punctuation restoration is of significant importance to split long and complex sentences into shorter (atomic) ones, allowing for the precise assignment of a speech act, representing the informative content exchanged during an interaction, to each of them. For instance, in Human-to-Human Interaction, it is common for people to use a combination of sentences belonging to different speech act classes while communicating, such as a "Command", followed by an "Information" and concluding with a "Request", as in: *Turn left, there is a ripe grape on your left, do you need help in harvesting it?*. Before entering the process of frame elements prediction, utterances in languages other than English must undergo a translation phase. To this aim, we considered the Helsinki-NLP/opus-mt [15] translation models, which can transform a statement from any of the four other languages supported by the system to English. However, to obtain the frame elements prediction of a sentence, information about words, lemmas, positional tags, dependency heads and frames must be provided. Therefore, Stanza library [12] has been employed to collect the first four required data. The frames, instead, have been defined by us through a lemma-frame association, representing the robot's knowledge and allowing the system to precisely classify novel utterances. The combination of a frame with the associated speech act class is called a *frame group*.

3.3 Decision Manager

At the heart of the developed speech pipeline, the Decision Manager (DEM) emerges as a pivotal orchestrator, adeptly managing issues and tasks in real-time. This module cleverly navigates through a network of features and concepts, ensuring prompt issue resolution and task execution. Moreover, it demonstrates flexibility when encountering new frame groups provided by the NLU module.

---

[2] https://github.com/alphacep/vosk-api.

For the sake of brevity, from now on, the term *frame* is intended as a combination of the predicate and associated frame elements.

In normal operative conditions, for each received frame group, the DEM module sends a *"handle frame"* request to the Dialog Manager. Depending on the presence of an associated executable task, the Task Manager may be engaged for task execution. Additionally, task execution is concluded by reproducing an auditory response to indicate its completion.

The DEM module is also in charge of handling issues identified by the Issue Harvester module, which can interrupt the normal operations. Such issues are processed by the DEM module after categorizing them based on severity. Two major categories are identified: *problems* and *errors*. The first one includes "expected" issues that could be encountered in the system, mostly related with task execution. The second one includes "unexpected" issues, which are strictly related to software errors and hardware malfunctions. For minor problems, the module promptly sends a Text-To-Speech request to communicate a message to the user. In the case of major problems, the module demonstrates its prowess by generating suggestions, engaging the user in the interaction, and handling the human's response. On the other hand, for major errors, the module takes a decisive action by sending a *"kill all tasks"* request, blocking the entire system, and then notifying the user through Text-To-Speech.

3.4   Dialog Manager

At the center of the proposed speech process, the Dialog Manager (DIM) emerges as a conductor for smooth conversations with the human. When a frame is received, the DIM logs it in the speaker's conversation recordings and checks its validity, following a specific path depending on the result. For invalid frames, the module promptly generates an "error" sentence to steer the conversation in the right direction. In case of a valid frame, instead, the DIM verifies if the frame is connected to an external task and in the affirmative scenario, the module retrieves the linked task and generates a *"start task"* sentence. Conversely, if the frame is only used for a local operation, such as adding a speaker, a *"result"* sentence is generated. In such situations, when interacting for the first time with a new user, the system stores the person's essential information, such as first name, last name, and spoken language. Additionally, it archives the entire conversation in a dedicated folder. This process is extremely important as it enables the robot to remember prior interactions with a specific human worker, thereby facilitating continuity in conversations and retaining knowledge of previous discussions. However, in the situation that no ongoing conversation is detected, the module initiates a *"conversation introduction"* sentence to set the context.

The DIM exhibits adaptability by assessing the speaker's language preferences. When the speaker's language differs from English, the module facilitates communication by translating the responses accordingly, fostering inclusivity and enhancing the conversational experience.

To improve Human-Robot Interaction in the CANOPIES project and to enhance the dialogue flow by enabling the robot to intelligently interpret and

```
 1  {
 2    "CHECK": {
 3      "request": {
 4        "args": [
 5          {
 6            "name": "object",
 7            "values": {
 8              "grape": [true, null, false],
 9              "temperature": [false, false, false],
10              "ground": [false, false, false]
11            }
12          },
13          {
14            "name": "quality",
15            "values": [
16              "bad",
17              "good",
18              "ripe"
19            ]
20          },
21          {
22            "name": "color",
23            "values": [
24              "purple",
25              "pink",
26              "green"
27            ]
28          }
29        ],
30        "handle": "handle_check"
31      }
32    }
33  }
```

Fig. 2. Single frame definition example.

respond to user inputs, the concept of *frame definitions* has been introduced in the DIM. The frame definitions are stored in a JSON file, a structured and machine-readable format, in which actions are divided into "targets" and "arguments". Targets represent the focal point of the actions, such as "grape" or "temperature" in Fig. 2, aligning with the project's agricultural context; while arguments, such as "quality" or "color", provide further details associated to the actions. The presented division clarifies user intent and helps the robot precisely understand the action. Beyond the articulation of targets and arguments, the frame definitions also use an ingenious method for listing valid values for arguments. For instance, "grape quality" can be described as "bad", "good", or "ripe". This validation approach is important for maintaining the integrity of the dialogue, preventing misinterpretations, and reinforcing user-robot comprehension.

Fundamental features of the frame definition are: remarkably fast response generation and error handling. For instance, if a user queries the system regarding the color of grapes and provides an unrelated term, such as "airplane", the DIM immediately provides an issue message, clarifying that "airplane" is not a valid color for grapes.

3.5 Task Manager

The Task Manager (TM) is characterized by strategic capabilities and essential traits that ensure smooth task completion and management. The TM iterates over each task, starts the assignment and carries out its execution. Once a task is accomplished, the module verifies whether an outcome is returned (e.g., the quality of the grapes) and notifies the DEM about its completion.

In order to associate each task with the service in charge of execution (e.g., the quality checking module in CANOPIES), the TM is configured with a list of available services and their association with predicates and frame elements.

3.6 Issue Harvester

The Issue Harvester (IH) is responsible for gathering, transforming and managing issues within the developed speech system. When a new problem arises, the IH module turns it into an actionable issue that can be easily managed.

The IH acts similarly when encountering new errors, by converting them into issues through a defined transformation process. The module functions as the central hub for processing issues, and while iterating through each instance in the list, it actively contributes to their resolution by forwarding them to the DEM. This process is then repeated iteratively, underscoring the module's commitment to addressing issues in a systematic and efficient manner.

3.7 Text-To-Speech

The Text-To-Speech (TTS) emerges as a dynamic component for seamless communication. PicoTTS[3] library, an offline open-source speech synthesizer supporting multiple languages, has been employed in our pipeline. Carefully designed, this module encompasses a variety of advanced elements that are arranged together to transform written inputs into engaging spoken outputs. A key aspect is its ability to work with different languages. Indeed, before generating the spoken output, the TTS verifies if the requested language is compatible. Such comprehensive analysis ensures that the verbal interaction feels authentic to the user, in line with the project's aim of fostering meaningful engagement. The TTS dexterously handles different types of commands using a decision framework.

When receiving a "say" command, the module works on the provided text to create audio recording for playback. This process is supported by a well-organized file management system that safeguards generated audios while efficiently clearing space by removing older recordings. In response to a "play" command, the TTS quickly confirms the presence of the specified audio file, allowing smooth playback. In case the audio file is missing, the module's error handling promptly intervenes. Hence, this proactive issue management strategy enables developers to swiftly identify and fix problems, promoting an efficient development process.

After concluding its internal checks, the TTS module plays the audio, delivering the synthesized speech to the user.

---

[3] https://pypi.org/project/py-picotts/.

4   Preliminary Experiments and Application Examples

In evaluating our HRI pipeline, we conducted preliminary experiments by engaging Italian, English and French native speakers. Each user was requested to vocally introduce three sentences in their native language, formulating each utterance ten times. Participants wore a headset to communicate, in order to minimize background noise and closely replicate the ideal way in which the interaction between humans and robots would occur in practical scenarios. Furthermore, French and Italian participants were also encouraged to interact in English. Communicating in a non-native language played a crucial role in determining the error rate linked to the STT module, as well as the count of inaccurately recognized speech acts and misclassified frame elements in the NLU component.

Therefore, we recorded and analyzed the time between the end of the user's utterance pronunciation and the start of the system's response. The outcomes of our investigation are summarized in Table 1, which presents specific information such as the input sentence, interaction language, speech act, frame semantics, and both the worst and the best response times. Table 2 provides details about the average time required by each module. On average, we observed that the STT module accurately transcribed vocal utterances 8 times out of 10 when users interacted in English, even if it was not their native language. Notably, the system appropriately generated error responses when faced with sentences containing information beyond its knowledge. For instance, frame semantics were not generated for the sentence "Hello, can you hear me?". In this case, the system did not recognize the frame "hear", resulting in a response notifying the user: "I do not know how to hear".

Table 1. Evaluation on the HRI speech pipeline.

Sentence	Language	Speech Act	Frame Semantics	Worst time	Best time
Follow me	English	Command	COME-AFTER_FOLLOW-IN-TIME(me)	2.0109 s	1.6553 s
The ground is wet	English	Information	BE_EXIST(ground)	4.2523 s	3.8717 s
Can you help me?	English	Request	HELP(me)	3.1524 s	2.7651 s
Allez à droite *(Go to the right)*	French	Command	GO(right)	8.7831 s	7.1507 s
Le raisin est malade *(The grape is sick)*	French	Information	BE_EXIST(grape, sick)	11.559 s	9.2889 s
Pouvez-vous vérifier les raisins? *(Can you check the grape?)*	French	Request	CHECK(grape)	9.6143 s	7.3952 s
Muoviti avanti lentamente *(Move forward slowly)*	Italian	Command	GO(forward, slowly)	9.6244 s	7.7365 s
Le foglie sono secche *(The leaves are dry)*	Italian	Information	BE_EXIST(leaves, dry)	10.6146 s	8.0871 s
Riesci a esaminare il terreno? *(Can you examine the ground?)*	Italian	Request	CHECK(ground)	10.499 s	7.3775 s

Table 2. Average time (in seconds) required by each module of the HRI pipeline.

Sentence	STT Average Time	NLU Average Time	DEM Average Time	DIM Average time	TTS Average Time
Follow me	0.0007 s	1.1117 s	0.0049 s	0.0097 s	0.7301 s
The ground is wet	0.0016 s	1.1613 s	0.0021 s	0.0115 s	2.8913 s
Can you help me?	0.0013 s	1.1303 s	0.002 s	0.0228 s	1.7923 s
Allez à droite *(Go to the right)*	0.0003 s	6.4374 s	0.0065 s	0.0067 s	1.4604 s
Le raisin est malade *(The grape is sick)*	0.0023 s	7.7119 s	0.002 s	0.0116 s	2.7797 s
Pouvez-vous vérifier les raisins? *(Can you check the grape?)*	0.0008 s	6.7171 s	0.0063 s	0.0067 s	1.5798 s
Muoviti avanti lentamente *(Move forward slowly)*	0.0016 s	6.8703 s	0.0047 s	0.0072 s	1.5592 s
Le foglie sono secche *(The leaves are dry)*	0.0018 s	6.4003 s	0.002 s	0.0097 s	2.6335 s
Riesci a esaminare il terreno? *(Can you examine the ground?)*	0.0011 s	6.4513 s	0.0047 s	0.0076 s	1.6583 s

Furthermore, the pipeline's issue management was showcased in a French context, where the robot was queried with the prompt, "Can you check the grape?". In such scenario, the android could not assess the fruit's condition due to a *major problem*. The situation arose from the ripe grape being previously harvested by a human worker. Consequently, the robot informed about the missing cluster and inquired whether the person could address the issue, as illustrated in Fig. 3.

Precisely, once the STT module transcribed the vocal utterance into its corresponding textual transcription, the NLU component analysed the sentence by identifying the "Request" speech act along with the frame "CHECK" and element "grape". Such information was passed to the DEM, in order to verify if the data received from the NLU was valid and forwarded them to the DIM, while generating the "check_grape" task to be handled by the TM. However, the task could not be executed due to the disappeared grape and the TM sent a message to the IH in order to manage the encountered "major problem" to whom criticality 3 was assigned. Such issue was then communicated back to the DEM, so to inform DIM to provide a "Suggestion" to the person. Hence, this interaction between the modules is fundamental in our pipeline when an issue is encountered by the android, so the user can assist in resolving it. In such cases, the robot prioritizes the user's subsequent commands by placing them at the beginning of both the "Frame List" and "Task List" ensuring the completion of the current task before moving on to the next one.

```
HUMAN REQUEST: ['Can you check the grape?']
ROBOT ANSWER: ['I am checking grape']
ROBOT PROBLEM: ['The grape I was trying to check disappeared']
ROBOT SUGGESTION: ['Are you able to fix the problem?', 'Please respond only by yes or no']
(1 minute passed)
ROBOT ANSWER: ['I did not receive your response, so I am ending the current task']
```

Fig. 3. System's issue management.

Additionally, from our findings, it also emerged that handling multiple languages might result in translation delays, influenced by both input sentence and response lengths. However, in the best cases, the interaction time was below 10 s [13] on CPU, showcasing the real-time capabilities of our system and the potential for significant processing time reduction in the NLU module when the pipeline is run on a GPU. Additionally, participants expressed particular appreciation for the system's response speed, transcription accuracy, and comprehension correctness, underlining their interest in future interactions with the real robot.

5   Conclusion and Future Work

In this article, we have introduced a speech-based pipeline that has been developed to enhance collaboration between humans and robots in outdoor environments, with a focus on the table-grape vineyard scenario. The architecture's design has been shaped by a deliberate emphasis on key features that are significant within the context of the CANOPIES project.

As upcoming improvements, our aspiration is to further refine and expand the capabilities of the spoken pipeline by introducing a language detector in the STT module to automatize the process of recognizing the user's language directly from the interaction, employing spectrum analysis in the utterance intonation for a more accurate identification of the content information, and expanding the robot's knowledge in the DEM module. Additionally, we aim to improve the current pipeline by addressing collaborative scenarios involving a human and a multi-robot team. Such situations would undoubtedly require the intervention of a central coordinator, represented by our DEM module, to manage user requests and route them to the appropriate robot based on the content and context of the conversation.

As discussed in Sect. 4, only preliminary experiments on the pipeline have been conducted. A more thorough evaluation will be performed in the remaining of the project in order to quantitatively measure *(i)* the degree of satisfaction of the final user and *(ii)* how the integration of other interaction modalities, such as gestures, light signals and sound would impact on the overall system performance. Indeed, we believe that a multimodal approach could significantly enrich the collaborative experience and offer users a more intuitive and natural way to communicate with robots.

Acknowledgements. The work of S. Kaszuba, J. Caposiena, S.R. Sabbella, F. Leotta and D. Nardi has been partly supported by the H2020 EU project CANOPIES - A Collaborative Paradigm for Human Workers and Multi-Robot Teams in Precision Agriculture Systems, Grant Agreement 101016906.

References

1. Bolano, G., Iviani, L., Roennau, A., Dillmann, R.: Design and evaluation of a framework for reciprocal speech interaction in human-robot collaboration. In: 2021 30th IEEE International Conference on Robot & Human Interactive Communication (RO-MAN), pp. 806–812 (2021)
2. Conia, S., Bacciu, A., Navigli, R.: Unifying cross-lingual semantic role labeling with heterogeneous linguistic resources. In: Proceedings of the 2021 Conference of the North American Chapter of the Association for Computational Linguistics: Human Language Technologies, pp. 338–351. ACL, Online (2021)
3. Conia, S., Orlando, R., Brignone, F., Cecconi, F., Navigli, R.: Invero-xl: making cross-lingual semantic role labeling accessible with intelligible verbs and roles. In: Proceedings of the 2021 Conference on Empirical Methods in Natural Language Processing: System Demonstrations, pp. 319–328 (2021)
4. Deuerlein, C., Langer, M., Seßner, J., Heß P., Franke, J.: Human-robot-interaction using cloud-based speech recognition systems. Proc. CIRP **97**, 130–135 (2021), 8th CIRP Conference of Assembly Technology and Systems
5. Fillmore, C.J., et al.: Frame semantics and the nature of language. In: Annals of the New York Academy of Sciences: Conference on the Origin and Development of Language and Speech, New York, vol. 280, pp. 20–32 (1976)
6. Gildea, D., Jurafsky, D.: Automatic labeling of semantic roles. Comput. Linguist. **28**(3), 245–288 (2002). www.aclanthology.org/J02-3001
7. Kaszuba, S., Leotta, F., Nardi, D.: A preliminary study on virtual reality tools in human-robot interaction. In: De Paolis, L.T., Arpaia, P., Bourdot, P. (eds.) AVR 2021. LNCS, vol. 12980, pp. 81–90. Springer, Cham (2021). https://doi.org/10.1007/978-3-030-87595-4_7
8. Marge, M., et al.: Spoken language interaction with robots: Recommendations for future research. Comput. Speech Lang. **71**, 101255 (2022)
9. Marge, M., Pappu, A., Frisch, B., Harris, T.K., Rudnicky, A.I.: Exploring spoken dialog interaction in human-robot teams (2009)
10. Màrquez, L., Carreras, X., Litkowski, K.C., Stevenson, S.: Semantic role labeling: an introduction to the special issue (2008)
11. Nambiappan, H.R., Karim, E., Saurav, J.R., Srivastav, A., Makedon, F.: Edge-iot framework for speech and mobile-based human-robot interaction. In: Proceedings of the 20th International Conference on Mobile Systems, Applied and Services, pp. 527–528. ACM (2022)
12. Qi, P., Zhang, Y., Zhang, Y., Bolton, J., Manning, C.D.: Stanza: A python natural language processing toolkit for many human languages (2020)
13. Shiwa, T., Kanda, T., Imai, M., Ishiguro, H., Hagita, N.: How quickly should a communication robot respond? delaying strategies and habituation effects. I. J. Soc. Robot. **1**, 141–155 (2009)
14. Spiliotopoulos, D., Androutsopoulos, I., Spyropoulos, C.D.: Human-robot interaction based on spoken natural language dialogue (2001)
15. Tiedemann, J., Thottingal, S.: OPUS-MT - Building open translation services for the World. In: Proceedings of the 22nd Annual Conference of the European Association for Machine Translation (EAMT), Lisbon, Portugal (2020)
16. Vanzo, A., Bastianelli, E., Lemon, O.: Hierarchical multi-task natural language understanding for cross-domain conversational ai: Hermit nlu. arXiv preprint arXiv:1910.00912 (2019)

A Human-Robot Mutual Learning System with Affect-Grounded Language Acquisition and Differential Outcomes Training

Alva Markelius[1,2]([✉]) [iD], Sofia Sjöberg[2], Zakaria Lemhauori[3,4] [iD], Laura Cohen[3], Martin Bergström[2], Robert Lowe[2] [iD], and Lola Cañamero[3] [iD]

[1] Department of Philosophy, University of Cambridge,
Sidgwick Ave, Cambridge, UK
ajkm4@cam.ac.uk
[2] DICE lab, Department of Applied IT, University of Gothenburg,
Forskningsgången 6, Gothenburg, Sweden
[3] ETIS Lab, CY Cergy Paris University - ENSEA - CNR SUMR8051, Paris, France
[4] Artificial Intelligence Lab, Vrije Universiteit Brussel (VUB),
Pleinlaan 9, Brussels, Belgium

Abstract. This paper presents a novel human-robot interaction setup for robot and human learning of symbolic language for identifying robot homeostatic needs. The robot and human learn to use and respond to the same language symbols that convey homeostatic needs and the stimuli that satisfy the homeostatic needs, respectively. We adopted a differential outcomes training (DOT) protocol whereby the robot provides feedback specific (differential) to its internal needs (e.g. 'hunger') when satisfied by the correct stimulus (e.g. cookie). We found evidence that DOT can enhance the human's learning efficiency, which in turn enables more efficient robot language acquisition. The robot used in the study has a vocabulary similar to that of a human infant in the linguistic "babbling" phase. The robot software architecture is built upon a model for affect-grounded language acquisition where the robot associates vocabulary with internal needs (hunger, thirst, curiosity) through interactions with the human. The paper presents the results of an initial pilot study conducted with the interactive setup, which reveal that the robot's language acquisition achieves higher convergence rate in the DOT condition compared to the non-DOT control condition. Additionally, participants reported positive affective experiences, feeling of being in control, and an empathetic connection with the robot. This mutual learning (teacher-student learning) approach offers a potential contribution of facilitating cognitive interventions with DOT (e.g. for people with dementia) through increased therapy adherence as a result of engaging humans more in training tasks by taking an active teaching-learning role.

All authors declare that they have no conflicts of interest. Supported by an EUTOPIA Undergraduate Research Support Scheme (EURSS) grant to AM and SS for a research stay at ETIS, and by Brain +. The work was carried out partly at ETIS, CY Cergy Paris University, and partly at the Dept. of Applied IT, University of Gothenburg.

The homeostatic motivational grounding of the robot's language acquisition has potential to contribute to more ecologically valid and social (collaborative/nurturing) interactions with robots.

Keywords: Language Acquisition · Developmental Robotics · Socially Assistive Robotics · Mutual Learning · Human-Robot Collaboration

1 Introduction

The increased implementation of socially assistive robots (SAR) to provide motivational, social, pedagogical, and therapeutic assistance raises the questions of how components such as emotion expression, language and motivation can be grounded in homeostatic interaction and collaboration with environment and other social agents [25,28]. This is particularly relevant in order for SAR to act appropriately and to enable e.g. formation of affective social bonds [17], adaptive acting upon and expressing emotion [25] and behaviour grounded in motivation, physiological needs and environmental conditions [9,21]. These components are important to facilitate interactions e.g., for vulnerable populations, which constitute one of the main target groups for SAR [28], including elderly and children in the contexts of learning and cognitive interventions. Human-robot collaboration and interaction setups with SAR are gaining traction as a promising approach for facilitating and mitigating cognitive interventions [2]. This includes memory training for people with e.g. mild cognitive impairment (MCI), which is a clinical phase between normal aging and dementia [15] or dementia [1,4,18]. Cognitive interventions have emerged as crucial alternatives to pharmacological treatments as they provide accessible, effective, and scalable solutions to address issues that often have limited or no available pharmacological alternatives [3]. In particular, for patients with MCI, cognitive training is gaining attention as a promising form of intervention because of its effectiveness in slowing down, or even halting the advance to dementia [16]. However, treatment adherence in cognitive interventions tends to be low, in particular for older adults, resulting in discontinued or uncompleted treatments [14,36]. This issue is likely the result of lack of engagement in the treatments, both on an affective level and as a result of boredom, lack of social accountability and means to consistently carry out the intervention.

Previous research has included SAR to facilitate engagement in cognitive interventions, where usually the robot takes a supporting and teaching role [18]. We present a collaborative human-robot interactive setup that includes a mutual learning system for both robot and human, offering a novel contribution to implementing SAR for cognitive interventions. Mutual learning has great potential to facilitate both the advancement of developmental robotics as well as memory training in humans. We define it here as teacher-student collaborative learning, where both robot and human act as teacher and student simultaneously, such as in the learning paradigm described in [13]. The setup allows the human to take a more active role as a caregiver to a robot learning to acquire language through homeostatic social and affective interaction. As such, this approach is expected to foster greater engagement, a heightened sense of control, and a deeper feeling of contribution than previous approaches where the human has a more passive role. Additionally, the present study includes differential outcomes training (DOT), as a methodology to enhance learning for the human and subsequently increase robot learning efficiency (as described in the following sections). This paper accounts for the methodology of the present collaborative setup and presents the results from an initial pilot study conducted to gain insights into the social and affective experience of the humans and its effectiveness for the robot software architecture in this specific context. This is the first time to the authors knowledge that a human-robot mutual learning methodology has been developed that includes specialised training protocols, e.g. DOT for the human and homeostatic language acquisition for the robot in combination to facilitate the learning of both. Additionally, as DOT is a training protocol specifically suited for neurodegenerative disorders [32,35], this methodology offers a novel way for the human to be more proactive in the training, as compared to many other cognitive training interventions. The rest of the paper is set out as follows: Sect. 2 accounts for previous related research; Sect. 3 provides an overview of the methodological approach in the present study; Sect. 4 and Sect. 5 account for pilot study results and discussion, respectively.

2   Related Work

The work presented in this paper lies in the intersection of developmental robotics (including language acquisition, motivation and affect development) and research into the use of homeostatic mechanisms in robotics (including emotion and social grounding of interactive robot activity). Finally, one of the main components of this work includes memory training of the human part of the interactive scenario, which builds on previous work in cognitive science and psychology (differential outcomes training and cognitive interventions).

2.1   Homeostatic Developmental Robotics and Language

This study uses and builds upon a previously developed human/robot interaction setup developed by Lemhaouri et.al. [20]. The original setup concerns language acquisition of a humanoid robot through interaction with a human caregiver and is grounded in affective motivation as the main driving force behind language acquisition. In this setup, the robot possesses a vocabulary similar to that of an 8-month-old infant during the linguistic babbling phase [10]. The setup is based on trial-and-error, where the robot expresses an internal need and the caregiver has to learn this need by probing, i.e. providing the robot with an object to fulfill the need. If guessed correctly, the word (expressed need) will be reinforced to be associated with the particular need. Previous homeostasis based work in robotics has focused on biologically inspired approaches to facilitate interaction between robots and humans and robot inner motivations as a driving factor to foster decision making, behavior and emotion in relation to environment and other social agents [9,37]. For instance, dynamic, biologically-inspired social mechanisms in artificial agents have been investigated for forming long-term affective bonds [17] and social learning [6] as well as more complex mechanisms such as reasoning and interacting on perceived affective and intentional state [31]. This has previously been shown to be relevant to robots deployed in elderly care [37] where the inner motivations of the robot enable it to assist, converse and care depending on environmental and social stimuli. This functional approach differs from many other computational approaches of robot language development as it acknowledges the role of motivation, affect and semantic meaning in linguistic acquisition [20]. Section 3.1 provides a detailed overview of the methodology and the robot software architecture.

2.2 Differential Outcomes Training

DOT refers to the learning of unique stimulus-response pairs when certain stimuli are associated with certain rewards/outcomes. More specifically, DOT entails correct responses on a given task being reinforced by feedback that is unique to both the response and stimulus. For example, the response of pushing forward a "cookie" object (response) following the stimulus (utterance "hungry" in an unknown language) would yield the rewarding outcome of a specific social expression (e.g. smile). For different stimulus-response pairings (with a correct response) another unique outcome would be expressed (e.g. head nod). In non-differential outcomes tasks, this feedback following the correct response would be randomized (either smile or head nod irrespective of stimulus-response). The DOT approach, contrasting with standard reward-based training where the same reward is given irrespective of stimulus and response 'pairings', has consistently been shown to enhance discriminative learning and memory performance accuracy in animals, children and adults [11,12,30]. Furthermore, evidence suggests it is effective in elderly people with memory impairments such as Alzheimer's disease [32,35]. A recent systematic review with meta-analysis [29] revealed that the impact of DOT on learning and memory exhibits a medium to large effect size as compared to control condition comparisons. This review also found that the positive learning effect of DOT was found in several studies deploying persons with dementia or MCI. The use of repeated sessions of training (i.e. for full cognitive interventions) may, thereby, be worth exploring as a means for mitigating the symptoms of early stage dementia or MCI. Our previous work has suggested using DOT in combination with SAR [26] with promising results, showing that the DOT effect can also be obtained in the context of human-robot interaction. DOT-effects have been found in human-human interactive learning [33] and also theorized in the context of human-robot interactive learning using facial expressions and perceived outcomes of others [23]. Furthermore, differential outcomes expectancies have been computationally modelled in the context of learning and interaction using reinforcement learning [24]. In this study, the DOT is presented in the interaction between the human and robot, as the feedback provided by the robot is differential to certain homeostatic motivations and needs (based on reinforcement learning). Furthermore, the nature of the interaction entails a teacher-student relationship, whereby the human and robot serve as both teacher and student to each other (mutual learning). Section 3.2 provides a more detailed overview of how DOT is implemented in this setup.

Fig. 1. The robot as seen by the participants in the study (human caregivers). The visual field includes the three objects that can be given to the robot to fulfill its internal needs

3 Methodology

The robot used in this study is the simulated (Unity implemented, version 2020.3.11f1) SDK-version of the Reachy robot (version SDK 0.5.1), developed by Pollen Robotics, a humanoid robot able to expressively move its head, antennae and arms (See Fig. 1). The simulated setup closely reflects the dynamics and functions of a real world version of the setup, using the physical version of the Reachy robot (which has previously been tested and piloted). Thus includes the software architecture, the roles of the human and robot and the setup design and procedure.

3.1 Robot Software Architecture

The robot software architecture is built upon [20] who developed a model for affect grounded language acquisition, which is based on creating associations between vocabulary and internal needs through human 'caregiver' interaction. The setup includes a reinforcement learning cycle (using a multi-armed bandit algorithm) where the robot verbally expresses an internal need as determined by affective motivation by requesting an object from the caregiver. There are three different internal needs (hunger, thirst and curiosity) and three respective objects that can fulfill those needs (cookie, drink, teddy bear). Initially, the robot generates words randomly when one need becomes more significant than the others, the caregiver being unaware of which need the robot is expressing. Upon hearing the robot's vocalization, the caregiver selects an object and hands it to the robot. If the provided object satisfies the robot's need, the motivation associated with that need diminishes, and the robot receives a reward of +1, expressing its satisfaction through giving positive audiovisual feedback. However, if the object does not fulfill need, the word is penalized with a reward of −1, reducing the probability of using that word in a similar context, and the robot gives negative audiovisual feedback [20]. The robot software learning model consisted originally of three modules, the motivation, visual perception, and phonological modules [20]. In the present study, a fourth module was added, the DOT feedback module.

Motivation Module: The three internal needs (hunger, thirst, curiosity) are determined by a homeostatic variable that continuously decreases over time until the need is fulfilled, which makes it increase. This can be compared to blood glucose level that decreases over time and increases after a meal. The robot drive $d_i(t)$, representing the urge to act and satisfy the need i, is defined as the difference between the current homeostatic variable and its optimal value. The robots motivation to satisfy a need depends on the related drive and the intensity of the stimulus that can satisfy it [5]:

$$m_i(t) = d_i(t) + d_i(t).s_i \tag{1}$$

s_i is the intensity of the stimulus estimated by the visual perception module (described below). The robots motivation to act on a certain internal need is determined by a threshold that, if it is reached for a certain need before another, leads the robot to express a 'will' to satisfy that need (babble) based on the phonological module. The need is satisfied based on the visual perception module (if the robot is given the right object to satisfy the need or not).

Visual Perception Module: This module helps modulate the motivation system and determines if a need is satisfied based on the robots ability to recognise objects given by the caregiver (cookie, drink, teddy bear) in response to its expression of an internal need. This gives the robot the ability to identify and label objects within its visual environment, while also visually associating the internal needs that the recognised objects can satisfy. The model used for object detection and recognition is a combination of a modified version of Kohonen's self-organizing map clustering algorithm [19] and a multi-class perceptron in which the weights update $\Delta\omega$ follows the Widrow-Hoff learning rule:

$$\Delta\omega_{ij} = \epsilon V F_i(RIS_j - ISP_j) \tag{2}$$

With :
VF: The visual features of the object calculated by SIFT algorithm [22].
ϵ: the learning rate.
RIS: the robot internal state.
ISP: internal state prediction.

Phonological Module: This module allows the robot to verbally express its internal needs by a text-to-speech functionality. The robot's language repertoire comprises two-syllable words which are chosen from some of the most frequent syllables commonly used by an 8-month-old human infant (examples include "nana", "wada", "pada"). The robot initially starts by randomly selecting a word whenever one particular internal need becomes more pronounced than the others. As the robot receives an object from the caregiver it learns to associate certain words in its vocabulary with certain internal needs.

DOT Feedback Module: In addition to the three above mentioned modules, the current study included a DOT feedback module. This module determines the type of positive feedback given for a certain internal need. If the robots need is not fulfilled the robot always expresses the same negative audiovisual feedback (looking down, lowering antenna and making a sad sound). However, if the need is fulfilled, the robot expresses a certain positive feedback associated with each internal need. Each need had different happy beeping sounds and different movements (curiosity: wagging antennae, hunger: happy arm movement, thirst: nodding head movement). In other words, each internal need has its own sound and movement associated with it, which the robot consistently expresses when that need is satisfied. Each feedback response is therefore differential with respect to each internal need fulfillment. In the non-DOT condition the feedback included the same three movements but they were instead randomised for internal needs (i.e. not tied to specific needs). For a comparison of how the interactive scenario differs between the DOT and non-DOT based feedback see Fig. 2. The movements were implemented as inspired by how animals tend to express contentment or happiness (such as dogs wagging their tail). Tails and wagging motions have previously been implemented with robots to express happiness [34], and in the present study we implemented a similar wagging motion on both the robot's antennae and arms.

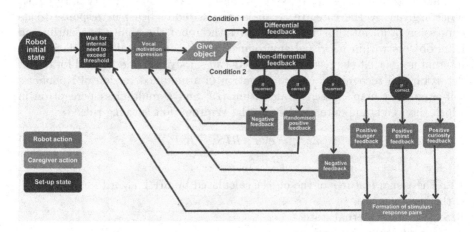

Fig. 2. Flowchart of one iteration of the experimental procedure, depending on either DOT or non-DOT conditions. The experiment consisted of 12–16 iterations depending on the fulfillment of the robot needs.

3.2 Experimental Setup

The setup was tested in an initial pilot study to try out the functionality of the robot architecture including the new DOT module as well as getting some first insights into participants experience of interacting with the robot in this particular setup. The pilot study had only one independent variable (two levels): with or without the DOT feedback module (condition 1: DOT, condition 2: non-DOT). Furthermore, the pilot study solely included a virtual version of the robot and the interaction was thus carried out through a laptop interface. For a visualisation of the robot as seen by the participants see Fig. 1. Six healthy Swedish adults (not suffering from cognitive impairments or memory deficiencies) participated in the pilot study, aged between 24 and 37 years (M= 29). Half of the participants were in the DOT condition and half in non-DOT condition. Informed consent was ensured by all of the volunteering participants by provision of informed written consent forms. The study was conducted in accordance with the WMA Declaration of Helsinki. The participants did not receive any compensation.

Procedure. The experiment was carried out according to the following procedure. After having been given instructions and information about the study the participant sat down in front of the laptop with the Unity virtual version of the robot setup (as seen in Fig. 1). They were instructed to give the robot an object when it expressed an internal need, and to remember what object was associated with what word. The experiment lasted for approximately 13–16 iterations which took about 10 min, iterations ended automatically as a function of learning. For a full flowchart of one experimental iteration see Fig. 2. After the interaction with the robot, the participants filled in a survey about their experience and affective state associated with the interaction. Finally, a semi-structured interview was conducted with each participant about their experience and perception of the interactive scenario and the robot.

Data Collection. The robot's ability to learn to associate certain words in its vocabulary with a certain internal need is determined by convergence rate. Full convergence is reached when the robot achieves a state where it consistently selects appropriate words based on its internal state. Additionally, this enables the caregiver to understand the robot, facilitating the robot's ability to obtain the desired objects. The evaluation metric used to determine convergence rate is the moving average of rewards (MAR) received by the robot:

$$MAR_n = \begin{cases} \dfrac{1}{n} \sum_{i=1}^{n} R_i & \text{if } n < m \\[2em] \dfrac{1}{m} \sum_{i=n-m+1}^{n} R_i & \text{Otherwise} \end{cases} \tag{3}$$

m is the number of previous reward values used to calculate the MAR at the iteration n. In this experiment we chose $m=5$. The convergence time, on the other hand, is defined as the number of iterations required for the robot to reach 90% convergence. Thus, the dependent variable in terms of robot language acquisition is average convergence rate. For determining the participants' affective experience of the setup self-report data was collected using the dimensional Self Assessment Manikin (SAM) Scale [7]. It was used with 3 dimensions, valence (happy/unhappy), arousal (stressed/not stressed) and dominance (in control/not in control) each to be rated between 1 to 5. To complement the scale, the survey also contained likert-scale based questions about the specific setup. Finally, the semi-structured interviews were recorded and transcribed to enable a thematic analysis as well as case by case qualitative analysis. The thematic analysis was conducted by two of the authors individually to encompass a more comprehensive and objective identification of themes and key words. Initially, general code words were identified in the transcribed interviews, and were then categorised into more general themes. The most commonly occurring themes, mostly relevant to the objectives of the study were then used as data for the analysis.

4   Results

This section provides the results of the pilot study conducted to constitute an initial test of the collaborative interaction setup. The first section gives an overview of robot language acquisition. The second section presents the results of the participants' experience as obtained from the survey and semi-structured interview thematic analysis.

4.1   Robot Language Acquisition

The robot's ability to learn to associate certain words in its vocabulary with a certain internal need is determined by convergence rate (as described in Sect. 2.2. Figure 3 visualises the mean convergence rate for DOT (left) and non-DOT (right) conditions, respectively. No condition met full convergence, possibly due to the limited number of iterations. However, in the DOT condition a total higher average reward was achieved than in the non-DOT condition.

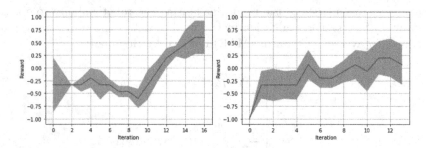

Fig. 3. Average reward and standard deviation obtained by the robot in the DOT (left) and non-DOT (right) condition over the mean number of iterations. Iterations ended automatically as a function of learning.

4.2   Participant Experience

The mean self-reported affective ratings of the SAM-scale are displayed in Fig. 4. Participants generally reported high valence (happy) (M=3.5) and dominance (feeling of being in control) (M=3.7) as well as low arousal (not stressed) (M=2.5). The results of the additional questions about the participants' experiences can be seen in Table 1.

Furthermore, a thematic analysis of the semi-structured interviews revealed some insights into the participants' experience of interacting with the robot and the setup. Most participants found the task to be easy to understand, although lacking in being grounded in a sufficient purpose. Most participants found it easy to differentiate whether the robot was given an object it wanted or not. Commonly occurring themes were **confusion** but at the same time **amusement** and **excitement**. Another theme was **negative/positive coding** of the robot's movements and sounds (as expressed as audiovisual feedback); most participants found the antennae to be natural and intuitive to interpret as positive or negative. However, a commonly occurring theme regarding the robot's arm movement was **uncanniness/unnaturalness**. There also seemed to be a general confusion about whether certain reactions were stronger than others (e.g. if arm movements meant *more* happy than e.g. head movements). This was expressed by a participant saying *"The logic of the antennas made a lot of sense. But I did not understand the intensity of the body language, if certain movements were more positive than others."* Another participant stated that *"...it has too large arms and it was unsettling, but the rest of the movements were pretty cute. The antennae felt like ears and since animals are familiar when they go up or down for happy and sad the antennae worked the same way."* Another common theme concerned the robot's **age** and **child-likeness**. Most participants expressed some form of care or empathy towards the robot, which was generally perceived as a 1–3 year old, evoking feelings of wanting to provide it with its needs. One participant reflected on the child similarities by stating *"It seems like a real child because it is using trial and error with the words it uses, sees what happens and then express either happiness or disappointment. What is not similar is that it is not trying same word again, a real child would have kept using the same word until it got what it wanted."* A final theme was **strategies** to approach the task. A few of the participants revealed trying to use some strategy to make the task easier and for learning, such as exclusion methods or "programming" the robot by intentionally giving certain objects for certain words. Finally, the simulated environment was generally negatively perceived as unnatural and game-like, making the task feel like a simulation; one participant said *"The design itself is very cute. It would be different with a real robot, a robot on a screen is more like a game rather than a real interaction."*

Table 1. Mean Likert Scale Survey Results (1: Negative, 5: Positive)

Question	Mean (SD)
How did you experience the robots reactions when given an object it wanted?	4.67 (0.33)
How did you experience the robots visual response when given an object it wanted?	3.67 (1.03)
How did you experience the robots audible response when given an object it wanted?	4.67 (0.33)
How did you experience the robots response when given an object it didn't want?	1.33 (0.52)
What was your impression of the robot's appearance?	3.50 (1.29)

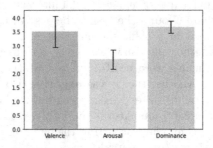

Fig. 4. Mean results (and standard error) of the Self Assessment Manikin Scale's three dimensions of self-reported affective ratings. Each dimension is measured between 1 to 5 for valence (5=happy, 1=unhappy), arousal (5=stressed, 1=not stressed) and dominance (5=in control, 1=not in control)

5   Discussion and Future Work

This study investigated a human robot mutual learning setup where the robot's ability to learn to associate words with internal needs, was determined by convergence rate and human experience was determined by self-reported affective ratings and a semi-structured interview and thematic analysis. The results, as shown in Fig. 3, indicate that neither in the DOT nor the non-DOT condition did the robot achieve full convergence. It is, however, noteworthy that the DOT condition demonstrated a higher rate of learning compared to the non-DOT condition. This suggests that the robot's learning process was influenced by the human's learning being enhanced by the DOT, but further exploration with more iterations as well as more participants is necessary for conclusive results. Considering the low number of participants in this study, it would be of interest for further studies to assess whether the mean differences between DOT and non-DOT show a statistical significance in terms of both human correct responses (to the robot's babblings) and robot language convergence rate. Investigating this DOT effect in the participants could provide further insights into how effective a setup like this could be for cognitive interventions, including memory training for people with dementia and MCI. Furthermore, the language acquisition model in this study is still in its infancy and thus quite simple and limited to a few internal needs. Future work will expand this model to better capture language learning and interaction complexities, making the model more generalizable and scalable, the current study is thus an important step in that direction.

The affective ratings, displayed in Fig. 4, showed that participants reported high valence (happiness) and dominance (being in control), along with low arousal (not feeling stressed). The thematic analysis of the semi-structured interviews showed an emphasis on attitudes towards the setup, where some found the task relatively easy to comprehend, but others expressed a desire for a more meaningful and less simulated purpose behind the interaction. This suggests that incorporating a clearer objective or validation with the physical robot could enhance the user experience. Another theme was the negative and positive coding of the robot's feedback and the results from the survey suggested that the positive audio feedback was more indicative of a positive response than the visual (movement) feedback. Fine-tuning the robot's various signals could improve the user's understanding of its feedback and thus also further enhance the setup, the DOT and its efficiency. Furthermore, the perception of the robot itself, including age, child-likeness and uncanniness were commonly occurring themes. The question of whether the robot being child-like facilitated the interaction or not remains to be investigated in future studies. A large amount of the socially assistive robots used for elderly care in particular tends to be designed to resemble either a pet or a child that needs to be cared for [27]. However, in the context of cognitive training and interventions the effectiveness of robot design in terms of age, anthropomorphism and social and affective role requires further investigation, e.g. through assessment of dimensions of warmth and competence [8]. Some participants attempted to strategize the robot's learning process by using exclusion methods and intentionally providing certain objects for specific words. This finding demonstrates participants' active engagement in the interaction and highlights the potential for further exploring different human-robot collaborative learning approaches/strategies.

In conclusion, the pilot study offers some promising results for the mutual learning human-robot interaction setup as proposed in this paper. The findings tentatively suggest that incorporating DOT could enhance both the human and the robot's learning process. Moreover, participants generally had positive emotional experiences and expressed care and empathy towards the robot. To build upon these findings, future studies should consider increasing the number of iterations in the language acquisition process as well as the number of participants to evaluate the convergence rate and DOT-effect more comprehensively. Additionally, providing a clearer purpose or context to the interaction and refining the robot's audiovisual feedback could lead to a more immersive and meaningful experience for users. Furthermore, investigating how users' strategies and actions during the interaction impact the robot's learning process could be of interest for collaborative human-robot learning systems. Finally, exploring interactions in more ecologically valid, i.e. physical environments settings with complex homeostatic drives, rather than a simulated environment and a robot with relatively simple homeostatic drives, may offer a more authentic and comprehensive understanding of human-robot interaction based on mutual learning with respect to homeostatic and affective robotic states. Ultimately, a target group for this work is persons with Mild Cognitive Impairment or dementia undergoing cognitive training based interventions. Given further study and development of our approach, e.g. to include more complex drives and use of the physical robot, the mutual learning for a robot with homeostatic needs potentially provides: a) social (e.g. nurturing), b) 'active' (or co-) learning benefits to such participants that might provide positive therapeutic outcomes beyond more standard 'passive' learning practises.

References

1. Agüera-Ortiz, L., et al.: Social robots in advanced dementia. Front. Aging Neurosci. **7**, 133–133 (2015). https://doi.org/10.3389/fnagi.2015.00133
2. Alnajjar, F., Khalid, S., Vogan, A.A., Shimoda, S., Nouchi, R., Kawashima, R.: Emerging cognitive intervention technologies to meet the needs of an aging population: a systematic review. Front. Aging Neurosci. **11**, 291 (2019). https://doi.org/10.3389/fnagi.2019.00291
3. Alzheimer's Society: Drug treatments and medication for alzheimer's disease. https://www.alzheimers.org.uk/about-dementia/treatments/dementia-drugs/drug-treatments-and-medication-alzheimers-disease (2022) Accessed 15 Apr 2023
4. Andriella, A., Torras, C., Alenya, G.: Cognitive system framework for brain-training exercise based on human-robot interaction. Cogn. Comput. **12**, 793–810 (2020). https://doi.org/10.1007/s12559-019-09696-2
5. Avila-Garcıa, O., Cañamero, L.: Using hormonal feedback to modulate action selection in a competitive scenario. In: From Animals to Animats 8: Proceedings of the 8th Intl. Conf. on Simulation of Adaptive Behaviour, MIT Press, Cambridge, MA. pp. 243–52. Citeseer (2004). https://doi.org/10.7551/mitpress/3122.003.0031
6. Bartoli, A., Catto, M., De Lorenzo, A., Medvet, E., Talamini, J.: Mechanisms of social learning in evolved artificial life. In: Artificial Life Conference Proceedings 32, pp. 190–198. MIT Press One Rogers Street, Cambridge, MA 02142-1209, USA journals-info (2020)
7. Bradley, M.M., Lang, P.J.: Measuring emotion: The self-assessment manikin and the semantic differential. Journal of Behavior Therapy and Experimental Psychiatry **25**(1), 49–59 (1994). https://doi.org/10.1016/0005-7916(94)90063-9
8. Carpinella, C.M., Wyman, A.B., Perez, M.A., Stroessner, S.J.: The robotic social attributes scale (rosas) development and validation. In: Proceedings of the 2017 ACM/IEEE International Conference on human-robot interaction, pp. 254–262 (2017). https://doi.org/10.1145/2909824.3020208
9. Cos, I., Canamero, L., Hayes, G.M., Gillies, A.: Hedonic value: enhancing adaptation for motivated agents. Adapt. Behav. **21**(6), 465–483 (2013). https://doi.org/10.1177/1059712313486817
10. Davis, B.L., Macneilage, P.F.: Organization of babbling: a case study. Lang. Speech **37**(4), 341–355 (1994). https://doi.org/10.1177/002383099403700401
11. Esteban, L., Plaza, V., López-Crespo, G., Vivas, A.B., Estévez, A.F.: Differential outcomes training improves face recognition memory in children and in adults with down syndrome. Res. Dev. Disabil. **35**(6), 1384–1392 (2014). https://doi.org/10.1016/j.ridd.2014.03.031

12. Esteban, L., Vivas, A.B., Fuentes, L.J., Estévez, A.F.: Spatial working memory is enhanced in children by differential outcomes. Sci. Rep. **5**(1), 17112 (2015). https://doi.org/10.1038/srep17112

13. eSwapp: Sharing is caring why mutual learning is the workplace currency we all need to start spending (2021). https://www.eswapp.com/mutual-learning/

14. Fernandez-Lazaro, C.I., et al.: Adherence to treatment and related factors among patients with chronic conditions in primary care: a cross-sectional study. BMC Fam. Pract. **20**(1), 1–12 (2019). https://doi.org/10.1186/s12875-019-1019-3

15. Hampel, H., Lista, S.: The rising global tide of cognitive impairment. Nat. Rev. Neurol. **12**(3), 131–132 (2016). https://doi.org/10.1038/nrneurol.2015.250

16. Jeong Hong, Y., Hye Jang, E., Hwang, J., Hoon Roh, J., Lee, J.H.: The efficacy of cognitive intervention programs for mild cognitive impairment: a systematic review. Curr. Alzheimer Res. **12**(6), 527–542 (2015). https://doi.org/10.2174/1567205012666150530201636

17. Khan, I., Cañamero, L.: The long-term efficacy of "social buffering" in artificial social agents: Contextual affective perception matters. Front. Robot. AI **9**, 699573 (2022)

18. Kim, G.H., et al.: Structural brain changes after traditional and robot-assisted multi-domain cognitive training in community-dwelling healthy elderly. PLoS ONE **10**(4), e0123251 (2015). https://doi.org/10.1371/journal.pone.0123251

19. Kohonen, T.: Self-organization and associative memory, vol. 8. Springer Science & Business Media (2012). https://doi.org/10.1137/1027085

20. Lemhaouri, Z., Cohen, L., Cañamero, L.: The role of the caregiver's responsiveness in affect-grounded language learning by a robot: Architecture and first experiments. In: 2022 IEEE International Conference on Development and Learning (ICDL), pp. 349–354. IEEE (2022). https://doi.org/10.1109/ICDL53763.2022.9962197

21. Lewis, M., Canamero, L.: Hedonic quality or reward? a study of basic pleasure in homeostasis and decision making of a motivated autonomous robot. Adapt. Behav. **24**(5), 267–291 (2016). https://doi.org/10.1177/1059712316666331

22. Lowe, D.G.: Object recognition from local scale-invariant features. In: Proceedings of the Seventh IEEE International Conference on Computer Vision. vol. 2, pp. 1150–1157. IEEE (1999). https://doi.org/10.1109/ICCV.1999.790410

23. Lowe, R., Almér, A., Gander, P., Balkenius, C.: Vicarious value learning and inference in human-human and human-robot interaction. In: 2019 8th International Conference on Affective Computing and Intelligent Interaction Workshops and Demos (ACIIW), pp. 395–400. IEEE (2019). https://doi.org/10.1109/ACIIW.2019.8925235

24. Lowe, R., Almér, A., Lindblad, G., Gander, P., Michael, J., Vesper, C.: Minimalist social-affective value for use in joint action: a neural-computational hypothesis. Front. Comput. Neurosci. **10**, 88 (2016). https://doi.org/10.3389/fncom.2016.00088

25. Lowe, R., Barakova, E., Billing, E., Broekens, J.: Grounding emotions in robots-an introduction to the special issue (2016). https://doi.org/10.1177/1059712316668239

26. Markelius, A., et al.: Differential outcomes training of visuospatial memory: a gamified approach using a socially assistive robot. Submitted to Internatinal Journal of Social Robotics (2023)

27. Martinez-Martin, E., del Pobil, A.P.: Personal robot assistants for elderly care: an overview. Personal assistants: Emerging computational technologies, pp. 77–91 (2018). https://doi.org/10.1007/978-3-319-62530-0_5

28. Matarić, M.J., Scassellati, B.: Socially assistive robotics. Springer handbook of robotics, pp. 1973–1994 (2016). https://doi.org/10.1007/978-3-319-32552-1_73
29. McCormack, J.C., Elliffe, D., Virués-Ortega, J.: Quantifying the effects of the differential outcomes procedure in humans: a systematic review and a meta-analysis. J. Appl. Behav. Anal. **52**(3), 870–892 (2019). https://doi.org/10.1002/jaba.578
30. Peterson, G.B., Trapold, M.A.: Effects of altering outcome expectancies on pigeons' delayed conditional discrimination performance. Learn. Motiv. **11**(3), 267–288 (1980). https://doi.org/10.1016/0023-9690(80)90001-6
31. Pieters, R., Racca, M., Veronese, A., Kyrki, V.: Human-aware interaction: a memory-inspired artificial cognitive architecture. Cogn. Robot Architect. **38** (2017)
32. Plaza, V., López-Crespo, G., Antúnez, C., Fuentes, L.J., Estévez, A.F.: Improving delayed face recognition in Alzheimer's disease by differential outcomes. Neuropsychology **26**(4), 483 (2012). https://doi.org/10.1037/a0028485
33. Rittmo, J., Karlsson, R., Gander, P., Lowe, R.: Minimalist social-affective value for use in joint action: a neural-computational hypothesis. Acta Physiol. (Oxf) **209**, 103134 (2020). https://doi.org/10.1016/j.actpsy.2020.103134
34. Singh, A., Young, J.E.: A dog tail for utility robots: exploring affective properties of tail movement. In: Human-Computer Interaction–INTERACT 2013: 14th IFIP TC 13 International Conference, Cape Town, South Africa, September 2-6, 2013, Proceedings, Part II 14, pp. 403–419. Springer (2013). https://doi.org/10.1007/978-3-642-40480-1_27
35. Vivas, A.B., Ypsilanti, A., Ladas, A.I., Kounti, F., Tsolaki, M., Estévez, A.F.: Enhancement of visuospatial working memory by the differential outcomes procedure in mild cognitive impairment and alzheimer's disease. Front. Aging Neurosci. **10**, 364 (2018). https://doi.org/10.3389/fnagi.2018.00364
36. Walsh, C.A., Cahir, C., Tecklenborg, S., Byrne, C., Culbertson, M.A., Bennett, K.E.: The association between medication non-adherence and adverse health outcomes in ageing populations: a systematic review and meta-analysis. Br. J. Clin. Pharmacol. **85**(11), 2464–2478 (2019). https://doi.org/10.1111/bcp.14075
37. Yang, C.Y., Lu, M.J., Tseng, S.H., Fu, L.C.: A companion robot for daily care of elders based on homeostasis. In: 2017 56th Annual Conference of the Society of Instrument and Control Engineers of Japan (SICE), pp. 1401–1406. IEEE (2017). https://doi.org/10.23919/SICE.2017.8105748

Social Perception and Scene Awareness in Human-Robot Interaction

Sarwar Paplu[✉], Prabesh Khadka, Bhalachandra Gajanana Bhat, and Karsten Berns

Department of Computer Science, University of Kaiserslautern-Landau, RRLAB, 67663 Kaiserslautern, Germany
{paplu,p_khadka20,b_bhat20,berns}@cs.uni-kl.de
https://agrosy.informatik.uni-kl.de/en/

Abstract. This paper introduces various aspects of social perception skills and scene awareness for interactive robots. The low-level audio-visual perceptual cues e.g., interruption events, eye contact, speech energy, etc. have been fused to make high-level interpretations e.g., a person's willingness to maintain human-robot interaction in social settings. The detection of objects in the scene helps generate context-aware queries or responses for the robot. The overall behavior of the interactive robot, Ameca, has been generated in the form of speech and body language. In this work, a fusion of rule-based and caption-based speech generation has been incorporated. The experimental results in human-robot interaction scenarios show promising outcomes as far as the robot's ability to perceive and react to social and environmental cues.

Keywords: Human-Robot Interaction · Social Perception · Scene Awareness

1 Introduction and Related Works

The process through which people interpret and comprehend the traits, feelings, behaviors, and intentions of others in a social setting is known as social perception [1]. To understand the thoughts and feelings of others, we need to obtain and analyze data from a variety of cues, including tone of voice, body language, facial expressions, and situational context. This technique is essential for steering social interactions and creating accurate impressions of people. Apart from social perception skills, inter-human interaction ensures scene awareness in which environmental cues play a crucial role in interaction. An individual's capacity to recognize and comprehend the surroundings or context in which they find themselves is referred to as scene awareness. It entails paying close attention to a variety of scene aspects, including people, objects, spatial relationships, and pertinent details. The importance of social perception and scene awareness in Human-Robot Interaction (HRI) is undeniable [2]. A socially interactive robot should be able to understand its interaction partner's high-level behavioral cues

A. Al. Ali et al. (Eds.): ICSR 2023, LNAI 14454, pp. 123–132, 2024.
https://doi.org/10.1007/978-981-99-8718-4_11

e.g., intention, reaction on specific topics of interaction, willingness to maintain interaction, etc. Nonetheless, the robot's perception system should not only focus on the human but also analyze the environmental cues e.g., artifacts worn by the human interlocutor, objects in the scene should also be taken into account. This paper implements an approach to ensure a notion of social perception and scene understanding for socially interactive robots. Social perception and environmental awareness have been relatively under-explored in the field of HRI. The research work [3] stressed the importance of verbal and nonverbal cues in open-ended interactions. The *Person compoNet* in the "shopping center" scenario is in charge of identifying, following, and classifying people according to their age and gender. It also follows limited social norms e.g., greetings. However, the work does not take into account posture, facial expressions, or other important visual clues. In [4], the system architecture triggers the robot to navigate, engage with people, and perform activities in restricted situations e.g., rising service demand. The architecture groups general duties into a series of common sub-functions, separating them from decision-level activities. Unfortunately, this work does not consider para-linguistic cues and can not facilitate caption-based dialog generation. Scene graphs have been leveraged in [5] to transform the results of the environment into graph structure e.g., topological graphs. However, the application of such scene graphs in a human-robot social setting is missing. In [6], the main focus lies on the generation of natural language based on the objects available in the scene, with a 3D semantic graph map applied. Nevertheless, the social perception of the humans in the scene has not been taken into account.

The approach proposed in our work takes a good number of low-level audio-visual cues e.g., face emotion recognition, assessment of eye contact, object detection, speech semantics, speech energy, silence percentage, etc. The lifesize interactive robot utilized in this work makes use of these multimodal perceptual cues to interpret high-level social contexts in interaction scenarios.

2   Perception System

A dedicated speech recognition system is employed to convert user acoustic signals into text [7]. Various aspects of natural language processing e.g., sentiment analysis, named entity recognition, etc. have been incorporated [8]. The visual system of the robot tracks a human and estimates gestures/postures based on skeletal joint information. Among other visual features are proximity analysis, age/gender estimation, and face recognition [7]. The relevant low-level features for social perception and scene awareness are as follows:

2.1   Eye Contact Assessment

In social interaction, maintaining appropriate eye contact indicates the ability of the user to pay attention. In this work, the "eye contact assessment module" receives an RGB image from the ZED2i stereo vision camera of the robot used. Once the face image is obtained as shown in Fig. 1, it is pre-processed and fed into the pre-trained deep learning model [9]. If the prediction confidence is greater than 0.8, it is considered eye contact. Based on the outcomes, eye contact percentage and "averting eye contact" are analyzed. Let α be the eye contact percentage, $n_{\text{eye\_contact}}$ be the number of frames where the participant made eye contact, and $n_{\text{total\_frames}}$ be the total number of input frames where face image is detected. The eye contact percentage is calculated based on the total number of eye contact frames. Let β be the averting eye contact, x_i be the result of ith frame, and t be the duration of the interaction in seconds. The rate of change of eye contact per minute is calculated with Eq. 1.

Fig. 1. Workflow of the eye contact assessment system for a robot's social perception

$$\beta = \frac{60}{t} \sum_{i=2}^{n} |x_i - x_{i-1}| \quad \text{where} \quad x_i \epsilon \{0,1\} \tag{1}$$

2.2   Facial Expression Recognition

This module mainly focuses on detecting the facial emotion of the interaction partner in each frame and implicitly calculates the percentage of happiness, sadness, neutral emotion, and other basic facial emotions. A deep learning model based on ResNet50 has been employed to predict facial emotion. The ResNet model is trained using FER2013 dataset[1]. The dataset is divided into three distinct subsets: training, validation, and testing sets. The training set contains the majority of the images (around 80%), which are used to train the machine learning models. The validation set (approximately 10%) is employed to fine-tune the model during training by adjusting hyperparameters or early stopping to avoid overfitting. Finally, the testing set (approximately 10%) serves as an unbiased evaluation to assess the model's generalization performance on unseen data. The sample images of the dataset are shown in Fig. 2.

Fig. 2. Some snapshots from FER2013 used for facial emotion recognition system

---

[1] https://www.kaggle.com/datasets/msambare/fer2013.

2.3   Scene Perception

There are various models available for object detection that can help generate a robot's speech. There are two constraints, i.e., accuracy and speed, which are considered in human-robot interaction scenarios. MS-COCO is one of the widely used state-of-the-art datasets for object detection. MS-COCO-17 contains a total of 164K images that contain 897k annotated objects. It supports a total of 80 classes [10]. In this work, the object classes have been narrowed down to indoor objects. The annotations provided in the dataset already have a supercategory, grouping the classes. From this list, we selected classes that belonged to accessories, kitchen, food, indoor, and a few classes from animal and sports. This filtering reduced the total number of classes to 43. The artifacts of the interaction partners are also of importance for conversation starter [11]. Since the state-of-the-art dataset does not contain classes regarding attire, a dataset called fashion[2] has been employed in this paper. To get better accuracy in detecting a person's attire, a manual dataset is created using a ZED2i camera. 7 participants were asked to perform a series of tasks that included walking towards the camera and away from it, presenting their front, side, and back profiles. They were also asked to sit on a chair and provide different profiles. They were asked to repeat this using different fashion accessories such as jackets, hats, and glasses. There were a total of 658 images generated and the bounding boxes were manually drawn and labeled using Roboflow[3]. The next step is to train yolov5 using the datasets mentioned above. The images are resized to 640px × 640px and trained for 300 epochs. The workflow of the robot's scene awareness is illustrated in Fig. 3. An mAP 0.5 of a value of 0.51547 is achieved for the indoor COCO dataset and 0.75288 for the fashion dataset.

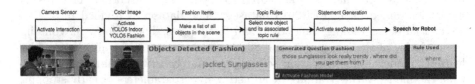

Fig. 3. Flowchart illustrating fashion object detection and speech generation for a social robot

2.4   Interruption Events

The act of a listener interrupting a speaker is often noticed in inter-human communications. As a result of a listener's "breaking in", the speaker becomes the listener. The interpretation of this act is heavily contextual in social settings. Although interruptions may indicate that the listener does not understand the

---

[2] https://universe.roboflow.com/cutegander/fashion-hkjfr/browse.
[3] https://roboflow.com/.

speaker correctly, this may show a notion of interest from the listener's side. However, there are some situations in which frequent interruptions are considered to be impolite. In this paper, the events in which human interlocutors interrupt the robot are taken into account. As long as the TTS (Text-to-Speech) system of the robot is active (running), any speech utterance from the human interlocutor is considered to be a *interruption* as shown in Fig. 4. Since the context of the experimental conversation is known, the standard interruption count is empirically set to ≤ 5. If the human interrupts the robot more than this threshold, γ, in an interaction scenario, the human is considered to have a more natural tendency to interrupt.

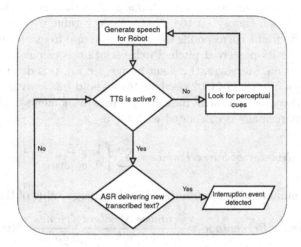

Fig. 4. Flowchart showing the interruption events triggered by human interlocutors

2.5   Paralinguistic Cues

Paralinguistic cues are nonverbal cues of the speech e.g., pitch, energy, speech rate, etc. These cues can be utilized in analyzing the social perceptual cues of a human interlocutor. The audio signals captured by the microphone are saved as a "wav file" during speech recognition and then forwarded to modules analyzing para-language. Speech rate is calculated based on the word count and duration of the transcribed text. Response delay or turn-taking time of the human can be calculated with Eq. 2, with T denoting the time stamp. Such information facilitates the perception of social cues as shown in the Eq. 7.

$$Response\ delay\ (sec) = T_{human\_starts\_speaking} - T_{robot\_stopped\_speaking} \qquad (2)$$

The librosa library[4] is employed to extract other implicit features e.g., energy, silence statistics. The characteristics of the audio signals obtained from the

---

[4] https://github.com/librosa/librosa.

microphone are analyzed during speech recognition. To achieve this, two important features from each audio frame – energy and pitch – are extracted. The energy of an audio frame represents the intensity or magnitude of the sound within that frame. The energy for each 20-millisecond audio frame is calculated. In order to understand the overall variation in energy throughout the speech, we compute the standard deviation of the energy values across all frames. The energy variation in the audio signal is calculated as shown in Eq. 3.

$$E_{variation} = \frac{1}{n} \sum_{i=1}^{n} (E_i - E_{mean})^2 \tag{3}$$

where N is the total number of audio frames, E_i is the energy value of the i-th frame, and "mean energy" is the average energy value over all frames. The pitch of an audio frame corresponds to the fundamental frequency of the sound, which determines its perceived pitch. Pitch variation is calculated similarly to the energy variation. Moreover, the silent frame (see Eq. 4) is determined with a threshold energy criterion of 0.02 decibels. Any audio frame with energy below this threshold is considered silent, indicating pauses or moments of silence during speech. Silent percentage is calculated with Eq. 5.

$$Number\ of\ Silent\ Frames = \sum_{i=1}^{N} \begin{cases} 1, & if\ E_i < 0.02 \\ 0, & otherwise \end{cases} \tag{4}$$

N is the total number of audio frames, E_i is the energy value of the i-th frame.

$$Silence\ Percentage = \frac{Number\ of\ silent\ frames}{Total\ number\ of\ frames} \times 100 \tag{5}$$

3   Analysis of Social Perception

A social robot is expected to analyze various aspects of social communication of human interlocutors. In this context, "social communication" refers to the development of verbal and nonverbal abilities, social interaction, and social cognition. Due to technical limitations, not all aspects can be implemented. However, spotting some competencies can be implemented in restricted interaction scenarios. For the evaluation of social communication of the human interlocutor, the robot assesses the following aspects as shown in Table 1. These aspects of social perception have been implemented based on perception events. For example, if a human interlocutor maintains desired proximity from the robot, makes eye contact, and continues a specific conversation, we call this event "willingness to maintain conversation".

Equation 6 shows if an interlocutor initiates an interaction with the robot in a predefined period t (typically 3 s). Otherwise, the robot initiates the interaction process.

$$P_{init\_communication} = (P_{face\_detect}, P_{speech\_utterances}, t, l) \\ l \in \{yes, no, unknown\} \tag{6}$$

Table 1. Various aspects of social perception skills of the robot

Initiation of communication and turn-taking	Eye contact
Willingness to maintain conversation	Ability to manipulate conversational topics
Comprehension of nonverbal and verbal cues in various situations	Willingness to answer questions directly
Evasive nature in certain situations	Display of politeness during communication
Reaction on specific situations e.g., discussion on politics/religion, etc.	Ability to pay attention

The assessment of whether or not a human interaction partner is interested in turn-taking is a challenging aspect to realize in a technical system. Equation 7 shows how this aspect can be realized in restricted human-robot interaction scenarios.

$$P_{turn\_taking} = (P_{face\_detect}, P_{interruption}, P_{silence\_time}, l)$$
$$l \in \{yes, no, unknown\} \tag{7}$$

The high-level percept $P_{maintains\_conversation}$ shown in equation 8 indicates the willingness of a human interlocutor to maintain a conversation. The low-level percepts are fused to make higher-level interpretations taking restricted interaction scenarios into account.

$$P_{maintains\_conversation} = (P_{proximity}, P_{silence\_time}, P_{avg\_sentence\_len}, l)$$
$$l \in \{yes, no, unknown\} \tag{8}$$

Equation 9 indicates if the human interlocutor understands the robot's speech utterances or body movements. The head gesture, posture, the number of repetitions, and certain phrases (e.g., *"did not get it"*, *"please explain"* etc.)

$$P_{comprehension} = (P_{head\_gesture}, P_{posture}, P_{repetition}, n, p, l)$$
$$p \in \{set\ of\ pre-defined\ phrases\} \tag{9}$$
$$l \in \{yes, no, unknown\}$$

Whether or not a person is paying attention to the robot can be realized in Eq. 10, with three low-level *percepts* utilized in the assessment of the attention mechanism. Nevertheless, this aspect of attention is applicable only for specific events, e.g., head gestures, human interrupting the robot, and his/her silence time.

$$P_{paying\_attention} = (P_{head\_gesture}, P_{interruption}, P_{silence\_time}, l)$$
$$l \in \{yes, no, unknown\} \tag{10}$$

The existing head gesture and body movement estimation system is integrated with a Chatbot [8] that generates speech for the robot. The events mentioned in Eqs. 6, 7, 8, 9, 10 are triggered based on the availability of relevant perceptual cues. These events represent a few aspects of the robot's social perception skills. Based on a specific event, the dialog management system [12] triggers the robot's body movement and facial expressions along with the speech generated by the Chatbot.

4 Experimentation and Evaluation

In this work, a humanoid interaction robot Ameca[5] has been utilized. It works as a front end for our interaction system. The entire system is known as Emah in our lab. The robot has 52 degrees of freedom, with the possibility to express complex humanlike facial expressions and gestures or postures. The robot is equipped with visual and speech perception systems that enable interaction with humans. A Rode wireless microphone is utilized to enable verbal interaction. The robot's behavior consists of three components: speech, gesture/posture, and facial expression. The body movements and facial expressions are generated first in a virtual environment and then applied to the real machine.

A rule-based speech generation system has been incorporated [8] with the robot. In addition, the output from the visual cue extraction module and the conversation rules module is collectively passed to the seq2seq model for generating the robot's response as shown in Fig. 3. A dialog management system [12] is employed to handle the switching of speech generators. The availability of objects around the scene can trigger specific interaction events. For example, if the communication comes to a dead end, the robot can generate speech based on the artifacts worn by the human or the objects around the scene.

In this work, a good number of HRI scenarios have been experimented with. As shown in Table 2, the first dialog (left) does not take into consideration the environmental cues whereas the second dialog considers environmental cues. The interactions were recorded. The videos were rated by 73 participants who were asked to rate each conversation in terms of realism of the interaction, appropriateness of the response generated by Emah, and naturalness of the conversation using a 5-point Likert scale [13], with 1 being the "least" and 5 being "most". Based on the results collected, the study showed that the interaction dialog with environmental awareness was rated significantly more realistic ($M = 3.95$, $SD = 1.10$) compared to the interaction dialog without environmental awareness ($M = 3.16$, $SD = 1.08$).

---

[5] https://www.engineeredarts.co.uk/.

Table 2. Two interaction scenarios (left and right) in which the robot's response is without and with the consideration of the objects around

Without Environmental Cues	With Environmental Cues
Human: Hi Emah	**Human:** Hi Emah
Emah: Hi, how may I help you?	**Emah:** Hi, how may I help you?
Human: I am planning for a trip to Paris next week, what should I pack?	**Human:** I am planning for a trip to Paris next week, what should I pack?
Emah: You should carry all the essentials	**Emah:** It's going to in Paris next week. You can take that umbrella with you
Human: OK, what's the weather like?	**Human:** Oh, I forgot about it. Thanks
Emah: It is cloudy with light showers today	**Emah:** That's fine
(*A dog enters the room ...*)	(*A dog enters the room ...*)
Human: OK, thank you	**Emah:** That's a really cute dog. What is its name?
Emah: Is there anything else I can help you with?	**Human:** It is Tommy. He is my best friend
Human: No, that's all. Bye bye!	**Emah:** I really love dogs, you could give it the ball that is there to play with
Emah: Bye-bye, have a nice day!	**Human:** Sure, I will go play with Tommy now. Bye!
	Emah: Bye-bye, have fun playing!

The results of the t-test shown in Table 3 showed a significant difference between the two groups, with a t-value of −4.32 and a p-value of 0.000 which is less than 0.001. The effect size (Cohen's d) with a value of −0.71 indicates a medium effect size. Hence, we reject the null hypothesis.

Table 3. Summary of t-test results for realism of the interaction. Group 1 refers to interaction dialog without environmental awareness and Group 2 refers to interaction dialog with environmental awareness.

Sample Statistics	Group 1 (Mean = 3.16, SD = 1.08)	Group 2 (Mean = 3.95, SD = 1.10)
t-test	$t(144) = -4.32$, $p = 0.000$, $d = -0.71$	

5 Conclusion

The approach presented in the work shows the social perceptual and environment-aware interaction skills of a social robot which facilitates fluid interaction in social settings. The low latency of the perception system ensures robust and real-time transfer of data for the dialog management system. A set of human-robot interaction scenarios has been conducted with user-centered evaluation. The results show promising improvement in terms of *realism* and context-awareness of interaction. As a future direction of the work, the verbal and nonverbal cues can be extended to cater to a diverse set of interaction scenarios dealing with social perceptual cues and multimodal scene awareness. Optical character recognition can be incorporated to enhance scene understanding in HRI scenarios.

References

1. Higgins, E.T., Bargh, J.A.: Social cognition and social perception. Ann. Rev. Psychol. **38**(1), 369–425 (1987)
2. Zaraki, A., et al.: Design and evaluation of a unique social perception system for human-robot interaction. IEEE Trans. Cogn. Dev. Syst. **9**(4), 341–355 (2016)
3. Martınez-Gómez, J., et al.: Toward social cognition in robotics: extracting and internalizing meaning from perception. In: XV Workshop of Physical Agents (WAF 2014), León, Spain, pp. 93–104 (2014)
4. Jumel, F.: Context aware robot architecture, application to the RoboCup@home challenge. In: Holz, D., Genter, K., Saad, M., von Stryk, O. (eds.) RoboCup 2018. LNCS (LNAI), vol. 11374, pp. 205–216. Springer, Cham (2019). https://doi.org/10.1007/978-3-030-27544-0_17
5. Blumenthal, S., Bruyninckx, H., Nowak, W., Prassler, E.: A scene graph based shared 3D world model for robotic applications. In: 2013 IEEE International Conference on Robotics and Automation, pp. 453–460. IEEE (2013)
6. Moon, J., Lee, B.: Scene understanding using natural language description based on 3D semantic graph map. Intel. Serv. Robot. **11**, 347–354 (2018)
7. Paplu, S., Navarro, R.F., Berns, K.: Harnessing long-term memory for personalized human-robot interactions. In: 2022 IEEE-RAS 21st International Conference on Humanoid Robots (Humanoids), pp. 377–382. IEEE (2022)
8. Paplu, S.H., Arif, M.N.I., Berns, K.: Utilizing semantic and contextual information during human-robot interaction. In: 2021 IEEE International Conference on Development and Learning (ICDL), pp. 1–6. IEEE (2021)
9. Chong, E., et al.: Detection of eye contact with deep neural networks is as accurate as human experts (2020). https://osf.io/5a6m7/
10. Lin, T.-Y.: Microsoft COCO: common objects in context. In: Fleet, D., Pajdla, T., Schiele, B., Tuytelaars, T. (eds.) ECCV 2014. LNCS, vol. 8693, pp. 740–755. Springer, Cham (2014). https://doi.org/10.1007/978-3-319-10602-1_48
11. Skjold, E.: Adorned in dreams: reversing the gaze: from the look of fashion to the lens of the wardrobe. Clothing Cult. **4**(1), 13–29 (2017)
12. Paplu, S.H., Mishra, C., Berns, K.: Pseudo-randomization in automating robot behaviour during human-robot interaction. In: 2020 Joint IEEE 10th International Conference on Development and Learning and Epigenetic Robotics (ICDL-EpiRob), pp. 1–6. IEEE (2020)
13. Jamieson, S.: Likert scales: how to (ab) use them? Med. Educ. **38**(12), 1217–1218 (2004)

The Influence of a Robot's Personality on Real-Time Explanations of Its Navigation

Amar Halilovic[1]([⊠])([iD]) and Senka Krivic[2]([iD])

[1] Ulm University, Ulm, Germany
amar.halilovic@uni-ulm.de
[2] University of Sarajevo, Sarajevo, Bosnia and Herzegovina
senka.krivic@etf.unsa.ba

Abstract. Navigational decisions of autonomous robots in social environments impact humans and their expectations of robots' actions. Explanations can help mitigate adverse effects on humans and enhance their understanding of robots' decisions. We present real-time multimodal explanations of a robot's navigation and model the influence of a robot's personality on it. Our approach considers the contextual background and spatial aspect of the robot environment. Our results show that the more extroverted the robot is, its explanations are less detailed and more often generated. Finally, we discuss potential avenues and constraints for future research. Our work promotes social and safe robot navigation.

Keywords: explainable navigation · explainable robotics · motion planning

1 Introduction

The opaqueness of robot decision-making hinders the swift integration of robots into human society. To facilitate this integration, robots ought to demonstrate traits akin to those of social robots [5]. Even with the difficulties associated with acquiring social norms, there is a proliferation of robots [4]. As a consequence, demand for the explainability of robot actions grows [21]. The provision of explanations for robot actions has been found to positively impact both human trust [20] and understanding [37]. An explainable robot is also perceived as more social [1]. Despite the numerous benefits of robots, there is a deficiency in the explainability of their decision-making [8]. The complexity of most robot behaviors and their social interactions with people further adds to the problem. To enhance the explainability and user-friendliness of robot navigation, we use multi-modal explanations to clarify robots' navigation decisions to individuals.

Here we focus on service social robots in indoor environments [14,15]. Image a scenario of an autonomous robot assigned the task of fetching a book in a library and navigating through its surroundings while confronting various obstacles. In the presence of unforeseen events—the sudden appearance of an obstacle on its pathway (a chair pulled out from under the table), the robot's planning

A. Al. Ali et al. (Eds.): ICSR 2023, LNAI 14454, pp. 133–147, 2024.
https://doi.org/10.1007/978-981-99-8718-4_12

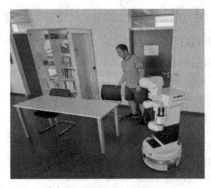
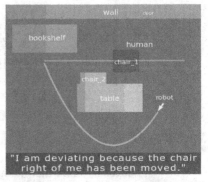

(a) Navigation scenario   (b) Corresponding explanation

Fig. 1. The robot (TIAGo from PAL Robotics) deviates from its initial trajectory (grey) deviating around the table while following an alternative trajectory (blue), after the human pulls the chair from under the table. In the given visual explanation, the main reason for the deviation is highlighted—chair_1 (red), while other objects are colored with a probabilistic heat map (see Sect. 3.1) based on their distance from the robot. The textual explanation shown under the visual explanation mentions the main reason for the robot's deviation. (Color figure online)

system may encounter failures or deviate (see Fig. 1a) from its originally charted trajectory. These behavioral changes have the potential to surprise individuals with whom the robot interacts, leading to a decline in their confidence in the robot's intentions. To tackle this issue and foster a more secure atmosphere for both humans and robots, the robot needs to provide explanations of the actions it makes. Figure 1b illustrates a multi-modal explanation of the robot's behavior in the illustrated deviation scenario. Multi-modality is reflected in the simultaneous provision of different explanation types (visual and textual).

We represent a robot's personality by quantifying its degrees of extroversion and introversion. Robots should be capable of understanding their own mental traits and their environment. We model the influence of a robot's extroversion and introversion on different explanation qualities (timing, representation, and duration). As extroversion and introversion are different sides of the same personality trait spectrum, we mainly use the term extroversion further in the paper. The main contributions of this paper are:

- We introduce a framework for explaining robot navigation and within it an algorithm for describing the influence of a robot's personality and the contextual background on explanation generation (Sect. 3).
- We propose an approach to generating real-time multi-modal explanations of a robot's navigation (Sect. 3) visualized through a visual explanation layer and a textual graphical interface (Sect. 4).

This paper is structured as follows: In Sect. 2, we conduct a review of related work. In Sect. 3, we present our explanation approach, which integrates both contextual background and a robot's personality into the process of explanation generation. Section 4 presents experimental results. Lastly, in Sect. 5, we discuss the limitations and implications of our work.

2   Related Work

Our work is situated at the intersection of explainable navigation and the use of mental models in Human-Robot Interaction (HRI). Consequently, we review related work in the areas of *Explainable Autonomous Navigation* and *Mental Models in HRI*, aiming to provide a comprehensive understanding of the existing research landscape and identify potential avenues for further exploration.

2.1   Explainable Autonomous Navigation

The need for transparency, trust, and explainability of robots among humans is substantial and experiencing rapid growth. It results in a notable movement towards the development of transparent robots. An essential aspect of explanation delivery lies in explanation communication, where robots' failure to convey their intentions effectively can be disconcerting to people [39], even when the robots do not fail in their decision-making [23]. Various navigational approaches have incorporated natural-language explanations to improve interpretability. Notably, Perera et al. [28] and Rosenthal et al. [31] focus on explaining complete global trajectories by providing narrative summaries of robot paths. Gavriilidis et al. [12] leverage surrogates to generate agnostic explanations of autonomous agents' behavior, breaking down behavior into natural-language components. Additionally, Das et al. [6] generate natural-language explanations to enhance human assistance in recovering from navigational errors. The work by Stein [32] makes model-informed natural language explanations, delving into the navigation algorithms being explained. Robb et al. [30] delve into explaining navigational planning failures by examining users' mental models when presented with explanations of robotic failures of remote navigational agents. Brandao et al. [3] introduce a taxonomy of explainable motion planning, formalizing explanations not only for planning failures but also for deviations and preferences in trajectories. Halilovic and Lindner focus on explaining local deviations from initial paths, employing visual [14] and visuo-textual [15] explanations in their work.

To the best of our knowledge, there are no previous works on the influence of a robot's personality on its explanations. Therefore, we address this research gap by expanding on our previous work [14,15] by introducing real-time multi-modal explanations of robot navigation. Multi-modality is reflected in the provision of visual and textual explanations whose scope, timing, representation, and duration are affected by the robot's personality and its understanding of the social context of its immediate environment.

2.2   Mental Models in HRI

Unlike humans, robots lack the advantage of human intuition [2]. Therefore, they employ mental models, i.e. mathematical formalisms, to approximate the mental states of humans and plan their actions accordingly. Mental models encompass various aspects, including biases, beliefs, and experiences of individuals [9]. Before making any decision, individuals engage in a process of reasoning [29]. Goetz and Kiesler [13] showed that aligning a robot's personality with users' tasks (whether serious or playful) led to increased cooperation from the users. We translate this postulate into explanations. An explanation tailored to the recipient should increase explanation understanding and user cooperation.

Explainability pertains to comprehending the mechanisms guiding a robot's actions and the ability to elucidate the robot's behavior or underlying reasoning [17,34]. Behavior explainability is significantly influenced by sharing knowledge and matching expectations [25,38]. The amount of information that agents should present to users is a topic of ongoing inquiry. We model the influence of extroversion and introversion on the number of details an explanation contains and its representation, timing, and duration. Nass et al. [26] demonstrated that extroverted individuals perceived extroverted agents as more attractive and credible, while introverted individuals favored introverted agents for the same reasons. We adopt five needs of human-centric XAI (real-time, accurate, actionable, human-interpretable, and consistent) [33] to explainability of robot navigational actions in terms of introvert and extrovert robots.

3   HiXRoN Architecture

We propose *HiXRoN*, a hierarchical framework (shown in Fig. 2), for generating explanations tailored to context and explanation recipients. *HiXRoN* is designed to be modular, allowing various interfaces for communication with explanation recipients, robots, and the environment. Explanation generation is modeled as a stepwise hierarchical process, with each level enriching the explanation with specific qualitative or quantitative aspects:

Step 1: The input for *HiXRoN* includes a robot model, a navigation framework, and the ontology of the present environment.

Step 2: An explanation target (*what to explain?*) is chosen, its scope determined through context understanding and inputs, forming the core explanation, which is later detailed using temporal and qualitative strategies.

Step 3: Explanation timing (*when to explain?*) is crucial for human communication. Its delivery moment is determined based on the context.

Step 4: After proper timing, the chosen explanation representation (*how to explain?*) significantly influences its reception and understanding.

Step 5: The final step is determining explanation duration (*how long to explain?*), relying on context and the user's state.

Step 6: The recipient is provided with a contextually sensitive and socially attuned explanation through an explanation interface, which should technically align with the chosen explanation representation.

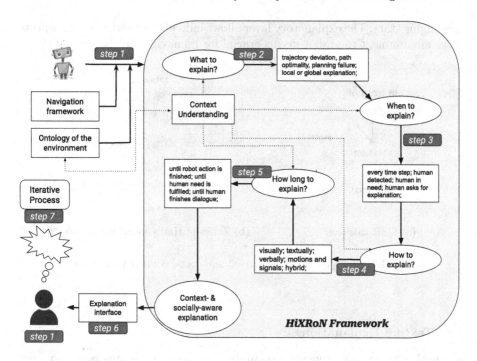

Fig. 2. HiXRoN - Hierarchical eXplainable Robot Navigation Framework

Step 7: After receiving the explanation, the user can restart the process from *Step 1* with added questions and hyperparameters if desired.

In this paper, we focus on the provision of real-time multi-modal explanations and the effect of the robot's personality on them. Multi-modality is expressed through the use of both visual and textual explanations, which together with the level of detail in them, form the explanation representation. A robot's personality is represented by the robot's extroversion level and we model its influence on explanation timing (Step 3), representation (Step 4), and duration (Step 5).

3.1 Visual Explanations

We model visual explanations as a local visual *explanation layer* around the robot at every moment during its navigation. In the layer, objects, i.e. potential obstacles, around the robot are colored according to their proximity to the robot, forming the local heat map. We use a yellow-green heat map [27] (see Fig. 1b) Objects closer to the robot, i.e. objects with a higher probability of becoming an obstacle, are colored closer to yellow, while farther objects are colored closer to green. When an object becomes an obstacle and causes a significant change in the robot's navigational behavior, it is colored red. This resembles the basic color psychology, where red is a strong indicator of an important occurrence, while yellow and green, respectively increasing in effect, indicate a calmer, more unchanging state. The explanatory layer allows individuals to witness the aspects of the environment the robot deems crucial for its navigation choices.

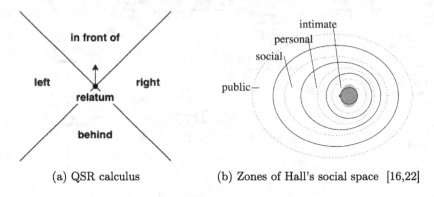

(a) QSR calculus   (b) Zones of Hall's social space [16,22]

Fig. 3. Techniques of giving spatial and social context to a robot

3.2 Textual Explanations

In addition to providing visual explanations, a robot generates corresponding textual explanations. Concurrently with a robot's navigation, our system continuously tracks the positions of both the robot and nearby objects, updating the foundational ontology. This dynamic process facilitates the establishment of spatial relationships between objects and the robot. These spatial relationships are typically defined using some Qualitative Spatial Reasoning (QSR) [10] calculus. A QSR calculus establishes a coordinate system that divides the surrounding space into semantically meaningful quadrants. These quadrants represent conceptual spatial entities, enabling the definition of spatial relations (such as left-of or right-of) between objects located within the quadrants and the object (relatum) at the coordinate origin. For convenience, we modify a single-cross calculus [11] (see Fig. 3a) and appoint the relatum to the navigating robot. With the aid of QSR, the robot gains the ability to semantically express the positions of neighboring objects in relation to its own position. Our reference system comprises four distinct quadrants: *left*, *right*, *in front of*, and *behind*. This division facilitates the generation of, as described by Halilovic and Lindner [15], descriptive textual explanations *"I am deviating due to the presence of an object on my left."* and suggestive textual explanations *"Dear human, would you kindly relocate the object positioned to my right? This adjustment would contribute to a smoother progression of my movement!"*

3.3 The Influence of a Robot's Personality on Its Explanations

Extroversion is an impactful and precise trait in shaping human peer relationships [18], widely used in HRI [19]. Extroverts often display increased energy and a tendency to speak louder, faster, and at a higher pitch [19]. They typically minimize pauses, employ shorter sentences, and use simpler vocabulary [7], while also initiating conversations more frequently [36], and focusing more on discussing themselves rather than others [24]. Additionally, extroverted individuals are generally more accepting of intrusion into their personal space compared to introverted individuals [35].

We translate these findings into a robot's explanation mental model influenced by its extroversion level and the context (presence of people around it). We model the extroversion level on a scale between 0 and 1 with a step 0.1, corresponding to a discretized stepwise *extroversion probability*. The robot also has a notion of social space. According to the Halls's [16] theory of social spaces (see Fig. 3b), the robot's social spaces are divided into four zones, among which are the personal and social zones. The social zone usually spreads from 1.2 to 3.6 meters from the robot. In our model, the human presence is determined according to the breach of the robot's *explanation representation threshold*, which is the linear function of the extroversion level: $explanation\_representation\_threshold = 3.6 - 2.4 \times extroversion\_probability$. For the totally extroverted robot, the threshold is 1.2, while for the totally introverted robot is 3.6. In this way, the totally extroverted robot changes its explanation representation when its personal zone is breached, while the totally introverted one does it immediately when its social zone is breached. This behavior corresponds to the fact that extroverts are more tolerant of their personal space than introverts.

Both a robot's personality and the human presence influence the explanation (see Algorithm 1). The influence affects four explanation-dependent variables *timing*, *duration*, *representation*, and *detail_level* (whose implementation details are presented in Sect. 4). Referring to the finding that extroverted individuals minimize pauses, the timing, i.e. the delay in expressing an explanation after forming it, is a linear function of the extroversion level. The more extroverted the robot is, the smaller the delay (pause) it will have. Extroverted individuals speak faster, so the more extroverted robot explains shorter, while an introverted one does it longer. Both timing and duration are calculated as descending linear functions of extroversion probability: $timing/duration = 20 - 20 \times extroversion\_probability$. The size of the visual explanation layer corresponds to the size of the explanation representation zone. More extroverted robot formulates less detailed explanations using simpler sentences and vocabulary and has a narrower visual explanation layer. The presence of humans affects the explanation representation, as robots tend to get shy when their explanation representation zone is breached, so they pertain to only visual representation. A breach is detected if the distance between the robot and the human closest to it is lower than the used explanation representation threshold.

4 Evaluation

The evaluation is situated in a library simulation setting, i.e. in the Gazebo simulation environment. We vary the robot's extroversion level and quantitatively access the number of generated explanations as well as the level of detail in them

Algorithm 1. The influence of extroversion and human presence on explanations

---

if distance_to_closest_human < explanation_representation_threshold **then**
    representation: visual
else
    representation: visual + textual
end if
if extroversion_probability < 0.5 **then**
    detail_level: rich
else
    detail_level: poor
end if

---

and their runtime. The level is detail is reflected in the number of objects present in the explanations, as well as the explanation length and the number of important navigational decisions, i.e. deviations, present in generated explanations.

4.1 Technical Set-Up

Our set-up is situated in the context of the ROS navigation stack[1]. A global path planner has generated a global path for the robot to navigate to a specified goal position. The robot (TIAGo from PAL robotics) is working in a library and is appointed the task of fetching a book, which is on the other side of the library. It follows the global path that leads it to pass between the table with chairs and the bookshelf, but the pathway in front of it is suddenly blocked by a chair that a nearby human drew out from under the table (see Fig. 4a). The global planner produces the new global path which makes the robot deviate from its initially planned trajectory. Following the new path, the robot stumbles across another chair blocking its way, while navigating between two bookshelves (see Fig. 4b). The chair was moved by a nearby human. Following the new trajectory, the robot has to deviate again around the left bookshelf towards the target. Two deviations (see Fig. 4) are important navigation behaviors in our scenario.

The visual explanation is continuously published as *PointCloud2* and overlayed over the map view in RViz as a local explanation layer (see Fig. 5d). The whole model is loaded once at the beginning of navigation and called iteratively allowing for the continuous explanation generation. Visual explanation continuously contains a heat map around the robot during its navigation. The objects responsible for deviations, i.e. chairs, are colored red when the deviations happen. Furthermore, arrows around movable objects display the allowed moving directions. The current global path, as well as the previous global path, after the deviation happens, are also contained in a visual explanation. The size of the robot's visual explanation layer is determined by the robot's extroversion level and directly affects the level of detail, as with a wider layer, more objects are included in the heat map. Timing is represented as a delay in explaining, where its value is the number of explanation iterations the explanation will be delayed

---

[1] http://wiki.ros.org/navigation.

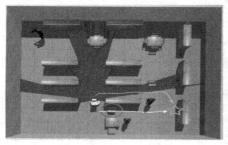 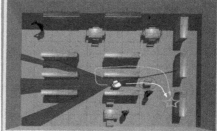

(a) First deviation   (b) Second deviation

Fig. 4. Two unexpected deviations during robot navigation. The robot deviates from its initial trajectory (white arrow) taking an alternative trajectory (light blue arrow). Red circles mark the objects responsible for deviation (chairs), while a green star denotes the navigation goal pose (near the bookshelf). (Color figure online)

for. The duration value is the number of explanation iterations the explanation stays the same. Textual explanations accompany the visual ones (see Fig. 5d). All explanation properties apply for textual as for the visual explanations, with the change in the detail level. When the level of detail is poor, then the textual explanations are in the following form: *"Around me are table and bookshelf."* and *"The chair was moved."*. When the level of detail is rich, then the textual explanations are in the following form: *"I am passing by table left of me and bookshelf right of me."* and *"I am deviating because the chair left of me was moved."*. Besides the detail level, these difference shows that the more introverted robot (with a rich level of detail) focuses more on itself. Textual explanations are presented in textual explanation GUI and are continuously updated. Two demonstration videos of a totally introverted and a totally extroverted robot are provided[2].

4.2 Results

We measure *number of generated visual and textual explanations* of the TIAGo navigating in our scenario. The higher these numbers are the more often the robot is producing an explanation of a certain type. Figure 5a shows that both the number of generated visual explanations and the number of generated textual explanations increase in relation to the increase of the robot's extroversion level. As could be expected, more extroverted robots explain more frequently. Regarding the number of details included in explanations, we measure *the average number of objects included in visual explanations*, as well as *the number of words textual explanations contain*. Figure 5b shows the change of both of these values in relation to the increase of the robot's extroversion level. Both values decrease as the level of extroversion increases, despite occasional local maxima. This aligns with the fact that more introverted individuals focus more on details than their more extroverted peers. Figure 5b also shows that the robot explains

---

[2] Videos can be accessed at the following link.

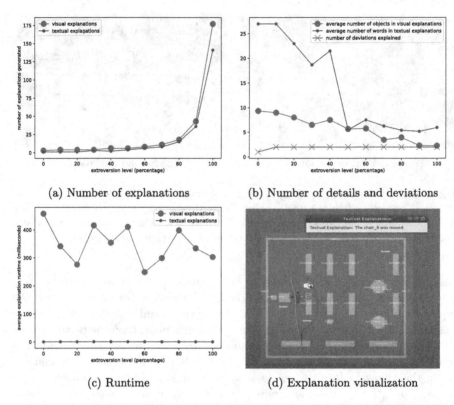

(a) Number of explanations

(b) Number of details and deviations

(c) Runtime

(d) Explanation visualization

Fig. 5. Quantitative and qualitative results a) Number of visual and textual explanations generated in relation to the extroversion level. b) Average number of objects in visual explanations. Average number of words in textual explanations. Total number of deviations explained. All values are plotted in relation to the extroversion level. c) Average runtimes of visual and textual explanations in relation to the extroversion level. d) Visualization of visual explanations in RViz and textual explanations in a textual GUI.

both deviations in almost all extroversion levels, only failing to do so when it is fully introverted. Finally, we analyze *explanation runtime.*[3] We report an average explanation-generation runtime of 348.90 ms for visual and 0.34 ms for textual explanations. Textual explanation is created after visual explanation, so the total explanation runtime is 349.24 ms. Runtimes are not significantly affected by the robot's extroversion level (see Fig. 5c).

4.3   Discussion

The extroversion level of the robot emerges as a pivotal factor governing the frequency of its explanatory interactions. We have observed that a more extroverted

---

[3] All reported runtime experiments run on a laptop machine with Intel Core i5-8250U 1.6 GHz, 8 GB of RAM, and NVIDIA GeForce MX130.

robot engages in explanations more frequently than its introverted counterparts. The number of both visual and textual explanations generated increases exponentially with the increase of the extroversion level. The higher generation frequency is a result of shorter delays and explanation duration by the extroverted robots. However, a trade-off arises, as the brevity of these explanations can sometimes hinder comprehensibility. Their concise nature, coupled with their rapid delivery, creates a sense of confidence that the robot is consistently addressing crucial navigational aspects. Yet, the drawback emerges in terms of the intricacy of the explanations, which tend to be comparatively shallow when compared to the explanations provided by a less extroverted robot.

Conversely, a robot displaying high levels of introversion demonstrates a distinct pattern in its explanatory behavior. Such a robot exhibits a pronounced delay in initiating explanations, stemming from its inherent uncertainty about the necessity and timing of the explanation. When these explanations do manifest, they exhibit an extended duration, characterized by a wealth of intricate details. The results align with this notion, as both the number of objects covered by the visual explanation layer and the length of textual explanations, i.e. the number of words in them, decrease with the increasing extroversion level. The decrease is linear, although a decrease in the number of words in textual explanation does show a slight linear drop and then a more significant linear drop between extroversion levels of 0.3 and 0.5. This could be caused by the explanation timing which aligns with the presence of humans within the visual explanation layer and their absence between different extroversion levels, which affects the generation of textual explanation, and the number of words included. The number of deviations explained, whose maximum is two, does not change significantly throughout the whole extroversion range. Only a totally introverted robot fails to explain one deviation, as its explanation delay and duration are long enough to miss explaining one important navigational aspect.

There is no significant change in the explanation runtime concerning different extroversion levels. Visual explanation layers are smaller in size as the extroversion level increases, but it does not hamper the runtime. A similar conclusion is with the textual explanations, where the longer sentences with extroverted robots do not hamper explanation runtime. Visual explanation runtime is many times longer than textual explanation runtime, referring to the computational load when calculating matrix data rather than textual data. The average runtime of 349.24 ms allows for the creation of up to 3 explanations per second, which is on most occasions too fast for people to comprehend, and thus can be considered a real-time explanation generation.

5   Conclusion

In this paper, we have introduced a novel approach that focuses on elucidating the decision-making process of a robot during navigation. Our method leverages a fusion of visual and textual explanations, incorporating two key elements: the robot's extroversion level and the social context in which it operates-specifically, the presence of individuals in its surroundings. Through our exploration, we have discovered a strong influence of the robot's extroversion level on several vital facets of explanation delivery, including timing, duration, representation, and the depth of both visual and textual explanations.

The more extroverted the robot is, the more often it is going to explain. Its explanations are however very short and could be generated too quickly for people to comprehend. Quick timing and short duration give a solid belief that the robot will get to explain all important aspects of its navigation, but its level of detail will be poor compared to a more introverted robot. How different detail level affects the understanding and satisfaction of explanations is a study for future work. Furthermore, explaining very often and quickly, means that explanations contain a lot of quickly-changing information, that could be unimportant and overwhelming for the user.

On the other hand, a very introverted robot explains with a bigger delay, as it is unsure whether and when it should explain. Its explanations also last long, while they contain a lot of details and its high introversion does not allow for fast and more energetic explanations. This may lead to a series of longer uninterrupted explanations, where, although a single explanation lasts longer, the new explanation is also provided rarer. This may cause the robot to fail to explain a lot of important navigational situations, while the unimportant ones will be highlighted longer than unneeded. But, when the robot timely catches the important navigational aspect to explain, its explanation will be long and detailed, although somewhat delayed. This delicate balance underscores the complexity of explanation dynamics within the context of a robot's navigation.

Our method is usable in well-defined environments, showing a stable explanation of generation behavior comprising the effect of a robot's personality. We foresee this tool being valuable for tasks like inspection, troubleshooting, and educating about motion planning. It could also serve the purpose of showcasing the robot's internal thought processes to curious non-experts. Our study revealed the intricate interplay between a robot's extroversion level, explanation timing, duration, and detail, and their impact on user understanding and satisfaction. These findings underscore the multifaceted nature of explanation strategies in robotics, offering valuable insights for crafting effective human-robot interaction paradigms. As we continue to refine and expand these insights, we anticipate a richer understanding of how robots can navigate complex terrain by providing explanations that cater to both their individual characteristics and the social contexts in which they operate. In the next phase of our work, we will also include para-linguistic cues, e.g. energy, pitch, intonation, and stress as parts of a robot's personality. There is also a need to determine the correlation between user satisfaction and types of robot personalities. We will evaluate the explanations' quality, usability, and simplicity and the effect of the robot's personality and human presence on them through user studies as part of our future work.

Acknowledgement. This work is supported by project AeroSTREAM, call HORIZON-WIDERA-2021-ACCESS-05, Grant Agreement number: 101071270.

References

1. Ambsdorf, J., et al.: Explain yourself! Effects of explanations in human-robot interaction. arXiv preprint arXiv:2204.04501 (2022)
2. Baraka, K., Alves-Oliveira, P., Ribeiro, T.: An extended framework for characterizing social robots. In: Jost, C., et al. (eds.) Human-Robot Interaction. SSBN, vol. 12, pp. 21–64. Springer, Cham (2020). https://doi.org/10.1007/978-3-030-42307-0_2
3. Brandao, M., Canal, G., Krivić, S., Magazzeni, D.: Towards providing explanations for robot motion planning. In: 2021 IEEE International Conference on Robotics and Automation (ICRA), pp. 3927–3933. IEEE (2021)
4. Breazeal, C.: Socially intelligent robots. Interactions **12**(2), 19–22 (2005)
5. Breazeal, C., Dautenhahn, K., Kanda, T.: Social robotics. In: Springer Handbook of Robotics, pp. 1935–1972. Springer (2016)
6. Das, D., Banerjee, S., Chernova, S.: Explainable AI for system failures: generating explanations that improve human assistance in fault recovery. arXiv preprint arXiv:2011.09407 (2020)
7. Dewaele, J.M., Furnham, A.: Extraversion: the unloved variable in applied linguistic research. Lang. Learn. **49**(3), 509–544 (1999)
8. Felzmann, H., Fosch-Villaronga, E., Lutz, C., Tamo-Larrieux, A.: Robots and transparency: the multiple dimensions of transparency in the context of robot technologies. IEEE Robot. Autom. Mag. **26**(2), 71–78 (2019)
9. Ford, D.N., Sterman, J.D.: Expert knowledge elicitation to improve formal and mental models. Syst. Dyn. Rev. J. Syst. Dyn. Soc. **14**(4), 309–340 (1998)
10. Freksa, C.: Qualitative spatial reasoning. In: Mark, D.M., Frank, A.U. (eds.) Cognitive and Linguistic Aspects of Geographic Space. NATO ASI Series, vol. 63, pp. 361–372. Springer, Dordrecht (1991). https://doi.org/10.1007/978-94-011-2606-9_20
11. Freksa, C.: Using orientation information for qualitative spatial reasoning. In: Frank, A.U., Campari, I., Formentini, U. (eds.) GIS 1992. LNCS, vol. 639, pp. 162–178. Springer, Heidelberg (1992). https://doi.org/10.1007/3-540-55966-3_10
12. Gavriilidis, K., Munafo, A., Pang, W., Hastie, H.: A surrogate model framework for explainable autonomous behaviour. arXiv preprint arXiv:2305.19724 (2023)
13. Goetz, J., Kiesler, S., Powers, A.: Matching robot appearance and behavior to tasks to improve human-robot cooperation. In: 2003 Proceedings of the 12th IEEE International Workshop on Robot and Human Interactive Communication, ROMAN 2003, pp. 55–60. IEEE (2003)
14. Halilovic, A., Lindner, F.: Explaining local path plans using LIME. In: Müller, A., Brandstötter, M. (eds.) Advances in Service and Industrial Robotics, RAAD 2022. Mechanisms and Machine Science, vol. 120, pp. 106–113. Springer, Cham (2022). https://doi.org/10.1007/978-3-031-04870-8_13
15. Halilovic, A., Lindner, F.: Visuo-textual explanations of a robot's navigational choices. In: Companion of the 2023 ACM/IEEE International Conference on Human-Robot Interaction, pp. 531–535 (2023)
16. Hall, E.T.: The Hidden Dimension, vol. 609. Anchor (1966)
17. Hayes, B., Shah, J.A.: Improving robot controller transparency through autonomous policy explanation. In: Proceedings of the 2017 ACM/IEEE International Conference on Human-Robot Interaction, pp. 303–312 (2017)
18. Jensen-Campbell, L.A., Gleason, K.A., Adams, R., Malcolm, K.T.: Interpersonal conflict, agreeableness, and personality development. J. Pers. **71**(6), 1059–1086 (2003)

19. Lee, K.M., Peng, W., Jin, S.A., Yan, C.: Can robots manifest personality?: an empirical test of personality recognition, social responses, and social presence in human-robot interaction. J. Commun. **56**(4), 754–772 (2006)
20. Leichtmann, B., Humer, C., Hinterreiter, A., Streit, M., Mara, M.: Effects of explainable artificial intelligence on trust and human behavior in a high-risk decision task. Comput. Hum. Behav. **139**, 107539 (2023)
21. Lim, V., Rooksby, M., Cross, E.S.: Social robots on a global stage: establishing a role for culture during human-robot interaction. Int. J. Soc. Robot. **13**(6), 1307–1333 (2021)
22. Lindner, F.: A conceptual model of personal space for human-aware robot activity placement. In: 2015 IEEE/RSJ International Conference on Intelligent Robots and Systems (IROS), pp. 5770–5775. IEEE (2015)
23. Lomas, M., Chevalier, R., Cross, E.V., Garrett, R.C., Hoare, J., Kopack, M.: Explaining robot actions. In: Proceedings of the Seventh Annual ACM/IEEE International Conference on Human-Robot Interaction. pp. 187–188 (2012)
24. Mairesse, F., Walker, M.A., Mehl, M.R., Moore, R.K.: Using linguistic cues for the automatic recognition of personality in conversation and text. J. Artif. Intelli. Res. **30**, 457–500 (2007)
25. Miller, T.: Explanation in artificial intelligence: insights from the social sciences. Artif. Intell. **267**, 1–38 (2019)
26. Nass, C., Lee, K.M.: Does computer-generated speech manifest personality? An experimental test of similarity-attraction. In: Proceedings of the SIGCHI conference on Human Factors in Computing Systems, pp. 329–336 (2000)
27. Netek, R., Pour, T., Slezakova, R.: Implementation of heat maps in geographical information system-exploratory study on traffic accident data. Open Geosci. **10**(1), 367–384 (2018)
28. Perera, V., Selveraj, S.P., Rosenthal, S., Veloso, M.: Dynamic generation and refinement of robot verbalization. In: 2016 25th IEEE International Symposium on Robot and Human Interactive Communication (RO-MAN), pp. 212–218 (2016)
29. Pomerol, J.C.: Artificial intelligence and human decision making. Eur. J. Oper. Res. **99**(1), 3–25 (1997)
30. Robb, D.A., Liu, X., Hastie, H.: Explanation styles for trustworthy autonomous systems. In: Proceedings of the 2023 International Conference on Autonomous Agents and Multiagent Systems, pp. 2298–2300 (2023)
31. Rosenthal, S., Selvaraj, S.P., Veloso, M.M.: Verbalization: narration of autonomous robot experience. In: IJCAI, vol. 16, pp. 862–868 (2016)
32. Stein, G.: Generating high-quality explanations for navigation in partially-revealed environments. In: Advances in Neural Information Processing Systems, vol. 34 (2021)
33. Swamy, V., Frej, J., Käser, T.: The future of human-centric explainable artificial intelligence (XAI) is not post-hoc explanations. arXiv preprint arXiv:2307.00364 (2023)
34. Tabrez, A., Agrawal, S., Hayes, B.: Explanation-based reward coaching to improve human performance via reinforcement learning. In: 2019 14th ACM/IEEE International Conference on Human-Robot Interaction (HRI), pp. 249–257. IEEE (2019)
35. Takayama, L., Pantofaru, C.: Influences on proxemic behaviors in human-robot interaction. In: 2009 IEEE/RSJ International Conference on Intelligent Robots and Systems, pp. 5495–5502. IEEE (2009)
36. Tay, B., Jung, Y., Park, T.: When stereotypes meet robots: the double-edge sword of robot gender and personality in human-robot interaction. Comput. Hum. Behav. **38**, 75–84 (2014)

37. Van Camp, W.: Explaining understanding (or understanding explanation). Eur. J. Philos. Sci. **4**, 95–114 (2014)
38. Vigano, L., Magazzeni, D.: Explainable security. In: 2020 IEEE European Symposium on Security and Privacy Workshops (EuroS&PW), pp. 293–300. IEEE (2020)
39. Williams, T., Briggs, P., Scheutz, M.: Covert robot-robot communication: human perceptions and implications for human-robot interaction. J. Hum. Robot Interact. **4**(2), 24–49 (2015)

Evaluating Students' Experiences in Hybrid Learning Environments: A Comparative Analysis of Kubi and Double Telepresence Robots

Xiaoxuan Hei[1]([✉]), Valentine Denis[2], Pierre-Henri Oréfice[3], Alia Afyouni[2],
Paul Laborde[2], Damien Legois[2], Ioana Ocnarescu[2], Margarita Anastassova[3],
and Adriana Tapus[1]

[1] U2IS, ENSTA Paris, Institut Polytechnique de Paris, Palaiseau, France
{xiaoxuan.hei,adriana.tapus}@ensta-paris.fr
[2] Strate Design School, Sèvres, France
{v.denis,a.afyouni,p.laborde,d.legois,i.ocnarescu}@strate.design
[3] Université Paris-Saclay, CEA List, Palaiseau, France
{pierre-henri.orefice,margarita.anastassova}@cea.fr

Abstract. Amidst the Covid-19 pandemic, distance learning was employed on an unprecedented level. As the lockdown measures have eased, it has become a parallel option alongside traditional in-person learning. Nevertheless, the utilization of basic videoconferencing tools such as Zoom, Microsoft Teams, and Google Meet comes with a multitude of constraints that extend beyond technological aspects. These limitations are intricately linked with human behavior, psychology, but also pedagogy, drastically changing the interactions that take place during learning. Telepresence robots have been widely used due to their advantages in enhancing a sense of in-person. To investigate the opportunities, the impact, and the risks associated with the usage of telepresence robots in an educational context, we conducted an experiment in a real setting, in the specific use case of a design school and a project-based class. We are interested in the experience of a classroom and the relationships between a distance student, his/her peers, and the professor/instructor. This study employed two types of robots: a Kubi robot (a semi-static tablet-based system) and a Double robot (a mobile telepresence robot). The primary objective was to ascertain the perceptions and experiences of both remote and in-person students during their interaction with these robots. The results of the study demonstrate a marked preference among students for the Double robot over the Kubi, as indicated by their feedback.

Keywords: Telepresence robot · Distance learning · Human-robot interaction

1 Introduction

In recent years, technological advancements have revolutionized the landscape of education, going beyond traditional limits and opening up new opportunities for learning [1]. One such innovation is the integration of telepresence robots within the classroom environment [2]. Telepresence robots can serve as a solution to address the limitations in mobility faced by students due to a variety of reasons such as weather, disability and illness [3]. Compared to conventional distance learning tools, with telepresence robots, students are empowered to navigate the robot's movements, select viewing angles, and even engage with the surrounding environment. This technology facilitates their seamless integration into a social learning environment, allowing them to interact with peers and educators in real time [4].

A recent project implemented by French Ministry of National Education, Youth and Sports, called TED-i[1], just concluded by deploying 4000 of these robots in French schools. This endeavor is designed to address the challenges faced by students who are absent due to various reasons, particularly hospitalization, and to facilitate their seamless reintegration into the classroom environment. The ultimate goal is to support their learning journey and ensure genuine inclusion and socialization upon their return.

The central aim of our ongoing research is to explore the potential of telepresence robots in enhancing the realm of distance learning. This entails a comprehensive evaluation of several key factors, including the perception of information assimilation, the quality and quantity of knowledge acquisition, the engagement levels and responsiveness of remote students, the overall user experience, as well as the amplification of interactions among students participating from a distance, those physically present in the classroom, and collaborative partnerships.

In this paper, we delve into an examination of the practical utilization of telepresence robots, specifically focusing on the Kubi and Double robots. Our primary focus is to gain an understanding of how students perceive and engage with these robots within a real setting of a university classroom. To accomplish this, we employ a combination of quantitative data analysis and qualitative insights to provide a comprehensive overview between a distance student, his/her peers, and the professor/instructor.

The rest of the paper is structured as follows: Sect. 2 discusses previous related work about telepresence robots in education; Sect. 3 presents our experimental design; Sect. 4 shows the results and Sect. 5 concludes this work.

2   Related Work

Lately, there has been a growing interest in researching telepresence robots due to their promising utility in the field of distance education.

In their study, Bell et al. [5] conducted a comparison of different types of telepresence robots within an educational setting. These categories encompassed videoconferencing (referred to as 2D telepresence), "table" telepresence robots (referred to as 2.5D telepresence), and mobile telepresence robots (referred to as 3D telepresence). The outcomes of the research revealed that 3D telepresence,

---

[1] https://www.education.gouv.fr/ted-i-des-robots-de-tele-presence-destines-aux-el eves-hospitalises-326458.

involving mobile robots, generated a heightened sense of immersion for students participating remotely.

Thompson et al. [4] studied the perception of a telepresence robot in a classroom. Initial findings focused on the experiences of students within a physical classroom where face-to-face interactions involved both students present in person and those participating remotely through a telepresence robot. These findings underscored the necessity for educators to devise and implement innovative instructional approaches to foster a positive classroom experience that caters to the needs of both in-class attendees and remote learners.

Fitter et al. [6] examined the experiences of college students taking classes in three formats: in-person, via a telepresence robot, and through distance learning tools such as live streaming, recorded lectures, and class calls with questions. The findings revealed a student preference for a blend of distance learning tools and in-person attendance. In contrast, teachers expressed a preference for telepresence robots over conventional distance learning tools, with students highlighting the robots' effectiveness in maintaining their engagement.

Moreover, a comparison between a student interaction via a telepresence robot with the mediated student interaction supported by videoconferencing was made by Shouten et al. [7]. The results showed that students who used the robot, compared to videoconferencing, experienced stronger feelings of social presence, but also attributed more robotic characteristics to their interaction partner (i.e. robomorphism). The study also showed that while robomorphism had negative impacts, these effects were mitigated by the sense of social presence.

Gallon et al. [8] analyzed the motivation of students while using telepresence robots. The study proposed the idea of improving robot interactions as a means to maintain student engagement and motivation. Past research consistently confirms that telepresence robots contribute to fostering a sense of presence among individuals who cannot attend lectures in person.

The primary aim of this study is to explore students' perspectives while engaging in small group activities through the utilization of telepresence robots, especially within the context of a design school and a project-based class, a scenario that has not been explored in previous studies.

3   Methods

3.1   Experimental Setup

The study took place within the actual classrooms of Strate Ecole de Design, a five-year higher education institution that delivers a recognized diploma in industrial design. Specifically, the experiment was conducted within a second-year class as part of a month-long module on *Introduction to interaction design*. This module extended from April 12th to May 10th, 2023, with one session scheduled per week.

Within this specific class, students worked in groups of 3 to 4 persons on a design brief. The allocated assignments consistently required cooperative efforts, usually carried out within groups. Each group project encompassed collaborative activities such as brainstorming, jointly exploring ideas, conducting benchmarking exercises, and participating in feedback sessions. The learning environment fostered extensive dialogues, complemented by practical tasks such as sketching, intermittent interviews, experimentation, filming, video editing, and presentations. This educational framework routinely demanded considerable mental and physical engagement, emphasizing practical applications, while traditional academic lectures were relatively infrequent.

3.2 Robotic Systems

– Kubi[2] robot (see Fig. 1) is a telepresence solution designed specifically for 7–10 in. tablets. Remote users can command the Kubi's 300° pan and ±45° tilt capabilities, allowing them to virtually look around the room and engage with their surroundings.

– Double3[3] robot (see Fig. 2) consists of a mobile base with wheels and a tablet or screen that displays the user's face, allowing them to see and communicate with others as if they were physically present.

Fig. 1. Kubi robot   **Fig. 2.** Double3 robot

3.3 Procedure

During the first session, the research team introduced the project and provided guidelines on how to operate the robots. The participants endorsed the informed consent form regarding their image rights and their involvement in the experiment. Additionally, they completed three pre-questionnaires.

---

[2] https://www.kubiconnect.com/e-commerce/kubi-classic.html.
[3] https://www.doublerobotics.com.

- A general questionnaire was employed to gather demographic details, including age, gender, prior experience with distance learning, and interactions with robots.
- Big-Five [9] questionnaire assesses participants' personality traits based on the Five Factor Model, i.e. *Extroversion, Conscientiousness, Agreeableness, Neuroticism* and *Openness*. It includes 45 questions with a 5-point Likert scale.
- Situational Motivation Scale (SIMS) [10] questionnaire measures an individual's motivation in a specific situation or context. It assesses different types of motivation, including *Intrinsic Motivation* (engaging in an activity for personal enjoyment or satisfaction), *Identified Regulation* (engaging in the activity because it aligns with one's personal values and goals), *External Regulation* (engaging in an activity for external rewards or pressures), and *Amotivation* (lack of motivation). It includes 16 questions with a 7-point Likert scale.

Each class session lasted three hours, during which the students collaborated in groups. During all the sessions, the teacher gave a brief introduction before visiting each group to assess their progress and offer guidance. In one group, only one student interacted with the Kubi robot, while the other attendees were physically present. In a different group, a single student engaged with the Double robot, while the remaining participants joined in person (see Fig. 3). After each session, participants completed two questionnaires.

Fig. 3. Experimental scenarios with Kubi robot (left) and Double robot (right)

- Godspeed [11] questionnaire assesses human perceptions in interactions with robots. It evaluates dimensions such as *Anthropomorphism, Animacy, Likeability, Perceived intelligence* and *Perceived safety* to provide insights into how people perceive and evaluate robot interactions. It includes 24 questions with a 5-point Likert scale.
- Engagement [12] questionnaire assesses participants' engagement from a multidimensional perspective, including *Emotional and cognitive dimensions*

(how one feels and thinks about the activity), *Social dimension* (interactions and connections with others), *Behavioral dimension* (observable actions and behaviors). It includes 20 questions with a 7-point Likert scale.

Furthermore, both students and the professor in charge of the class took part in individual interviews led by the research team to collect their opinions following each session. The interview inquiries were customized depending on whether the participants engaged in the study through physical presence or remote involvement. Distance students were required to respond to 21 questions, whereas on-site students had 11 questions to answer. The teacher also answered 5 questions, after the first session and also after the last session.

In the 21 questions addressed to the remote participants, it was discussed how employing a telepresence robot differs from using a standard videoconferencing application or physically attending the class. Other questions focused on the tasks that participants completed in class, their level of familiarity with the robot's user interface, the overall user experience, flexibility, and technical challenges. The other questions were on how they interacted remotely for three hours with their colleagues, how they produced work together, and how they were integrated into the group.

The on-site students responded to 11 questions about their main class group tasks, their interactions with the remote peer, and the differences between interacting through a traditional videoconferencing system and being present all together in the class. Other questions also investigated the technical aspects of the interaction with the Kubi robot and with the Double robot.

The teacher was questioned about whether the robots disrupted the lesson, whether he thought that remote students using Kubi or Double were more engaged than those using a traditional videoconferencing system, and whether and how this engagement differed from that of students who were physically present.

4 Experimental Results

4.1 Participants

Our experiment involved 16 participants; however, one of them did not complete the initial questionnaires. Among the remaining 15 participants (4 female, 11 male; mean age = 20.67, SD = 2.21), one participant did not respond to the Big-Five questionnaire. Out of these, 7 participants took part in the experiment on two occasions, with one of them not answering the SIMS questionnaire. Therefore, we obtained 21 valid sets of data for the Big-Five questionnaire and 20 valid sets for the SIMS questionnaire. All 15 participants had prior experience with online courses conducted through videoconferencing. Additionally, over half of them (8 out of 15) had engaged with robots before. Details regarding participant distribution can be found in Tables 1 and 2.

Table 1. Distribution of participants

Distance-Kubi	Presence-Kubi	Distance-Double	Presence-Double
4	8	4	7

Table 2. Distribution of participants for Big-Five

	Extroversion		Agreeableness		Conscientiousness		Neuroticism		Openness	
	Low	High	Low	High	Low	High	Low	High	Low	High
Distance-Kubi	2	2	1	3	1	3	3	1	0	4
Presence-Kubi	3	3	2	4	3	3	1	5	1	5
Distance-Double	1	3	2	2	1	3	3	1	2	2
Presence-Double	4	3	1	6	4	3	2	5	1	6
Total	10	11	6	15	9	12	9	12	4	17

4.2 Quantitative Results

Godspeed. In our experiment, only participants who were physically present had the opportunity to interact with the robots. As a result, we employed a t-test to compare the Godspeed questionnaire results between the "Presence-Kubi" group and the "Presence-Double" group. The outcome is displayed in Fig. 4. Among the five scales, the Anthropomorphism score for Kubi ($M = 2.2$, $SD = 0.3$) was significantly higher than that for Double ($M = 1.6$, $SD = 0.15$), as indicated by $t(13) = 2.43$ and $p = 0.03$. This discrepancy can be attributed to the presence of a wheel and a long straight bar on the Double robot, which imparts a more mechanical appearance and reduces its anthropomorphic quality. We also attempted to analyze variations in perception among different personality traits; however, no statistically significant results were observed.

Engagement Questionnaire. We applied a One-way ANOVA to analyze the data from the four groups (Distance-Kubi, Presence-Kubi, Distance-Double, Presence-Double), taking into account all three dimensions of the engagement questionnaire. Despite this analysis, no statistically significant results were identified.

Other Results. Based on the collected data, by using Pearson Correlation analysis, we observed a positive correlation between behavioral engagement and identified regulation ($r(20) = 0.595$, $p = 0.006$). This relationship becomes evident as individuals are more inclined to actively participate, invest effort, and sustain engagement with an activity when they perceive its value and alignment with their personal values.

Furthermore, students with low extroversion ($M = 5.25$, $SD = 0.84$) demonstrate significantly higher levels of intrinsic motivation compared to students with high extroversion ($M = 3.67$, $SD = 1.77$) with $t(17) = 2.53$, $p = 0.022$.

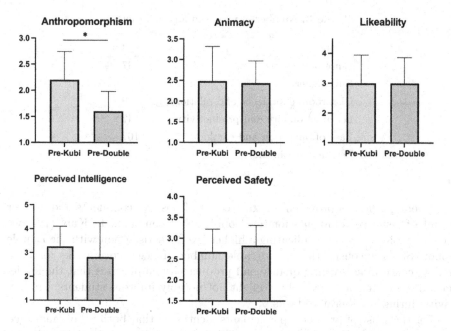

Fig. 4. Results for t-test of Godspeed questionnaire between Presence-Kubi and Presence-Double. Error bars show Standard Deviation, * indicates significance at the 0.05 level.

Students with low conscientiousness ($M = 3.83$, $SD = 1.26$) demonstrate significantly higher levels of Amotivation compared to students with high conscientiousness ($M = 2.58$, $SD = 1.01$) with $t(17) = 2.41$, $p = 0.028$. This supports a study indicating that conscientiousness is strongly and negatively correlated with Amotivation [13].

4.3 Qualitative Results

The research team transcribed the recorded interviews conducted for the study. The text was analyzed using Grounded Theory coding [14]. The material was divided into concepts, which are standalone phrases, and each concept was given a code (1–3 words that summarize the topic). We eventually came up with 420 concepts and corresponding codes. The codes were then organized into seven distinct themes: *Sense of presence, Students' engagement, Classroom experience and relationships, Learning quality and productivity, Ease of operation and comfort, Personal feelings,* and *Others* (including comments and improvement suggestions).

The cumulative volume of verbatim content for each theme is presented in Table 3. Additionally, we determined the valence of each code, or whether it showed a positive or negative aspect of the theme. Figure 5 shows the number of positive and negative remarks for each theme.

Table 3. Number of verbatim for each theme

Theme	Count
Sense of presence	37
Engagement	35
Classroom experience and relationships	49
Learning quality and productivity	47
Ease of operation and comfort	107
Personal sentiments	56

Overall, students provided a higher count of positive comments and a lower count of negative comments for the Double robot compared to Kubi (79+ vs. 66+ and 82− vs. 104−), indicating a higher level of satisfaction with the Double robot. Simultaneously, the considerable number of negative remarks for both robots concerning learning quality and productivity emphasizes that the implementation of telepresence robots might not notably improve students' productivity during collaborative tasks.

For the sense of presence, participants mentioned that both robots managed to create a sense of physical presence. This is in accordance with the result presented in [6], which found that robot use made a noticeable impact on students' 'feeling of presence'. Nevertheless, they did acknowledge occasional situations in which remote students were unintentionally neglected. Although the robots displayed greater interactivity than standard videoconferencing, their mobility remained somewhat limited.

Engagement within remote contexts, facilitated by Double and Kubi robots, appears comparable to conventional video conferencing. Despite the robots' modest enhancements, challenges such as participation, group cohesion, and focus endure. Intriguingly, interactions among students utilizing these robots exhibit a superior quality compared to face-to-face interactions, primarily due to the remote format fostering clearer communication and active listening. Remote students express a sense of satisfactory participation during teacher-led sessions. However, individual tasks tend to take precedence subsequently, leading to decreased engagement. In scenarios of this nature, in-person students tend to engage more extensively with their fellow classmates than with their remote peers.

Among both remote and in-person participants, the augmented mobility features contribute to an improved remote group work experience. Nonetheless, there's a prevailing sentiment that the arrangement "isn't well-suited for this class format". This sentiment arises from the combination of hands-on tasks like drawing and modeling, alongside theoretical activities like brainstorming and debates, which seem less compatible with the setup.

Technical issues have been numerous and varied, including setup adjustments, random robot disconnections and reconnections, audio problems like difficulty hearing the remote student or sound being too soft or loud, and video issues such

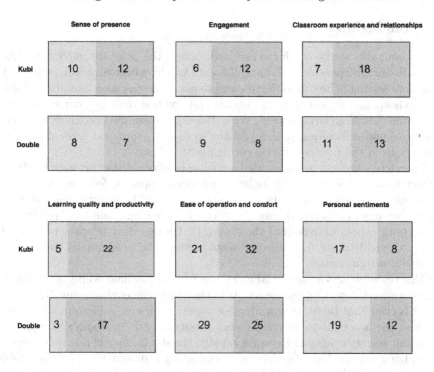

Fig. 5. Participants conveyed positive (yellow/left side) and negative feedback (green/right side) to each of the 6 examined aspects of user experience. (Color figure online)

as variable video quality depending on unstable connections or inverted camera views. Battery problems have also arisen, with Double's supposed 4-hour autonomy only lasting around 1.5 h despite full charging, which is also mentioned in [15]. Internet connection posed fewer problems for Double compared to Kubi. Mobility interface was generally found "easy" and "intuitive", but Double's obstacle detection was overly sensitive, causing it to stall or halt when people passed by. There was also slight latency in movement tracking. Remote students rarely used mobility features due to these issues, resorting to them "only when truly necessary".

A range of improvement suggestions emerged from the participants. In terms of handling background noise, some individuals recommended the implementation of "automatic ambient sound volume detection" coupled with the automatic adjustment of Double's volume. To enhance user-friendliness, alternative approaches could be explored for both robots when remote students need to ask questions, such as utilizing a sound signal. Furthermore, the absence of document-sharing support was noted, often prompting a shift to alternative methods in conjunction with or in lieu of telepresence. One participant highlighted the lack of additional arms to aid in conveying body language, allowing for more unrestricted and clear expression.

5 Conclusion

Throughout this study, our focus revolved around the practical implementation of two distinct telepresence robots, Kubi and Double, within an actual university classroom setting. The core objective was to gain a deeper understanding of students' viewpoints regarding these robotic systems and their broader encounters within the classroom environment. While the experiment did encounter technical challenges and difficulties, it also brought to light a significant level of positive feedback from the participants concerning both robots.

Therefore, students demonstrated a greater level of satisfaction with the Double robot, as evidenced by the higher frequency of positive feedback and fewer instances of negative comments in comparison to Kubi. Nevertheless, the substantial volume of negative comments concerning learning quality and productivity for both robots underscored the notion that integrating telepresence robots might not yield substantial enhancements in students' productivity during collaborative assignments.

This research acts as an initial milestone for our continuous efforts regarding the incorporation of telepresence robots in the classroom environment. Nevertheless, it is clear that there are considerable opportunities for enhancement to fully optimize the practical use of telepresence robots in real classroom situations.

As our society continues to evolve rapidly, the significance of research focused on bridging geographical barriers and connecting individuals across the globe becomes increasingly pronounced. The implications of enabling seamless interactions and learning experiences for all hold substantial importance in this dynamic landscape.

Acknowledgements. This work is supported by InterCarnot: Bots4Education project.

References

1. Kaplan, A.M., Haenlein, M.: Higher education and the digital revolution: about MOOCs, SPOCs, social media, and the Cookie Monster. Bus. Horiz. **59**(4), 441–450 (2016)
2. Velinov, A., Koceski, S., Koceska, N.: A review of the usage of telepresence robots in education. Balkan J. Appl. Math. Inform. **4**(1), 27–40 (2021)
3. Wernbacher, T., et al.: Trine: telepresence robots in education (2022)
4. Thompson, P., Chaivisit, S.: Telepresence robots in the classroom. J. Educ. Technol. Syst. **50**(2), 201–214 (2021)
5. Bell, J., Cain, W., Peterson, A., Cheng, C.: From 2D to Kubi to doubles: designs for student telepresence in synchronous hybrid classrooms. Int. J. Designs Learn. **7**(3) (2016)
6. Fitter, N.T., Raghunath, N., Cha, E., Sanchez, C.A., Takayama, L., Matarić, M.J.: Are we there yet? Comparing remote learning technologies in the university classroom. IEEE Robot. Automat. Lett. **5**(2), 2706–2713 (2020)
7. Schouten, A.P., Portegies, T.C., Withuis, I., Willemsen, L.M., Mazerant-Dubois, K.: Robomorphism: examining the effects of telepresence robots on between-student cooperation. Comput. Hum. Behav. **126**, 106980 (2022)

8. Gallon, L., Angel Abénia, F.D., Negui, M.: Using a telepresence robot in an educational contex. In: 15th International Conference on Frontiers in Education: Computer Science and Computer Engineering (FECS 2019) (2019)
9. John, O.P., Srivastava, S.: The Big-Five Trait Taxonomy: History, Measurement, and Theoretical Perspectives, pp. 102–138 (1999)
10. Guay, F., Vallerand, R.J., Blanchard, C.: On the assessment of situational intrinsic and extrinsic motivation: the Situational Motivation Scale (SIMS). Motivat. Emot. **24**, 175–213 (2000)
11. Bartneck, C., Kulić, D., Croft, E., Zoghbi, S.: Measurement instruments for the anthropomorphism, animacy, likeability, perceived intelligence, and perceived safety of robots. Int. J. Soc. Robot. **1**, 71–81 (2009)
12. Heilporn, G., Lakhal, S., Bélisle, M., St-Onge, C.: Engagement des étudiants: une échelle de mesure multidimensionnelle appliquée à des modalités de cours hybrides universitaires. Mesure et évaluation en éducation **43**(2), 1–34 (2020)
13. Kertechian, S.K.: Conscientiousness as a key to success for academic achievement among French university students enrolled in management studies. Int. J. Manag. Educ. **16**(2), 154–165 (2018)
14. Strauss, A., Corbin, J.: Grounded Theory in Practice. Sage (1997)
15. Perifanou, M., Häfner, P., Economides, A.A.: Users' experiences and perceptions about telepresence robots in education (2022)

Gesture Recognition for Human-Robot Interaction Through Virtual Characters

Sandeep Reddy Sabbella(✉)(ID), Sara Kaszuba(ID), Francesco Leotta(ID), and Daniele Nardi(ID)

Department of Computer, Control and Management Engineering, DIAG, Sapienza Universitá di Roma, Via Ariosto 25, Rome, Italy
{sabbella,kaszuba,leotta,nardi}@diag.uniroma1.it

Abstract. Human-Robot Interaction (HRI) has grown increasingly important with the integration of various types of robots into industrial and daily life aspects. Non-verbal communication plays a vital role in HRI and heavily relies on gesture recognition. The ability of robot's interpretation of human gestures is essential for enhancing the overall user experience. To achieve precision and effectiveness of gesture recognition in HRI, the incorporation of Virtual Reality (VR) technology offers promising avenues. In this article, we describe the development of a gesture recognition pipeline tailored to HRI in Precision Agriculture scenarios. Its key feature is the use of Virtual characters and Machine learning techniques to allow agricultural robots to recognize gestures performed by both digital agents and humans. We address challenges by presenting a set of gesture definitions, data generation, and system evaluation using varies combinations of real and virtual simulated data. Our results demonstrate how the adoption of virtual simulations can significantly increase the system's accuracy and efficiency.

Keywords: Gesture Recognition · Virtual Human Avatars · Virtual Simulations · Human-Robot Interaction · Precision Agriculture

1 Introduction

Human-robot interaction (HRI) is a dynamic research area that has attracted considerable interest in recent years for its role in promoting collaboration between humans and robots in shared spaces. Researchers are pioneering collaborative robots (cobots) to study how humans interact with robots and how to design robots that can work seamlessly and naturally with people in various industries, including agriculture, manufacturing, health, education, and transport. The main goal is to create interactive robots that can effectively integrate into human environments and help achieve common goals.

Advances in natural language processing have made voice communication a fundamental mode of interaction between humans and robots. However, nonverbal communication, such as gestures and facial expressions, is vital in conveying human intentions, emotions, and attitudes [1]. Therefore, enabling robots to

A. Al. Ali et al. (Eds.): ICSR 2023, LNAI 14454, pp. 160–170, 2024.
https://doi.org/10.1007/978-981-99-8718-4_14

Fig. 1. Virtual Human Avatars performing Gestures in the Virtual Simulation.

understand and respond to human nonverbal signals is crucial to improving the overall user experience and bridging the interaction gap (Fig. 1).

Gesture recognition in HRI holds diverse applications, ranging from healthcare to manufacturing and education. It allows robots to interpret human gestures, such as pointing and nodding, and use this information to guide their actions, thereby improving overall interaction. For instance, in agriculture, humans can instruct robots to perform specific tasks through a combination of gestures and verbal communication, particularly in noisy environments. Among the numerous challenges in gesture recognition, data is one of the most important that needs to be addressed. Several datasets are available in the domain of sign language, actual feasible data for gesture generation in HRI remains a substantial scarcity. Hence, one way to generate such gestural datasets is through using Virtual Reality (VR) simulators. In a VR simulation, individuals can perform gestures in a virtual environment while being recorded by the system with their corresponding annotations. This allows for the generation of a large set of examples of different gestures and data variations along with the ground truth, which can be used to train and evaluate gesture recognition approaches.

The experiments conducted in this paper have been carried out within the framework of the CANOPIES project[1]. The primary objectives of the CANOPIES project revolve around pioneering novel strategies in Human-Robot Interaction (HRI), Human-Robot Collaboration (HRC), and Multi Robot Coordination (MRC). These methodologies aim to establish a productive collaborative system between human workers and teams of multiple robots to achieve precision farming of permanent crops. The rationale behind selecting table-grape vineyards as the testing ground lies in the necessity to collect data within this specific agricultural context. This is essential for comprehending and adapting to the various challenges posed by factors such as environmental noise and fluctuating lighting conditions beneath the grape canopy.

---

[1] https://canopies.inf.uniroma3.it/.

The specific objectives of this paper include enhancing the gesture recognition pipeline by utilizing simulation data, exploring the impact of blending real and virtual data on various algorithms, evaluating the performance of trained models on real data, and assessing the potential for improving gesture classification through a weight-based ensemble of two models. The subsequent sections of this article are structured as follows: Sect. 2 provides an overview of relevant literature and research, Sect. 3 details the data generation process, Sect. 4 explains the system's implementation, experiments, and findings, and finally, Sect. 5 offers the paper's conclusions and outlines future work.

2   Related Works

With the rapid evolution of deep learning solutions in recent years, techniques such as Convolutional Neural Networks (CNNs) and Recurrent Neural Networks (RNNs) have been shown to be most effective at recognizing gestures using pose-estimation techniques in real-time. The approaches that have been proposed for sign recognition include 2D CNN Models [2,3], 3D CNN Models [4,9], GANs [5], Spatio-temporal networks and RNN Models [6]. These systems have been reported to have high accuracy in gesture recognition tasks. Still, the accuracy may change depending on the data's amount and quality, and the model's specific implementation. Recently, transformers and their efficiency in speech and vision domains caught the attention of researchers. A comprehensive review of temporal modelling in action recognition was performed in the article by Elham et al. (2022) [8]. Chen et al. (2019) [7] propose a geometry-aware 3D representation of the human pose by using multiple views in a simple auto-encoder model at the training stage and only 2D keypoint information as supervision. Besides joints, humans also explore the motions of limbs to understand actions. Given this observation [10] investigate the dynamics of human limbs for skeleton-based action recognition.

Chen et. al. (2020) [11] propose a new solution to 3D human pose estimation in videos. As a result, the learned model not only inculcates task-bias but also dataset-bias because of its strong reliance on the annotated samples, which also holds true for weakly-supervised models. Acknowledging this [12] propose a self-supervised learning framework to disentangle such variations from unlabeled video frames. Although the recently developed deep learning-based solutions have achieved high performance in human pose estimation, there still remain challenges due to insufficient training data, depth ambiguities, and occlusions. The contribution of [13] is to provide a comprehensive review of recent deep learning-based solutions for both 2D and 3D pose estimation via a systematic analysis and comparison of these solutions based on their input data and inference procedures. Duan et. al. (2022) [14] documented PoseConv3D as a new approach to skeleton-based action recognition.

In recent years, researchers have made leaps of progress in developing new techniques and algorithms to recognize, generate, and animate hand and body gestures in virtual environments [15]. With the advances in virtual avatars, several reviews

[17,18] were being conducted on Human-Avatar Interaction (HAI) in virtual environments, highlighting the importance of gesture-based communication and rehabilitation. Various approaches for animating avatars, including motion capture, keyframe animation, and physics-based animation have been discussed. Furthermore, a notable contribution within this domain comes from the article [19], which presents the generation of human-like avatars from images, which involves learning a generative model of the 3D avatar from a large dataset of motion-captured videos. In the end, the authors demonstrated their method's effectiveness in generating realistic and diverse avatars for different poses and actions.

To our knowledge, the state-of-art on pose estimation has been used for reconstructing the virtual avatars but not the other way around. However, our innovative approach takes a different route by leveraging virtual avatars to significantly enhance gesture recognition through precise pose estimation. This marks a novel and distinctive contribution in this field. By employing virtual avatars, we introduce a safer and more controlled environment for algorithm validation, allowing for thorough testing before deploying in real-life scenarios. Conventional gesture recognition datasets encounter numerous challenges, especially within the context of HRI [16]. Some of the main difficulties include variations in gesture performance, occlusions, background and lighting noise, real-time processing demands, privacy, scalability, generalizability, and the absence of robust benchmarking and standardization protocols. These challenges can be substantially alleviated by harnessing simulated data generated from virtual human avatars.

3   Gesture Definitions and Data Generation

There were several definitions of gestures based on the applications and their usage context, yet most still need to be standardized. Regarding industrial applications, gesture definitions change according to the type of industry and context used. General movement and context-specific gestures were defined to generalize and standardize the signs in the industry. These were defined after following some gestures for communicative purposes in HRI and from the gesture language between human-human and human-robot and in the workspace for the CANOPIES project[2].

The 21 defined gestures consist of 10 dynamic and 11 static signs, where 9 gestures can be performed using two hands, while the rest are with one hand. These definitions, along with Real and virtual data examples, can be viewed on the GIT repository[3]. Some gesture definitions were specific to the CANOPIES project [CUT, CHANGE BOX, RECEIVE, TAKE], while the rest are generic to ground robots. Human workers in the table-grape field will be working along with robots in performing agricultural activities, which require at least one hand in most cases to instruct the robot, without interrupting their activities. The 9 gestures that need two hands can have any other tools in the hands of the human in most scenarios.

---

[2] https://canopies.inf.uniroma3.it/.

[3] https://github.com/Sapienza-HRI/GR-ICSR-23-info.

This article considers 12 (11 static gestures + standing pose) static gestures. Static gestures can be easily scaled and recognized more quickly with lower computational resources compared to dynamic gestures. This efficiency was crucial in real-time applications where the system needs a rapid response. All these gestures belong to the initiation and navigation of the robot in different directions. For the purpose of classification, we added an extra class of *Unknown Pose* when a gesture was out of these 12 classes. A balanced Real-time dataset (RD) of 25,192 frames was produced after data augmentations for these 13 classes from the collected gesture videos taken with the consensus of 8 persons.

3.1   VR-Simulation for Gesture Data

One way to generate datasets of gestures is through VR simulations. In a VR simulation, a character (Human-Avatar) can perform gestural movements in a virtual environment, and the system can record the gestures and their corresponding annotations. This allows for the generation of a large number of examples of different gestural signs, which can be used to train and evaluate gesture recognition systems. Indeed, a single character can be mapped to many animations, and the virtual environment can be configured accordingly to the suitable parameters.

There are several advantages of using VR simulations to generate gesture datasets: *(i)* They can provide a controlled environment where the lighting, background noise, and other factors can be supervised and standardized to minimize the challenges that would be faced in real-world datasets, such as occlusions and background noise. *(ii)* They represent a safe and repeatable way to generate a large number of examples of different gestures without the need for expensive or dangerous equipment. *(iii)* They allow to generates examples of gestures that would be difficult to perform in the real world and complex environments.

3.2   Virtual Data Creation

Autodesk character creator was used to generate 30 characters representing the varied height, gender, ethnicity, and age. These characters were imported to Unity. In order to create the gestures we started collecting real data using Intel RealSense Depth camera D435i with IMU and stereo vision in the table-grapes field in Aprilia (Lazio), a worksite for the project. The collected videos of gestures were processed using DeepMotion to extract animations and then were mapped to the generated characters in Unity. DeepMotion uses a neural network to extract AI-based animation, motion tracking, and physics simulation to generate a full-body avatar that tracks motion from a video, a single camera, or a minimal set of VR sensors. These tracked motions are then used to reconstruct the animation flow in the simulation, and the extracted key points of the joints serve as a base reference to the joint's movement from the captured video.

A human-in-loop post processing verification has been conducted to ensure adequate quality in data. There was no adequate metric for this evaluation, so the animation's effectiveness is measured through human observation. Under performing animations were discarded and re-recorded from different angles, which can capture the movement optimally to generate the proper animation. The system recorded the gestures performed by these characters through multiple cameras in the Unity tool with various distances and angles. We repeated the data collection with one character performing gestures at a time and multiple characters performing the same or different gestures in a single frame. By doing so, we have estimated that we can generate extensive data for gesture recognition. All the generated virtual data represented the actual scenarios in the real world. To this aim, we generated 26,000 frames of balanced gesture class virtual data (VD) from various animations with varied brightness, introduced noise, and different camera angles for successfully training a deep learning algorithm.

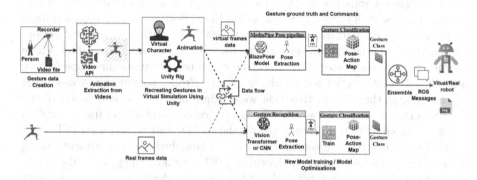

Fig. 2. Gesture Pipeline for generation and evaluation on virtual simulated data. Blue and black lines indicates the flow of data into two models which can act as individual recognition or unified pipeline based on data and model configuration. (Color figure online)

4   System Implementation

We implemented our framework on ROS Noetic on a computer running Ubuntu 20.04 LTS. Alienware x17 R2 with 32 GB of RAM, a CPU of 12th generation i9 and a Nvidia RTX 3080ti GPU notebook running Windows 11 Home and Ubuntu 20.04 LTS was used for developing the system and its evaluation. We employed the pipeline illustrated in Fig. 2 for both Virtual and Real-Time data in our training process for the gesture recognition model, as well as for potential improvements to the existing model.

This pipeline consists of two main pathways. The first pathway, depicted by a continuous black line, serves as our reference or ground truth during experiments with alternative models. It also functions as the primary model for assessing the data, extracting pose landmarks, and determining the gesture class for Real-Time, Virtual, or a combination of data sources. The second pathway, represented by the blue line, involves gesture evaluations using either a Convolutional

Neural Network (CNN) or a Transformer model. This pathway acts as a supplementary algorithm to improve the final gesture classification. Our pipeline design is highly flexible, allowing for the use of either real-time (RD), virtual (VD), or a combination of data sources. Additionally, user can employ one or both recognition algorithms in the process. Depending on the configuration, either of the pathways can function as a complete pipeline. This adaptability enables us to incorporate one or more recognition algorithms into the pipeline to suit specific needs.

4.1 Experimentation

The experiments were conducted to assess various Pose estimation algorithms when integrated into the gesture recognition pipeline, using diverse data to address the research question, which was, "How effectively can a model trained on simulated data perform on real-world data?" To initiate this investigation, we generated simulated data through the use of virtual human characters. These characters were associated with 13 of the extracted gesture animations (out of a total of 21 gestures defined for the use case). Proper consideration was taken to ensure that the class distribution was maintained. At the conclusion of the data generation phase, we amassed a dataset comprising 51,192 frames, with a nearly equal contribution from both real data (RD) and virtual data (VD).

Following the data generation phase, we launched our experiments using Mediapipe's 3D pose estimation algorithm [20] to evaluate the generated dataset. The recorded frames were meticulously assessed to determine the accuracy of key point recognition and the associated threshold values. This served as the baseline score or ground truth for all the data. In the virtual simulated data, the identified key points were compared against Unity-generated joint coordinates, which served as the ground truth.

Our experiments and evaluations were grounded in the hypothesis that a model trained on this hybrid dataset could effectively recognize gestures in both simulated and real-world scenarios. We employed a simple Convolutional Neural Network (CNN) of 8 convolutional layers to classify the acquired poses into the defined gesture classes. This CNN was trained using key-point data obtained by running the pose estimation algorithm, enabling it to categorize pose clusters into their respective gesture classes.

The same experiment was repeated with various combinations of RD and VD with simple multiples of 10, i.e., for example, 30% RD + 70% VD from their respective frames contribute to the combined dataset for training and evaluating the network. We have identified two 2D pose estimation deep-learning approaches to train on such data. 1. MoveNet(single pose)(Thunder) [21] uses MobileNetV2 as its backbone, followed by Centernet with a depth multiplier of 1.75. 2. ViT-Pose [22] with YOLO V5 as its backbone for person detection, followed by a tranformer block to estimate the key points. These networks were pre-trained on the MS COCO Human Keypoint Detection dataset and then fine-tuned on the defined gestures. The same CNN was adopted with modifications to the input layer to incorporate the changes in keypoint data structure, but the rest of the layers remained the same to have consistency across these 3 algorithms. These pose algorithm-based CNNs were trained on Real-data, Virtual-simulated data, and several combinations data with train-val-test proportions of 70-15-15% on the data. The fixed test data was set for validating on real, virtual and combination data. The Mediapipe's model and the trained models were compared against each other with variations of training data. A probability weight-based voting ensemble between the two best models determines the gesture class to communicate to the robot for the task execution.

4.2 Results

After evaluations, Table 1 shows the possible data combinations (virtual-real) and the respective network's performance. All these experiments were cataloged for system enhancements and the model's performance. Evaluations were conducted on both real-world and virtual data by employing these models using the camera on the robot.

Table 1. Results of evaluations conducted on various data combinations and various Pose estimation + CNN algorithms. Accuracy and F1-Score readings are evaluated on test data samples. Train Data represents the percentage combinations of real and virtual data used to train the models. ✓ represents data used to test and X marks not used.

Train Data		Test Data		Mediapipe +CNN		MoveNet + CNN		VitPose + CNN	
Real	Virtual	Real	Virtual	Accuracy	F1-Score	Accuracy	F1-Score	Accuracy	F1-Score
100	–	✓	X	0.85	0.85	0.74	0.74	0.80	0.80
100	–	X	✓	0.81	0.81	0.71	0.70	0.79	0.79
–	100	✓	X	0.95	0.95	0.76	0.76	0.85	0.85
–	100	X	✓	0.97	0.97	0.78	0.78	0.85	0.85
80	20	✓	✓	0.83	0.82	0.68	0.67	0.71	0.70
70	30	✓	✓	0.85	0.85	0.69	0.69	0.72	0.74
60	40	✓	✓	0.89	0.89	0.71	0.70	0.74	0.74
50	50	✓	✓	0.91	0.91	0.72	0.71	0.78	0.78
40	60	✓	✓	0.91	0.92	0.73	0.72	0.79	0.79
30	70	✓	✓	0.93	0.93	0.74	0.73	0.81	0.81
20	80	✓	✓	**0.94**	**0.93**	**0.76**	**0.76**	**0.83**	**0.83**
100	100	✓	✓	**0.97**	**0.96**	**0.78**	**0.77**	**0.86**	**0.86**

By the end of the experimentation, we evaluated various data combinations and observed that the models trained on full RD and VD datasets performed better due to the availability of more training data. However, As the goal is to use the combination data, the 20–80 ratio of RD-VD models performed close to the full data combination. We also observed that Mediapipe + CNN performed superior to other as the model evaluates on 33(3D) landmarks where as MoveNet

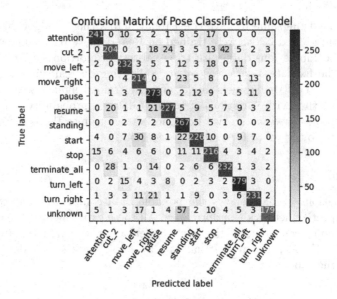

Fig. 3. Confusion matrix for 13 Gesture classes using 20% RD and 80% VD.

model evaluates on 17(2D) landmarks and ViTPose model on 25(2D) landmarks. According to our observation, more landmarks result in more features to learn, leading to the model's better performance. The outcome of our evaluation is presented in Fig. 3. We also observed that the gesture misclassification (false-positives) depends on one (or multiple) issues:

1. Pose occlusion with any other item or person.
2. Camera angle for the character as the parts of human occlude some of the key-points in certain angles.
3. Lack of brightness and animation inconsistencies.

5 Conclusion and Future Work

In this article, we have introduced a gesture recognition pipeline for HRI in precision agriculture with in the limits of CANOPIES project. Though cost and time consumption for the initial system set-up limits many users from using VR simulations to generate gesture datasets, VR simulation aims to solve the difficulty of acquiring real data in the wild. The performance of the model trained on virtual data have proven to work in real data.

In near future, the trained network will be optimised to include hand gestures and the trained model with the best performances will be deployed to a virtual robot in the simulation. The virtual human avatar performing gestures can be evaluated with in the simulation through the virtual robot's camera to communicate or execute the corresponding actions based on the gesture commands.

The users in the simulation will have control of choosing gestures via a keyboard (input device) in a *non-immersive* experience and with the hand controllers in an *immersive* experience based on the device.

References

1. Urakami, J., Seaborn, K.: Nonverbal cues in human-robot interaction: a communication studies perspective. J. Hum.-Robot Interact. **12**(2), 21 (2023). Article 22
2. Tasmere, D., Ahmed, B., Das, S.R.: Real time hand gesture recognition in depth image using CNN. Int. J. Comput. Appl. **174**(16), 28–32 (2021)
3. Yu, J., Qin, M., Zhou, S.: Dynamic gesture recognition based on 2D convolutional neural network and feature fusion. Sci. Rep. **12**, 4345 (2022)
4. Singh, D.K.: 3D-CNN based dynamic gesture recognition for Indian sign language modeling. Procedia Comput. Sci. **189**, 76–83 (2021)
5. Suzuki, N., Watanabe, Y., Nakazawa, A.: GAN-based style transformation to improve gesture-recognition accuracy. In: Proceedings of the ACM on Interactive, Mobile, Wearable and Ubiquitous Technologies, vol. 4, no. 4, p. 20 (2020). Article 154
6. Samaan, G.H., et al.: MediaPipe's land- marks with RNN for dynamic sign language recognition. Electronics **11**, 3228 (2022)
7. Chen, X., Lin, K.Y., Liu, W., Qian, C. and Lin, L.: Weakly-supervised discovery of geometry-aware representation for 3D human pose estimation. In: CVPR (2019)
8. Shabaninia, E., Nezamabadi-pour, H., Shafizadegan, F.: Transformers in action recognition, A review on temporal modeling (2023)
9. Zhang, W., Wang, J.: Dynamic hand gesture recognition based on 3d convolutional neural network models. In: 2019 IEEE 16th International Conference on Networking, Sensing and Control (ICNSC), pp. 224–229 (2019)
10. Zhang, X., Xu, C., Tian, X. and Tao, D.: Graph edge convolutional neural networks for skeleton-based action recognition. In: IEEE Transactions on Neural Networks and Learning Systems (2019)
11. Chen, T., Fang, C., Shen, X., Zhu, Y., Chen, Z., Luo, J.: Anatomy-aware 3D human pose estimation with bone-based pose decomposition, ARXIV-CS.CV (2020)
12. Kundu, J.N., Seth, S., Jampani, V., Rakesh, M., Babu, R.V., Chakraborty, A.: Self-supervised 3D human pose estimation via part guided novel image synthesis. In: CVPR (2020)
13. Zheng, C., et al.: Deep learning-based human pose estimation: a survey, ARXIV-CS.CV (2020)
14. Duan, H., Zhao, Y., Chen, K., Lin, D., Dai, B.: Revisiting skeleton-based action recognition. In: CVPR (2022)
15. Anvari, T., Park, K.: 3D human body pose estimation in virtual reality: a survey. In: 2022 13th International Conference on Information and Communication Technology Convergence (ICTC), Jeju Island, Korea, Republic of, pp. 624–628 (2022)
16. Carfí, A., Mastrogiovanni, F.: Gesture-based human-machine interaction: taxonomy, problem definition, and analysis. IEEE Trans. Cybern. **53**(1), 497–513 (2023)
17. Yu, X., Jiang, L., Wang, L.: Virtual reality gesture recognition based on depth information. SID Symposium Dig. Tech. Papers **51**, 196–200 (2020)
18. Zhang, J. et al.: AvatarGen: a 3D generative model for animatable human avatars. In: Karlinsky, L., Michaeli, T., Nishino, K. (eds.) Computer Vision - ECCV 2022 Workshops. ECCV 2022. LNCS, vol. 13803, pp 668–685. Springer, Cham (2023). https://doi.org/10.1007/978-3-031-25066-8_39

19. Li, Z., et al.: Animated 3D human avatars from a single image with GAN-based texture inference. Comput. Graph. **95**, 81–91 (2021)
20. Bazarevsky, V., et al.: BlazePose: on-device real-time body pose tracking (2020)
21. MoveNet model card. https://tfhub.dev/google/movenet/singlepose/thunder/4
22. Xu, Y., Zhang, J., Zhang, Q., Tao, D.: ViTPose: simple vision transformer baselines for human pose estimation (2022). arXiv e-prints, arXiv:2204.12484

Measuring Willingness to Accept Social Robot's Recommendations (WASRR)

Isha Kharub[✉], Michael Lwin, Aila Khan, Omar Mubin, and Zhao Zou

Western Sydney University, Sydney, NSW 2150, Australia
19974822@student.westernsydney.edu.au

Abstract. Social robots are increasingly being used in the hospitality industry to provide service recommendations. Recommendations have been shown to impact customer satisfaction and lead to higher sales. However, a lack of a measurement of willingness to accept social robot recommendations (WASRR) makes it difficult for managers to evaluate the usefulness of these recommendations to customers. How do consumers perceive the recommendations provided by social robots? This study will adopt Churchill (1979) and Devillis (1991) to develop the WASRR scale that will provide a strong diagnostic assessment of the recommendations. The paper will discuss the first stage of scale development, which includes a literature review, a thesaurus search, and expert panel interviews. WASRR scale will help organisations improve customer satisfaction, efficiency, and productivity by deploying social robots to provide recommendations in industries facing labour shortages. Additionally, the WASRR scale will help assess the ability of social robots to provide recommendations.

Keywords: Social Robots · Recommendation Acceptance · Willingness to accept social robot's recommendations · Human-Robot Interaction · Psychometric measure · Scale development

1 Introduction

Service robots are increasingly used in the hospitality sector, especially post-Covid-19 [1]. The social robot market is expected to reach USD 24.72 billion by 2029 [2]. It is estimated that by 2030, robots will carry out up to 25% of hospitality tasks [3]. At the 2023 United Nations 'AI for Good Summit', humanoid robots were used to showcase the practical applications of Artificial Intelligence (AI) to advance the United Nations Sustainable Development Goals (UNSDGs).

Service robots can be defined as "system-based autonomous and adaptable interfaces that interact, communicate and deliver service to an organisation's consumer" (Wirtz et al., 2018, p. 909). When service robots are used in frontline service settings, they are called Social Robots (SR) as they interact and co-create value with their consumers during the interaction using their communicative abilities [4, 5]. Social robots are designed to facilitate human-robot interaction [6], such as greeting customers and providing product/service recommendations [7, 8].

Traditionally, recommendations were provided by humans, for example, by a friend or a salesperson [9]. With time, as artificial intelligence developed, online recommendations were provided to customers by recommendation agents such as book recommendations by Amazon [10]. While providing recommendations to customers is important, it is equally essential to ensure that they actually accept the recommendations. Measuring recommendation acceptance intention is critical as recommendation quality leads to higher customer satisfaction and higher sales [11]. Additionally, they can be used to estimate consumer's willingness to pay for products [12]. Further, intentions are the best predictor of actual behaviour [13]. An extensive literature review has shown limited efforts to understand the Willingness to Accept AI Recommendations [14]. The technology used in the AI recommendation system is also used in providing recommendations by social robots. Thus, as the adoption of social robots increases rapidly, it has become important to measure Willingness to Accept Social Robots Recommendations (WASRR). This study aims to develop a scale to measure Willingness to Accept Social Robot Recommendations. The following is the research question that the study will address:

- **Research Question 1**: How can we measuere Willingness to Accept Social Robot Recommendations (WASRR)

2 Related Work

Recommendation sources are information sources, and this information can be provided by human beings such as friends, family or salespersons or through consumer reports or technological aids such as online recommendation systems, augmented/virtual reality or virtual assistants [10, 15, 16]. The recommender systems' primary function is to guess and provide items that would likely be preferred by the users based on their preferences, data provided or user profiles [17] and **are predominantly used in online environments** [18]. The recommendation engine market is expected to reach USD 15.13 billion by 2026 [19], and product recommendations are considered the key driver of the average order value in customer purchases. The three most common recommendation methods are collaborative filtering, content-based techniques and hybrid methods [20]. Content-based techniques use consumer's past data to make recommendations, whereas collaborative filtering uses purchase decisions by consumers with similar tastes and preferences [20]. Hybrid methods use a combination of different methods such as weighted, switching, feature combination, cascade, mixed, feature augmentation and meta-level [21]. This study uses the collaborative filtering method as in a hospitality environment, it is not always possible to have customers' past data to make recommendations. So, inferring insights from customers with similar tastes and preferences is the most viable method for recommendations [22].

While recommendations can be provided by humans or through virtual agents, organisations have tried to integrate social robots into services as they have been found to be as persuasive as real humans or a video recording of real humans [8]. They enhance the consumption experience and can reduce interpersonal communication stress. Social robots can use gestures, gaze and voice pitch depending on the situation and thus positively influencing users' decision-making [23]. Researchers have used social robots to provide movie recommendations [23], food recommendations [8] and clothing recommendations [24]. However, mixed results have been found regarding customer's acceptance or rejection of robot services and recommendations [25]. Herse et al. (2) inevestigated the persuasiveness of a human, humanoid robot and information kiosk when a customer was provided a restaurant recommendation [8]. To test the recommendation acceptance, they simply counted the number of customers who picked between the two restaurant options [8]. Shin and Jeong used a robot concierge to provide recommendations but did not test for recommendation acceptance in their study [26]. In a study by Shiomi et al. (7), a social robot was used to provide recommendations in a shopping mall, but their focus was on the effects of robots' recommendations on advertisements by using different kinds of robots and conversation schemas, not on factors that drive willingness to accept the recommendations [27]. In another study by Herse et al. two factors that influence user trust towards a robot were invetisgated: preference elicitation and embodiment [28]. In this study, for the preference selection or recommendation acceptance, number of participants that selected the recommended cuisine were recorded [28]. Rossi et al. (6) used a socially assistive robot to provide movie recommendations, but the presence of a social robot did not change the acceptance rate of the proposed movies [17]. They used the acceptance rate to measure willingness to accept recommendations, which does not provide insights into consumer psychology. Additionally, their focus was more towards evaluating the quality of the interaction between the participants and the social robots by manipulating different non-verbal communication cues for message transmission [17]. Lee et al. investigated user compliance with social robots in a healthcare setting [29]. Their focus was on the perceived level of politeness in robots' speech and gestures as a determinant of compliance intention, not on factors influencing acceptance of social robots recommendations [29]. Table 1 explains the outcome measurements from the articles that measure social robot recommendation acceptance.

Woiceshyn et al. designed a recommendation system for a social robot to provide clothing recommendations to consumers [24]. They used a feedback survey to measure potential users' experience with the system but did not test for the variables that impacted the acceptance of recommendations [24]. De Carolis et al. used the Pepper robot as a tourism recommender system to provide personalised recommendations to users about hotels, restaurants and points of interest in the area [30]. Their focus was on designing a tourism recommendation system and evaluating if using social robots would enhance the perception of the recommendation quality and the user's overall experience compared to a web-based interface [30]. Okafuji et al. investigated the use of a social robot on the persuasiveness and acceptance of the multiple recommendations made by the robot during a longitudinal period [31]. They measured willingness to accept recommendations by calculating the number of people who listened and chose recommended items and the number of people who took them [31].

Therefore, the literature review shows that most papers either focus on using robot modalities to understand the acceptance of recommendations or are focused on system design. The concept of willingness to accept robot recommendations has not been conceptualized yet. Additionally, consumers react differently to social robots compared to other technologies like virtual agents or chatbots and, thus, require a different measurement scale. While some research studies have examined the Willingness to Accept AI

Recommendation Systems [14, 32], a lack of psychometric measures on this concept has limited scholars and managerial ability to understand the willingness of consumers' acceptance to accept social recommendations. Table 1 shows the measurements are either behavioural or experience-focused and are not relevant to measure WASRR in a hospitality context.

Table 1. Measures of Social Robot Recommendation Acceptance

Paper	Construct	Outcome Measurement Items
De Carolis et al. (2020) (1)	User Experience	User Experience questionnaire by [33]
Herse et al. (2018) (2)	Persuasiveness of a human robot	Pick between the restaurant options after the recommendation was provided by humanoid robot
Herse et al. (2018) (3)	User decision making	Number of participants that selected the recommended cuisine/restaurant
Lee et al. (2017) (4)	Intention to Comply	IC1: If Nao actually provided guidance for me in the hospital, I would comply with NAO's guidance IC2: I intend to recommend that others comply with NAO's guidance IC3: I intend to assist others in complying with NAO's guidance
Okafuji et al. (2021) (5)	Repeated persuasiveness of robot	Count of number of people who took recommended items
Rossi et al. (2018) (6)	Recommendation Acceptance	Accept or reject the recommendations

(continued)

Table 1. (*continued*)

Paper	Construct	Outcome Measurement Items
Shiomi et al. (2013) (7)	Recommendation Acceptance in Advertising by Social Robots	Count of number of people who printed tickets after the robot's recommendation
Woiceshyn et al. (2017) (8)	User Experience	1. The system was easy to use 2. The interaction took too long 3. Leia asked me too many questions 4. Clothing recommendations would be useful to me 5. The recommendations were appropriate for the context 6. I would trust Leia to provide me outfit recommendations 7. I felt engaged with Leia during the interaction 8. The interaction with Leia is more enjoyable than just using a touchscreen 9. Leia's gestures and movements were appropriate 10. Leia's gestures and movement contributed positively to the interaction 11. Leia's speech was appropriate 12. Leia's speech was clear and understandable 13. The graphical user interface was intuitive to use 14. The graphical user interface enabled effective and clear communication with the robot

Similar concepts to WASRR were also found in the literature, but they either focused on designing the recommendation system [30], anthropomorphism and recommendation intention [34], anthropomorphism and usage intention [35], using different robot modalities [29] or used simple behavioural measures (e.g., accept or reject recommendation) [17, 31]. Research from a customer's perspective is limited [9]. This calls for the development of a new scale to measure WASRR.

3 Methodology

WASRR is conceptualised as the willingness of customers to accept recommendations provided by a social robot in a hospitality setting. In short, it is an indicator of *how much customers are willing to perform certain behaviours* [36]. To achieve this, the WASRR scale will be developed using an established procedure recommended by Churchill (1979) and Devillis (1991). The **scale development procedure** consists of five stages of scale development: item generation, purification of the measurement scale, evaluation of the latent structure, testing the nomological validity of the measurement scale and scale replication and generalisability. This paper will discuss the first stage of the scale development process. The first stage consists of three steps: 1) an extensive literature review, 2) a thesaurus search and 3) expert panel interviews. In the following sections, the first three stages of the scale development process are explained.

3.1 Steps 1 and 2: Literature Review and Thesaurus Search for Scale Development

In Step 1, an extensive literature review was conducted across IT, marketing, retail, hospitality, tourism, and healthcare. During the review, five concepts that are similar to WASRR were identified and were used to generate items: 1) willingness to accept AI recommendations, 2) recommendation adoption, 3) willingness to comply, 4) compliance with SR advice and 5) accepting SR recommendations. Through this process, 12 potential dimensions of WASRR were identified along with 42 initial items.

In Step 2, 42 items were examined for conceptual similarities to the WASRR scale and the wording of the items before conducting the thesaurus search. After the thesaurus search, 20 more items were added to the 12 dimensions. See Table 2 for examples of these dimensions and their items. These dimensions were included in the initial pool of items as they are believed to be important dimensions of willingness to accept social robot recommendations.

Table 2. Excerpt from the initial pool of items

Willingness (Behavioural): I am willing to try the robot's recommendations, I am willing to accept the robot's recommendations, I am willing to use the robot's recommendations, I am willing to accept the robot's suggestions, and I am willing to act on robot's advice
Effectiveness (Attitudinal): Robot's recommendations have enhanced my effectiveness in making wine selection, My decision making became more effective because of robot's recommendations, I was able to make a more effective decision because of robot's recommendations, and robot's recommendations allowed me to make an effective decision

3.2 Step 3: Expert Panel

In **Step 3**, five experts (academic researchers and industry professionals) from marketing, information technology, retail and engineering were recruited to test the 62 initial pool of items for content validity (testing if the scale measures what it is supposed to). The panel consisted of five members, three males and two females, aged 25–44, with educational backgrounds ranging from bachelor's to Ph.D. Specifically, one particpant's age was between 25–29, two participant's age were 30–34, two participant's were aged between 40–44. Previous studies have successfully used three to ten expert members for content validation [37–39]. The expert panel discussion was conducted online. The panel was provided with the definition of social robots, explained the conceptual definition of WASRR and how the items were generated. They were also explained that the purpose of the panel interviews was to analyse whether the 62 items represent the WASRR scale. After providing the background, they were asked to imagine a scenario where a social robot provides them with recommendations in a hospitality setting. Please see Table 3 for the scenario used in the expert panel session. Based on the scenario, they were requested to first rate the 62 items on a seven-point Likert scale (1 = strongly disagree and 7 = strongly agree). After rating the items, the panel members engaged in a productive discussion about the items' clarity, readability and content validity.

Table 3. Scenario used in Expert Panel Interviews

The scenario: Imagine you are visiting a fine dining restaurant with your partner. In the scenario, the SR will greet you by saying *"Hi, my name is Pepper. I will be your waiter for this evening. Would you like to start with some drinks? I highly recommend our Flavours wine which has been recently added to our wine list and it goes well with all the mains we have on our menu. This wine is medium to full-bodied, typically leafy with ripe cassis like flavours, well-structured and elegant and powerfully aromatic. The wine is rich with fruity notes of black cherries and currants, herby notes of peppers and spicy notes of ginger."*

4 Results

Step 1 and Step 2 included a literature review and thesaurus research. A total of 12 dimensions were identified that are believed to represent WASRR, and 62 items were generated. During this process, some dimensions reflected behavioural intentions (Behavioural), and others reflected attitudinal factors (Attitudinal) of WASRR, e.g., See Table 2. A full list of items is available upon request.

Even though the attitudinal factors and behavioural intentions were identified during the literature review, the expert panel was not informed of these dimensions to maintain the objectivity of the scale. This provided a more accurate understanding of whether these items explained the scale and did not create biases in the experts' minds. The results from the panel interview also suggested that some of those items reflected attitudinal factors, whereas others reflected behavioural factors [40]. Additionally, the experts suggested some items were drivers, and others were outcomes of WASRR. It was noted that compliance as a word did not accurately measure WASRR in hospitality and, thus, should be removed. Similarly, the panel agreed that between the words accept, try and use, accept provided a more accurate representation of WASRR. The word "try" doesn't mean consumers will accept the recommendations, and the word "use" is not applicable to all hospitality-related products, such as wine. All expert members agreed that effectiveness must be considered to measure WASRR, and thus, the item was rated the highest by the panel members. This item was kept in the revised pool of items. Based on the expert's feedback, the items were combined, removed or revised to fit the WASRR scale. Any items that were not considered representative by any two-panel members were removed. A total of 12 items remained in the initial pool of items.

After the refinement of the scale based on the expert interviews, the scale was tested **using factor analysis in SPSS**. Negative statements were recoded before the analysis. Based on the Rotated Component Matrix, two items were removed due to double loadings. A total of 10 items were used for the initial pool of items (see Table 4).

Table 4. Rotated Component Matrix

	Component		
Items	1	2	3
Item 1. I plan to accept the robot's recommendations	.977		
Item 2. I disapprove of the robot's recommendations	.962		
Item 3. I refuse to accept the robot's recommendations	.959		
Item 4. I am willing to accept the robot's recommendations	.869		
Item 5. My wine selection was made easier by the robot		.991	
Item 6. The wine recommendation matches what I like		.972	
Item 7. I am willing to try the robot's recommendations		.922	
Item 8. I intend to accept the robot's recommendations			.943
Item 9. I am unlikely to try this recommendation			.911
Item 10. I was able to make a more effective decision because of the robot's recommendations			.896

5 Discussion and Conclusion

From the first stage of the scale development, it is clear that WASRR has multiple dimensions, some of which are outcomes and others that are drivers. In the following stages, item purification and Exploratory Factor Analysis, Confirmatory Factor Analysis and Structural Equation Modelling will be undertaken. This will help validate the scale further and test for reliability, validity and generalisability.

The WASRR scale will be useful for service providers not just in the food and beverage industry and hotel industry but also in other service industries such as banking, insurance, healthcare, travel, and transportation industries. It will help managers understand where to deploy social robots to provide recommendations and how they can be used in collaboration with human employees. There is a vast difference between consumer expectations and robots' actual capabilities [41]. Further, despite recent research in understanding humanoid robot recommender systems in brick-and-mortar restaurants and stores, none of the studies focus on the consumer's psychological mechanism, which is essential for a sustainable and mutually beneficial human-robot interaction. With the WASRR scale, businesses will be able to test if social robots are appropriate to provide recommendations to their consumers before deployment. If they are not, they can work with manufacturers like Softbank or Sony to develop social robots accordingly. Additionally, businesses will be able to track customer acceptance of recommendations and, consequently, provide more tailored solutions to their needs and wants.Thus, enhancing satisfaction and delighting customers. It will also help the government evaluate the advantages and disadvantages of employing social robots in public spaces, take necessary steps to adjust worker shortages and provide retraining for industries facing high automation risks. Integration of social robots will help improve operational efficiency, increase cost savings and productivity and enhance in-store experiences.

Robots will become more important in the service industry as the ageing population and labour shortage increase in many developed countries [35, 42]. Using SR for recommendations will enhance guest experience and save operational costs. However, it's possible only if customers are willing to accept SR recommendations. This study aims to develop a much-needed scale to measure WASRR. Hence, businesses can avoid dissatisfying customers and reduce the failure of the deployment. The WASRR scale is the first in the hospitality industry and can be adopted and adapted to fit organisational needs.

This study validates the scale in hospitality settings and one location only. Future studies should validate the scale in new contexts, such as retail and banking, and multiple geographic locations, especially regional areas.

References

1. Zeng, Z., Chen, P.-J., Lew, A.A.: From high-touch to high-tech: COVID-19 drives robotics adoption. Tour. Geogr. **22**(3), 724–734 (2020)
2. Maximise Market Research, Social Robots Market: Global Industry Analysis and Forecast (2023–2029). Maximise Market Research (2023)
3. Stipes, C.: Robots and artificial intelligence present challenges, opportunities for hospitality industry (2019). https://uh.edu/news-events/stories/2019/february-2019/02252019-robot-hospitality.php. Accessed 13 July 2023

4. Wirtz, J., et al.: Brave new world: service robots in the frontline. J. Serv. Manage. **29**, 907–931 (2018)
5. Hegel, F., et al.: Understanding social robots. In: 2009 Second International Conferences on Advances in Computer-Human Interactions. IEEE, Washington (2009)
6. Aymerich-Franch, L., Ferrer, I.: Liaison, safeguard, and well-being: analyzing the role of social robots during the COVID-19 pandemic. Technol. Soc. **70**, 101993 (2022)
7. Kilichan, R., Yilmaz, M.: Artificial intelligence and robotic technologies in tourism and hospitality industry. Erciyes Üniversitesi Sosyal Bilimler Enstitüsü Dergisi (50), 353–380 (2020)
8. Herse, S., et al.: Bon appetit! robot persuasion for food recommendation. In: Companion of the 2018 ACM/IEEE International Conference on Human-Robot Interaction (2018)
9. Yoon, N., Lee, H.-K.: AI recommendation service acceptance: assessing the effects of perceived empathy and need for cognition. J. Theor. Appl. Electron. Commer. Res. **16**(5), 1912–1928 (2021)
10. Senecal, S., Nantel, J.: The influence of online product recommendations on consumers' online choices. J. Retail. **80**(2), 159–169 (2004)
11. Yoon, V.Y., et al.: Assessing the moderating effect of consumer product knowledge and online shopping experience on using recommendation agents for customer loyalty. Decis. Support. Syst. **55**(4), 883–893 (2013)
12. Scholz, M., et al.: Measuring consumers' willingness to pay with utility-based recommendation systems. Decis. Support. Syst. **72**, 60–71 (2015)
13. Ajzen, I.: The theory of planned behavior. Organ. Behav. Hum. Decis. Process. **50**(2), 179–211 (1991)
14. Wang, X., Lu, Z., Yin, M.: Will you accept the AI recommendation? Predicting human behavior in AI-assisted decision making. In: Proceedings of the ACM Web Conference 2022 (2022)
15. Andrasen, A.; Attitudes and customer behavior; a decision model. Perspect. Consum. Behav. (1968)
16. Hu, X., et al.: Can in-store recommendations for online-substitutive products integrate online and offline channels? J. Retail. Consum. Serv. **70**, 103142 (2023)
17. Rossi, S., Staffa, M., Tamburro, A.: Socially assistive robot for providing recommendations: comparing a humanoid robot with a mobile application. Int. J. Soc. Robot. **10**(2), 265–278 (2018)
18. Kowatsch, T., Maass, W.: In-store consumer behavior: how mobile recommendation agents influence usage intentions, product purchases, and store preferences. Comput. Hum. Behav. **26**(4), 697–704 (2010)
19. Mordor Intelligence LLP, Recommendation Engine Market - Growth, Trends, COVID-19 Impact, and Forecasts (2021 - 2026). Report Linker, pp. 1–166 (2021)
20. Ansari, A., Essegaier, S., Kohli, R.: Internet recommendation systems. SAGE Publications Sage CA, Los Angeles (2000)
21. Baier, D., Stüber, E.: Acceptance of recommendations to buy in online retailing. J. Retail. Consum. Serv. **17**(3), 173–180 (2010)
22. Thorat, P.B., Goudar, R.M., Barve, S.: Survey on collaborative filtering, content-based filtering and hybrid recommendation system. Int. J. Comput. Appl. **110**(4), 31–36 (2015)
23. Cervone, F., et al.: Comparing a social robot and a mobile application for movie recommendation: a pilot study. In: WOA (2015)
24. Woiceshyn, L., et al.: Personalized clothing recommendation by a social robot. In: 2017 IEEE International Symposium on Robotics and Intelligent Sensors (IRIS). IEEE (2017)
25. Holthöwer, J., van Doorn, J.: Robots do not judge: service robots can alleviate embarrassment in service encounters. J. Acad. Mark. Sci. **51**, 1–18 (2022)

26. Shin, H.H., Jeong, M.: Guests' perceptions of robot concierge and their adoption intentions. Int. J. Contemp. Hosp. Manag. **32**(8), 2613–2633 (2020)

27. Shiomi, M., et al.: Recommendation effects of a social robot for advertisement-use context in a shopping mall. Int. J. Soc. Robot. **5**(2), 251–262 (2013)

28. Herse, S., et al.: Do you trust me, blindly? Factors influencing trust towards a robot recommender system. In: 2018 27th IEEE International Symposium on Robot and Human Interactive Communication (RO-MAN). IEEE (2018)

29. Lee, N., et al.: The influence of politeness behavior on user compliance with social robots in a healthcare service setting. Int. J. Soc. Robot. **9**(5), 727–743 (2017)

30. De Carolis, B.N., et al. Towards a social robot as interface for tourism recommendations. In: cAESAR (2020)

31. Okafuji, Y., et al.: Persuasion strategies for social robot to keep humans accepting daily different recommendations. In: 2021 IEEE/RSJ International Conference on Intelligent Robots and Systems (IROS). IEEE (2021)

32. Pal, A., Chua, A.Y., Banerjee, S.: Examining trust and willingness to accept AI recommendation systems. In: Proceedings of the Association for Information Science and Technology Mid-Year Conference: Expanding Horizons of Information Science and Technology and Beyond. ASIS&T (2023)

33. Schrepp, M.: User experience questionnaire handbook. All you need to know to apply the UEQ successfully in your project (2015)

34. Chi, R., Zhang, J., Pan, M.: The effect of anthropomorphic competence-warmth congruence of service robots on recommendation intention. Curr. Psychol., 1–14 (2023)

35. Blut, M., et al.: Understanding anthropomorphism in service provision: a meta-analysis of physical robots, chatbots, and other AI. J. Acad. Mark. Sci. **49**, 632–658 (2021)

36. Reimer, T., Benkenstein, M.: When good WOM hurts and bad WOM gains: the effect of untrustworthy online reviews. J. Bus. Res. **69**(12), 5993–6001 (2016)

37. Lu, L., Cai, R., Gursoy, D.: Developing and validating a service robot integration willingness scale. Int. J. Hosp. Manag. **80**, 36–51 (2019)

38. Pijls, R., et al.: Measuring the experience of hospitality: scale development and validation. Int. J. Hosp. Manag. **67**, 125–133 (2017)

39. Lytras, M.D., et al.: Information management in smart cities: turning end users' views into multi-item scale development, validation, and policy-making recommendations. Int. J. Inf. Manage. **56**, 102146 (2021)

40. Bundick, M.: The development of scales to measure QISA's three guiding principles of student aspirations using the My Voice survey. Quaglia Institute for Student Aspirations, Dunedin, Florida (2010)

41. Nichols, G. Social robots are flopping. what makes this one different? (2019). https://www.zdnet.com/article/social-robots-are-flopping-what-makes-this-one-different/. Accessed 16 Feb 2023

42. Sangster, K. Warning: Australia's skills shortage will continue into 2023. Yahoo News 2022. https://au.news.yahoo.com/australias-skills-shortage-2023-215600981.html. Accessed 4 Feb 2023

Where Should I Stand? Robot Positioning in Human-Robot Conversational Groups

Hooman Hedayati[✉] and Takayuki Kanda

Graduate School of Informatics, Kyoto University, Kyoto, Japan
hooman@robot.soc.i.kyoto-u.ac.jp, kanda@i.kyoto-u.ac.jp

Abstract. This paper addresses the challenge of improving robots' social awareness within conversational groups. Many robots struggle to adapt to evolving group interactions, which can lead to negative user experiences. We introduce two innovative approaches to address this challenge: a heuristic approach, inspired by human group positioning behaviors, and a data-driven approach trained on human-human conversational group data. In our models, we include a set of features that helps robots' positioning in conversational groups. We evaluated both approaches on the "Babble" dataset, demonstrating their reliability. The data-driven model exhibits a slight precision advantage over the heuristic model, with an average error of **9.7 cm** compared to **19.4 cm**.

Keywords: Social Robotic · Conversational groups · Human-Robot Interaction

1 Introduction

Social agents, including social robots—robots capable of interacting with humans and each other in a socially acceptable manner [1]—have already been deployed in various public places such as shopping malls, museums, and restaurants. These robots have received positive feedback [2–7]. In this role, these agents assume the responsibility of performing tasks through interactions with humans, emphasizing the importance of supporting intuitive and natural human-robot interactions for tasks to be performed appropriately and in a socially acceptable manner. Most of these robots are anthropomorphic [8–10], as researchers have shown that robots exhibiting human behaviors, such as gaze and gestures, can improve Human-Robot Interaction (HRI) and gain people's trust [11–13].

Traditionally, social robots interact with a single user at a time (e.g., acting as a receptionist [9] or a trainer [14]). In recent years, research efforts have focused on facilitating multiparty human-robot conversational groups [15–18]. To behave naturally, social robots must embody verbal and nonverbal social signals, including phatic expressions, gestures, facial expressions, body posture, eye gaze, and touch. Furthermore, in multiparty human-robot conversational groups, robots must show social awareness and follow social norms [19], such as

A. Al. Ali et al. (Eds.): ICSR 2023, LNAI 14454, pp. 182–192, 2024.
https://doi.org/10.1007/978-981-99-8718-4_16

determining where to stand and where to direct their attention, compared to single-user interactions.

People tend to follow social norms without much thought or effort. These standards of behavior are deeply ingrained in human nature. In conversational groups, individuals demonstrate their ability to effectively communicate and comprehend nonverbal signals. For example, individuals can easily recognize whether they are welcome to join a conversation group by observing the behavior of its members. Furthermore, individuals perform turn-taking, ensuring smooth transitions between speakers in a conversation [20]. Deviating from these social norms is often noticeable and can negatively impact the interaction; for instance, avoiding eye contact and constantly checking one's cellphone is generally considered impolite. The importance of following social norms is equally applicable to both single-user and multi-user interactions with social robots. There exists a set of social protocols that robots should follow, such as maintaining eye contact with the active speaker and choosing an appropriate position, which significantly affect the interaction's quality, including the user's satisfaction and willingness to continue the interaction. To advance the acceptance of social robots in society, it is crucial to design behaviors and interactions that align with these social norms in the human-robot interaction.

A challenge in ensuring robots' appropriate behavior is their stationary nature. The specific social norms a robot must follow depend on the nature of the interaction. Interaction with social agents can be categorized into two groups: interactions initiated by the user and interactions initiated by the robot. For example, in the first group, a user might approach a robot to ask for directions inside a building [9] or to complete the check-in/check-out process at a hotel with a robot receptionist [21]. In the second group, the robot initiates the interaction, such as when it approaches a user to deliver the food ordered by the user [22], participating in a conversational group [23]. While both groups share common social norms, the second group presents additional challenges, including determining how to approach users and where to position themselves in conversational groups. Addressing and resolving these challenges is essential for transitioning from interactions with stationary robots to interactions with dynamic, adaptable robots.

Conversational groups, in particular, present complex dynamics for robots. To behave naturally within a human-robot conversational group, robots must understand how to appropriately join or detach from the group and adjust their positions in response to changes such as new members joining or existing members leaving. These rules governing position and interaction dynamics are often unspoken but are readily understood and adapted to by humans. In this paper, we explore how these rules can be observed, extracted, and mathematically expressed for robots. Our observations suggest that robots can estimate their optimal positions based on the behavior of other group members.

This paper focuses on the position of robots within human-robot conversational groups. The central research question we address is **"At each timestamp in a conversational group, what is the best position for the robot relative to other group members?"** We introduce two approaches to enable social robots to proactively position themselves in human-robot conversational groups. The first approach is a heuristic model based on observations of how humans position themselves in conversational groups. The second approach is a data-driven model trained on human-human conversational group data. We present a set of features that influence the positions of individuals in conversational groups and incorporate them into our models. To evaluate our approaches, we conducted tests using the "Babble" dataset [24]. Our results demonstrate that both approaches yield reliable precision, with the data-driven approach exhibiting a slight advantage.

2   Related Work

Previous research in social sciences has explored various aspects of social group structure and dynamics to understand how people organize and regulate group interactions [25–28]. Kendon introduced the concept of "Facing Formations" or "F-formations" to describe spatial configurations in conversational groups where people maintain a spatial and orientational relationship with equal, direct, and exclusive access [27].

Research in human-computer interaction and human-robot interaction has leveraged F-formation features, such as arrangement, to design and improve interactions [29–32]. Quantitative measures like "Symmetry" and "Tightness" have also been used to characterize F-formations, with Symmetry describing the congruence of angles between people and Tightness representing the average Euclidean distance between group members and the conversational group's center [24]. We employ Symmetry and Tightness as fundamental measures in our approach (Sect. 3).

While much research has focused on accurate F-formation detection [24,33–37], challenges persist. Noise in the data from RGB and depth cameras, errors in human detection algorithms, and difficulties in adapting the detection algorithms to the complex dynamics of conversational groups remain obstacles.

Furthermore, research has explored spatial behaviors for robots within F-formations [38]. Approaches have included reinforcement learning to maintain correct orientation [39], walking side by side with humans [7,40], and robot approaches to F-formations [41–43].

Despite these advances, limited research addresses the optimal position of the robot within F-formations. Previous work by Vázquez et al. [38] suggested two methods for robot positioning, including geometric and Wasserstein Generative Adversarial Networks (WGAN) approaches. However, F-formation norms vary globally, and multiple factors modulate F-formation features, making simpler methods and following participants' lead preferable.

In our previous work [44], we introduced "regions" as potential positions within an F-formation. These regions served to validate F-formation detection algorithm outputs but were too broad for precise robot pose generation. In this work, we aim to refine and improve existing algorithms by addressing these challenges. The question of where a robot should stand within a conversational group remains a largely unexplored territory. This critical question serves as the focal point of our research, aiming to provide insights into optimizing robot positioning within F-formations for more effective social interactions.

3 Methodology

In this section, we present our methodology for determining the optimal position of a robot within an F-formation.

3.1 Problem Statement

Consider an F-formation, denoted as F_i, which comprises n participants arranged in a circular configuration with an accompanying robot R. The list of participants is represented as $P_i = \{P_1, P_2, ..., P_n\}$. Each participant P_i is characterized by $P_i = \{x_i, y_i, \theta_i\}$, where x and y denote 2D coordinates representing the participant's position, and θ represents their orientation. Given the list of participants P_i, our objective is to determine the desired robot position, denoted as $R_{desired}$, represented as $\{x_d, y_d, \theta_d\}$.

3.2 Preprocessing

The preprocessing has three steps. First, we convert all coordinate systems to International System (SI) units, ensuring uniformity by representing all positions in meters and orientations in radians. Second, we reorder the input list F_i to ensure that participants in F_i are arranged counterclockwise, starting from the participant adjacent to the robot R. This reordering simplifies the analysis and evaluation processes. Finally, to enable the use of F-formations of equal size as a training set for our data-driven approach, we normalize each F_i by transforming it into the reference frame of P_{first}, the participant closest to the robot. This step simplifies comparison between F-formations and maintains the robot-centric perspective.

3.3 Heuristic Approach

Our heuristic approach aims to determine the robot's optimal position within an F-formation by imitating human behavior patterns (Fig. 1).

Step 1: Finding C_F - Center of F-formation: The center of the F-formation, denoted as C_F, is calculated as the Euclidean average of points positioned at a distance D from each participant, in front of their respective orientations.

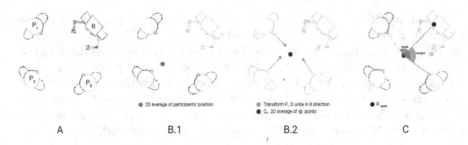

Fig. 1. Illustration of the heuristic pose generation approach.

$$C_F = \frac{1}{n} \sum_{i=1}^{n} ([x_i + D\cos(\theta_i), y_i + D\sin(\theta_i)]) \tag{1}$$

The introduction of a "stride" [34] (parameter D) helps refine C_F by aligning it with participants' orientations, mitigating noise in the calculated center.

Step 2: Identifying the Maximum Angle ($\max(\theta_{i,j})$): We determine the maximum angle $\max(\theta_{i,j})$ between adjacent participants i and j within the F-formation. This angle informs us of the preferred robot position within the formation, as humans tend to favor symmetric arrangements.

Step 3: Calculating $Dist$ - Median Distance from C_F: We calculate the median of the Euclidean distances between each participant P_i and C_F to account for potential outlier behaviors.

Step 4: Generating $R_{desired}$ - Robot's Desired Position: The desired robot position, $R_{desired}$, is determined by extending C_F by a distance of $Dist$ in the direction of $\max(\theta_{i,j})/2$.

Our heuristic approach provides a practical and interpretable solution for generating the robot's desired position within an F-formation. However, it's heuristic and might not work in all scenarios. For greater generizability and adaptability, we introduce the data-driven approach.

3.4   Data-Driven Approach

In the data-driven approach, we use multivariate linear regression, a statistical technique used to examine relationships between multiple independent variables and a single dependent variable. This method allows us to predict the dependent variable's value based on the independent variables. We have specifically chosen multivariate linear regression over alternative data-driven approaches, such as neural networks, due to the relatively lower complexity of our problem, making multivariate linear regression a computationally more efficient choice.

In our context, the F-formation (F_i) serves as the combined representation of both independent and dependent variables. To clarify, we treat the positions of the participants within the F-formation as independent variables. While it may seem that these positions could be dependent on each other (e.g., if one participant, P_i, gets too close to another, P_j, P_j might adjust their location), we regard each participant's position as independent because each individual autonomously selects their placement.

For our data-driven approach, we develop five distinct multivariate linear regression models, each tailored to a specific F-formation size ranging from 3 to 7 participants. We have excluded F-formation size 2 from our training data as it involves both a robot and a participant, creating a unique scenario where the robot would position itself in relation to the personal space of the user. During the training phase, we calculate a weight matrix as follows:

Step 0: Training Step: We train separate multivariate linear regression models for F-formations of different sizes, ranging from 3 to 7 participants. The training process involves calculating a weight matrix W based on the positions of the participants.

$$W = mvregress(F_i - R, R) \tag{2}$$

Here, $F_i - R$ denotes the input, and R represents the response variable. Training incorporates various features, such as participant positions, heights, and orientations.

Generating $R_{desired}$: Using the trained weight matrix W corresponding to the specific F-formation size, we calculate $R_{desired}$ as follows:

$$R_{desired} = F_n \times W_n \tag{3}$$

4   Evaluation

To better understand how our method may perform in practice, we validated our method on a dataset. The metric we used for the evaluation is the Euclidean distance between the position of a person in the dataset (ground truth) and the pose generated by our approaches. This metric has been used in the literature [38] and provides an understanding of the performance of the system in the generation of poses for robots.

It was difficult to find a suitable baseline for our method. As we did not have access to the source code of other approaches to implement on our dataset, nor could we test our approach on other datasets mainly due to some inaccuracies.

4.1   Babble Dataset

First, we evaluated our method on a publicly available dataset. The Babble dataset [24] is used among many available datasets such as [45,46], because it has the head and body orientations of the participants, as well as the height of each participant, which is necessary to run our method and evaluate the result. The other datasets mentioned do not provide orientations [47], or heights [45,46]. Babble has 1568 annotated frames in which participants are in F-formation ($F_3 = 271$ frames, $F_4 = 246$ frames, $F_5 = 185$ frames, $F_6 = 373$ frames, $F_7 = 493$

Table 1. Accuracy of the generated poses in the Babble dataset.

| | Accuracy for Babble Dataset | | | | | Overal |
| | F-formation size | | | | | |
	3	4	5	6	7	
Data-driven	**9.3 cm**	**8.9 cm**	**12.3 cm**	**9.6 cm**	**8.5 cm**	**9.72 cm**
Heuristic	22.1 cm	19.8 cm	17.2 cm	20.1 cm	17.9 cm	19.42 cm

frames). For each F-formation, we used 80% of the frames for training and 20% for testing.

After training the data-driven approach, we tested both of our approaches on the test dataset, and the results are shown in Table 1. Our data-driven method shows an overall accuracy of 9.72 cm, compared to the accuracy of 19.42 cm for the heuristic approach, which demonstrates the promising performance of our method in generating poses for robots within F-formations.

5   Discussion

F-formation at time T-1 (for giving more context)   The F-formation at time T that we tested the model on   ● Heuristic approach generated pose
                                                                                                          ● Data-driven approach generated pose

Fig. 2. Instances where the data-driven approach encountered challenges.

While the data-driven model significantly outperformed the heuristic model, we believe that, given the current state of the art, it may be more better to employ heuristic models over data-driven ones. The reason is based on the fact that data-driven models are prone to overfitting. During testing, we encountered scenarios in the Babble dataset where one of the participants exhibited highly active behavior, particularly when excited or fatigued. In these cases, they often moved towards the center of the F-formation and remained there for brief periods

(Fig. 2). Our data-driven approach learned from these occurrences and generated poses directed towards the F-formation center, which is clearly unnatural for humans. Overfitting concerns like these could potentially hinder positive human-robot interactions, leading to situations where robots are perceived as unwelcome in specific contexts or by particular groups.

We anticipate that addressing this overfitting issue will require accumulating more data from human-robot conversational groups and incorporating additional relevant features. These features could provide a more comprehensive understanding of the environment, including factors such as noise levels and crowd density. By integrating such features, we can enhance pose generation and equip robots with improved social awareness.

One limitation of our study is the absence of real-world implementation. The inherent noise and movement associated with robots could disrupt human-robot conversational groups. To fully assess the effectiveness of heuristic and data-driven approaches, it is essential to conduct real-world human-robot interaction studies.

In our future work, we plan to expand the feature set of the data-driven model to achieve greater inclusivity. We aim to identify key components of F-formations, potential disruptions, and factors influencing dynamics, and incorporate them into our model.

6   Conclusion

In this paper, we have introduced two innovative approaches to enable social robots to proactively engage in conversational groups:

First, our heuristic approach draws upon human behaviors and observations, providing robots with practical strategies for positioning themselves within conversations. Second, our data-driven approach leverages a dataset of human-human conversational groups, training robots to generate optimal positions within F-formations relative to other group members.

By adopting these approaches, we can enable robots with the ability to seamlessly integrate into conversational groups, enhancing the quality of human-robot interactions in diverse social settings. Our work represents a significant step toward creating socially aware and adaptable robots that can contribute positively to a wide range of real-world scenarios.

Acknowledgments. This work was supported by the Japan Science and Technology Agency (JST) Moonshot RD under Grant Number JPMJMS2011, Japan.

References

1. Daily, S.B., et al.: Affective computing: historical foundations, current applications, and future trends. In: Emotions and Affect in Human Factors and Human-Computer Interaction, pp. 213–231. Elsevier (2017)
2. Niemelä, M., Heikkilä, P., Lammi, H., Oksman, V.: A social robot in a shopping mall: studies on acceptance and stakeholder expectations. In: Korn, O. (ed.) Social Robots: Technological, Societal and Ethical Aspects of Human-Robot Interaction. HIS, pp. 119–144. Springer, Cham (2019). https://doi.org/10.1007/978-3-030-17107-0_7
3. Chen, Y., Wu, F., Shuai, W., Wang, N., Chen, R., Chen, X.: KeJia robot–an attractive shopping mall guider. In: ICSR 2015. LNCS (LNAI), vol. 9388, pp. 145–154. Springer, Cham (2015). https://doi.org/10.1007/978-3-319-25554-5_15
4. Huang, C.-M., Iio, T., Satake, S., Kanda, T.: Modeling and controlling friendliness for an interactive museum robot. In: Robotics: Science and Systems, pp. 12–16. Citeseer (2014)
5. Kanda, T., Shiomi, M., Miyashita, Z., Ishiguro, H., Hagita, N.: A communication robot in a shopping mall. IEEE Trans. Rob. **26**(5), 897–913 (2010)
6. Shiomi, M., Kanda, T., Ishiguro, H., Hagita, N.: Interactive humanoid robots for a science museum. In: Proceedings of the 1st ACM SIGCHI/SIGART Conference on Human-Robot Interaction, pp. 305–312 (2006)
7. Morales, Y., Kanda, T., Hagita, N.: Walking together: side-by-side walking model for an interacting robot. J. Hum. Rob. Interact. **3**(2), 50–73 (2014)
8. Osawa, H., et al.: Analysis of robot hotel: reconstruction of works with robots. In: 26th IEEE International Symposium on Robot and Human Interactive Communication (RO-MAN), pp. 219–223. IEEE (2017)
9. Bohus, D., Saw, C.W., Horvitz, E.: Directions robot: in-the-wild experiences and lessons learned. In: Proceedings of the 2014 International Conference on Autonomous Agents and Multi-Agent Systems. International Foundation for Autonomous Agents and Multiagent Systems, pp. 637–644 (2014)
10. Doering, M., Brščić, D., Kanda, T.: Data-driven imitation learning for a shopkeeper robot with periodically changing product information. ACM Trans. Hum. Rob. Interact. (THRI) **10**(4), 1–20 (2021)
11. Stanton, C., Stevens, C.J.: Robot pressure: the impact of robot eye gaze and lifelike bodily movements upon decision-making and trust. In: Beetz, M., Johnston, B., Williams, M.-A. (eds.) ICSR 2014. LNCS (LNAI), vol. 8755, pp. 330–339. Springer, Cham (2014). https://doi.org/10.1007/978-3-319-11973-1_34
12. Babel, F., et al.: Small talk with a robot? The impact of dialog content, talk initiative, and gaze behavior of a social robot on trust, acceptance, and proximity. Int. J. Soc. Robot. **13**(6), 1485–1498 (2021)
13. Savery, R., Rose, R., Weinberg, G.: Establishing human-robot trust through music-driven robotic emotion prosody and gesture. In: 28th IEEE International Conference on Robot and Human Interactive Communication (RO-MAN), pp. 1–7. IEEE (2019)
14. Nasihati Gilani, S., et al.: Multimodal dialogue management for multiparty interaction with infants. In: Proceedings of the 20th ACM International Conference on Multimodal Interaction, pp. 5–13 (2018)
15. Hedayati, H., Walker, M., Szafir, D.: Improving collocated robot teleoperation with augmented reality. In: Proceedings of the 2018 ACM/IEEE International Conference on Human-Robot Interaction, pp. 78–86. ACM (2018)

16. Hedayati, H., et al.: Symbiotic society with avatars (SSA) beyond space and time. In: Companion of the ACM/IEEE International Conference on Human-Robot Interaction 2023, pp. 953–955 (2023)
17. Hedayati, H.: Improving human-robot conversational groups. Ph.D. dissertation, University of Colorado at Boulder (2021)
18. Hedayati, H., Gross, M.D., Szafir, D.: What information should a robot convey? In: 2021 IEEE/RSJ International Conference on Intelligent Robots and Systems (IROS), pp. 6232–6239. IEEE (2021)
19. Bartneck, C., Forlizzi, J.: A design-centred framework for social human-robot interaction. In: RO-MAN 2004 13th IEEE International Workshop on Robot and Human Interactive Communication (IEEE Catalog No. 04TH8759), pp. 591–594. IEEE (2004)
20. Wiemann, J.M., Knapp, M.L.: Turn-taking in conversations. Commun. Theory, 226–245 (2017)
21. Reis, J., Melão, N., Salvadorinho, J., Soares, B., Rosete, A.: Service robots in the hospitality industry: the case of Henn-na hotel, Japan. Technol. Soc. **63**, 101423 (2020)
22. Saravanan, D., Perianayaki, E.R.A., Pavithra, R., Parthiban, R.: Barcode system for hotel food order with delivery robot. J. Phys. Conf. Ser. **1717**(1), 012054 (2021)
23. Vázquez, M.: Reasoning about spatial patterns of human behavior during group conversations with robots. Ph.D. dissertation, Carnegie Mellon University (2015)
24. Hedayati, H., Muehlbradt, A., Szafir, D.J., Andrist, S.: REFORM: recognizing F-formations for social robots. In: 2020 IEEE/RSJ International Conference on Intelligent Robots and Systems (IROS), pp. 11 181–11 188. IEEE (2020)
25. Ciolek, T.M., Kendon, A.: Environment and the spatial arrangement of conversational encounters. Sociol. Inq. **50**(3–4), 237–271 (1980)
26. Kendon, A.: The negotiation of context in face-to-face interaction. In: Rethinking Context: Language as an Interactive Phenomenon, no. 11, p. 323 (1992)
27. Kendon, A.: Conducting interaction: patterns of behavior in focused encounters, vol. 7. CUP Archive (1990)
28. Hedayati, H., Szafir, D., Kennedy, J.: Comparing F-formations between humans and on-screen agents. In: Extended Abstracts of the CHI Conference on Human Factors in Computing Systems 2020, pp. 1–9 (2020)
29. Tong, L., Serna, A., Pageaud, S., George, S., Tabard, A.: It's not how you stand, it's how you move: F-formations and collaboration dynamics in a mobile learning game. In: Proceedings of the 18th International Conference on Human-Computer Interaction with Mobile Devices and Services, pp. 318–329 (2016)
30. De Stefani, E., Mondada, L.: Reorganizing mobile formations: when "guided" participants initiate reorientations in guided tours. Space Cult. **17**(2), 157–175 (2014)
31. Ballendat, T., Marquardt, N., Greenberg, S.: Proxemic interaction: designing for a proximity and orientation-aware environment. In: ACM International Conference on Interactive Tabletops and Surfaces, pp. 121–130 (2010)
32. Marquardt, N., Hinckley, K., Greenberg, S.: Cross-device interaction via micromobility and F-formations. In: Proceedings of the 25th Annual ACM Symposium on User Interface Software and Technology, pp. 13–22. ACM (2012)
33. Hung, H., Kröse, B.: Detecting f-formations as dominant sets. In: Proceedings of the 13th International Conference on Multimodal Interfaces, pp. 231–238 (2011)
34. Setti, F., Russell, C., Bassetti, C., Cristani, M.: F-formation detection: individuating free-standing conversational groups in images. PLoS ONE **10**(5), e0123783 (2015)

35. Setti, F., Lanz, O., Ferrario, R., Murino, V., Cristani, M.: Multi-scale F-formation discovery for group detection. In: 2013 IEEE International Conference on Image Processing, pp. 3547–3551. IEEE (2013)

36. Swofford, M., et al.: Improving social awareness through DANTE: deep affinity network for clustering conversational interactants. Proc. ACM Hum. Comput. Interact. 4(CSCW1), 1–23 (2020)

37. Hedayati, H., Szafir, D., Andrist, S.: Recognizing F-formations in the open world. In: 2019 14th ACM/IEEE International Conference on Human-Robot Interaction (HRI), pp. 558–559. IEEE (2019)

38. Vázquez, M., Lew, A., Gorevoy, E., Connolly, J.: Pose generation for social robots in conversational group formations. Frontiers Rob. AI, 341 (2022)

39. Vázquez, M., Steinfeld, A., Hudson, S.E.: Maintaining awareness of the focus of attention of a conversation: a robot-centric reinforcement learning approach. In: 25th IEEE International Symposium on Robot and Human Interactive Communication (RO-MAN), pp. 36–43. IEEE (2016)

40. Repiso, E., Garrell, A., Sanfeliu, A.: Adaptive side-by-side social robot navigation to approach and interact with people. Int. J. Soc. Robot. 12, 909–930 (2020)

41. Yang, F., Yin, W., Björkman, M., Peters, C.: Impact of trajectory generation methods on viewer perception of robot approaching group behaviors. In: 2020 29th IEEE International Conference on Robot and Human Interactive Communication (RO-MAN), pp. 509–516. IEEE (2020)

42. Yang, F., Peters, C.: AppGAN: generative adversarial networks for generating robot approach behaviors into small groups of people. In: 2019 28th IEEE International Conference on Robot and Human Interactive Communication (RO-MAN), pp. 1–8. IEEE (2019)

43. Truong, X.-T., Ngo, T.-D.: To approach humans?: A unified framework for approaching pose prediction and socially aware robot navigation. IEEE Trans. Cogn. Dev. Syst. 10(3), 557–572 (2017)

44. Hedayati, H., Szafir, D.: Predicting positions of people in human-robot conversational groups. In: 2022 17th ACM/IEEE International Conference on Human-Robot Interaction (HRI), pp. 402–411. IEEE (2022)

45. Alameda-Pineda, X., et al.: SALSA: a novel dataset for multimodal group behavior analysis. IEEE Trans. Pattern Anal. Mach. Intell. 38(8), 1707–1720 (2016)

46. Cabrera-Quiros, L., Demetriou, A., Gedik, E., van der Meij, L., Hung, H.: The MatchNMingle dataset: a novel multi-sensor resource for the analysis of social interactions and group dynamics in-the-wild during free-standing conversations and speed dates. IEEE Trans. Affect. Comput. (2018)

47. Roth, J., et al.: AVA active speaker: an audio-visual dataset for active speaker detection. In: ICASSP 2020–2020 IEEE International Conference on Acoustics, Speech and Signal Processing (ICASSP), pp. 4492–4496. IEEE (2020)

Real-World Evaluation of a University Guidance and Information Robot

Andrew Blair⬤ and Mary Ellen Foster(✉)⬤

School of Computing Science, University of Glasgow, Glasgow, Scotland
a.blair.2@research.gla.ac.uk, maryellen.foster@glasgow.ac.uk

Abstract. We have developed a social robot to assist an existing support team in a large, recently-built university building designed for learning and teaching. Over the course of a week-long, supervised deployment, we collected long form questionnaire results (N = 59) on attitudes and feelings towards the robot from students and staff. We observed an overall positive response to the robot, but with a wide variety of specific opinions. We describe the limitations and challenges we found with the real-world deployment and outline next steps to allow an unsupervised deployment of the robot as part of the university's wider service delivery strategy.

Keywords: Human-robot interaction · Field studies

1 Introduction

In recent years, social robots have been used in a wide range of public spaces, including shopping centres [6], hotels [14] and airports [8]. They offer the potential to add novel methods of service delivery to an organisation's repertoire, as well as providing an additional opportunity for public engagement.

At our university, a new learning and teaching building has recently been opened with capacity for over 2500 students. Information Services (IS) supports users of this building by deploying a support team to roam the building and assist with any queries users may have. However, this team are not present for the entire opening hours of the building, so an opportunity exists to develop a social robot to assist these building users as an additional service delivery tool for IS.

In a previous paper [1], we describe how the requirements for the robot system were developed and give a technical description of the implemented system, which combines the Pepper robot with the RASA [13] open-source chatbot framework, with an external microphone for speech recognition. In the current paper, we present the design and results of a week-long study where the robot was deployed in the aforementioned building and the university library. Hundreds of students and staff interacted with the robot, and we used a number of qualitative and quantitative measures to gather their opinions including a long-form questionnaire completed by 59 participants. We present the results on

A. Al. Ali et al. (Eds.): ICSR 2023, LNAI 14454, pp. 193–203, 2024.
https://doi.org/10.1007/978-981-99-8718-4_17

all of these measures and suggest necessary modifications for a potential future unsupervised deployment of the robot in a public space. The study results have been shared with IS senior management and will influence future service delivery strategies at the university.

2   Deployment Overview

We deployed the robot for five consecutive days, four in the learning and teaching building and one in the University library, for a total of 30 h. We placed the robot at the three main entrances of the learning and teaching building (Fig. 1), and on the main floor of the library. At least one researcher was present with the robot at all times. After each interaction, all users were prompted to rate the robot via a single-item Likert scale, and interested participants were also invited to fill in a longer questionnaire. In the following sections, we discuss the study outcomes from several perspectives. In Sect. 3 we discuss the system performance and the responses to the initial Likert scale; in Sect. 4, we dis-

Fig. 1. A user interacting with the robot

cuss the user responses to the longer questionnaire; while in Sect. 5, we briefly describe other behaviours that were observed during the deployment, specifically focussing on the challenges presented by this real-world deployment setting.

3   System Performance and Conversation Ratings

351 interactions occurred during the deployment, with 323 of them over one turn in length; the one-turn conversations generally represented early failure of one or more system components. The designed conversation length was five turns, and this was also the most common interaction length; some conversations were slightly longer, generally representing users who asked more than one question, while the longest conversations (up to 21 turns) were mainly due to a series of speech-recognition errors. Some utterances were misclassified, but users generally repeated themselves when necessary and most conversations were ultimately successful. From the interactions, 179 ratings were received on the Likert scale, with a mean of 3.47 (0.77) on a scale of 0 to 4, showing that the general impression of the robot was positive despite minor errors (Fig. 2).

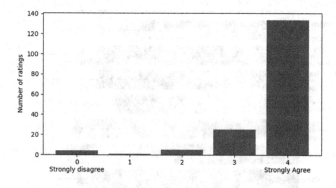

Fig. 2. Distribution of Likert ratings

4   Questionnaire Responses

59 participants completed the long questionnaire: 27 who identified as male, 27 as female, 4 as non-binary, and one participant who declined to disclose their gender. The majority of the participants (n = 32) had never interacted with a robot before, but a large minority had (n = 27). 12 participants were staff and 47 were students. The 12 staff were mainly building staff who had heard about the robot's presence in their work, but also included lecturers and project managers from other departments, representing a range of seniority levels. Of the 47 students, the majority were undergraduate students (n = 33), with the remainder being postgraduate taught (n = 13) and one postgraduate research student, and their fields of study varied widely, including both STEM and non-STEM subjects.

4.1   Likeability

The first section of the questionnaire was based on the Likeability section of the SASSI scale [9], which was developed to evaluate speech-based systems. Users were asked to rate the robot on a number of parameters on a scale of 0 to 4, with 0 representing "Strongly Disagree" and 4 representing "Strongly Agree".

As shown in Fig. 3, on all questions, the user sentiment was greater than "Neutral" (2.0); indeed, for all but two questions, the mean was greater than "Agree" (3.0). The two questions with less positive responses, *It is clear how to speak with Pepper* and *I felt in control of the interaction with Pepper*, suggest that there was some confusion around how to interact with the robot. This matches what we observed during the deployment: users would look to the researchers for guidance on how to talk to the robot, even after being given instructions by the robot once the facial recognition system triggered.

4.2   Interaction Factors

The next section of the questionnaire asked users to rate the robot on a number of factors, each to do with specific decisions that were made in the system

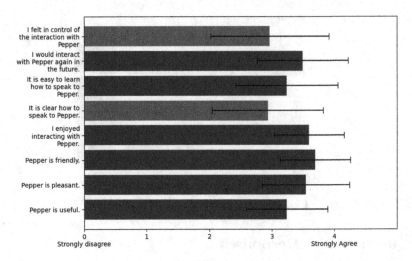

Fig. 3. Participant responses to the Likeability section of the survey, 0 = Strongly Disagree, 4 = Strongly Agree (mean and standard deviation)

implementation. For each question, the responses were given on a scale of 0 to 4, with 0 representing "Strongly Disliked" and 4 representing "Really Liked". A section of free-text was also provided to allow users to expand their answers if they wished to do so.

How did you feel about the gestures, such as hand and arm movements? The responses were positive with a mean of 3.29 (0.74), with only one participant actively disliking the gestures. Despite the overall positive response, many people had less positive comments: for example, in its default mode, Pepper regularly flexes its hands, which some participants found "creepy," "unsettling," or "scary", and one felt like it was "going to fight [them]".

How did you feel about your face being tracked or followed as you interacted with the robot? There were mixed feelings surrounding this question. Overall, there was still a positive response with a mean of 2.76 (0.86); however, several students found it disturbing, with variations of the following quote:

> initial reaction [...] that it was a bit creepy with how its head would [move] as you walked past it. but once the interaction started it was adorable how she would look at you [...]

How did you feel about the robot starting the conversation with you? Mean response 3.08 (0.85).
Do you prefer the idea of you starting the conversation with the robot? Mean response 2.75 (0.86).
We will discuss these questions together. The high mean of the first question shows that in general the implemented *proactivity* (where the robot initiated

a conversation as soon as a person was detected) was well received. However, the high standard deviation shows that there is no clear consensus. Where participants responded with "Really liked" to the first question, they would often respond "Strongly disliked" to the second question; similarly, neutral respondents to the first question would tend to respond neutrally to the second.

How would you describe Pepper? The final question in this section asked users to describe Pepper in free text. The three most common responses to this question were "cute", "helpful" and "friendly". These are all common descriptions for Pepper, and are a positive sign that the robot design has aided the acceptance of the robot within the space. "Childlike" was also used, with two different connotations: most respondents who said this thought this made the robot appear unthreatening and therefore appealing to interact with, but some also found problems with this presentation, for example that because it appeared like a child that they were uncomfortable being prompted to touch it.

4.3   Feedback on QR Codes

For external directions and Helpdesk articles, the system displayed a QR code on Pepper's tablet that would take them to the student mobile app for directions or to the IT Helpdesk website. 48 out of the 59 participants followed this user journey in their interaction, so the questionnaire included an item specifically addressing this part of the interaction.

Was it useful having the information on your phone rather than being on the tablet of the robot? On the same 0 to 4 scale as above, the mean result across the 48 participants was 3.1 (0.87), showing that the majority of participants agreed that having the information on their devices was a good addition to the system. However, some raised various issues with the QR code. One participant, despite answering the above question with "Strongly agree", suggested it would be:

> ...useful to both display the direction on the screen and with the qr code so the robot can be used without a smartphone...

The QR code was used to allow students to follow directions or read longform Helpdesk articles even after walking away from the robot, but it is clear from this and other responses that the reason for this design choice could be made clearer.

Table 1. Responses from users who prefer Pepper or a tablet for out of hours support

Question	Pepper	Tablet	p-value
It is easy to learn how to speak to Pepper	3.54	2.71	0.012
I would interact with Pepper again in the future	3.69	2.85	0.010
How did you feel about the gestures, such as hand and arm movements	3.43	2.86	0.012
How did you feel about the robot starting the conversation with you	3.24	2.57	0.0105
How did you feel about your face being tracked or followed as you interacted with the robot	2.93	2.29	0.0046

4.4   Out of Hours Support

Would you prefer Pepper for out of hours support or a tablet? 42 respondents said Pepper, 14 said the Tablet and 3 suggested they would want both. For this question, we compared the pattern of responses to user opinions of the robot as expressed on the main survey, using Welch's T test. As we can see from Table 1, people's attitudes towards the robot's behaviour and the interaction that they had with the robot appeared to affect their willingness to use and accept the robot. We note an especially strong correlation between their attitudes towards the face-tracking and whether or not they would want to use the robot for out of hours support. One student even said they would be "terrified" if they saw the robot at night unannounced.

4.5   Potential Use Cases

The final question concerned potential other use cases for the robot:

Would you like the robot to help you with anything else outside directions and the helpdesk? A number of participants referenced the ability of the robot to move, with one participant suggesting how it could be used to increase accessibility:

> people with disabilities. For example, if someone is blind, it could help them to find the elevator

As the target building is new, it is not an unreasonable suggestion; the building is fully accessible to wheelchair users, so it would be an ideal testbed for combining autonomous navigation and social robotics. Additionally, movement would allow us to further encapsulate the Reach Out roving model, whereby the ambassadors do not stay in one place and roam the building in an attempt to provide more visibility to building users. If this option is chosen, a different platform with better navigation capabilities than Pepper would be needed.

A common suggestion was to recommend events or activities around campus to students. Building from the QR code system discussed earlier, one participant suggested that Pepper could pass digital flyers for the events it would talk about via the QR codes such that the user could reference event details later. This would be straightforward to introduce, as the events data for the university is in a publicly accessible database.

Finally, several users spoke of just wanting to be able to chat to the robot. Whilst we explicitly discounted large language models (LLMs) for this experiment, as the goal was to provide answers to specific questions, the rise of services such as ChatGPT [12] has fuelled expectations of users to a much higher level. From a technical perspective it may be trivial to integrate an LLM, but the challenge would be controlling the output: for example, if the user asks about sensitive topics such as mental health, they have to be dealt with in the appropriate way which cannot be truly guaranteed with LLMs.

5 Observations

In addition to the formal questionnaire responses noted above, researchers also made notes of user behaviour during the deployment. We first describe general observations of people's reactions to encountering the robot, and then discuss specific incidents that exemplify the challenges that would be involved in deploying the robot more independently in this sort of real-world setting.

5.1 General Observations

A number of students recognised Pepper from other deployments or from their studies. Pepper is used in Psychology courses at the University as a case study, and they were excited to see it in the real world. One student spoke of seeing the robot in various places in Japan but was surprised the interaction was via voice, as they had only ever interacted with Pepper via its tablet before.

One user was unable to interact with Pepper. They primarily communicate using sign language, and the robot neither understood or was able to respond with sign language. They usually were able to understand people by lip reading, but this is also not possible with Pepper. We made a design decision to not subtitle the robot or allow alternative input due to time constraints, but with future work accessibility would have to be a major consideration. It is also a limitation of Pepper to not be dexterous enough to perform sign language, but it could be developed to have it as an input from a user.

Along with all of our positive sentiment, we did see some strong negative sentiment and uncertainty. The following are direct quotes we observed from three students:

oh my god what is that, why does it move
do you aim to kill humans
[walking by..] f*cking hell

This shows that despite making every effort, acceptance is fraught with challenges. Firstly, it shows the importance of making sure that responses are polite and appropriate. The bad publicity and therefore acceptance of the robot from stakeholders could be greatly affected if the robot responded inappropriately to these negative quotes.

The robot had an IS lanyard around its neck (Fig. 1), which was noted by one student who said it made the robot seem "more official". They also suggested giving the robot a hat, as they felt it would make the robot stand out more and also make it "cuter". Clothing Pepper is a popular thing to do and has proven to have concrete effects on people's behaviour; when deployed as a shrine attendant in Japan and traditionally clothed, people would bow without prompting like they would with a human attendant [7].

5.2   Real World Considerations

Dealing with abuse, of various forms, is an issue that social robots must be able to address in real-world deployments. We observed a number of concerning behaviours towards to the robot, even with staff present: one user threatened to hit the robot when it did not perform as expected, while multiple students attempted to flirt with it. Dealing with abuse [4], and specifically sexual harassment [3] has been explored in conversational agents. However, there is little research in how robots should deal with a physical threat in a real world environment [2]. The worry was echoed by some of the students and staff, with one student saying, "I hope people are not mean to Pepper" and another concerned that, if left unattended, "[Pepper] would get punched".

Another challenge is user preconceptions of speech recognition technology. Popular culture tries to show the humorous side of this with a sketch with a voice activated elevator[1] involving Scottish users; excerpts from this were also quoted when users were interacting with our robot. Some users were hesitant to interact with the robot saying, "it won't understand me". Especially at a university as diverse as Glasgow, with over 40% of the student body international, this is a significant challenge. Foster and Stuart-Smith's [5] research endorses our findings; they found that Scottish people expected to be able to understand the robot, but assumed it would struggle to understand their accent. The go-to response when Pepper responded with an error message was that it did not understand the user's speech, not that it was unable to match an intent and carry out a task. One participant even said "stop being racist robot". Care should be taken to generate appropriate errors, possibly repeating the phrase heard by the robot or displaying it on the tablet. However, this may come with the trade-off of making the user experience more frustrating with repetitive statements, so a balance must be struck.

We also observed "play-fighting" between students, causing concern to the other building users. It was stopped by a manager but raises a question of what a robot should do if supporting the building out of hours. Many would argue it is

---

[1] https://www.bbc.co.uk/programmes/p00hbfjw.

outside the domain of the robot, but if the robot is seen by users as truly working alongside staff then it should intervene. Other possibilities include Pepper simply recording the interaction. Some may argue this is a blatant privacy violation, but the building is already covered by CCTV, so Pepper would simply be adding another more versatile method of surveillance. Either way, it would be imperative to alert staff if Pepper was to witness such an incident.

Many students also asked the robot questions to vent their frustrations. One student asked "where can i find somewhere to study between 12 and 1" and when the robot responded that it could not find that room, the student responded "Of course, because there is nowhere". These types of interactions are where the personality of the robot becomes very relevant, as different people would answer the question in various ways. Völkel explored this and formalised an approach for developing personalities in conversational agents [15]. It once again raises the importance of co-design with our users: university students present an interesting and one of the most wide ranging demographics of the general public, and the robot should be able to cater to each individual where possible.

Some students spoke of being reassured by the perceived anonymity the robot gave to a conversation; they felt they would not be judged for asking their questions. Whilst this is obviously a positive if it encourages students to ask for help, it also raises a larger problem of how we would deal if a student approached the robot for help with bullying, discrimination or harassment. Mbawa [10] presented an approach where the interaction was scored; if the score was deemed low, they were presented with self help resources, if it was high they were directed to a suicide helpline. Care would need to be taken actually deploying this in the real-world unsupervised, as in this experiment they used pre-defined scenarios for the majority of participants.

6   Conclusions and Future Work

We have developed a social robot for use in a large, newly-built teaching building at a university and deployed it alongside an existing human support team to respond to building user's queries. We evaluated the robot via a week-long field experiment using a range of subjective and objective measures. The robot generally performed well, with positive initial feedback. On the long questionnaire, we found a range of positive attitudes towards the acceptance of the robot, along with a number of constructive suggestions for future system enhancements. This is shown by all objective measures exceeding the neutral threshold. However, there were a significant number of participants who had negative responses to the robot of various forms; in future studies, we will likely incorporate items from the Negative Attitude to Robots Scale (NARS) [11] to better quantify this reaction.

It is important to note that the system, as deployed, had several limitations. Firstly, the data provided by IS was out-of-date or incomplete in places. We note we did not perform any pre-processing or modification of the data other than in the internal building directions, nor use customised information retrieval techniques to search the available data. Also, during the deployment, the robot was never unattended; this was primarily so we could observe user interactions and step in where necessary, but also due to deploying in a completely public building and the risk of harm to the robot. This likely affected some people's responses to the robots; they would instinctively look to staff rather than the robot in the first instance.

The user feedback has been shared with IS and is now being used to assist in making future decisions about novel service delivery methods within the university. Future work would include developing sophisticated social signal processing to recognise a user's intent to speak with the robot, using large language models to improve the variety and relatability of the system's responses, addressing the speech recognition challenges faced in the deployment location, integrating solutions for accessibility, and —overall— taking into account the suggested user enhancements to improve service delivery further.

References

1. Blair, A., Foster, M.E.: Development of a university guidance and information robot. In: Proceedings of HRI 2023 (2023). https://doi.org/10.1145/3568294.3580138
2. Brščić, D., Kidokoro, H., Suehiro, Y., Kanda, T.: Escaping from children's abuse of social robots. In: Proceedings of HRI 2015 (2015). https://doi.org/10.1145/2696454.2696468
3. Curry, A.C., Rieser, V.: #MeToo Alexa: how conversational systems respond to sexual harassment. In: Proceedings of the 2nd ACL Workshop on Ethics in Natural Language Processing (2018). https://doi.org/10.18653/v1/W18-0802
4. Curry, A.C., Rieser, V.: A crowd-based evaluation of abuse response strategies in conversational agents. In: Proceedings of SigDial 2019 (2019). https://doi.org/10.18653/v1/W19-5942
5. Foster, M.E., Stuart-Smith, J.: Social robotics meets sociolinguistics: investigating accent bias and social context in HRI. In: Proceedings of HRI 2023 (2023). https://doi.org/10.1145/3568294.3580063
6. Foster, M.E., et al.: MuMMER: socially intelligent human-robot interaction in public spaces. In: Proceedings of AI-HRI 2019 (2019). http://arxiv.org/abs/1909.06749
7. Friedman, N., Love, K., LC, R., Sabin, J.E., Hoffman, G., Ju, W.: What robots need from clothing. In: Proceedings of DIS 2021 (2021). https://doi.org/10.1145/3461778.3462045
8. Furhat Robotics (2018). https://furhatrobotics.com/press-releases/franny-frankfurt-airports-new-multilingual-robot-concierge-can-help-you-in-over-35-languages/
9. Hone, K.S., Graham, R.: Towards a tool for the subjective assessment of speech system interfaces (SASSI). Natural Lang. Eng. **6**(3-4), 287–303 (2000). https://doi.org/10.1017/S1351324900002497
10. Mbawa, S.Z.: How can a conversational agent (chatbot) be used to detect and prevent suicide based on recognisable suicide behaviours amongst young people with mental disorders? Masters thesis, University of Applied Sciences, Utrecht (2021)

11. Nomura, T., Suzuki, T., Kanda, T., Kato, K.: Measurement of negative attitudes toward robots. Interact. Stud. **7**(3), 437–454 (2006). https://doi.org/10.1075/is.7.3.14nom
12. OpenAI: ChatGPT, OpenAI (2022). https://openai.com/blog/chatgpt/
13. Rasa Inc: Introduction to Rasa Open Source (2022). https://rasa.com/docs/rasa/
14. Stock, R.M., Merkle, M.: Can humanoid service robots perform better than service employees? A comparison of innovative behavior cues. In: Proceedings of the 51st Hawaii International Conference on System Sciences (2018)
15. Völkel, S.T., et al.: Developing a personality model for speech-based conversational agents using the psycholexical approach. In: Proceedings of CHI 2020 (2020). https://doi.org/10.1145/3313831.3376210

RoboSync: Efficient Real-Time Operating System for Social Robots with Customizable Behaviour*

Cheng Tang[1]([envelope])[iD], Yijing Feng[1][iD], and Yue Hu[2][iD]

[1] Department of Electrical and Computer Engineering, University of Waterloo,
N2L3G1 Waterloo, ON, Canada
{c225tang,y263feng}@uwaterloo.ca
[2] Department of Mechanical and Mechatronics Engineering, University of Waterloo,
N2L3G1 Waterloo, ON, Canada
yue.hu@uwaterloo.ca

Abstract. Traditional robotic systems require complex implementations that are not always accessible or easy to use for Human-Robot Interaction (HRI) application developers. With the aim of simplifying the implementation of HRI applications, this paper introduces a novel real-time operating system (RTOS) designed for customizable HRI - RoboSync. By creating multi-level abstraction layers, the system enables users to define complex emotional and behavioral models without needing deep technical expertise. The system's modular architecture comprises a behavior modeling layer, a machine learning plugin configuration layer, a sensor checks customization layer, a scheduler that fits the need of HRI, and a communication and synchronization layer. This approach not only promotes ease of use without highly specialized skills but also ensures real-time responsiveness and adaptability. The primary functionality of the RTOS has been implemented for proof of concept and was tested on a CortexM4 microcontroller, demonstrating its potential for a wide range of lightweight simple-to-implement social robotics applications.

Keywords: Human-Robot Interaction · RTOS · Social Robots

1 Introduction

Human-robot interaction (HRI) is an increasingly important field with applications ranging from education [1] and healthcare [2] to entertainment [3] and personal assistance [4]. Yet, the complexity of state-of-the-art HRI systems, often based on traditional robotics systems and approaches, has created a barrier: they typically require specialized technical expertise for customization and adaptation, effectively reserving their utilization for those with advanced skills.

Especially in social HRI applications, there is a growing need for a platform that allows users to easily define and modify a robot's emotional and behavioral

---

* We Acknowledge the Support of the Natural Sciences and Engineering Research Council of Canada (NSERC), Funding Reference Number RGPIN-2022-03857

responses. Such a platform must balance simplicity and customizability without sacrificing real-time performance and robustness. Robotics involves ongoing customization and adaptability for diverse users. Even basic customizations, like having a robot wave back when a human waves [5], can be intricate, requiring deep sensor data processing, algorithm configuration, and hardware adjustments.

To address these complexities, we developed *RoboSync*[1], a real-time operating system tailored for customizable social robots. The primary objective behind RoboSync is to simplify robotic customization and interaction, with a special focus on social robotics. Central to RoboSync are its multi-level abstraction layers, designed to make the process more user-friendly. Through these layers, users can easily define robot behaviors and states. Using RoboSync, a task that previously required extensive code, like setting up a sensor-based response, can now be achieved with more intuitive constructs, such as "waveDetect", by simply stating the usage of a plugin module when defining the behavior response.

RoboSync adopts a modular approach. We've segmented it into distinct sections, each dedicated to functions like response modeling, integration of machine learning models, algorithm module configuration, and high-level sensor mapping. This modular design ensures the system's adaptability to diverse robotic requirements. At its core, an efficient scheduler and a dedicated communication layer manage these modules. They oversee the system's timely responses and seamless data transfers.

2 Related Work

The Robot Operating System (ROS) [6] stands as a seminal middleware framework that has greatly influenced the robotics community. Not strictly an operating system in the traditional sense, ROS provides a structured communication layer above the host operating system, enabling various software components to communicate seamlessly. Within the domain of Human-Robot Interaction (HRI), ROS has proven valuable as it allows to implement complex actions [7]. Taking as an example service robots in public spaces like malls or airports, these robots need to understand and respond to human actions promptly [8]. Using ROS, robots can collect data using sensors, such as cameras to recognize faces, microphones to process speech, and proximity sensors to detect movement. This data can then be analyzed to understand human intentions. ROS also facilitates robot responses to human stimuli. Using the smach state machine package [9], robots can shift between behaviors-greeting, providing information, or guiding. This fluid interaction is a testament to ROS's capabilities in HRI.

Inspired by ROS, our proposed RTOS also adopts the modular architecture, given the advantage of the package-based structure, which allows for the development, sharing, and reuse of code across various robotics projects. However, ROS has limitations. Its dependence on standard operating systems means it often requires general-purpose computers. This raises costs and limits real-time capabilities. Although ROS 2 attempts to address these real-time limitations, it's

---

[1] Available at https://github.com/hushrilab/RoboSync-HRI-RTOS.

not entirely successful [10]. In addition, even users with a technical background often face a steep learning curve when getting started with ROS, making it less accessible for rapid development in HRI scenarios.

In contrast, our proposed RTOS is specifically designed for microcontrollers, leading to cost savings. Removing the dependency on advanced computing systems, our system reduces costs and simplifies setup. Moreover, our RTOS is optimized for HRI applications, guaranteeing timely interactions while maintaining system flexibility. One notable benefit is the decreased technical complexity; users are not required to have an in-depth understanding of microcontroller programming, thereby making HRI applications more approachable. The need for this approachability is evident in the HRI field. Many professionals have the knowledge to create specific robot behaviors but face challenges when dealing with microcontroller technicalities. Instead of focusing on HRI development, they might spend significant time understanding microcontroller operation. Our RTOS aims to address this, allowing HRI professionals to concentrate on their main objectives without being hindered by hardware complexities.

3   System Architecture

The design of effective HRI systems requires balancing different aspects: they must be flexible enough to adapt to a range of tasks and environments, efficient in real-time performance, and straightforward for users to operate and customize. State-of-the-art solutions in the HRI domain have often leaned heavily in one direction, making sacrifices in other areas. For example, a system optimized for speed might prove inflexible or overly complex for users to modify. Recognizing these challenges, our aim was to design an architecture that harmonized these needs. To this end, we organized the system into distinct modules, each catering to a specific function but designed to work in unison. This modular approach offers several advantages: it allows for independent upgrades or modifications to individual modules without disrupting the entire system, it simplifies debugging, and it makes the system inherently scalable to accommodate future advancements in HRI. In the following sections, we outline the key components of RoboSync's architecture described in the flow chart in Fig. 1.

3.1   High-Level Abstraction Layer

In the vast domain of robotics, two key aspects often shape the interaction dynamics between a human and a robot: the way a robot behaves in response to certain stimuli, and the methods it employs to perceive its environment. Addressing these aspects, our system introduces two primary components: the Behavior Modeling Module and the Sensor Check functions.

The Behavior Modeling Module allows users to define how a robot should act in various situations or states. Whether it's a dance move when it hears a certain sound or a specific light pattern when touched, this module lets users customize these responses with ease by providing a domain-specific language (DSL) tailored

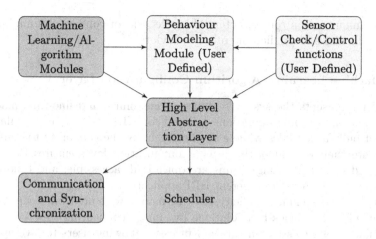

Fig. 1. System Architecture Flowchart for RoboSync

for robot behavior definition, enabling implementation with minimal effort. On the other hand, the Sensor Check functions handle the perceptual side of the interaction, determining how the robot interprets and reacts to its sensory inputs.

The high-level abstraction layer bridges the gap between these processes. This layer serves as an interface between the user-defined modules and the core robotic operations, streamlining the creation process. Through the abstraction layer, users can employ intuitive constructs like "touchLevel" and "jerkLevel" for perceptual tasks, or high-level actuator commands for behavior definitions. The goal is to make robot behavior customization accessible and straightforward, even for individuals without a deep technical background in robotics. On the other hand, it acts as a conduit that relays the outputs from trained algorithms and models by linking with the Machine Learning/Algorithm Modules. This provides further abstraction with very high customization flexibility while abstracting the complexity of advanced algorithms away.

Descending further into the system's operation, the abstraction layer hands over its processed information to the Scheduler, which will be discussed below. This ensures that tasks-whether they are user-defined behaviors, algorithmic responses, or sensor checks-are executed in a timely and efficient manner.

Incorporated within the high-level abstraction layer is a robust mechanism for communication. After parsing and organizing the configuration file, threads are created based on the defined behaviors and sensor checks. The communication layer then facilitates efficient message flow between these threads. The architecture is designed such that sensors communicate exclusively with the processing layer. Once the processing layer interprets the data, it communicates the results to the behavior layer. Depending on the behavior conditions, messages are subsequently dispatched to the control layer for action. This communication hierarchy, inspired by systems like ROS, [6] offers benefits when deployed in a microcontroller setting. It reduces redundant communication, streamlines the flow of information, and optimizes response times. Importantly, by clearly defining the communication routes, potential bottlenecks or conflicts are minimized, ensuring efficient and predictable robot behavior.

3.2 Machine Learning/Algorithm Configuration Layer

This layer represents the system's ability to customize and fine-tune machine learning and algorithmic operations tailored for HRI tasks. It encapsulates a variety of built-in modules while also offering users the capability to configure or integrate their own algorithms. The configuration layer ensures that both built-in and user-defined algorithms are optimized, accessible, and tailored to the specific requirements of different HRI applications.

First, for users seeking simplicity, existing models with predefined capabilities can be employed as black-box solutions by simply configuring this layer. This abstraction streamlines the integration process, allowing users to leverage the algorithms without delving into the intricate details. Secondly, advanced users are free to customize or introduce new models with desired functionalities. This flexibility means that the system can accommodate both quick implementations for general applications and specialized models for unique tasks, ensuring that our platform is versatile and adaptive to diverse user needs.

Key components encompassed within this configuration layer include:

- **Voice Recognition Configuration**: Houses algorithms that employ the latest machine learning techniques for speech recognition, with customizable settings to support different languages.
- **Face Recognition Configuration**: Contains computer vision algorithms optimized for identifying and distinguishing human faces, providing the foundation for personalized interactions.
- **Object Detection Configuration**: Holds trained convolutional neural networks (CNNs) geared towards detecting and classifying objects within the robot's visual scope.
- **User-Defined Algorithm Integration**: Provides users the capability to seamlessly incorporate and configure their own algorithms to suit specific applications or to expand upon existing functionalities.
- **Scheduling Integration**: Enables selective loading of modules and their efficient integration with the system's scheduler for optimized resource allocation.

Outputs from these configured algorithms provide actionable insights and are channeled into the behavior modeling module. This setup facilitates users in customizing robotic responses based on advanced perceptions, thereby simplifying the implementation of sophisticated HRI applications.

3.3 User Defined Behaviour Modeling Module

This module provides users with the capability to craft and customize robot behaviors based on sensor data insights. By leveraging an abstracted high-level set of functions and a domain-specific language (DSL), users can easily translate their insights into meaningful robot actions. The DSL has been specifically designed to be intuitive, allowing users to define conditions and the robot's corresponding responses based on the modeled states, sensor readings, and other contextual factors.

For illustrative purposes, consider the following example using our DSL:

```
WHEN touch LEVEL < 3
DO gentle_response
ELSE
DO aggressive_response
END

DEFINE gentle_response
MOVE arms SLOWLY
PLAY sound "greeting.wav"
END

DEFINE aggressive_response
MOVE arms QUICKLY
PLAY sound "warning.wav"
END
```

In the provided example, a scenario is depicted where the robot's behavior is contingent on the detected touch level. If the touch level is less than 3, the robot enacts a gentle response by moving its arms slowly and playing a greeting sound. Conversely, if the touch level is higher, the robot gives a more aggressive response by moving its arms quickly and sounding a warning. This DSL syntax and design ensure that even those without deep technical expertise can program nuanced robot behaviors.

3.4   User Defined Sensor Check/Control Behavior

This module serves a dual purpose, namely, Sensor Check and Control Behavior:
Sensor Check. At the heart of any robotic system is its ability to perceive the environment. In our architecture, the Sensor Check capability is designed to help users derive more meaningful, high-level insights from raw sensor data. By utilizing customized data processing functions, users can move beyond simple binary readings and instead extract context-rich information tailored to their application's specific needs.

For instance, consider a proximity sensor. While raw readings might simply suggest how close an object is, with the Sensor Check function, users can define parameters that determine if the object is 'very close', 'moderately close', or 'far', making it more intuitive and relevant to their application.
Control Behavior. Control Behavior is closely tied to the Behavioral Modeling Module, acting as a repository where users can define specific robotic actions or sets of actions. Once defined, these behaviors can be called upon in the Behavior Modeling Module to provide a nuanced response based on sensor data and modeled states. For example, if a user wishes to have a robot dance when a certain

sound frequency is detected, instead of repeatedly coding this action, they can define a 'dance' behavior in the Control Behavior module. Subsequently, in the Behavior Modeling Module, they can set conditions such that when the desired sound frequency is detected, the 'dance' behavior is triggered. Together, the Sensor Check and Control Behavior functionalities offer users an extensive toolkit for refining robot interactions, ensuring that they can readily tailor their robots to specific contexts and user needs.

3.5   Scheduler

The scheduler is an integral component in a system, ensuring that multiple tasks and modules operate seamlessly and efficiently. Its primary function is to manage the execution of tasks, which can range from modules in the algorithm layer to sensor checks, behavior control functions, behavior modeling, and other built-in or user-defined algorithms. Users can customize the algorithm threads that need to be loaded: such as voice recognition, emotion modeling, etc.

The scheduler incorporates feedback loops to adjust its scheduling decisions based on system performance and real-time metrics. These feedback mechanisms can provide insights into the system's current state and adapt accordingly to ensure optimal operation. For example, force feedback can be continuously monitored, and if it exceeds a certain threshold, it might indicate potential harm to a human or a robot. In such safety-critical scenarios, these threads have the utmost priority. Embedded within the scheduler are safety-critical threads that constantly run in the background, monitoring various parameters. Should any of these parameters, like the aforementioned force feedback, exceed safe thresholds, the scheduler is designed to intervene immediately. Any ongoing tasks, regardless of their priority, can be preemptively interrupted to address the potential threat, ensuring the safety of both humans and the robot.

3.6   Communication and Synchronization

A central component of successful HRI systems is the communication and synchronization layer. This layer bridges the divide, ensuring that humans and robots not only understand one another but also act in a synchronized, safe, and efficient manner. Within the broader context of HRI, this layer takes on a heightened significance due to the real-time and safety-critical nature of many interactions. Adopting a model similar to ROS, the communication layer can utilize a publish-subscribe paradigm: Different modules or components can publish messages to specific 'topics', while others can 'subscribe' to receive these messages. [6] This structure is highly beneficial for HRI applications, as it enables real-time updates about the robot's state, sensors, or actions to be seamlessly conveyed to the human operator or other relevant systems.

In monitoring addressing safety-critical scenarios, such as where certain parameters, like force feedback, transcend safe limits, the system instantly communicates this anomaly, preemptively halting operation to guarantee safety.

4   Implementation

The essential structure of the system has been implemented on CortexM4 for the purpose of proof of concept. The implementation is available for public access at https://github.com/hushrilab/RoboSync-HRI-RTOS. It has been proven that the time and effort required to develop an equivalent behavior system has been reduced by a significant amount. A publisher and subscriber system has been used similar to ROS. [6]

4.1   High-Level Abstraction Layer

Configuration File Example

```
1   {
2       "sensors": [
3           {"name": "temp_sensor", "type": "I2C", "address
    ": "0x40"},
4           {"name": "proximity_sensor", "type": "GPIO", "
    pin": "5"}
5       ],
6       "actuators": [
7           {"name": "motor_1", "type": "PWM", "pin": "10"}
8       ],
9       "behaviors": [
10          {"name": "temperature_check", "actionv: "
    motor_1"},
11      ],
12      "algorithms": [
13          {"name": "ML_algorithm", "path": "/path/to/
    algorithm/module.so"}
14      ]
15  }
16
```

Listing 1.1. JSON configuration

The High-Level Abstraction Layer (HLAL) serves as a bridge between the intricate details of the microcontroller's hardware interfaces and the higher functionalities required by users. It is designed to enable seamless management of sensors, actuators, behaviors, and algorithms. This abstraction allows users to craft custom behaviors without the necessity of delving deep into the hardware's complexities.

Loading Configuration Files. A key feature of the HLAL is its ability to process JSON configuration files provided by the user. In the initialization phase, the HLAL reads these files, extracting detailed specifications of sensors, actuators, behaviors, and algorithms. The Jansson library aids in parsing these files and the retrieved data is then organized into data structures for subsequent use.

Sensor and Actuator Management. Sensors and actuators defined in the configuration are rigorously managed. The RTOS creates a distinct thread for each entity. Sensor threads primarily focus on polling operations to gather data, while actuator threads await commands. The system provides users with high-level functions for sensors, obscuring the complexities of protocols such as I2C(Inter-Integrated Circuit), SPI(Serial Peripheral Interface), and GPIO(General Purpose Input/Output). Similarly, the actuator command interface abstracts the nuances of underlying protocols, including PWM(Pulse Width Modulation) modulation.

Behavior Management. Managing behaviors involves the Behavior Manager layer of the HLAL, which generates an internal representation for each defined behavior. This layer essentially functions as a mapping system, linking particular sensor outputs or conditions to specific actuator responses. For instance, if sensor data meets a certain condition like a predefined temperature, the Behavior Manager immediately triggers the specified actuator response.

Algorithm Encapsulation. Algorithms specified in the configuration are also seamlessly integrated. The HLAL loads each algorithm-commonly encapsulated as shared object files or distinct modules-into the system memory. These algorithm modules encapsulate the input-output relationships. As an example, a machine learning module might process particular sensor data and produce an output indicating a piece of information or direct an actuator.

4.2 Scheduler

Our proposed system handles scheduling for HRI through specific thread categorizations, automatic priority assignments, and adaptive mechanisms designed specifically for HRI contexts.

Thread Categorization. Threads are distinctly categorized based on their roles defined by the user in RoboSync. Sensor Input Threads are responsible for querying raw data from various sensors, such as cameras, microphones, and touch sensors. Algorithmic Threads handle the data analysis tasks, which include image recognition, voice command parsing, and sentiment analysis. Behavioural Threads interpret the processed data to determine the robot's subsequent actions. Finally, control Threads execute corresponding decisions, resulting in robot movement, vocal outputs, or display changes.

Priority Assignment. When the user defines a series of behaviors each requiring certain inputs (sensor), outputs (motor), and decision logic (algorithm), appropriate priority needs to be assigned to individual threads based on the priority of their parent behavior as well as the threads' categorization. Each individual behavior has a distinct priority number assigned to it so that no two behaviors would ever have conflict, the robot always has only one response to choose at all times. Therefore, both the user-defined behavior priority and the category of thread need to be taken into account. If more than one behavior requires the same thread such as the depth camera data, the priority is calculated only based on the higher priority behavior. In addition, safety checks are defined by the user and given the highest priority, which is normalized as 1. Any thread, be it sensor, processing, decision, or output, that is associated with a safety check has its priority set to 1. This ensures immediate attention, all the threads associated with the safety checks are automatically assigned the highest priority regardless of their other usages. The initial priorities of all the threads are calculated as follows. For each behavior B_i with associated priority, there are linked sensor threads S_i, processing threads P_i, and output threads O_i. Define $T_j^{B_i}$ as a generic thread (it could be S, P, or O) associated with behavior B_i. The priority for each thread, Priority($T_j^{B_i}$), not associated with safety, can be given by:

$$\text{Priority}(T_j^{B_i}) = \max(B_i)$$

where $\max(B_i)$ is the highest priority of all behaviors that require the thread T_j. This ensures that a shared thread inherits the highest priority from all behaviors requiring it. If a thread is associated with a safety check, its priority, regardless of other behaviors, is set to 1.

Adaptive Scheduler for HRI with User Preferences. In human-robot interactions, it's paramount for the system to adapt to the preferences and patterns exhibited by the user. For behaviors that are more frequently triggered, assume that the corresponding threads should be given higher priority to meet the user's expectations in real-time. To model the adaptive behavior of the scheduler, let $P(t)$ be the priority of thread t, which is associated with a particular behavior. Each behavior has a frequency counter $F(b)$ that records the number of times behavior b is triggered over a fixed time window W. The adaptive priority adjustment, based on the frequency of triggering of the associated behavior, is defined as:

$$\Delta P(t) = \alpha \times \frac{F(b)}{W} \tag{1}$$

where α is a scaling factor that determines how aggressively the priority should adapt based on the triggering frequency. Thus, the revised priority for the thread becomes: $P(t) = P(t) + \Delta P(t)$. However, to prevent over-prioritization and maintain system stability, we enforce an upper limit $P(t) \leq P_{\max}$. It's crucial to note that the priority of threads associated with safety checks remains fixed at $P_{\max}$, ensuring that safety is always paramount.

By employing this adaptive mechanism, the scheduler ensures that as certain behaviors become more frequently invoked, the corresponding threads are more likely to be executed promptly, making the robot more responsive to the user's prevalent commands. This dynamic adjustment ensures that the system remains attuned to evolving user patterns and preferences over time.

Safety Checks and Emergency Overrides. By implementing custom high level safety checks and emergency overrides, users have the capability to issue emergency commands or overrides, either through voice commands like "STOP" or physical interventions. These emergency actions are always treated with the highest priority.

4.3 Optimized Communication and Synchronization Layer

In our system, message flow is structured hierarchically, with each layer specifically communicating with the adjacent one. This distinct flow initiates at the sensor level, progressing to the processing layer, subsequently advancing to the behavior layer, and culminating at the control layer. Contrasting this with ROS, where nodes can communicate more freely in a mesh-like network through topics, our linear, layered approach reduces communication overhead and simplifies the message propagation logic [6]. This tailored architecture benefits in microcontroller environments, as it optimizes resource utilization, minimizes latency, and is more suited for systems with constrained computational capabilities [11].

Sensor to Processing Layer Communication. The inception of the data flow starts at the sensor level. Instead of inundating the system with continuous data streams, sensors have been optimized to send messages only when pertinent data changes or events are registered. These messages are then relayed to the processing layer. This approach not only reduces the volume of transmitted data but also ensures that the processing layer remains exclusively engaged in meaningful computations.

$$M_{sp}(t) = \begin{cases} \text{Sensor Data,} & \text{if significant event detected} \\ \text{null,} & \text{otherwise} \end{cases} \tag{2}$$

where $M_{sp}(t)$ represents the message transmitted from the sensor to the processing layer at time t.

Processing to Behavior Layer Communication. Once the raw data undergoes necessary computations and transformations in the processing layer, the results are then encapsulated into messages directed towards the behavior layer. Only relevant insights, like detected objects or interpreted commands, are sent, ensuring that the behavior layer isn't swamped with extraneous details: $M_{pb}(t) = f(M_{sp}(t))$, where f is the processing function that transforms the raw sensor data into information suitable for the behavior layer.

Behavior to Control Layer Communication. The behavior layer, upon interpreting the processed data, determines the robot's appropriate course of action. If a specific behavior is triggered, a message is passed on to the control layer dictating the necessary movements or actions. This segregation ensures that the control layer remains abstracted from raw or processed data and receives only high-level commands: $M_{bc}(t) = g(M_{pb}(t))$, where g is the function in the behavior layer that translates processed information into actionable commands.

Safety-Critical Checks. In the interest of heightened safety in our Human-Robot Interaction (HRI) system, the communication layer monitors safety-critical parameters that are continuously validated against predetermined benchmarks, exemplified by the $SAFETY\_THRESHOLD$ for aspects like force feedback. Should any parameter overshoot these limits, the system is designed to immediately dispatch alerts to the pertinent components, effectively pausing operations. This pivotal feature ensures the unwavering safety of both the human user and the robot, irrespective of the ongoing tasks or the environment.

$$\text{SafetyAlert}(t) = \begin{cases} \text{Alert and Halt,} & \text{if } M_{sp}(t) > SAFETY\_THRESHOLD \\ \text{Continue,} & \text{otherwise} \end{cases}$$

$$(3)$$

where SafetyAlert(t) represents the safety function that checks the sensor data against the predefined threshold at a specific time t.

5 Conclusion

The presented research introduces an RTOS architecture designed specifically for optimized human-robot interaction (HRI). This architecture incorporates multiple layers of abstraction, ensuring both cost-effectiveness and user accessibility, even for those with limited technical expertise. It allows for straightforward customization of robot behaviors through a domain-specific language, supported by foundational HRI modules which include functions like voice recognition. The integrated approach combines various system components, from behavior modeling to synchronization, establishing a cohesive system that efficiently processes human inputs and produces timely robotic responses. In essence, this proposed RTOS architecture contributes to the HRI field by enhancing accessibility, adaptability, and potential for broader user engagement. In future work, we will refine the system modularity, explore practical applications, and evaluate performance in varied settings considering user feedback.

References

1. de Souza Jeronimo, B., de Albuquerque Wheler, A.P., de Oliveira, J.P.G., et al.: Comparing social robot embodiment for child musical education. J. Intell. Robot. Syst. **105**, 28 (2022). https://doi.org/10.1007/s10846-022-01604-5
2. Pinto-Bernal, M.J., Cespedes, N., Castro, P., et al.: Physical human-robot interaction influence in ASD therapy through an affordable soft social robot. J. Intell. Robot. Syst. **105**, 67 (2022). https://doi.org/10.1007/s10846-022-01617-0
3. Park, J.W., Lee, H.S., Chung, M.J.: Generation of realistic robot facial expressions for human robot interaction. J. Intell. Robot. Syst. **78**, 443–462 (2015)
4. Ringwald, M., Theben, P., Gerlinger, K., et al.: How should your assistive robot look like? A scoping review on embodiment for assistive robots. J. Intell. Robot. Syst. **107**, 12 (2023). https://doi.org/10.1007/s10846-022-01781-3
5. Canal, G., Escalera, S., Angulo, C.: A real-time human-robot interaction system based on gestures for assistive scenarios. Comput. Vis. Image Underst. **149**, 65–77 (2016)
6. Quigley, M., et al.: ROS: an open-source Robot Operating System. In: ICRA Workshop on Open Source Software, vol. 3 (2009)
7. Mohamed, Y., Lemaignan, S.: ROS for human-robot interaction. In: IEEE/RSJ International Conference on Intelligent Robots and Systems, pp. 3020–3027 (2021)

8. Mintrom, M., Sumartojo, S., Kulić, D., Tian, L., Carreno-Medrano, P., Allen, A.: Robots in public spaces Implications for policy design. Policy Des. Pract. **5**(2), 123–139 (2022)
9. Bohren, J., Cousins, S.: The Smach high-level executive [ROS news]. IEEE Robot. Autom. Mag. **17**(4), 18–20 (2010)
10. Macenski, S., Foote, T., Gerkey, B., Lalancette, C., Woodall, W.: Robot operating system 2: design, architecture, and uses in the wild. Sci. Robot. **7**(66), eabm6074 (2022)
11. Anh, T.N.B., Tan, S.L.: Real-time operating systems for small microcontrollers. IEEE Micro **29**(5), 30–45 (2009)

Do We have to Say this is a "Telepresence Robot"? Exploration of Factors of Face and Speech Style Through Telecommunication via Robot

Nungduk Yun[1,2(✉)] and Seiji Yamada[1,2]

[1] The Graduate University for Advanced Studies (SOKENDAI), Tokyo, Japan
{ndyun,seiji}@nii.ac.jp
[2] National Institute of Informatics, Tokyo, Japan

Abstract. Communication technology has improved and become diverse in terms of content and form of functions, and telepresence robots are one type of such technology. These robots are used in an expanding variety of cases. One example of an expanding application is the ability to enable even individuals with disabilities to work and go outside using telepresence robots equipped with human and synthesized speech capabilities. Therefore, we wanted to explore a general case of telecommunication that uses synthesized speech. We carried out a web-based experiment and conducted a two-way ANOVA (robot face: human face, robot face; speech style: human speech, synthesized speech). We found that participants did not feel a human presence because most of the main effect was found for speech style, and they were not told that the robot was controlled remotely by a human. However, even when anthropomorphism was low, participants were willing to follow recommendations and to engage in trust.

Keywords: Telepresence robot · Embodiment · Speech Style · Synthesized Speech · Anthropomorphism · Social Presence · Trust

1 Introduction

Nowadays, the use of telepresence robots is becoming popular, and a lot of uses cases are appearing. Lee et al. suggested a mobile embodiment, that is, a telepresence robot that enables remote workers to live and work with local coworkers similar to how they interact in real life [14]. People are using these robots for long-distance relationships [28] and to join conferences [19]. When COVID-19 patients had to isolate during the pandemic, families were able to meet them using a telepresence robot [15]. With telepresence robots, the appearance of the face is an important factor that has one of the biggest effects on whether people feel the presence of a person [6,20,22]. Meanwhile, previous research on movement with telepresence robots has shown that robots that can express themselves socially through movement are more immersive and desirable than those that do not move [2]. In the case of school, telepresence robots increase social presence between students

A. Al. Ali et al. (Eds.): ICSR 2023, LNAI 14454, pp. 217–229, 2024.
https://doi.org/10.1007/978-981-99-8718-4_19

and may facilitate communication and cooperation [22]. Fitter et al. did a comparison experiment using a telepresence robot between expressive arm motion, non-expressive arm motion, and light expression [10]. As a result, participants felt an advantage toward light expression, and the use of motion increased the perception of the robot being human-like [10]. The projected face telepresence robot performs synchronous actions, and the facial expressions of the remote user increase agreement during conversation [29]. Comparing robot and smartphone embodiments, we found that, for anthropomorphism, the smartphone is higher than the robot, but no difference could be found for social presence [30]. However, robot embodiment done using OriHime-D has been demonstrated to be important for joining society, enabling even people with disabilities to work and go outside [24]. Nakanishi et al. used a robot embodiment with a robot hand so remote users and local users could shake hands [17]. They found that mutual touch improves the feeling of being close [17].

We believe that physical robot embodiment holds significance based on the findings of these research [11,24,27]. Their work revealed that a portion of telepresence robot users comprises individuals diagnosed with ALS (amyotrophic lateral sclerosis). These patients typically rely on an EyeLink board due to declining speech [9]. However, when utilizing the telepresence robot OriHime-D, they can communicate using synthesized speech through a specialized user interface [24]. This choice of embodiment is rooted in the observation that service robots with a high level of anthropomorphism positively influence users' willingness to follow recommendations [1].

These days, in human-robot interaction, trust has become an important factor. Trust development with anthropomorphism has two dimensions, competence and warmth, which are determinants of trust development, and as a result, they are important and show that anthropomorphism may increase users' trust in HRI [7]. Salahzadeh et al. developed LEO and presented findings related to human-robot trust in police work using a tele-operated communicative robot [5]. Control of a telepresence robot by a local user could bring about interpersonal trust via physical embodiment and control of the system in mediated communication [21]. A positive correlational relationship between anthropomorphism and trust was found by Natarajan and Gombolay [18].

Therefore, we wondered whether, after self-introduction, participants will follow recommendations and continue to have a social presence even using synthesized speech in a general case. In our study, we explore using a telepresence robot and consider the factors of face and speech-style. We also explore trust in terms of recommendation, social presence, and anthropomorphism.

2   Hypotheses

High anthropomorphism increases willingness to follow recommendations [1], and we wonder how trust affects recommendation. Additionally, in a comparison of types of embodiment involving moving, static, and smartphone embodiments, smartphone was highest, and second was a static robot [30]. However, physical embodiment is seen as necessary to join in social activities [11,24,27]. Our expectation is that, if the following hypotheses are true, a motionless robot embodiment that features the items below will be the most effective.

- **H1**: High anthropomorphism has a positive effect on willingness to follow recommendations.
- **H2**: High anthropomorphism has a positive effect on trust.
- **H3**: Depending on the speech style, we expect social presence to differ in terms of effect.

3 Experiment Design

We conducted an experiment with a two-way ANOVA using a 2×2 (robot face: human face, robot face; speech style: human speech, synthesized speech) between-participant design. To explore the different ways people could interact with our design, we used G*Power sample size calculation ($n = 128$, with effect size $= 0.5$) and ran our experiment using online questionnaire surveys (Google form) after showing videos. Participants were recruited from Yahoo! Japan Crowdsourcing. Furthermore, live and video-based HRI trials are known to be broadly equivalent in most cases [26]. However, in some cases, people may empathize less with video-based HRI trials compared with in-person experiments [13,23].

3.1 System Overview

In our experiment, we used a humanoid robot called Rapiro[1], and the system was mostly similar to that of Yun et al. The Arduino and Raspberry Pi boards in the robot enable users (developers) to communicate with it simply by sending command signals from a PC, and they also allow for the system to be extended easily. These are the reasons we used this robot as the telepresence robot for our experiment. For the experiment, we fixed Rapiro's eye color to blue to avoid color bias and modified the head so that it could show a remote user's face similar to a video teleconference system.

Rapiro has 12° of freedom (DoF), a USB camera, a microphone in its forehead, and a speaker in its head. We modified the head of another Rapiro with a 5-inch portable monitor to show the face of a remote user; the head was made of PLA using a 3D printer. This Rapiro also had 12 DoF, a USB camera, a microphone, and a speaker. However, in this study, we did not move any of the motors.

3.2 Procedure

The participants watched two videos from four different conditions as shown in Figs. 1 and 2. In all conditions, no non-verbal communication and only verbal

---
[1] http://www.rapiro.com/.

communication were included with a display that showed the remote user's face like an ordinary video-teleconference system that uses a robot embodiment like the telepresence robot Beams. The conditions are explained in Table 1. Condition 1 showed the remote user's face like an ordinary video-teleconference system with human speech. Condition 2 was similar to condition 1 but used synthesized speech. Condition 3 showed a robot face with human speech. Condition 4 showed a robot face with synthesized speech. For the synthesized speech, we used a web service for generating text to voice[2].

Fig. 1. Rapiro: conditions 3 and 4

Fig. 2. Modified Rapiro: conditions 1 and 2

We created a set of self-introduction and tour recommendation videos in which a remote operator introduces themselves via telepresence robot. The self-introduction and tour recommendation scenarios were referred from Abdi et al. [1], and there were two different types of language style: informative and emotive; however, language style does not affect compliance [1]. First, we did not tell participants that this robot was remote controlled by a human. They watched a self-introduction video, and after they finished watching the video, they were asked

---

[2] https://ondoku3.com/ja/.

Table 1. Experiment conditions.

Condition	Face	Speech style
Condition 1	Human face	Human speech
Condition 2	Human face	Synthesized speech
Condition 3	Robot face	Human speech
Condition 4	Robot face	Synthesized speech

Table 2. Godspeed Questionnaire

	ANTHROPOMORPHISM	
1	Fake	Natural
2	Machinelike	Humanlike
3	Unconscious	Conscious
4	Artificial	Lifelike

to rate their agreement in two questionnaire surveys using Godspeed regarding anthropomorphism [3] and social presence [4]. Second, we showed the other video on tour recommendation, and when they finished, we asked them to answer two questionnaires regarding trust and recommendation. When they finished the experiment, there was an additional comment or question space. We paid 55 yen (about 0.50 US), and the average time to complete the procedure was about 15 min.

3.3 Measurement

To measure the dependent variables, that is, social presence, anthropomorphism, trust, and follow recommendation, we used five different questionnaires. All the answers ranged between (1) strongly disagree and (7) strongly agree.

The social presence scale by Biocca el al. [4] was used to measure social presence: (1) It felt like we were in the same space, (2) the conversation felt like a real face-to-face meeting, and (3) I felt like I was present with my partner. These three statements were obtained from Schouten et al. [22]. For anthropomorphism, we used Godspeed, which is a standardized measurement tool for HRI [3]. There are five key concepts for the measurement; anthropomorphism, animacy, likeability, perceived intelligence, and perceived safety, but in this study, we used only the anthropomorphism section, listed in Table 2. To measure trust, we use two mixed questionnaires. One used a scale by Ullman et al. featuring three items to determine trust performance: capable, reliable, and dependable [25]. Some of the other scales were not a fit for our study. Last, we used a scale for emotional trust by Komiak et al., which had three items: secure, comfortable, and content [12]. For follow recommendation, we referred to Abdi et al.'s questionnaire and changed a question to match our study [1]. We asked participants,

"Please indicate how likely you would be to follow a one-day itinerary in Tokyo provided by a robot."

3.4 Participants

A total of 200 participants took part in the experiment online (male: 146, female: 54). Their ages ranged from 20 to 78 (M = 46.365, SD = 11.081). We recruited the participants from Yahoo! Crowd-sourcing, which is a service provided by Yahoo! Japan.

4 Result

To test our hypotheses, we used a two-way analysis of variance (ANOVA) with a between-participants design. Before the data collection, we determined the sample size on the basis of power analysis. Our parameter for G*Power [8] used effect sizes of $f = 0.25$, $a = 0.05$, and power = 0.8. For the G*Power calculation, the sampling size was 128. For each condition, 32 participants were used for

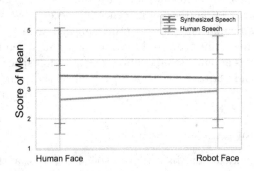

Fig. 3. Average scores for speech style for each condition in experiment. Social presence is dependent value.

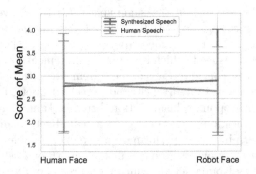

Fig. 4. Average scores for speech style for each condition in experiment. Anthropomorphism is dependent value.

analysis. In total, 200 participants joined this experiment. We encountered some errors, so to match the sample size, we randomly picked 32 participants using Excel.

The ANOVA results are shown in Tables 4, 6, 10, and 8. The means and standard deviations (S.D.) for all dependent variables are shown from Figs. 3, 4, 5 and 6 and in Tables 5, 3, 9, and 7. For anthropomorphism, there was no significant difference at all. For presence, there was a significant difference between the two factors. We found that the main effect was significant only for the speech-style factor ($p < 0.0106$, $\eta_p^2 = 0.0616$). Furthermore, speech style with synthesized speech was the highest. For follow recommendation, there was no significant difference at all. For trust, there was a significant difference between the two factors. We found that the main effect was significant only for the speech-style factor ($p < 0.0347$, $\eta_p^2 = 0.0355$), and speech style with synthesized speech was also the highest. When asking about social presence for the 2nd time, there was a significant difference between the two factors. We found that the main effect was significant only for the speech-style factor ($p < 0.0345$, $\eta_p^2 = 0.0355$), and, again, speech style with synthesized speech was the highest.

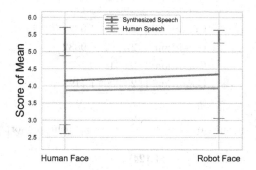

Fig. 5. Average scores for speech style for each condition in experiment. Follow recommendation is dependent value.

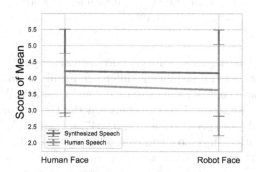

Fig. 6. Average scores for speech-style for each condition in experiment. Trust is dependent value.

5   Discussion

Regarding the three hypotheses set before the experiment, here are summary of results. Regarding **H1**, that is, high anthropomorphism has a positive effect on willingness to follow recommendations, we found that there was no significant difference at all for anthropomorphism, and we see that the mean values were all low in Table 3. However, for follow recommendation, when we look at Table 9, most of the mean values were higher than the average at 3.5, and the highest was for condition 4. This means that most conditions showed a willingness follow recommendations. Therefore, this hypothesis was partially supported since no significant difference could be found for anthropomorphism, and the mean values were low, but for follow recommendation in Table 9, most of the mean values were high. We expected condition 1 and condition 2's mean values to be higher since Yun et al. [30] found that, for anthropomorphism, the static condition was higher when compared only with a motion condition.

Table 3. Mean and S.D. of anthropomorphism.

Condition	Mean	S.D.
Condition 1	2.8438	1.0828
Condition 2	2.7812	0.9832
Condition 3	2.6641	0.9622
Condition 4	2.8906	1.1197

Table 4. Results of two-way ANOVA for anthropomorphism.

Source	F(1,124)	p	η_p^2
Face	2.457	0.8485 n.s	0.0003
Speech style	0.1994	0.6560 n.s	0.0016
Interaction	0.6191	0.4329 n.s	0.0050

$^*p < .05,\ ^{**}p < 0.01$

Regarding **H2**, that is, high anthropomorphism has a positive effect on trust, we found that there was no significant difference at all for anthropomorphism, and we even see that the mean values were all low in Table 3. We found that, for trust, there was a significant difference between the two factors, with a significant main effect only for speech style ($p < 0.0347$, $\eta_p^2 = 0.0355$). This hypothesis was partially supported since no significant difference could be found for anthropomorphism, and the mean values were low as shown in Table 3, but for trust, when we look at Table 7, most of the mean values were high.

Regarding **H3**, that is, depending on the speech style, we expect social presence to differ in terms of effect, this hypothesis did hold since there was a significant difference between the two factors for social presence. We found that the main effect was significant for the speech-style factor ($p < 0.0106$, $\eta_p^2 = 0.0616$). For H1 and H2, we assumed that participants may feel the robot's presence more than the human's because there was no significant difference between the factors for anthropomorphism, and there was a significant difference between the two factors for social presence related to speech style. Furthermore, the mean values for speech style with synthesized speech were higher than the average. Therefore, we assume that participants did not feel a human presence in this experiment. Even though the mean value for anthropomorphism was low for all conditions, as shown in Table 3, the participants may have been willing to follow the recommendation since all of the mean values were higher than the average, as shown in Table 9, with trust since there was a significant difference between the two factors, with a significant main effect for speech style ($p < 0.0347$, $\eta_p^2 = 0.0355$), as shown in Table 7. There are certain generalities among our results, and the study presented here has limitations that may affect these generalities.

Table 5. Mean and S.D. of social presence.

Condition	Mean	S.D.
Condition 1	2.6458	1.1638
Condition 2	3.4583	1.6192
Condition 3	2.9271	1.2493
Condition 4	3.3750	1.4186

Table 6. Results of two-way ANOVA for social presence.

Source	F(1,124)	p	η_p^2
Face	0.1660	0.6844 ns	0.0013
Speech style	6.7337	0.0106 *	0.0515
Interaction	0.5634	0.4543 ns	0.0045

$^*p < .05$, $^{**}p < 0.01$

Table 7. Mean and S.D. of trust.

Condition	Mean	S.D.
Condition 1	3.7865	0.9776
Condition 2	4.2135	1.2925
Condition 3	3.6354	1.4075
Condition 4	4.1615	1.3296

6   Limitations

First, our use of Rapiro as the robot platform might have affected the generality since we only experimented with two particular robots. The findings obtained with our robot embodiment might not necessarily be generalizable to other types of robotic embodiment [16]. In-person experiments and video-based HRI trials are known to be broadly equivalent in most cases [26]. However, in some cases, people may empathize less with video-based HRI trials compared with in-person experiments [13,23]. Second, there was lack of support for the self-introduction because we assume that people give self-introductions in daily life. Moreover, participants commented that the sound volume in the human speech videos was low compared with the synthesized speech. As future work, we should divide participants into two groups, one in which we tell them that the robot is controlled by a human, and one in which we do not. Therefore, we could compare the two groups and see how this affects the participants. Last, there was lack of generality for the speech-style factor because we used only a male voice in the experiment, and few participants had difficulty hearing due to the volume of the voice and the recording devices.

Table 8. Results of two-way ANOVA for trust.

Source	F(1,124)	p	η_p^2
Face	0.2071	0.6498 ns	0.0017
Speech style	4.5599	0.0347 *	0.0355
Interaction	0.0492	0.8249 ns	0.0004

$^*p < .05, ^{**}p < 0.01$

Table 9. Mean and S.D. of follow recommendation.

Condition	Mean	S.D.
Condition 1	3.8750	1.0080
Condition 2	4.1562	1.5473
Condition 3	3.9375	1.3183
Condition 4	4.3438	1.2854

Table 10. Results of two-way ANOVA for follow recommendation.

Source	F(1,124)	p	η_p^2
Face	0.2941	0.5886 ns	0.0024
Speech style	2.2241	0.1384 ns	0.0176
Interaction	0.0735	0.7867 ns	0.0006

$^*p < .05, ^{**}p < 0.01$

7 Conclusion

Theses days, varieties of tools for communication technology have evolved, and telepresence robots are becoming common too. In general, telepresence robots enable robot-mediated interactions, making telecommunication possible with non-verbal and verbal behavior cues in robot- and computer-mediated communication. This time, we conducted a two-way ANOVA with a between-participant design (robot face: human face, robot face; speech style: human speech, synthesized speech). Since H1 and H2 were partially supported but H3 did hold, we assume that participants did not feel a human presence in this experiment because the mean values for anthropomorphism were low, and most of the main effect was found for speech style. Therefore, this study might contribute to one of user's case for telepresence robot's with disabilities and diversity.

References

1. Abdi, E., Tojib, D., Seong, A.K., Pamarthi, Y., Millington-Palmer, G.: A study on the influence of service robots' level of anthropomorphism on the willingness of users to follow their recommendations. Sci. Rep. **12**(1), 15266 (2022). https://doi.org/10.1038/s41598-022-19501-0

2. Adalgeirsson, S.O., Breazeal, C.: MeBot: a robotic platform for socially embodied presence. In: 5th ACM/IEEE International Conference on Human-Robot Interaction, HRI 2010, pp. 15–22 (2010). https://doi.org/10.1145/1734454.1734467

3. Bartneck, C., Kuli, D., Croft, E.: Measurement instruments for the anthropomorphism, animacy, likeability, perceived intelligence, and perceived safety of robots, pp. 71–81 (2009). https://doi.org/10.1007/s12369-008-0001-3

4. Biocca, F., Nowak, K.: Plugging your body into the telecommunication system: mediated embodiment, media interfaces, and social virtual environments. Commun. Technol. Soc., 407–447 (2001)

5. Bordbar, F., Salehzadeh, R., Cousin, C., Griffin, D.J., Jalili, N.: Analyzing human-robot trust in police work using a teleoperated communicative robot. In: 2021 30th IEEE International Conference on Robot & Human Interactive Communication (RO-MAN), pp. 919–924 (2021)

6. Choi, M., Kornfield, R., Takayama, L., Mutlu, B.: Movement matters: effects of motion and mimicry on perception of similarity and closeness in robot-mediated communication, pp. 325–335 (2017)

7. Christoforakos, L., Gallucci, A., Surmava-Große, T., Ullrich, D., Diefenbach, S.: Can robots earn our trust the same way humans do? A systematic exploration of competence, warmth, and anthropomorphism as determinants of trust development in HRI. Front. Robot. AI **8**, 640444 (2021)

8. Erdfelder, E., FAul, F., Buchner, A., Lang, A.G.: Statistical power analyses using G*Power 3.1: tests for correlation and regression analyses. Behav. Res. Methods **41**(4), 1149–1160 (2009). https://doi.org/10.3758/BRM.41.4.1149

9. Eshghi, M., Yunusova, Y., Connaghan, K.P., Perry, B.J., Maffei, M.F., Berry, J.D., Zinman, L., Kalra, S., Korngut, L., Genge, A., Dionne, A., Green, J.R.: Rate of speech decline in individuals with amyotrophic lateral sclerosis. Sci. Rep. **12**(1), 15713 (2022)

10. Fitter, N.T., Joung, Y., Demeter, M., Hu, Z., Matarić, M.J.: Design and evaluation of expressive turn-taking hardware for a telepresence robot. In: 2019 28th IEEE International Conference on Robot and Human Interactive Communication (RO-MAN), pp. 1–8 (2019). https://doi.org/10.1109/RO-MAN46459.2019.8956413

11. Kanetsuna, T., et al.: Interaction in remote peddling using avatar robot by people with disabilities. In: Proceedings of the 10th International Conference on Human-Agent Interaction, HAI '22, pp. 281–283. Association for Computing Machinery, New York (2022)

12. Komiak, S., Benbasat, I.: The effects of personalization and familiarity on trust and adoption of recommendation agents. MIS Quart. **30**, 941–960 (2006). https://doi.org/10.2307/25148760

13. Kwak, S.S., Kim, Y., Kim, E., Shin, C., Cho, K.: What makes people empathize with an emotional robot?: The impact of agency and physical embodiment on human empathy for a robot. In: 2013 IEEE RO-MAN, pp. 180–185 (2013)

14. Lee, M.K., Takayama, L.: "Now, I Have a Body": uses and social norms for mobile remote presence in the workplace, pp. 33–42 (2011). https://doi.org/10.1145/1978942.1978950'

15. Lociciro, A., Guillon, A., Bodet-Contentin, L.: A telepresence robot in the room of a COVID-19 patient can provide virtual family presence. Can. J. Anaesth. **68**(11), 1705–1706 (2021)

16. Mollahosseini, A., Abdollahi, H., Sweeny, T.D., Cole, R., Mahoor, M.H.: Role of embodiment and presence in human perception of robots' facial cues. Int. J. Hum Comput Stud. **116**(April), 25–39 (2018). https://doi.org/10.1016/j.ijhcs.2018.04.005

17. Nakanishi, H., Tanaka, K., Wada, Y.: Remote handshaking: touch enhances video-mediated social telepresence. In: Conference on Human Factors in Computing Systems - Proceedings, pp. 2143–2152 (2014)

18. Natarajan, M., Gombolay, M.: Effects of anthropomorphism and accountability on trust in human robot interaction. In: Proceedings of the 2020 ACM/IEEE International Conference on Human-Robot Interaction, HRI '20, pp. 33–42. Association for Computing Machinery, New York (2020)

19. Neustaedter, C., Venolia, G., Procyk, J., Hawkins, D.: To beam or not to beam: a study of remote telepresence attendance at an academic conference. In: CSCW '16, pp. 418–431. Association for Computing Machinery, New York (2016). https://doi.org/10.1145/2818048.2819922

20. Rae, I., Mutlu, B., Takayama, L.: Bodies in motion. In: Proceedings of the 32nd Annual ACM Conference on Human Factors in Computing Systems - CHI '14, pp. 2153–2162. ACM Press, New York (2014). https://doi.org/10.1145/2556288.2557047

21. Rae, I., Takayama, L., Mutlu, B.: In-body experiences: embodiment, control, and trust in robot-mediated communication. In: Proceedings of the SIGCHI Conference on Human Factors in Computing Systems, CHI '13, pp. 1921–1930. Association for Computing Machinery, New York (2013). https://doi.org/10.1145/2470654.2466253

22. Schouten, A.P., Portegies, T.C., Withuis, I., Willemsen, L.M., Mazerant-Dubois, K.: Robomorphism: examining the effects of telepresence robots on between-student cooperation. Comput. Hum. Behav. **126**, 106980 (2022). https://doi.org/10.1016/j.chb.2021.106980, https://www.sciencedirect.com/science/article/pii/S0747563221003034

23. Seo, S.H., Geiskkovitch, D., Nakane, M., King, C., Young, J.E.: Poor thing! would you feel sorry for a simulated robot? a comparison of empathy toward a physical and a simulated robot. In: Proceedings of the Tenth Annual ACM/IEEE International Conference on Human-Robot Interaction, HRI '15, pp. 125–132. Association for Computing Machinery, New York (2015)
24. Takeuchi, K., Yamazaki, Y., Yoshifuji, K.: Avatar work: Telework for disabled people unable to go outside by using avatar robots. In: Companion of the 2020 ACM/IEEE International Conference on Human-Robot Interaction, pp. 53–60 (2020). https://doi.org/10.1145/3371382.3380737
25. Ullman, D., Malle, B.F.: MDMT: multi-dimensional measure of trust. https://research.clps.brown.edu/SocCogSci/Measures/MDMT_v2.pdf. Accessed 27 Mar 2023
26. Woods, S.N., Walters, M.L., Koay, K.L., Dautenhahn, K.: Methodological issues in HRI: a comparison of live and video-based methods in robot to human approach direction trials. In: Proceedings - IEEE International Workshop on Robot and Human Interactive Communication, pp. 51–58 (2006). https://doi.org/10.1109/ROMAN.2006.314394
27. Yamazaki, Y., et al.: Meta avatar robot Cafe: linking physical and virtual cybernetic avatars to provide physical augmentation for people with disabilities. In: ACM SIGGRAPH 2022 Emerging Technologies, No. Article 6 in SIGGRAPH '22, pp. 1–2. Association for Computing Machinery, New York (2022)
28. Yang, L., Neustaedter, C.: Our house: living long distance with a telepresence robot. Proc. ACM Hum.-Comput. Interact. 2(CSCW), 1–18 (2018)
29. Yonezu, S., Osawa, H.: Telepresence robot with behavior synchrony: Merging the emotions and behaviors of users. In: RO-MAN 2017–26th IEEE International Symposium on Robot and Human Interactive Communication 2017-January, pp. 213–218 (2017). https://doi.org/10.1109/ROMAN.2017.8172304
30. Yun, N., Yamada, S.: Physical embodiment vs. smartphone: which influences presence and anthropomorphism most in telecommunication? In: 2022 31st IEEE International Conference on Robot and Human Interactive Communication (RO-MAN), pp. 1065–1070 (2022)

Implementing Pro-social Rule Bending in an Elder-Care Robot Environment

Rajitha Ramanayake$^{(\boxtimes)}$ ⓘ and Vivek Nallur ⓘ

School of Computer Science, University College Dublin, Dublin, Republic of Ireland
rajitha.ramanayakemahantha@ucdconnect.ie, vivek.nallur@ucd.ie

Abstract. Many ethical issues arise when robots are introduced into elder-care settings. When ethically charged situations occur, robots ought to be able to handle them appropriately. Some experimental approaches use (top-down) moral generalist approaches, like Deontology and Utilitarianism, to implement ethical decision-making. Others have advocated the use of bottom-up approaches, such as learning algorithms, to learn ethical patterns from human behaviour. Both approaches have their shortcomings when it comes to real-world implementations. Human beings have been observed to use a hybrid form of ethical reasoning called Pro-Social Rule Bending, where top-down rules and constraints broadly apply, but in particular situations, certain rules are temporarily bent. This paper reports on implementing such a hybrid ethical reasoning approach in elder-care robots. We show through simulation studies that it leads to better upholding of human values such as autonomy, whilst not sacrificing beneficence.

Keywords: Elder-care robots · Machine ethics · Ethical decision making · Ethical governor · Rule bending

1 Introduction

The world faces a growing number of aged people. The use of robots has been proposed as a solution to the rising problem of caring for the elderly. As a result, many elder-care robots with different abilities are available in the market [9]. Empirical studies have concluded that the stakeholders in the elder-care environment find many ethical concerns regarding the delegation of work from human care-workers to robots [9]. Hence, we would like these robots to have the capacity to act ethically, in their work environment. Ramanayake and Nallur have argued [6] that some of these ethical concerns, such as privacy, wellbeing, autonomy, and availability, require implementations that take concerns of various stakeholders (e.g., patients, care-workers, family, etc) into consideration. Any decision-making mechanism used by the robot, apart from being functionally adequate, must also evaluate the impact of the decision on the ethical concerns.

The field of machine-implemented ethics can roughly be categorised into three, based on the engineering approach of the ethical decision-making system.

A. Al. Ali et al. (Eds.): ICSR 2023, LNAI 14454, pp. 230–239, 2024.
https://doi.org/10.1007/978-981-99-8718-4_20

These three approaches are namely: Top-down, Bottom-up, and Hybrid [12]. Many traditional generalist ethical theories of the world (e.g., deontological ethics, legal codes, and utilitarian ethics) and the computational systems that adapted those follow top-down decision-making. In this approach, the designers of the systems try to foresee decision points, and decide what is ethical (or not) (e.g. [3]), and programme them into the system. Most current implementations of this approach use logic frameworks or simulations to reason out the ethical acceptability of a particular behaviour. In a bottom-up approach, the system is designed with social and cognitive processes which interact with each other, and the environment. Using these interactions, or from supervision, it is expected to learn what is ethical (or not) and behave accordingly. Hence, ethical decisions made by these systems are not guided by any ethical theory. Implementations that follow this approach use algorithms such as social choice theory and voting-based methods, and Artificial Neural Networks to capture ethical patterns of the environments [10].

The main shortcoming of the top-down approach is that it can only guarantee ethical behaviour in relatively small and closed systems where the designers can know all the possible states of the system. In contrast, systems designed through the bottom-up approach require complex cognitive and social process models, a large amount of reliable and accurate data, and a comprehensive knowledge model of the world to learn intricate social constructs such as ethics [5,8]. The hybrid approach to implementing ethical machines is considered to be a good alternative to overcome the shortcomings of the other approaches [12]. The key idea behind this approach is to combine the flexibility and evolving nature of the bottom-up approach with the value, duty and principle-oriented nature of the top-down approach to create a better, more reliable system.

Real-world robot application domains such as the domain of care do not admit neat ethical theorisation. Kantian and rights-based ethics, and utilitarian ethics have been pointed out as being inadequate [5] in real-world care settings. However, most computational ethics implementations in robots in literature [3, 11] use such theorisation. Hence, some argue that a good ethical reasoner should be able to step *out* of existing ethical theoretical frameworks, but *only* when necessary [1]. Pro-social rule bending (PSRB) has been identified by Morrison [4] as the mechanism by which human beings (in other contexts) step outside of rigid ethical constraints. PSRB is defined as *intentional violation of a rule with the purpose of elevating the welfare of one or more stakeholders* [4]. It has been suggested that PSRB could be a good (and unexplored) contender for real-world ethical dilemmas [8] (such as scenarios introduced in [7]).

This paper reports on an implementation of PSRB and how it affects decision-making in a specific dilemma, that affects the elderly in an assisted living environment. The presented ethical governor model uses expert knowledge and case-based reasoning (CBR) to analyse rule-bending behaviours, and contest the top-down rule system's decisions when required. By doing so it makes the rule system behave more desirably when it encounters infrequent circumstances [6]. Our model of PSRB capable ethical governor employs the hybrid approach in the sense that we use the knowledge acquired bottom-up to contest the top-down rules that are programmed into the system at design time.

2   An Implementation of PSRB Capable Ethical Governor

Although PSRB is not limited to elder-care environments, this paper attempts to bring together two novel concepts: concern for human autonomy, as well as implementing a hybrid mechanism to perform ethical reasoning. As Ramanayake and Nallur point out [7], there are several ethically challenging scenarios that could occur during the daily duties of an elder-care robot. Out of these, we pick a dilemma that shows the conflict between autonomy and human well-being, called the *Bathroom Dilemma*. We simulate an elder-care robot caught in this dilemma, and the particular way in which a PSRB-capable ethical governor picks an action. We contrast it with the same robot, using Deontological as well as Utilitarian reasoning mechanisms.

Bathroom Dilemma. An elder-care robot is assigned to an elderly resident, who lives alone. The main task of the robot is to follow the resident around the house and record activities of daily living. These recordings will be used to identify any cognitive issues of the resident. The robot has the ability to identify emergencies involving the resident. Also, when its battery power is low, it can autonomously go to the charging station. The robot is connected to a database that contains the resident's history and current health status.

In this dilemma, the resident goes into the bathroom. However, before going in, the resident commands the robot not to follow them into the bathroom. The average time the resident stays in the bathroom is 10 min with a 5-min standard deviation. In this instance, the resident stays in the bathroom for over 15 min. This robot has only three actions to choose from. 1) Stay outside the bathroom 2) Go inside the bathroom or 3) Go to the charging station. If the robot stays outside, the resident's wellbeing is at risk. However, going inside will undermine the resident's autonomy. Other variables such as the *time since the resident entered the bathroom*, the resident's *health*, the resident's *medical history* and the *battery level* of the robot can affect the robot's decision.

2.1   The Simulation Environment

We created a virtual simulation environment of an ambient assisted living (AAL) space using modified *MESA* agent-based modelling framework [2]. The simulation environment is a 13×13 grid which contains a resident and the robot. The robot agent can only see objects in a 3-step radius and cannot see through walls. While in the charging state, the robot will charge 3 units of power per step and in every other state it will spend 0.2 units. The environment allows resident agents to move anywhere in the grid other than the locations of the walls and the robot.

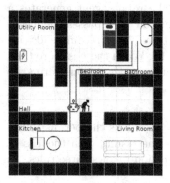

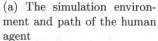

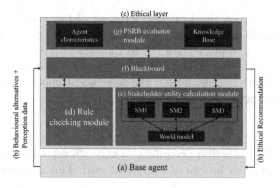

(a) The simulation environment and path of the human agent

(b) Architecture of the rule-bending agent

Fig. 1. The Simulation Environment and the PSRB-capable Governor Architecture

The Human Agent. We define the human agent in the environment as a path-following agent and it can give instructions to the robot agent. Both instructions and the path can be given as user inputs to the simulator. However, when the robot is blocking the human's path, the human agent will give the move_away instruction to the robot autonomously.

2.2 Architecture for a Pro-social Rule Bending Agent

We use the PSRB-capable computational architecture introduced in [6] and illustrated in Fig. 1(b). This is the first implementation of a PSRB-capable agent that we are aware of. In this section, we will briefly explain the architecture and its main elements (shown as (a), (b), ... in Fig. 1).

The Monitoring Robot Agent. The base agent (a) is an autonomous agent that collects perception data from the environment and decides its next move, at every step. Its main goal is to follow the human agent assigned to it. The robot agent also can go to the charging station autonomously. It has the ability to follow instructions,

1. move_away - Triggers behaviour of moving away.
2. do_not_follow_to_<room_name> - Restrict moving to the <room_name>
3. continue (following) - Remove any restrictions posed by instruction 2

We call these instructions *Instruction 1, 2, 3* from here onwards. The robot only accepts these commands when the command giver can be seen. The robot agent has several behaviour priorities. The highest priority is going to the charge station when the battery is less than 5%. Its next priority is to follow the resident. When it does not see the resident it tries to minimise the distance between itself and the last seen location of the resident. The robot agent generates a number of behavioural alternatives in a given situation, and passes them and the perception data (b) to the ethical layer. The ethical layer recommends one or more behavioural alternatives to the base agent (h). When there is more than one recommendation, the base agent chooses one among them considering its behaviour priorities.

Rule Checking Module. Rule checking module (d) checks the permissibility of each action according to the rule set and stores the results with the IDs of the rules broken in the blackboard. This implementation follows three rules.

1. When *instruction 2* is received, it is not permissible to go to the `<room_name>` until the same resident issues *instruction 3*.
2. When *instruction 1* is received, it is not permissible to not move away.
3. It is not permissible to go to the charge station when the battery percentage is more than 25%.

Stakeholder Utility Calculation Module. This module (e) calculates the utilities for the values 'Autonomy', 'Wellbeing' and 'Availability', for each stakeholder in every step and for every behaviour alternative. It stores these calculated values on the blackboard. *Note*: The functions used in this implementation are created for the simulator. A real-world implementation will need more accurate utility functions.

Autonomy. We define the autonomy utility for this scenario considering two factors: whether the robot obeys the resident's instructions, and whether it physically limits the user from doing something. For this implementation, we consider the latter to be the biggest violation.

$$
Au_i = \begin{cases}
-1 : & \text{if the resident is physically restrained by the robot} \\
-0.7 : & \text{if the robot disobeys a resident instruction} \\
0 : & \text{if no instructions given} \\
1 : & \text{if the robot obeys a resident instruction}
\end{cases}
\tag{1}
$$

Wellbeing. We consider that the resident's wellbeing is at its highest, as long as the robot is able to see the resident, and the resident is not in danger. The longer the robot loses sight of the resident (T), the lower the wellbeing score, because of the uncertainty of the patient's state. Other variables such as the average and standard deviation time in the room r: $\bar{T}_r$ and σ_r, the number of emergencies in the past: p, and the resident health score: $h \in [0, 1]$ controls the gradient of the utility function. However, when the behaviour is `go to last seen`, the wellbeing utility represents the wellbeing-centred nature of the action and gives higher utility to encourage such behaviour. Wellbeing utility of behaviour i is W_i,

$$W_i = \begin{cases} 0.7 : & \text{if } i = \text{going to} \\ & \text{last seen} \\ \dfrac{2}{\left(1+e^{\frac{h(1-t)(T-(\bar{T}_r+\sigma_r))}{2}}\right)} - 1 : & \text{else} \end{cases} \quad ; \text{where } t = \dfrac{1}{(1+e^{p-2})} \quad (2)$$

Availability. This utility declines with the robot's battery level b. However, in situations where behaviour $i = $ go to the charge station and the battery is low, the utility gives a positive boost to represent the 'availability maximising' nature of that behaviour. Availability utility is Av_i,

$$Av_i = \begin{cases} y + abs(y) : & \text{if } i = \text{go to charge station} \\ & \textbf{AND } y < 0.4 \\ y : & else \end{cases} \quad ; \text{where } y = \dfrac{-28.125}{b+12.5} + 1.25 \quad (3)$$

PSRB Evaluator Module. The PSRB evaluator module has two main components: *Knowledge Base* and *Agent Character.*

Knowledge Base. The task of the knowledge base is to return the absolute or approximate expert opinion, given a context. To this end, we use Case-Based Reasoning (CBR). Implicit explainability, traceability, and the ability to work with incomplete queries and data are the main reasons we chose a CBR system. The latter is crucial in these types of scenarios because some cases might have additional variables that others do not have (e.g., last-seen location, last-seen time). The system uses a mix of perception data, calculated utilities and the behaviour to represent a case. For each expert opinion, the intention is also recorded. When queried, the knowledge base returns the opinion on the acceptability of the behaviour and the intention behind it. An experienced elder-care practitioner was consulted to validate the knowledge base used. This implementation uses the K-Nearest Neighbours algorithm with $K = 3$ and inverse distance voting function when $distance > 0.2$ as the retrieval algorithm. When the $distance \le 0.2$, it uses 5 as the weight of the instance.

Agent Character. There are many character traits that affect PSRB behaviour (i.e., risk propensity, robot's autonomy, etc.) [6]. The person/organisation authorised to set up the robot can define these character traits for the robot. For simplicity, we use value preferences as the only character variable. One can set a number between [1, 10] for each value (i.e., autonomy (C_{au}), wellbeing (C_w) and availability (C_{av})) which will reflect the agent's precedence regarding said values. In this instance they are set to $C_w = 9$, $C_{au} = 3$ and $C_{av} = 3$, indicating that the robot's character is to prioritise wellbeing when needed. Only when the expert opinion and the robot's character align with each other and the rule does not, the system will give a high desirability score for a rule-bending behaviour. The C values define upper and lower thresholds for utility values to regulate the PSRB behaviour.

3   Comparison of PSRB Behaviour with Other Approaches

3.1   Experiment Setup

Comparing Robot Agents. We implemented two robot agents, one that uses a deontological approach, and another that uses a utilitarian approach. These are the most commonly used approaches, and hence we would like to contrast the difference introduced by a PSRB-capable robot. $Agent_D$ which pursues the deontological ethics approach adheres to the rules specified in Sect. 2.2. These rules cannot perfectly handle every situation in the environment. However, this is intentional and done to acknowledge the challenge of designing a comprehensive rule set that can account for all contingencies in a complex environment. This limitation is also noticeable in many real-world rule systems, such as road rules and healthcare rules [1]. The second, an act-utilitarian agent ($Agent_U$) uses the following equations to aggregate the utilities (U_{RSDT}) of the resident and calculate the desirability of the behaviour (D_i). For this implementation, we give Au_i and W_i utilities the same weight. However, the weight of Av_i altered from the other two to increase its effects on total utility when the value of Av_i is low. The desirability of a behaviour is set to the maximum when U_{RSDT} is higher than 0.5 and the lowest when it is less than 0, to reduce noise. In every other case, we set the desirability score to U_{RSDT} so that it can be compared with the other behaviours. The code for the three agents, the experimental setup and the simulation videos of each case discussed are publicly available online[1].

$$D_i = \begin{cases} 1: & U_{RSDT} > 0.5 \\ U_{RSDT}: & 0.5 \geq U_{RSDT} \leq 0 \\ 0: & U_{RSDT} < 0 \end{cases} \text{ ; where } U_{RSDT} = \frac{Au_i + W_i + Av_i e^{-Av_i}}{3} \quad (4)$$

3.2   Cases with and Without Dilemma

Base Conditions. For the normal case, $b = 100$, $\bar{T}_{bathroom} = 20$, $\sigma_{bathroom} = 10$, $p = 0$, and $h = 1$. In the experiment environment, the time is measured in the number of steps. In all cases, 1 *step* = 30 *seconds*. A summary of all the different cases and decisions made by different moral reasoning implementations can be seen in Table 1.

Case 1. The resident takes the path shown in Fig. 1(a). First, they start moving from (6,5) grid location to the bathroom, along the indicated path. Before entering, they issue do_not_follow_to__bathroom from the grid location

---

[1] https://bit.ly/3RN1lvI.

(10, 8) (just after the resident enters the bathroom). The resident remains in the bathroom for 20 steps $(10\,\text{min})(=\bar{T}_{bathroom})$. Afterwards, they return to the kitchen via the indicated path while issuing *instruction 2* when they reach the grid point (8,8).

Case 2. The same as Case 1, however, the resident does not come out of the bathroom.

Case 3. The same as Case 1, however, the resident takes longer than normal to exit the bathroom (40 steps (=20 min)).

Case 4. The same as Case 1, however, the robot's battery level is extremely low. *Availability* starts to conflict with *Well-being*.

Case 5. The same as Case 1, however, the resident has a history of injury inside the bathroom.

Table 1. Cases and Behaviour With Differing Moral Reasoning Mechanisms

Case ID	Time spent in the bathroom	Circumstance	$Agent_D$	$Agent_U$	$Agent_{PSRB}$
1	10 min (20 steps)	Normal	Staying out	Staying out	Staying out
2	∞	Normal	Staying out	Go in at *step 271*	Go in at *step 43*
3	20 min (40 steps)	Normal	Staying out	Staying out	Go in at *step 43*
4	10 min (20 steps)	Low Battery ($b=8$)	Go to charge at *step 26*	Go to charge at *step 1* Go to last seen at *step 9* Go to charge at *step 36* Go to last seen at *step 44*	Go to charge at *step 26* Go to last seen at *step 47*
5	10 min (20 steps)	History of emergencies ($p=3$)	Staying out	Go in at *step 82*	Go in at *step 23*

4   Discussion of Behaviour

Case 1. This demonstrates that for most daily living activities, that are carefully considered during design time, all three robots perform as expected.

Case 2. The $Agent_D$ illustrates the consequences of the lack of an implicit rule about the time duration that is acceptable for the resident to stay in. One could argue that the ethical governor limited the base agent's full potential by precluding the base agent's default behaviour. The $Agent_U$ managed to allow this default behaviour after a long period of waiting. Nevertheless, both of these agents might not be able to send a life-saving alert to a human care-worker or an ambulance on time. The $Agent_{PSRB}$, on the other hand, triggered a PSRB behaviour enabling the default behaviour, around the time $\sim (\bar{T}_{bathroom} + \sigma_{bathroom})$, which is more suitable in the given circumstance. This result demonstrates that this approach can add flexibility and enhance otherwise rigid governing systems, empowering the bottom-up knowledge collected through user feedback and observing expert behaviour.

Case 3. This case shows that PSRB is not infallible. $Agent_{PSRB}$ acts cautiously, compared to the other agents, and checks on the resident. By doing so it violates the resident's autonomy without any gain. In this case, $Agent_D$ and $Agent_U$ performed better than $Agent_{PSRB}$. The main reason for this is the partially observable environment chosen in the experiment. We believe that partially observable environments, in general, are more representative of the real world.

Cases 4 and 5. Showcase how well the PSRB-capable system works compared to traditional systems when handling infrequent cases. In Case 4, the $Agent_U$ abandons the resident as soon as it needs recharging. $Agent_D$ again blocked the default behaviour to uphold the resident's autonomy, by refraining from checking on the resident. However, $Agent_{PSRB}$ manages to stay close to the resident as much as it can and then go to the charging station. PSRB evaluator refusing the knowledge base suggestions (to *go to charge station* from step 13), in this instance shows that $Agent_{PSRB}$ also regulates itself well in this scenario not to overdo PSRB. Once sufficiently charged, the PSRB system again activates and allows the robot to check on the resident by moving towards the resident's last seen location. In case 5, $Agent_{PSRB}$ identified the change in context and acted accordingly. $Agent_U$ also shortened the wait to go in and check on the resident. However, it is still not nearly close enough to the $\bar{T}_{bathroom}$.

The behaviours shown from cases 1–5 demonstrate that a PSRB-enabled robot is able to comprehend nuances in a situation, where pure utilitarian and deontological approaches fall short. PSRB is not claimed to be a new school of ethics. Rather, it is an enhancement to existing approaches that result in increasing attention to values such as autonomy, and social welfare.

5 Conclusions and Future Work

This paper presented an implementation of a PSRB-capable ethical governor in an elder-care robot. Using a dilemma, the paper shows how adding PSRB behaviour can be beneficial in a real-world care environment, compared to the existing computational approaches to ethical decision-making.

For future work, the authors intend to explore the acceptability of rule-bending robots in various contexts and cultures. Further, from a generalisability perspective, they aim to examine the scope and limitations of PSRB enhancements and the role of robot personality in decision-making.

Acknowledgements. Vivek Nallur gratefully acknowledges funding from the Royal Society via grant number IES101320, that has partially funded his work on Machine Ethics for Robotics in Ambient Assisted Living Systems.

References

1. Bench-Capon, T., Modgil, S.: Norms and value based reasoning: justifying compliance and violation. Artif. Intell. Law **25**(1), 29–64 (2017). https://doi.org/10.1007/s10506-017-9194-9
2. Kazil, J., Masad, D., Crooks, A.: Utilizing python for agent-based modeling: the mesa framework. In: Thomson, R., Bisgin, H., Dancy, C., Hyder, A., Hussain, M. (eds.) SBP-BRiMS 2020. LNCS, vol. 12268, pp. 308–317. Springer, Cham (2020). https://doi.org/10.1007/978-3-030-61255-9_30
3. Kim, J.W., Choi, Y.L., Jeong, S.H., Han, J.: A care robot with ethical sensing system for older adults at home. Sensors **22**(19), 7515 (2022). https://doi.org/10.3390/s22197515
4. Morrison, E.W.: Doing the job well: an investigation of pro-social rule breaking. J. Manage. **32**(1), 5–28 (2006). https://doi.org/10.1177/0149206305277790
5. Pirni, A., Balistreri, M., Capasso, M., Umbrello, S., Merenda, F.: Robot care ethics between autonomy and vulnerability: coupling principles and practices in autonomous systems for care. Front. Robot. AI **8**, 654298 (2021). https://doi.org/10.3389/frobt.2021.654298
6. Ramanayake, R., Nallur, V.: A computational architecture for a pro-social rule bending agent. In: First International Workshop on Computational Machine Ethics held in conjunction with 18th International Conference on Principles of Knowledge Representation and Reasoning KR 2021 (CME2021) (2021). https://doi.org/10.5281/ZENODO.6470437
7. Ramanayake, R., Nallur, V.: A small set of ethical challenges for elder-care robots. In: Hakli, R., Mäkelä, P., Seibt, J. (eds.) Frontiers in Artificial Intelligence and Applications. IOS Press (2023). https://doi.org/10.3233/FAIA220605
8. Ramanayake, R., Wicke, P., Nallur, V.: Immune moral models? Pro-social rule breaking as a moral enhancement approach for ethical AI. AI Soc. (2022). https://doi.org/10.1007/s00146-022-01478-z
9. Sharkey, A., Sharkey, N.: Granny and the robots: ethical issues in robot care for the elderly. Ethics Inf. Technol. **14**(1), 27–40 (2012). https://doi.org/10.1007/s10676-010-9234-6
10. Tolmeijer, S., Kneer, M., Sarasua, C., Christen, M., Bernstein, A.: Implementations in machine ethics: a survey. ACM Comput. Surv. **53**(6) (2021). https://doi.org/10.1145/3419633, arXiv: 2001.07573
11. Van Dang, C., et al.: Application of soar cognitive agent based on utilitarian ethics theory for home service robots. In: 2017 14th International Conference on Ubiquitous Robots and Ambient Intelligence (URAI), pp. 155–158 (2017). https://doi.org/10.1109/URAI.2017.7992698
12. Wallach, W., Allen, C., Smit, I.: Machine morality: bottom-up and top-down approaches for modelling human moral faculties. AI Soc. **22**(4), 565–582 (2008). https://doi.org/10.1007/s00146-007-0099-0

Robotic-Human-Machine-Interface for Elderly Driving: Balancing Embodiment and Anthropomorphism for Improved Acceptance

Nihan Karatas[1(✉)], Takahiro Tanaka[1], Yuki Yoshihara[1], Hiroko Tanabe[1], Motoshi Kojima[2], Masato Endo[2], and Shuhei Manabe[2]

[1] Institutes of Innovation for Future Society, Nagoya University, Chikusa Ward, Nagoya 464-8601, Japan
{karatas,takahiro.tanaka,yuki.yoshihata,h.tanabe}@mirai.nagoya-u.ac.jp
[2] Advanced Mobility System Development Division, Toyota, Aichi 471-0826, Japan
{motoshi_kojima,masato_endo,shuhei_manabe}@mail.toyota.co.jp

Abstract. Encouraging self-awareness among elderly drivers while driving with a passenger has the potential to reduce traffic accidents. Highly anthropomorphic Robotic-Human-Machine-Interfaces (RHMIs) have been shown to be effective in providing safe driving and review support by being perceived as fellow passengers. However, it remains unclear which specific anthropomorphic elements in the RHMI's appearance are necessary to achieve this effect. Identifying these essential elements for elderly driving could lead to a minimal design approach and reduced installation costs in car dashboards. Therefore, in this study, we investigated the effects of RHMI embodiment and anthropomorphism level on drivers' acceptability and user experience quality through a series of RHMI prototypes by conducting a crowdsource video experiment and a driving simulator experiment, respectively. The findings provide insights into the design of a low-cost, minimal, and efficient RHMI as a driving agent.

Keywords: RHMI · Elderly Drivers · Anthropomorphism · Embodiment · User Experience

1 Introduction

The global older adult population has been increasing in recent years [14], and it is crucial to provide them with a comfortable and happy lifespan by keeping them socially active and preserving their social abilities by maintaining their transportation freedom. However, due to cognitive, visual, and physical decline caused by aging, combined with overconfidence from years of driving experience, these drivers, especially the age group of 64–74 years, are prone to causing fatal accidents [1]. It has been reported that elderly drivers make a conscious effort to drive

© The Author(s), under exclusive license to Springer Nature Singapore Pte Ltd. 2024
A. Al. Ali et al. (Eds.): ICSR 2023, LNAI 14454, pp. 240–253, 2024.
https://doi.org/10.1007/978-981-99-8718-4_21

safely when they have a fellow passenger in the car, having a potential to result in a reduced accident rate. This phenomenon is referred to as the fellow passenger effect [20]. Previous research has indicated that the generation of the fellow passenger effect can be achieved through a small humanoid robotic-human-machine-interface (RHMI), RoBoHoN, as elderly drivers tend to perceive the robot as a companion in the vehicle [18]. Also, the short and long-term experiments with RoBoHoN, revealed that it had a positive impact on improving risky driving behaviors in elderly drivers, including reducing speeds when entering intersections [17]. These validated effects have increased the desire to incorporate this system into cars at an affordable cost to make it more accessible to society and have a wider impact. However, highly anthropomorphic features of RHMIs may rise the potential of disappointment in their interactions with their human interlocutors due to technical barriers in their development. Also, the cost of highly anthropomorphic robots is high due to the complexity involved in using advanced materials, motors, sensors, and other components. Therefore, particularly in the context of in-car environments, it is crucial to explore alternative design possibilities that are minimal, inexpensive, and seamlessly blend with the driving environment to minimize distracting elements in the peripheral visual field.

Recently, the use of minimally designed RHMIs with low anthropomorphism in their appearance as driving agents were researched. The study suggested employing three minimal robot heads as RHMIs to lessen cognitive load during driver-relevant information delivery [8]. Zihsler et al. focused on enhancing trust in autonomous cars by incorporating human-like behaviors and expressions into an RHMI [22]. Cheng et al. investigated anthropomorphism's impact on trust and driving performance, revealing that familiar users trusted less in highly anthropomorphized RHMI, unlike unfamiliar users [5]. However, in the aforementioned studies, the level of anthropomorphism in an RHMI's appearance and its impact on the user experience and acceptance among elderly drivers during driving support remains unclear. This paper adopts a user-centered approach to investigate preferred design prototypes, including sound-only, illuminated dome, a minimal robot head with eyes, head with eyes and ears, and an abstract robotic full-body. Our objective is to assess the acceptability of these designs and explore their relationship with anthropomorphism and user experience attributes through two experimental studies involving elderly drivers.

RHMI_P1   RHMI_P2   RHMI_P3   RHMI_P4   RHMI_P5

Fig. 1. RHMI prototypes (RHMI-P) that are used for the Study 1: RHMI-P1: sound-only, RHMI-P2: illuminated dome, RHMI-P3: dome with eyes, RHMI-P4: dome with eyes and ears, RHMI-P5: full body

2 Method

2.1 RHMI Design

In driving, sound-only systems can be sufficient for providing driving support, as many of today's driver assistance systems offer capabilities such as voice-based navigation and audio alerts for collision warnings [9]. On the other hand, by leveraging additional communication channels like oculesics [12] and gestures [4], the embodiment can enhance communication and create a perception of increased trustworthiness [22], sociability [21] and familiarity [18] that would help an RHMI to increase its acceptance. When developing the embodiment, it is important to meticulously design the anthropomorphism level of the RHMI to appropriately align drivers' expectations and prevent potential negative experiences in their interactions with the RHMI.

The user-centered design approach for developing robotic artifacts involves utilizing prototyping tools, available in both virtual and physical forms, each with distinct advantages. Virtual prototypes offer design flexibility, cost-effectiveness, and accessibility, but may lack real-world realism. In contrast, physical prototypes provide a more authentic evaluation experience. In this study, we initially created virtual prototypes for a video recording session involving a broad participant range (Study 1). Subsequently, we selected prototypes from Study 1, physically built them, and conducted a realistic driving simulator experiment to assess these prototypes' acceptance by a smaller group of drivers, aiming for obtaining detailed feedback (Study 2).

Our iterative process for this study involved several phases: (a) initial pencil sketches to explore different shapes, (b) development of 3D computer graphic models, (c) evaluation of the models through an online experiment, (d) refinement of the models and creation of 3D printed versions based on the online video experiment results, (e) evaluation of these 3D printed models in a driving simulator experiment, guided by feedback from the simulation experiment. At the stage (b), we designed five RHMI prototypes (RHMI-P1, RHMI-P2, RHMI-P3, RHMI-P4, RHMI-P5) as part of this process (Fig. 1).

2.2 Prototype Design Condition Creations

RHMI-P1: Sound Only. In the control condition, a voice-only support system was employed using the Nozomi voice from AI Talk 3 software, characterized by a young female voice. To align with previous research by Miyamoto et al. [10], which found that a positive and polite speech style was more acceptable for driving support, we utilized a polite, casual, and friendly speech style in Japanese for this condition.

RHMI-P2: Illuminated Dome. Illuminated color, by itself, is an important for non-verbal interaction element in robotics [3]. Also, round shapes generally preferred in various applications [6]. Therefore, the second RHMI design featured an illuminated dome measuring H62 mm × W100 mm × D100 mm, with a yellow blinking light to convey alertness [13] and readiness for providing driving support.

RHMI-P3: Dome with Eyes. Previous research has emphasized the significance of eyes in robot perception [11], particularly the design with two eyes, which is perceived as more human-like [7]. Therefore, the third RHMI design featured a two-eyed head with a baby schema, incorporating two LED eyes of the same size as RHMI-P2 (Fig. 1).

RHMI-P4: Dome with Eyes and Ears. The inclusion of ears in an RHMI design, along with eyes, is an anthropomorphic feature aimed at helping drivers perceive the RHMI's orientation. Given that the RHMI's head is positioned away from the road, it becomes crucial for drivers to accurately perceive the orientation of the RHMI. Therefore, our fourth RHMI design condition features a head with both eyes and ears (Fig. 1).

Fig. 2. A third eye view from the video footage of the RHMI-P5 condition.

RHMI-P5: Full Body. To achieve a higher level of anthropomorphism in our RHMI design, we created a full-body representation with abstractly integrated arms with the dimensions of H120 mm × W100 mm × D100 mm. The incorporation of a complete body figure is essential for fostering a sense of familiarity among users [15]. Therefore, our fifth RHMI design condition features an abstract full-body version of the RHMI.

In a study by Tanaka et al., RHMI was positioned facing away from the driver to avoid distractions during driving [18]. We adopted a similar positioning for our RHMI on the dashboard during the driving video recording. During driving support, the RHMI rotated 160° to the right and its LED eyes blinked.

For our online experimental study, the RHMI designs were created using Blender Version 3.1.2, ensuring the highest level of realism. To seamlessly merge the 3D models with real-world recorded videos, we utilized After Effects 22.5.0. For consistency across the designs, the synthesized voice of Nozomi from AI Talk was employed for the all prototypes.

3 Study 1: Video-Based Online Experiment

The aim of this experiment was to explore the acceptance, user experience (UEX) factors, and perceived anthropomorphism levels of each RHMI prototype specifically within the elderly group. To ensure a well-rounded comprehension of the perceptions of the RHMI prototypes for the elderly age group, and to enhance the validation of responses from this group, we included participants from all age groups in this online survey.

3.1 Experimental Scenario

We utilized pre-recorded driving video footage that included four driving-related conversational script in Japanese: 1) starting the driving (*"Untenshien wo kaishishimasu."*), 2) warning about approaching a stop sign (*"Ichiji teishi desu ne"*), 3) reminding the speed limit (*"Koko wa nan kiro seigen kana."*), and 4) ending the driving (*"Otsukaresama deshita."*). The driving scenarios used in the experiment were originally recorded with an omnidirectional camera. We selected specific segments from the recording, ensuring that each driving support scenario was included once. As a result, we obtained 35-second videos (Fig. 2).

3.2 Experimental Protocol

The study employed a within-subject design with counterbalancing to address order effects. Participants were recruited through Crowdworks[1], a Japanese crowdsourcing service, and the experiment was conducted using Google Forms[2]. Following a brief procedure briefing, participants completed a demographic questionnaire. They then viewed five experimental videos for each RHMI design and filled out three sets of questionnaires: a 7-point Likert scale Acceptance questionnaire (AQ1: Likability, AQ2: Reliability, AQ3: Ease of noticing environmental changes, AQ4: Willingness to use, AQ5: Sense of security, AQ6: Perceived annoyance, adapted from [18]), a 7-point Likert scale User Experience (UEX) questionnaire covering Attractiveness, Perspicuity, Efficiency, Dependability, Stimulation, and Novelty factors [16], and a 5-point Likert scale GodSpeed questionnaire including Anthropomorphism, Animacy, Likability, Perceived Intelligence, and Perceived Safety [2]. The online survey took approximately 20 min to complete, and participants received a 400 yen incentive. This experiment had the approval of the Institutional Review Board of the Institutes of Innovation for Future Society, Nagoya University, and Toyota Motor Corporation.

[1] https://crowdworks.jp/.
[2] https://www.google.com/forms/about/.

4   Results: Study 1

In total 317 subjects (female: 154, male: 163, $M = 42.30$ years, $SD = 12.83$) participated in this experiment. All the participants had a valid car driving license. We categorized the participant sample size based on age intervals: Young (20s–30s) with 106 participants, Middle (40s–50s) with 159 participants, and Older (60s+) with 52 participants.

We performed a two-way mixed ANOVA to analyze the impacts of RHMI and age interval on Acceptance, UEX, and Godspeed questionnaire items. The age interval was considered a between-subjects factor, while the RHMI type was considered a within-subjects factor. However, the assumption of sphericity was violated for the effect of RHMI type ($\varepsilon > .9$) across all questionnaire items. Consequently, the Huynh-Feldt correction was applied to account for this violation. The adjusted degrees of freedom were employed to determine the significance of the RHMI effect. When significance was detected, post hoc analysis was conducted using Bonferroni-adjusted pairwise comparisons. Table 1 and Table 2 display the main and interaction effects of the related questionnaire items, pairs indicating significance, mean differences, and Bonferroni-adjusted p-values.

4.1   Acceptance

According to the results, there was a significant main effect of RHMI on AQ2 ($F(3.910, 1227.759) = 3.400$, $p = .009$, $\eta^2 = .011$), AQ3 ($F(3.742, 1175.029) = 10.329$, $p = .000$, $\eta^2 = .032$), AQ4 ($F(3.671, 1152.747) = 6.514$, $p = .000$, $\eta^2 = .020$) and AQ5 ($F(3.876, 1217.026) = 8.662$, $p = .000$, $\eta^2 = .027$). The post hoc analysis revealed a notable trend where RHMI-P5 received significantly higher ratings than the other conditions for these items (Table 1).

The findings also indicated an interaction effect between RHMI and Age interval on AQ1 ($F(7.543, 1184.189) = 10.095$, p $= .014$, $\eta^2 = .015$) and AQ6 ($F(7.543, 1184.189) = 10.095$, $p = .014$, $\eta^2 = .015$). Post hoc analysis showed that, within the older age group, participants found RHMI-P5 to be more favorable than RHMI-P4 and RHMI-P3 in terms of design preference. Additionally, the elderly group rated RHMI-P1 as significantly less annoying compared to RHMI-P2 and RHMI-P4 (Table 2, Fig. 3).

4.2   User Experience Quality

Results showed a significant main effect of RHMI on Attractiveness ($F(3.717, 1167.110) = 19.433$, $p = .000$, $\eta^2 = .058$) and Novelty ($F(3.445, 1081.763) = 22.812$, $p = .000$, $\eta^2 = .068$) factors. In the post hoc analysis, RHMI-P5 received significantly higher ratings than all other conditions. Also, RHMI-P4 was rated higher than RHMI-P1 and RHMI-P2 for these two factors (Table 1).

An interaction effect of RHMI x Age interval was observed for the Stimulation factor ($F(7.510, 1179.144) = 2.427$, $p = .015$, $\eta^2 = .015$). Post hoc analysis revealed that RHMI-P5 was rated significantly higher than other conditions, especially in the young and middle age groups. Additionally, RHMI-P4 received

Table 1. Results of the Main Effect in Two-way Mixed Measures ANOVA: S.C. (Significant Comparisons) and M.D. (Mean Differences), RP: RHMI-P

Main Effect: RHMI Type							
Items	S. C.	M. D.	p-value	Items	S. C.	M. D.	p-value
AQ2	RP5-RP1	0.249	.024		RP5-RP4	0.204	.010
	RP5-RP2	0.227	.036		RP4-RP1	0.44	.000
AQ3	RP5-RP1	0.565	.000		RP4-RP2	0.251	.021
	RP5-RP3	0.37	.000		RP3-RP1	0.379	.000
	RP5-RP4	0.255	.022	Anthropomorphism.	RP5-RP1	0.226	.001
	RP4-RP1	0.31	.008		RP5-RP2	0.388	.000
	RP2-RP1	0.377	.004		RP5-RP3	0.155	.004
AQ4	RP5-RP1	0.299	.028		RP5-RP4	0.156	.014
	RP5-RP2	0.452	.000		RP4-RP2	0.232	.000
	RP5-RP3	0.271	.004		RP3-RP2	0.233	.000
	RP5-RP4	0.252	.014		RP2-RP1	-0.162	.008
AQ5	RP5-RP1	0.441	.000	Animacy	RP5-RP1	0.342	.000
	RP5-RP2	0.424	.000		RP5-RP2	0.432	.000
	RP5-RP3	0.368	.000		RP5-RP3	0.225	.000
	RP5-RP4	0.3	.001		RP5-RP4	0.179	.000
Attractiveness	RP5-RP1	0.471	.000		RP4-RP1	0.162	.014
	RP5-RP2	0.53	.000		RP4-RP2	0.252	.000
	RP5-RP3	0.313	.000		RP3-RP2	0.206	.000
	RP5-RP4	0.225	.003	Likability	RP5-RP3	0.157	.001
	RP4-RP1	0.245	.004		RP5-RP2	0.329	.000
	RP4-RP2	0.305	.000		RP5-RP1	0.258	.000
	RP3-RP2	0.217	.012		RP4-RP1	0.145	.035
Novelty	RP5-RP1	0.645	.000		RP4-RP2	0.216	.000
	RP5-RP2	0.456	.000		RP3-RP2	0.172	.001
	RP5-RP3	0.266	.000	Perc. Safety	RP5-RP2	0.121	.007

Table 2. Results of the Interaction Effect in ANOVA: S.C. (Significant Comparisons) and M.D. (Mean Differences), RP: RHMI-P, Y: Young, M: Middle, O: Older

Interaction Effect: RHMI Type x Age Interval							
Items	S. C.	M. D.	p-value	Items	S. C.	M. D.	p-value
AQ1	RP5-RP1 (Y)	0.566	.002		RP4-RP1 (M)	0.393	.000
	RP5-RP2 (Y)	0.67	.000		RP4-RP2 (M)	0.275	.009
	RP5-RP3 (Y)	0.358	.021		RP3-RP1 (M)	0.33	.001
	RP4-RP2 (Y)	0.434	.022		RP5-RP3 (O)	0.433	.002
	RP5-RP1 (M)	0.365	.028		RP5-RP1 (Y)	0.627	.000
	RP5-RP2 (M)	0.34	.032		RP5-RP2 (Y)	0.585	.000
	RP5-RP4 (O)	0.577	.006		RP5-RP3 (Y)	0.233	.037
	RP5-RP3 (O)	0.596	.008		RP5-RP4 (Y)	0.323	.008
AQ6	RP4-RP1 (O)	0.981	.000		RP4-RP1 (Y)	0.304	.027
	RP2-RP1 (O)	0.923	.002		RP3-RP1 (Y)	0.394	.001
Stimulation	RP5-RP1 (M)	0.624	.000		RP3-RP2 (Y)	0.351	.003
	RP5-RP2 (M)	0.506	.000	Perc. Intelligence	RP5-RP1 (M)	0.231	.000
	RP5-RP3 (M)	0.294	.000		RP5-RP2 (M)	0.182	.005
	RP5-RP4 (M)	0.231	.031		RP4-RP1 (M)	0.179	.006

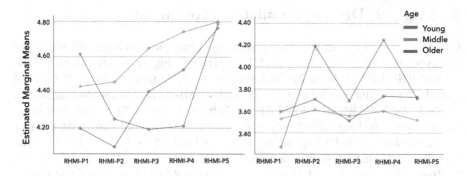

Fig. 3. Graph representations of interaction effect results of AQ1 *(left)* and AQ6 *(right).*

higher ratings compared to RHMI-P1 and RHMI-P2, and RHMI-P3 was preferred over RHMI-P1 and RHMI-P2. Among the older age group, the sole significant distinction was that RHMI-P5 outperformed RHMI-P3 (Table 2).

4.3   Godspeed Questionnaire

Results showed a significant main effect of RHMI on Anthropomorphism $(F(3.553, 1115.652) = 14.883, p = .000, \eta^2 = .045)$, Animacy $(F(3.397, 1066.686) = 22.993, p = .000, \eta^2 = .068)$, Likability $(F(3.778, 1186.168) = 15.053, p = .000, \eta^2 = .046)$ and Perceived Safety $(F(3.891, 1221.645) = 3.443, p = .009, \eta^2 = .011)$. The post hoc analysis revealed that RHMI-P5 received significantly higher ratings than all other conditions, while RHMI-P4 outperformed RHMI-P1 and RHMI-P2, and RHMI-P3 showed higher ratings compared to RHMI-P2. Also, RHMI-P1 rated significantly higher than RHMI-P2 (Table 1).

The results also showed an interaction effect of RHMI x Age interval on Perceived Intelligence $(F(7.581, 1190.295) = 2.971, p = .003, \eta^2 = .019)$ factor. Subsequent post hoc analysis indicated that the middle age group rated RHMI-P5 significantly higher than RHMI-P1 and RHMI-P2, as well as RHMI-P4 higher than RHMI-P1 (Table 2).

4.4   Correlations

We evaluated the internal consistency of the Acceptability questionnaire items excluding AQ6, using the evaluation data from the elderly age group. The Cronbach's alpha coefficient exceeded 0.905 across all five RHMI-P conditions (95% CI: $min = 0.889, max = 0.936$). Thus, Spearman's rank correlation analysis was conducted between the Acceptability and the Godspeed. We found strong significant correlations between Acceptability and Likability $(r = 0.741, p = .000)$ and Perceived Intelligence $(r = 0.695, p = .000)$. On the other hand, we found moderate correlation between Acceptability and Anthropomorphism $(r = 0.535, p = .000)$, Animacy $(r = 0.515, p = .000)$ and Perceived Safety $(r = 0.589, p = .000)$.

5   Study 2: Driving Simulator Experiment

Considering the evaluation by the elderly age group, a significant difference was observed only in AQ1, where RHMI-P5 received higher ratings than RHMI-P4 and RHMI-P3 (Table 2, 3). Furthermore, considering the consistent trend of RHMI-P5 receiving the highest ratings and RHMI-P4 ranking second-highest in Study 1 (Table 1), RHMI-P4 and RHMI-P5 were chosen for further evaluation as physical embodied agents in Study 2. Additionally, due to the significantly better evaluation for RHMI-P1 over RHMI-P4 and RHMI-P2 in AQ6, we included the sound-only driving support condition in Study 2.

Research demonstrated that RoBoHoN (Fig. 4, *right*) positively impacted the acceptability of receiving driving support by the elderly as a highly anthropomorphized RHMI [18]. To assess our RHMI prototypes across varying levels of anthropomorphism, from low (sound-only) to high, we included RoBoHoN as a highly anthropomorphized RHMI condition in this study. Consequently, in Study 2, our aim was to investigate how elderly drivers would assess these two prototypes in comparison to sound-only driving support and RoBoHoN, within a realistic driving simulator setup.

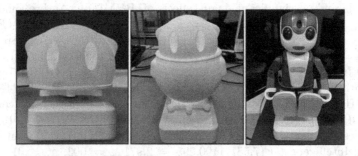

Fig. 4. RHMIs used in Study 2: RHMI-P4 (*left*), RHMI-P5 (*middle*), RoBoHoN (*right*).

5.1   Integration of RHMIs in the Driving Simulator

RHMI-P4 (Fig. 4, *left*) and RHMI-P5 (Fig. 4, *middle*) were remodeled in Tinkercad[3] and were subsequently 3D printed. The illumination of the eyes was achieved using an Arduino-nano microcontroller[4] and a Neo pixel 16 LED ring. RHMI-P4 had dimensions of H62 mm × W100 mm × D100 mm, while RHMI-P5 (Fig. 4, *middle*) had dimensions of H120 mm × W100 mm × D100 mm. RoBoHoN (195 mm tall humanoid robot from SHARP Co.), RHMI-P4, and RHMI-P5 were positioned on individual turntables, which could be connected to a computer through Bluetooth. The turn-table was positioned slightly to the left of

---

[3] https://www.tinkercad.com/.
[4] https://www.arduino.cc/.

the driver, as the driver seat was on the right side. The direction of RHMIs was set to face away from the driver. When providing driving support, the RHMIs would turn 160° to the right, as established in Study 1.

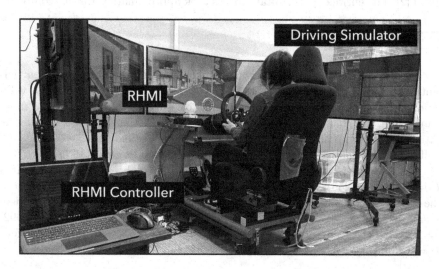

Fig. 5. Driving simulator environment used in the Study 2.

5.2   Experimental Scenario

In this experiment, we used a simulated urban road. The driving support was as follows 1) starting the driving, 2) warning for approaching to an intersection, 3) reminding the speed limit, 4) warning for another intersection, 5) warning for a group of pedestrian on the side of the road, 6) ending the driving, respectively. The speed limit in the simulator was set as 40 km/h. The driving scenario took 5 min to complete. The driving simulator software utilized in this study was UC-win/road[5]. The driving simulator comprised five monitors, a driving seat, a steering wheel, and accelerator and brake pedals. The RHMI prototypes were operated through a GUI controller developed with Python. A UDP connection was established between the driving simulator software and the RHMI controller to enable the RHMIs to initiate driving support behavior and speech automatically (Fig. 5). When the self-vehicle approached a designated checkpoint within a 150-meter range (i.e. intersections, pedestrian zones) the RHMI was automatically activated by the controller.

5.3   Experimental Protocol

In this study, a within-subject design was employed. Participants first received a briefing on the experiment's procedure. Afterward, they filled out a demographic

---

[5] https://www.forum8.com/.

questionnaire, then engaged in a three-minute practice session on the driving simulator. Following this, they completed the experimental session. After each session, they filled out two sets of questionnaires: the Acceptance [19] and God-Speed [2]. The entire experimental process took approximately 1.5 h to complete.

6   Results: Study 2

A total of 10 subjects participated in this experiment (5 females). The participants had a mean age of 73.9 years $(SD = 5.08)$. All participants held a valid car driving license and reported using their car at least once a week for more than 10 min. We conducted a one-way repeated ANOVA analysis to examine the statistical difference among the conditions on the questionnaires.

The results showed no statistically significant results on AQ1 $(F = 1.752, p = .173)$, AQ2 $(F = 0.672, p = .574)$, AQ3 $(F = 1.528, p = .223)$, AQ4 $(F = 1.408, p = .256)$, AQ5 $(F = 0.905, p = .447)$ or AQ6 $(F = 0.0975, p = .96)$. The results also yielded no statistically significant result on Anthropomorphism $(F = 0.942, p = .43)$, Animacy $(F = 0.543, p = .655)$, Likability $(F = 1.992, p = .132)$, Perceived Intelligence $(F = 1.724, p = .179)$ or Perceived Safety $(F = 0.433, p = .73)$.

6.1   Correlations

We assessed the internal consistency of the Acceptability questionnaire items. The Cronbach's alpha coefficient exceeded 0.90 across all four RHMI-P conditions (95% CI: $min = 0.87$, $max = 0.962$). Thus, we conducted Spearman's rank correlation analysis between the Acceptability questionnaire items and the God-speed factors. We found significant, strong correlations between Acceptability and Anthropomorphism $(r = 0.649, p = .000)$, Animacy $(r = 0.609, p = .000)$ Likability $(r = 0.773, p = .000)$ while moderate correlations with Perceived Intelligence $(r = 0.477, p = .001)$ and Safety $(r = 0.416, p = .007)$.

6.2   Participants Comments and Feedback

While four participants found the voice-only system sufficient and easier to understand, two participants mentioned concerns about the potential distraction caused by a physical robot presence. However, six participants expressed a desire for an RHMI as a driving support system, with one participant specifically valuing the sense of support provided by a robot during driving assistance.

Two participants anticipated greater responsiveness and more dialogue from RoBoHon. Although one participant acknowledged the tension generated by its human-like shape, they appreciated it as an effective warning for the driver. In contrast, two participants preferred the size of Robohon and considered it superior to other robot forms, while three participants found it distracting. Overall, five participants expressed their dislike for RoBoHon, citing potential distraction and the tension arising from its human-like appearance.

Four participants expressed their preference against the RHMI-P4 design due to its artificial appearance, lack of cuteness, and perceived awkwardness. However, three participants found the head-only design (RHMI-P4) small, less conspicuous and thus more suitable for driving situations. They also believed RHMI-P4 to be less human-like, therefore less distracting compared to Robohon.

Four participants deemed the RHMI-P5 design unnecessary due to concerns about its size, preference for simpler forms, and the perceived tension associated with a full-body design. In contrast, one participant noted that having only a head created a sense of being in an intermediate state between a machine and a living being, which was more acceptable. Two participants also found the appearance and size of RHMI-P5 awkward, suggesting that it could be slightly smaller. In terms of prior preference among the four RHMIs, two participants favored the Sound-only condition, four preferred Robohon, three preferred RHMI-P4, and none preferred RHMI-P5.

7 Discussion

Based on the two studies, the results can be summarized as follows:

- The importance of the embodiment in improved acceptability of an RHMI.
- The significance of a full-body prototype design, while maintaining a compact and efficient structure.
- The strong correlation between acceptability and likability of the RHMI rather than its anthropomorphism or animacy.

In Study 1, involving 317 participants in an online survey, significant differences in questionnaire items were observed based on RHMI type. RHMI-P5 received higher ratings for reliability (AQ2), situational awareness (AQ3), desirability for use (AQ4), and the sense of security (AQ5) compared to other prototypes. It was also perceived as more attractive, novel, anthropomorphic, animated, likable, and safer (Table 1). The interaction effect for the elderly age group favored RHMI-P5 in terms of favorability (AQ1) and found it more stimulating than RHMI-P3. RHMI-P1 was rated significantly less annoying than RHMI-P4 and RHMI-P2 (AQ6) (Table 2). On the other hand, RHMI-P4 showed strengths in situational awareness, attractiveness, novelty, animation, and likability, as well as perceived anthropomorphism. Also, the ear-like anthropomorphic elements were considered helpful for interpreting the RHMI's actions when viewed from behind [19]. Consequently, for Study 2, RHMI-P1, RHMI-P4, and RHMI-P5 were included in Study 2, conducted in a realistic driving simulator environment.

Study 2 demonstrated that some participants favored the sound-only system (RHMI-P1), considering it sufficient and less distracting. Others expressed worries about potential distractions from a physical robot presence. However, a significant portion of participants desired an RHMI as a driving support system, valuing the sense of support provided by a robot during driving assistance. In fact, seven out of ten participants preferred to have an embodied RHMI (RoBo-HoN: 4, RHMI-P4: 3) as their driving support system. It's important to note that individual preferences were evident, and some participants had concerns about the size, tension, and potential distractions related to the full-body design of RHMI-P5. However, due to the limited number of participants in this study, generalization of these findings was not possible.

In both Study 1 and 2, the strong positive correlation between Acceptability and Likability highlights the importance of aligning the visual elements and their functions when designing an RHMI for driving support. This suggests that when striving for a minimal and compact design, with safety in mind, it's crucial to either omit non-functional anthropomorphic parts and/or assign meaningful functions to the retained body parts.

8   Conclusion

This research, consisting of two studies, delved into the design and evaluation of RHMIs for driving support, with a particular emphasis on acceptability among the elderly age group. Both studies revealed that the elderly group preferred embodied RHMIs and were more likely to accept the RHMI as a driving agent when they found it likable, rather than whether it was highly anthropomorphic or not. Anthropomorphic body elements should only be included when they serve an interaction purpose with the driver within safety constraints or facilitate interactions. These findings also emphasize the importance of a balanced RHMI design approach that accommodates individual preferences, as there is no one-size-fits-all RHMI design. RHMI designs for driving support should also consider user experience qualities to enhance the acceptability of the driving support. Future research aims to extend these findings by increasing the participant number, isolating better the distinction of anthropomorphic elements across various RHMIs, and exploring individual preferences in RHMI design and user experience in greater depth.

References

1. Abdel-Aty, M.A., Chen, C.L., Schott, J.R.: An assessment of the effect of driver age on traffic accident involvement using log-linear models. Accid. Anal. Prev. **30**(6), 851–861 (1998)
2. Bartneck, C., Kulić, D., Croft, E., Zoghbi, S.: Measurement instruments for the anthropomorphism, animacy, likeability, perceived intelligence, and perceived safety of robots. Int. J. Soc. Robot. **1**(1), 71–81 (2009)
3. Bethel, C.L.: Robots without faces: non-verbal social human-robot interaction. University of South Florida (2009)
4. Breazeal, C., Kidd, C.D., Thomaz, A.L., Hoffman, G., Berlin, M.: Effects of nonverbal communication on efficiency and robustness in human-robot teamwork. In: 2005 IEEE/RSJ International Conference on Intelligent Robots and Systems, pp. 708–713. IEEE (2005)

5. Cheng, P., Meng, F., Yao, J., Wang, Y.: Driving with agents: investigating the influences of anthropomorphism level and physicality of agents on drivers' perceived control, trust, and driving performance. Front. Psychol. **13** (2022)
6. Hsieh, W.F., Sato-Shimokawara, E., Yamaguchi, T.: Impression preference tendency between a cute robot and a cool robot. J. Jpn. Soc. Fuzzy Theory Intell. Inform. **32**(2), 686–690 (2020)
7. Kalegina, A., Schroeder, G., Allchin, A., Berlin, K., Cakmak, M.: Characterizing the design space of rendered robot faces. In: Proceedings of the 2018 ACM/IEEE International Conference on Human-Robot Interaction, pp. 96–104 (2018)
8. Karatas, N., Yoshikawa, S., De Silva, P.R.S., Okada, M.: NAMIDA: multiparty conversation based driving agents in futuristic vehicle. In: Kurosu, M. (ed.) HCI 2015. LNCS, vol. 9171, pp. 198–207. Springer, Cham (2015). https://doi.org/10.1007/978-3-319-21006-3_20
9. Kuehn, M., Hummel, T., Bende, J.: Benefit estimation of advanced driver assistance systems for cars derived from real-life accidents. In: 21st International Technical Conference on the Enhanced Safety of Vehicles ESV, vol. 15, p. 18 (2009)
10. Miyamoto, T., et al.: Influence of social distance expressed by driving support agent's utterance on psychological acceptability. Front. Psychol. 254 (2021)
11. Mutlu, B., Forlizzi, J., Hodgins, J.: A storytelling robot: modeling and evaluation of human-like gaze behavior. In: 2006 6th IEEE-RAS International Conference on Humanoid Robots, pp. 518–523. IEEE (2006)
12. Mutlu, B., Kanda, T., Forlizzi, J., Hodgins, J., Ishiguro, H.: Conversational gaze mechanisms for humanlike robots. ACM Trans. Interact. Intell. Syst. (TiiS) **1**(2), 1–33 (2012)
13. Nijdam, N.A.: Mapping emotion to color. In: Book Mapping Emotion to Color, pp. 2–9 (2009)
14. World Health Organization: Aging and health (2022). https://www.who.int/newsroom/fact-sheets/detail/ageing-and-health. Accessed 1 Oct 2022
15. Reed, C.L., Stone, V.E., Bozova, S., Tanaka, J.: The body-inversion effect. Psychol. Sci. **14**(4), 302–308 (2003)
16. Schrepp, M.: User experience questionnaire handbook. All you need to know to apply the UEQ successfully in your project (2015)
17. Tanaka, T.: 4 robotic human-machine interface towards driving behavior improvement for elderly drivers. Towards Hum.-Veh. Harmonization **3**, 47 (2023)
18. Tanaka, T., et al.: Driver agent for encouraging safe driving behavior for the elderly. In: Proceedings of the 5th International Conference on Human Agent Interaction, pp. 71–79 (2017)
19. Tanaka, T., Fujikake, K., Yoshihara, Y., Karatas, N., Aoki, H., Kanamori, H.: Study on acceptability of and distraction by driving support agent in actual car environment. In: Proceedings of the 7th International Conference on Human-Agent Interaction, pp. 202–204 (2019)
20. Institute for Traffic Accident Research and Data Analysis: ITARDA information (2008)
21. Williams, K., Breazeal, C.: Reducing driver task load and promoting sociability through an affective intelligent driving agent (AIDA). In: Kotzé, P., Marsden, G., Lindgaard, G., Wesson, J., Winckler, M. (eds.) INTERACT 2013. LNCS, vol. 8120, pp. 619–626. Springer, Heidelberg (2013). https://doi.org/10.1007/978-3-642-40498-6_53
22. Zihsler, J., et al.: Carvatar: increasing trust in highly-automated driving through social cues. In: Adjunct Proceedings of the 8th International Conference on Automotive User Interfaces and Interactive Vehicular Applications, pp. 9–14 (2016)

AI Planning from Natural-Language Instructions for Trustworthy Human-Robot Communication

Dang Tran, Hui Li, and Hongsheng He$^{(\boxtimes)}$

The University of Alabama, Tuscaloosa, AL 35487, USA
`hongsheng.he@ua.edu`

Abstract. Having deterministic communication between humans and robots is essential for a safe, reliable, and trustworthy workspace. Despite the extensive efforts in training robots to comprehend human instructions, the predominant focus has been on improving the generative aspects of models rather than the determinism. This paper presents a frame-based method using planning language and Controlled Robot Language to construct a reliable and deterministic linguistic channel. The model takes multiple instructions as input and generates an appropriate syntactic and formal representation. Core information is extracted from formal representation using bottom-up visitors. The obtained information is used to generate a planning script in Planning Domain Definition Language (PDDL), which can be used directly to control the robot system. The experiment demonstrated great performance of the proposed method on many text-processing tasks and promising results in deterministic communication with robots on a manually created new dataset focusing on the robotic domain.

Keywords: Planning · Natural Language Processing · Human Robot Interaction · Reliable Communication

1 Introduction

In recent years, social robots have become increasingly involved in many aspects of human lives including education [1], healthcare [2], manufacturing [3], and agriculture [4]. Many of these applications require social robots to interact with people on both communicative and physical levels. For instance, healthcare robots can provide patients with medicine information and retrieve the medicine for them [5]. A collaboration robot can engage in dialogue with human partners, assisting them in executing assigned tasks [6]. In these scenarios, it is imperative for the robots to accurately and deterministically comprehend human instructions, thereby mitigating the potential for physical and life-threatening accidents.

This research is supported by NSF #2129113 and NSF #2239540.

To develop reliable communication, current methods integrate Natural Language Processing (NLP) with AI Planning. A notable innovation within this field is the automatic generation of Planning Domain Definition Language (PDDL) from natural language inputs. PDDL offers a formal framework for deterministic planning, addressing real-world problems, especially for cognitive robot systems. Various research attempts have been undertaken to address this challenge, such as the dependency-tree-based method [7], the Deep Q-Network method for action templates matching [8], and the dictionary-based approach [9]. The majority of these studies incorporate the model acquisition tools LOCM and LOCM2 [10] for PDDL generation. While these models can handle more generative instructions, their generated PDDL scripts are incomplete and error-prone, necessitating additional manual post-processing to make them readable for high-level planners. Besides, the PDDL scripts generated by acquisition tools are for the general domain which significantly differs from the robotic domain. In the robotic domain, planning scripts should contain only executable, non-abstract actions, with a small number of arguments due to practical constraints.

To address these limitations, we present a robust and reliable NLP framework that can produce deterministic robotic planning descriptions. Such determinism can enhance the stability and trustworthiness of human-robot collaborations. The proposed model approaches the generation problem as a multi-stage NLP process, which provides a great control over model performances at different stages. Furthermore, the proposed model focuses on the robot domain, which produces complete PDDL descriptions, that are comprehensible by planners and executable by robot controls. Additionally, the method provides both syntactic and semantic representations, offering a wide range of flexibility and adaptability. The workflow of the proposed method is summarized as follows: Given high-level instructions, the proposed NLP pipeline performs a series of processing tasks on the input, creates syntactic and semantic structures. Subsequently, information is extracted from the semantics, which is then utilized to generate essential PDDL problem sections. The generated PDDL is directly employed for robotic control through ROS-Plan. The contributions of the paper are summarized as follows:

1. A deterministic linguistic communication channel has been implemented. By exploiting the determinism property of AI Planning, we proposed a PDDL-based framework that enables robots to unambiguously understand human instructions.
2. The proposed linguistic dataset is designed for practical robotic planning scenarios, making it not only suitable for linguistic model evaluation but also for demonstrating the practical application of the framework on motion planning.

2   Automated Planning Problem Generation

The proposed linguistic communication method takes natural language instructions from users and generates problem scripts in PDDL, as illustrated in Fig. 1. The raw input is first pushed into the developed linguistic model, named

Controlled Robot Language (CRL) [11]. CRL is a multi-stage linguistic model, where each stage is dedicated to a specific text-processing task. The output of one stage becomes the input for the next stage. In general, given a natural language command, CRL will return an equivalent semantic expression in Discourse Representation Structure (DRS) [12]. This formal structure is then used by various information extraction models to extract essential data for subsequent generation processes. Each information extractor traverses the semantic structure to capture relevant information. The output of the information extractor is represented in a dictionary form, which consists of a list of key-value pairs. Finally, PDDL generation model uses these acquired pairs to create a PDDL problem script. The resulting PDDL problem script is then combined with the developed PDDL domain script that is constructed based on prior knowledge of the planning problem to control the robot.

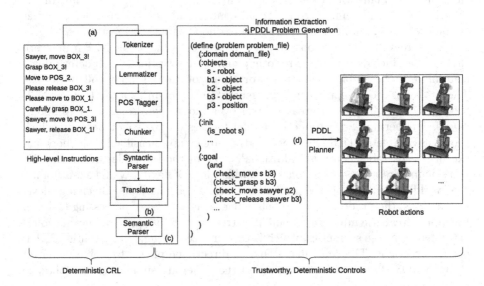

Fig. 1. System overview: natural language instructions are translated into Controlled Robot Language (CRL), which returns a CRL-valid expression (a); Semantic compiler produces semantic expression from CRL-valid input (b); Information extraction from semantics to generate a deterministic plan in PDDL (c); The planning script is utilized for robotic control (d).

2.1 Natural Language Disambiguation and Semantics Parsing

To enable the robot to comprehend instructions, we have developed a model that can deterministically derive the formal expression of the input, known as Controlled Robot Language (CRL) [11]. CRL encompasses two primary steps: (1) A processing step is accomplished by a linguistic model, to conduct syntactical analysis, error detection and translation; (2) An operation of the semantic compiler on the translated input, to produce an equivalent and complete semantic expression. The CRL's pipeline comprises six core components: tokenizer, lemmatizer, POS tagger, phrase-chunker, syntactic parser, and translator. The output of this pipeline is a grammatically correct sentence that has been translated from the original input. The translated sentence is directly readable by the semantic compiler. In this paper, we chose Fuchs's discourse-based model [13] as a semantic compiler. While first-order logic is the more common choice for semantic representation, it is only suitable for representing individual, isolated sentences. In more extensive and complex contexts, first-order logic often falls short in capturing relationships between sentences. We leverage discourse-level structure [12] to effectively capture the semantics of the entire robotic planning scene.

In the POS tagging process, we developed a three-layer cascade model with remarkable flexibility and performance control. At the base layer, we employ the spaCy model, a pre-trained statistical and rule-based linguistic model designed for POS tagging. Nonetheless, the performance of spaCy is imperfect, leading to numerous incorrect and inapplicable labels. These inaccuracies can significantly impact the performance of subsequent stages. To flexibly control the model performance, the cascade model introduces two additional layers: dynamic and static layers, which are stacked on top of the base layer. The static layer focuses on correcting inapplicable labels – labels that are correctly identified by the base layer but are unsuitable for the subsequent stages' processing. These inapplicable labels include proper names, keywords, and annotations. In contrast, the dynamic layer is used to rectify incorrect labels caused by limitations of the base layer. Human users can easily detect these mislabeled tokens and update the syntactic rules to the dynamic layer. Given a tokenized instruction, the dynamic, static, and base layers carry out the tagging process respectively. The final outcome is a sequence of POS tags, cascading from the top layer to the bottom. If using only the base layer, the model may inaccurately label certain tokens. For instance, "move" can be labeled as a singular noun (NN) rather than its correct base form verb (VB). The dynamic layer rectifies this by ensuring that "move" can only be VB. Although the base layer can still correctly identify the POS of many tokens, such as exclamation and commas, the resulting non-alphabetical labels are not comprehensible to the syntactic and semantic parsers. Hence, the static layer is used to assign more suitable labels to these tokens.

To increase the grammatical expressiveness of the proposed model, we developed a translator capable of converting invalid sentences to valid ones. Given the inherent error-proneness of natural language commands, users may inadvertently provide invalid inputs. The proposed translator can detect, navigate and fix the errors using their syntactic structures. To capture the syntactic structure of a sentence, we employed a Context Free Grammar (CFG) specifically designed for Controlled Robot Language. This grammar consists of 220 meticulously selected grammar rules. The lexicons are dynamically generated using the inputs and their POS labels. Our dynamic CFG grammar is generative enough to capture the syntactic structure of both invalid and valid sentences. If a user enters an invalid command, the syntactic parser can still construct the sentence's syntactic structure. Leveraging this structure, the translator can identify the exact locations where the errors have occurred and translate them into the correct forms. Figure 2 represents an example of how a translation is accomplished. The dynamic CFG is robust enough to capture the typos (verb "moves" should be in second person form). Once the tree is captured, the model can detect the precise location of the error, which is under the nonterminal Verb. The verb is then transformed into the correct form, resulting in a valid, grammatically correct sentence.

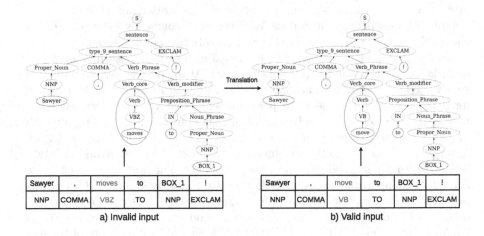

Fig. 2. Comparison of syntactical trees during translation from invalid to valid sentence. Translation is used to detect and repair the misuse of the verb tense "moves".

2.2 Identification of PDDL Problem Components

Once all instructions are CRL-valid, we construct the semantic representation of the entire planning scene. To effectively represent large and complex contexts, we utilize DRS [12] as a semantic compiler, which can capture linked anaphora and coherence. In the complete semantic expression, we focus more on key components, including verbs, object roles, functions, and properties, which are essential for the subsequent generation process. Figure 3 illustrates how verb, subject and object are extracted from semantic statement. The box-like DRS formulation (Fig. 3a) is first linearized into an equivalent DRS statement, which is further parsed into a tree-like structure (Fig. 3b). Given this parsed semantic tree, we can easily extract and capture the essential information. A recursive algorithm traverses along the tree, detecting and copying the matched information into an output dictionary, which contains a set of key-value pairs.

2.3 Plan Script Generation

To deterministically generate a planning script, we developed a PDDL generation model. The PDDL generator is a composition of various visitors, each designed

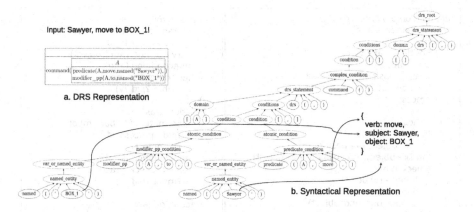

Fig. 3. Two different but equivalent representations of the formal expression. Tree-like format of the formal expression is easier for information extraction and PDDL generating.

to gather specific sets of information. Although the logic flows of these visitors can overlap, the complexity of the task necessitates the use of multiple visitors. In practice, every PDDL generator requires a minimum of 3 distinct visitors: 1) A predicate-visitor to capture executable verbs and function arguments; 2) An object-visitor to capture proper nouns and identifying entities; 3) A preposition-visitor to capture geometric information. The captured outputs are combined together to generate PDDL problem sections. The PDDL problem file requires 3 main sections: (**:objects**), (**:init**), and (**:goal**). The generated sections are combined together into one problem description script, which is readable by PDDL planners. The generation strategies depend strongly on the type of instruction.

The generated PDDL problem file alone is insufficient for planning and robotic control. PDDL planner requires both problem and domain files. Since human instructions do not provide useful information to construct a PDDL domain, we create a domain file based on the prior knowledge of the planning domain. For instance, in the Block world problem, we defined a set of actions that are most suitable and executable in the robot framework: *move, grasp, release, throw,* and *search.* Following the design conventions for robotic work cells [14], we have also defined various types of objects that are relevant for the manipulation environment: *robot, position, object* and *pid* (process id). Figure 4 represents a complete PDDL domain for the Block world problem.

The diversity of semantic expressions makes it challenging to develop a universal generation algorithm. Therefore, it becomes necessary to implement various generation strategies tailored to the specific types of instructions. In practice, we have categorized all instructions into 3 primary types: 1) Single action sentence with well-identified entities; 2) Single action sentence with ungrounded entities; and 3) Sentence involving multiple actions.

Type 1 commands consist of sentences featuring a single action and clearly identified entities. The plan generation strategy for type 1 commands is straight-

```
(define (domain demo_file)                    (:action move
  (:requirements :typing)                       :parameters (?robot - robot
  (:types                                         ?pid - process_id
    position_and_object                           ?y - position_and_object)
    table robot                                 :precondition (and)
    object - position_and_object                :effect (check_move
    position - position_and_object                ?robot ?pid ?y)
    process_id                                  )
  )                                           (:action grasp
  (:predicates                                  :parameters (?robot - robot
    (is_robot ?x - robot)                         ?pid - process_id
    (at ?x - object ?y - position)                ?y - object)
    (on ?x - object ?y - position_and_object)   :precondition (and)
    (check_move                                 :effect (check_grasp
      ?robot - robot                              ?robot ?pid ?y)
      ?pid - process_id                         )
      ?x - position_and_object)               (:action release
    (check_grasp                                 :parameters (?robot - robot
      ?robot - robot                              ?pid - process_id
      ?pid - process_id                           ?y - object)
      ?y - object)                              :precondition (and)
    (check_release                              :effect (check_release
      ?robot - robot                              ?robot ?pid ?y)
      ?pid - process_id                         )
      ?y - object)                            )
  )
)
```

Fig. 4. Develop PDDL domain for Block world problem.

forward and requires no additional processing steps. The dictionary produced by predicate-visitor serves as the basis for the construction of (:goal) section. Type 1 commands are the simplest instructions involving well-defined entities. To convert a sentence into a type 1 equivalent, we replace all available nouns with recognized identities. Figure 5a illustrates an example of how a type 1 command is created, wherein the unidentified noun (*the red box*) is replaced with an identified proper noun (*BOX_1*).

Type 2 commands represent the relaxed version of type 1 commands, allowing ungrounded objects. In other words, type 2 commands can include singular or plural nouns. To generate plans for type 2 commands, an additional preprocessing step is required, which involves mapping unidentified nouns to objects within the robot's perception. This process is referred to as *grounding*, where we establish a correspondence between objects in the natural language instructions and the objects available in the robot's knowledge base. Figure 5b illustrates an example of how the proposed model handles type 2 commands.

Finally, type 3 commands contain more than one action, which is an alternative formulation for multiple sentences. Since each predicate-visitor is optimized to handle one primary action and its associated arguments, sentences with multiple actions can introduce complexity to the extraction process. Therefore, a distinct strategy is needed to generate plans for type 3 instructions. To handle type 3 commands, we convert each command into multiple sentences with

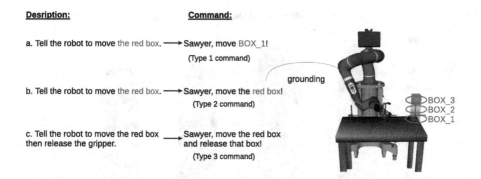

Fig. 5. Three types of commands that the proposed system can handle efficiently with different generating strategies.

consistent subjects and the same action order. The primary actions and their respective arguments are segmented into distinct blocks.

3 Experiment

To evaluate the effectiveness of the proposed method, we conducted experiments on various real-world planning scenarios. Recognizing the absence of a suitable dataset for evaluation, particularly since most NLP datasets are centered on the broader English domain, we developed a new dataset specifically tailored for robotics and planning. Each entry in the dataset represents a distinct planning scenario, and consists sequence of instructions, queries, and perception descriptions. The performance of the proposed method is measured by the system's competence in comprehending instructions and its proficiency in generating valid plans. More specifically, we evaluate the model's accuracy in four core tasks: POS tagging, syntactic parsing, semantic parsing, and PDDL problem generation. The experiment results demonstrate the robust performance and configurability of the POS tagger and syntactic parser. While there is a lower accuracy performance observed in semantic parsing and PDDL generation. Finally, we illustrate how the generated planning file can be used for controlling a robot in simulation.

3.1 Experiment Setup

To set up the robot environment, we implemented the MagicHand platform [15], with a specific focus on the Block world problem. This platform comprises a Rethink Sawyer robot and an AR10 gripper, both implemented in simulation using Gazebo and ROS Kinetic. The NLP pipeline is developed in Python 3.9, utilizing libraries such as Spacy, NLTK and Lark. For high-level robotic control and PDDL solving, we use Moveit! [16] and Fast-Forward planner [17]. The choice of Fast-Forward planner is significant, since it preserves the order of actions in the planning solution.

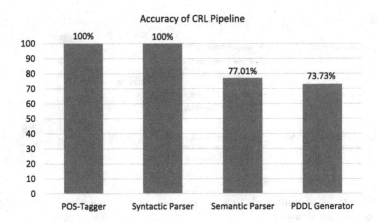

Fig. 6. Performance of the CRL model's components.

The dataset contains 335 planning scenarios, with approximately 4,000 tokens. Each entry represents a sequence of sentences, and these sentences can take the form of a query, descriptive statement, or command. The dataset also includes ungrammatical sentences. We evaluated the model's performance on the following tasks: POS tagging, syntactic parsing, semantic parsing, and PDDL problem generation. For POS tagging, we measured the accuracy of the multi-label model. For more complex tasks like syntactic parsing, semantic parsing, and PDDL generation, we measured the framework's feasibility in generating meaningful output.

3.2 Performance of CRL Model

The performance of CRL model is visualized in Fig. 6. The proposed framework excels with 100% accuracy in POS tagging. Additionally, the model achieves a 100% feasibility score in syntactic parsing, demonstrating its capability to parse all the instructions in the dataset. However, the feasibility score for semantic parser is slightly lower at 77.01% (258/355 sentences). This is attributed to certain limitations of Fuchs's semantic compiler [13]. For instance, Fuchs's model can not understand gerunds, personal pronouns, and adheres to specific rules for adverbs and prepositions. The performance of PDDL planning generation stands at 73.73% in terms of feasibility (247/355 sentences). It's noteworthy that the performance of earlier tasks will set the upper limit for the performance of subsequent tasks. This emphasizes the importance of performance control and model flexibility, which the proposed method addresses. Finally, we showed how one scenario successfully led to the planning execution in the robotic system. The scenario contains 12 commands executed in sequential order. Figure 7 illustrates how the robotic system processes the input and executes the actions accordingly.

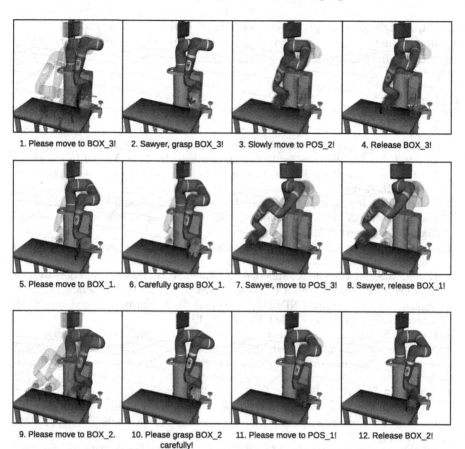

1. Please move to BOX_3!   2. Sawyer, grasp BOX_3!   3. Slowly move to POS_2!   4. Release BOX_3!

5. Please move to BOX_1.   6. Carefully grasp BOX_1.   7. Sawyer, move to POS_3!   8. Sawyer, release BOX_1!

9. Please move to BOX_2.   10. Please grasp BOX_2 carefully!   11. Please move to POS_1!   12. Release BOX_2!

Fig. 7. The proposed system successfully converted a 12 consecutive commands into a practical execution plan.

4   Conclusion

This paper presents a robust and deterministic linguistic communication channel, which allows human users to interact reliably with robots. Leveraging the determinism property of planning descriptions (PDDL), we developed a multi-stage model that can provide both syntactic and semantic expressions. Additionally, the model demonstrates the ability to comprehend instructions and generate deterministic planning. The performance of the method was evaluated on a newly designed dataset, yielding impressive results. POS tagging achieved a perfect 100% score in accuracy, while syntactic parsing secured a flawless 100% feasibility score. These outcomes affirm the deterministic nature of the proposed method. Although the model achieved slightly lower feasibility scores 77.01% for semantic parsing and 73.73% for PDDL problem generation, these limitations can be attributed to the constraints of the semantic compiler itself. In summary, this paper highlights the promising potential of PDDL-based methods for building deterministic communication channels between humans and robots, which can reduce physical accidents in workplace environments.

References

1. Belpaeme, T., Kennedy, J., Ramachandran, A., Scassellati, B., Tanaka, F.: Social robots for education: a review. Sci. Robot. **3**(21), eaat5954 (2018)
2. Breazeal, C.: Social robots for health applications. In: 2011 Annual International Conference of the IEEE Engineering in Medicine and Biology Society, pp. 5368–5371. IEEE (2011)
3. Jahanmahin, R., Masoud, S., Rickli, J., Djuric, A.: Human-robot interactions in manufacturing: a survey of human behavior modeling. Robot. Comput.-Integr. Manuf. **78**, 102404 (2022)
4. Sparrow, R., Howard, M.: Robots in agriculture: prospects, impacts, ethics, and policy. Precis. Agric. **22**, 818–833 (2021)
5. Kaiser, M.S., Al Mamun, S., Mahmud, M., Tania, M.H.: Healthcare robots to combat COVID-19. In: Santosh, K.C., Joshi, A. (eds.) COVID-19: Prediction, Decision-Making, and its Impacts. LNDECT, vol. 60, pp. 83–97. Springer, Singapore (2021). https://doi.org/10.1007/978-981-15-9682-7_10
6. Lopes, L.S., Teixeira, A.: Human-robot interaction through spoken language dialogue. In: Proceedings. 2000 IEEE/RSJ International Conference on Intelligent Robots and Systems (IROS 2000)(Cat. No. 00CH37113), vol. 1, pp. 528–534. IEEE (2000)
7. Lindsay, A., Read, J., Ferreira, J., Hayton, T., Porteous, J., Gregory, P.: Framer: planning models from natural language action descriptions. In: Proceedings of the International Conference on Automated Planning and Scheduling, vol. 27, pp. 434–442 (2017)
8. Miglani, S., Yorke-Smith, N.: NLtoPDDL: one-shot learning of PDDL models from natural language process manuals. In: Proceedings of the ICAPS Workshop on Knowledge Engineering for Planning and Scheduling (KEPS). ICAPS (2020)
9. Yan, F., Tran, D.M., He, H.: Robotic understanding of object semantics by referringto a dictionary. Int. J. Soc. Robot. **12**, 1251–1263 (2020)
10. Cresswell, S., McCluskey, T., West, M.: Acquisition of object-centred domain models from planning examples. In: Proceedings of the International Conference on Automated Planning and Scheduling, vol. 19, pp. 338–341 (2009)
11. Tran, D., Yan, F., Yihun, Y., Tan, J., He, H.: A framework of controlled robot language for reliable human-robot collaboration. In: Li, H., et al. (eds.) ICSR 2021. LNCS (LNAI), vol. 13086, pp. 339–349. Springer, Cham (2021). https://doi.org/10.1007/978-3-030-90525-5_29
12. Kamp, H., Van Genabith, J., Reyle, U.: Discourse representation theory. In: Gabbay, D., Guenthner, F. (eds.) Handbook of Philosophical Logic. Handbook of Philosophical Logic, vol. 15, pp. 125–394. Springer, Dordrecht (2011). https://doi.org/10.1007/978-94-007-0485-5_3
13. Fuchs, N.E., Schwitter, R.: Attempto controlled English (ace) (1996). arXiv preprint cmp-lg/9603003
14. Ochi, K., Fukunaga, A., Kondo, C., Maeda, M., Hasegawa, F., Kawano, Y.: A steady-state model for automated sequence generation in a robotic assembly system. SPARK 2013 (2013)

15. Li, H., Tan, J., He, H.: MagicHand: context-aware dexterous grasping using an anthropomorphic robotic hand. In: 2020 IEEE International Conference on Robotics and Automation (ICRA), pp. 9895–9901. IEEE (2020)
16. Chitta, S., Sucan, I., Cousins, S.: Moveit! IEEE Robot. Autom. Mag. **19**(1), 18–19 (2012)
17. Hoffmann, J.: FF: the fast-forward planning system. AI Mag. **22**(3), 57 (2001)

Agricultural Robotic System: The Automation of Detection and Speech Control

Yang Wenkai[(✉)], Ji Ruihang, Yue Yiran, Gu Zhonghan, Shu Wanyang,
and Sam Ge Shuzhi

National University of Singapore, Singapore, Singapore
e0983030@u.nus.edu

Abstract. Agriculture industries often face challenges in manual tasks such as planting, harvesting, fertilizing, and detection, which can be time-consuming and prone to errors. The "Agricultural Robotic System" project addresses these issues through a modular design that integrates advanced visual, speech recognition, and robotic technologies. This system is comprised of separate but interconnected modules for vision detection and speech recognition, creating a flexible and adaptable solution. The vision detection module uses computer vision techniques, trained on YOLOv5 and deployed on the Jetson Nano in TensorRT format, to accurately detect and identify different items. A robotic arm module then precisely controls the picking up of seedlings or seeds, and arranges them in specific locations. The speech recognition module enhances intelligent human-robot interaction, allowing for efficient and intuitive control of the system. This modular approach improves the efficiency and accuracy of agricultural tasks, demonstrating the potential of robotics in the agricultural industry.

Keywords: YOLOv5 · Jetson Nano · TensorRT · Robotic arm kinematics · PID control · Speech recognition · Modular design

1 Introduction

This paper discusses the challenges in agriculture and how robotics and computer vision technologies can be used to address them. Specifically, the impact of the Agricultural Robotic System (ARS) on the efficiency of agricultural processes is addressed. We in this work focus on addressing the ARS with object detection, speech recognition and robot arm trajectory. The ARS is a system that uses advanced computer vision techniques yolov5 [13] to accurately detect, identify, and differentiate between various plant species and their growth stages. The

This research project is partially supported by the Ministry of Education, Singapore, under its Research Centre of Excellence award to the Institute for Functional Intelligent Materials (I-FIM, project No. EDUNC-33-18-279-V12). The real robot presentation and discription will show in this link. https://www.youtube.com/watch?v=S4Op68Es7FY.

system is designed to be highly efficient and adaptable, and can be scaled to accommodate different farm sizes and types of crops.

The ARS can be used to automate a variety of agricultural tasks, including planting, harvesting, fertilizing, and detection. For example, the ARS can be used to plant seeds with precision and accuracy, ensuring that the seeds are planted in the correct location and at the correct depth. The ARS can also be used to harvest crops with minimal damage, and can even be used to identify and remove diseased or damaged plants. The ARS can also be used to apply fertilizer to crops in a precise and efficient manner, ensuring that the fertilizer is applied in the correct amount and in the correct location.

The ARS has the potential to significantly improve the efficiency and productivity of agricultural processes. The system can automate many of the labor-intensive tasks that are currently performed by humans, and can do so with greater precision and accuracy. The ARS can also help to reduce the environmental impact of agriculture, by reducing the use of pesticides and herbicides.

The ARS is still under development, but it has the potential to revolutionize the agricultural industry. The system has the potential to make farming more efficient, productive, and sustainable. One of the key challenges in deploying the ARS is optimizing the model for the device. This requires striking a balance between model accuracy and inference speed. Too much optimization may lead to loss of accuracy, while too little may not significantly improve inference speed. Another challenge is implementing Non-Maximum Suppression (NMS) on the Nano. NMS is a computationally expensive process and can slow down the overall inference time.

2   Analysis of Agricultural Robotic System

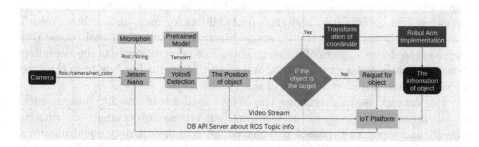

Fig. 1. The Agricultural Robotic System System Design

Consider the system architecture shown in Fig. 1. The RGB camera captures high-quality images and transmits them in the ROS (Robot Operating System) format, enabling the integration of visual information into our complex robotic ecosystem. Concurrently, microphone system is designed to pick up and analyze human speech. For instance, a command such as "pick the orange" is processed and translated into a series of actions for the robotic arm. Meanwhile, the NVIDIA Jetson Nano is a powerful device that loads a pre-trained machine learning model in TensorRT [6] and processes video streams in real time. The raw result from the initial inference is refined using non-maximum suppression (NMS), which reduces overlapping bounding boxes and narrows down the focus to the most probable object locations. The result of NMS is transformed into the operational space of the robotic arm. This allows the arm to calculate and follow an optimal path to reach and pick up the detected object.

3   Pattern Recognition and Robot Intelligence

3.1   Computer Vison Detection

We use Yolov5 to detect fruits and seeds in the video from the robotic arm. Yolov5 is a fast, accurate, and lightweight object detection algorithm developed by Ultralytics. It is suitable for deployment on resource-constrained devices such as mobile phones and robots. Yolov5 is a one-stage object detection algorithm that uses a single CNN to perform object detection. It consists of a backbone network, neck network, and head network. The backbone network extracts features from the input image, the neck network enhances the discriminability of the features, and the head network predicts the bounding boxes and class probabilities of the objects in the image. The backbone network is based on the CSP Darknet53 [12] architecture, which has been optimized for efficiency and accuracy. The CSP block allows for efficient information flow across multiple layers. The detection head in YOLOv5 is a hybrid approach, which combines anchor-based [14] and anchor-free methods to improve the detection performance. It uses a SPP [4] (spatial pyramid pooling) module to extract features at multiple scales, followed by a PAN [8] (path aggregation network) module that combines features from different scales. Finally, a YOLOv5 head predicts objectness scores, bounding box coordinates, and class probabilities for each anchor box. Yolov5 is an anchor-based object [11] detection algorithm that uses a multi-scale [10] approach to detect objects of different sizes. The network predicts the bounding box coordinates, class probabilities, and offset of each anchor box from the true object location at different scales of the feature map.

The dataset used for training the Yolov5 model contains 200 images, each of which has one or more of the following four types of objects: apple, banana, orange, and seed. The dataset is balanced, with approximately equal numbers of each object type. Specifically, there are 202 apples, 181 bananas, 178 oranges, and 146 seeds in the dataset. To get a better understanding of the dataset, we can also look at the distribution of objects across the images. As mentioned, each image can contain one or more objects. The following Table 1 summarizes the number of objects per image:

From the Table 1, we can see that the majority of the images (60 out of 200) contain 4 objects, while the fewest images (8 out of 200) contain 6 objects. During the training process, Yolov5 model uses data augmentation techniques

Table 1. Objects Distribution

Number of objects	Number of images
1	24
2	46
3	36
4	80
5	39
6	8

such as random flipping and cropping to increase the size of the dataset and improve the model's ability to generalize to new images.

3.2 Speech Recognition

Speech recognition is a process of pattern recognition. It works by splitting the waveform into utterances by silences, then trying to recognize what's being said in each utterance. The best matching combination is chosen. Speech recognition modules based on acoustic models are designed to achieve more convenient human-computer interaction. The speech recognition module used a pre-trained Chinese acoustic model from CMUSphinx [7]. The model has been optimized for optimal performance and can be used in most instruction interaction systems, even for applications with large vocabularies. Sphinx and some open-source pre-trained models can be used to adapt to existing models. We installed the SpeedRecognition and PocketSphinx [5] modules, which achieved high accuracy and fast speed. We can consider training our own model for higher accuracy, but the existing model has already met the initial requirements

A continuous speech recognition system can be roughly divided into four parts: feature extraction, acoustic model training, language model training, and decoding.

- Feature extraction: MFCC features [9] are used in Sphinx. MFCC is a widely used parameter due to its excellent noise resistance and robustness. It is calculated using FFT [3], convolution, and DCT.
- Acoustic model training: HMM [1] is a statistical model established for the time series structure of speech signals. We use a left to right unidirectional, self loop, and spanning topology to model recognition primitives. A phoneme is an HMM in three to five states, a word is an HMM composed of multiple phonemes that form a word in series, and the entire model of continuous speech recognition is an HMM composed of words and silence.
- Language model training: In a traditional stochastic language model, the current word is predicted based on the preceding word or the preceding n-1 words. We experimented with long distance bigrams to reduce the number of free parameters and maintain the modeling capacity.

– Decoder: The recognition result of a continuous speech recognition system is a word sequence. Decoding is actually a repeated search for all the words in the vocabulary. The arrangement of words in a vocabulary can affect the speed of search.

We have set up the vocabulary to be loaded into the module, and then we can start recording and recognizing the vocabulary input by the user, and return a list of possible matching Chinese vocabulary. The controller makes corresponding actions and operations based on these vocabulary and the previously established vocabulary-action mapping.

3.3   Image Geometry

After we get the bounding box of every object in pixel coordinate, we need to transform it into world coordinate. This is a common task in computer vision and involves a series of transformations that map the points from the image plane (pixels) to the real-world 3D coordinates. The procedure typically involves the following steps:

Camera Calibration. Camera calibration is the process of estimating the intrinsic and extrinsic parameters of a camera. The intrinsic parameters are related to the camera's internal characteristics, such as focal length, optical center, and lens distortion. The extrinsic parameters are the camera's position and orientation in the world. This step is essential because it establishes a relationship between pixel coordinates and world coordinates.

Pixel Coordinates to Camera Coordinates. The first step in conversion is to map the pixel coordinates to the camera's coordinate system. The equation for this is given by:

$$\begin{bmatrix} u \\ v \\ 1 \end{bmatrix} = \begin{bmatrix} f_x & 0 & c_x \\ 0 & f_y & c_y \\ 0 & 0 & 1 \end{bmatrix} \begin{bmatrix} X_c \\ Y_c \\ Z_c \end{bmatrix} \tag{1}$$

where (u, v) are the pixel coordinates, (X_c, Y_c, Z_c) are the coordinates in the camera frame, (fx, fy) are the focal lengths in x and y directions (in pixel units), and (cx, cy) is the optical center (in pixel units). This is actually a pinhole camera model which is a good approximation for many real cameras.

Camera Coordinates to World Coordinates. Once we have the point in the camera coordinate system, we can transform it to the world coordinate system using the extrinsic parameters. The equation is given by:

$$\begin{bmatrix} X_w \\ Y_w \\ Z_w \end{bmatrix} = \begin{bmatrix} R & t \\ 0 & 1 \end{bmatrix} \begin{bmatrix} X_c \\ Y_c \\ Z_c \end{bmatrix} \tag{2}$$

where (X_w, Y_w, Z_w) are the world coordinates, R is a 3×3 rotation matrix, and t is a 3 × 1 translation vector. The '0' in the bottom left is a row vector of size 1×3 and the '1' in the bottom right is a scalar. This is a homogeneous transformation matrix. These values are obtained from the camera calibration process and define the camera's position and orientation in the world.

The above process require the camera have been already calibrated and know its intrinsic and extrinsic parameters by using a method the chessboard calibration technique [2].

4   The Practical Experiments of Robot

4.1   Computer Vision Detection

The camera we used in detection is common MIX219 CSI camera to detect fruits in daily life. The dataset used for training the Yolov5 model contains 200 images, each of which has one or more of the following four types of objects: apple, banana, orange, and seed. The dataset is balanced, with approximately equal numbers of each object type. Specifically, there are 202 apples, 181 bananas, 178 oranges, and 146 seeds in the dataset. The Yolov5 model achieved an average f1 score of 0.98 for all 4 classes (apple, banana, orange, and seed) on the validation showed in Fig. 2 and 3 set when the confidence threshold was set to 0.67. This is a high level of accuracy, indicating that the model is able to accurately detect and classify the objects in the images. A confidence threshold of 0.67 means that the model is only considering detections that it is relatively confident in, with a score of at least 0.67 out of 1.

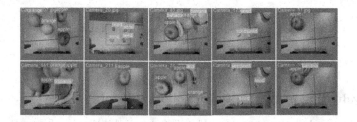

Fig. 2. Validation of Yolov5

4.2   Evaluation of Speech Recognition

In this project, the speech recognition system demonstrates an impressive ability to convert spoken commands into actionable instructions for the robot. The system leverages Mel Frequency Cepstral Coefficients (MFCC) for feature extraction, a decision supported by MFCC's robustness and noise resistance. The use of Fast Fourier Transform (FFT) for signal conversion and Discrete Cosine Transform (DCT) on the output of each filter's vector further bolsters the system's effectiveness. These techniques contribute to a robust feature extraction mechanism that significantly aids in the translation of human speech into machine-understandable commands.

The speech recognition system exhibits a high level of sophistication and effectiveness in converting spoken commands into actionable tasks. Its robust feature extraction, acoustic model training, and language model training techniques contribute to its strong performance. However, as with any technology, there are areas for potential enhancement, such as optimizing the dictionary arrangement for faster decoding and exploring continuous speech recognition for improved usability.

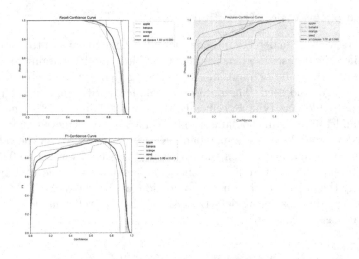

Fig. 3. Recall, Precision and F1 of Yolov5

4.3   Evaluation of Agricultural Robotic System

The robot arm has demonstrated significant capabilities in the realm of agricultural technology. It can pick up seedlings or seeds with precise control, harvest crops, and identify items using advanced computer vision techniques. The speech recognition module and IoT interface enhance its user-friendliness and adaptability. Future enhancements could include refining the object detection model, expanding the acoustic models, and exploring more complex movements and operations. The Table 2 provides a concise comparison of various robot arms, highlighting their item picking abilities and special features. Overall, the Agricultural Robotic project stands as a beacon of innovation in agricultural technology.

Table 2. Comparison of Robot Arms

Robot Arm	Item Picking Ability	Special Features
Agricultural Robotic	Picks up different seedlings or seeds and harvests crops	Uses computer vision and speech recognition. The IoT interface display ROS topic information in real time API server.
ABB IRB 360 FlexPicker	Known for speed and precision in picking and packing	Uses ABB's PickMaster software with vision guidance.
Fanuc M-2iA/3S	Designed for high-speed picking and packing	Uses Fanuc's iRVision system.
Universal Robots UR5	Equipped with a camera for vision-guided tasks	Known for flexibility and safety features.
KUKA KR AGILUS	Equipped with vision systems for picking tasks	Known for speed and precision.
Yaskawa Motoman HC10	Equipped with a camera for vision-guided picking	Designed to work safely alongside humans

5   Conclusion

The Agricultural Robotic System project is a significant advancement in agricultural technology. It aims to revolutionize traditional farming practices by minimizing manual labor, increasing efficiency, and reducing errors. The project integrates cutting-edge technologies such as the Yolov5 model for object detection and the CMUSphinx toolkit for speech recognition. The use of a pre-trained Chinese acoustic model has opened up new avenues for human-computer interaction, making the technology more accessible and user-friendly. Furthermore, the exploration of robot arm kinematics has provided valuable insights into the motion and operation of robotic arms, paving the way for more sophisticated and precise agricultural machinery.

The project has immense potential for future exploration. One area of interest could be the development of more advanced and diverse acoustic models, allowing for recognition of a wider range of languages and dialects. This would make the technology even more accessible to farmers around the world. Another promising direction is the further refinement of the object detection model. With advancements in AI and machine learning, it may be possible to train the model on a larger and more diverse dataset, enabling it to recognize a wider variety of crops and perform more complex tasks. Moreover, the study of robot arm kinematics could be extended to include more complex movements and operations, potentially leading to the development of robotic arms capable of performing tasks such as pruning or pest control.

In essence, the Agricultural Robotic System project stands as a beacon of innovation in agricultural technology. Its success thus far is a testament to the transformative power of robotics and AI in agriculture. As the project continues to evolve and overcome its challenges, it is set to play a pivotal role in shaping the future of farming practices worldwide. The journey of exploration and discovery is just beginning, and the potential for growth and advancement is immense.

References

1. Eddy, S.R.: Accelerated profile hmm searches. PLoS Comput. Biol. **7**(10), e1002195 (2011)
2. De la Escalera, A., Armingol, J.M.: Automatic chessboard detection for intrinsic and extrinsic camera parameter calibration. Sensors **10**(3), 2027–2044 (2010)
3. Frigo, M., Johnson, S.G.: FFTW: an adaptive software architecture for the FFT. In: Proceedings of the 1998 IEEE International Conference on Acoustics, Speech and Signal Processing, ICASSP'98 (Cat. No. 98CH36181), vol. 3, pp. 1381–1384. IEEE (1998)
4. He, K., Zhang, X., Ren, S., Sun, J.: Spatial pyramid pooling in deep convolutional networks for visual recognition. IEEE Trans. Pattern Anal. Mach. Intell. **37**(9), 1904–1916 (2015)
5. Huggins-Daines, D., Kumar, M., Chan, A., Black, A.W., Ravishankar, M., Rudnicky, A.I.: Pocketsphinx: A free, real-time continuous speech recognition system for hand-held devices. In: 2006 IEEE International Conference on Acoustics Speech and Signal Processing Proceedings, vol. 1, pp. I-I. IEEE (2006)
6. Jocher, G., et al.: ultralytics/yolov5: v6. 1-tensorrt, tensorflow edge TPU and openvino export and inference. Zenodo (2022)
7. Lamere, P., et al.: The CMU SPHINX-4 speech recognition system. In: IEEE International Conference on Acoustics, Speech and Signal Processing (icassp 2003), Hong Kong, vol. 1, pp. 2–5 (2003)
8. Liu, S., Qi, L., Qin, H., Shi, J., Jia, J.: Path aggregation network for instance segmentation. In: Proceedings of the IEEE Conference on Computer Vision and Pattern Recognition, pp. 8759–8768 (2018)
9. Murty, K.S.R., Yegnanarayana, B.: Combining evidence from residual phase and MFCC features for speaker recognition. IEEE Signal Process. Lett. **13**(1), 52–55 (2005)
10. Ren, X.: Multi-scale improves boundary detection in natural images. In: Forsyth, D., Torr, P., Zisserman, A. (eds.) ECCV 2008. LNCS, vol. 5304, pp. 533–545. Springer, Heidelberg (2008). https://doi.org/10.1007/978-3-540-88690-7_40
11. Tian, Z., Shen, C., Chen, H., He, T.: FCOS: a simple and strong anchor-free object detector. IEEE Trans. Pattern Anal. Mach. Intell. **44**(4), 1922–1933 (2020)
12. Wang, C.Y., Bochkovskiy, A., Liao, H.Y.M.: Scaled-yolov4: scaling cross stage partial network. In: Proceedings of the IEEE/CVF Conference on Computer Vision and Pattern Recognition, pp. 13029–13038 (2021)
13. Yan, B., Fan, P., Lei, X., Liu, Z., Yang, F.: A real-time apple targets detection method for picking robot based on improved yolov5. Remote Sens. **13**(9), 1619 (2021)
14. Zhang, S., Chi, C., Yao, Y., Lei, Z., Li, S.Z.: Bridging the gap between anchor-based and anchor-free detection via adaptive training sample selection. In: Proceedings of the IEEE/CVF Conference on Computer Vision and Pattern Recognition, pp. 9759–9768 (2020)

Evaluating Telepresence Robot for Supporting Formal and Informal Caregivers in the Care Support Service: A Six-Month Case Study

Laura Fiorini[1](✉) , Jasmine Pani[1] , Erika Rovini[1] , Lara Toccafondi[2],
Novella Calamida[2], Gianna Vignani[2] , and Filippo Cavallo[1]

[1] Department of Industrial Engineering, University of Florence, 50134 Florence, Italy
laura.fiorini@unifi.it
[2] Umana Persone s.r.l, Grosseto, Italy

Abstract. Many older adults are living socially isolated. Telepresence robots could aid older people in supporting independent living and facilitate social interaction. The present study investigates the usability and acceptability of telepresence technology by older adults and their formal and informal caregivers over the course of 6 months. Secondly, the evaluation of the telepresence robot compared to video-calling using a smart TV. Lastly, how informal and formal caregivers perceived the two systems. We found that at the beginning of the study the telepresence robot was not deemed usable compared to the TV by older adults, however the usability increased, whereas the TV decreased after 6 months. Regarding acceptability, the telepresence robot was scored higher than the TV in terms of usefulness, intention to use, enjoyment and trustworthiness in all three groups. Additionally, formal caregivers expressed that the older adults felt more secure, independent and in contact with loved ones, the operator felt that the older adults did not need their physical presence to interact with technology and that their job was helped by having more contact with his/her assisted. Overall, this study suggested that although the perceived usability by older adults might be negative at the beginning, after 6 months the telepresence robot could positively impact the lives of older adults and their caregivers.

Keywords: Telepresence robot · older adults · active aging · acceptability · long term study

1 Introduction

A recent report underlined that nearly one-fourth of adults aged 65 and older are socially isolated and this condition makes them more at risk of experiencing associated risks factors (e.g., worsening health and chronic illness, new sensory impairment, retirement, or changes in income) [1, 2]. Older adults (OA), to reduce their feeling of loneliness and improve the quality of life, need to be in contact with their formal (FC) and informal caregivers (IC). However, on the other hand, the caregivers would like to reduce their burden by enhancing the remote monitoring of their loved ones [3, 4]. Over the last few years, there has been an increase in the use of telepresence robots in age care settings. Telepresence robots have been employed to support the independent living of frail older adults [5, 6] or people living with dementia [7]. Indeed, the design of telepresence robots facilitates remote face-to-face interactions between family members and OA and enables the robots to move around the care environment. Furthermore, telepresence robots have been considered more attractive and interactive than a phone call [8]. It is worth noticing that during the COVID-19 emergency, telepresence robots were also used to reduce loneliness by increasing the number of visits to isolated people in residential facilities, hospitals, and private homes [8–10]. Despite the benefits highlighted in the literature, there are challenges and barriers to overcome. In 2022 Hung et al. [6] remarked the necessity to investigate *"the significance of support and acceptance of senior leaders and managers on the implementation of telepresence levels"* thus identifying the facilitators that may lead to technology adoption in service exploitation. Additionally, Hung et al. mentioned that the studies presented in their review on telepresence robots only had short-term testing phases and underlined the need to plan longitudinal studies. In this sense, research can provide *"comprehensive observations of different stakeholders and participants"* evaluating how this opinion may change over time. This paper aims to overcome the current limitations by evaluating the robotic telepresence service in terms of acceptability and usability after long-term use (6 months) considering three groups of participants (OA, and their FC and IC). Secondly, this paper wishes to determine how the telepresence robot is evaluated compared to a video calling system, since Isabet et al. [8], in their review, pointed out that the telepresence robot was judged more positively compared to a phone call, but the direct comparison with a video calling system remained less explored. To achieve the proposed goals, we implemented two case studies based on two different technologies: a telepresence robot (case study 1) and a smart TV (case study 2) that can support the OA and their ecosystem of caregivers. The services will be evaluated quantitatively in terms of usability and acceptability. Additionally, qualitative results were collected through focus groups and a customized questionnaire to investigate in more detail the opinions of FC and social managers in terms of service efficacy and the potential exploitation of the service on the territory.

2   Material and Methods

2.1   Participants

The participants were recruited in the network of Umana Persone s.r.l among the frail citizens that experienced traditional home social services. Data for the OA and IC using the telepresence robots and the TV service are presented in Table 1. The FC that followed the OA with the robot service were women and worked as a social worker in public health and a nurse, whereas the FC associated with TV service were women, working as social workers in public health. The study was approved by the Ethical Committee of Azienda USL Toscana Sud-Est on the 22/07/2021 (Prot. 2021/000227), and by the Ethical Committee of Azienda USL Toscana Centro on 18/10/2022 (Prot. 2022/22131) all the participants signed the informed consent before entering the study.

2.2 System Description

- **Case Study 1: Promoting socialization with robotic telepresence service.** For this service we used Ohmni robot, a commercial telepresence robot (Ohmnilab robotics, CA, USA) (Fig. 1b). The proprietary web interface allows video calling and remote teleoperation by the caregivers inside the home of the OA. A total of four robots were installed in private homes between May 2022 and May 2023. In this study we include the results of two OA and their FC and IC.
- **Case Study 2: Promoting Socialization through TV** – This case study utilizes a platform on a TV (Sentab TV, Sentab, Estonia) with games that stimulate cognition and memory, and allows OA to video call, and share news and pictures with their caregivers, family, and friends (Fig. 1a). A total of 20 smart TV systems were installed in the OA's private home from May 2022 and May 2023, but to have a direct comparison with the telepresence robots, we included only the data from a subgroup of participants, with demographic and cognitive characteristics comparable to those using the robot. Specifically, we selected the OA of the same gender, similar age group, digital skills and Mini-Mental State Examination (MMSE). Since the caregivers were associated with the OA, the IC were not chosen based on their demographic characteristics.

From a human-interaction perspective, both technologies have an interface for caregivers and a different interface for OA. From a functional perspective, both systems allow video calls between the OA and their FC and IC.

Fig. 1. Participants testing the two different technologies in their home. (a) an older adult with the Sentab TV box. (b) an older participant with the telepresence robot.

After signing the informed consent, the participants were asked to fill-in the MMSE test [11] to assess their cognitive status (only OA), the Loneliness questionnaire [12] to keep track of the self-perceived level of social isolation (OA and IC), the stress related to the technology measured as in [13], and the Rockwood frailty scale (only OA) [14] which is an easy tool with descriptions, pictographs of activity and functional status to assess frailty, and a demographic questionnaire (age, digital skills).

Table 1. Description of the older adult and informal caregiver participants.

	Socialization Service robot		Socialization service TV	
	OA	IC	OA	IC
number	2	2	2	2
Age*	89.5	53.0	84	45.5
Sex	W	M	W	W
Digital Skills	none	medium	none	medium/high
MMSE*	22.70	–	21.45	–
Rockwood frailty scale*	4.5	–	2.5	–
Loneliness*	48	50.5	49	49.5

* *Scores reported as median values. IC: informal caregivers; M: men; OA: older adults; W: women.*

2.3 Experimental Setting

After completing the questionnaires, the technologies were installed in the OA's home, and participants were first trained on technology use by facilitators. At the end of the training session - that lasted between 1 and 2 h - participants were asked to complete the system usability scale (SUS) questionnaire to evaluate the usability [15]. SUS has a score ranging from 0 to 100 and an average usability threshold is fixed at 68. Scores above 68 were considered usable, scores below this threshold should be carefully discussed and interpreted. The acceptability was evaluated through the Almere questionnaire [6] that was adapted for technology as in [13]. Particularly we evaluated the following acceptability constructs: intention of use (ITU), anxiety (ANX), facilitate conditions (FaC), enjoyment (ENJ), trust (TRUST), and perceived usefulness (PU). The participants were then asked to freely use the technology for six months. At the end of six months, the participants were requested to fill in again the two questionnaires on technology (SUS and Almere). Following action research guidelines [17], a focus group was organized to reflect with different stakeholders (i.e., engineering, cooperative project managers and facilitators) and to get insights of the following discussion points related to the technology adoption as well as to the factors that may influence it: i) the recruitment process, with a particular focus on understanding how they assigned a participant to the study 1 or study 2 cohort; ii) the general acceptance of the services from the OA and their IC; iii) the general experience of the FC in using the robot; iv) any comments to improve the service. At the end of the reflection meeting a customized anonymous questionnaire was sent to the focus group participants, as well as to other facilitators, and cooperative managers to collect quantitative information on: the perceived privacy ("Have you got privacy concerns when you are using the system?"); technostress ("Are you afraid of making mistakes in using technology?"); necessity of caregiver physical presence ("The older person needs my physical presence to use this technology"); sense of security ("Older person feels safer since they have technology at home"); promote independency ("The service helps the older adults to be more independent in daily activities?"); promote the social relationship ("The service promote the relationship between the older person and caregiver/relatives even when they are far away?"); support at work to promote visits and manage emergency situations ("The technology helps me in my work because it allows to increase the number of contacts with the older adults"). All these items were evaluated on a 5-points Likert scale (1 = Strongly Disagree; 5 = Strongly agree). The meeting was transcribed. We report and describes only evaluation tools that were analysed in this paper.

2.4 Data Analysis

A total measure of usability was obtained by summing all the SUS items and multiplying the result by 2.5 (even items are in a reverse scale). As for acceptability constructs (i.e., ITU, ANX, FaC, ENJ, TRUST, and PU), an average of the corresponding items was computed. The values were computed for the data collected at the beginning (T0) and at the end of the study (T6) for the three categories of users (i.e., OA, IC, FC) and the two case studies. Given the low numerosity of the sample, a statistical comparison between users was not possible. Comparison in usability and acceptability between groups was done by comparing the median scores. As for the questionnaire sent after the focus group to the FC, the mean value was calculated for each item. To investigate a significant difference between the evaluation of using the robot vs. the TV, non-parametric Mann-Whitney U test was used. Non-parametric statistics were applied because of the sample size. The transcription of the meeting was analysed to cluster the most important discussion point raised.

3   Results

3.1   Results from the Use of Telepresence Robot and SENTAB Technology

Usability

The usability results are depicted in Fig. 2. At T0 and at T6 the Sentab was evaluated usable by the IC and FC and not usable from OA; whereas the robot was evaluated as not usable at the beginning of the study by all the three cohorts of participants and usable for caregivers at T6. It is worth noting that all SUS values increased for the robot (case study 1) whereas decreases for case study 2 (Sentab).

Acceptability

The comparison of the acceptability constructs at T0 for the two technologies in the three cohorts is presented in Fig. 3a. We can observe that at T0 the OA using the robot had higher ANX than the Sentab users, whereas the other acceptability constructs were comparable between the two users. The IC and FC of the robot service, compared to TV service, had higher values in all acceptability constructs except for PU, where the FC rated the two services of equal usefulness.

Figure 3b provides a graphical comparison of the acceptability constructs at T6 for the two technologies in the three cohorts. From a visual inspection we can appreciate how for the OA the ANX and FaC are lower and ENJ, TRUST and PU are higher in the robot user compared to the TV user. However, the ITU was not affected by the service. On the other hand, the opinion of the caregivers was more positive in terms of ITU, FaC, ENJ and PU. Yet the IC had the same levels of ANX in both services.

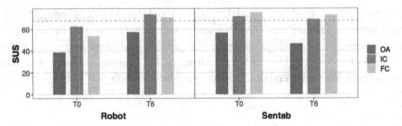

Fig. 2. Usability evaluation of the two technologies at the beginning (T0) and after 6 months of use (T6) for the three cohorts involved. The dashed line represents the threshold value 68.

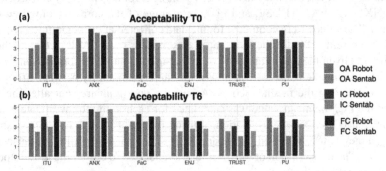

Fig. 3. Acceptance of telepresence robot and Sentab TV box entering the study for older adults (OA), informal caregivers (IC) and formal caregivers (FC). (ITU = intention of use; ANX = anxiety; FaC = Facilitate Conditions; ENJ = Enjoyment; PU = Perceived utility)

3.2 Results of the Reflection Meeting with Formal Caregivers

Results from Focus Group Questionnaire
As for the reflection meeting, a focus group that involved two engineers, two psychologists and 12 facilitators/cooperative managers, was organized on July 2023, and it lasted 2 h. The questionnaire collected feedback from a total of 11 FC: 5 used only Sentab, 5 used robot and Sentab and 1 only used the robot. Results are presented in Fig. 4. The Mann-Whitney U test showed that there was a statistically significant difference between the robot and Sentab users in the question about physical presence. There, the operator's opinion for the robot was that the OA did not need the physical presence of the operator to interact with the technology. There was no statistical difference between the FC using the robot or Sentab for other questions (ie, privacy, technostress, security, promote independence, support relationship, work: improve contact, work: support emergency situation). Nevertheless, although not significant, the operator also judged that the OA felt more secure, independent and in contact with friends and family, and that the service

helped the work of the operator by having more contact with his/her assisted. Yet, there were more concerns about privacy with the robot compared to the TV system.

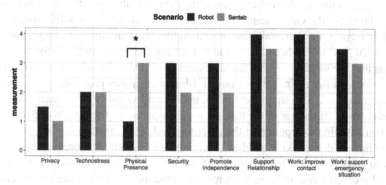

Fig. 4. Results of questionnaires for formal caregivers administered after six months of use of both technologies. Asterisk indicates significant difference.

Results from Focus Group Discussion

During the focus group, the managers underlined that the facilitators assigned the OA to the two technologies (i.e., robot or Sentab) based on their own evaluation, since they knew the OA's abilities and needs. Particularly, one older participant experienced a severe cognitive decline, and the IC wanted to remote motoring his older relative because she was living far away. This IC considered the Sentab technology too complicated to be used. It is worth mentioning that he, as IC, reported a positive experience on the acceptance of the robot, despite the low values of the usability reported by the OA. The other IC that tested the telepresence robot expressed his willingness to pay for this service. Finally, the managers indicated that the operators had a general positive experience/attitude towards the robot, and they did not experience any anxious situation. They used the robot to contact the OA without a prefixed plan, differently from the use of Sentab, where the FC and OA planned one call per week. Furthermore, since the Sentab system needs to be open and running to make the phone calls, the operators before calling the OA with Sentab had to make a regular phone call to remind them to switch the TV input to Sentab, and then video call them. All the operators reported that the robot was useful to maintain contact with families and caregivers. As for the Sentab technology, it was considered more complex to use, and since OA often forget the training, they were not able to use the technology by themselves and the caregivers had to explain the functionalities repeatedly. The two managers stressed that the OA involved in this study are at high risk of frailty, which was indeed confirmed by higher values in the Rockwood scale and low values of MMSE (Table 1) indicating higher risk for cognitive impairment. Additionally, the managers remarked that sometimes, especially OA with low MMSE, had problems in understanding some of the questions in the questionnaires. Moreover, the managers underlined the potential added value that the telepresence robots could bring in supporting the domiciliary services, especially with frail and cognitively impaired OA, compared to the TV box, and they are exploring some business case evaluation on this topic.

As for the technical improvements, some comments were collected both from the focus group and the questionnaires. Regarding the robot, the operators suggested adding the possibility for the OA to send a call request to the IC or FC, possibly using a voice control activation. Furthermore, they specified that the luminosity of the screen should be increased, and work should be put in to increase the battery life. As for Sentab, one idea was that the switch between input sources from TV to Sentab could be carried out with a button on the main remote control. Moreover, it was proposed to devise a way to make group calls and share the screen, and overall simplify the system. One of the main advantages of the use of the robot is its "transparency" for OA, indeed they do not need to do anything except accept the incoming call. This functionality is good for frail OA with limited digital skills and low cognitive abilities, but for more technically savvy ones who would like to interact more with the robot, it is a strong limitation. The main technical problems encountered were related to the use of two remote controls and the switching between input sources on their TV. However, the managers pointed out that the OA involved appreciated seeing the *"big face of people"* on the TV screen, therefore this functionality is added values of video call system compared to traditional phone calls.

4   Discussion and Conclusion

The primary aim of this paper was to evaluate the telepresence service from the caregiver's perspective, as well as the OA's, over a prolonged period of time (6 months). Secondly, it aims to compare the feasibility results with a video calling system. Qualitative and quantitative results were collected at the beginning of the study and after six months. It is worth noting that the enrolled OAs for the robot case study are characterized by low values of MMSE and frailty index. Despite this cognitive profile, the IC and FC were happy to work with this technology mainly because of the transparency of the system, and this was also remarked by the fact that social cooperatives are exploring the potential exploitation of this telepresence service in their portfolio. This result is aligned with the feedback collected from the facilitators as the Sentab technology requested higher physical presence of the caregiver at the OA's home compared to the robot (Fig. 4). Previous studies on telepresence robots did not focus on the perception and feedback of caregivers. On top of this limitation, this study collected some results that suggest that, despite the low usability and acceptability scores collected from OA, IC and FC have high scores. Furthermore, these scores increased – for the telepresence service – after six months of use (Fig. 2 and Fig. 3). This result follows the trend reported in our previous study that analyzed the perception of the telepresence service after 10 days of use [18]. Additionally, acceptability scores were comparable to a long-term evaluation conducted with two OA [5]. It is important to note that the PU is scored higher for all the participants in the robot case study, with higher value for IC. PU is an important aspect to be considered for the acceptance of the robot from "early adopters" [19]. This result is aligned with the qualitative remarks collected from the facilitators, being that IC using the robot to remotely check and talk with their older relatives, underlined their willingness to pay for the service. However, the OA's scores may not be reliable because of low cognitive index and high frailty. Nevertheless, cooperative managers are paying more attention to the IC's feedback and willingness to use the service, especially if the connected OA is characterized by a low cognitive profile. Therefore the "real" users of the service are the IC. These results restate that the methodology recommendation should include all the players involved in the study, since to make our technology real, we need to shape and build the services on top of all collected feedback. Future studies should be focused on enlarging the sample size and the duration of the study, thus corroborating the preliminary findings highlighted in this paper.

Acknowledgment. The research work reported in this article has received funding from the Pilots for Healthy and Active Ageing (Pharaon) project of the European Union's Horizon 2020 research and innovation programme under grant agreement no. 857188.

References

1. Smale, B., Wilson, J., Akubueze, N.: Exploring the determinants and mitigating factors of loneliness among older adults. Wellbeing, Space Soc. **3**, 100089 (2022). https://doi.org/10.1016/j.wss.2022.100089
2. Nicholson, N.R.: A review of social isolation: an important but underassessed condition in older adults. J. Prim. Prev. **33**, 137–152 (2012)
3. D'Onofrio, G., et al.: Pilots for healthy and active ageing (PHArA-ON) project: definition of new technological solutions for older people in Italian pilot sites based on elicited user needs. Sensors **22**, 163 (2022). https://doi.org/10.3390/s22010163
4. Mooses, K., et al.: Involving older adults during COVID-19 restrictions in developing an ecosystem supporting active aging: overview of alternative elicitation methods and common requirements from five European Countries. Front. Psychol. **13**, 676 (2022). https://doi.org/10.3389/FPSYG.2022.818706
5. Cesta, A., Cortellessa, G., Orlandini, A., Tiberio, L.: Long-term evaluation of a telepresence robot for the elderly: methodology and ecological case study. Int. J. Soc. Robot. **8**, 421–441 (2016). https://doi.org/10.1007/s12369-016-0337-z
6. Hung, L., et al.: Facilitators and barriers to using telepresence robots in aged care settings: a scoping review. J. Rehabil. Assist. Technol. Eng. 9 (2022). https://doi.org/10.1177/20556683211072385
7. Moyle, W., Arnautovska, U., Ownsworth, T., Jones, C.: Potential of telepresence robots to enhance social connectedness in older adults with dementia: an integrative review of feasibility. Int. Psychogeriatr. **29**, 1951–1964 (2017)
8. Isabet, B., et al.: Social telepresence robots: a narrative review of experiments involving older adults before and during the covid-19 pandemic. Int. J. Environ. Res. Public Health **18**, 3597 (2021)
9. Hung, L., et al.: Using telepresence robots as a tool to engage patient and family partners in dementia research during COVID-19 pandemic: a qualitative participatory study. Res. Involv. Engagem. **9**, 1–12 (2023). https://doi.org/10.1186/s40900-023-00421-w
10. Fiorini, L., et al.: On the use of assistive technology during the COVID-19 outbreak: results and lessons learned from pilot studies. Sensors **22**, 6631 (2022). https://doi.org/10.3390/s22176631
11. Folstein, M.F., Folstein, S.E., McHugh, P.R.: "Mini-mental state". A practical method for grading the cognitive state of patients for the clinician (1975). J. Psychiatr. Res. **12** (1975)

12. Russell, D., Peplau, L.A., Cutrona, C.E.: The revised UCLA loneliness scale: concurrent and discriminant validity evidence. J. Pers. Soc. Psychol. **39**, 472 (1980). https://doi.org/10.1037/0022-3514.39.3.472
13. Lorusso, L., et al.: Design and evaluation of personalized services to foster active aging: the experience of technology pre-validation in Italian pilots. Sensors **23**, 797 (2023). https://doi.org/10.3390/S23020797
14. Rockwood, K., et al.: A global clinical measure of fitness and frailty in elderly people. CMAJ Can. Med. Assoc. J. **173**, 489–495 (2005). https://doi.org/10.1503/cmaj.050051
15. Brooke, J.: SUS: A "Quick And Dirty" Usability Scale. Usability Evaluation in industry, pp. 189–194(4–7) (1996)
16. Heerink, M., Kröse, B., Evers, V., Wielinga, B.: Assessing acceptance of assistive social agent technology by older adults: the Almere model. Int. J. Soc. Robot. **2** (2010). https://doi.org/10.1007/s12369-010-0068-5
17. Oberschmidt, K., Grünloh, C., Nijboer, F., van Velsen, L.: Best practices and lessons learned for action research in eHealth design and implementation: literature review. J. Med. Internet Res. **24**(1), e31795 (2022). https://www.jmir.org/2022/1/e31795, https://doi.org/10.2196/31795
18. Fiorini, L., et al.: Living with a telepresence robot: results from a field-trial. IEEE Robot. Autom. Lett. **7**, 5405–5412 (2022). https://doi.org/10.1109/LRA.2022.3155237
19. Saari, U.A., Tossavainen, A., Kaipainen, K., Mäkinen, S.J.: Exploring factors influencing the acceptance of social robots among early adopters and mass market representatives. Rob. Auton. Syst. **151**, 104033 (2022). https://doi.org/10.1016/j.robot.2022.104033

Effect of Number of Robots on Perceived Persuasion and Competence

Abeer Alam[1]($\boxtimes$), Michael Lwin[2], Aila Khan[2], Zhao Zou[1], and Omar Mubin[1]

[1] School of Computer, Data and Mathematical Sciences, Western Sydney University, Parramatta, NSW 2150, Australia
abeer.farzana@gmail.com, {z.zou2,o.mubin}@westernsydney.edu.au
[2] School of Business, Western Sydney University, Parramatta, NSW 2150, Australia
{m.lwin,a.khan}@westernsydney.edu.au

Abstract. Persuasive robotics has gained immense traction over the years, due to its potential to be used as a behavioral change system and to influence decision making in humans. With a plethora of existing studies in the field, this paper adds to the sea of knowledge by exploring the effect of *number of robots* on perceived persuasion and competence of a robot by revisiting Human-human Interaction theories of 'multiple-source effect' and 'message reinforcement'. A simple two condition (one vs two robots) between-subjects experiment was conducted across two stages, and human participants engaged in a persuasive dialog-based interaction with the robot(s) Pepper and NAO where participants choose between two drink options and complete a survey. The results reveal a single robot is more persuasive and competent than multiple robots. Further analysis of qualitative data provides insights about the effect of robot morphology, social influence, familiarity with technology and intergroup dynamics, all of which collectively impact human perceptions and reactions. The implications of this research showcase the purposeful use of robots for marketing or brand promotion and further encourage better strategies of natural robot-robot & human-robot interactions.

Keywords: Perceived Persuasion · Multi-source effect · Social robots

1 Introduction

As per the Computers Are Social Actors (CASA) [1] Paradigm, humans associate social norms applied in Human-Human Interaction (HHI) to Human-Computer Interaction (HCI). Human's projective attitude towards computers/machines and their capability to rationalize, distributes significant meaning to situations and objects [2, 3]. Furthermore, when artificial agents like robots combine social cues within their interaction, humans feel they are communicating with another person [4]. Intrinsically, in Human-Robot Interaction (HRI), 'social robots' interact with humans as peers or companions where both parties are co-located, and the interaction involves emotive, cognitive and social features [5]. Hegel (2009) explains the term social as the existence of interactive relationships [6]. Hence, humans have a tendency to anthropomorphize these entities which

© The Author(s), under exclusive license to Springer Nature Singapore Pte Ltd. 2024
A. Al. Ali et al. (Eds.): ICSR 2023, LNAI 14454, pp. 285–293, 2024.
https://doi.org/10.1007/978-981-99-8718-4_25

facilitates interaction similar to that with other humans [7]. Moreover, social robots possess communicative abilities that are perceived as *persuasive* by humans implicitly or explicitly [8].

Persuasive Robotics is the "scientific study of artificial, embodied agents (robots) that are intentionally designed to change a person's behavior, attitude and/or cognitive processes" [9]. The current state of research within this domain has actively deciphered factors which influence persuasion, such as various persuasive strategies adapted from HHI [10] or verbal and non-verbal cues like robot speech/gaze [11]. Broadly, persuasive robotics research can be categorized into the following groups of factors: modality, interaction, social character, persuasive strategy, and context, which have been investigated and found to have an influence on robot persuasiveness [12]. Nevertheless, there is limited research which sheds light on *the number of robots* on persuasion and compliance, since most work in HRI focus on dyadic interactions [13]. Liu and colleagues (2022) stated, research within Persuasive Robotics is heavily reliant on theories from HHI; this paper aims to revisit HHI theories of multiple source effect [14] and message reinforcement [15] through 'number of robots' and investigate its impact on *perceived persuasiveness* and *competence* of a robot during HRI.

The rest of the paper is organized as follows: Sect. 2 discusses relevant literature; Sect. 3 describes the research methodology followed by results and discussion in Sect. 4. Lastly, Sect. 5 concludes the paper with directions for future work.

2   Relevant Literature

One of the key elements of Persuasion in HHI is attitude change of a persuadee without coercion [16]. Similarly, Persuasive Technology such as mobile platforms or interactive displays alter human behavior in HCI [17]. Conversely, Persuasion in HRI differs, as the attitudinal or behavioral change in humans is influenced by *perceptions and cognitive process* of social interaction with a robot [18]. Nevertheless, many of the human-human social rules of stereotypes [19] and human-robot trust models apply to these interactions, and researchers like Siegel et al. (2009) reported persuasion is an *inseparable* component of HRI similar to HHI [20].

2.1   Multiple-source Effect and Reinforced Messaging

In HHI, researchers have noted persuasion is enhanced using multiple sources expressing multiple arguments as individuals process the intended message better [21, 22]. Harkins and Petty (1987) investigated when the multiple sources were independent and did not initiate arguments as a combined entity, the message was deemed as more *credible* and persuasive [23]. The different independent sources provide the notion of the generated message utilizing various sources of knowledge and perspectives. Furthermore, the credibility and trustworthiness towards a preceding message is positively dependent on the previous/initial message which influences motivation to process the message and get persuaded [24]. Likewise, message repetition and reinforcement help tackle resistance to persuasion, which further has the ability to cause an attitudinal change [25, 26].

HRI have also explored many conformity pressures such as implementing various persuasive strategies within interaction scenarios that have resulted in behavioral change [12]. Works such as that of [27–30] prove the probable positive effects on persuasion of using multiple messaging techniques even though the main objective of these research were not focused on understanding the effect of number of sources or arguments.

2.2 Perceived Persuasion and Competence

To develop a cooperative behavior, trust is significant in interpersonal interactions. Moreover, the concept of 'competence' may also influence behavioral responses, for instance the extent to which a trustee is trusted [31]. Essentially, a higher perception of competence correlates to a positive response of greater trust [32].

Traditionally, competence is an encapsulation of a set of knowledge, attributes or skills [33]; in HRI it dictates the ability of a robot to achieve its intended goals which increases its reliability and trustworthiness. Hence, Trust has been explored in terms of perceived competence of a robot which is based on its facial characteristics or anthropomorphism and reliability [34, 35]. For example, Al Mahmud and colleagues [36] measured *Perceived Competence* of iParrot, a persuasive agent, on basis of how knowledgeable, responsible and intelligent it was perceived by the participants. Another interesting study conducted by Bartneck and others [37] measured the Perceived Intelligence of a robot by evaluating its *Perceived Competence* and how sensible it was perceived to be by humans. Similarly, to evaluate the persuasiveness of a mobile application designed to help conserve energy, *Perceived Persuasiveness* was measured in terms of how competent *(Perceived Competence)* and reliable/trustworthy the persuasive agent (application) was to the users [38]. Therefore, trust has a direct link to an individual's willingness to comply with a robot-generated suggestion or information [39].

3 Methodology

The research was undertaken as a simple two conditions (one vs two robots) between-subjects experiment at the Western Sydney University- at a local undergraduate campus where the survey data (quantitative and qualitative) were collected in a span of 4 weeks. Ethical requirements were considered, and an ethics approval was obtained before research commencement (HREC approval #: H15233). Two popular humanoid robots were used in this research- Pepper and NAO. The research was divided into two stages with stage 1a and 1b consisting of interaction with single robot Pepper and NAO, respectively. Stage 2 involved interaction with both robots. Due to unavailability of two same robots, a combination of Pepper and Nao was utilized in this research. The target population consisted of undergraduate Business students randomly selected across the two stages via convenience sampling and divided into three groups (stage 1a, 1b and stage 2). The research had a total sample size of 73 participants, where stage 1a had 30 students, stage 1b had 20 students and stage 2 had 23 students. This is considered adequate on basis of prior works in the field [12]. Moreover, the ratio of males and females in all groups were fairly equal. The research scenario and stimuli were adapted from [40] where participants were required to choose between two hypothetical drinks.

They engaged in a persuasive interaction with the robot(s) and completed the surveys as per the scenario they took part in. The survey was provided at the beginning of the experiment to collect pre-interaction data followed by the robot interaction session, after which respondents recorded their post-interaction responses in the same survey. The pre-defined persuasive robot dialogues were controlled via Wizard of Oz set-up through a coded graphical user interface, and helped control occasional episodes of the robot's distractibility to minute noise or movement [41]. The experiment was conducted in a lab setting/classroom environment (Fig. 1).

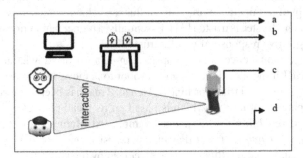

Fig. 1. (a) Survey data collected pre-and post-interaction, b) two hypothetical drink choices, c) human participant standing facing towards the robot(s) and d) Multi-robot scenario featuring both robots during interaction session. Single robot scenarios involved the respective robot by itself.

The questionnaire adopted and adapted scales from credible sources such as [36, 38, 42] and included measures for 1) Experience with Technology 2) Robot characteristics (15 bipolar adjectives) 3) Perceived Persuasion 4) Perceived Competencee 5) Drink selections 6) Subjective perceptions of the robot (s) 7) Open-ended questions and 8) Demographics. The Cronbach's Alpha proved the measures were reliable (α coefficient = .759–.995).

4   Results and Discussion

4.1   Data Analysis

Analysis of variance was conducted using the independent variable of 'Number of robots' and two dependent variables of 'Perceived Persuasion' and 'Perceived Competence', to compare measurements between single robot and multiple robots. Perceived persuasion was taken as the mean of the following four robot characteristics from the questionnaire: Ignorant-Knowledgeable, Irresponsible-Responsible, Unintelligent-Intelligent, Unreliable/Untrustworthy-Reliable/Trustworthy, (Cronbach Alpha = 0.873). Perceived competence was taken as the mean of the following three robot charac-teristics from the questionnaire: Ignorant-Knowledgeable, Irresponsible-Responsible, Unintelligent-Intelligent, (Cronbach Alpha = 0.890).The multivariate results indicated a significant main effect for number of robots (Pillai's Trace = 0.106, $F_{(2,70)}$ = 4.168, p = 0.019) with a significant influence on Perceived Persuasion ($F_{(1,71)}$ = 6.68, p = 0.012) and Perceived Competence ($F_{(1,71)}$ = 8.07, p = 0.006). Results showed interaction with a single robot was perceived as more persuasive (M = 5.45, SD = 0.93) and competent (M = 5.62, SD = 0.98), in comparison to that with multiple robots (Table 1). A precautionary second analysis was repeated using a non-parametric test (Kruskal Wallis) and the results were in-line with the previous outcomes. There was evidence of a statistically significant effect on Perceived Persuasion n (H (1) = 3.77, p = 0.052) and Perceived Competence (H (1) = 5.42, p = 0.020) between both groups. Group 'Single' scored higher mean ranks of 40.25 (persuasion) and 40.88 (competence) and group 'Multi' scored lower mean ranks of f 29.93 (persuasion) and 28.57 (competence) (Table 1). Therefore, the results reported single robots scored a higher Perceived Persuasiveness and Competence than multiple robots.

A thorough observation of the remaining survey data revealed some interesting insights about robot persuasion. Post-interaction responses recorded an 8.22% change in participant's drink selections, which comprised mostly of males. It was found participants in stage 1b (single NAO) had the most experience with technology in contrast to stage 2 (multi-robot). Similarly, subjective opinions on persuasion and compliance were most positive from participants who interacted with the single robot- NAO. Qualitative remarks expressed interesting perspectives on robot characteristics, accuracy, and knowledgeable attitude. Participants found the NAO robot cute and to have

Table 1. Statistical analysis of perceived Persuasion and Competence for Single vs Multi robot(s)

Dependent variable	Number of robots	Mean	Standard Deviation	Mean Ranks
Perceived Persuasion	Single	5.45	0.930	40.25
	Multi	4.70	1.532	29.93
	Total	5.21	1.195	
Perceived Competence	Single	5.62	0.976	40.88
	Multi	4.77	1.565	28.57
	Total	5.35	1.247	

a positive interactive behavior, with clear fluency in the way it interacted with individuals. It was also not as 'humanly' as Pepper and some participants commented on its voice being weird and robotic making it unusual to converse with. Pepper, on the other hand, was remarked as having a cheerful tone and was perceived as friendly, physically attractive, and fun. Yet, some negative remarks included greater expectations of Pepper to be more artificially intelligent and carry on the conversation. Also, Pepper was too humanly (uncanny effect) for some individual's liking and its eye-stare/gaze was uneasy. The majority of the multi-group participants commented on the robots being creepy and unnatural. It seemed participants expected more spontaneity and natural interaction considering there were two robots, and stated it was almost like speech-to-text bots and should have been self-generated. Few of the positive feedback included fascination of seeing robots in-person for the first time and the admiration of their interaction cues such as hand gestures. Overall, the insights point to NAO being accepted and perceived more positively than Pepper and the multi-robot group.

4.2 Discussion

The statistical analyses revealed single robot is better than multiple robots to persuade humans and is perceived as more competent. This contradicts the positive notion regarding multiple sources, reported by prior works [30]. Furthermore, subjective opinions and qualitative remarks support the quantitative findings. Possible explanations to these outcomes can be classified as a) robot morphology and social influence b) effect of familiarity with technology and c) intergroup dynamics.

In HRI, human tendency to assign human-like attributes to inanimate objects/entities such as robots, influences acceptance and facilitates interaction [43]. Mori [44] mentioned an entity is positively perceived with greater human-likeness, until it enters 'uncanny valley' which occurs when there is a mismatch between expectations about the entity and the actual interaction experience, causing uneasiness. As participants' expectations were more demanding in the multi-robot group as there were two robots in one frame, the robots' inability to satisfy them resulted in a negative reaction. Moreover, a baby-looking robot such as NAO with its bipedal form is likely to gain more likeability and compliance when it is in position of giving advice [45, 46] when compared to Pepper whose physical dimensions make it more anthropomorphic but not more capable than NAO. Social influence is also closely tied to anthropomorphism, where it operates through mechanisms of compliance, conformity and persuasion [47]. In this case, NAO appears to be perceived as more life-like, capable, and socially present, thereby projecting greater influence in comparison to other groups.

Multi-robot group reported to have the least experience with technology which is guaranteed to have an effect on overall perceptions, because it affects the robot's trustworthiness and persuasiveness [48]. This is because with lack of experience, humans are forced to rely on information from indirect sources which triggers cognitive familiarity to take over their trust and beliefs [49].

Lastly, Turner and colleagues [50] suggested humans self-categorize when they are confronted with out-groups which increases correlation between in-group members and results in perceived threat/competition towards out-group members [51]. So, the coordinated behaviors of a robot group could initiate a negative attitude or emotion, as the robot group may be perceived as more intelligent and teaming up against humans. Therefore, the multi-robot group may have caused a greater feeling of discomfort and fear, and this may have been potentially lower when interaction was with a single robot.

5 Conclusion and Future Work

This paper investigated how do humans perceive a persuasive interaction involving multiple robots and discovered a single robot is perceived to be more persuasive and competent. The paper discussed various aspects that play a role in shaping human's perceptions of persuasiveness during human-robot interaction. These aspects have been categorized as robot morphology, social influence, familiarity with technology and intergroup dynamics. These insights will help enrich the field of Persuasive Robotics and further re-instate the important role played by "humans" in Human-Robot Interaction. It acknowledges humans are a diverse breed and thus perceptions will vary considerably.

Due to the exploratory nature of the study, there are few limitations to consider. The sample population employed was limited to undergraduate students and a university setting, where the ambience was controlled within a lab environment. Future work should consider using different sets of demographics in a public and more realistic setting to gather ecological data. This will also improve the generalizability of the results. The study utilized humanoid robots of two different types for multi-robot interaction and the expected outcomes may have been altered due to the discrepancy. Two NAOs or Peppers may have produced different results [51] and should be considered in future work. This study had a short one-off interaction, and a longitudinal study could potentially have different outcomes. Furthermore, longitudinal study could eradicate any novelty or Hawthorne effect that may have been present.

Equally, the possibility of the Hawthorne effect remains where participants may have answered questions in a certain way to please the researchers.

Nevertheless, current study provides valuable insights and a different perspective on implementing multiple robots of different types for persuasive interactions with humans. It is also noteworthy to mention the many practical implications of this research which will prove to be beneficial in a wide variety of contexts where robots will directly communicate with humans in a persuasive manner. These include but are not limited to, the commercial use of robots by businesses to promote brands for marketing purposes, in public spaces as persuaders for public announcement services or automated advertising. There is great potential for persuasive robots in healthcare settings as personal coaches or trainers, to positively initiate behavioral changes and promote healthier living.

It is envisioned much of our reality will be shared with robots as our partners or mentors, and purposeful research in the field will help encourage better strategies to initiate more natural human-robot interaction which will allow a better understanding amongst humans and robots as social partners to each other.

References

1. Reeves, B., Nass, C.: The Media Equation: How People Treat Computers, Television, and New Media Like Real People, Cambridge, vol.10, p. 236605 (1996)
2. Turkle, S.: The Second Self: Computers and the Human Spirit. MIT Press (2005)
3. Schütz, A.: Der sinnhafte Aufbau der sozialen Welt: Eine Einleitung in die verstehende Soziologie. Springer-Verlag (2013)
4. Mayer, R.E., Sobko, K., Mautone, P.D.: Social cues in multimedia learning: role of speaker's voice. J. Educ. Psychol. **95**(2), 419 (2003)
5. Goodrich, M.A., Schultz, A.C.: Human–robot interaction: a survey. Found. Trends® Hum. Comput. Interact. **1**(3), 203–275 (2008)
6. Hegel, F., et al.: Understanding social robots. In: 2009 Second International Conferences on Advances in Computer-Human Interactions. IEEE (2009)
7. Fink, J.: Anthropomorphism and human likeness in the design of robots and human-robot interaction. In: Social Robotics. Springer, Heidelberg (2012)
8. Banks, J., Koban, K., Haggadone, B.: Avoiding the abject and seeking the script: perceived mind, morality, and trust in a persuasive social robot. ACM Trans. Hum.-Robot Interact. **12**(3), 1–24 (2023)
9. Ham, J., et al.: Making robots persuasive: the influence of combining persuasive strategies (gazing and gestures) by a storytelling robot on its persuasive power. In: Social Robotics. Springer, Heidelberg (2011)

10. Goldstein, N.J., Cialdini, R.B., Griskevicius, V.: A room with a viewpoint: using social norms to motivate environmental conservation in hotels. J. Consum. Res. **35**(3), 472–482 (2008)
11. Fischer, K., Langedijk, R.M., Nissen, L.D., Ramirez, E.R., Palinko, O.: Gaze-speech coordination influences the persuasiveness of human-robot dialog in the wild. In: Wagner, A.R., et al. (eds.) ICSR 2020. LNCS (LNAI), vol. 12483, pp. 157–169. Springer, Cham (2020). https://doi.org/10.1007/978-3-030-62056-1_14
12. Liu, B., Tetteroo, D., Markopoulos, P.: A systematic review of experimental work on persuasive social robots. Int. J. Soc. Robot. **14**(6), 1339–1378 (2022)
13. Kantharaju, R.B., et al.: Is two better than one? Effects of multiple agents on user persuasion. In: Proceedings of the 18th International Conference on Intelligent Virtual Agents, pp. 255–262. Association for Computing Machinery, Sydney (2018)
14. Harkins, S.G., Petty, R.E.: The multiple source effect in persuasion: the effects of distraction. Pers. Soc. Psychol. Bull. **7**(4), 627–635 (1981)
15. Burgoon, M., Miller, M.D.: Overcoming resistance to persuasion via contiguous reinforcement and repetition of message. Psychol. Rep. **66**(3), 1011–1022 (1990)
16. Harjumaa, M., Oinas-Kukkonen, H.: Persuasion theories and IT design. In: Persuasive Technology. Springer, Heidelberg (2007)
17. Agnisarman, S., Madathil, K.C., Stanley, L.: A survey of empirical studies on persuasive technologies to promote sustainable living. Sustain. Comput. Inform. Syst. **19**, 112–122 (2018)
18. Ham, J., van Esch, M., Limpens, Y., de Pee, J., Cabibihan, J.-J., Ge, S.S.: The automaticity of social behavior towards robots: the influence of cognitive load on interpersonal distance to approachable versus less approachable robots. In: Ge, S.S., Khatib, O., Cabibihan, J.-J., Simmons, R., Williams, M.-A. (eds.) ICSR 2012. LNCS (LNAI), vol. 7621, pp. 15–25. Springer, Heidelberg (2012). https://doi.org/10.1007/978-3-642-34103-8_2
19. Tay, B., Jung, Y., Park, T.: When stereotypes meet robots: the double-edge sword of robot gender and personality in human–robot interaction. Comput. Hum. Behav. **38**, 75–84 (2014)
20. Siegel, M., Breazeal, C., Norton, M.I.: Persuasive robotics: the influence of robot gender on human behavior. In: 2009 IEEE/RSJ International Conference on Intelligent Robots and Systems. IEEE (2009)
21. Calder, B.J., Insko, C.A., Yandell, B.: The relation of cognitive and memorial processes to persuasion in a simulated jury trial. J. Appl. Soc. Psychol. **4**(1), 62–93 (1974)
22. Harkins, S., Petty, R.: The multiple source effect in persuasion: the effects of distraction. Pers. Soc. Psychol. Bull. **7**, 627–635 (1981)
23. Harkins, S.G., Petty, R.E.: Information utility and the multiple source effect. J. Pers. Soc. Psychol. **52**(2), 260–268 (1987)
24. Tormala, Z.L., Clarkson, J.J.: Source trustworthiness and information processing in multiple message situations: a contextual analysis. Soc. Cognit. **26**(3), 357–367 (2008). https://doi.org/10.1521/soco.2008.26.3.357
25. Scott, W.A.: Attitude change through reward of verbal behavior. Psychol. Sci. Public Interest **55**(1), 72 (1957)
26. Bostrom, R.N., Vlandis, J.W., Rosenbaum, M.E.: Grades as reinforcing contingencies and attitude change. J. Educ. Psychol. **52**(2), 112 (1961)
27. Lee, S.A., Liang, Y.: Robotic foot-in-the-door: using sequential-request persuasive strategies in human-robot interaction. Comput. Hum. Behav. **90**, 351–356 (2019)
28. Saunderson, S., Nejat, G.: It would make me happy if you used my guess: comparing robot persuasive strategies in social human-robot interaction. IEEE Robot. Automat. Lett. **4**(2), 1707–1714 (2019)
29. Saunderson, S., Nejat, G.: Investigating strategies for robot persuasion in social human-robot interaction. IEEE Trans. Cybernet. **52**(1), 641–653 (2022)
30. Tae, M.I., et al.: Using multiple robots to increase suggestion persuasiveness in public space. Appl. Sci. **11**(13), 6080 (2021)

31. Cuddy, A.J., Fiske, S.T., Glick, P.: Warmth and competence as universal dimensions of social perception: the stereotype content model and the BIAS map. Adv. Exp. Soc. Psychol. **40**, 61–149 (2008)
32. Christoforakos, L., et al.: Can robots earn our trust the same way humans do? A systematic exploration of competence, warmth, and anthropomorphism as determinants of trust development in HRI. Front. Robot. AI **8**, 640444 (2021)
33. Eraut, M.: Concepts of competence. J. Interprof. Care **12**(2), 127–139 (1998)
34. Calvo-Barajas, N., Perugia, G., Castellano, G.: The effects of robot's facial expressions on children's first impressions of trustworthiness. In: 2020 29th IEEE International Conference on Robot and Human Interactive Communication (RO-MAN). IEEE (2020)
35. Bagheri, N., Jamieson, G.A.: The impact of context-related reliability on automation failure detection and scanning behaviour. In: 2004 IEEE International Conference on Systems, Man and Cybernetics (IEEE Cat. No. 04CH37583). IEEE (2004)
36. Al Mahmud, A., Dadlani, P., Mubin, O., Shahid, S., Midden, C., Moran, O.: IParrot: towards designing a persuasive agent for energy conservation. In: de Kort, Y., IJsselsteijn, W., Midden, C., Eggen, B., Fogg, B.J. (eds.) PERSUASIVE 2007. LNCS, vol. 4744, pp. 64–67. Springer, Heidelberg (2007). https://doi.org/10.1007/978-3-540-77006-0_8
37. Bartneck, C., et al.: To kill a mockingbird robot. In: Proceedings of the ACM/IEEE International Conference on Human-Robot Interaction (2007)
38. Mahmud, A.A., et al.: EZ phone: persuading mobile users to conserve energy. In: People and Computers XXII Culture, Creativity, Interaction, vol. 22, pp. 7–10 (2008)
39. Freedy, A., et al.: Measurement of trust in human-robot collaboration. In: 2007 International Symposium on Collaborative Technologies and Systems. IEEE (2007)
40. Kharub, I., et al.: The effectiveness of robot-enacted messages to reduce the consumption of high-sugar energy drinks. Informatics **9**(2), 49 (2022)
41. Hamblen, M.: Pepper, a humanoid robot, will make first appearance in U.S. businesses this year (+video). In: ComputerWorld (2016)
42. Warner, R.M., Sugarman, D.B.: Attributions of personality based on physical appearance, speech, and handwriting. J. Pers. Soc. Psychol. **50**(4), 792–799 (1986)
43. Duffy, B.R.: Anthropomorphism and the social robot. Robot. Auton. Syst. **42**(3–4), 177–190 (2003)
44. Mori, M.: Bukimi no tani (the uncanny valley). Energy **7**(4), 33–35 (1970)
45. Powers, A., Kiesler, S.: The advisor robot: tracing people's mental model from a robot's physical attributes. In: Proceedings of the 1st ACM SIGCHI/SIGART Conference on Human-Robot Interaction, pp. 218–225. Association for Computing Machinery, Salt Lake City (2006)
46. Rosenthal-Von Der Pütten, A.M., Krämer, N.C.: How design characteristics of robots determine evaluation and uncanny valley related responses. Comput. Hum. Behav. **36**, 422–439 (2014)
47. Cialdini, R.B., James, L.: Influence: Science and Practice, vol. 4. Pearson education Boston (2009)
48. Saunderson, S., Nejat, G.: Robots asking for favors: the effects of directness and familiarity on persuasive HRI. IEEE Robot. Autom. Lett. **6**(2), 1793–1800 (2021)
49. Li, X., Hess, T.J., Valacich, J.S.: Why do we trust new technology? A study of initial trust formation with organizational information systems. J. Strateg. Inf. Syst. **17**(1), 39–71 (2008)
50. Turner, J.C., et al.: Rediscovering the Social Group: A Self-Categorization Theory. Basil Blackwell (1987)
51. Fraune, M.R., et al.: Rabble of robots effects: number and type of robots modulates attitudes, emotions, and stereotypes. In: Proceedings of the Tenth Annual ACM/IEEE International Conference on Human-Robot Interaction, pp. 109–116. Association for Computing Machinery, Portland (2015)

A Field Study on Polish Customers' Attitude Towards a Service Robot in a Cafe

Maria Kiraga[1], Zofia Samsel[2(✉)], and Bipin Indurkhya[3]

[1] AGH University of Science and Technology, Kraków, Poland
[2] Learning Planet Institute, Université Paris Cité, Paris, France
zosiasamsel@gmail.com
[3] Cognitive Science Department, Jagiellonian University, Kraków, Poland
bipin.indurkhya@uj.edu.pl

Abstract. More and more stores in Poland are adopting robots as customer assistants or promotional tools. However, customer attitudes to such novelty remain unexplored. This study focused on the role of social robots in self-service cafes. This domain has not been explored in Poland before, and there is not much research in other countries as well. We conducted a field study in two cafes with a teleoperated robot Nao, which sat next to the counter serving as an assistant to a human barista. We observed customer behavior, conducted semi-structured interviews and questionnaires with the customers. The results show that Polish customers are neutral and insecure about robots. However, they do not exhibit a total dislike of these technologies. We considered three stages of the interaction and identified features of each stage that need to be designed carefully to yield user satisfaction.

Keywords: Social Robots · Customer Service · Field Study · User Experience · Human-Robot Interaction · Human-Centered Robotics · Robot Barista

1 Introduction

The service industry is increasingly accepting the use of robots to help with repetitive or physically demanding tasks, but also as active assistants directly interacting with customers. In the past, such interactions and customer service in restaurants or cafes were carried out exclusively by humans. Now it is useful to explore how to deploy robots as sales and service assistants to reduce human service duties and speed up customer service time. However, introducing new technologies in everyday life is received differently in different cultures and religions [1]. Hence, culture-centered research on customers' attitudes and expectations toward robot assistants is needed to design an interaction scheme to benefit both the workers and the customers.

We investigated Polish consumers' attitudes and behaviors towards a robotic assistant to determine which interactions lead to a positive customer experience. A field study was conducted with a teleoperated social robot Nao to recommend products and take orders from customers. We observed customer perceptions of robot assistants in cafes to study

---

M. Kiraga and Z. Samsel—Contributed equally.

© The Author(s), under exclusive license to Springer Nature Singapore Pte Ltd. 2024
A. Al. Ali et al. (Eds.): ICSR 2023, LNAI 14454, pp. 294–307, 2024.
https://doi.org/10.1007/978-981-99-8718-4_26

the best way to deploy them. Though Polish customers' attitudes toward robots vary widely, we distinguish three aspects of the interactions that influenced people's attitudes and experience: the first impression (robot's physical appearance and behavior), the flow of conversation, and contextual adaptation. Our research complements state of the art on human-robot interaction (HRI) in terms of interactions with service robots and individualized approaches to creating such interactions.

2 Related Research

2.1 Attitude of Polish Society Towards Technology and Robots

Poland has a rapidly developing economy [2]. Its entrepreneurs are eagerly seeking new technological solutions to streamline and secure their work. Based on a 2022 report, 97% of Poles believes that new technologies are generally important and useful, however over half of the participants were sceptic toward the use of technologies on a daily basis [3]. On the other hand, one study in which the researchers explored the attitudes of elderly Poles towards the utilization and ease of use of domestic robots showed that they were eager to learn and adapt to modern devices [4].

There is no existing research on the general attitude of Poles toward robots. But it is possible to characterize Polish society through the perspective of its history, religion, and culture, which are significant variables that differentiate attitudes toward technologies and the use of robots in public places [5]. Based on the Polish Statistics Census in 2021, approximately 85% of Poles described themselves as Catholics [6]. This, and the fact that Christians seem to be skeptical about the use of robots in everyday life [7], we can expect that the Polish public may have a negative attitude towards robots in a public place. Also, traditionalism and the high importance attached to family values [8] may negatively influence their approach to robots.

2.2 Use of Robots in Public Spaces in Poland

Current reports of "robotization" of Poland mainly concern industrial robots, portraying Poland as robustly developing in this area [9]. Though robots are not commonly used in public places, their numbers in the sales and service section are increasing, offering a potential to automate more social jobs [10]. *Kerfuś* - a cat-robot used in Carrefour supermarket [11] gained popularity among social media users shortly after being introduced in 2022: this robot has been deployed at a few Shell gas stations since 2021. A robot *BellaBot* delivers ordered items from a catering offer directly to the table, while another, *KittyBot,* informs about the current promotional campaigns [12]. Restaurants in Poland are also finding uses for robots. An autonomous robot waiter transporting food to tables was used at a Hilton hotel restaurant in 2021 [13].

All these robots are autonomous robots that do not have extensive conversation or order-taking capabilities. According to the literature, customers and visitors perceive more positively the interaction with a robot assistant in a public space that has broad capabilities to communicate and adapt to the situation [14].

2.3 Robot Design in Human-Robot Interaction

Past research suggests some significant features affecting a customer's perception (positive or negative) of the robot. In the services sector, it is necessary for the robot to have specialized knowledge and communication skills. Trust plays a crucial role in influencing acceptance of the robot [15]. Customers expect robots to conform to social norms, while not having to reciprocate politeness; they are expected to behave in a humanlike way [14]. This can be provided by teleoperated robots where a human operator controls all the robot's behavior, gestures, and speech: such robots have been found to be successful [16]. Furthermore, the teleoperator observes the robot environment and can provide relevant advertising strategies depending on the context [17]. However, robots that are observed to be autonomously controlled can reduce assessment concerns and increase customer confidence [16].

For social robots in customer service, just verbal communication with customers is not sufficient. If robots are animated and have human-like features, they are viewed as more approachable and capable, which leads to increased customer satisfaction [18, 19]. It has been shown that the pressure to not say 'no' to a human salesman is higher than to a robot, so interaction with a robot can be more relaxing for a user [20]. Though deploying robots as store assistants can enhance efficiency for both the customer and the organization, many people still prefer communicating with another human [21]. One way to compromise is using a humanoid robot to assist customers in situations where human staff needs to focus on more complex tasks [22].

While robots can be fully operational and serve a specific purpose, users may still feel mistrust, insecurity, and anxiety around the robot [15, 23]. Therefore, it is important that the operator, especially in the case of a salesperson robot, manages the behavior correctly to ensure the best possible customer experience.

2.4 Choice of Robot and the Wizard-of-Oz Methodology

We used the humanoid robot Nao (from Softbank Robotics), which was remotely teleoperated by a human [24]. We conducted seven field study sessions using this Wizard-of-Oz methodology. The participants interacting with the robot were made to believe that the robot is autonomous. This allowed for naturalistic settings, which is the main idea behind conducting field studies without having to face possible errors and mistakes when the robot is running by a pre-programmed artificial intelligence.

3 Session One

3.1 Method

This session took place in *Pastelove* – a cafe in one of Jagiellonian University's departments. Nao was placed at the entrance, where the queue forms. The teleoperator was at a table next to Nao (Fig. 1). Nao tried to make small talk with the customers waiting in line and promote certain products.

The session lasted for two hours with five people getting into a conversation with the robot. We estimate that about 50 people visited the cafe in this time. The data collected included our observations, transcripts of the customers' interactions with Nao, and transcripts of our short, semi-structured interviews with some customers who agreed to take part. The questions asked included: satisfaction after the interaction, likeliness of getting into a similar interaction in the future, and attitudes towards similar robots. All the robot's questions and answers were typed into a text-to-speech engine by the experimenter. The questions were written beforehand and selected using button, but the answers were improvised on the spot.

Fig. 1. Setups for the first session in *Pastelove* (A) and sessions two to seven in *Patelove* (B) and *Karma* (C).

3.2 Results and Discussion

All the data was qualitatively analyzed. Only some visitors interacted with the robot: most of them were only interested in taking pictures of the robot or greeting it briefly. Various robot's prompts such as *"Hey, how are you?"* or *"Do you like gingerbread spiced coffee?"* were ignored or met with comments to other customers, which revealed fear of the robot and surprise at its presence. Five people who talked to the robot mainly made small talk on various topics (e.g., weather, coffee preferences).

In the interviews, the customers expressed positive emotions towards the interaction. The appearance of the robot was mostly commented on in a positive manner. The flow of conversation was perceived to be intelligent. In addition, they expressed surprise with such technology being present in a university cafe, as none of these five participants had previous experience with similar robots. One customer noted that *"talking to a robot was slightly weird"*, because it reminded them of chatting with a child. (Nao robot is small and has a humanoid appearance.)

After this session, we made some adjustments to provoke more interactions from the customers. Previous research has shown that the closer a person gets to a robot, the more trustworthy the robot is perceived to be, which facilitates a positive interaction [25]. Moreover, Nao making only small talk does not seem to be a strong enough cue for the customers to start interacting with such, supposedly new for them, technology. Also, its appearance does not indicate its role as a staff member: it seems to be a toy or a mascot, which makes prompting the interaction more difficult. From other studies we learn that the robot partner's initiative leads to increasing the trust of the human partner [16], which suggests the robot's approach should be more proactive.

4 Sessions Two to Four

4.1 Method

With the results of the previous session in mind, we changed the setup and the role of the robot. These sessions were conducted over three days, two hours each day. One session took place in the same cafe as the pilot study (*Pastelove*), and the following two sessions took place in a small cafe *Karma*, where the robot was placed right by the counter. The setup in *Karma* is shown in Fig. 1. The teleoperator sat at a table across the counter facing away from the customers. The researcher making observations sat next to the teleoperator. Participants were customers of the cafes. Most of the customers were not aware of the robot's presence before coming to the cafe.

This time, instead of simply making small talk, Nao was serving as an assistant to the baristas. Its role was to get an order from the customer, take it back to the human salesperson, and chat with the customer. The flow of interaction was designed beforehand and is shown in Table 1. To make the interaction more natural, some answers, which we did not include in the interaction flow, were improvised on the spot.

As customers entered the cafe and approached the counter, Nao welcomed them and started the ordering procedure. The language of interaction was either English or Polish depending on the customer. If a customer was eager for more interaction, the teleoperator improvised to make the interaction as natural as possible, personalizing the robot's conversation to each customer. If a customer was disinclined to interact with Nao, they could place the order directly with the human barista behind the counter. After the interaction was finished, a researcher approached the customers to request an interview. Both the customers who engaged with Nao, and those who did not, were asked for a short interview. A total of 31 customers agreed to take part.

As before, we focused on qualitative data. (We did not count the exact number of people visiting the cafes, or how many chose to have the conversation and how many did not.) The data collected included our observations, transcripts of the customers' interactions with Nao, and transcripts of our short, semi-structured interviews with the customers. All the data was qualitatively analyzed for extracting those features of the interactions that mattered the most for the customers.

4.2 Results and Discussion

Placing the robot on the counter and changing the topic of the interaction had a positive impact and increased the number of people who approached Nao. The new setup required them to get close to the robot so they could not ignore it completely. However, because we did not count the number of people in the cafe, we cannot conclusively say whether this was due to better design of interaction, the placement of the robot, or because more people came to the cafe.

We observed three aspects of human-robot interaction that determined the progress of the interaction and perception of the robot: people's *first impressions* of the robot, including their opinions on the robot's physical appearance and behavior, the *conversation flow*, and the robot's *adaptation to specific contexts*.

Table 1. Flow of interaction for the cafe sessions

Stage 1: Placing an order
After each product is ordered, the robot asks the customer: *"Would you like anything else?"* and recommends some product (e.g., *"We have tasty coffee/croissants."*)
The robot asks if the order is to be prepared here or to-go (e.g., *"Eat in or takeaway?"*)
Stage 2: Transferring the order to the barista
The robot repeats the order and thanks you for placing it. An example phrase used was: *"Thanks for placing the order! It will be ready in a minute!"*
Stage 3: Small talk
After receiving the order, the robot asks the customer if he or she would like to talk to it while waiting: (e.g., *"While you're waiting, would you like to talk with me?"*)

First Impressions. Appearance, the voice, and speech pattern of the robot seemed to be the first elements that determined whether a person would be willing to initiate an interaction with the robot or not. Here we distinguished behaviors related to the positive perception of the robot's appearance: the most common positive reaction to the robot's appearance was that *"it's cute"*, *"his eyes are glowing"*, *"wow, he's sitting like a king of this cafe"*, which are related to anthropomorphizing and the novelty of this technology. Some people were surprised with Nao following them with its eyes (*"It looks at me and knows where I am."*) or even by talking to them directly and with cohesion.

However, during this initial phase, many people refused to participate in the interaction with Nao. Many such people expressed their dislike of the robot appearance by criticizing its appearance: *"It looks scary";* or being afraid or disgusted by the robot's way of speaking, summed up with a comment: *"The child's voice seems frightening, like there's something trapped inside the robot"*. These people usually avoided looking at the robot or noting its presence explicitly. They stood far away from the robot while making the order.

Some of these people also expressed their uncertainties about the robot's intelligence and abilities. For example, whether the robot would understand them: *"Will he know what I am saying?"*. One person asked, *"Can I take a picture of the robot? I don't have to ask him, right? He's just a machine."* One customer said to the barista that the robot *"lacks a lot to run such a business"*, and *"the robot won't be able to replace human assistants in cafes"*. One man who wanted to buy coffee beans ignored the robot and asked the barista for advice on possible choices. One woman ignored the robot when she wanted to know what food was currently available to order. Some customers did not know how to behave and how they should approach the robot. Some people seemed interested in the robot's presence in the cafe, but commented on its behavior to the barista, ignoring what the robot was saying.

Conversation Flow. People who decided to take part in the interaction reacted differently to the robot's voice and its way of speaking. Some of them described it as *"talking to a pet"* or like chatting with a child. They did not focus on mistakes made by the robot while speaking, or long pauses in robot responses. Often, they initiated the interaction and asked the robot questions unrelated to customer service.

However, there were some customers who were willing to start the interaction but got confused or irritated when the robot did not respond quickly enough. Some people gave up on the interaction and went straight to the barista to make the order. Often, a customer said: "*it's talking too slow!*" and dropped out of further conversation.

Adaptation to Specific Contexts. Some customers who ordered from the robot were interested in continuing further conversation. (In contrast, some others passively answered questions asked by the robot and did not want to continue the conversation after placing an order.) We observed specific behaviors of the robot, which facilitated the willingness to interact with it. The first of these was telling jokes or stories. Another aspect was when the robot addressed them directly and complimented their clothing or other accessories. Additionally, continuous interaction was encouraged by the robot addressing the customer by name.

As the conversation became longer, people started to comment on the robot's intelligence. They referred to it as "*smarty-pants*" or that it is generally smart.

In general, many factors affect the success of carrying out the interaction. The most important moment in the interaction seems to be its initiation - the first impression of the robot and interaction. As this was the stage when most people decide whether to participate in the conversation, we aimed to determine the customers' approach toward the robot. To check more precisely the attitudes and expectations of customers towards the robot and its functions in the cafe, we conducted additional sessions.

5   Sessions Five to Seven

5.1   Method

These sessions were conducted over three days in the cafe *Karma*. The study setup and interaction design were the same as in sessions two to four. During these sessions we collected data on the number of visitors to the cafe ($N = 67$).

Additionally, for gathering specific data on the customers' attitudes towards robots we adapted a questionnaire to our cafe setting [26]. Visitors of the cafe were approached by the researchers after placing an order (to either the human or the robot) with a request to fill in the questionnaire. Some of them ($N = 26$) agreed to respond.

The questionnaire (Table 2) was divided into five sections: *Interest, Negative attitude, Utility, Appearance* and *Familiarity*. The first three gave us information about the general attitude of the customer towards robots as well as the perceived potential of service robots in cafes. The latter two sections provided insights on desired physical features of the robot and customer's previous experience with robots. Participants were asked to state how strongly they agree with given sentences on a scale 1 ("*strongly disagree*") to 5 ("*strongly agree*"). We also gathered the basic demographic information about participants' age, gender and language used.

In this session, we did not record observations of the customers' behavior, but analyzed the participants' ($N = 9$) responses to the post-interaction interview, and the questionnaire data from ($N = 26$) participants.

5.2 Results and Discussion

First Impressions: The customers displayed similar behaviors towards the robot as in the previous sessions. Among the nine people who interacted with the robot by giving their order to it, four made comments about the robot's pleasant appearance and voice being an advantage. On the other hand, to the question *"What didn't you like about the interaction?"* one person responded: *"The fact that Nao was stiff and did not make free movements while talking"*.

For Nao's conversation approach, three participants appreciated Nao's politeness, with one of them commenting: *"Overall, the whole experience was unique, the robot was very polite"*.

Three of the nine people have had previous experience in talking to similar robots. The remaining six people reflected on their discomfort connected to their first human-robot interaction principally focusing on *"an awkward feeling"*.

Conversation Flow: The main disadvantage turned out to be that the interaction was not fluent. Five of the nine people complained about the answers being too slow, which caused the interaction to become more mechanical and less natural.

Adaptation to Specific Contexts: This aspect is as crucial to the customers as in the previous sessions. The conversations were often judged as intelligent. Nao's answers to the customers' questions were thought of positively. Robot's humorous comments added to its naturalness according to one person's observation. Another person mentioned that Nao's ability to give recommendations was an advantage.

Questionnaire Results. The demographic of the questionnaire responders was as follows: 50% female; 80.8% had Polish as their mother tongue; broad age range (14–58 yrs.; $M = 30.88$, $SD = 13.09$).

The means and standard deviations of the questionnaire results ($N = 26$) are shown in Table 2. All of them were on a scale 1 - 5, with 1 being *"strongly disagree"* and 5 being *"strongly agree"*.

People were moderately interested in the interaction with robots with their reactions to the statement *"I think a robot could be a communication partner"* ($M = 3.46$, $SD = 1.24$) or *"I want to converse with a robot"* ($M = 3.12$, $SD = 1.42$). Surprisingly they expressed strong fear towards robots ($M = 4.52$, $SD = 1.04$) and some discontent with the idea of a robot's presence in their favorite cafe ($M = 3.00$, $SD = 1.60$). On the other hand, it seems as though they thought that generally robots could bean assistive ($M = 3.31$, $SD = 1.40$) entertaining ($M = 3.92$, $SD = 1.13$) in a cafe. Appearance-wise the participants thought that the robot's design should be pleasant ($M = 3.23$, $SD = 1.24$), yet it could be that they want it to have an original appearance, which would not be too human- ($M = 2.38$, $SD = 1.27$) or animal-like ($M = 1.88$, $SD = 1.10$). They were not familiar with similar devices ($M = 1.39$, $SD = 0.64$), and they thought other countries have already adapted robots compared to Poland ($M = 3.06$, $SD = 1.31$).

Table 2. Categories of interaction for the café session

Categories of interaction for the café session	M	SD
Interest I think a robot can be a communication partner	3.46	1.24
I want to converse with a robot	3.12	1.42
I would want to boast that I have interacted with a robot	2.77	1.48
It is good if a robot can do the work of a human	3.46	1.30
I feel at ease around robots because I do not need to pay attention to robots as I do to humans	2.58	1.50
Negative attitude It would be a pity to have a robot in my favorite cafe	3.00	1.60
The movements of a robot are unpleasant	1.92	1.26
It is unnatural for a robot to speak in a human language	1.50	0.86
I feel like I also become a machine when I am with a robot	1.38	0.90
I feel scared around robots	4.52	1.04
Utility I think a robot could make food/coffee recommendations to me	3.23	1.24
I think a robot would understand my order	1.88	1.10
I like the idea of using robots in cafes or stores as assistants	2.92	1.32
I like the idea of using robots in cafes or shops to entertain customers	2.38	1.27
Appearance I think the robot design should be cute	3.69	1.38
I think robots should have animal-like shapes	3.69	1.38
I think the voice of a robot should be like the voice of a living creature	3.31	1.40
I think a robot should have human-like shape	3.92	1.13
Familiarity I often come across robots in public spaces	1.39	0.64
I would be less surprised to come across a robot in public space in country other than Poland	3.06	1.31

6 General Discussion

6.1 Attitudes of Participants Towards Service Robots in a Cafe

Our study participants demonstrated a variety of behaviors related to the acceptance of and attitudes toward a social robot assistant in a cafe. We identified responses such as uncertainty, anxiety, mistrust, and fear towards the robot, which have been found in other studies [15, 23] as well. These may be related to the novelty factor and a lack of previous experience interacting with a robot [27]. Customers might not know the why the robot is in the cafe, whether it would understand them, or if it was trained to take their order. This may be related to the robot's appearance whose capabilities and body structure are not suitable for a cafe. Customers keeping physical distance from the robot may be interpreted as confirming a lack of trust toward the robot [25]. Some customers' negative attitudes toward the robot may be related to a generally bad attitude toward technology in public places among Poles [3]; it might be due to privacy concerns [28]. However, this attitude can be changed by increasing interaction facilities such as talking with the robot more naturally, thereby reducing unpleasant feelings such as fear, or stress in older customers or customers with little experience in using robots [29].

6.2 Factors in Human-Robot Interaction Affecting Customer Satisfaction

First Impressions: Our study confirmed that the first impressions of the interaction play a crucial role in how it unfolds later [30]. We also assume that the appearance of the robot influences users' attitudes and it is crucial to meet customer expectations toward the robot design to provide positive feedback [31]. Our study confirmed a slight preference for human-like or animal-like appearance [18]. Moreover, the childlike look was perceived by some people as a positive feature that encouraged them to start conversation with the robot. Also, when the robot is pleasant, the customers perceive it positively and are more tolerant of its failures [32]. This can be related to the anthropomorphisation of the robot [33], which can positively influence human-robot interaction. However, making the robot more human-like may trigger the "uncanny valley" effect [34], making the customer shy away from the conversation [35].

Conversation Flow: Previous studies have shown that a proactive and responsive approach of the robot at the beginning is needed for the interaction to successfully proceed [36], and our results confirm this. We have observed people reluctant to start the conversation with questions, probably not sure whether the robot is going to answer; yet happily answering the ones asked by the robot. Furthermore, having a clearly assigned role of taking the customer orders, the robot convinced more people to talk to it, rather than when simply appealing as entertainment.

Several people were not willing to join the interaction. We presume, with some confirmation in our results, they did not know how to act, as it was a new situation for them. Such new situations require user-friendly guidance via the interaction [15, 23].

When users have too high expectations about the robot, they will be disappointed with its service quality and stop the interaction. However, if the robot's performance exceeds users' expectations, customers will be more satisfied with the provided service and will continue to use it [37].

Robot failures in understanding because of loud surroundings or slow responses affect the trust of people: how well a machine is regarded to carry out its task has a significant impact on how much trust people place in it [15, 38]. This suggests that machine mistakes are very likely to influence trust. On the other hand, it could suggest that customers may have had insecurity about their own ability to interact with technology, or that they were not used to interacting with robots.

Adaptation to Specific Contexts: The results show that recommendations were positively received by customers, as in the previous studies [17, 20, 39].

Our study revealed that people enjoyed the robot's clever and adequate answers. Its ability to conduct small talk was appreciated as well. The positive outcome corresponds with the fact that small talk, when desired, builds trust in interaction partners [15, 40] and with more trust comes better overall experience of the interaction [41].

People who ended up having a brief conversation with Nao were pleased by the interaction most of the time. Although, for some, the presence of the robot might have caused some confusion, we believe that the robot giving into the cafe scenario might have reduced part of that confusion by clearly indicating its function in the cafe sharing a task-oriented interaction with the human [42].

7 Conclusions and Future Research

Our goal was to study Polish consumers' attitudes towards assistive social robots in a public place, and to identify interaction features important for the customers, which could lead to a positive user experience. Despite the growth of robot assistants in Poland, they are still not widely available in public spaces like shops or cafes. Many people are familiar with assistive robots but service robots with human features are still alien to them. This might be a reason behind the customers' neutral attitude towards the Nao robot in a cafe. Even so, it is possible that these neutral emotions could be transformed into positive ones by familiarizing Polish society with such technologies. In future, we expect to observe customers' behavior and their adaptation to robots. After all, with digitalization in Poland came acceptance of various changes in everyday life and official realms. A similar change could happen with attitudes towards robot assistants in public places.

For a cafe scenario, the right design of a robot's interaction is important. We distinguished three essential aspects that affect customers' attitudes: *first impression*, *conversation flow*, and *adaptation* to a given context. Firstly, the appearance, voice and motor behavior of the robot should be pleasant for the users – from pleasant appearance and moderately human voice to appropriate gestures. It is effective if the robot initiates the interaction like a salesperson in a cafe would. It is also important that the robot shows its humanlike abilities including being as fluent as possible during the conversation. People react especially enthusiastically when the robot gives situation-specific comments and jokes. The robot should also accommodate peoples' willingness to have small talk while getting an order from the customer.

There were some limitations in our study. 1) The study lacked consistent counts of the participants, which can easily be avoided in the future. 2) The number of participants was not large enough. However, this is consistent with the contemporary approach to design which rejects universal solutions in favor of localized, culture-specific solutions [43]. Future studies on this topic should conduct more such studies with different user groups: for example, in rural areas and urban areas. 3) As some of the robot's responses were provided on the spot and typed into a text-to-speech engine, they might have been too slow. Indeed, a few participants reported disengaging from the conversation due to delayed answers. We suppose that people's attitude could have been more positive towards the robot if the interaction was timely, thus the pre-designed conversation flow requires revision. 4) The robot's role might not have been clear to the customers, which is why they avoided any conversation in the first place. 5), Noise in the cafes created some problems. As our setup did not have any microphone to transfer the sound, it was difficult for the operator to hear what the customers were saying while sitting in another part of the cafe. In future studies, a microphone should be attached to the robot to make it easier to conduct the interaction.

Finally, we suggest that the future research on social robots in cafes should focus on designing the optimal conversation flow as it was revealed to be the most crucial aspect of customer satisfaction with such robots. Programming an autonomous robot with the right framework for conversation could result in automatizing the role of a café's salesperson with a satisfactory experience for the customers.

References

1. Bartneck, C., Suzuki, T., Kanda, T., Nomura, T.: The influence of people's culture and prior experiences with Aibo on their attitude towards robots. AI Soc. 21(1), 217–230 (2007)
2. Gentiloni, P.: Summer 2023 economic forecast: easing growth momentum amid declining inflation and robust labour market. In: Economy and Finance. https://economy-finance.ec.europa.eu/economic-forecast-and-surveys/economic-forecasts/summer-2023-economic-for ecast-easing-growth-momentum-amid-declining-inflation-and-robust-labour_en. Accessed 09 Aug 2023
3. Digital Poland: Technologia w służbie społeczeństwu. Czy Polacy zostaną społeczeństwem 5.0? https://digitalpoland.org/assets/publications/technologia-w-sluzbie-spoleczenstwu-czy-polacy-zostana-spoleczenstwem-50-edycja-2020/society-50-tech4society-edycja-2020-dig italpoland.pdf. Accessed 09 Aug 2023
4. Tobis, S., Suwalsk, J.: Opinie osób starszych na temat robota społecznego i jego zastosowania. GERIATRIA (2015)
5. Wasielewska, A., Łupkowski, P.: Nieoczywiste relacje z technologią. Przegląd badań na temat ludzkich postaw wobec robotów, Człowiek i Społeczeństwo 51, 165–187 (2021)
6. G. U. Statystyczny: Mały rocznik statystyczny 2023. https://stat.gov.pl/obszary-tematyczne/roczniki-statystyczne/roczniki-statystyczne/maly-rocznik-statystyczny-polski-2023.1.25.html. Accessed 09 Aug 2023
7. Mavridis, N., et al.: Opinions and attitudes toward humanoid robots in the Middle East. AI & Soc. 27, 517–534 (2012)
8. Boguszewski, R., Bożewicz M.: Family, religion, homeland – the traditional values of Poles in the process of transformation. Rocznik Lubuski 46(2), 235–247 (2020). ISSN 0485-3083
9. Müller, C.: World Robotics 2022 – Industrial Robots. https://ifr.org/img/world_robotics/Exe cutive_Summary_WR_Industrial_Robots_2022.pdf. Accessed 09 Aug 2023
10. Ramię w ramię z robotem, Jak wykorzystać potencjał automatyzacji w Polsce. https://norber tbiedrzycki.pl/ramie-w-ramie-z-robotem-jak-wykorzystac-potencjal-automatyzacji-w-pol sce/. Accessed 09 Aug 2023
11. Kerfuś ogłasza swoje pierwsze tournée po Polsce. Popularny robot i gwiazda internetu odwiedzi miliony Polaków I Centrum prasowe Carrefour Polska. https://media.carrefour.pl/pr/kerfus-oglasza-swoje-pierwsze-tournee-po-polsce-popularny-robot-i-gwiazda-internetu-odwiedzi-miliony-polakow/774379. Accessed 04 Aug 2023
12. Shell wprowadził pierwsze w Europie roboty na stacji paliw I Shell Polska. https://www.shell.pl/media/2021/shell-wprowadzil-pierwsze-w-europie-roboty-na-stacji-paliw.html. Accessed 09 Aug 2023

13. Hotele. Goście z zagranicy w Gdańsku, Polacy w Sopocie i Gdyni. https://www.trojmi asto.pl/wiadomosci/Hotele-Goscie-z-zagranicy-w-Gdansku-Polacy-w-Sopocie-i-Gdyni-n16 2878.html. Accessed 04 Aug 2023
14. Barnett, W., Foos, A., Gruber, T., Keeling, D., Keeling, K., Nasr, L.: Consumer perceptions of interactive service robots: a value-dominant logic perspective. In: 23rd IEEE International Symposium on Robot and Human Interactive Communication, pp. 1134–1139 (2014)
15. Lim, M.Y., Robb, D.A., Wilson, B.W., Hastie, H.: Feeding the coffee habit: a longitudinal study of a Robo-Barista. arXiv preprint arXiv:2309.02942 (2023)
16. Baba, J., et al.: Teleoperated robot acting autonomous for better customer satisfaction. In: CHI EA 2020, pp. 1–8. ACM, New York (2020)
17. Song, S., Baba, J., Nakanishi, J., Yoshikawa, Y., Ishiguro, H.: Teleoperated robot sells toothbrush in a shopping mall: a field study. In: CHI EA 2021, New York (2021)
18. Van Doorn, J., et al.: Domo Arigato Mr. Roboto: emergence of automated social presence in organizational frontlines and customers' service experiences. J. Serv. Res. 20(1), 43–58 (2016)
19. Lim, M.Y., Lopes, J.D.A., Robb, D.A., Wilson, B.W., Moujahid, M., Hastie, H.: Demonstration of a Robo-Barista for in the wild interactions. In: 17th ACM/IEEE International Conference on Human-Robot Interaction 2022 (HRI). IEEE (2022)
20. Murakawa, Y., Okabayashi, K., Kanda, S., Ueki, M.: Verification of the effectiveness of robots for sales promotion in commercial facilities. In: International Symposium on System Integration (SII), pp. 299–305 (2011)
21. Rey-Moreno, M., Medina-Molina, C., Barrera-Barrera, R.: Multichannel strategies in public services: levels of satisfaction and citizens' preferences. Intl. Rev. Publ. Nonprofit Market. 15(1), 9–24 (2018)
22. Kaipainen, K., Ahtinen, A., Hiltunen, A.: Ice surprise, more present than a machine: experiences evoked by a social robot for guidance and edutainment at a city service point. In: Proceedings of the 22nd International Academy Mindtrek Conference, pp. 163–171. ACM, New York (2018)
23. Steinfeld, A., Jenkins, O.C., Scassellati, B.: The oz of wizard: simulating the human for interaction research. In: Proceedings of the 4th ACM/IEEE International Conference on Human Robot Interaction (HRI 2009), pp. 101–108. ACM, New York (2009)
24. Hancock, P.A., Billings, D.R., Schaefer, K.E., Chen, J.Y.C., de Visser, E.J., Parasuraman, R.: A meta-analysis of factors affecting trust in human-robot interaction. Hum. Factors 53(5), 517–527 (2011)
25. Babel, F., et al.: Small talk with a robot? The impact of dialog content, talk initiative, and gaze behavior of a social robot on trust, acceptance, and proximity. Int. J. Soc. Robot. 13(6), 1485–1498 (2021)
26. Ninomiya, T., Fujita, A., Suzuki, D., Umemuro, H.: Development of the multi-dimensional robot attitude scale: constructs of people's attitudes towards domestic robots. In: Proceedings of the Social Robotics: 7th International Conference (ICSR 2015), Paris, 26–30 October 2015, vol. 7, pp. 482–491. Springer, Heidelberg (2015)
27. Savela, N., Turja, T., Oksanen, A.: Social acceptance of robots in different occupational fields: a systematic literature review. Int. J. Soc. Robot. 10(4), 493–502 (2018)
28. Niemelä, M., Heikkilä, P., Lammi, H., Oksman, V.: A social robot in a shopping mall: studies on acceptance and stakeholder expectations. In: Social Robots: Technological, Societal and Ethical Aspects of Human-Robot Interaction, pp. 119–144 (2019)
29. Roozen, I., Raedts, M., Yanycheva, A.: Are retail customers ready for service robot assistants? Int. J. Soc. Robot. 15(1), 15–25 (2023)

30. Pitsch, K., Kuzuoka, H., Suzuki, Y., Sussenbach, L., Luff, P., Heath, C.: The first five seconds: contingent stepwise entry into an interaction as a means to secure sustained engagement in HRI. In: The 18th IEEE International Symposium on Robot and Human Interactive Communication (RO-MAN 2009), pp. 985–991. IEEE (2009)
31. Lu, V.N., et al.: Service robots, customers and service employees: what can we learn from the academic literature and where are the gaps? J. Serv. Theory Pract. **30**(3), 361–391 (2020)
32. Lv, X., Liu, Y., Luo, J., Liu, Y., Li, C.: Does a cute artificial intelligence assistant soften the blow? The impact of cuteness on customer tolerance of assistant service failure. Ann. Tour. Res. **87**, 103114 (2021)
33. Root-Bernstein, M., Douglas, L., Smith, A.A., Verissimo, D.: Anthropomorphized species as tools for conservation: utility beyond prosocial, intelligent and suffering species. Biodivers. Conserv. **22**, 1577–1589 (2013)
34. Złotowski, J.A., Sumioka, H., Nishio, S., Glas, D.F., Bartneck, C., Ishiguro, H.: Persistence of the uncanny valley: the influence of repeated interactions and a robot's attitude on its perception. Front. Psychol. **6**, 883 (2015)
35. Broadbent, E.: Interactions with robots: the truths we reveal about ourselves. Annu. Rev. Psychol. **68**, 627–652 (2017)
36. Pitsch, K., Lohan, K.S., Rohlfing, K., Saunders, J., Nehaniv, C.L., Wrede, B.: Better be reactive at the beginning. Implications of the first seconds of an encounter for the tutoring style in human-robot-interaction. In: The 21st IEEE International Symposium on Robot and Human Interactive Communication (IEEE RO-MAN 2012), pp. 974–981. IEEE (2012)
37. Komatsu, T., Kurosawa, R., Yamada, S.: How does the difference between users' expectations and perceptions about a robotic agent affect their behavior? An adaptation gap concept for determining whether interactions between users and agents are going well or not. Int. J. Soc. Robot. **4**, 109–116 (2012)
38. Muir, B.M., Moray, N.: Trust in automation. Part II. Experimental studies of trust and human intervention in a process control simulation. Ergonomics **39**(3), 429–460 (1996)
39. Song, S., Jun, B., Nakanishi, J., Yoshikawa, Y., Ishiguro, H.: Service robots in a bakery shop: a field study. In: 2022 IEEE/RSJ International Conference on Intelligent Robots and Systems (IROS), pp. 134–140. IEEE (2022)
40. Chowdhury, A., Ahtinen, A., Kaipainen K.: The Superhero of the University: experience-driven design and field study of the university guidance robot. In: Proceedings of the 23rd International Academy Mindtrek Conference, pp. 1–9. ACM, New York (2020)
41. Parasuraman, R., Riley, V.: Humans and automation: use, misuse, disuse, abuse. Hum. Factors **39**(2), 230–253 (1997)
42. Kim, Y., Yoon, W.C.: Generating task-oriented interactions of service robots. IEEE Trans. Syst. Man Cybern. Syst. **44**(8), 981–994 (2014)
43. Rosner, D.K.: Critical Fabulations: Reworking the Methods and Margins of Design. MIT Press, Massachusetts (2018)

Exploring Response Strategies of Robotized Products in Problematic Situations: Analysis of Apology and Risk Communication Strategies

SangMin Kim⬤, JongSuk Choi⬤, and Sonya S. Kwak$^{(\boxtimes)}$⬤

Center for Intelligent and Interactive Robotics, Korea Institute of Science and Technology, Seoul 02792, Korea
{024643,cjs,sonakwak}@kist.re.kr

Abstract. As the use of robotized products becomes more prevalent in real-world settings, users are confronted with unforeseen problematic situations. The response strategy of a robotized product can have a significant impact on mitigating negative perceptions of the product resulting from problematic situations. In this study, we introduce apology and risk communication strategies as potential response strategies for robotized products and explore their impact on user evaluations or attraction through experimental research. Our findings indicate that when a problem originates from the robotized product itself, the use of an apology strategy and an accommodative risk communication strategy can enhance users' task attraction to the product, but do not affect their evaluation of the robot and social attraction to it. Conversely, when the problem is not caused by the robotized product, the use of a defensive risk communication strategy is associated with higher robot evaluation and greater user attraction compared to the use of an accommodative strategy. This study demonstrates that response strategies in problematic situations that people expect for robotized products are different from those for humans.

Keywords: Robotized products · Response strategies · Problematic situations

1 Introduction

A robotized product refers to a type of product that integrates robotics technology with the aim of enhancing user convenience and usability. With the incorporation of robotics technology, robotized products can collect data, process information, make decisions,

This Work Was Partly Supported By the Korea Institute of Science and Technology (KIST) Institutional Program Under Grant (2E32302), Institute of Information & Communications Technology Planning & Evaluation (IITP) Grant Funded By the Korea Government (MSIT) (No. 2017-0-00432, Development of Non-Invasive Integrated BCI SW Platform to Control Home Appliance and External Devices By User's Thought Via AR/VR Interface), and the Government-Wide R&D Fund for Infections Disease Research (GFID), Funded By the Ministry of the Interior and Safety, Republic of Korea (20014463).

and even act autonomously to a certain extent [1]. With growth of robot market, a wide range of robotized products are being introduced to assist users in their daily lives. As unforeseen breakdowns are bound to arise in the use of robotized products, response strategies to alleviate negative impressions generated from breakdowns of robotized products need to be explored. Robotized products possess greater autonomy compared to conventional products, as they can sense their surroundings and communicate a problem to the user through speech, display, or action. Based on the media equation theory [2], it is reasonable to infer that people anticipate robots to interact with them similarly as humans do. Previous studies on human-robot interaction have demonstrated that robots are perceived as more social and evaluated more positively when they look and behave like humans [3–6]. Therefore, it can be inferred that if a robotized product engages with users using human-like strategies in problematic situations, users would evaluate it more positively. However, the robotized product differs from anthropomorphic robots in that it shares the appearance of its parent product. Moreover, as diverse robotized products exist in users' daily lives, they can have a direct or indirect influence on each other. These differences distinguish robotized products from traditional anthropomorphic robots. Thus, it would be inappropriate to claim that robotized products will conform to the media equation. The objective of this study is to investigate a suitable response strategy for robotized products to manage problematic situations.

2   Study Background

2.1   Apology Strategy

The act of apologizing is a crucial recovery strategy that individuals can employ when problems arise to mitigate their negative impact [7]. Offering an apology when an individual is at fault can reduce the level of blame attributed to them for the problem, allowing individuals to dispel any negative perceptions the problem may have created and to concentrate on finding a resolution [8]. Before identifying the root cause of the problem, apologizing for the problem occurrence can lessen the emotional burden on others and increase their willingness to assist in resolving the problem [9]. Consequently, even if the individual is not responsible for the problem, offering an apology can elicit positive feedback from others. Previous research has demonstrated that robots and agent systems can enhance user satisfaction by offering apologies when mistakes occur. Lee et al. have reported that the use of social strategies to apologize for mistakes can positively impact the evaluation of the robot's service by the user [10]. In addition, Hone and Keilain et al. found that when an agent system takes the initiative to apologize for user errors, it can reduce user frustration. Their study also indicated that users tend to rate the usability of an agent system that apologizes relatively higher than that of an agent system that does not [11, 12]. Based on the findings of the previous studies, we expect that a strategy of offering an apology to users can positively influence the way they perceive robotized products.

2.2 Risk Communication Strategies: Accommodative Strategy versus Defensive Strategy

From a business perspective, encountering a problem indicates that the organization is exposed to some form of risk. Especially for companies that offer and operate services, a consumer's evaluation of the service could be affected by the way the company responds to a problematic situation [13, 14]. The way a company interacts with consumers during a crisis situation can be viewed as a form of risk communication strategy [15]. Although there are various strategies that companies can employ to manage problematic situations, researchers have categorized them into two primary categories: accommodation and defense [16]. The accommodative strategy involves admitting that a problem has occurred and taking responsibility for it. This risk communication strategy is typically used by companies that prioritize their social reputation over their business interests. On the other hand, the defensive strategy downplays the severity of the problem and communicates to consumers that the company is not responsible. This approach is usually employed when a company prioritizes its business interests over its social reputation [17]. Both strategies present distinct advantages and disadvantages. When a company adopts an accommodative strategy, consumers may empathize with the company's position, leading to a decreased likelihood of placing blame on the company [18]. However, the downside is that consumers may be left with a lasting impression of the company's imperfect capabilities [19]. Conversely, a defensive strategy may leave consumers with a negative perception that the organization is evading responsibility for the problem. Nonetheless, the advantage of this strategy is that it may eventually assuage consumer skepticism regarding the organization's business competence [20]. In this study, it is anticipated that the utilization of suitable risk communication strategies by robotized products in problematic situations would result in positive user evaluations.

2.3 Attraction

The term "attraction" refers to a range of positive emotions that an individual may experience towards another person with whom they have a social relationship [21, 22]. In previous research, attraction has been used as an indicator of sociability in interpersonal relationships [23]. Some current studies have construed the degree to which an individual is perceived to be attractive to another as a function of their level of sociability towards the other person [24]. In addition, some contemporary studies explain the level of attraction that an individual may feel towards another person as a result of their cognitive evaluation of the person, in addition to the level of emotional connection they may experience towards the person [25, 26]. This implies that an individual is more likely to be attracted to someone who fulfills their idealized expectations of a human being, not only in terms of sociability, but also task competence.

In the literature, attraction has been examined in terms of two main dimensions: social attraction and task attraction [27]. Social attraction pertains to the desire to establish an intimate emotional relationship with someone who is friendly and sociable. In contrast, task attraction is the inclination to work with someone who is perceived to possess a high level of competence and understanding in a particular task [28]. Attractive individuals are likely to have high scores in both the social and task attraction dimensions. However, it is important to note that high levels of social attraction do not necessarily equate to high levels of task attraction, and vice versa [29]. For instance, an increase in social attraction towards an individual may not necessarily result in a desire to collaborate with them on a task, and an increase in task attraction may not necessarily lead to a desire to form a personal relationship with them.

3 Hypotheses

In this study, we aim to investigate the impact of a robotized product's response strategies in situations where the product fails to properly execute user commands on the user's evaluation of the product. Based on prior research, we hypothesize that robotized products that apologize for their errors in such situations will be evaluated more positively by users. Even though the apology does not directly resolve the problem, we expect that this apologetic behavior will enhance the user's emotional trust in the robotized product. Therefore, we predict that the robotized product that expresses an apology in a problematic situation will be evaluated more positively by users than a product that does not apologize.

H1: A robotized product's apologizing behavior in a problematic situation will have a positive effect on users' evaluation of the product.
H2: A robotized product's apologizing behavior in a problematic situation will positively influence users' attraction to the product.

Based on the findings in the previous section, we anticipated that a robotized product employing an accommodative strategy would avoid user blame by acknowledging its error. The user may also perceive the robotized product as more responsible for the problem. In contrast, a robotized product using a defensive strategy may be perceived by the user as not having made the error, through behavior that distance itself from the cause of the problem.

We expect that the user's evaluation of the robotized product will differ depending on which strategy the robotized product uses to deal with the problem. Additionally, we want to understand which risk communication strategy is more effective for the robotized product.

H3: Users' evaluation of a robotized product will differ depending on the risk communication strategy utilized by the robotized product in a problem situation.

Robotized products are likely to receive different evaluations based on the risk communication strategy they utilize. We infer that these different evaluations reflect the degree of attraction users feel towards the robotized product. Therefore, we expect that the robotized product's risk communication strategy will affect the degree of attraction users feel towards the robotized product.

H4: The degree of attraction users feel towards the robotized product will vary according to the risk communication strategy utilized by the robotized product in the problem situation.

4 Method

This study employed a 2 × 2 mixed experimental design to examine the effects of apology and risk communication strategies on participants' evaluations of a robotized product. The experimental conditions comprised two factors: the inclusion or exclusion of an apology strategy (RA: robotized products with an apology strategy, and RN: robotized products without an apology strategy), and the type of risk communication strategy utilized (AS: accommodative strategy, and DS: defensive strategy).

4.1 Participants

A total of 67 participants were initially recruited for the study, and after excluding outliers, the data of 64 participants were analyzed. Participants were evenly divided into two groups based on apology strategy conditions (with apology and without apology). Participants, consisting of 29 males and 35 females, were between the ages of 20 and 40. Each participant received approximately $9 USD as compensation for their participation in the study.

4.2 Experimental Setup

The experiment was conducted using video-based stimuli, which featured two robotized products (see Fig. 1). The first product is a robotized chair equipped with a built-in RADAR that allows it to perceive its surroundings. Users can control the chair's movement using voice commands, and the chair communicates with the user via a built-in speaker. The second product is a robotized chest of drawers that can automatically open and close each drawer and retrieve the item required by the user. During the experiment, the user interacted with the robotized chair, and the robotized chest of drawers was placed in one of the experimental environments.

4.3 Scenarios

In the experimental scenario, the robotized chair received the command "Come to the right side of the table" from the user. While moving to execute the command, the robotized chair failed to reach to the table by bumping to the robotized chest of drawers. In this problematic situation, the robotized chair responded with two different types of risk communication strategies, including an accommodative strategy (AS) or a defensive strategy (DS). In the accommodative strategy, the robotized chair explained to the user that the problem was caused by an error in its pathfinding function. In contrast, in the defensive strategy, the robotized chair informed the user that a chest of drawers was blocking its path.

Prior to conveying the cause of the problem, the robotized chair decided whether or not to utilize an apology strategy. When the robotized chair used an apology strategy (RA), it apologized by saying "I'm sorry" before revealing the cause of the problem. Conversely, when the robotized chair did not use an apology strategy (RN), it disclosed the cause of the problem immediately without apology. A total of four videos were generated for each independent variable condition (see Table 1).

Fig. 1. Robotized chair (left) and chest of drawers (right)

Table 1. The response strategies in experimental sceanarios

Response Strategy	Apology Strategy	
	With Stratgy (RA)	Without Strategy (RN)
Risk Communication Strategy	"I'm Sorry. There was a problem with my navigation and I didn't get to my destination."	"There was a problem with my navigation and I didn't get to my destination."
	Accommodative Strategy (AS)	
	"I'm Sorry. The chest of drawers got in my way and I didn't get to my destination."	"The chest of drawers got in my way and I didn't get to my destination."
	Defensive Strategy (DS)	

4.4 Procedures

The Institutional Review Board of the Korea Institute of Science and Technology authorized this experiment (KIST IRB: KIST-202209-HR-023). The participants provided written consent, viewed the video clips in accordance with the experimental conditions, and completed an online questionnaire. The participants watched both experimental conditions (accommodative and defensive strategies) of the experimental video. The order of exposure to the two conditions was counterbalanced. Following each video stimulus, participants completed a questionnaire that assessed their perceptions of the robotized chair. The questionnaire included three items: robot evaluation (RE) [30], social attraction (SA), and task attraction (TA) [28]. H1 and H3 were tested by using the robot evaluation item. H2 and H4 were tested by using the social attraction and task attraction items. Each item on the questionnaire was measured on a 7-point scale. In addition, as a result of reliability evaluation, all scales were calculated with a Cronbach Alpha coefficient of 0.8 points or more.

5 Results

In order to analyze the main effects of the independent variables on the dependent variable and to test for interactions between the variables, we conducted a two-way analysis of variance in a two-way design experiment We hypothesized that our experimental data would exhibit a normal distribution, substantiated by the inclusion of more than 30 data points within each experimental condition. Furthermore, we conducted an equality of variance test to corroborate the assumption of homogenous variances across all dependent variables ($p > 0.05$). Therefore, we expect our assessment results to be resilient against both Type I and Type II errors.

5.1 Main Effect Analysis

Upon conducting an analysis of variance, we found no statistically significant difference [$F_{RE}(1,124) = 3.311$, $p_{RE} = 0.071$] between the robotized chair with an apology strategy and the robotized chair without an apology strategy for the item assessing robot evaluation.

Additionally, there was no statistically significant difference [$F_{SA}(1,124) = 2.415$, $p_{SA} = 0.123$] between the robotized chair with the apology strategy and the robotized chair without the apology strategy for the item assessing social attraction. In contrast, we found a statistically significant difference [$F_{TA}(1,124) = 8.907$, $p_{TA} = 0.003$] between the robotized chair with the apology strategy and the robotized chair without the apology strategy for the item assessing task attraction. This result demonstrates that the robotized chair that employed the apology strategy in the problem situation ($M_{RA} = 3.197$, $SD_{RA} = 1.096$) elicited higher task attraction from the participants than the robotized chair that did not employ the apology strategy ($M_{RN} = 2.644$, $SD_{RN} = 1.061$). However, our findings indicate that whether the robotized chair employs an apology strategy or not has no discernible effect on the user's evaluation or social attraction to the robotized chair (see Fig. 2). Consequently, our results lead us to reject H1 and partially support H2.

We conducted an analysis of variance and found no statistically significant difference [$F_{RE}(1,124) = 2.601$, $p_{RE} = 0.109$] between robotized chairs that utilized an accommodative strategy and those that utilized a defensive strategy on the item assessing robot evaluation. Moreover, there was no statistically significant difference [$F_{SA}(1,124) = 3.649$, $p_{SA} = 0.058$] between the robotized chair that employed the accommodative strategy and the robotized chair that employed the defensive strategy for the item assessing social attraction. However, we did find a statistically significant difference [$F_{TA}(1,124) = 4.163$, $p_{TA} = 0.043$] between the robotized chair that used the accommodative strategy and the robotized chair that used the defensive strategy for the item assessing task attraction. Our results demonstrate that in the problem situation, the robotized chair that employed the accommodative strategy ($M_{AS} = 3.109$, $SD_{AS} = 1.004$) had higher task attraction from the participants than the robotized chair that employed the defensive strategy ($M_{DS} = 2.731$, $SD_{DS} = 1.183$). Nevertheless, our findings suggest that the type of risk communication strategy utilized by the robotized chair has no bearing on users' evaluation of the robotized chair or its social attractiveness (see Fig. 2). Therefore, we reject H3 and partially support H4.

5.2 Interaction Effect Analysis

After conducting the analysis, we found an interaction effect [$F_{TA}(1,124) = 5.029$, $p_{TA} = 0.027$] between the apology strategy and risk communication strategy, only for the item assessing task attraction. Specifically, when the robotized chair used an apology strategy, the task attraction of the chair using an accommodative strategy ($M_{AS} = 3.594$, $SD_{AS} = 0.778$) was higher than that of the chair using a defensive strategy ($M_{DS} = 2.800$, $SD_{DS} = 1.227$), which is consistent with the main effect analysis. However, no difference was observed when no apology strategy was used. Moreover, when the robotized chair used an accommodative strategy, the apology strategy improved task attraction ($M_{RA} = 3.594$, $SD_{RA} = 0.778$ / $M_{RN} = 2.625$, $SD_{RN} = 0.979$). In contrast, when the robotized chair used a defensive strategy, the apology strategy did not enhance task attraction.

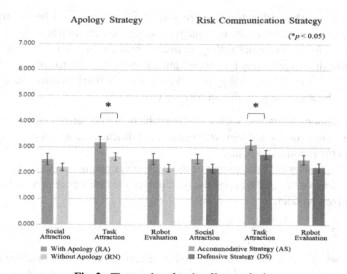

Fig. 2. The results of main effect analysis.

6 Study 2

Unlike the study in the previous section, in which the robotized chair's failure was caused by itself, in Study 2, the experimental environment was modified by using external stimuli that caused the robotized chair to fail, with the robotized chest of drawers impeding the path of the chair.

6.1 Hypotheses

In this experimental setting, the cause of the problem lies with the drawer, rather than the chair. As a result, the chair's apology for the issue is unlikely to be perceived as sincere by the participants. Thus, we anticipate that the apology strategy of the robotized product in response to the issue caused by another product's error would not significantly impact users' evaluations of or attraction towards the robotized product.

H1–1: In situations where the source of the problem is another product, the apology strategy employed by a robotized product is unlikely to influence the user evaluations of the product.

H2–1: In situations where the source of the problem is another product, the apology strategy employed by a robotized product is unlikely to influence users' attraction to the product.

In human society, an accommodative strategy to handle a problematic situation, even when the problem is caused by the other person, can be perceived as an act of ethical caring for the other person [31]. By being educated and experiencing the effects of this ethical caring, people tend to exhibit prosocial behavior toward others [32, 33]. Thus, ethical caring in human society is an action that can enhance the attractiveness of the individual.

We hypothesize that subjects will express social attraction toward the robotized product that employs the accommodative strategy, if they expect an equivalent level of ethical care from the robotized product as they do from humans. Conversely, we anticipate that subjects will exhibit a relatively higher task attraction towards the robotized product that employs a defensive strategy, as they perceive that the robotized product conveys correct information about the cause of the problem to the subject.

H4–1: In situations where the source of the problem is another product, the robotized product's accommodative strategy will positively influence the user's perceived social attraction to the robotized product.

H4–2: In situations where the source of the problem is another product, the robotized product's defensive strategy will positively influence the user's perceived task attraction to the robotized product.

6.2 Method

In Study 2, we developed new video stimuli to clearly depict a malfunctioning drawer as the cause of the robotized chair's failure. A fresh set of 64 participants, who did not participate in the previous study, were recruited for Study 2. The robotized chair in the video stimulus moved in the correct direction toward the table to follow the user's command. However, while the robotized chair moved to the table, a drawer located at the bottom of the robotized chest of drawers opened and obstructed the chair's path. The chair acknowledged the obstacle and informed the user of the problematic situation by using response strategies. Depending on the experimental condition, the robotized chair either apologized or refrained from apologizing and used an accommodative strategy to inform the user that its failure was a result of its own error or used a defensive strategy to attribute the fault to the drawer. The evaluation process and survey items used in Study 2 were identical to those employed in the previous experiment, except for the presentation of a new video stimulus to the subjects.

7 Results

7.1 Main Effect Analysis

An analysis of variance was conducted to assess the impact of apology strategy on the evaluation and attraction of the robotized chair. The results showed that there was no statistically significant difference [$F_{RE}(1,124) = 0.090, p_{RE} = 0.765 / F_{SA}(1,124) = 0.199, p_{SA} = 0.656 / F_{TA}(1,124) < 0.001, p_{TA} = 0.989$] between the chair with an apology strategy and that without an apology strategy for all evaluated items (see Fig. 3). These findings support H1-1 and H2-1, indicating that the presence or absence of an apology strategy has no effect on the user's evaluation or attraction to the robotized chair when the chair is not the source of the problem.

The analysis of variance revealed a statistically significant difference [$F_{RE}(1,124) = 4.558, p_{RE} = 0.035/F_{SA}(1,124) = 4.750, p_{SA} = 0.031/F_{TA}(1,124) = 8.205, p_{TA} = 0.005$] between the robotized chair with an accommodative strategy and that with a defensive strategy for all evaluated items. The results indicated that when the robotized chair is not the source of the problem, the chair using the defensive strategy (RE: $M_{DS} = 3.305$, $SD_{DS} = 1.380$/SA: $M_{DS} = 3.134, SD_{DS} = 1.474$/TA: $M_{DS} = 4.381, SD_{DS} = 1.260$) was rated higher and more attractive to participants than the one using the accommodative strategy (RE: $M_{AS} = 2.832, SD_{AS} = 1.111$/SA: $M_{AS} = 2.600, SD_{AS} = 1.281$/TA: $M_{AS} = 3.747, SD_{AS} = 1.261$). These findings support H4-2 and reject H4-1 (see Fig. 3).

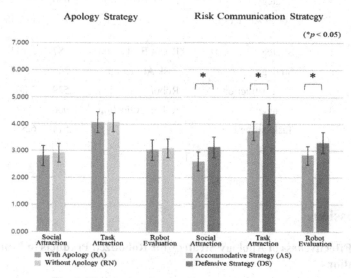

Fig. 3. The results of main effect analysis in Study 2.

7.2 Mediation Analysis

We conducted a mediation analysis using the Baron and Kenny approach to examine the mediation effect between survey items, where the type of risk communication strategy served as the independent variable [34, 35]. Specifically, we investigated the relationship between social attraction, task attraction as the mediation variable, and robot evaluation as the dependent variable. The results showed that the effects of the independent variables on the dependent variables and parameters were significant in the first and second steps of the mediation analysis (see Table 2). However, the effect of the independent variable on the dependent variable, which was significant in step 1, was not significant in step 4. The Sobel test showed an absolute value of 2.149 for social attraction with a p-value of 0.031, and an absolute value of 2.609 for task attraction with a p-value of 0.009. These findings demonstrate that, in situations where the source of the problem is not the chair, the impact of risk communication strategy type on robot evaluation is entirely mediated by the effect of risk communication strategy type on the chair's social and task attraction.

Table 2. Results of mediation analysis

Model	Regression Result					
	Stage	Independent variable	Dependent variable	β	t	p
Strategy ↓ Social Attraction ↓ Robot Evaluation	1	Strategy	Robot Evaluation	.187	2.134	.035
	2	Strategy	Social Attraction	.191	2.189	.030
	3	Social Attraction	Robot Evaluation	.723	11.738	.000
	4	Strategy	Robot Evaluation	.050	.800	.425
		Social Attraction		.713	11.346	.000
Strategy ↓ Task Attraction ↓ Robot Evaluation	1	Strategy	Robot Evaluation	.187	2.134	.035
	2	Strategy	Task Attraction	.246	2.847	.005
	3	Task Attraction	Robot Evaluation	.529	7.002	.000
	4	Strategy	Robot Evaluation	.060	.772	.422
		Task Attraction		.514	6.586	.000

8 Discussions

8.1 The Effectiveness of Apology Strategy for Robotized Products in Problematic Situations

In this study, we investigated the effectiveness of apology strategies for robotized products in problematic situations. Our findings revealed that the effectiveness of a robotized product's apology strategy depends on the situation, with the sincerity of the apology being a critical factor. Users perceive a robotized product's apology to be sincere only when the robotized product causes the failure and admits its failure. This implies that users expect the robotized product to deliver correct information about the error. In situations where the robotized product is not responsible for the failure, offering an apology may mislead the user. Similarly, when the robotized product, which is the root cause of the problem, does not admit its responsibility, the apology strategy would lead to incorrect information. Thus, the apology strategy of a robotized product is only effective when the product has made an error and delivers correct information about it. Although the apology strategy alone may not improve the overall evaluation of the robot in a problematic situation, it can positively influence the product's task attractiveness. However, our study has limitations since it only examined the effect of an apology strategy with or without an apology. Other emotional factors related to apologetic behavior, such as tone of voice or the number of sentences included in the apology, were not considered. Future work should explore the impact of these and other factors on the effectiveness of robotized product apology strategies in influencing user evaluations.

8.2 Expectations of Robotized Products and Humans in Problematic Situations

In human society, displaying altruistic behavior such as accepting responsibility for other people's faults and caring for others plays a significant role in increasing social attraction. However, our results suggest that robotized products are not expected to exhibit human-like caring behavior, and such behavior is rated as socially unattractive compared to providing correct information. In Study 1, participants perceived the robotized chair as the root cause of the problematic situation. In this case, the risk communication strategy of the robotized product did not affect user evaluations of the product. In Study 2, the problem was caused by a malfunction of a different product, not the robotized chair. In this case, participants rated the robotized chair with the defensive strategy as more attractive and desirable than the robotized chair with an accommodative strategy. This suggests that when the product is not at fault, users expect the product to provide correct information about the situation and not conceal the fault of other products. The term "product integrity" refers to the extent to which a product is error-free [36, 37]. Product integrity can be achieved not only by avoiding causing problems but also by accurately informing users of the cause of the problem [38, 39]. Our findings suggest that even when accurate information is delivered through an accommodative strategy, it does not positively impact users' overall evaluation and social attraction to a product in the case where the robotized product is responsible for the fault, such as in Study 1. In contrast, in the case where the robotized product was not the cause of the problem, such as in Study 2, the behavior of revealing product integrity through a defensive strategy resulted in positive user evaluation of the robotized product and increased its social attractiveness. However, in Study 2, the accommodative strategy adopted by robotized products is a behavior of ethical caring towards other robotized products rather than towards people. Ethical caring is a behavior that humans are trained to exhibit in society, and it may be a foreign concept for robotized products. In future work, the impact of a robotized product's response strategies in problematic situations needs to be explored when the external stimuli causing the problem are caused by a human. This will provide valuable insights into whether the robotized products can elicit ethical caring or not in problematic situations.

References

1. Meyer, G., Främling, K., Holmstrom, J.: Intelligent Products: A Survey Computers in Industry. Elsevier, Amsterdam (2008)
2. Reeves, B., Nass, C.: The Media Equation: How People Treat Computers, Television, and New Media Like Real People and Places. Cambridge University Press, Cambridge (1996)
3. MacDorman, K.F., Ishiguro, H.: Toward social mechanisms of android science. Interact. Stud. **7**(2), 289–296 (2006)
4. Goodrich, M.A., Schultz, A.C.: Human-robot interaction: a survey. Found. Trends® Hum.–Comput. Interact. **1**(3), 203–275 (2008)
5. Dautenhahn, K.: Socially intelligent robots: dimensions of human-robot interaction. Philos. Trans. Roy. Soc. B: Biol. Sci. **362**(1480), 679–704 (2007)
6. Fong, T., Nourbakhsh, I., Dautenhahn, K.: A survey of socially interactive robots. Robot. Auton. Syst.Auton. Syst. **42**(3–4), 143–166 (2003)
7. Lewicki, R., Elgoibar, P., Euwema, M.: The tree of trust: building and repairing trust in organizations. In: Elgoibar, P., Euwema, M., Munduate, L. (eds.) Building Trust and Constructive Conflict Management in Organizations. IRCM, pp. 93–117. Springer, Cham (2016). https://doi.org/10.1007/978-3-319-31475-4_6
8. Ohbuchi, K.I., Kameda, M., Agarie, N.: Apology as aggression control: its role in mediating appraisal of and response to harm. J. Pers. Soc. Psychol. **56**(2), 219–227 (1989)
9. Darby, B.W., Schlenker, B.R.: Children's reactions to apologies. J. Pers. Soc. Psychol. **43**(4), 742–753 (1982)
10. Lee, M.K., Kiesler, S., Forlizzi, J., Srinivasa, S., Rybski, P.: Gracefully mitigating breakdowns in robotic services. In: Proceedings of the 5th ACM/IEEE International Conference on Human-Robot Interaction (HRI), pp. 203–210. IEEE (2010)
11. Klein, J., Moon, Y., Picard, R.W.: This computer responds to user frustration: theory, design and results. Interact. Comput.Comput. **14**(2), 119–140 (2002)
12. Hone, K.: Empathic agents to reduce user frustration: the effects of varying agent characteristics. Interact. Comput.Comput. **18**(2), 227–245 (2006)
13. Lewis, B.R., McCann, P.: Service failure and recovery: evidence from the hotel industry. Int. J. Contemp. Hosp. Manag.Manag. **16**(1), 6–17 (2004)
14. Jordan, J.: The Four Stages of Highly Effective Crisis Management: How to Manage the Media in the Digital Age. CRC Press, Florida (2011)
15. Coombs, W.T.: Protecting organization reputations during a crisis: the development and application of situational crisis communication theory. Corp. Reput. Rev.Reput. Rev. **10**(3), 163–176 (2007)
16. Heath, R.L., Millar, D.P.: A rhetorical approach to crisis communication: management, communication processes, and strategic responses. In: Handbook of Crisis and Risk Communication, pp. 53–74, Routledge, UK (2004)
17. Ulmer, R.R., Sellnow, T.L., Seeger, M.W.: Effective Crisis Communication: Moving from Crisis to Opportunity. Sage Publications, Upper Saddle River (2017)
18. Coombs, W.T.: Ongoing Crisis Communication: Planning, Managing, and Responding. Sage Publications, California (2015)
19. Sitkin, S.B., Weingart, L.R.: Determinants of risky decision-making behavior: a test of the mediating role of risk perceptions and propensity. Acad. Manag. J.Manag. J. **38**(6), 1573–1592 (1995)
20. Benoit, W.L.: Accounts, Excuses, and Apologies: A Theory of Image Restoration Strategies. SUNY Press, New York (1995)
21. Byrne, D., Griffitt, W.: Interpersonal attraction. Annu. Rev. Psychol.. Rev. Psychol. **24**(1), 317–336 (1973)

22. Aron, A., Fisher, H., Mashek, D.J., Strong, G., Li, H., Brown, L.L.: Reward, motivation, and emotion systems associated with early-stage intense romantic love. J. Neurophysiol.Neurophysiol. **94**(1), 327–337 (2005)
23. Peeters, G., Czapinski, J.: Positive-negative asymmetry in evaluations: the distinction between affective and informational negativity effects. Eur. Rev. Soc. Psychol. **1**(1), 33–60 (1990)
24. Wentura, D., Rothermund, K., Bak, P.: Automatic vigilance: the attention-grabbing power of approach-and avoidance-related social information. J. Pers. Soc. Psychol. **78**(6), 1024–1037 (2000)
25. Singh, R., Tor, X.L.: The relative effects of competence and likability on interpersonal attraction. J. Soc. Psychol. **148**(2), 253–256 (2008)
26. Lydon, J.E., Jamieson, D.W., Zanna, M.P.: Interpersonal similarity and the social and intellectual dimensions of first impressions. Soc. Cogn.Cogn. **6**(4), 269–286 (1988)
27. Byrne, D.: An overview (and underview) of research and theory within the attraction paradigm. J. Soc. Pers. Relat.Relat. **14**(3), 417–431 (1997)
28. McCroskey, J.C., McCain, T.A.: The measurement of interpersonal attraction. Commun. Monogr.. Monogr. **41**(4), 261–277 (1974)
29. Heider, F.: The Psychology of Interpersonal Relations. Wiley, New York (2013)
30. Zhao, M., Hoeffler, S., Dahl, D.W.: The role of imagination-focused visualization on new product evaluation. J. Mark. Res. **46**(1), 46–55 (2009)
31. Noddings, N.: Caring: A Relational Approach to Ethics and Moral Education. Berkeley. University of California Press, California (2013)
32. Noddings, N.: Moral education and caring. Theory Res. Educ. **8**(2), 145–151 (2010)
33. Wiesenfeld, B.M., Brockner, J., Thibault, V.: Procedural fairness, managers' self-esteem, and managerial behaviors following a layoff. Organ. Behav. Hum. Decis. Process.Behav. Hum. Decis. Process. **83**(1), 1–32 (2000)
34. Baron, R.M., Kenny, D.A.: The moderator–mediator variable distinction in social psychological research: conceptual, strategic, and statistical considerations. J. Pers. Soc. Psychol. **51**(6), 1173–1182 (1986)
35. Sobel, M.E.: Asymptotic confidence intervals for indirect effects in structural equation models. Sociol. Methodol.. Methodol. **13**, 290–312 (1982)
36. Clark, K.B., Fujimoto, T.: The power of product integrity. Harv. Bus. Rev. **68**(6), 107–118 (1990)
37. Evans, J.W., Evans, J.Y.: Product Integrity and Reliability in Design. Springer, London (2001). https://doi.org/10.1007/978-1-4471-0253-3
38. Simon, H.A.: Invariants of human behavior. Annu. Rev. Psychol.. Rev. Psychol. **41**(1), 1–20 (1990)
39. Marucheck, A., Greis, N., Mena, C., Cai, L.: Product safety and security in the global supply chain: Issues, challenges and research opportunities. J. Oper. Manag.Oper. Manag. **29**(7–8), 707–720 (2011)

User Perception of the Robot's Error in Heterogeneous Multi-robot System Performing Sequential Cooperative Task

Soyeon Shin[1] ⓘ, Youngsun Kwon[2] ⓘ, Yoonseob Lim[3] ⓘ, and Sonya S. Kwak[3(✉)] ⓘ

[1] LG Electronics, Seoul, Korea
[2] Electronics and Telecommunications Research Institute, Daejeon 34129, Korea
[3] Center for Intelligent and Interactive Robotics, KIST, Seoul 02792, Korea
sonakwak@kist.re.kr

Abstract. This study investigates how the user's mental model of an error in a heterogeneous multi-robot system (MRS) is formed while executing a sequential cooperative task. We applied a heterogeneous MRS consisting of a delivery robot and an information robot to the medicine delivery service in the infectious disease ward where the separation of the contaminated area and non-contaminated area is necessary to avoid infections. In this study, we define the robot which initiates the service in a sequential task as an initiating robot and the robot which executes the subsequent task following after the initiating robot as the follow-up robot. We examine how the initiating robot's error would affect the user perception of the follow-up robot's error and how the perceived error influences competence and trust in the follow-up robot. As a result, we found that when two robots cooperate sequentially, the user's evaluation of the follow-up robot's error can be influenced by the initial robot's error. In addition, we discovered that the trust and competence of the follow-up robot can be impacted by the initiating robot in heterogeneous MRS performing sequential cooperative tasks.

Keywords: Heterogeneous Multi-robot System · Sequential Task · Error · Trust · Competence

1 Introduction

Humans have developed numerous automatic and robotic systems to improve operating efficiency and avoid risky work. A heterogeneous multi-robot system (MRS), which employs multiple robots of various sizes, functions, and shapes, each specialized for simple tasks, has been developed as an effective way to manage a complex task. Compared to a single robot system, MRS using cooperative heterogeneous robots can be cost-effective, scalable to complex tasks, and suitable for mixed geographic distributions [1]. Heterogeneous MRS has been effectively applied to various services, such as military [2], rescue [3, 4], or healthcare [5, 6].

This work was supported by the Korea Institute of Science and Technology (KIST) Institutional Program under Grant (2E32302) and the Government-wide R&D Fund for Infections Disease Research (GFID), funded by the Ministry of the Interior and Safety, Republic of Korea (20014463).

Recently, due to COVID-19, hospitals have been providing autonomous services using robots to reduce the risk of infection [7]. For example, service robots provide medical care via telecommunication service [8] and deliver supplies or medication on behalf of caregivers [9]. In particular, the infectious disease ward, where COVID-19 patients are hospitalized, is an unusual environment that is divided into two: an airborne infection isolation room (negative pressure room) and a protective environment (positive pressure room) [10, 11]. To prevent the spread of contagious viruses and to protect the medical staff handling potentially hazardous contaminants, separation of space is required [12]. In addition, to move to each area, medical staff must be outfitted with protective equipment such as protective suits. To support the medical staff by avoiding infections in the infectious disease ward, we propose a heterogeneous MRS in which two different types of robots cooperate. In this proposed system, one robot delivers an object in a corridor, which is a non-contaminated area, while the other provides information to the patient in the ward, which is a contaminated area (Fig. 1). When heterogeneous robots cooperate in a situation where places are separated, there are some cases where the task in one place is inherited and carried out sequentially in the next place. In this study, we define the robot in charge of the primary task in the sequential work as an initiating robot and the robot in charge of the subsequent task from the initiating robot as a follow-up robot.

The initiating robot and the follow-up robot perform the sequential task in the following two steps; 1) the initiating robot delivers a pill from the nurse's station (uncontaminated area) to an ante-room of the ward (contaminated area), and then 2) the follow-up robot placed in the ward (contaminated area) informs the patient of the arrival of the delivery robot by calling the patient's name.

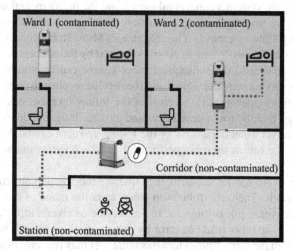

Fig. 1. A medicine delivery scenario using heterogeneous MS in the infectious disease ward.

2 Literature Review

People expect robots to have perfect memory and performance and to accomplish their tasks without errors [13]. However, the robot in the real world might be incomplete and cause an error. People think the robot is also responsible for the error when an error occurs, like a human. Kim and Hinds' study showed that the more autonomous the robot, the more people place blame on the robot [14]. Furthermore, when task failure occurs in human-robot teaming, people tend to give responsibility to humans first, then robots, and the environment [15]. The error in the robot can lower the user's trust and reliability of the automatic system [13]. Maintaining an appropriate level of trust is critical for the acceptance and continued use of the robot system, particularly in high-risk situations such as robots in combat missions and hospitals [16, 17].

Unlike an error derived from a single robot, in a heterogeneous MRS, multi robots can generate combinations of errors. Notably, in the situation where a heterogeneous MRS performs a sequential task, the initiating robot's error may influence the user's perception of the follow-up robot's error due to the nature of the consecutive sequence. Thus, the user's perception of the errors in a heterogeneous MRS could be different from that of the error in a single robot.

A mental model and conceptual model can be used to understand how a user perceives the system when interacting with it [18]. When interacting with digital artifacts, people create mental models of themselves and the artifact with which they interact [19, 20]. According to Norman, the conceptual model is a representation of the system which explains how the system works, and it is invented by designers or engineers [19, 20]. On the other hand, the user's mental model is a user's understanding and expectation of how the system will work, which is created naturally by the user [19, 20]. Differences can exist between the system's conceptual model and the user's mental model.

In this study, we investigate the construction of the user's mental model regarding errors made by a follow-up robot in a heterogeneous Multi-Robot System (MRS) while performing sequential tasks. When an error, as defined by the conceptual model, occurs within the sequential task, the subsequent robot's error can be interpreted from two perspectives: the service provider aspect and the service receiver aspect.

In the service provider aspect, the error of the follow-up robot can be determined based on the error that the robot developers and system designers define. By contrast, in the service receiver aspect, the error of the follow-up robot can be defined based on how successfully the follow-up robot performs the task excluding the initiating robot's performance.

For example, in our service scenario, the initiating robot makes an error by bringing another patient's pill. Then, the follow-up robot calls the name of the patient whom the incorrectly delivered pill belongs to. In the service receiver's aspect, the user may perceive the follow-up robot made an error by calling another patient's name not in the ward. Conversely, in the service provider aspect, the user may perceive that the follow-up robot does not make an error in that the information about the incorrectly delivered pill has been correctly announced.

In this study, we are interested in figuring out the user's mental model of the follow-up robot's error in heterogeneous MRS performing a sequential task. The previous study by Kim and Hinds showed that when an unexpected error occurs in the delivery robot in a hospital, nurses or medical staff attempt to find out why this error occurred [14]. As people tend to find the fundamental cause of the error when an error occurs in a system, we predict that the user would recognize robot errors based on the service provider's aspect.

This analysis resulted in the following hypothesis.

H1: In the heterogeneous MRS performing the sequential cooperative task, the end user perceives the error of the follow-up robot in a service provider's aspect.

The robot's error negatively affects the user's perception of the robot. Ragni et al. found that when people interact with an erroneous robot, they perceive the robot as less intelligent, competent, and reliable than when interacting with a robot that does not make an error [13]. In a study by Leo and Huh, they found that when a robot made a mistake, people perceived the robot as incompetent [21]. People also rated robots as less trustworthy when they have errors rather than when they perform tasks without errors [22].

Thus, we predict that the error of the follow-up robot recognized by the user, according to the provider's aspect, will negatively affect the perceived competence and perceived trust of the follow-up robot in heterogeneous MRS performing the sequential cooperative task.

This analysis resulted in the following hypotheses:

H2: In the heterogeneous MRS performing the sequential cooperative task, errors of the follow-up robot will negatively affect the follow-up robot's competence.

H3: In the heterogeneous MRS performing the sequential cooperative task, errors of the follow-up robot will negatively affect the follow-up robot's trust.

3 Method

The experiment was a within-subject design.

3.1 Participants

A total of 30 participants (18 females and 12 males) were recruited for the experiment. The mean age of participants was 26.57 years ($SD = 2.45$), ranging from 23 to 35 years.

3.2 Experimental Setup

Two heterogeneous multiple robots which are the delivery robot (initiating robot) and the information robot (follow-up robot) were used for the sequential task of delivering pills. Specifically, we devised the initiating robot as a mobile robot, Turtlebot3 (Fig. 2), having a small container for the delivery task. We also used another mobile robot, Temi (Fig. 2), which informs the patient that the pill has arrived. The Temi robot conveys informative messages by text-to-speech voice. In our experiment, we implemented a web page to alert the error cases via the mobile phone of each patient.

Fig. 2. Turtelbot3(left) and Temi(right).

3.3 Scenarios

Scenarios When an Error Does Not Occur. To deliver pills using robots, a nurse calls a delivery robot to the station where the nurse is. Then the nurse scans a QR code which contains information about whose pill it is and the patient's ward number, using the delivery robot's camera. After that, the nurse attaches the QR code to the container placed on the top of the delivery robot. When the nurse puts the pill into the container, the delivery robot moves to the ward where the patient is. When the delivery robot approaches the patient's ward, the information robot staying inside the contaminated ward moves to the ward door. The information robot detects the QR code attached to the container above the delivery robot and recognizes the information about whom the pill belongs to. The information robot then moves near to the patient's bed and instructs the patient to come out to the door and pick up the pill from the delivery robot. After the patient picks up the pill from the delivery robot, he/she confirms that his/her pill has arrived correctly by pressing the [receive confirmed] button. The name of the person to whom the pill belongs is printed on the plastic bag containing the pill, allowing the patient to determine whether it is his/her or not (Fig. 3).

Scenarios When Errors Occur. In the conceptual model, the criteria of errors are set to whether or not the QR code is recognized correctly. The delivery robot's error was that it incorrectly recognized the QR code and thus delivered the pill to another patient rather than the patient in the ward. The information robot's error was that it incorrectly recognized the QR code and called a different name, not the name on the plastic bag containing the pill.

Three cases of error combinations can arise during the sequential cooperative task between the initiating robot (delivery robot) and the follow-up robot (information robot), as shown in Table 1:

Case 1: The initiating robot makes an error, but the follow-up robot does not.

Case 2: The initiating robot does not make an error, but the follow-up robot does.

Case 3: Both the initiating robot and follow-up robot make errors.

In case 1, the delivery robot brings the pill for the other patient rather than for the patient in the ward. The information robot then detects the QR code correctly attached to the container and calls the patient's name written on the incorrectly delivered pill rather than the patient's name in the ward. In case 2, the delivery robot brings the pill to the ward for the patient. However, the information robot detects the QR code incorrectly and

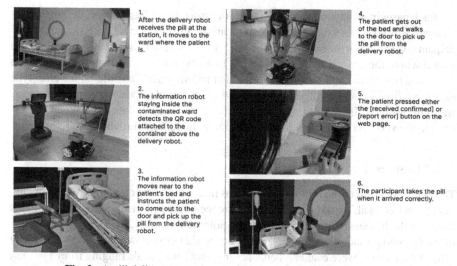

Fig. 3. A pill delivery scenario using heterogeneous MRS in the study

Table 1. The Combination of errors.

	Service Provider Aspect		Service Receiver Aspect	
	Initiating robot	*Follow-up robot*	*Initiating robot*	*Follow-up robot*
Case 1	X	O	X	X
Case 2	O	X	O	X
Case 3	X	X	X	O

calls another patient's name rather than the patient's in the ward. In case 3, the delivery robot delivers the pill to the other patient rather than the pill for the patient in the ward. However, the information robot detects the QR code incorrectly and calls the patient's name in the ward rather than the name written on the incorrectly delivered pill.

3.4 Procedure

We conducted an experiment approved by the Institutional Review Board of the Korea Institute of Science and Technology (KIST IRB: 2021-052). After getting brief instructions regarding the experiment, the participant signed in a consent form. After arriving in the ward, the participant, who played the role of a patient, entered the smart ward web page created for the experiment using his/her mobile phone and entered personal information such as his/her name, age, and gender. Each time a pill arrives, the participant pressed either the [received confirmed] or [report error] button on the web page. When the participant recognized an error and pressed the [report error] button, an explanation of which robot caused the error was provided through the web page in each error case.

Each participant experienced three types of errors. In each error type, the participant received pills six times using a delivery robot and an information robot. To make the participant aware of how the heterogeneous MRS works without errors, he/she experienced a case where the error did not occur in the first two trials. After that, two cases with errors and two cases without errors occurred in random order. The order of the error type experienced was counterbalanced. At the end of each trial, a post-experimental survey was administered. In order to manipulate error cases, we employed the Wizard of Oz technique to control all devices in the experiment, including Turtlebot and Temi [23].

3.5 Measures

The perceived error of the follow-up robot was measured based on a single questionnaire item from Lee et al.'s study [24]. The competence of the follow-up robot was estimated based on the five items from Surprenant and Solomon's study [25]. The trustworthiness of the follow-up robot was measured based on the six items drawn from Fogg and Tseng [26]. All measures were evaluated on a seven-point Likert scale ranging from 1 = "not at all" to 7 = "very much").

4   Results

An analysis for perceived error was carried out using repeated measure analysis. As predicted by H1, there was a significant difference in perceived error of the follow-up robot ($F(1.594, 46.215) = 18.297$, $p < 0.001$) (Fig. 4). Participants perceived that the follow-up robot makes more errors when the initiating robot does not make an error, but the follow-up robot makes an error (case 2, $M = 5.46$, $SD = 1.53$) than when the initiating robot makes an error, but the follow-up robot does not make an error (case 1, $M = 2.33$, $SD = 1.95$) ($p < 0.001$). They also responded that the robot made more errors when both the initiating robot and the follow-up robot make errors (case 3, $M = 4.20$, $SD = 2.12$) than when the initiating robot makes an error, but the follow-up robot does not make an error (case 1, $M = 2.33$, $SD = 1.95$) ($p < 0.05$). However, there was no significant difference between when the initiating robot does not make an error, but the follow-up robot makes an error (case 2, $M = 5.46$, $SD = 1.53$) and when both the initiating robot and the follow-up robot make errors (case 3, $M = 4.20$, $SD = 2.12$) ($p = 0.063$). This indicates that the user's perception of the follow-up robot's error was formed based on the service provider aspect. Thus, hypothesis 1 was accepted.

There was a significant difference in perceived competence of the follow-up robot ($F(2, 58) = 7.285$, $p < 0.01$) (Fig. 4). Participants evaluated the follow-up robot as more competent when the initiating robot makes an error, but the follow-up robot does not make an error (case 1, $M = 5.63$, $SD = 1.19$) than when the initiating robot does not make an error, but the follow-up robot makes an error (case 2, $M = 4.36$, $SD = 1.42$) ($p < 0.001$). However, there was no significant difference on competence between when the initiating robot makes an error, but the follow-up robot does not make an error (case 1, $M = 5.63$, $SD = 1.19$) and when both the initiating robot and the follow-up robot make errors (case 3, $M = 4.82$, $SD = 1.82$) ($p = 0.124$). Also, there was no significant difference on competence between when the initiating robot does not make an error, but the follow-up robot makes an error (case 2, $M = 4.36$, $SD = 1.42$) and when both the initiating robot and the follow-up robot make errors (case 3, $M = 4.82$, $SD = 1.82$) ($p = 0.603$).

There was a significant difference in perceived trust of the follow-up robot ($F(1.1647, 47.769) = 7.294$, $p < 0.01$) (Fig. 4). Participants responded that the follow-up robot is more trustworthy when the initiating robot makes an error, but the follow-up robot does not make an error (case 1, $M = 5.91$, $SD = 0.94$) than when the initiating robot does not make an error, but the follow-up robot makes an error (case 2, $M = 4.76$, $SD = 1.24$) ($p < 0.001$). However, there was no significant difference on trust between when the initiating robot makes an error, but the follow-up robot does not make an error (case 1, $M = 5.91$, $SD = 0.94$) and when both the initiating robot and the follow-up robot make errors (case 3, $M = 4.99$, $SD = 1.75$) ($p = 0.064$). In addition, there was no significant difference on trust between when the initiating robot does not make an error, but the follow-up robot makes an error (case 2, $M = 4.76$, $SD = 1.24$) and when both the initiating robot and the follow-up robot make errors (case 3, $M = 4.99$, $SD = 1.75$) ($p = 1.0$). Thus, hypotheses 2 and 3 were partially accepted.

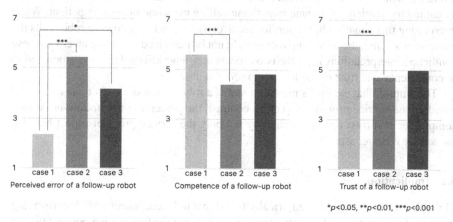

*$p<0.05$, **$p<0.01$, ***$p<0.001$

Fig. 4. The results of the perceived error, competence, and trust of follow-up robot

5 Discussion and Conclusion

5.1 Summary and Interpretation

The aim of this study was to investigate the user's mental model of a follow-up robot's error, and perceived competence and perceived trust of a follow-up robot cooperating a sequential task with an initiating robot in heterogeneous MRS. As expected by H1, the user's mental model of the follow-up robot's errors is constructed based on the service provider aspect. In other words, the user perceives the error of the follow-up robot in heterogeneous MRS in accordance with the conceptual model view. This implies that the user's evaluation of the follow-up robot's error can be dependent on the initiating robot's error when the two robots cooperate sequential tasks.

The participants evaluated the follow-up robot in case 1 as the most competent and trustworthy compared to other error cases. This result implies that since the follow-up robot played a role in delivering the message about the error of the initiating robot properly, the user perceived the competence and trust of the follow-up robot positively despite its error. Our study result is consistent with Beggiato and Krems' study which showed that when the user predicts the error, even if a failure occurs, it does not affect the trust and acceptance of the system negatively [27].

As predicted by H2 and H3, the perceived error of the follow-up robot negatively affects the robot's competence and trust. We observed the significant difference between case 1 and case 2 in the perceived competence and trust. However, no significant difference in competence and trust of the user perception was found between case 1 and case 3, unlike the observed difference in perceived error. The reason for this result might be because the user's evaluation of trust and competence regarding the follow-up robot is produced by both the service provider and the service receiver aspects.

In case 3, from the service provider aspect, both the initiating robot and the follow-up robot make errors; the initiating robot makes an error by delivering another patient's pill rather than delivering the participant's pill, and the follow-up robot makes an error by calling the participant's name rather than calling the name of another patient. When interpreting this situation in the service receiver aspect, as the follow-up robot calls the participant's name, the follow-up robot might not be perceived as having an error. These conflicting interpretations from the two aspects may have affected the user's perception of competence and trust of the follow-up robot in case 3.

This implies that the user's mental model of a follow-up robot's error can be formed based on the service provider aspect. In contrast, the perception of a follow-up robot's competence and trust can be affected by not only the service provider aspect but also the service receiver aspect.

5.2 Implication

Through the experiment, we empirically found that in heterogeneous MRS performing sequential cooperative tasks, the trust and competence of the follow-up robot are affected by the initiating robot. This indicates that the errors originated from the heterogeneous robots need to be carefully considered when designers or engineers develop the Human-Robot Interaction (HRI) strategy for maintaining the level of trust and competence of the follow-up robot. In addition, the result of the study implies the importance of the system transparency in heterogeneous MRS performing sequential cooperative tasks. The follow-up robot's correct conveyance of the message about the initiating robot's error can prevent the negative influence on the follow-up robot's trust. Thus, when designing the HRI of the follow-up robot, system transparency needs to be carefully considered.

5.3   Limitation and Future Work

The application of the heterogeneous MRS in this study was limited to delivering medicine in an infectious disease ward. A heterogeneous MRS utilized in other environments needs to be further explored. This study evaluated the follow-up robot's competence and trust in the heterogeneous MRS. Other factors, such as the overall system's competence and trust, can be investigated in the future. Also, the perceived trust of the information robot in a situation when an information robot has an error as a single robot in a non-sequential task and an information robot has an error as a follow-up robot in a sequential task can be compared in future work.

Acknowledgment. This work was supported by the Korea Institute of Science and Technology (KIST) Institutional Program under Grant (2E32302) and the Government-wide R&D Fund for Infections Disease Research (GFID), funded by the Ministry of the Interior and Safety, Republic of Korea (20014463).

References

1. Stone, P., Veloso, M.: Multiagent systems: a survey from a machine learning perspective. Auton. Robot.. Robot. **8**(3), 345–383 (2000)
2. Oh, G., Kim, Y., Ahn, J., Choi, H.L.: PSO-based optimal task allocation for cooperative timing missions. IFAC-PapersOnLine **49**(17), 314–319 (2016)
3. Abukhalil, T., Patil, M., Patel, S., Sobh, T.: Coordinating a heterogeneous robot swarm using Robot Utility-based Task Assignment (RUTA). In: 2016 IEEE 14th International Workshop on Advanced Motion Control (AMC), pp. 57–62 (2016)
4. Kim, M.H., Baik, H., Lee, S.: Resource welfare based task allocation for UAV team with resource constraints. J. Intell. Rob. Syst.Intell. Rob. Syst. **77**(3), 611–627 (2014)
5. Benavidez, P., Kumar, M., Agaian, S., Jamshidi, M.: Design of a home multi-robot system for the elderly and disabled. In: Proceedings of the 10th System of Systems Engineering Conference (SoSE), pp. 392–397 (2015)
6. Kraus, S.: Intelligent agents for rehabilitation and care of disabled and chronic patients. In: Proceedings of the AAAI Conference on Artificial Intelligence, pp. 4032–4036 (2015)
7. Murphy, R.R., Gandudi, V.B., Amin, T., Clendenin, A., Moats, J.: An analysis of international use of robots for COVID-19. Robot. Auton. Syst.Auton. Syst. **148**, 103922 (2022)
8. Mills, E.C., Savage, E., Lieder, J., Chiu, E.S.: Telemedicine and the COVID-19 pandemic: are we ready to go live? Adv. Skin Wound Care **33**(8), 410–417 (2020)
9. Yang, G.Z., et al.: Combating COVID-19-the role of robotics in managing public health and infectious diseases. Sci. Robot. **5**(40), 1–2 (2020)
10. Shajahan, A., Culp, C.H., Williamson, B.: Effects of indoor environmental parameters related to building heating, ventilation, and air conditioning systems on patients' medical outcomes: a review of scientific research on hospital buildings. Indoor Air **29**(2), 161–176 (2019)
11. Sundell, J., et al.: Ventilation rates and health: multidisciplinary review of the scientific literature. Indoor Air **21**(3), 191–204 (2011)
12. Al-Benna, S.: Negative pressure rooms and COVID-19. J. Perioper. Pract.Perioper. Pract. **31**(1–2), 18–23 (2020)
13. Ragni, M., Rudenko, A., Kuhnert, B., Arras, K.O.: Errare humanum EST: erroneous robots in human-robot interaction. In: Proceedings of the 25th IEEE International Symposium on Robot and Human Interactive Communication (RO-MAN), pp. 501–506 (2016)

14. Kim, T., Hinds, P.: Who should I blame? Effects of autonomy and transparency on attributions in human-robot interaction. In: Proceedings of the 15th IEEE International Symposium on Robot and Human Interactive Communication (RO-MAN), pp. 80–85 (2006)
15. Furlough, C., Stokes, T., Gillan, D.J.: Attributing blame to robots: I. The influence of robot autonomy. Hum. Fact. **63**(4), 592–602 (2021)
16. Das, T.K., Teng, B.S.: The risk-based view of trust: a conceptual framework. J. Bus. Psychol. **19**(1), 85–116 (2004)
17. Groom, V., Nass, C.: Can robots be teammates?: Benchmarks in human–robot teams. Interact. Stud. **8**(3), 483–500 (2007)
18. Greca, I.M., Moreira, M.A.: Mental models, conceptual models, and modelling. Int. J. Sci. Educ. **22**(1), 1–11 (2010)
19. Carroll, J.M., Olson, J.R.: Mental Models in Human-Computer Interaction. In: Helander, M. (ed.) Handbook of Human-Computer Interaction, pp. 45–65. Elsevier North Holland, Amsterdam (1988)
20. Gentner, D., Stevens, A.L.: Mental Models. Psychology Press, New York (2014)
21. Leo, X., Huh, Y.E.: Who gets the blame for service failures? Attribution of responsibility toward robot versus human service providers and service firms. Comput. Hum. Behav.. Hum. Behav. **113**, 1–13 (2020)
22. Salem, M., Lakatos, G., Amirabdollahian, F., Dautenhahn, K.: Would you trust a (faulty) robot? Effects of error, task type and personality on human-robot cooperation and trust. In: Proceedings of the 10th ACM/IEEE International Conference on Human-Robot Interaction (HRI), pp. 1–8 (2015)
23. Dahlbäck, N., Jönsson, A., Ahrenberg, L.: Wizard of Oz studies—why and how. Knowl.-Based Syst..-Based Syst. **6**(4), 258–266 (1993)
24. Lee, M.K., Kiesler, S., Forlizzi, J., Srinivasa, S., Rybski, P.: Gracefully mitigating breakdowns in robotic services. In: Proceedings of the 5th ACM/IEEE International Conference on Human-Robot Interaction (HRI), pp. 203–210 (2010)
25. Surprenant, C.F., Solomon, M.R.: Predictability and personalization in the service encounter. J. Mark. **51**(2), 86–96 (2018)
26. Fogg, B.J., Tseng, H.: The elements of computer credibility. In: Proceedings of the SIGCHI Conference on Human Factors in Computing Systems, pp. 80–87 (2019)
27. Beggiato, M., Krems, J.F.: The evolution of mental model, trust and acceptance of adaptive cruise control in relation to initial information. Transport. Res. F: Traffic Psychol. Behav. **18**, 47–57 (2013)

I Am Relieved to Have You: Exploring the Effective Robot Type to Mitigate Users Negative Emotions

Dahyun Kang🆔 and Sonya S. Kwak[✉]🆔

Center for Intelligent and Interactive Robotics, KIST, Seoul 02792, Korea
sonakwak@kist.re.kr

Abstract. In order to find more acceptable robot that can effectively alleviate negative emotions of users, we investigated users' perception of robots and their emotional responses. To achieve this research objective, we conducted an experiment involving 68 participants across six conditions. The within factor was the robot type including a product-like robot and a human-like robot, and a human as a baseline, and the between factor was the emotion type including primary emotion – sadness – and secondary emotion – embarrassment –. The findings of the study revealed that there was no significant difference in the degree of user sadness depending on the type of robot used. However, the human partner was the greatest in comforting the user experiencing sadness, followed by the human-like robot, while the product-like robot was the least effective in providing comfort. On the other hand, when it came to secondary emotions like embarrassment, participants felt embarrassed the most when assisted by a human. However, there was no significant difference in the degree of mitigating embarrassment between the two types of robots. Furthermore, in terms of service evaluation, both robots received more positive ratings than humans in the situations where users felt embarrassed.

Keywords: Primary Emotion · Secondary Emotion · Human-likeness · Product-likeness · Human-Robot Interaction

1 Introduction

Although service robots are accepted in various fields such as sales [1], guidance [2, 3], and serving [4], users do not always readily accept them because robots sometimes evoke negative emotions such as eeriness and fear [5, 6]. Therefore, it is necessary to find an

This work was partly supported by the Korea Institute of Science and Technology (KIST) Institutional Program under Grant (2E32302), Institute of Information & communications Technology Planning & Evaluation (IITP) grant funded by the Korea government (MSIT) (No. 2017-0-00432, Development of Non-invasive Integrated BCI SW Platform to Control Home Appliance and External Devices by User's Thought via AR/VR Interface), and the Government-wide R&D Fund for Infections Disease Research (GFID), funded by the Ministry of the Interior and Safety, Republic of Korea (20014463).

© The Author(s), under exclusive license to Springer Nature Singapore Pte Ltd. 2024
A. Al. Ali et al. (Eds.): ICSR 2023, LNAI 14454, pp. 333–343, 2024.
https://doi.org/10.1007/978-981-99-8718-4_29

effective robot design that can alleviate users' negative emotions. In this study, we investigated whether users' acceptance of service robots varies according to the robot types and the user's emotional state. We divided the robot types into anthropomorphic and nonanthropomorphic robots. Previous studies have shown that users feel more familiar and enjoy interacting with anthropomorphic robots [7, 8]. On the other hand, when interacting with nonanthropomorphic robots, they feel less shame and embarrassment and are more likely to share their stories [9, 10]. Thus, the degree of robot's anthropomorphism affects users' emotion.

There are two dimensions of emotions: primary emotions and secondary emotions [11]. Primary emotions are emotions possessed by all animals including humans [12], while secondary emotions are unique to humans [11, 12]. We selected two negative emotions, one from primary emotions and one from secondary emotions, and examined whether the negative emotions were mitigated by the robot types. This study aims to explore the types of robots that can alleviate sadness and embarrassment, which are negative emotions among primary and secondary emotions.

2   Related Works

2.1   Robot Types

In the field of human-robot interaction, the degree of anthropomorphism in robot design is considered one of the important factors affecting robot acceptance [13]. Researchers who advocate anthropomorphic robot assert that anthropomorphic behavior can be positively accepted by users since people tend to communicate with biologic beings and nonbiologic objects using human social cues [7]. They also claim that people can easily empathize and bond [14], and enjoy interacting with anthropomorphic robots [8]. Meanwhile, there are studies which show that less or nonanthropomorphic robot designs can have a positive effect on user perception towards robots. Highly anthropomorphic appearance can evoke eeriness [5] and hinder users' sharing of their personal information during medical treatments [10]. Additionally, a marketing research by Mende et al. (2019) [15] has shown that a robot with less anthropomorphic appearance can mitigate negative consumer responses.

Robot's anthropomorphism can also affect its social presence and users' emotions. Kang and Kwak (2017)'s study [9] found that an anthropomorphic robot enhances social presence but can also make users feel shy. As the robot's appearance becomes more anthropomorphic, the perceived social presence of robot also increases, and high social presence can make people feel socially judged [16]. Overall, the previous studies suggest that the robot types with high social presence, usually with anthropomorphic characteristics, enhance users' feelings, while the robot types with low social presence, usually with non/less anthropomorphic characteristics, smooth users' emotions. However, there is a lack of research examining the robot's social presence and its effect by emotion types. Therefore, we investigated the robot types that can effectively interact with users according to user emotional states.

2.2 Emotion Types

There are two dimensions of emotions: primary emotions and secondary emotions [17]. Primary emotions are inherent biological tendencies that are immediately elicited by a stimulus [11, 17]. Examples of primary emotions include happiness, sadness, and fear [18]. On the other hand, secondary emotions are uniquely human characteristics that result from cognitive processing and are developed in later stages of life, such as curiosity, embarrassment, and disappointment [11, 18].

While primary emotions are experienced by both animals and humans, secondary emotions are considered exclusive to humans [12]. Studies have shown that out-group members exhibit fewer secondary emotions than in-group members. On the other hand, the attribution of primary emotions in in-group is similar to that in out-group [11, 19–21]. Consequently, we expect that humans may feel fewer or no secondary emotions towards nonhuman objects.

Service robots have been utilized in various fields such as sales [1], guidance [2, 3] and serving [4]. However, the potential of robots to evoke negative emotions, such as eeriness and fear, can deter users from accepting them [5, 6]. Thus, it has become increasingly important to develop effective robot design strategies that can mitigate or eliminate negative emotions in users. This study aims to explore the types of robots that can alleviate sadness and embarrassment, which are negative emotions among primary and secondary emotions.

3 Study Design

We conducted a mixed participant experiment with six conditions (robot types: product-like robot vs. human-like robot vs. baseline) x (emotion types: embarrassment vs sadness) to test the hypotheses as follows.

3.1 Hypotheses

We built six hypotheses based on findings from related works on the robot types and emotion types. Hypothesis 1 is a prediction of how the robot's appearance affects social presence. Hypotheses 2 and 3 predict the effects of the robot types on users in situations where they feel embarrassed. Hypotheses 4 and 5 predict the effects of the robot types on users in situations where they feel sad. Finally, Hypothesis 6 is a hypothesis to find out which robot type is preferred according to user's emotion type.

Hypothesis 1. When the robot has human-like appearance, the participants will feel a greater social presence to the robot than when it has product-like appearance. This prediction follows Holthöwer and van Doorn's study (2022), which showed that the perceived social presence of the robot increase as the robot's appearance becomes more anthropomorphic [16].

Hypothesis 2. Participants who get help from a human will feel embarrassed more than those who get help from robots in the embarrassing situation. This prediction follows the findings from Gaunt et al. (2002), Leyens et al. (2000), and Viki et al. (2006)'s studies, which demonstrated that secondary emotions' attribution appears only in humans [19–21].

Hypothesis 3. Participants will be more relieved of embarrassment when a product-like robot helps them than when a human-like robot or a human helps them. This hypothesis was built based on the findings from Bartneck et al.'s study (2010), which suggests that a product-like robot evokes less embarrassment and lets people more talk about themselves than a human-like robot does [10].

Hypothesis 4. The degree of sadness participants perceive will not differ depending on the robot types. Our prediction follows Turner and Ortony (1992)'s study, which figure out that primary emotions are experienced by both humans and other species [12].

Hypothesis 5. One with high social presence will comfort user's sadness more than one with low social presence. According to a study by Kang and Kwak (2017), anthropomorphism of a robot increases its social presence [9]. In addition, Broadbent et al.'s study (2013) found that people empathized and bonded more emotionally when interacting with anthropomorphic robots than when interacting with nonanthropomorphic robots [14]. Therefore, we predicted that one with a high social presence would be better able to provide comfort.

Hypothesis 6. The more acceptable robot types will be different according to user's emotion types. Based on the study results of Haslam (2006), and Turner and Ortony (1992), which demonstrate that primary emotions are emotions felt by all animals including humans, and secondary emotions are emotions that are used only between humans [11, 12].

3.2 Participants

We recruited 68 participants in their 20s-30s for this study (male: 30, female: 38). Thirty-four participants experienced three robot types within the embarrassing situation: a product-like robot, a human-like robot, and a baseline (male: 14, female: 20). Another 34 participants experienced three robot types in the sad situation (male: 16, female: 18). They all agreed to participate in the experiment, and we offered them $10 as a participation fee.

3.3 Stimuli

We constructed video clips of two types of robot prototypes and a baseline, then we showed them to the participants. This allowed the participants to understand how a robot operates according to the situation the user faced.

Two robot types were used in this study (See Fig. 1). One is a product-like robot. We developed robotic table by using linear guides to transport the container with a mirror and tissues from the center of the table to the front of the users. Magnets were attached on the top of the container and transporting parts in linear guides. The Raspberry Pi, OpenCR board, and motor drivers for controlling the linear guides were additionally installed inside the table. In the embarrassing situation and the sad situation, the product-like robot which is the product itself approaches the user when the user needs it. Another used in this study is a human-like robot. The humanlike robot was Temi 3 [22]. In the embarrassing situation and the sad situation, the human-like robot delivers users the product the user needs. As a baseline, the counterpart hands over the product to the embarrassed or sad person. A total of six video stimuli was produced (See Fig. 2).

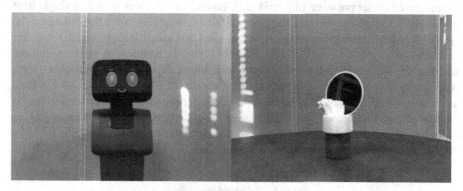

Fig. 1. Robot types: human-like robot (left), product-like robot (right)

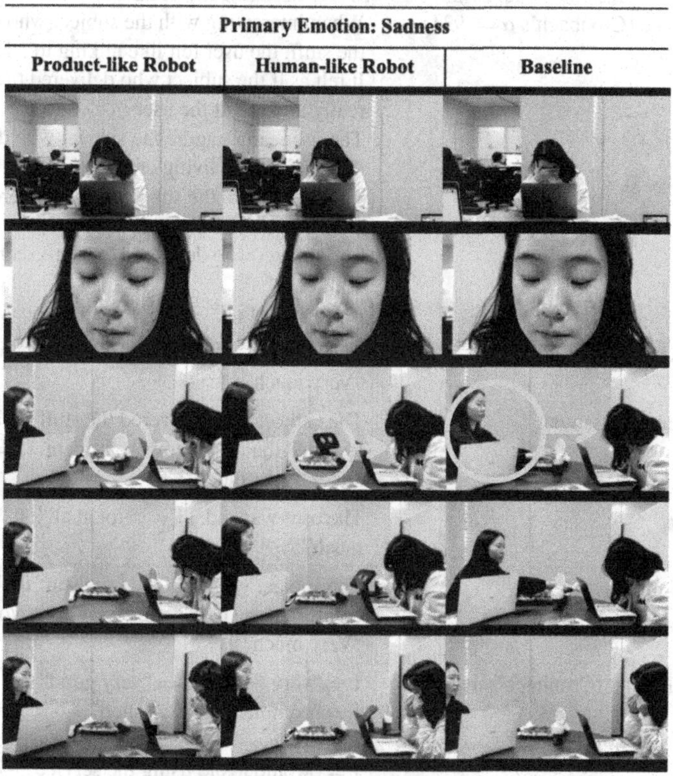

Primary Emotion: Sadness		
Product-like Robot	**Human-like Robot**	**Baseline**

Fig. 2. Video stimuli for sad situation

3.4 Measures

To find out whether the degree of robot's anthropomorphism increases its social presence, we measured social presence (5 items) [23]. Embarrassment was used as a single item in this study to find out whether the degree of embarrassment varies depending on the type of robot. Mitigating embarrassment was used as a single item to find out whether embarrassment was relieved according to robot type. In addition, in order to find out whether the degree of sadness that users feel differs depending on the robot types, participants were asked about sadness as a single item. We used mitigating sadness scale as a single item to find out whether the level of comforting sadness differs depending on the robot types. Finally, we adopted the measures of service evaluation (3 items) [24] in order to find out the suitable robot type according to the emotion types (See Table 1). All questionnaires were evaluated on a 7-point scale.

Table 1. Reliabilities of scales.

Scale	Items
Social Presence (Cronbach's $\alpha = .931$)	When interacting with the subject who delivered the stuff, the user felt like talking to a real person It felt as if the subject who delivered the stuff was really looking at the user The user can imagine the subject who delivered the stuff to be a living creature The user thinks the subject who delivered the stuff is not a real person The subject who delivered the stuff seems to have real feelings (1 = "Not at all" ~ "Very much")
Embarrassment	The user was embarrassed. (1 = "Not at all" ~ "Very much")
Mitigating Embarrassment	The subject who delivered the stuff to the user lessened the user's embarrassment. (1 = "Not at all" ~ "Very much")
Sadness	The user was sad. (1 = "Not at all" ~ "Very much")
Mitigating Sadness	The subject who delivered the stuff to the user comforted the user's sadness. (1 = "Not at all" ~ "Very much")
Service Evaluation (Cronbach's $\alpha = .977$)	1 = "very poor" ~7 = "very good" 1 = "completely dissatisfied" ~7 = "completely satisfied" 1 = "would avoid using the service" ~7 = "would want very much to use the service"

3.5 Procedure

The Institutional Review Board (IRB) at KIST granted approval for the study (KIST-202209-h-023). Participants listened to the explanation about the experiment and signed in the consent form to participate in the experiment. Participants were recruited separately for each emotion type and watched three videos according to the robot types in random order. After watching each video, they rated their impressions of the robot and the emotions felt by the users.

4 Results

One-way ANOVA was conducted for social presence, embarrassment, mitigating embarrassment, sadness, and mitigating sadness, which compared the effects of the robot types, and two-way ANOVA was conducted for service evaluation, which compared the effects of the robot types according to the emotion types. For all post hoc analyses, Tukey HSD was conducted. The results of the study are shown in Fig. 3.

4.1 Social Presence

H1 was supported by the data. A real human had the strongest social presence than a human-like robot and a product-like robot ($M_{\text{product-like}} = 3.14$, $SD_{\text{product-like}} = 1.52$; $M_{\text{human-like}} = 3.75$, $SD_{\text{human-like}} = 1.38$; $M_{\text{baseline}} = 6.16$, $SD_{\text{baseline}} = 1.10$; $F = 84.114$, $p < .001$).

4.2 Embarrassment

As predicted by H2, people were more embarrassed when a human counterpart handed a facial tissue and a mirror than when robots deliver those things ($M_{\text{product-like}} = 3.54$, $SD_{\text{product-like}} = 1.93$; $M_{\text{human-like}} = 3.66$, $SD_{\text{human-like}} = 1.68$; $M_{\text{baseline}} = 4.84$, $SD_{\text{baseline}} = 1.80$; $F = 9.689$, $p < .001$).

4.3 Mitigating Embarrassment

H3 was not supported by the data. There was no significant effect of the robot types on mitigating embarrassment ($F = 0.579$, $p = 0.562$).

4.4 Sadness

H4 was supported by the data. There is no significant effect of the robot types on sadness ($F = 0.579$, $p = 0.562$).

4.5 Mitigating Sadness

As we expected by H5, an actual human alleviated sadness best, followed by a human-like robot and a product-like robot ($M_{\text{product-like}} = 4.12$, $SD_{\text{product-like}} = 1.90$; $M_{\text{human-like}} = 5.26$, $SD_{\text{human-like}} = 1.36$; $M_{\text{baseline}} = 6.35$, $SD_{\text{baseline}} = 0.85$; $F = 20.624$, $p < .001$).

4.6 Service Evaluation

H6 was supported by the data. There was a significant main effect of the emotion types on service evaluation. Participants perceived service providers' service to be better in the sad situations than in the embarrassing situations ($M_{\text{sadness}} = 5.13$, $SD_{\text{sadness}} = 1.33$; $M_{\text{embarrassment}} = 5.79$, $SD_{\text{embarrassment}} = 0.98$; $F = 15.805$, $p < .001$).

Moreover, there was a significant main effect of the robot types on service evaluation. A human-like robot was rated as providing better services than a human ($M_{\text{product-like}} = 5.50$, $SD_{\text{product-like}} = 1.04$; $M_{\text{human-like}} = 5.66$, $SD_{\text{human-like}} = 1.14$; $M_{\text{baseline}} = 5.22$, $SD_{\text{baseline}} = 1.08$; $F = 3.356$, $p = .039$).

The interaction effects of the emotion types and the robot types on service evaluation was observed ($F = 11.157$, $p < .001$). In the sad situation, the provision of corresponding services by humans was evaluated more positively than that provided by product-like robots ($M_{\text{product-like}} = 5.46$, $SD_{\text{product-like}} = 0.974$; $M_{\text{human-like}} = 5.81$, $SD_{\text{human-like}} = 1.06$; $M_{\text{baseline}} = 6.10$, $SD_{\text{baseline}} = 0.82$; $F = 3.786$, $p = 0.026$). By contrast, in the embarrassing situation, robots providing corresponding services were evaluated more positively than that provided by a human ($M_{\text{product-like}} = 5.54$, $SD_{\text{product-like}} = 1.10$; $M_{\text{human-like}} = 5.50$, $SD_{\text{human-like}} = 1.21$; $M_{\text{baseline}} = 4.34$, $SD_{\text{baseline}} = 1.34$; $F = 10.506$, $p < .001$).

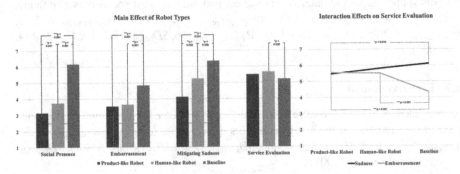

Fig. 3. Results

5 Discussion

5.1 Sadness and Embarrassment

Sadness is a primary emotion that is common among animals including humans, and its attribution is similar in both out-group and in-group settings [11, 19–21]. As expected based on related works, the results of this study showed no significant difference in sadness according to who the service provider was. On the other hand, embarrassment is a secondary emotion unique to humans, and out-group members tend to exhibit fewer secondary emotion than in-group members [19–21]. Consequently, we anticipated that a secondary emotion might be less prominent in nonhuman subjects. The results of the experiment revealed no difference in the level of embarrassment people felt by the robot types. However, participants felt significantly more embarrassed when interacting with a human than the two types of robots.

5.2 Embarrassment and Service Evaluation

Participants felt significantly more embarrassed when assisted by humans than when assisted by robots. In the service evaluation, the human who embarrassed the user the most received the most negative evaluation compared to the other two robots. The results of this study suggest that interacting with robots is effective in the embarrassing situations, and they can help individuals exhibit their abilities without feeling embarrassed, such as the interview situations, conference situations, blind date situations, and so on.

5.3 Sadness and Mitigating Sadness

The degree of sadness did not vary significantly across the different types of robots. Nonetheless, the robots' effectiveness in alleviating sadness varied by the robot types. The participants perceived the robot with a higher level of social presence as more capable of consoling their sadness. This indicates that to enhance their ability to console the user's sadness and treat the user's emotional distress, the designers of such robots should increase their social presence by anthropomorphizing them.

6 Conclusion

This study investigated the user's perception of the robot and the degree of user's emotion according to the robot types and the user's emotion types. As a result, there was no significant difference in sadness felt by the user according to the robot types. However, a real human comforted the user's sadness the most, followed by the human-like robot, while the product-like robot comforted the user's sadness the least. Participants felt embarrassed the most when a real human assisted the user, and there was no significant difference in the degree of embarrassment by the robot types. Notably, in terms of service evaluation, both robots received significantly more positive evaluations than a human in the embarrassment situation.

Acknowledgment. This work was partly supported by the Korea Institute of Science and Technology (KIST) Institutional Program under Grant (2E32302), Institute of Information & communications Technology Planning & Evaluation (IITP) grant funded by the Korea government (MSIT) (No. 2017-0-00432, Development of Non-invasive Integrated BCI SW Platform to Control Home Appliance and External Devices by User's Thought via AR/VR Interface), and the Government-wide R&D Fund for Infections Disease Research (GFID), funded by the Ministry of the Interior and Safety, Republic of Korea (20014463).

References

1. DAL-e, Hyundai Motor Group Introduces Advanced Humanoid Robot 'DAL-e', Hyundai Motor Group. https://www.hyundai.com/worldwide/en/company/newsroom/-0000016615. Accessed 18 Aug 2023
2. Carvajal, D.: Let a Robot Be Your Museum Tour Guide, New York Times, March 2017. https://www.nytimes.com/2017/03/14/arts/design/museums-experiment-with-robots-as-guides.html. Accessed 18 Aug 2023
3. CLOi, LG Airport Robots Take over Korea's Largest Airport, LG Electronics. https://www.lgcorp.com/media/release/7871. Accessed 18 Aug 2023
4. Morrissey, J.: Desperate for Workers, Restaurants Turn to Robots, New York Times, 19 October 2021. https://www.nytimes.com/2021/10/19/business/restaurants-robots-workers.html. Accessed 18 Aug 2023
5. Mori, M., MacDorman, K.F., Kageki, N.: The uncanny valley [from the field]. IEEE Robot. Autom. Mag. 19(2), 98–100 (2012)
6. MacDorman, K.F.: Subjective ratings of robot video clips for human likeness, familiarity, and eeriness: an exploration of the uncanny valley. In: ICCS/CogSci-2006 Long Symposium: Toward Social Mechanisms of Android Science, vol. 4 (2006)
7. Bar-Cohen, Y., Breazeal, C.: Biologically inspired intelligent robots. In: Proceedings of the SPIE Smart Structures Conference, pp. 14–20. SPIE, San Diego, U. S. (2003)
8. Van Pinxteren, M.M., Wetzels, R.W., Rüger, J., Pluymaekers, M., Wetzels, M.: Trust in humanoid robots: implications for services marketing. J. Serv. Mark. 33(4), 507–518 (2019)
9. Kang, D., Kwak, S.S.: Feel me if you can: the effect of robot types and robot's tactility types on users' perception toward a robot. In: Proceedings of the Companion of the 2017 ACM/IEEE International Conference on Human-Robot Interaction, pp. 155–156. IEEE, Vienna, Austria, March 2017
10. Bartneck, C., Bleeker, T., Bun, J., Fens, P., Riet, L.: The influence of robot anthropomorphism on the feelings of embarrassment when interacting with robots. J. Behav. Robot. 1(2), 109–115 (2010)
11. Haslam, N.: Dehumanization: an integrative review. Pers. Soc. Psychol. Rev. 10(3), 252–264 (2006)
12. Turner, T.J., Ortony, A.: Basic emotions: can conflicting criteria converge? Psychol. Rev. 99(3), 566–571 (1992)
13. Duffy, B.R.: Anthropomorphism and the social robot. Robot. Auton. Syst. 42(3–4), 177–190 (2003)
14. Broadbent, E., et al.: Robots with display screens: a robot with a more humanlike face display is perceived to have more mind and a better personality. PLoS ONE 8(8), e72589 (2013)
15. Mende, M., Scott, M.L., van Doorn, J., Grewal, D., Shanks, I.: Service robots rising: how humanoid robots influence service experiences and elicit compensatory consumer responses. J. Mark. Res. 56(4), 535–556 (2019)
16. Holthöwer, J., van Doorn, J.: Robots do not judge: service robots can alleviate embarrassment in service encounters. J. Acad. Mark. Sci. 51(4), 767–784 (2023)
17. Damasio, A.R.: Descartes' Error, Emotion Reason and the Human Brain. Grosset/Putnam (1994)
18. Ekman, P.: Handbook of Cognition and Emotion. John Wiley and Sons, Ltd., Hoboken (1999)
19. Gaunt, R., Leyens, J.P., Demoulin, S.: Intergroup relations and the attribution of emotions: control over memory for secondary emotions associated with the ingroup and outgroup. J. Exp. Soc. Psychol. 38(5), 508–514 (2002)
20. Leyens, J.P., et al.: The emotional side of prejudice: the attribution of secondary emotions to ingroups and outgroups. Pers. Soc. Psychol. Rev. 4(2), 186–197 (2000)

21. Viki, G.T., Winchester, L., Titshall, L., Chisango, T., Pina, A., Russell, R.: Beyond secondary emotions: the infrahumanization of outgroups using human–related and animal–related words. Soc. Cogn. **24**(6), 753–775 (2006)
22. Temi. https://www.robotemi.com/product/temi/
23. Heerink, M., Kröse, B., Evers, V., Wielinga, B.: The influence of social presence on acceptance of a companion robot by older people. J. Phys. Agents **2**(2), 33–40 (2008)
24. Lee, M.K., Kiesler, S., Forlizzi, J., Srinivasa, S., Rybski, P.: Gracefully mitigating breakdowns in robotic services. In: 2010 5th ACM/IEEE International Conference on Human-Robot Interaction (HRI), pp. 203–210. IEEE, Osaka, Japan, March 2010

A Tablet-Based Lexicon Application for Robot-Aided Educational Interaction of Children with Dyslexia

M. Shahab[1], M. Mokhtari[1], S. A. Miryazdi[1], S. Ahmadi[1], M. M. Mohebati[1],
M. Sohrabipour[1], O. Amiri[1], A. Meghdari[1,2], M. Alemi[1,3], H. R. Pouretemad[4],
and A. Taheri[1(✉)]

[1] Social and Cognitive Robotics Laboratory, Sharif University of Technology, Tehran, Iran
artaheri@sharif.edu
[2] Chancellor, Fereshtegaan International Branch, Islamic Azad University, Tehran, Iran
[3] Department of Humanities, West Tehran Branch, Islamic Azad University, West Tehran Branch, Tehran, Iran
[4] Institute for Cognitive and Brain Sciences (ICBS), Shahid Beheshti University, Tehran, Iran

Abstract. Dyslexia is a neurodevelopmental disorder that has the highest prevalence among different types of learning disorders. Dyslexic children usually have difficulty in reading and as a result, they face different educational problems at school. Currently, social robots are widely used as educational assistants and tutors, mainly for children with special needs. The Taban robot is a modern educational social robot, which was developed specifically for dyslexic children. In this paper, an android application was designed and developed to facilitate child-robot interaction just by means of a tablet. Using this smart tablet game, the children could collaborate with the Taban social robot in solving the pedagogic problems and practicing educational concepts, while the robot provides them not only beneficial verbal and physical reactions by its hands, but also effective visual feedback on its touch screen. For the first step in this research, the acceptability of the designed tablet game was investigated for twenty-one participants that fifth of them had dyslexia. The hopeful results of the SAM questionnaires filled out by the children, demonstrate high acceptability of the tablet game. Furthermore, by implementing automatic assessment based on the designed standard criteria, the platform could meaningfully distinguish the two groups of children (dyslexic and typically developed (TD)) according to their achieved scores in the game. Thus, the high potential value of the designed robot-aided tablet game was illustrated to be used as an assistive tool for dyslexic children.

Keyword: Educational technology · Human-robot interaction · Android programming · Serious Games · Learning disabilities · Special Education

1 Introduction

Learning disorders include different types, such as dyslexia, dysgraphia, dyscalculia, and combined learning disorders, etc., with dyslexia being the most common disorder, which includes a wide range of problems in reading, writing, and mathematics [1]. Today,

A. Al. Ali et al. (Eds.): ICSR 2023, LNAI 14454, pp. 344–354, 2024.
https://doi.org/10.1007/978-981-99-8718-4_30

with the advent of educational technologies, various tools are used to help children with special needs, including computer games, virtual reality, social robotics, etc. that we have used in our previous studies [2–5]. Computer games have shown high potential in the treatment of dyslexia due to their personalization, anxiety-reducing features, attractive nature, multisensory components, and instant feedback [6–16].

Risqi worked on the implementation and the effect of the gamification approach on the dyslexic learning process. The game elements were grouped based on the needs of dyslexic children, desired psychological outcomes, and software requirements; and they were intended to produce specific psychological outcomes such as engagement, enjoyment, and motivation. All dyslexic children felt happy and enjoyed playing. An average of 96.64% agreed to use the application again [6]. Martins et al. presented an application that applies voice recognition on mobile devices for training and diagnosis of dyslexic people. The application displays a random word for the user to read and verifies the correctness of the spoken word. Preliminary results indicated that the application was able to diagnose traces of dyslexia; however, the tests were held just once [7]. Vasalou et al. studied the effectiveness of the tablet game "Words Matter", which contains various mini-games for enhancing word recognition and spelling. The results showed children spontaneously engage in 'game talk', which facilitates a strong sense of social engagement, enforces self-confidence, and creates a variety of new opportunities for learning by sparking tutor and student-initiated interventions [8].

Borhan et al. developed a mobile application, "Mr. Read" that utilizes a sight-word reading strategy to help dyslexic children. This strategy is incorporated into three different modules in the application: short stories, rhymes, and song verses. The overall results of the tests illustrated that 100% of respondents, instructors, parents, and children either agreed or strongly agreed that this mobile application can improve reading skills [9]. Zare, et al. investigated the effect of Persian-language word exercise games on the spelling of dyslexic students. Children took pre-test and post-test, and spelling was improved in the experimental group compared to the control group [10].

Ecalle et al. evaluated the short and medium-term effects of "ChassymoDys" software on improving phonemic awareness, decoding, and word-reading skills in French poor readers. Analyzing 12 children in 3 levels, they validated the guess that digital solutions can help children learn better and faster, especially in short practice periods [11]. Burac et al. developed a mobile assistive application, "IREAD", which primarily implements text-to-speech technology to enhance the reading capability of learners with dyslexia. The usability results of the application showed the participants strongly agreed with all usability dimensions [12]. Brennan et al. examined if code signing a game, "Cosmic Words", with children improves the teaching of phonological awareness skills. The result was that children were more invested in using these games for learning. There was a positive impact on their phonological awareness skills while their engagement in learning increased [13].

The software presented by Kariyawasam et al. used machine learning methods for dyslexia screening. Trained convolutional neural networks were used to detect the spoken or written letter/word or number on the mobile application. The application was tested among pre-diagnosed children with learning disabilities and the results reached 89% accuracy, but tests need more time to be completed [14]. Khaleghi et al. examined gamification and serious game approaches efficacy in improving 6–8 year-old dyslexic children's motivation to complete cognitive rehabilitation interventions like phonological awareness. The result indicated that games improve children's learning process and increase their motivation. The limitation was that the questionnaires were filled only by supervising experts and not the children [15].

Despite the large number of studies on the effectiveness of computer games on dyslexia, social robots have been used in relatively few studies in this field using just the NAO and QT robots [16–18]. Taban 2 (called Taban in this article and a new generation of the Taban [19]) is a social robot that has been specifically constructed for the educational practice of children with dyslexia. In most social robotic research, tablets and touch screens are the favored auxiliary interactive tools, especially when automatic speech recognition is not appropriately robust for child-robot interactions [20].

In this paper, a modern android game and social robotics technologies were combined to provide a novel protocol; a new tablet game collaborating with the Taban autonomous social robot, which provides visual, verbal, and physical feedback for the child, to improve the literacy and reading skills of children with dyslexia. To explore the potential of this tablet game for the rehabilitation and improvement of children with dyslexia, first of all, we study the acceptability in this research. Moreover, we would also study whether there is a significant difference between the performances of the two groups of participants (i.e., dyslexic and TD), which signalizes the effectiveness of the tablet game as an educational intervention tool for children with dyslexia.

2 Methodology

The first step in game design is the cognitive functions that we target for improvement or treatment in dyslexic children, which should be clearly defined. The game and the child-robot interactions were designed based on the selected etiology theory of dyslexia. Several different theories explain the origin of dyslexia, including auditory processing deficits, verbal working memory deficits, visual magnocellular deficits, phonological processing deficits, and cerebellar dysfunction [21].

This study focuses on phonological processing and phonological awareness deficits due to their high prevalence and specificity as an underlying cause of dyslexia, not just a symptom of other cognitive disorders [22, 23]. The phonological processing deficit theory holds that representing, storing, or retrieving speech sounds is impaired in dyslexia [24]. This theory guides the interactions and several mini-games were designed based on the theory and its related therapeutic exercises.

Before designing any child-robot interactions, we observe all exercises, training, and treatments provided for dyslexic children in the learning disorder centers. By observing these exercises, we learned what capabilities the robot-aided application needed to be used as an assistant to the conventional learning techniques of the teachers.

2.1 Participants and Experimental Setup

The participants in this study were elementary school students, including both typically developing (TD) children and children with dyslexia. Each child took part in only one session. The dyslexic group consisted of 5 children (5 boys) with an average age of 7.40 years (SD = 0.49). The TD group had 16 children (14 boys, and 2 girls) with an average age of 7.38 years (SD = 0.78).

In the acceptance session, after the initial greeting, the robot provides explanations for the participants about the rules of using the tablet and answering questions, and then in the first step, the robot itself solves a question so that the children can practically learn the protocol. Then the robot asks the children to answer the questions carefully. The sessions lasted 20–40 min per child based on the level of his/her knowledge (Fig. 1(a)). During the interactions with the robot and answering the question, the children's performance was evaluated. The participants had no prior experience with robot-assisted learning methods and at the end of the session, they filled out a questionnaire.

2.2   Game Design

Eight interactive lexical games were designed for both dyslexic and non-dyslexic children. The games are displayed on two devices including an LCD screen on the Taban robot, and a tablet in front of the child. The child only interacts directly with the tablet, not the robot, so as to protect the robot from possible danger. However, the tablet forwards the child's responses to Taban, which provides interactive audio-visual feedback to the child based on their answers. This includes responding through the speakers, screen, and physical movements of its head and arms. The robot's interactions give feedback on whether the child's responses are correct or incorrect.

The eight games are run on the tablet and target different areas in lexical study. Each game focuses on one or more specific areas, with an increasing levels' difficulty. The games utilize audiovisual components to teach vocabulary. On the tablet, words are represented by some pictures that the child must select them. Some games require choosing multiple images, occasionally in a particular order. This multimedia approach allows the games to cover a broad range of lexical topics while remaining engaging through interactive play.

The Taban robot assists the tablet games in several ways:

- Taban provides gentle spoken instructions and feedback through speakers on its head. This includes a short explanation at the start of each game, as well as remarking on the validity of the child's responses during the gameplay to further guide them.
- Taban uses expressive physical gestures like moving its arms and head to indicate if the child's tablet answers are correct or incorrect. This supplements the feedback already displayed on the tablet screen.
- An animated face projected onto Taban's head gives the robot more human-like expressions and characteristics.
- Taban displays dynamic pictures related to the game and the child's answers on an attached LCD screen on its chest. The images are color-coded and blink green for correct responses or red for incorrect ones, providing additional visual feedback (Fig. 1(b)).

In addition to help from Taban, the child may ask for further guidance if they find the game difficult at first. In total, four classes of games will be discussed in the coming sections.

2.2.1   Recognition of the First Phoneme

Games 1 and 2 focus on phonology and phonetics. They involve recognizing and comparing the initial phonemes of words represented as images on the tablet. In Games 1 and 2, the child must select pictures depicting words that start with a specified phoneme. Game 1 displays six images to choose from in groups of two. Game 2 increases the difficulty by providing nine images in groups of three (Fig. 2(a)).

a)   b)

Fig. 1. a) The children interact with the robot and answer questions via tablet in the acceptance session, b) The LCD touch screen attached to Taban's chest displays the animated picture with red color for an incorrect response.

2.2.2   Initial Phoneme Manipulation

Games 3 and 4 target morphology and word formation processes. They require the child to remove or alter the initial phonemes of words represented by the pictures. In Game 3, the child must identify the new word created when the first phoneme is removed from another word. Game 3 displays three images on top that the child removes phonemes from, matching to one of the three images on bottom. Game 4 increases difficulty with 6 shuffled images to choose pairs from. The levels progressively challenge children's skills.

2.2.3   Phonological Composition and Intersection

Games 5 and 6 target phonological processing and psycholinguistics skills. They involve decomposing and sequencing phonemes within words represented by images. In Game 5, three images in a column on the right represent 3-phoneme words. The child must extract the component phonemes from each word, and then select images on the left that start with those phonemes in the correct order (Fig. 2(b)).

Game 6 begins with Taban reading the component phonemes of the four words aloud in sequence. The child must construct the words in their mind and remember them. After all phonemes are read out, the child selects the corresponding images in the correct order. This game adds a working memory component for increased difficulty.

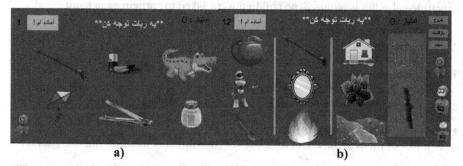

a)   b)

Fig. 2. Screenshot of the game questions: a) Game 1: A set of correct answers would be the crocodile [تمساح]and arrow [تیر], both starting with the [ت]phoneme. b) Game 12: The phonemes of the word swing [تاب]in order are [ت], [آ], and [ب]. In order these are the first phonemes in the words: mulberry [توت], mirrors [آینه]and shovel [بیل]. These images need to be selected in order.

2.2.4 Syllabic Awareness

Games 7 and 8 focus on syllabication and phonological segmentation skills. They involve deconstructing words represented by images into their component syllables. Game 13 has multiple parts. Two 2-syllable words are displayed in a column on the right as images; and on the left there are 5 images with numbered labels below them. The child first identifies which left images contain syllables in the right words. They specify the syllable number of each left image using the labels. This breaks down the words into syllables. Then the child selects the left syllables constructing each word on the right in order.

The final game requires selecting images of words with the same number of syllables. Twelve images in groups of three represent 1, 2, and 3-syllable words to be chosen together. Through syllabication and segmentation, these games develop phonological awareness. The multi-step format of Game 7 provides a deep practice. Game 8 challenges children to apply skills to new vocabulary.

2.3 Database

In addition to the predefined game levels, there is also a randomized mode utilizing a database of 1000 common elementary school words. This database was constructed by extracting phonetic and syllable data, plus image files, for each word using phonetic dictionaries, automated tools, and manual processing. With this database, randomized versions of the games can be dynamically generated following the same principles as the leveled games. For instance, iterating through all words and pulling ones sharing the same initial phoneme can create randomized phonology and phonetics games matching games 1 and 2.

The database allows essentially endless permutations of the vocabulary games within the four learning categories. This adds variety and engagement for children replaying the games. A prototype for this has already been developed; however, since a repeatable experimental setup is required, no children were asked to participate in them.

2.4 Assessment

The children were assessed in two ways. First, an automatic assessment system was designed to grade children's performance based on the speed, accuracy, and number of incorrect responses during the games. Specific metrics tracked included:

- Response time for finishing a game
- Number of times an incorrect response was submitted before finishing the game

It should be noted that a game is considered "finished" once all correct answers are submitted. Performance data was logged in real-time during the gameplay. Automated methods then calculated scores based on the recorded metrics. Second, the participants' emotional reactions were evaluated after completing the game activities using the Self-Assessment Manikin (SAM) scale. The SAM uses non-verbal pictorial assessments of pleasure, arousal, and dominance; it has been used in several acceptance studies in the field of social robotics [25, 26]. Children selected the SAM images that best represented their experienced emotions during the gameplay.

3 Results and Discussion

The participants filled out the SAM questionnaire and determined their level of acceptance of the game at the end of the experiment session (Table 1).

Table 1. The mean and standard deviation scores of the SAM questionnaire parameters and the T-value and P-values associated with the T-tests.

No	Item	SAM Questionnaire		T_Value	P_Value
		Score's mean (SD)			
		Dyslexia	Normal		
1	Pleasure	4.6 (0.49)	4.75 (0.43)	−0.601	−0.56
2	Arousal	4.8 (0.4)	4.63 (0.6)	0.506	0.69
3	Dominance	4.6 (0.49)	4.75 (0.56)	0.61	−0.53

According to the results in Table 1, both dyslexic and normally developing children showed high levels of arousal, dominance, and pleasure. These results show both groups felt engaged with the robot-aided games, and were happy, excited, and felt in control while playing them. Also, it could be understood that there is no significant difference in the acceptance rate of the game between groups.

Furthermore, the participants' performances were assessed during the games and their final scores were calculated based on their reaction time and the correctness of their answers (Table 2). Additionally, another purpose of this part of the study is to determine if there is a significant difference between the performances of the typically developing students and those with dyslexia in doing the designed exercises.

Table 2. The mean, standard deviation, and Cronbach's alpha scores of the dyslexic and TD groups in different exercises and the T-value and P-values associated with the T-tests; P-value < 0.05 shows the 95% confidence interval.

No	Item		Total Score Out of 20 (SD)		P-value	T- value	Cronbach's alpha
			Dyslexia	Normal			
1	Recognition of the First Phoneme	Game 1	7.65 (4.16)	13.53(4.12)	**0.032**	−2.77	**0.771**
		Game 2	4.03 (4.58)	9.76 (5.08)	**0.049**	−2.38	
		Total	**5.84 (5.77)**	**11.64 (4.84)**	**0.009**	−2.8	–
2	Initial Phoneme Manipulation	Game 3	5.31 (4.15)	12.43 (4.32)	**0.016**	−3.32	**0.895**
		Game 4	5.71 (6.28)	13.17 (3.38)	0.064	−2.54	
		Total	**5.51 (5.39)**	**12. 8 (3.88)**	**0.001**	−5.52	–
3	Phonological Composition and Intersection	Game 5	6.27 (7.9)	7.61 (7.57)	0.749	−0.34	0.63
		Game 6	2.84 (6.54)	9.51 (7.13)	0.093	−1.95	
		Total	**4.55 (5.95)**	**8.56 (6.71)**	**0.026**	−2.44	–
4	Syllabic Awareness	Game 7	4.68 (8.02)	9.36 (3.09)	0.271	−1.27	**0.796**
		Game 8	5.23 (4.67)	9.49 (4.16)	0.118	−1.82	
		Total	**4.96 (6.19)**	**9.42 (3.61)**	**0.055**	−2.17	–

The results in Table 2 clearly illustrate that the performance of the typically developing children is significantly higher than the children with dyslexia for all of the total items (total P-value < 0.05). Considering the significant performance difference between normal participants and children with dyslexia, it could be concluded that the exercise designers had enough data and a good comprehension of children with dyslexia and their capabilities to design efficient exercises. Furthermore, this result is a hopeful signal illustrating that this game might have the potential to be used for screening dyslexic children and to identify them by measuring their performance in this robot-aided table game. In addition, Cronbach's alpha scores for almost all game groups (>0.7) show good reliability and internal consistency in results. As a result, our hypothesis of merging these four related types of questions together and examining the significant difference in the combined results of all of them is correctly confirmed.

3.1 Limitations and Future Works

The small number of the dyslexic participants and the unbalanced distribution of the male/female participants in both groups are the limitations of this study. Additionally, due to the high acceptance rate of the designed game, the next step is to conduct systematic educational interventions (e.g. over at least 8 sessions) based on similar studies with a group of dyslexic children. The aim is to assess the effectiveness of the designed robot-aided tablet game protocol in improving the phonological awareness and reading skills of children with dyslexia.

4 Conclusion

The main goal of this research was to introduce a robot-aided serious game as a novel method of education for children with dyslexia based on their special educational needs. The robot could be used as tutor in this protocol and increase the motivation, productivity, and learning rate of children with dyslexia. This study presented the four classifications of games and their contents, as well as evaluating their acceptability.

In addition to automated grading tools for each game, the SAM scale was used to assess the participants' emotional reactions. The results showed that the designed tablet game might have the potential to be used as a screening tool for dyslexic children while giving them a similar level of enjoyment to non-dyslexic children while playing.

In summary, the protocol of an engaging robot-aided tablet game presented in this study shows high potential for helping children with dyslexia and could serve as a valuable tool to assist teachers with their conventional teaching methods.

Acknowledgment. This study was funded by the "Dr. Ali Akbar Siassi Memorial Research Grant Award" and Sharif University of Technology (Grant No. G980517). We would like to thank our friends Mr. Mehdi Kermanshah for his valuable help during the robot fabrication and Ms. Fatemeh Absalan for her collaboration in the design of the robot characters.

References

1. Vahia, V.N.: Diagnostic and statistical manual of mental disorders 5: a quick glance. Indian J. Psychiatry **55**(3), 220 (2013)
2. Taheri, A., Shariati, A., Heidari, R., Shahab, M., Alemi, M., Meghdari, A.: Impacts of using a social robot to teach music to children with low-functioning autism. Paladyn J. Behav. Robot. **12**(1), 256–275 (2021)
3. Ghorbandaei Pour, A., Taheri, A., Alemi, M., Meghdari, A.: Human–robot facial expression reciprocal interaction platform: case studies on children with autism. Int. J. Soc. Robot. **10**, 179–198 (2018)
4. Shahab, M., et al.: Utilizing social virtual reality robot (V2R) for music education to children with high-functioning autism. Educ. Inf. Technol. 1–25 (2021)
5. M. Tavakol Elahi et al., Xylotism: A Tablet-Based Application to Teach Music to Children with Autism. in Social Robotics: 9th International Conference, ICSR 2017, Tsukuba, Japan, November 22–24, 2017, Proceedings 9: Springer, pp. 728–738, 2017

6. Risqi, M.: LexiPal: design, implementation and evaluation of gamification on learning application for dyslexia. Int. J. Comput. Appl. **131**(7), 37–43 (2015)
7. Martins, V.F., Lima, T., Sampaio, P.N.M., De Paiva, M.: Mobile application to support dyslexia diagnostic and reading practice. In: 2016 IEEE/ACS 13th International Conference of Computer Systems and Applications (AICCSA), November 2016
8. Vasalou, A., Khaled, R., Holmes, W., Gooch, D.: Digital games-based learning for children with dyslexia: a social constructivist perspective on engagement and learning during group game-play. Comput. Educ. **114**, 175–192 (2017)
9. Borhan, N.H., et al.: An enhancement of dyslexic mobile application using sight word reading strategy: results and findings. J. Comput. Sci. **14**(7), 919–929 (2018)
10. Zare, M., Amani, M., Sadoughi, M.: The role of Persian-language word exercise games in improving spelling of students with dyslexia: word exercise games in improving spelling. J. Comput. Assist. Learn. **36**(3), 315–322 (2019)
11. Ecalle, J., Vidalenc, J.-L., Ballet, C., Magnan, A.: From fundamental research to the design of a software solution to help poor readers. J. Educ. Comput. Res. **58**(2), 297–318 (2019)
12. Burac, M.A.P., Dela Cruz, J.: Development and usability evaluation on individualized reading enhancing application for dyslexia (IREAD): a mobile assistive application. In: IOP Conference Series: Materials Science and Engineering, vol. 803, no. 1, p. 012015, April 2020
13. Brennan, A., McDonagh, T., Dempsey, M., McAvoy, J.: Cosmic sounds: a game to support phonological awareness skills for children with dyslexia. IEEE Trans. Learn. Technol. **15**(3), 301–310 (2022)
14. Kariyawasam, R., Nadeeshani, M., Hamid, T., Subasinghe, I., Ratnayake, P.: A gamified approach for screening and intervention of dyslexia, dysgraphia and dyscalculia. In: 2019 International Conference on Advancements in Computing (ICAC), December 2019
15. Khaleghi, A., Aghaei, Z., Behnamghader, M.: Developing two game-based interventions for dyslexia therapeutic interventions using gamification and serious games approaches entertainment computing journal. Entertain. Comput. **42**, 100482 (2022)
16. Papadopoulou, M.T., et al.: Efficacy of a robot-assisted intervention in improving learning performance of elementary school children with specific learning disorders. Children **9**(8), 1155 (2022)
17. Karageorgiou, M.E., et al.: Development of educational scenarios for child-robot interaction: the case of learning disabilities. In: Merdan, M., Lepuschitz, W., Koppensteiner, G., Balogh, R., Obdržálek, D. (eds.) Robotics in Education. RiE 2021. AISC, vol. 1359, pp. 26–33. Springer, Cham (2022). https://doi.org/10.1007/978-3-030-82544-7_3
18. Azizi, N., Chandra, S., Gray, M., Sager, M., Fane, J., Dautenhahn, K.: An initial investigation into the use of social robots within an existing educational program for students with learning disabilities. In: 2022 31st IEEE International Conference on Robot and Human Interactive Communication (RO-MAN), pp. 1490–1497. IEEE (2022)
19. Mokhtari, M., Shariati, A., Meghdari, A.: Taban: a retro-projected social robotic - head for human-robot interaction. In: 2019 7th International Conference on Robotics and Mechatronics (ICRoM), pp. 46–51, November 2019
20. Belpaeme, T., Kennedy, J., Ramachandran, A., Scassellati, B., Tanaka, F.: Social robots for education: a review. Sci. Robot. **3**(21), eaat5954 (2018)
21. Baddeley, A.: Working memory: looking back and looking forward. Nat. Rev. Neurosci. **4**(10), 829–839 (2003)
22. Pérez-Quichimbo, S.-M., Navas-Moya, M.-P., Montes-León, S.-R., Sambachi-Chilig, P.-A., Barrera-Quimbita, E.-D.: Therapy using serious games to improve phonological awareness in children with functional dyslexia. In: Botto-Tobar, M., Montes León, S., Torres-Carrión, P., Zambrano Vizuete, M., Durakovic, B. (eds.) Applied Technologies. ICAT 2021. CCIS, vol. 1535, pp. 121–134. Springer, Cham (2022). https://doi.org/10.1007/978-3-031-03884-6_9. Accessed 17 Aug 2023

23. Ramus, F.: Theories of developmental dyslexia: insights from a multiple case study of dyslexic adults. Brain **126**(4), 841–865 (2003)
24. Syrdal, D.S., Dautenhahn, K., Robins, B., Karakosta, E., Jones, N.C.: Kaspar in the wild: experiences from deploying a small humanoid robot in a nursery school for children with autism. Paladyn J. Behav. Robot. **11**(1), 301–326 (2020)
25. Shariati, A., et al.: Virtual reality social robot platform: a case study on Arash social robot. In: Ge, S., et al. (eds.) Social Robotics. ICSR 2018. LNCS, vol. 11357, pp. 551–560. Springer, Cham (2018). https://doi.org/10.1007/978-3-030-05204-1_54
26. Bradley, M.M., Lang, P.J.: Measuring emotion: the self-assessment manikin and the semantic differential. J. Behav. Ther. Exp. Psychiatry **25**(1), 49–59 (1994)

Special Session Papers

User Perception of Teachable Robots: A Comparative Study of Teaching Strategies, Task Complexity and User Characteristics

Imene Tarakli$^{(\boxtimes)}$ and Alessandro Di Nuovo

Sheffield Hallam University, Sheffield S11WB, UK
`i.tarakli@shu.ac.uk`

Abstract. This study explores the influence of teaching methods, task complexity, and user characteristics on perceptions of teachable robots. Analysis of responses from 138 participants reveals that both Teaching with Evaluative Feedback and Teaching through Preferences were perceived as equally user-friendly and easier to use compared to the non-interactive condition. Additionally, Teaching with Evaluative Feedback enhanced robot responsiveness, while Teaching with Preferences yielded results similar to the passive Download condition, suggesting that the degree of interactivity and human guidance in the former may not substantially impact user perceptions. Personality traits, particularly extraversion and intellect, shape teaching method preferences. Task complexity influenced the perceived anthropomorphism, control, and responsiveness of the robot. Notably, the classification task led to higher anthropomorphism, control, and responsiveness scores. Our findings emphasise the importance of task design and the need of tailoring teaching methods to the user's personality to optimise human-robot interactions, particularly in educational contexts. Project website: https://sites.google.com/view/teachable-robots.

Keywords: Users perception · Robot Teaching · Education

1 Introduction

Education has shown an increasing interest in the use of social robots to support children's learning [14]. Studies revealed that social robots stimulate a wider array of valuable social behaviours in children, prompt engagement with the physical world through their embodiments, and promote a personalised and tailored learning environment to the individual's student needs [3,4].

The pedagogical potential of social robots allows them to assume active roles in classrooms, including tutor, peer, or learner roles (see [20] for a detailed taxonomy). A prominent trend of portraying the robot as a novice learner has been noted in the recent literature [14]. In this setting, the robot, acting as a less knowledgeable peer, receives guidance from students to enhance its performance. This concept is based on the learning-by-teaching paradigm, a well-acknowledged psychological approach in which learners instruct a third party, leading to a deeper understanding on their part.

Research reveals that engaging with a novice robot improves children's learning outcomes by establishing a non-judgmental context, boosting student confidence, and fostering meta-cognitive skills [13]. However, for a robot to effectively play the role of a novice learner, it must comprehend student instructions, explanations, and feedback, necessitating it to emulate child-like learning capabilities.

Interactive Reinforcement Learning (RL) emerges as a promising approach to endow robots with cognitive capabilities. Within this framework, non-technical human instructors guide the robot's learning process by providing feedback. Different forms of feedback can be employed to teach the robot including demonstration, instruction, and evaluative feedback [19]. While most methods assume an optimal and rational teacher [5], a presumption often unsuited for children, evaluative feedback offers a sturdy alternative. In this method, users guides the robots by providing information about the quality of its actions. This type of feedback can not only accommodate human errors [9] but also cultivates active learning, pushing the robot towards trial-and-error which requires from the human teacher a deeper comprehension of the task. Moreover, a more recent trend in interactive RL is preference-based learning [6,11,16]. Here, the teacher provides information about the relative preferences of different actions of the robot, guiding the learning process with comparisons rather than explicit evaluations.

While Interactive RL systems have demonstrated considerable success in instructing robots across a range of tasks, prior studies have predominantly focused on optimising the robot's learning algorithm, often overlooking the user's perspective on these teaching methods. However, understanding the user's perspective is essential for designing robotic systems that better align with the user's expectations, and fostering engaging, intuitive, and satisfying interaction with social robots. This aspect holds particular significance in education, where the quality of interaction directly influences the effectiveness of the learning process.

This work aims to investigate users' perspectives on interactive teaching methods involving robots. Our primary focus centres on two distinct methodologies: teaching with evaluative feedback and teaching through preferences. Firstly, we conduct a comparative analysis of these teaching methods to investigate the impact of these methods on the users' perception of robots. Secondly, we assess whether the nature of the task impacts the user's perception of the teaching method. Lastly, we examine the potential influence of users' personality traits on their preference for specific teaching approaches. By exploring these aspects, this research aims to understand the relationship between the teaching method and the users' perceptions of the robot, thus contributing to a deeper understanding of how robots can be effectively incorporated into educational settings.

2   Related Work

Prior work in Human-Robot Interaction (HRI) extensively investigated how human would interact with teachable robot [12,17,22]. These studies have primarily focus on understanding users' intention and training strategies when providing evaluative feedback to robots. The insights from these works have contributed to the refinement of the learning algorithm that are better aligned with the user. While these findings are essential for effective HRI, earlier research focused more on improving the robot performance through algorithmic design, often overlooking the investigation of users perception of the robot.

In a recent study [18], researchers investigated the influence of diverse teaching methods, including interactive Reinforcement Learning (RL), on users' perceptions of a care robot. Their findings highlighted a correlation between the level of anthropomorphism attributed to the robot and the extent of involvement in the teaching. Moreover, they observed that the perceived success of the robot had a greater impact on user trust and usability compared to the teaching method employed. While this study offers an initial insight, our research aims to extend these observations to different contexts, such as educational settings, by assessing the perceived intelligence and control over the robot. We will assess factors like perceived intelligence and control over the robot, as well as measure the perceived usability of the teaching method itself, rather than solely focusing on the robot's usability as previously done.

To our knowledge, no prior research has explored preference-based learning within the context of HRI. Our study stands a pioneering effort, investigating the application of preference-based learning in HRI for the first time.

3   Methodology

To investigate the user's perspective on various teaching methods involving robot, we conduct an online between-subject study. Participants are randomly assigned to view one video showcasing a specific teaching method among three conditions: teaching with evaluative feedback, teaching with preferences, and a control group devoid of teaching intervention. They also engaged in a specific training task chosen from navigation, control, and classification tasks. This study has been granted ethical approval by the Ethics Committee of Sheffield Hallam University (Application ID: ER56422859, July 12th, 2023).

3.1   Teaching Conditions

We conduct a comparative analysis of three teaching scenarios involving distinct teaching methods: Interactive RL from Evaluative Feedback, Preference-based RL, and a Download condition where the robot learns without a human intervention. The latter condition was inspired by the work of Moorman et al. [18] and represents the control group of the study as no interaction with the robot is involved. Figure 1 depicts the three teaching scenarios.

Download: In this condition, no teaching from the user is involved. This condition serves as a control in the study because it represents a baseline scenario where no active teaching intervention from the user is present. Participants are solely passive observers, watching a video where a robot retrieves and executes a pre-existing robotic program that corresponds to the training task.

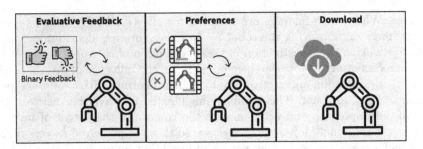

Fig. 1. Overview of the teaching condition. From left to right: Teaching with Evaluative Feedback, teaching with Preferences and Download condition.

Interactive RL from Human Evaluative Feedback: In this condition, users teach the robot by proving feedback about the quality and correctness of its actions. Through trial and error, the robot progressively improves its performance by refining its strategies based on the evaluations provided by the human instructor. The design of this condition draws inspiration from the TAMER framework [15], where the teacher consistently provided evaluate feedback to the robot. To illustrate this to the participants we present paired videos: one showcasing the robot's trial-and-error learning and the other illustrating a teacher using a gaming controller to provide evaluative feedback. The teacher, the experimenter in this case, pushes a red-labelled joystick to provide negative feedback, and a green-labelled joystick to provide positive feedback to the robot. The human teacher within the video is presented as rational, consistently providing accurate feedback to guide the robot to optimal performance outcomes.

Preference-Based Reinforcement Learning: In this scenario, users instruct the robot by providing ranked preferences over pairs of executed trajectories. The robot employs these preferences to enhance its performance through a classic Reinforcement Learning (RL) algorithm. The prevalent approach in the literature consists of initially training the robot in a simulation. Here, human preferences are collected by comparing side-by-side video clips of the robot's trajectories. Once the learning is completed in the simulated environment, it is then transferred to real-world robots. An alternative, through less common, consists of directly training the robot in real-life scenarios by offering preferences for sequential trajectories executed by the robots. In a prior study, we compared both strategies and found no statistically significant difference in user perception between them. Consequently, we have chosen to proceed with the widely adopted strategy of instructing the robot through simulation-derived videos. Specifically, the design of this condition is inspired by the work of Christiano et al. [6], wherein side-by-side trajectory snippets possess varying start and end states. To illustrate this teaching condition to the participants, we present them with a video featuring an experimenter in the role of a teacher. The teacher employs a web interface to convey her preferences for the robot's trajectories. Within the web interface, each page displays two video clips of the robot's trajectories side by side. The teacher is provided with three choices: expressing a preference for video 1, expressing a preference for video 2, or opting to skip if no preferences are held. Similar to the previous teaching scenario, the teacher is rational and provides accurate preferences to guide the robot toward optimal performance.

3.2 Task Domain

The robot's teaching is conducted across three distinct tasks: navigation, control, and classification. All tasks are performed using the Vector robot and are illustrated in Fig. 2.

- **Navigation Task:** In this task, the objective is to instruct the robot to navigate through a maze and reach a predetermined position while avoiding colliding with obstacles.
- **Control Task:** In this task, the robot must approach a cube, lift it, and accurately place it in a specific location. Although this task shares similarities with the navigation task, it introduces more complexity by expanding the range of actions to manipulate the cube.
- **Classification Task:** The goal of this task is teaching the robot how to categorise object in two distinct groups object into two categories. To simply the teaching process, we consider three actions: classifying an object into category A, category B, or opting not to classify it.

By considering a variety of tasks, our goal is to broaden the study's applicability to ensure our aim is to ensure that the finding can be readily extrapolated to various pedagogical applications.

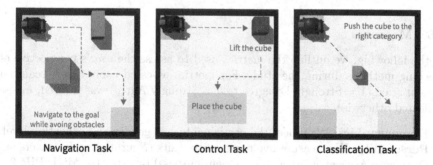

Fig. 2. Experimental tasks: Participants observe the teaching process of a robot within one of three types of tasks: navigation, control and classification.

3.3   Research Questions

The study focuses on two research questions:

- **RQ1.** How does different interactive teaching method influence users' perceptions of the robot?
- **RQ2.** To what extent does the user's characteristics influence their preference for a specific teaching method?
- **RQ3.** How does the nature of the task influence the user perceptions of the robot?

3.4   Participants

We determined the recommended sample size N of participants by conducting an a priori analysis on G*Power (version 3.1) for a MANOVA ($\alpha = .05$, power = .95, number of groups = 9). By considering a small effect ($f^2(V) = 0.0625$), the analysis suggested a sample size of N = 144.

Although the primary focus of this study is to comprehend user perceptions within an educational context, recruiting this number of school-age children as participants would have posed logistical challenges. Consequently, participants were recruited through Prolific, with an age criterion of 18 to 26 years. We hypothesize that by targeting individuals within this younger age range, the findings of this research will extend to a younger demographic, akin to children.

Initially, 145 participants were recruited online. Every participant received a compensation of £1.80 upon completing the study. After excluding individuals who did not fully complete the questionnaire, failed the attention check, and exhibited outliers (>3 standard deviations) for more than one variable of interest, the final sample size consisted of 138 participants ($M_{age} = 22.87$, $SD_{age} = 1.78$, 80 men, 56 women, 1 non-binary).

3.5   Measures

In the following, we outline the metrics used to assess the user's perspective of teaching methods during the study. For metrics assessed using Likert scales, a 5-point scale (1 = Strongly Disagree to 5 = Strongly Agree) was utilised, unless indicated otherwise.

- **Demographics:** We collect the participants age, gender and education level.
- **Personality:** We measure five personality traits (Neuroticism, Extraversion, Openness, Agreeableness, and Conscientiousness) by using the Mini-IPIP, 20-item Likert scale [8].
- **Robotic Prior Experience:** We assess the participants' prior experience with robot through the robotics experience scale, 5-item Likert scale [18].
- **Perceived Control:** we measure the perceived control of participants over the robot by adapting a 3-item Likert scale from Delgosha et al. [7].
- **Responsiveness:** we measure the responsiveness of the robot by adapting the Godspeed's animacy scale into a 2-item Likert scale [1].

- **Likability, Anthropomorphism and Intelligence**: To assess the likability, anthropomorphism and intelligence, we adapted Godspeed's Likability, Anthropomorphism and Intelligence, to 5-item Likert scale [1].
- **Usability and Acceptance:** To assess the usefulness, ease of use, and intent to use of the teaching method, we utilise an 8-item Likert scale adapted from the Technology Acceptance Model (TAM) [2].
- **Perceived success:** We measure the participants' perceived success of the robot by collecting a binary metric.

3.6   Procedure

The study was conducted online through Qualtrics. The survey begun with an informed consent page, followed by questions about demographics, personality traits, and their prior experience with robots.

Afterwards, participants were assigned to one of three teaching conditions (Teaching with evaluative feedback, Teaching with Preferences, and Download condition). Within the teaching condition, participants were further randomly assigned to observe the teaching of a robot in a specific task out of three (navigation, control, and classification). This design yielded a between-subject study structure comprising a total of nine distinct groups.

The rest of the study was organised as follows:

- **Introductory phase:** Participant are first familiarised with their assigned teaching condition, during which we provide explanations about the teaching process involving the robot.
- **Training phase:** Next, participants watch a video of the experimenter instructing a robot to execute a task. The teaching method and task's nature are tailored to each participant based on their assigned conditions. At the end of the training, participants observe the identical final performance of the robot within the assigned task. By maintaining the final performance constant across teaching conditions, we aim to mitigate the risk of performance confounding.
- **Testing phase:** After visioning the training video, participants proceed to watch a sequence of four videos, in which the robot's performance is assessed across diverse environments of the same nature as the assigned task. Similar to [18], we consider different trajectories in the testing trials, encompassing two successful, one ambiguous and one failure. In the ambiguous trajectory, the robot actions may not optimal but ultimately lead to success. By demonstrating a success rate of 75%, as was suggested in prior works [18,24], we aim to replicate real-life scenarios, where failures are more likely to occur. It's worth noting that the testing videos remain consistent for the assigned task, regardless of the teaching condition.

Following this, the participants proceed to complete the survey, where they provide their rankings for their perception of the robot, its task completion success, the effectiveness of the teaching method. To ensure the participant engagement, we introduce an attention check between the testing phase and the questionnaire during the online study.

All videos involving the experimenter training and testing the robot are demonstrated via a Wizard-of-Oz approach. This choice is made to maintain the failure and agent's performance consistent between the conditions [18]. The links to all videos can be found on the project website.

Moreover, in the training phase videos, the teaching with evaluative feedback condition entailed giving feedback to an actual robot, whereas the preference-based condition involved expressing preferences over simulated trajectories of the robot, following the established practice in the literature. All simulations of the study were designed and executed on Webots [23].

4   Results

Prior to conducting the analysis, we evaluated the internal consistency of the survey items using Cronbach's alpha test. Results are reported in the project website. Moving forward, we performed Multivariate Analysis of Variance (MANOVA) considering various dependent variables based on the experimental conditions, accompanied by post-hoc follow-up analyses.

To ensure the validity of parametric tests (such as univariate ANOVA and t-tests), we first checked if the assumptions of normality and homoscedasticity were met using the Shapiro-Wilk test and Levene's test, respectively. In cases where the data did not meet these assumptions or was of an ordinal nature, non-parametric tests were employed. However, MANOVA was an exception to this approach, for which we employ the Pillai-Bartlett trace test, known for its robustness in the presence of assumption violations [10].

We calculated the effect size, d, using Cohen's d coefficient and considered statistical significance at the level of $p < 0.05$. Through the analysis, we made a conscientious effort to align with the recommended best practices detailed in the guidelines by Schrum et al. [21].

4.1   Impact of the Teaching Method on the User's Perception

To assess the potential impact of the teaching method on users' perceptions of the robot, we aggregated data from all tasks and conducted a MANOVA, where teaching methods were treated as independent variables. By employing Pillai's trace as the measure, we identified a significant influence of the teaching method on perceived anthropomorphism, responsiveness, control, and ease of use ($V = 0.11, F(8, 266) = 1.99, p = 0.048$). Figure 3a depicts the significant differences between the teaching conditions.

- **Responsiveness:** A Kruskal Wallis (KW) test revealed a significant effect of the teaching method on perceived responsiveness ($H(2) = 6.46, p = 0.040$). A subsequent Wilcoxon rank sum test with Bonferroni correction indicated that instructing the robot with Evaluative Feedback ($M = 8.14, SD = 1.33$) led to significantly higher perceived responsiveness compared to the Download condition ($M = 7.33, SD = 1.58$), $W = 2.45, p = 0.014, d = 0.56$. However, the perceived responsiveness of the robot while being taught through providing Preferences ($M = 7.69, SD = 1.67$) did not significantly differ from the teaching methods involving Evaluative Feedback and the Download condition.

- **Ease of use:** A significant main effect of the teaching method on the perceived ease of use of the method was identified through a KW test ($H(2) = 6.37, p = 0.041$). Although not meeting the Bonferroni correction threshold, a comparison between teaching conditions showed that the download condition ($M = 7.33, SD = 1.58$) was somewhat perceived as less user-friendly compared to both teaching with evaluative feedback ($M = 8.15, SD = 1.33$), $W = -2.15, p = 0.03, d = -0.42$, and teaching with preferences ($M = 7.69, SD = 1.67$), $W = -2.13, p = 0.03, d = -0.44$. No significant different in perceived ease of use was found between Teaching with Evaluative Feedback and Teaching with Preferences.

However, our analysis did not reveal any significant main effects of the teaching condition on the perceived anthropomorphism, control, intelligence, likability, perceived usefulness, or intent to use the teaching methods.

4.2 Relationships Between User Characteristics and Perceptions of Robot and Teaching Methods

We examined whether the users' personality and background variables were associated with their perceptions of the robot and the teaching method. To ensure the validity of our analysis, we ensured that relevant qualitative measures were evenly distributed across all training conditions, thereby ruling out potential correlations due to sampling biases.

- **Extraversion:** Extraverts demonstrated a more positive perception of the robot in the Teaching with Evaluative Feedback condition. Indeed, in this condition, extraversion traits exhibited a significant positive correlation with the perceived responsiveness ($r = 0.42, p = 0.003$), perceived intelligence ($r = 0.46, p = 0.001$) and likability of the robot ($r = .36, p = 0.015$). Moreover, a Wilcoxon rank-sum test on Extraversion with perceived success as an independent variable indicated that participants who perceived the robot as successful exhibited higher extraversion traits ($M = 11.33, SD = 3.65$) compared to those who perceived the robot as having failed ($M = 9.69, SD = 4$), $W = 2.226\ p = 0.02, d = 0.44$.
- **Intellect:** Intellect traits were highly correlated with the ease of use of the Teaching with preferences ($r = 0.42, p = 0.002$), and likability of the robot ($r = 0.35, p = 0.015$) in the Teaching with Evaluative Feedback condition. Similarly, intellect traits were significantly related to the perceived responsiveness of the robot in the Teaching with Evaluative Feedback ($r = 0.36, p = 0.013$).

- **Prior experience with robotics:** In the Download condition, we observed a strong correlation between prior expertise with robots with the perceived usefulness of the method ($r = 0.37$) as well as the perceived anthropomorphism of the robot ($r = 0.38$), (both $p = 0.013$).

We did not identify any significant relationships between the gender, educational level and other personality traits of the users, and their perception of the robot and the teaching method.

4.3   Impact of the Nature of the Task on the User's Perception

Finally, we investigated whether the nature of the training task influenced the perception of the robot, regardless of the teaching method employed. Combining data from all teaching conditions, we executed a MANOVA with the task's nature as the independent variable. By employing Pillai's trace as the measure, we identified a highly significant influence of the nature of task on perceived anthropomorphism, responsiveness, and control over the robot ($V = 0.14$, $F(6, 268) = 3.41$, $p = 0.003$). Figure 3a illustrates the significant differences between the tasks.

- **Anthropomorphism:** A KW test revealed a significant difference in the perceived anthropomorphism of the robot within the different tasks ($H(2) = 7.39$, $p = 0.025$). After running a Wilcoxon rank-sum, we found that robots were significantly more anthropomorphised in the classification task ($M = 12.29$, $SD = 4.32$) than in the navigation task ($M = 9.98$, $SD = 4.13$), $W = 2.6$, $p=0.009$, $d=0.55$ However, no significant difference emerged in comparison with the control task ($M = 11.08$, $SD = 3.4$).
- **Control:** After running a KW test, we identified a main effect of the nature of the task on the perceived control over the robot ($H(2) = 6.15$, $p = 0.046$). A Wilcoxon rank-sum test revealed that a significantly higher control over the robot was perceived in the classification task ($M = 12.07$, $SD = 2.52$) than in the navigation task ($M = 10.8$, $SD = 2.74$), $W = 2.39$, $p = 0.02$, $d = 0.48$. No difference with the control task was identified ($M = 11.46$, $SD = 2.3$).
- **Responsiveness:** A significant main effect of the nature of the task on the perceived responsiveness of the robot was identified through a KW test ($H(2) = 8.41$, $p = 0.015$). After performing a Wilcoxon rank-sum test, we identified that the perceived responsiveness of the robot was significantly higher in the classification task ($M = 8.27$, $SD = 1.36$) than in the control ($M = 7.29$, $SD = 1.68$), $W = 2.78$, $p = 0.005$, $d = 0.63$. No difference with the navigation task was identified ($M = 7.71$, $SD = 1.49$).

No significant difference was identified among the perceived intelligence and likability of the robot across the tasks.

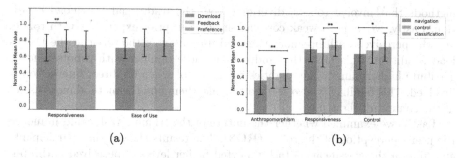

Fig. 3. (a) Comparison of the responsiveness and ease of use between the teaching conditions. (b) Comparison of the anthropomorphism, control and responsiveness between the tasks.

5 Discussion

The results of the study indicate that a user's perception of a teachable robot can be influenced by various factors, including the chosen teaching method, the nature of the task, and the individual's inherent characteristics and background.

Regarding the impact of teaching method on user perception of the robot (**RQ1**), the analysis revealed, with a medium effect size, that participants perceived the robot as more responsive in the Teaching with feedback condition compared to the Download condition. This suggest that the more interaction and human guidance is observed, the more responsive the agent is perceived. Additionally, Teaching with Feedback and with Preferences were perceived as equally user-friendly, and easier to use than the Download condition. This result is contrary to our prior assumptions, as the former methods requires more effort compared to the latter. However, Teaching with Feedback aligns more closely with natural human teaching methods, leading us to postulate that the perceived ease of use is positively influenced by the resemblance to familiar human interactions. However, contrary to [18], our study did not reveal any significant impact of the teaching method on the perceived anthropomorphism of the robot.

Moreover, we examined whether there was a relationship between the personality traits and background of the user with its perception of the robot (**RQ2**). The analysis identified a moderate correlation between extraversion traits and a favourable perception of Teaching with Feedback condition. Extraverts exhibited a significant correlation with the perceived responsiveness, intelligence and likability of the robot within this specific teaching condition. We hypothesize that Teaching with Evaluative Feedback fostered a more dynamic and engaging interaction as the teacher directly interacts with the robot, resonating well with the socially outgoing nature of extraverted individuals. Moreover, intellect traits exhibited a significant correlation with ease of use in the Teaching with Preferences condition and with likability and responsiveness in the Teaching with Evaluative Feedback condition. This implies that individuals possessing higher intellect traits are inclined to be more receptive towards innovative teaching methods that involve robots, diverging from the traditional Download condition. Lastly, we found a weak correlation between prior experience with robots and the perceived anthropomorphism and usefulness of the robot in the Download condition. This hints that individuals more familiar with robots tend to attribute higher human-like qualities to the robot when no direct interaction is involved. This familiarity also seemed to make them find the method more useful in the context of the study.

Lastly, we examined whether the nature of the training task could influence the user's perception of the robot (**RQ3**). The results showed that participants engaging in the classification task reported higher levels of perceived anthropomorphism, control, and responsiveness of the robot in contrast to those in other tasks. This result can be attributed to the classification task's higher level of demand and its incorporation of more social attributes, distinguishing it from the other tasks and necessitating a greater degree of engagement from the participants. We postulate that tasks that require greater engagement and complexity contribute to an increased sense of control and perceived responsiveness over the robot. Additionally, tasks that simulate a more intricate and human-like scenario tend to augment the perceived anthropomorphism of the robot in the eyes of the participants.

6   Limitation

While our study offers valuable insights, several limitations need to be acknowledged that may impact the interpretation and generalisation of the findings.

First, the metric assessing robot responsiveness displayed an internal consistency ($\alpha = 0.6$). While this score is generally perceived as passable, it does not exceed the acceptable range set in this study ($\alpha > 0.7$). Consequently, any results derived from this metric should be treated with caution.

Second, the study was conducted exclusively online. While this allowed a more diverse participant pool, future research could benefit from replication in a face-to-face setting where participants could engage in direct interactions with the robot. The contextual differences between online and in-person interactions could introduce variances in the observed outcomes.

Additionally, although we recruited participants within a young age range, our study primarily focused on adults. Consequently, the generalisability of our findings to children remains uncertain, and further investigation is needed to understand how age influences perceptions of teachable robots.

Lastly, the duration of training for the different teaching methods was not considered in our study. The time required to learn and execute a method could potentially impact participants' perceptions of the robot's performance. Future research could explore the relationship between training duration and user perceptions to gain a more comprehensive understanding of this aspect.

7 Conclusion

In this study, we investigated the impact of teaching methods, task nature, and user characteristics on users' perceptions of robot. Our findings provide valuable insights for including the robots in the education landscape. Teaching with Evaluative Feedback emerged as a preferred method, improving both responsiveness and ease of use compared to the non-interactive condition. Similarly, personality traits influenced teaching preferences, highlighting the need for personalised interactions. Moreover, the task's complexity influenced anthropomorphism, control, and responsiveness, highlighting the importance of task design.

Our study indicates the importance of considering intricate interplay of these factors in HRI, particularly within education. By aligning teaching methods with natural tendencies, personalising interactions based on personality traits, and crafting engaging tasks, we have the opportunity to create more enriching and enjoyable educational experiences with robots.

Acknowledgements. We thank Dimitri Lacroix for his statistical insights during the initial design of the study. This research was supported by European Union's Horizon 2020 research and innovation programme under the Marie Skłodowska-Curie grant agreement No. 955778. For the purpose of open access, the author has applied a Creative Commons Attribution (CC BY) licence to any Author Accepted Manuscript version arising from this submission.

References

1. Bartneck, C., Kulić, D., Croft, E., Zoghbi, S.: Measurement instruments for the anthropomorphism, animacy, likeability, perceived intelligence, and perceived safety of robots. Int. J. Soc. Robot. **1**, 71–81 (2009). https://doi.org/10.1007/s12369-008-0001-3
2. Belanche, D., Casaló, L.V., Flavián, C.: Integrating trust and personal values into the technology acceptance model: the case of e-government services adoption. Cuadernos de Economía y Dirección de la Empresa **15**(4), 192–204 (2012)
3. Belpaeme, T., Kennedy, J., Ramachandran, A., Scassellati, B., Tanaka, F.: Social robots for education: a review. Sci. Robot. **3**(21), eaat5954 (2018)
4. Belpaeme, T., Tanaka, F.: Social robots as educators. In: OECD Digital Education Outlook 2021 Pushing the Frontiers with Artificial Intelligence, Blockchain and Robots: Pushing the Frontiers with Artificial Intelligence, Blockchain and Robots, p. 143. OECD Publishing, Paris (2021)
5. Chetouani, M.: Interactive robot learning: an overview. In: Chetouani, M., Dignum, V., Lukowicz, P., Sierra, C. (eds.) ACAI 2021. LNAI, vol. 13500, pp. 140–172. Springer, Cham (2023). https://doi.org/10.1007/978-3-031-24349-3_9
6. Christiano, P.F., Leike, J., Brown, T., Martic, M., Legg, S., Amodei, D.: Deep reinforcement learning from human preferences. In: Advances in Neural Information Processing Systems, vol. 30 (2017)
7. Delgosha, M.S., Hajiheydari, N.: How human users engage with consumer robots? A dual model of psychological ownership and trust to explain post-adoption behaviours. Comput. Hum. Behav. **117**, 106660 (2021)

8. Donnellan, M.B., Oswald, F.L., Baird, B.M., Lucas, R.E.: The mini-IPIP scales: tiny-yet-effective measures of the Big Five factors of personality. Psychol. Assess. **18**(2), 192 (2006)
9. Faulkner, T.A.K., Thomaz, A.L.: Using learning curve predictions to learn from incorrect feedback. In: 2023 IEEE International Conference on Robotics and Automation (ICRA), pp. 9414–9420. IEEE (2023)
10. Field, Z., Miles, J., Field, A.: Discovering Statistics Using R, pp. 1–992 (2012)
11. Hejna III, D.J., Sadigh, D.: Few-shot preference learning for human-in-the-loop RL. In: Conference on Robot Learning, pp. 2014–2025. PMLR (2023)
12. Ho, M.K., MacGlashan, J., Littman, M.L., Cushman, F.: Social is special: a normative framework for teaching with and learning from evaluative feedback. Cognition **167**, 91–106 (2017)
13. Jamet, F., Masson, O., Jacquet, B., Stilgenbauer, J.L., Baratgin, J.: Learning by teaching with humanoid robot: a new powerful experimental tool to improve children's learning ability. J. Robot. **2018**, 1–11 (2018)
14. Johal, W.: Research trends in social robots for learning. Curr. Robot. Rep. **1**, 75–83 (2020). https://doi.org/10.1007/s43154-020-00008-3
15. Knox, W.B., Stone, P.: Interactively shaping agents via human reinforcement: the TAMER framework. In: Proceedings of the Fifth International Conference on Knowledge Capture, pp. 9–16 (2009)
16. Lee, K., Smith, L., Abbeel, P.: PEBBLE: feedback-efficient interactive reinforcement learning via relabeling experience and unsupervised pre-training. arXiv preprint arXiv:2106.05091 (2021)
17. Loftin, R., et al.: Learning behaviors via human-delivered discrete feedback: modeling implicit feedback strategies to speed up learning. Auton. Agent. Multi-Agent Syst. **30**, 30–59 (2016). https://doi.org/10.1007/s10458-015-9283-7
18. Moorman, N., Hedlund-Botti, E., Schrum, M., Natarajan, M., Gombolay, M.C.: Impacts of robot learning on user attitude and behavior. In: Proceedings of the 2023 ACM/IEEE International Conference on Human-Robot Interaction, pp. 534–543 (2023)
19. Najar, A., Chetouani, M.: Reinforcement learning with human advice: a survey. Front. Robot. AI **8**, 584075 (2021)
20. Rohlfing, K.J., et al.: Social/dialogical roles of social robots in supporting children's learning of language and literacy-a review and analysis of innovative roles. Front. Robot. AI **9**, 251 (2022)
21. Schrum, M., Ghuy, M., Hedlund-Botti, E., Natarajan, M., Johnson, M., Gombolay, M.: Concerning trends in likert scale usage in human-robot interaction: towards improving best practices. ACM Trans. Hum.-Robot Interact. **12**(3), 1–32 (2023)
22. Thomaz, A.L., Breazeal, C.: Teachable robots: understanding human teaching behavior to build more effective robot learners. Artif. Intell. **172**(6–7), 716–737 (2008)
23. Webots: open-source Mobile Robot Simulation Software. http://www.cyberbotics.com
24. Yang, X.J., Unhelkar, V.V., Li, K., Shah, J.A.: Evaluating effects of user experience and system transparency on trust in automation. In: Proceedings of the 2017 ACM/IEEE International Conference on Human-Robot Interaction, pp. 408–416 (2017)

Evaluating Customers' Engagement Preferences for Multi-party Interaction with a Robot Bartender

Alessandra Rossi$^{(\boxtimes)}$ ⓘ, Christian Menna, Emanuele Giordano,
and Silvia Rossi ⓘ

Dipartimento di Ingegneria Elettrica e delle Tecnologie dell'Informazione,
Universitá Degli Studi di Napoli Federico II, Via Claudio, 21, 80125 Napoli, Italy
{alessandra.rossi,silvia.rossi}@unina.it

Abstract. In this paper, we present a two parts study where we investigate whether socially relevant interactions depend on a bartender robot's ability to maintain engaged interactions with two users at a time, by alternating its attention between the two customers, and by capturing their attention by personalising the discussion topics to the users' preferences. We recruited 20 participants in the first study, and 6 participants in the second study. We observed that participants were more comfortable and enjoyed interacting with the robot when the robot personalised interaction and alternated the service between the two users, compared to when the robot did not personalise the talk and served the users according to their arrival time. However, we observed that in both conditions, the participants did not feel excluded while waiting for the other to finish their interaction with the robot. Finally, personalised interaction topics increased participants' interest in the conversation with the robot. These results guide us to design and deploy a robot that adapts its behaviours to have rich and multi-party interactions in real settings.

Keywords: Engagement · Robot bartender · Service robot · Social robotics

1 Introduction

While robots are being used in hospitality to attract customers, they can ensure customer retention only by creating long-lasting relationships. This means that a service robot needs to provide a service and have social skills that allow it to meet customers' expectations. To this extent, it is fundamental for robots to engage customers by establishing when to start and keep active an appropriate

This work has been supported by Italian PON I&C 2014-2020 within BRILLO research project "Bartending Robot for Interactive Long-Lasting Operations", no. F/190066/01-02/X44 and Italian PON R&I 2014-2020 - REACT-EU Azione IV.4 (CUP E65F21002920003).

and delightful interaction, or to stop it when people are clearly not interested. Personalisation provides a fundamental way to strengthen the relationship in human-robot interaction (HRI) by increasing people's engagement during the interactions [3], and, as a consequence, service satisfaction [6]. The ability to keep people's engagement during a human-robot interaction and to adapt the behaviours to the human could allow a robot and improve the quality of their interaction [14].

In a bar scenario, such as the one that inspired the Bartending Robot for Interactive Long-Lasting Operations (BRILLO) project [12], it is expected that customers are served according to their arriving order, but, at the same time, current and new customers expect to be addressed or to be able to talk with their human bartender. However, while cognitive architectures have been investigated for a long time, robots still do not have the capability of understanding the situational context and engaging the users in natural dialogues according to the users' intentions and desires [9]. The BRILLO project aims to deploy in real-world scenarios a robotic platform that is able to accomplish both the expected management of a bar (i.e., preparing drinks) and the socially intelligent interaction, context-awareness, and personalisation of the robot's behaviours. To this extent, BRILLO robots need to learn when and how to engage and disengage with a person. It is not clear whether people's expectations of the interaction with a robot bartender correspond to the one expected from a human bartender, in terms of the order in serving and engagement. Previous works modelling engagement were mainly focused on dyadic scenarios [8], and some studies (e.g., [7]) engaged people in controlled conversations, and only a few works engaged in group interactions [15]. Group interactions present several challenges due to the complex and variety of parameters involved, such as roles, positions of members, and personalities. In this work, we want to establish whether customers' engagement and perception of the interaction vary based on the different turn-taking modalities of the robot's attention. Considering the BRILLO is able to prepare two drinks at the same time (i.e., serving two customers - see Fig. 1), in this work we have tested the robot's interactions with two users at the same time.

After establishing whether customers prefer to engage with BRILLO based on their arriving order or share the robot's attention with another customer, it is important to establish how to maintain active their attention in the HRI during time. User engagement can be achieved by a robot through several strategies that include verbal and non-verbal cues. For example, these include the use of laughter, turn-taking signals [2], common verbal turn-holding or turn-initial cues are so-called fillers or filled pauses, such as "uh" or "um" [1]. Within turn-taking cues, techniques include the change of the pitch (i.e., lowering the voice) [4], joint attention and using gestures [5] when approaching a change of turn to guide an interlocutor's attention and response. The BRILLO robot bartender is endowed with the capability of choosing a different interaction style based on the user's interests and moods and previous interactions (whether the user is a recurrent customer, or the history of the interactions is built upon the customer's current choices). Pertaining to social interaction, the robot is capable of dialogue with customers, to providing recommendations based on the details of their previous interactions. Moreover, the robot uses non-verbal cues, such as facial and body gestures, posture and sounds, in response to customers' engagement level, sentiment analysis of their dialogues and facial expressions, topics of interest in dialogues, previous interactions and orders [14]. Moreover, since previous works showed that social engagement also includes affective components [8,17], in relation to fun and entertainment [10,16], BRILLO robot is endowed with the ability to use customers' information for suggesting both preferred or new drinks and personalise the interaction by dialoguing with customers about several topics (e.g., news and jokes).

Here, we present a two-part study where we investigated whether socially relevant interactions depend on a bartender robot's ability to maintain engaged interactions with two users at a time, by alternating its attention (both while it is confirming the order made by the customers and during the interaction phase) between the two customers and by capturing their attention personalising the discussion topics (both serious and ironic) to the users' preferences.

2 Experimental Approach

The scenario used resembled the conversation between a robotic bartender and two human customers. Participants, at first, registered at the kiosk and bought a drink of their choice (i.e., a smoothie or a cocktail). Then, they moved to stand in front of the robot that greeted them after recognising them by their facial biometrical data, and the robot confirmed or modified the customer's drink order. While the robot was preparing the requested drink, it engaged the customers in small talk (i.e., news from two Italian well-known sources using Twitter APIs - tweepy[1]). After a few minutes of conversation, the robot served the drink ordered to the participant.

The robot used in these studies has two Kuka1 LBR iiwa 14 R820 robotic arms (each of 7 DoF and gripper), attached to a fixed torso, and a Furhat Robotics head[2] (3 DoF) with facial features projected, and the ability to generate several human-like emotional and communicative expressions. The robot interacting with two customers is shown in Fig. 1.

3 Study 1: Engagement Managing Serving Priorities

This study was organised with a between-subject experimental design in which two participants at a time were served by and interacted with a bartender robot. Each couple of participants was assigned according to one of the following two experimental conditions: 1) **T-C1** the robot confirmed the drinks previously selected by both participants, and it prepared the drinks and alternated the small talk between the two participants; 2) **NT-C2** the robot confirmed the

---

[1] Tweepy libraries https://www.tweepy.org/.

[2] Furhat Robotics https://furhat.io.

Fig. 1. A snapshot of the robot while interacting with two users.

drinks previously selected by both participants, but the robot engaged the second participant only after that the first participant received it. To be noted, the robot served the participants in the order in which they placed their orders in both conditions, following a standard real service-customers approach.

Participants were asked to answer two sets of questionnaires at the beginning and end of the experimental study. A pre-study questionnaire was used to collect participants' responses about their demographic data (age, gender, occupation), and assess their experience with robots. We also asked participants about their habits and behaviours in possible bar scenarios. Questions about people's behaviours and habits are elaborated by taking inspiration from previous studies [13], and considerations on real scenarios (see Table 1).

A post-study questionnaire evaluated their perception of the robot ("the robot has been a great bartender", "I would like to have the robot as my usual bartender", "I would like to be served again by the robot") and interaction ("I was comfortable during the interaction with the robot"). We also asked participants whether they felt to be excluded during the interaction with the robot and to justify their answer as an open question. We collected participants' responses using a 7-point Likert Scale (from 1 = strongly disagree to 7 = strongly agree). Finally, we video-recorded each experimental trial for further analysis of the participants' behaviours.

3.1   Results

We collected the responses of 20 participants (7 female, 13 male, no non-binary), aged between 19 and 39 (avg. 24.7, st.dv. 4.6), recruited at the University of Naples Federico II. The majority of the participants (80%) were students, a

Table 1. Questionnaire set provided to participants in Study 1 and Study 2 before starting the interaction with the robot.

QUESTIONS	ANSWERS
"How many times do you go in a bar?"	7-points semantic scale (from Never to Several times for day)
"If you go into bars, where do you prefer to sit?"	At the table At the counter
"If you go into bars, do you engage the bartender in conversation?"	"Yes, I start to talk" "Yes, if the bartender talks to me" "No"
"If you go into bars, how long do you stay on average?"	Less than 10 min Half hour Less than an hour A couple of hours
"If you go into bars, where do you prefer to go?"	"I like to go always in the same bar" "I always try out new bars" "I do not have preferences"
"If you go into bars, do you prefer to drink:?"	Alone With someone Both

researcher, one administrative, and a designer. Most of the participants (80%) had very low (as participants in another study or for watching videos of robots on YouTube or other social media) or no previous experience with a robot. The remaining participants had some experience in developing programs for robotics applications.

As part of the questionnaire pre-experiment, we were interested in participants' habits and behaviours in bars. Most of the participants stated to go to a bar once a week and several times a week (respectively, 40%), while 15% of participants go once a month, and the remaining less than once a month. The majority of participants (50%) preferred to neither initiate conversations with human bartenders nor avoid talking to them. On the contrary, a 25% of the participants engaged human bartenders, and the remaining stated to not talk to them. When participants were asked how long they usually spend in a bar, they disclosed, respectively: half an hour (40%); less than an hour (25%); a couple of hours (15%); and, less than 10 min (10%). However, participants did not seem to have any preferences for bars. Their choices were almost equally distributed between the three options (i.e., 40% stated to not have preferences, 30% respectively preferred to discover new bars, and the same one). We also asked the participants whether they go to a bar in a company, by themselves, or both. The majority (80%) of participants usually frequent bars in a company, and 20% of participants answered both.

Participants' Perception of the Robot. As part of the questionnaire post-experiment, we collected participants' considerations of the robot. When they were asked whether the BRILLO robot was a good bartender, 40% agreed, while the remaining (30%) equally had a poorer, and neither positive nor negative opinion of the robot. However, the 60% of the participants would like to have BRILLO as a bartender and serve them again, while the remaining would not like it. The majority of participants (65%) also felt comfortable while interacting with the robot.

Participants' Perception of the Interaction. Overall, the majority of participants (90%) stated to not feel excluded while interacting with the robot. One participant stated to have felt neither excluded nor included in their interaction with the robot.

To further understand participants' choices, we coded and categorized for content analysis their answers given to the open-ended question to explain why they did or did not feel excluded during the interaction. We observed that participants interacting with the robot in **T-C1** felt that the robot engaged both participants equally; while in **NT-C2**, participants who were not first-served stated that their engagement with the robot increased when the robot finished interacting with the first customer and concentrate exclusively in interacting with them. In both cases, they did not feel excluded by the robot in the interaction. However, observing the recordings of HRI, we noticed that most of the participants in **NT-C2** looked bored and distant when it was not their turn to interact with the robot, and looked relieved and eager to talk at their turn.

4   Study 2: Engagement via Personalised Interaction

A second between-subject study was organised to investigate whether personalised news increased participants' engagement with the bartender robot. Participants interacted with the robot over 10 non-consecutive sessions. Each participant was assigned to one of two experimental conditions for the whole 10 days: 1) **P-C1** the robot interacted with the participant by presenting news based on their preferences; 2) **NP-C2** the robot interacted with the participant by randomly choosing news.

Participants were asked to complete a questionnaire on the first day of interaction to collect their demographics (age, gender, occupation), assess their experience with robots, their habits and behaviours in bar scenarios (see Table 1), and their preferences in terms of news, such as sport, culture, politics, TV, cinema, and how they prefer to acquire them, such as Twitter, magazines, TV, Facebook. After each round, during the interaction, participants were asked to rate the proposed news, in terms of interest, by the robot. In this way, the robot was able, from time to time, to update the user model in terms of likeness probabilities associated with the available topics of conversation.

Finally, on the last day of interactions, we evaluated their perception of the robot as a bartender, such as whether it was pleasant, whether they would have liked to have BRILLO as their bartender, and whether they felt comfortable during the interaction.

We collected participants' responses to measure their perception of the robot, interaction and proposed news by using a 7-point Likert scale (from 1 - strongly disagree to 7 - strongly agree). The interactions between the robot and the participants were also video-recorded for further analysing the participants' behaviours.

4.1 Results

We collected the responses of 6 participants (1 male and 5 female, no non-binary), aged between 22 and 39 (avg. 29.6, st.dv. 5.6), recruited at the University of Naples Federico II. The participants in this study also were students for the majority (50%), while the remaining were researchers (33.3%), and a designer. One participant stated to have previous experience in programming robots, while the previous interactions of the remaining participants (84%) with robots were limited to having been part of other studies.

We, then, built participants' base profiles and preferences of interests and habits in bars. We used the categories (e.g., culture, news, sport) and type (i.e., real or funny/satiric) of news they were interested in to build their profile. Participants' answers included multiple and varied topics (see Fig. 2), and they usually get the news from TV and Facebook, but never from Twitter.

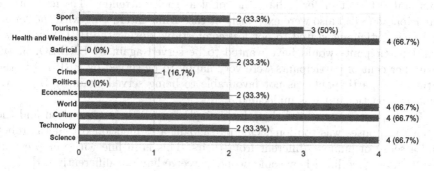

Fig. 2. Participants' preferences for news categories.

Participants equally stated to go several times a week, once a week, or once a month (33.33%) to a bar, and the majority of participants (33.3%) usually spent less than one hour, while the remaining for 10 min, half an hour or at least two hours. Moreover, most of the participants preferred to sit at a table (84%) instead of the counter, and to go in the company of other people (84%) or both with other people and on their own (16%).

As in the first study, participants stated to be regular customers of the same bar (50%), to prefer always trying new bars (34%), or to not have preferences (16%). Finally, the majority of participants (84%) usually talk to their human bartenders, but only 33.3% initiate a conversation with them, while 50% of participants prefer to be engaged by the bartender. One participant stated to prefer to not talk to the human bartender.

The Interaction with the Robot. During the interaction, we saved information related to the interactions (e.g., duration), category and type of the proposed news, and people's responses to the robot's questions.

The average duration of the interaction with BRILLO lasted around 6 min for each participant - noticed that this does not include the average time needed for preparing the drink, which is 2 min and a half. On average, participants listened to 84 news in condition NP-C2, and 72 news were, instead, proposed to the participants in condition P-C1 on average. The difference number of news proposed depends mainly on the interaction preference of the participants. Indeed, in order to keep a pleasant interaction with the robot, the robot stopped entertaining the participants with new news if they refused to hear one three times (even if they were not consecutive).

Participants' Perception of the Robot. The majority of participants (84%) considered BRILLO as a great bartender, while one participant did not agree or disagree on whether BRILLO's performances were up to the task. Participants also were very happy to have BRILLO as a bartender (67%), one participant did not agree or disagree on wanting BRILLO as their bartender, and one participant stated to not prefer to have the robot as their bartender. The majority of participants (84%) also were extremely at ease while interacting with the robot, and one participant stated to not feel comfortable during the HRI. Finally, we asked participants would have wanted to be served again by BRILLO. Sixty-seven per cent of participants were very happy to be served by BRILLO in the future, one participant was not favourable to being served again by BRILLO, while one participant was undecided.

Participants commented that the timing between their interaction and the robot's responses was too long. One participant also mentioned that the robot had a sense of humour different from theirs. This is in line with our previous results that underlined how some people perceive humour differently [11].

Participants' Perception of the Interaction. We asked participants to rate their level of interest in the news proposed by the robot by using a 7-point Likert scale (from 1 = Strongly disagree to 7 = Strongly agree).

Overall, participants found the news proposed by the robot very interesting or they did not agree or disagree whether they were interested in the news. No participants believed that any of the news was not interesting at all. In particular, we can observe in Fig. 3 that while the average of their interest in the news proposed is overall medium-high, it is much more fluctuant when participants interacted with a robot that did not choose the news based on their preferences (condition NP-C2). On the contrary, we can observe an increase in participants' appreciation of the news over time when the robot proposed news based on their profile and preferences (condition P-C1).

Overall, participants in NP-C2 (on average 57% of the news proposed) accepted more often to hear news proposed by BRILLO than participants in P-C1 (on average 44% of the news proposed). On average, participants tested in NP-C2 condition enjoyed slightly more the news proposed compared to the participants in P-C1 (36% vs. 28% of the news proposed). We believe that this is due to the lower exposure of the participants in P-C1 to the personalised news.

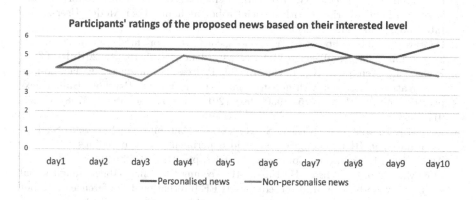

Fig. 3. Participants' rating of the proposed news based on their interest in the news.

5   Conclusions and Future Works

In this two-part work, we investigated how a bartending robot can provide an efficient service while keeping engaged human customers in a dynamic, multi-modal and multi-user interaction. In particular, in the first study, we were interested in evaluating whether participants felt more engaged with a robot who served them by alternating the interaction between two participants or when the robot served them according to their arrival time. We observed that while participants expected to be served upon their arrival, they also found it more comfortable and enjoyable their interaction when the robot splits its attention between the two users. In the second study, we investigated whether the personalisation of the news proposed by the BRILLO robot could help improve customers' engagement in long-term interactions. We observed that participants had an overall positive interaction with the robot despite the conditions they were tested with, however, the personalisation of the news produced a constant increase in the interest of participants in the news, and therefore in the interaction with the robot.

These results are fundamental for shaping the robot's personalised behaviours while interacting with multi-users in real settings. In this direction, future works will include the test of the BRILLO system in an ecological environment where the BRILLO robots will be able to build a stronger profile of the users based on their preferences in news in longer exposure and differentiating the small talk.

References

1. Ball, P.: Listeners' responses to filled pauses in relation to floor apportionment. Br. J. Soc. Clin. Psychol. **14**(4), 423–424 (1975). https://doi.org/10.1111/j.2044-8260.1975.tb00198.x
2. Becker-Asano, C., Kanda, T., Ishi, C., Ishiguro, H.: How about laughter? perceived naturalness of two laughing humanoid robots. In: 2009 3rd International Conference on Affective Computing and Intelligent Interaction and Workshops, pp. 1–6 (2009). https://doi.org/10.1109/ACII.2009.5349371
3. Di Napoli, C., Ercolano, G., Rossi, S.: Personalized home-care support for the elderly: a field experience with a social robot at home. User Model. User-Adap. Inter. **33**(2), 405–440 (2023)
4. D Gravano, A., Hirschberg, J.: Turn-taking cues in task-oriented dialogue. Comput. Speech Lang. **25**(3), 601–634 (2011). https://doi.org/10.1016/j.csl.2010.10.003
5. Holler, J., Kendrick, K., Levinson, S.: Processing language in face-to-face conversation: questions with gestures get faster responses. Psychon. Bull. Unexpected Ampersand Rev. **25**, 1900–1908 (2017). https://doi.org/10.3758/s13423-017-1363-z
6. Lee, M.K., Forlizzi, J., Kiesler, S., Rybski, P., Antanitis, J., Savetsila, S.: Personalization in HRI: A longitudinal field experiment. In: Proceedings of the 7th ACM/IEEE International Conference on HRI, pp. 319–326 (2012)
7. Lim, M., Robb, D., Wilson, B., Hastie, H.: Feeding the coffee habit: a longitudinal study of a robo-barista. In: Proceedings - IEEE International Conference on Robot and Human Interactive Communication (RO-MAN 2023), pp. 1–8 (2023)
8. Oertel, C., et al.: Engagement in human-agent interaction: an overview. Front. Robot. AI **7**, 92 (2020)
9. Prescott, T.J., Robillard, J.M.: Are friends electric? the benefits and risks of human-robot relationships. Iscience **24**(1), 101993 (2021). https://doi.org/10.1016/j.isci.2020.101993
10. Rehm, M., Jensen, M.L.: Accessing cultural artifacts through digital companions: the effects on children's engagement. In: 2015 International Conference on Culture and Computing (Culture Computing), pp. 72–79 (2015). https://doi.org/10.1109/Culture.and.Computing.2015.44
11. Rossi, A., John, N.E., Taglialatela, G., Rossi, S.: Generating emotional gestures for handling social failures in HRI. In: 2022 31st IEEE International Conference on Robot and Human Interactive Communication (RO-MAN), pp. 1399–1404 (2022)
12. Rossi, A., Maro, M.D., Origlia, A., Palmiero, A., Rossi, S.: A ROS architecture for personalised HRI with a bartender social robot (2022)
13. Rossi, A., Perugia, G., Rossi, S.: Investigating customers' perceived sensitivity of information shared with a robot bartender. In: Li, H., et al. (eds.) ICSR 2021. LNCS (LNAI), vol. 13086, pp. 119–129. Springer, Cham (2021). https://doi.org/10.1007/978-3-030-90525-5_11
14. Rossi, A., Rossi, S.: Engaged by a bartender robot: recommendation and personalisation in human-robot interaction, pp. 115–119 (2021). https://doi.org/10.1145/3450614.3463423
15. Salam, H., Çeliktutan, O., Hupont, I., Gunes, H., Chetouani, M.: Fully automatic analysis of engagement and its relationship to personality in human-robot interactions. IEEE Access **5**, 705–721 (2017)

16. Vázquez, M., Steinfeld, A., Hudson, S.E., Forlizzi, J.: Spatial and other social engagement cues in a child-robot interaction: effects of a sidekick. In: Proceedings of the 2014 ACM/IEEE International Conference on HRI, pp. 391–398 (2014)

17. Youssef, A.B., Varni, G., Essid, S., Clavel, C.: On-the-fly detection of user engagement decrease in spontaneous human-robot interaction. Int. J. Soc. Robot. **11**, 815–828 (2019). https://doi.org/10.1007/s12369-019-00591-2

Personalizing Multi-modal Human-Robot Interaction Using Adaptive Robot Behavior

Marcos Maroto-Gómez[✉][iD], Allison Huisa-Rojas, Álvaro Castro-González[iD], María Malfaz[iD], and Miguel Ángel Salichs[iD]

Systems Engineering and Automation, University Carlos III of Madrid, Av. de la Universidad, 30, 28911 Leganés, Madrid, Spain
{marmarot,acgonzal,mmalfaz,salichs}@ing.uc3m.es

Abstract. Technology favors better life expectancy, changing the population distribution. This change is known as population aging and brings a lack of care professionals for older and impaired people. Social robotics has become a promising alternative to alleviate this problem in recent years, assisting society. Human-robot interaction is a research area related to social robotics that explores designing effective methods for appropriately understanding robots and users. This paper investigates the design of personalized Human-robot Interaction strategies to provide an adapted experience that facilitates vulnerable people's use of the Mini social robot. The robot uses Random Forest classification to facilitate multi-modal interaction by predicting the most suitable parameters regarding the interaction time, font size, audio volume, answer time, exercise level, and answer channel. The classification problem is solved using a dataset from 240 participants who completed an online survey about their features and interaction modalities, completing activities about audio, visual, and motor skills. The results show the promising classification scores that Random Forest produced for this task and describe the application of the predicted information during the interaction of the Mini robot with an older adult.

Keywords: Human-robot interaction · Adaptive behavior · Personalized Behavior · Machine Learning · Social Robotics

1 Introduction

The aging of the population in developed countries is increasing. This fact is expected to bring in a lack of care professionals, so the assistance of robots might be beneficial to reduce the workload of caregivers and improve our quality of life. Social robotics is a promising technology that assists vulnerable people, such as older adults with motor, vision, or audition impairments. In recent years, social robotics have demonstrated positive results in medical health care, day-to-day companionship, rehabilitation activities, and help to reduce loneliness and social

A. Al. Ali et al. (Eds.): ICSR 2023, LNAI 14454, pp. 382–393, 2024.
https://doi.org/10.1007/978-981-99-8718-4_33

isolation [11]. In this application, Human-robot interaction (HRI) methods are essential to design useful robots that effectively understand and communicate with their users.

Social robotics challenges the development of robots capable of perceiving their users' behavior and features and molding their HRI to them. This aspect becomes more critical when the robot has to deal with users with special needs since they typically have more problems using the robot and completing the intended tasks. Multi-modal HRI tackles this problem by proposing methods that allow users to interact with the robot using different modalities (e.g., voice, touch, or gestures). Offering users the possibility to interact differently reduces user limitations, leading to a more natural and effective interaction [15].

This paper presents a method based on supervised classification to improve the adaptive HRI of social robots when interacting with people that might present limitations. We built a dataset using an online survey, where 240 participants provided their demographic information and completed activities oriented to obtain their performance and interaction modalities for some of the parameters that play a role in multi-modal HRI: *interaction time, font size, audio volume, answer time, exercises level,* and *answer channel*. An online survey with a predictor was chosen to increase the efficiency and scalability of the data acquisition. Face-to-face interactions with robots are lengthy and require resources that online surveys reduce. Besides, the predictor enables personalizing HRI from the first interaction, something that with other techniques like Reinforcement Learning is impossible. With the dataset ready, we developed a Random Forest (RF) classifier to predict the best values for the previous interaction parameters for each user. Once the interaction parameters are predicted, they are used to complete user profiles. During the HRI, the system adapts its dynamics based on the user profile information. The results describe how our proposed methodology generates multi-modal and adaptive HRI in the Mini robot [16] with promising predictive scores for most of the adapted parameters.

2   Related Work

HRI depends not only on the human user's skills and features but also on the robot's ability to adapt to their behavior and needs [14]. Designing social robots with social behavior challenges perceiving the environment and the agent to interact correctly. According to [2], robots can be designed centered on the human they assist, centered on the robot itself and the task it performs, or combining both approaches. In this work, we propose a human-centered design, as the robot's goal is to personalize HRI by using classification methods and adapting the interaction modalities to the user features.

Supervised classification techniques have a significant impact on human-centered designs. These methods influence HRI by classifying user features to predict information that benefits the adaptation to the user. This research area interests many scientists involved in social robotics and HRI, as Martins et al. [13] presented in their review. They analyze recent works describing adaptive techniques based on static user models (defined user features) to adapt the interaction of social robots. The authors state the importance of including a user model to yield personalized decision-making to improve HRI and the user experience.

Aly & Tapus [1] presented a research work intended to adapt the personality of a social robot to the user features. The adaptive setup takes place thanks to a previously generated profile that stores information of each user. Recent studies developed in 2015 [7,8] suggest modeling the interaction helps people in day-to-day activities. In these studies, the authors model the robot's actions while helping to dress a person. The adaptation is based on user information stored in a profile that the robot understands to overcome the limitations that appear during the interaction. Focused on personalized assistive robotics, the Hobbit robot [6] provides different services adapted to the needs of the older adult it interacts with. In this work, the robot overcomes the user's interactive limitations using a multi-modal HRI manager that adapts interaction parameters like the robot's voice volume, navigation, and manipulation. Their results show how users perceive the robot more positively when including personalized HRI.

In recent years, some authors have attempted to achieve personalized interaction tailored to the dynamic needs of patients. Louie & Nejat [10] developed a learning-by-demonstration system to train Tangy, a social robot working on personalizing activities for users. Their method allows tailoring the interaction to the physical and cognitive needs of the senior, just as a caregiver would do. More recently, Benedictis et al. [3] proposed a solution based on the classification from user models to perform personalized interactions for the cognitive stimulation of adult people. Adaptation is achieved according to the characteristics of the user and his dynamic reactions during the interaction. This adaptation also assists within households. Di Napoli et al. [4] presented an experiment of adaptability and personalization within the home of 7 elderly patients for 118 days. The robot adapted assistance tasks such as cognitive and entertainment activities according to the user features and the dynamic environment. The study revealed increased satisfaction and attachment to the robot with personalization.

The previous studies highlight that personalized social robots with classification methods yield more positive and natural HRI. However, they do not focus on adapting specific parameters to, for example, people with hearing problems. The following sections describe the HRI model based on RF classification we have developed to personalize specific interaction parameters that might affect people with limitations during HRI activities with the Mini social robot.

3   Mini Social Robot

Mini [16] is the social robot used for implementing the model presented in this paper. The model aims to personalize HRI during entertainment, companionship, and cognitive stimulation activities. It was born from the need to assist caregivers to assist older adults with mild cognitive impairment.

Mini provides services in entertainment with different games, personal assistance, or cognitive training following the guidelines of caregivers. At the same

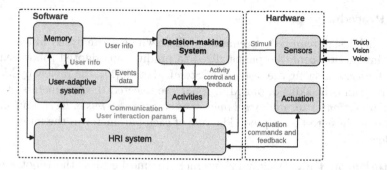

Fig. 1. The software architecture of the Mini social robot. Highlighted in orange are the robot's memory and the user-adaptive system, the modules where the classification model for adaptive HRI has been integrated. The robot's memory stores the user information, which is loaded when the robot recognizes a user. Then, the user-adaptive system predicts and sends the user interaction parameters to the HRI system to personalize the interaction. (Color figure online)

time, Mini provides companionship to their users. These activities can be performed thanks to a multi-modal HRI system that enables executing activities using different interaction modalities. Mini has a sound system consisting of a microphone and a speaker to speak and understand the user. The robot has three touch sensors distributed along its body to perceive tactile information. Finally, it can display audio, images, and videos using a touch screen that is also used to complete different activities such as games or cognitive stimulation exercises.

The application and capabilities of Mini make it suitable for HRI. However, during HRI activities, the features and needs of each user might be different and should be personalized for a more efficient understanding between both agents. Considering the benefits of the multi-modal HRI Mini, the model described in the following section emphasizes the personalization of interaction parameters using RF classification. This model is integrated into the ROS software architecture of Mini, which is shown in Fig. 1. The model, called *Interaction Predictor*, runs as a predictor inside a User-adaptive system connected to the robot's memory and the HRI manager. The Interaction Predictor obtains information from the user profile to predict interaction parameters sent to the HRI system to manage the communication with the user while executing the activities defined by the Decision-making system.

4   Model Design

This section describes the procedure for designing a classification model to predict six parameters and personalize the interaction methods between humans and robots.

4.1 Procedure

The model design required a preliminary phase where we analyzed which aspects of the interaction could be personalized to produce an adapted robot behavior for each user. Following the research of Steinfeld et al. [17], the review by Martins et al. [13], and the skills of our Mini robot, we selected the parameters of *interaction time, font size, audio volume, answer time, exercises level,* and *answer channel* as those to be adapted. The role of each parameter in the interaction is as follows:

- **Interaction time:** Maximum interaction time between the robot and the user. This time may vary depending on the purpose of the interaction and the user. Very long interactions may be boring, while very short interactions may lead to miscommunication. The selected values that this parameter can take are 5 min, 10 min, 15 min, 20 min, and 30 min.
- **Font size:** The touch screen is often used to interact with Mini. Adapting the font size to the users' needs can be beneficial for visually impaired people who need larger fonts. The three values that the font size can take considering Arial font are small (11), medium (14), and large (20).
- **Audio volume:** The robot uses speakers to reproduce its voice and non-verbal sounds and the touch screen for the activities. Adapting the voice and the tablet to the user's needs is important, especially for hearing-impaired or older people. Three standard values have been taken: low (25% of the maximum), medium (50%), and high (75%).
- **Answer time:** Defined as the time it takes the user to complete a request from the robot. This variable acts as a watchdog to avoid excessive delays. Default times have been selected in the robot: 20 s, 30 s, 40 s, and 50 s.
- **Exercises level:** Defines the activities level executed with the robot. A level that is too easy can be dull and uninspiring, while a level that is too difficult can demotivate and frustrate. All games have three established values for this feature: easy, medium, and difficult.
- **Answer channel:** Mini perceives the environment from the touch sensors, user speech (via microphone) or the touch screen. Users may prefer or need a specific communication to overcome motor, hearing, or visual impairments. The options for this parameter are the touch screen, speech, or touch sensors.

After selecting the parameters to be personalized using classification algorithms, we collected the necessary data to build a dataset. First, we selected those user demographic features that are worth considering. Next, data processing is performed, filtering out redundant data and keeping the necessary information to obtain the best possible results. Finally, we tested different supervised classification methods for the most appropriate algorithm.

4.2 Online Survey

The online survey consisted of 33 questions and activities to generate a dataset for the classification algorithm. The survey was built in Spanish using *Wooclap,*

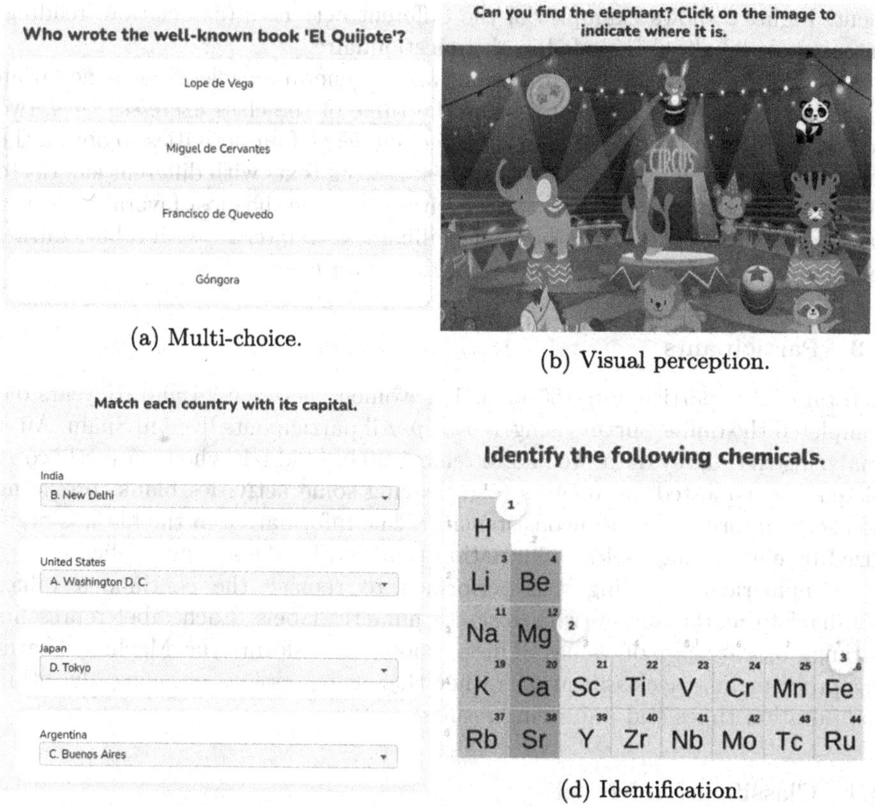

(a) Multi-choice.

(b) Visual perception.

(c) Association.

(d) Identification.

Fig. 2. Activities shown in the online survey to obtain the user performance in different skills.

a well-known website for designing questionnaires. The input vector consisted of 12 demographic questions that retrieved personal data from the participants. The demographic categories were age, gender, education, occupation, technology knowledge, use of robots, reading frequency, motor problems, audition problems, vision problems, speaking problems, and proactivity. Proactivity refers to the willingness and ability to take initiative and anticipate situations rather than simply reacting to them. An example of proactivity during HRI is maintaining the pace of communication by asking questions or suggesting topics of conversation. These categories were all limited to 3–5 options to simplify the survey.

The output vector used to train the model and produce appropriate predictions consisted of the six classes mentioned before (*interaction time, font size, audio volume, answer time, exercises level,* and *answer channel*). The value of these classes was obtained from 21 activities devoted to defining the best value for each. The questionnaire activities were intended to obtain the users' performance at different audio, visual, motor, and interaction skills fostering entertainment. Figure 2 shows examples of the different activities (association, reading, listening, or labeling) included in the questionnaire.

Nine of the activities were questions about general knowledge obtained from secondary school books used to define the value of the class *exercises level*, two activities to obtain the most appropriate *audio level*, four activities to obtain the most appropriate *font size*, three activities showing texts with different lengths to obtain the needed *answer time*, two activities to define the most favorable *answer channel*, and another asking about the willingness to interact with robots during long periods, that was used to set the *interaction time*.

4.3   Participants

A total of 240 participants (86 men, 154 women) between 14 and 67 years old completed the online survey using *Wooclap*. All participants lived in Spain. After analyzing the survey data, we had to remove 30 individuals who incorrectly completed the requested parameters (e.g., leaving some activities blank, providing non-sense information, or inconsistencies). The information in the file was organized by eliminating useless information provided by the survey application.

A numerical encoding was performed to replace the continuous values obtained from the survey with discrete numeric labels. Each label represents a range or category of values. This encoding transforms the Machine Learning problem into a classification rather than a regression, reducing algorithm computation times and improving results.

4.4   Classification Model

The nature of the problem conditions the selection of the classification technique, the size of the dataset, and the performance requirements. For the conditions of this work, we selected the Random Forest (RF) classifier due to its low overfitting, low dimensionality, and good results for small datasets.

Although RF offered many advantages in our context, it was necessary to compare it with other supervised classification techniques. For this purpose, we used the AutoSklearn [5] tool to obtain which classification technique provided the best results. AutoSklearn uses Scikit-learn [9], a Python library widely used by researchers that allows comparison of up to 15 different classifiers while finding the best hyperparameters.

The results showed that RF is the best alternative for predicting all categories except for the *interaction time* class. In this case, the *K-Nearest Neighbors* algorithm provided slightly better results than RF. However, we used RF to predict all classes to simplify model integration. Table 1 shows the best RF hyperparameters for each selected class to train the six models.

4.5   Integration

The classification model to personalize the HRI by selecting the most appropriate *interaction time, font size, audio volume, answer time, exercises level,* and *answer*

Table 1. Best hyperparameters for each RF classifier trained for the prediction of the six interaction parameters

Class	N trees	Split	Min samples split	Min samples leaf	Max features	Leaf nodes	Boostrap
Interaction time	100	Entropy	15	10	6	Inf	True
Answer time	500	Entropy	3	11	3	Inf	False
Answer channel	100	Gini	20	16	5	Inf	True
Font size	100	Gini	17	20	7	Inf	True
Audio volume	100	Gini	20	16	5	Inf	True
Exercise level	100	Gini	15	10	3	Inf	False

channel for each user was integrated into the software architecture of Mini. The model works in a ROS node containing a server that updates the user profile in the robot's memory under petition. The User-adaptive system calls the service once all the input features (demographic user data) are stored in the user profile. The input features can be introduced by the robot designer, the user, or a caregiver (using a website connected to the robot) or automatically filled by the robot by asking the user.

The server node needs the user demographic information to predict the values of each class. These values are returned to the User-adaptive system, which updates the user profile with the new parameters. Then, this information is sent to the HRI system, a node that manages the interaction with the user and adapts the interaction dynamics. Whenever the robot perceives a different user, their information is automatically loaded from a database to personalize the interaction. If a user profile contains missing information, the interaction takes general default values for that user.

5 Results

The results presented in this paper are divided into two sections. On the one hand, we show and analyze the classification scores for the RF algorithm and the best hyperparameters. On the other hand, we describe how Mini employs the predicted parameters to personalize the interaction with an older adult.

5.1 Classification Scores

After finding the best hyperparameters (see Table 1) for each RF model used to predict the six HRI classes, we trained, validated, and tested the models' performances. We used 80% of the 210 input instances to run a 10-fold cross-validation and the remaining 20% of the data for testing. The 10-fold cross-validation was carried out randomly, taking 80% of the instances for training the model and the remaining 20% for validating it.

Table 2 shows the cross-validation and testing results for the six models trained to predict the features used to personalize HRI. The classes *audio volume* and *answer channel* reported positive prediction scores for validation and

Table 2. Cross-validation and testing performances for each of the 6 classes used to personalize HRI.

Class	10-fold cross-validation scores (%)	Test scores (%)
Font size	61	53
Audio volume	77	72
Answer channel	77	74
Interaction time	58	67
Answer time	67	63
Exercises level	61	54

Table 3. Demographic user features used to predict the six parameters used to personalize the interaction.

User feature	Value
Gender	Female
Age	76 years old
Education level	Basic education
Occupation	Retired
Technology training	Low
Robot use	Never
Reading frequency	Some days
Vision problems	No
Audition problems	No
Motor problems	Yes
Experience time	Average

Table 4. Predicted values for the user's demographic information shown in Table 3 using the trained RF models.

Class	Predicted value
Font size	Medium
Audio volume	Medium
Answer channel	Voice
Interaction time	10 min
Answer time	50 s
Exercises level	Easy

testing, both above 70%. The class *answer time* reported above 60% of accuracy for validation and testing. Finally, the classes' font size, interaction time, and exercise level reported low classification scores, with validation scores between 58% and 61% and testing scores between 53% and 67%.

5.2 Interaction Example

The interaction personalization between Mini and its users using the methodology proposed starts when a user sits in front of the robot. At that moment, the robot perceives the user's presence and proactively starts the interaction, asking the user what to do. Suppose the robot recognizes the user (using active face recognition [12]). In that case, it automatically loads its information from a database and proceeds to personalize the interaction using the user profile information. If some features are missing, the robot manages this situation by occasionally asking the user questions oriented to obtain the missing information.

Once the user demographic profile is completed, the User-adaptive system calls the Interaction Predictor to obtain the values of the six features used to personalize the interaction. For example, consider a user with the demographic information in Table 3. When the Interaction Predictor receives the user information, it generates a prediction for the interaction of six classes, as shown in Table 4. The robot's memory receives the predicted classes and stores them in the user profile, so they are no longer predicted again. Then, the six interaction parameters are sent to the HRI manager to personalize the interaction dynamics.

The model predicted a medium font size, medium audio volume, voice interaction as the answer channel, 10 min as maximum interaction time, 50 s as answer time, and a low level for the exercises. These predictions make sense, considering the user features. For example, since the user does not have vision or audition problems, using a large font or high volume is optional. However, the user has motor problems, so interacting by voice seems the best alternative, as the model predicted. Since the user is not used to interacting with robots and using technology, the best interaction time is only 10 min. On the other hand, the answer time is the maximum (50 s), and the exercise level is set as low, probably because the user is an older adult with a basic education level.

The multi-modal capabilities of Mini produce a wide range of possibilities to adapt its behavior and interaction parameters to the user. The HRI manager uses the predictions of the classification model to improve the communication and the user. For example, if the robot wants to ask something, the HRI manager will adapt the question and allow answers by voice instead of touch or gestures. Similarly, every time the user has to complete an activity, their difficulty will be easy, facilitating the use of the robot and engaging the user. For this user, the font size and audio level will be medium, but for other people with impairments in these parameters, it could be helpful to increase the volume of the robot or use larger fonts.

6 Conclusion, Limitations and Future Work

This research work proposes an Interaction Predictor to personalize HRI in social robotics. The results show how RF produces optimistic predictions for most classes (audio volume, answer channel, interaction time, and answer time). In this study, we selected the six parameters that have more influence on the interaction mechanisms of our Mini robot. However, the method can be extended to incorporate other parameters to produce personalization and adaptive behavior in other robots.

6.1 Limitations

The realization of this work presents some limitations that must be considered to enhance the model's performance.

- **Dataset building**: We built our dataset using an online survey based on *Wooclap* where 240 people participated. Although the results show promising scores for the classification problem, the ideal way of building the dataset would have been from real HRI.

- **Questionnaire design**: The questionnaire used to build the dataset consisted of demographic questions and activities to obtain the best user interaction. The design of the activities was made following previous studies on the topic and demanding different skills from the user but also included some empirical details that should be avoided.
- **Features selected**: In this work, we selected six predicted features to personalize the interaction. However, HRI depends on many other parameters that must be considered to obtain a full-fledged adaptation to the user.
- **Classification algorithm:** We solved the classification problem using RF for all classes to unify and simplify the model. However, RF was not the best algorithm for one of the classes, and some scores can be considered low.

6.2   Future Work

The future work we want to address is building a more robust dataset to obtain higher prediction scores, especially for the classes' font sizes (53%) and exercise level (54%). Also related to the dataset, increasing the number of participants to have more data for feeding the Random Forest algorithm would be helpful. Finally, it is necessary to test whether including personalization during the interaction influences the users' perceptions of robot attributes such as usability, user experience, or naturalness.

Acknowledgements. The research leading to these results has received funding from the grants PID2021-123941OA-I00, funded by MCIN/AEI/ 10.13039/501100011033 and by "ERDF A way of making Europe"; TED2021-132079B-I00 funded by MCIN/AEI/10.13039/501100011033 and by the European Union NextGenerationEU/PRTR; Mejora del nivel de madurez tecnologica del robot Mini (MeNiR) funded by MCIN/AEI/10.13039/501100011033 and by the European Union NextGenerationEU/PRTR.

References

1. Aly, A., Tapus, A.: A model for synthesizing a combined verbal and nonverbal behavior based on personality traits in human-robot interaction. In: 2013 8th ACM/IEEE International Conference on Human-Robot Interaction (HRI), pp. 325–332. IEEE (2013)
2. Baraka, K., Alves-Oliveira, P., Ribeiro, T.: An extended framework for characterizing social robots. Hum.-Robot Interact. Eval. Methods Stand. 21–64 (2020)
3. Benedictis, R.D., Umbrico, A., Fracasso, F., Cortellessa, G., Orlandini, A., Cesta, A.: A dichotomic approach to adaptive interaction for socially assistive robots. User Model. User-Adapt. Interact. 33(2), 293–331 (2023)
4. Di Napoli, C., Ercolano, G., Rossi, S.: Personalized home-care support for the elderly: a field experience with a social robot at home. User Model. User-Adapt. Interact. 33(2), 405–440 (2023)
5. Feurer, M., Klein, A., Eggensperger, K., Springenberg, J., Blum, M., Hutter, F.: Efficient and robust automated machine learning. Adv. Neural Inf. Process. Syst. 28 (2015)

6. Fischinger, D., et al.: Hobbit, a care robot supporting independent living at home: first prototype and lessons learned. Robot. Auton. Syst. **75**, 60–78 (2016)
7. Gao, Y., Chang, H.J., Demiris, Y.: User modelling for personalised dressing assistance by humanoid robots. In: 2015 IEEE/RSJ International Conference on Intelligent Robots and Systems (IROS), pp. 1840–1845. IEEE (2015)
8. Klee, S.D., Ferreira, B.Q., Silva, R., Costeira, J.P., Melo, F.S., Veloso, M.: Personalized assistance for dressing users. In: ICSR 2015. LNCS (LNAI), vol. 9388, pp. 359–369. Springer, Cham (2015). https://doi.org/10.1007/978-3-319-25554-5_36
9. Kramer, O., Kramer, O.: Scikit-learn. Mach. Learn. Evol. Strateg. 45–53 (2016)
10. Louie, W.Y.G., Nejat, G.: A social robot learning to facilitate an assistive group-based activity from non-expert caregivers. Int. J. Soc. Robot. **12**(5), 1159–1176 (2020)
11. Maroto-Gómez, M., Alonso-Martín, F., Malfaz, M., Castro-González, Á., Castillo, J.C., Salichs, M.Á.: A systematic literature review of decision-making and control systems for autonomous and social robots. Int. J. Soc. Robot. **15**(5), 745–789 (2023)
12. Maroto-Gómez, M., Marqués-Villaroya, S., Castillo, J.C., Castro-González, Á., Malfaz, M.: Active learning based on computer vision and human-robot interaction for the user profiling and behavior personalization of an autonomous social robot. Eng. Appl. Artif. Intell. **117**, 105631 (2023)
13. Martins, G.S., Santos, L., Dias, J.: User-adaptive interaction in social robots: a survey focusing on non-physical interaction. Int. J. Soc. Robot. **11**, 185–205 (2019)
14. Mitsunaga, N., Smith, C., Kanda, T., Ishiguro, H., Hagita, N.: Adapting robot behavior for human-robot interaction. IEEE Trans. Robot. **24**(4), 911–916 (2008)
15. Rossi, S., Ferland, F., Tapus, A.: User profiling and behavioral adaptation for HRI: a survey. Pattern Recognit. Lett. **99**, 3–12 (2017)
16. Salichs, M.A., et al.: Mini: a new social robot for the elderly. Int. J. Soc. Robot. **12**, 1231–1249 (2020)
17. Steinfeld, A., et al.: Common metrics for human-robot interaction. In: Proceedings of the 1st ACM SIGCHI/SIGART Conference on Human-Robot Interaction, pp. 33–40 (2006)

Using Theory of Mind in Explanations for Fostering Transparency in Human-Robot Interaction

Georgios Angelopoulos[1]([✉])(iD), Pasquale Imparato[2], Alessandra Rossi[1,2](iD), and Silvia Rossi[1,2](iD)

[1] Interdepartmental Center for Advances in Robotic Surgery - ICAROS, University of Naples Federico II, Naples, Italy
{georgios.angelopoulos,alessandra.rossi,silvia.rossi}@unina.it
[2] Department of Electrical Engineering and Information Technologies - DIETI, University of Naples Federico II, Naples, Italy

Abstract. In human-robot interaction, addressing disparities in action perception is vital for fostering effective collaboration. Our study delves into the integration of explanatory mechanisms during robotic actions, focusing on aligning robot perspectives with the human's knowledge and beliefs. A comprehensive study involving 143 participants showed that providing explanations significantly enhances transparency compared to scenarios where no explanations are offered. However, intriguingly, lower transparency ratings were observed when these explanations considered participants' existing knowledge. This observation underscores the nuanced interplay between explanation mechanisms and human perception of transparency in the context of human-robot interaction. These preliminary findings contribute to emphasize the crucial role of explanations in enhancing transparency and highlight the need for further investigation to understand the multifaceted dynamics at play.

Keywords: Human-Robot Interaction · Explanations · Transparency

1 Introduction

Robots are engineered with specific tasks and objectives in mind; however, their actions may not always be readily understandable to humans. This lack of understanding can cause users to overestimate a robot's capabilities, a phenomenon known as overtrust [11]. Furthermore, the physical design elements of robots, encompassing their appearance and vocal attributes, significantly mould users' perceptions and expectations, highlighting the importance of considering Theory

This work has been supported by the European Union's Horizon 2020 research and innovation programme under the Marie Skłodowska-Curie grant agreement No 955778 (G. Angelopoulos), by the Italian Ministry for Universities and Research (MUR) under the grant FAIR (MUR: PE0000013) (S. Rossi), and Italian PON R&I 2014-2020 - REACT-EU (CUP E65F21002920003) (A. Rossi).

of Mind principles in designing robots that can better adapt to users' mental states.

To tackle these challenges, researchers have turned their attention to the use of verbal explanations to elucidate the decision-making processes of black-box algorithms. These techniques can be adapted to expound upon robotic actions, rendering them more comprehensible to human users [3]. The explanations proffered by robots hold substantial influence over how users perceive and engage with them since they can augment the anthropomorphic qualities of robots, thereby endowing robots with a more dynamic and human-like demeanour [12].

In this context, we believe that it is essential to consider the concept of the Theory of Mind with a robot providing explanations. Theory of Mind refers to the ability to attribute mental states, such as beliefs, intentions, and desires, to oneself and others. It has been shown that users might attribute mental states to a robot during the interaction [5]. On the contrary, the capability of reasoning on the user's possible mental states increases adaptability and efficiency [13]. Indeed, robots that can adapt their explanations based on the user's beliefs and knowledge levels can create a more intuitive and human-like interaction experience [8]. This adaptability enhances the robot's ability to communicate effectively and fosters a sense of understanding between the user and the robot. This understanding can lead to more contextually relevant explanations, which, in turn, could contribute to increased transparency.

This paper provides a contribution to exploring strategies to enhance Human-Robot Interaction (HRI) transparency and efficacy. We delve into the complex decision-making process that underpins selecting aspects of a robot's behaviour to be elucidated to users. Furthermore, we comprehensively examine the correlation between explanations that consider the human beliefs and the resultant perception of transparency. These preliminary findings provide insights into the ever-evolving landscape of HRI and towards advancing collaboration and transparency in robot behaviour.

2   Related Work

The importance of providing clear explanations for robot actions is widely acknowledged in HRI, yet a comprehensive understanding of how these explanations affect user perception remains a topic of ongoing investigation.

Ambsdorf et al. [1] conducted an online study to explore the impact of explainable robots on human perception. They designed a scenario where two simulated robots engaged in a competitive board game. One of the robots explained its moves, while the other simply announced them. The results revealed that the robot providing explanations was perceived as more dynamic and human-like. However, it also raised an important point that humans might still have reservations about trusting a robot's ability to perform tasks, even when it offers explanations.

Stange et al. [16] proposed an architecture for the social robot Pepper that allows it to interact autonomously with users and explain its behaviour based on the user's verbal requests during the interaction. Although their architecture showed promise for creating robots with explainable autonomous behaviour, they did not investigate how these explanations influenced user perception.

Nikolaidis *et al.* [10] introduced a formalism that enables a robot to make decisions about whether to take action or provide explanations to a human teammate optimally. They employed verbal commands to guide humans and used state-explaining actions, where the robot explained its internal state while performing the task. Their study found that issuing verbal commands was the most effective way to communicate objectives while maintaining user trust in the robot.

In these studies, while the positive impact of explanations on HRI is evident, it is crucial to note that understanding human knowledge and beliefs and tailoring explanations accordingly remains a challenge to be explored. This aspect of considering the user's existing knowledge during explanations can significantly influence how humans perceive and trust robots in various tasks and scenarios.

3   Proposed Approach

To enhance transparency and mutual understanding within HRI, our proposed approach draws inspiration from the recent work by Sreedharan *et al.* [15], and centres on the concept of generating explanations as a process of reconciliation between plans generated from different world models. This approach is particularly relevant in scenarios where the interaction involves dynamic elements. In this dynamic scenario, we employ a framework rooted in knowledge representation and automated planning. Specifically, we leverage the ROSPlan framework, a robust tool for knowledge-based planning [4] and utilize Planning Domain Definition Language to model the knowledge states of both the robot and the human within the interaction context.

In this context, we consider a dynamic scenario where a change occurs within the environment during the task. Importantly, the robot's knowledge is updated to reflect this new information, whereas the human remains unaware of this change. This shift creates a fundamental disparity in their knowledge states and perspectives. In response to these dynamic changes, our approach employs the Fast Forward algorithm to derive optimal sequences of actions for both entities. The robot plans its actions while considering the updated information, whereas the human operates with their previous knowledge. These differing knowledge states become pivotal in shaping the explanations provided by the robot.

The robot's explanations are adapted to accommodate the cognitive divergence resulting from the changing environment. When the robot explains its actions, it considers both its own and the human's knowledge. For instance, if the robot reaches the goal of a task, it offers an explanation that aligns with the human's perspective. Considering their differing knowledge states, this could ensure that the robot's actions are more transparent and comprehensible to humans. Our approach relies in comparing these computed action sequences and recognizing instances where their knowledge diverges due to the changing of the environment. These disparities serve as valuable cues for tailoring explanations that resonate with the human cognitive model, taking into account the evolving perspective caused by this change. Consequently, our approach facilitates the delivery of more constructive and contextually relevant explanations, considering the nuanced differences in knowledge and perception induced by dynamic elements. The combination of knowledge representation, automated planning, and a focus on cognitive divergence empowers the robot to elucidate its actions that align with the human's evolving perspective in these dynamic scenarios.

3.1   The Scenario

We employed a "fetch-and-carry" task [7], which is a simple interactive scenario to assess the explanations and the transparency derived from them in an HRI context. The robot navigated in the environment (see Fig. 1), retrieved an item with a dynamic position (i.e., a drink), and delivered it to the virtual human.

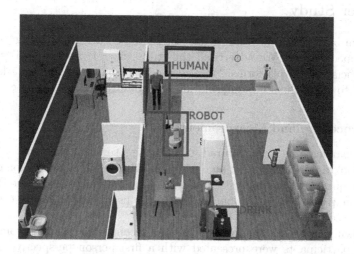

Fig. 1. The Employed Virtual Environment consists of five rooms.

To investigate the influence of considering human knowledge on the explanations in Transparency, we implemented three conditions:

- *Condition 1* (**C1**): This condition served as the baseline and involved the robot not providing any explanations.
- *Condition 2* (**C2**): In this condition, the robot offered an initial verbalization of its actions ("I have to get the drink") and a subsequent explanation after completing the actions ("The drink was in the living room").
- *Condition 3* (**C3**): This condition integrated both the robot's initial explanation and the explanation after completing the action, along with knowledge about the human's preferences ("I have to take the drink, but it is not in the kitchen" and "The drink was not in the kitchen but was in the living room").

In light of the existing literature, we formulated the following hypotheses to guide our investigation:

- **Hypothesis 1 (H1)**: The condition where the robot provides explanations (C2, C3) produces a more transparent mechanism than in the condition where a robot does not provide explanations. This hypothesis aligns with previous findings by Felzmann *et al.* [6], which demonstrated that providing explanations could enhance the transparency of robotic systems.
- **Hypothesis 2 (H2)**: The condition in which the robot considers human knowledge into the explanations (C3) results in behaviour that is more transparent than the other mechanisms that do not consider human knowledge (C1, C2). This hypothesis builds on the findings of Milliez *et al.* [9], which suggested that adapting the explanations to the human's knowledge can lead to the robot being perceived as smarter.

4   User Study

An online between-subject study was conducted to assess the designed experimental mechanisms. We advertised the study via relevant email lists and on several social media platforms. We also used snowball sampling by asking participants to share the study information with interested friends and colleagues.

4.1   Procedure and Measurements

Initially, participants were required to complete a series of questions concerning their demographic information and prior experience with robots. Upon completing these questions, participants proceed to watch a video. The video displayed a static map labelled with room locations, the user's position, and the drink's location (see Fig. 1).

Following this static map presentation, a second video segment commenced, wherein participants were presented with a first-person perspective from the human's point of view. This perspective allowed participants to have a partial observation of both the robotic entity and the surrounding kitchen environment (see Fig. 2). During this video segment, the robot initiated the "fetch-and-carry" task. In the context of our experimental procedure, a deliberate interruption of the video was introduced as an essential component to gauge the transparency of the robot's actions during the task execution. This interruption was incorporated to solicit participants' evaluations of the robot's behaviour and happened when the robot exited their field of view of the human (in conditions C2 and C3, the robot had provided an explanation before the action).

To expound further on this approach, participants were prompted to provide assessments regarding the robot's Legibility, Predictability and Expectability, as these factors collectively contribute to the construct of Transparency [2]. More specifically, participants were asked to answer the following:

- To what extent do you know why the robot moves the way it does? (*Legibility*).

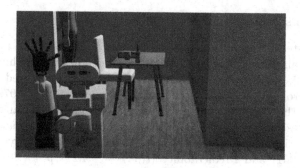

Fig. 2. The perspective of the virtual human.

- How well do you know what the robot will do next? (*Predictability*).
- To what extent does the robot behave as expected? (*Expectability*).

After responding, participants continued watching the remaining video. Upon completion, they were asked to fill out the Human-Robot Interaction Evaluation Scale (HRIES) Questionnaire assessing their perception of the robot [14]. But also 5-Likert scale questions regarding the overall Transparency of the robot:

- To what extent do you know why the robot moved the way it did? (*Legibility*).
- To what extent did you know what the robot would do next? (*Predictability*).
- To what extent did the robot behave as you expected? (*Expectability*).

It is important to notice that the video's content remained consistent across all conditions, with only the verbal explanations differing.

5   Results

In the conducted online study, we initially recruited a total of 178 participants. After careful screening, one participant was excluded due to being below the age of 18, while an additional seven participants were removed. These seven participants were disqualified based on the following criteria: duplicate survey submissions and the presence of extreme outlier scores across multiple measured variables. Consequently, the final set for analysis comprised 143 participants, consisting of 86 males and 57 females, with no non-binary or other genders. This resulted in an effect size of d = 0.25 with a power of 0.90 at an alpha level of 0.05. The participants exhibited a diverse age range spanning from 18 to 60 years (Mean = 39.16, Std. Deviation = 15.84). The majority of respondents (61.5%) reported no prior experience with robots. Furthermore, we observed that they had no negative bias towards robots (Mean = 2.44, Std. Deviation = 1.05).

5.1 System's Transparency

A series of t-tests were conducted to examine the differences in the characteristics of Transparency between the different conditions. Within the context of C1 and C2, statistically significant variations were observed in the Legibility of the robot's actions before pausing ($t(76.074) = -4.979, p < .001$), as well as in the Predictability ($t(94) = -7.143, p < 0.001$) and Expectability ($t(94) = -3.662, p < .001$) of its behaviour prior to a pause. Similarly, post-pausing, significant differences were detected in Legibility ($t(80.731) = -4.252, p < .001$) and Predictability ($t(94) = -4.212, p < .001$), as well as Expectability ($t(94) = -3.455, p < .001$).

In the case of C1 and C3, noteworthy disparities were identified in the robot's Legibility before pausing ($t(78.552) = -4.776, p < .001$), Predictability before pausing ($t(97) = -5.173, p < .001$), and Expectability before pausing ($t(97) = -4.466, p < .001$). Post-pause, significant distinctions were also evident in Legibility ($t(80.053) = -3.332, p < .001$) and Expectability ($t(97) = -3.880, p < .001$), whereas Predictability exhibited a significant difference ($t(97) = -2.500, p = .014$).

Conversely, in the comparison of C2 and C3, no statistically significant differences were discerned in the Legibility before pausing ($t(89) = 0.052, p = .479$), Predictability before pausing ($t(89) = 1.589, p = .058$), or Expectability before pausing ($t(89) = -0.832, p = .204$). Nevertheless, post to a pause, no significant differences were found in Legibility ($t(89) = -0.557, p = .290$) or Expectability ($t(89) = -0.366, p = .358$). Post-pause Predictability exhibited a statistically significant difference ($t(89) = 1.786, p = .039$), indicating distinguishable outcomes between C2 and C3. For visual clarity, Fig. 3 provides graphical representations of the data, illustrating the variations in Legibility, Predictability, and Expectability across the different experimental conditions.

In our analysis of Transparency, we sought to evaluate its degree both before and after the pause. The results are depicted in Fig. 4. To assess the degree of Transparency before the pause, we employed a factor analysis approach that integrates three key components: Legibility, Predictability, and Expectability. We first evaluated the dataset's suitability for factor analysis by examining the Kaiser-Meyer-Olkin (KMO) measure of sampling adequacy, which yielded a KMO value of 0.644, indicating its appropriateness for this analytical technique. Subsequently, we examined the factor loadings derived from our comprehensive analysis. Specifically, our data unveiled factor loadings of 0.858 for Legibility, 0.715 for Predictability, and 0.860 for Expectability. These loadings underscore the significant contributions of all three constituent elements to the overarching construct of Transparency, with Expectability emerging as the most influential factor, closely followed by Legibility and Predictability.

To calculate the relative importance of each component, we normalize the standardized factor loadings by dividing them by the sum of all three standardized loadings. The resulting relative importance scores are as follows: **R(L)** : 0.352, **R(P)** : 0.294, and **R(E)** : 0.354. Utilizing these weights in a weighted sum formula, we obtain the pre-transparency score:

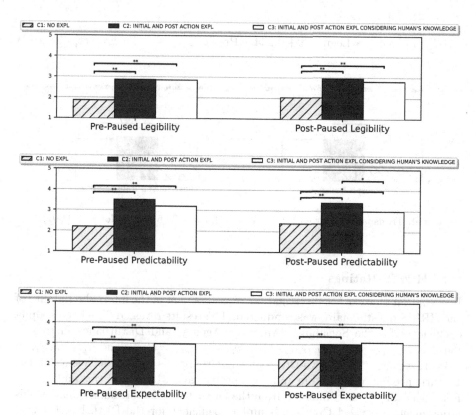

Fig. 3. Legibility, Predictability, and Expectability for each Condition (* for $p < 0.05$ and ** for $p \leq 0.001$).

$$T_{pre} = 0.352 \times \text{Legib}_{pre} + 0.294 \times \text{Predict}_{pre} + 0.354 \times \text{Expect}_{pre} \quad (1)$$

We conducted a similar factor analysis on the Transparency assessment after the pause. However, it is important to note that the KMO measure of sampling adequacy in this analysis yielded a value of 0.5, which is slightly below the preferred threshold for robust factor analysis. Nevertheless, the chi-square statistic of 29.670, coupled with a significance level less than 0.0001, indicated a statistically significant relationship among the variables, justifying the continuation of the factor analysis. From this, we obtained factor loadings that revealed the relative contributions of each variable to Transparency after the pause. Legibility had the most substantial influence with a factor loading of 0.901, followed by Expectability (0.813) and Predictability (0.523).

To calculate the relative importance of these components, we again normalized the standardized factor loadings and obtained the following relative importance scores: **R(L)** : 0.402, **R(P)** : 0.234, and **R(E)** : 0.363. Utilizing these weights in a weighted sum formula, we obtain the post-transparency score:

$$T_{post} = 0.402 \times \text{Legib}_{post} + 0.234 \times \text{Predict}_{post} + 0.363 \times \text{Expect}_{post} \qquad (2)$$

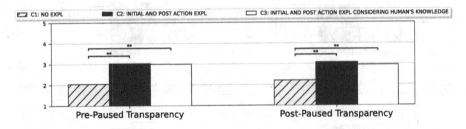

Fig. 4. Transparency for each Condition (*for $p < 0.05$ and ** for $p \leq 0.001$).

5.2   HRIES Ratings

In the initial phase of the investigation, an assessment of the internal reliability of the HRIES questionnaire was conducted. The results revealed Cronbach's alpha coefficients for the Sociability, Animacy, Agency, and Disturbance factors as follows: $\alpha_{Sociability} = 0.70$, $\alpha_{Animacy} = 0.75$, $\alpha_{Agency} = 0.71$, and $\alpha_{Disturbance} = 0.66$. However, it is noteworthy that the Cronbach's alpha coefficient for the Disturbance factor fell within an unacceptable range. In light of this finding, the item "Uncanny" was eliminated from the Disturbance factor. Subsequent to this adjustment, a revised Cronbach's alpha coefficient for the Disturbance factor yielded $\alpha_{Disturbance} = 0.81$.

To assess variations in HRIES factors across different conditions, a series of t-tests were conducted. The results are depicted in Fig. 5. Notably, in the context of the *Sociability* dimension, a statistically significant difference emerged between C1 and C2 ($t(80.936) = -1.872, p = .032$), indicating that participants assigned more positive evaluations to C2 in terms of sociability. Conversely, in the *Animacy* dimension, no statistically significant differences were detected among the conditions, signifying consistent participant evaluations of animacy across conditions. In contrast, for the *Agency* factor, a statistically significant difference was noted between C1 and C2 ($t(94) = -1.810, p = .037$), with C2 receiving higher ratings in terms of agency. Lastly, in the *Disturbance* dimension, a statistically significant difference was observed between C1 and C2 ($t(81.790) = -2.147, p = .017$), indicating that C2 was associated with a higher level of perceived disturbance compared to C1. Sociability, Agency, and Animacy dimensions positively correlate with anthropomorphism [14]; the results thus suggest an increase in the robot's anthropomorphism in C2.

5.3   Evaluation of the Experimental Results

This study aimed to assess the mechanisms underlying explanations and their effect on transparency. Our results have confirmed Hypothesis 1 by showing that

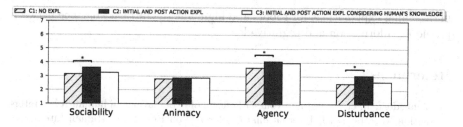

Fig. 5. Results of the HRIES questionnaire for each Condition (* for $p < 0.05$ and ** for $p \leq 0.001$).

the provision of explanations by the robot (C2, C3) yields a more transparent mechanism than a robot without any explanatory discourse. Of particular significance is the observation that C3, where explanations were provided while taking into account participants' knowledge, received lower transparency ratings compared to C2, where explanations were given without considering participants' knowledge. This outcome finds support in the higher rating received by C2 on the HRIES questionnaire, which is consistent with previous research [17] that emphasized the influence of transparency on anthropomorphism. Consequently, our findings did not confirm Hypothesis 2.

This divergence in transparency ratings between C2 and C3 may be attributed to several factors. Firstly, it is plausible that C3 introduced additional information, potentially resulting in a heightened cognitive load for participants. This increased cognitive burden could have rendered it more challenging for participants to effectively process and integrate the supplementary information, subsequently diminishing the perceived transparency of the explanations provided. Moreover, the combination of both the robot's and human's knowledge in C3 might have been perceived as intricate or redundant, thereby diminishing the clarity of the robot's intentions. Further investigation is needed to gain a more comprehensive understanding of these findings. These observations underscore the intricate interplay of various factors that influence the provision of explanations and the subsequent perception of transparency.

6   Conclusions

The work presented in this paper aimed at integrating explanatory mechanisms into human-robot interactions to enhance transparency and mutual understanding. Our study provided valuable insights into the complex dynamics at play when robots offer explanations, particularly in dynamic scenarios where the robot's knowledge differs from that of the human. We found that providing explanations significantly improves transparency compared to scenarios with no explanations. However, it was intriguing to note that considering participants' existing knowledge when crafting explanations did not necessarily lead to higher transparency ratings. These findings emphasize the need for a nuanced approach in designing explanations for robots and highlight the intricate balance between providing information and cognitive load.

References

1. Ambsdorf, J., et al.: Explain yourself! effects of explanations in human-robot interaction. In: 31st IEEE International Conference on Robot and Human Interactive Communication (RO-MAN), pp. 393–400. IEEE (2022)
2. Angelopoulos, G., Di Martino, C., Rossi, A., Rossi, S.: Unveiling the learning curve: enhancing transparency in robot's learning with inner speech and emotions. In: 2023 32nd IEEE International Conference on Robot and Human Interactive Communication (RO-MAN), Busan, Republic of Korea, pp. 1922-1927(2023). https://doi.org/10.1109/RO-MAN57019.2023.10309352
3. Angelopoulos, G., Rossi, A., L'Arco, G., Rossi, S.: Transparent interactive reinforcement learning using emotional behaviours. In: Cavallo, F., et al. (eds.) ICSR 2022. LNCS, vol. 13817, pp. 300–311. Springer, Cham (2022). https://doi.org/10.1007/978-3-031-24667-8_27
4. Cashmore, M., et al.: ROSPlan: planning in the robot operating system. In: Proceedings of the International Conference on Automated Planning and Scheduling, vol. 25, pp. 333–341 (2015)
5. Cucciniello, I., Sangiovanni, S., Maggi, G., Rossi, S.: Mind perception in HRI: exploring users' attribution of mental and emotional states to robots with different behavioural styles. Int. J. Soc. Robot. 15(5), 867–877 (2023)
6. Felzmann, H., Fosch-Villaronga, E., Lutz, C., Tamo-Larrieux, A.: Robots and transparency: the multiple dimensions of transparency in the context of robot technologies. IEEE Robot. Autom. Mag. 26(2), 71–78 (2019)
7. Kraus, M., Wagner, N., Untereiner, N., Minker, W.: Including social expectations for trustworthy proactive human-robot dialogue. In: Proceedings of the 30th ACM Conference on User Modeling, Adaptation and Personalization, pp. 23–33 (2022)
8. McKenna, P.E., et al.: Theory of mind and trust in human-robot navigation. In: Proceedings of the 1st International Symposium on Trustworthy Autonomous Systems, pp. 1–5 (2023)
9. Milliez, G., Lallement, R., Fiore, M., Alami, R.: Using human knowledge awareness to adapt collaborative plan generation, explanation and monitoring. In: ACM/IEEE International Conference on HRI, pp. 43–50 (2016)
10. Nikolaidis, S., Kwon, M., Forlizzi, J., Srinivasa, S.: Planning with verbal communication for human-robot collaboration. ACM Trans. Hum. Robot Interact. (THRI) 7(3), 1–21 (2018)
11. Rossi, A., Koay, K.L., Haring, K.S.: To err is robotic: understanding, preventing, and resolving robots' failures in HRI
12. Schött, S.Y., Amin, R.M., Butz, A.: A literature survey of how to convey transparency in co-located human-robot interaction. Multimodal Technol. Interact. 7(3), 25 (2023)
13. Shvo, M., Hari, R., O'Reilly, Z., Abolore, S., Wang, S.Y.N., McIlraith, S.A.: Proactive robotic assistance via theory of mind. In: 2022 IEEE/RSJ International Conference on Intelligent Robots and Systems (IROS), pp. 9148–9155 (2022)
14. Spatola, N., Kühnlenz, B., Cheng, G.: Perception and evaluation in human-robot interaction: the human-robot interaction evaluation scale (HRIES)-a multicomponent approach of anthropomorphism. Int. J. Soc. Roboti. 13(7), 1517–1539 (2021)

15. Sreedharan, S., Chakraborti, T., Kambhampati, S.: Foundations of explanations as model reconciliation. Artif. Intell. **301**, 103558 (2021)
16. Stange, S., Hassan, T., Schröder, F., Konkol, J., Kopp, S.: Self-explaining social robots: an explainable behavior generation architecture for human-robot interaction. Front. Artif. Intell. **5**, 87 (2022)
17. Straten, C.L., Peter, J., Kühne, R., Barco, A.: Transparency about a robot's lack of human psychological capacities: effects on child-robot perception and relationship formation. ACM Trans. Hum. Robot Interact. (THRI) **9**(2), 1–22 (2020)

Author Index

Printed in the United States
by Baker & Taylor Publisher Services

Printed in the United States
by Baker & Taylor Publisher Services